SUPERIOR SPORTS INV...

Always Buying Unopened Boxes and Singles

Call us at: 817-770-0804

Text us pictures of your cards

Check Out Our Website for Our Huge Inventory of Graded Cards, Singles, Boxes and Supplies!

We have purchased thousands of collections

THIS YEAR!

WE BUY WHAT OTHERS DON'T!

www.superiorsportsinvestments.com

BECKETT STAR WARS

COLLECTIBLES PRICE GUIDE-2023

THE HOBBY'S MOST RELIABLE AND RELIED UPON SOURCE™

FOUNDER: DR. JAMES BECKETT III

EDITED BY MATT BIBLE WITH THE BECKETT PRICE GUIDE STAFF

★BECKETT.

BECKETT is a registered trademark of BECKETT COLLECTIBLES LLC, PLANO, TEXAS
Manufactured in the United States of America | Published by Beckett Collectibles LLC

Beckett Collectibles LLC
2700 Summit Ave, Ste 100, Plano, TX 75074
(866) 287-9383 • beckett.com

First Printing
ISBN: 978-1-936681-60-0

We Buy Everything!

Kruk Cards is currently buying complete collections, inventories, and accumulations. What do you have for sale? We have four buyers traveling the country searching for sports and non-sports and gaming cards. Reach out, if you'd like us to stop by!

BUYING JUNK WAX BOXES

PER 36 COUNT WAX BOX

FOOTBALL pay $16	BASEBALL pay $13
HOCKEY (NHL) pay $8.50	BASKETBALL (NBA) pay $25

BUYING COMMONS

PER 5,000 COUNT BOX

FOOTBALL pay $30	BASEBALL pay $12
HOCKEY pay $20	BASKETBALL pay $15

For commons from the year 2000 to present we will pay a premium.
We have great shipping rates for groups of 500,000 commons and up.
Please call or email for the details.

www.krukcards.com

Check out our website for our available inventory!
We have over 25,000 auctions updated daily on eBay.

eBay User ID: Krukcards

Krause Publications 20
ebay POWER SELLER
Dealernet B²B

Kruk Cards
210 Campbell St.
Rochester, MI 48307
Email us:
George@krukcards.com

Hours: 5:30 AM - 5:30 PM EST
Phone: (248) 656-8803 • Fax: (248) 656-6547

2023 BECKETT STAR WARS PRICE GUIDE HOT LISTS

TOP 5 PRODUCTS 2021-22

2022 Star Wars Finest

2022 Star Wars Chrome Sapphire Edition

2021 Star Wars Masterwork

2021 Star Wars Bounty Hunters

2021 Star Wars Chrome Legacy

TOP 5 AUTOGRAPHS 2021-22

2021 Star Wars Stellar Signatures Autographs #ANP Natalie Portman

2021 Star Wars Chrome Legacy Age of Rebellion Autographs #ARBRD Rosario Dawson

2021 Star Wars Masterwork Autographs #MWAEC Emilia Clarke

2022 Star Wars Finest Book of Boba Fett Autographs #BATM Temuera Morrison

2021 Star Wars Stellar Signatures Autographs #ARD Rosario Dawson

TOP 5 ACTION FIGURES 2021-22

2020-22 Hasbro Star Wars Black Series Empire Strikes Back 6-Inch #4 Boba Fett Prototype (Amazon Exclusive)

2020-22 Hasbro Star Wars Black Series The Bad Batch 6-Inch #12 Cad Bane Bracca (Amazon Exclusive)

2010-22 Hasbro Star Wars The Vintage Collection #VC245 Obi-Wan Kenobi w/L0-LA59

2010-22 Hasbro Star Wars The Vintage Collection #VC234 R2-D2 w/sensorscope (Walmart Exclusive)

2010-22 Hasbro Star Wars The Vintage Collection #VC230 Koska Reeves (Target Exclusive)

TOP 5 FUNKO POPS 2021-22

2011-22 Funko Pop Vinyl Star Wars #474 Grogu Macy's Thanksgiving Day Parade

2011-22 Funko Pop Vinyl Star Wars #534A Cassian Andor SDCC

2011-22 Funko Pop Vinyl Star Wars #567A Anakin Skywalker w/Lightsabers NYCC

2011-22 Funko Pop Vinyl Star Wars #SE BB-8 Make-A-Wish

2011-22 Funko Pop Vinyl Star Wars #548A Krrsantan FLK SDCC

TOP 20 ALL-TIME AHSOKA COLLECTIBLES

TOP 5 AHSOKA TRADING CARDS

2008 Star Wars The Clone Wars #3 Ahsoka Tano

2008 Star Wars The Clone Wars Stickers #24 Ahsoka Tano

2020 Star Wars The Mandalorian Season 2 #21 In Search of Information/1,982*

2021 Star Wars Masterwork #4 Ahsoka Tano

2010 Star Wars The Clone Wars Rise of the Bounty Hunters Foil Insert #2

TOP 5 AHSOKA ACTRESS AUTOGRAPHED CARDS

2013 Star Wars Galactic Files 2 Autographs Ashley Eckstein

2021 Star Wars Chrome Legacy Age of Rebellion Autographs #ARBRD Rosario Dawson

2021 Star Wars Stellar Signatures Autographs #ARD Rosario Dawson

2017 Star Wars Journey to The Last Jedi Autographs #AAE Ashley Eckstein

2015 Star Wars Masterwork Autographs Ashley Eckstein

TOP 5 AHSOKA ACTION FIGURES

2010-22 Hasbro Star Wars The Vintage Collection #VC102 Ahsoka Tano

2020 Hasbro Star Wars Black Series Rebels 6-Inch #7 Ahsoka Tano

2008-13 Hasbro Star Wars The Clone Wars Blue and Black #CW44 Ahsoka

2010-22 Hasbro Star Wars The Vintage Collection #VC222 Ahsoka Tano (Corvus)

2020-23 Hasbro Star Wars Black Series The Mandalorian 6-Inch #19 Ahsoka Tano

TOP 5 AHSOKA FUNKO POPS

2011-22 Funko Pop Vinyl Star Wars #130A Ahsoka (2016 Hot Topic Exclusive)

2011-22 Funko Pop Vinyl Star Wars #464 Ahsoka (2021)

2011-22 Funko Pop Vinyl Star Wars #496 Ahsoka Pink

2011-22 Funko Pop Vinyl Star Wars #130C Ahsoka GITD (2017 Comikaze Exclusive)

2011-22 Funko Pop Vinyl Star Wars #467A Ahsoka (2021 Amazon Exclusive)

Beckett Star Wars Collectibles Price Guide – 2023

WHAT'S LISTED?

Products in the price guide typically:

- Are produced by licensed manufacturers
- Are widely available
- Have market activity on single items

WHAT THE COLUMNS MEAN

The LO and HI columns reflect current retail selling ranges. The HI column on the right generally represents the full retail selling price. The LO column on the left generally represents the lowest price one would expect to find with extensive shopping.

CONDITION

Prices in this issue reflect the highest raw condition (i.e. not professionally graded by a third party) of the card commonly found at shows, shops, online, and right out of the pack for brand new releases. This generally means NrMint to Mint condition. Action figure prices are based on Mint condition. Action figures that are loose (out-of-package) are generally sold for 50 percent of the listed price, but may list for less/more depending on popularity, condition, completeness, and market sales.

CURRENCY

This price guide is intended to reflect the entire North American market. While not all the cards/figures are produced in the United States, they will reflect the market value in U.S. dollars.

GLOSSARY/LEGEND

Our glossary defines terms most frequently used in the action figure/non-sports card collecting hobby. Some of these terms are common to other types of collecting. Some terms may have several meanings depending on the use and context.

ALB	Album exclusive card. This indicates that a card was only available in a collector album or binder that was devoted to a certain product.
AU	Certified autograph
BB	Box bottom - A card or panel of cards on the bottom of a trading card box.
BI	Box incentive
BN	Barnes & Noble exclusive
BT	Box topper - A card, either regulation or jumbo-sized, that is inserted in the top of a box of trading cards.
C	Common card
CI	Case-Incentive or Case Insert - A unique card that is offered as an incentive to purchase a case (or cases) of trading cards.
COA	Certificate of Authenticity - A certificate issued by the manufacturer to insure a product's authenticity.
COR	Corrected version of an error (ERR) card
CT	Case-topper exclusive card
D23	Disney D23 Convention
ECCC	Emerald City Comic Con
EE	Entertainment Earth exclusive - An exclusive that was offered for sale on Entertainment Earth's website.
EL	Extremely limited
ERR	Error card - A card with erroneous information, spelling, or depiction on either side of the card, most of which are not corrected by the manufacturer.
EXCH	Exchange card
FACT	Factory set exclusive
FLK	Flocked variant - This description applies exclusively to Funko products.
FOIL	holofoil
GCE	Galactic Convention Exclusive - This description applies specifically to Funko products.
GEN	General distribution - This term most usually applies to promotional cards.
GITD	Glow-in-the-Dark variant - This description usually applies to Funko products.
GS	GameStop exclusive
HOLO	hologram

HT	Hot Topic exclusive
L	Limited
LE	Limited Edition
LS	Limited Series
MEM	Memorabilia card
MET	Metallic variant - This describes a metallic version of a Funko product.
NNO	Unnumbered card
NSU	Non-Sports Update exclusive card
NYCC	New York Comic Con
OPC	O-Pee-Chee (a Canadian subsidiary of Topps)
R	Rare card
RED	Redemption card
SDCC	San Diego Comic Con
SI	Set-Incentive
SP	Single or Short Print - A short print is a card that was printed in less quantity compared to the other cards in the same series.
SR	Super Rare card
SWC	Star Wars Celebration
TW	Toy Wars exclusive
U	Uncommon card
UER	Uncorrected error
UNC	Uncut sheet or panel
UR	Ultra Rare card
VAR	Variation card - One of two or more cards from the same series, with the same card number, that differ from one another in some way. This sometimes occurs when the manufacturer notices an error in one or more of the cards, corrects the mistake, and then resumes the printing process. In some cases, one of the variations may be relatively scarce.
VAULT	This description applies specifically to Funko products and indicates a figurine that has been re-released by the company.
VL	Very Limited
VR	Very Rare card
WG	Walgreen's exclusive
WM	Walmart exclusive

As with any publication, we appreciate reader feedback. While there are many listings, not all collectibles may be priced due to market constraints. If you have any questions, concerns, or suggestions, please contact us at: **nonsports@beckett.com**

Action Figures and Figurines

PRICE GUIDE

VINTAGE

1977-78 Kenner Star Wars 12-Backs A

NNO	Ben Kenobi grey hair	600.00	1200.00
NNO	Ben Kenobi white hair	500.00	1000.00
NNO	Ben Kenobi (w/double telescoping lightsaber)	4000.00	8000.00
NNO	C-3PO	500.00	1000.00
NNO	Chewbacca	500.00	1000.00
NNO	Darth Vader	1000.00	2000.00
NNO	Darth Vader (w/double telescoping lightsaber)	5000.00	10000.00
NNO	Death Squad Commander	400.00	800.00
NNO	Han Solo (small head)	1000.00	2000.00
NNO	Jawa (plastic cape)	6000.00	12000.00
NNO	Luke Skywalker (blond hair)	1250.00	2500.00
NNO	Luke Skywalker/telescoping lightsaber	10000.00	20000.00
NNO	Princess Leia	1000.00	2000.00
NNO	R2-D2	500.00	1000.00
NNO	Stormtrooper	400.00	800.00

1977-78 Kenner Star Wars 12-Backs B

NNO	Ben Kenobi (grey hair)	500.00	1000.00
NNO	Ben Kenobi (white hair)	750.00	1500.00
NNO	C-3PO	400.00	800.00
NNO	Chewbacca	400.00	800.00
NNO	Darth Vader	1000.00	2000.00
NNO	Death Squad Commander	300.00	600.00
NNO	Han Solo (small head)	750.00	1500.00
NNO	Jawa	450.00	900.00
NNO	Luke Skywalker (w/blond hair)	750.00	1500.00
NNO	R2-D2	500.00	1000.00
NNO	Stormtrooper	350.00	700.00
NNO	Tusken Raider	300.00	600.00

1977-78 Kenner Star Wars 12-Backs C

NNO	C-3PO	300.00	600.00
NNO	Chewbacca	400.00	800.00
NNO	Darth Vader	750.00	1500.00
NNO	Death Squad Commander	450.00	850.00
NNO	Han Solo (large head)	600.00	1200.00
NNO	Jawa	400.00	800.00
NNO	Luke Skywalker (blond hair)	750.00	1500.00
NNO	Luke Skywalker (w/double telescoping lightsaber)	4000.00	8000.00
NNO	Princess Leia	400.00	800.00
NNO	R2-D2	400.00	800.00
NNO	Stormtrooper	350.00	700.00
NNO	Tusken Raider	300.00	600.00

1977-78 Kenner Star Wars 12-Backs D

NNO	C-3PO	400.00	750.00
NNO	Chewbacca	400.00	800.00
NNO	Luke Skywalker (blond hair)	500.00	1000.00
NNO	Princess Leia	350.00	700.00
NNO	R2-D2	300.00	600.00
NNO	Death Squad Commander	400.00	800.00

1977-78 Kenner Star Wars 12-Backs E

NNO	R2-D2	1000.00	2000.00

1977-78 Kenner Star Wars 20-Backs A

NNO	Ben Kenobi (white hair)	250.00	500.00
NNO	C-3PO	200.00	400.00
NNO	Chewbacca	200.00	400.00

NNO	Death Squad Commander	150.00	300.00
NNO	Han Solo (large head)	350.00	700.00
NNO	Jawa	200.00	400.00
NNO	Princess Leia	250.00	500.00
NNO	Stormtrooper	200.00	350.00
NNO	Tusken Raider	150.00	300.00

1977-78 Kenner Star Wars 20-Backs B

NNO	Chewbacca	150.00	300.00
NNO	Death Squad Commander	200.00	400.00
NNO	Death Star Droid	200.00	400.00
NNO	Greedo	600.00	1200.00
NNO	Hammerhead	750.00	1500.00
NNO	Luke X-Wing Pilot	300.00	600.00
NNO	Power Droid	750.00	1500.00
NNO	R5-D4	750.00	1500.00
NNO	Snaggletooth (red)	1000.00	1500.00
NNO	Stormtrooper	125.00	250.00
NNO	Walrus Man	300.00	600.00

1977-78 Kenner Star Wars 20-Backs C

NNO	Chewbacca	200.00	400.00
NNO	Death Squad Commander	150.00	300.00
NNO	Jawa	200.00	400.00
NNO	Stormtrooper	150.00	300.00
NNO	Hammerhead	200.00	400.00
NNO	Luke X-Wing Pilot	150.00	300.00

1977-78 Kenner Star Wars 20-Backs D

NNO	Jawa	225.00	450.00
NNO	Death Star Droid	200.00	400.00
NNO	Luke X-Wing Pilot	200.00	350.00
NNO	R5-D4	200.00	350.00

1977-78 Kenner Star Wars 20-Backs E

NNO	Ben Kenobi (white hair)	200.00	400.00
NNO	Chewbacca	300.00	600.00
NNO	Darth Vader	350.00	700.00
NNO	Death Squad Commander	150.00	300.00
NNO	Jawa	225.00	450.00
NNO	Luke Skywalker (blond hair)	400.00	800.00
NNO	Princess Leia	300.00	600.00
NNO	Stormtrooper	200.00	400.00
NNO	Tusken Raider	200.00	350.00
NNO	Greedo	300.00	600.00
NNO	Hammerhead	200.00	400.00
NNO	Luke X-Wing Pilot	300.00	600.00
NNO	Power Droid	300.00	600.00
NNO	R5-D4	250.00	500.00
NNO	Snaggletooth (red)	250.00	500.00
NNO	Walrus Man	200.00	400.00

1977-78 Kenner Star Wars 20-Backs F

NNO	Darth Vader	250.00	500.00
NNO	Princess Leia	200.00	400.00

1977-78 Kenner Star Wars 20-Backs G

NNO	Death Squad Commander	200.00	400.00
NNO	Han Solo (large head)	200.00	350.00
NNO	Jawa	125.00	250.00
NNO	Luke Skywalker (blond hair)	600.00	1200.00
NNO	Tusken Raider	200.00	400.00

1977-78 Kenner Star Wars 20-Backs H

NNO	Tusken Raider	150.00	300.00

1977-78 Kenner Star Wars 20-Backs I

NNO	Jawa	150.00	300.00

1977-78 Kenner Star Wars 20-Backs J

NNO	Jawa	150.00	300.00
NNO	Stormtrooper	250.00	500.00
NNO	Walrus Man	200.00	400.00

1977-78 Kenner Star Wars 20-Backs K

NNO	Jawa	150.00	300.00
NNO	Stormtrooper	200.00	400.00
NNO	Tusken Raider	150.00	300.00

1977-78 Kenner Star Wars 21-Backs A1

NNO	Ben Kenobi (white hair)	200.00	350.00
NNO	Darth Vader	300.00	600.00
NNO	Han Solo (large head)	300.00	600.00
NNO	Jawa	150.00	300.00

1977-78 Kenner Star Wars 21-Backs A2

NNO	Luke Skywalker (blond hair)	300.00	600.00
NNO	R2-D2	250.00	500.00
NNO	Greedo	225.00	450.00
NNO	Hammerhead	150.00	300.00
NNO	Luke X-Wing Pilot	250.00	500.00
NNO	Power Droid	200.00	350.00
NNO	R5-D4	200.00	400.00
NNO	Snaggletooth (red)	200.00	400.00
NNO	Walrus Man	200.00	350.00

1977-78 Kenner Star Wars 21-Backs B

NNO	Boba Fett	4000.00	8000.00
NNO	C-3PO	225.00	450.00
NNO	Darth Vader	300.00	600.00
NNO	Death Squad Commander	250.00	500.00
NNO	Greedo	250.00	500.00
NNO	Hammerhead	150.00	300.00
NNO	Han Solo (large head)	300.00	600.00
NNO	Luke Skywalker (blond hair)	350.00	700.00
NNO	Luke X-Wing Pilot	250.00	500.00
NNO	Power Droid	200.00	400.00
NNO	Princess Leia	300.00	600.00
NNO	R2-D2	150.00	300.00
NNO	R5-D4	250.00	500.00
NNO	Snaggletooth (red)	225.00	450.00
NNO	Tusken Raider	150.00	300.00
NNO	Walrus Man	150.00	300.00

1977-78 Kenner Star Wars 21-Backs C

NNO	Ben Kenobi (white hair)	125.00	250.00
NNO	C-3PO	150.00	300.00
NNO	Chewbacca	225.00	450.00
NNO	Darth Vader	300.00	600.00
NNO	Death Squad Commander	125.00	250.00
NNO	Han Solo (large head)	200.00	350.00
NNO	Luke Skywalker (blond hair)	300.00	600.00
NNO	Princess Leia	250.00	500.00
NNO	R2-D2	200.00	400.00
NNO	Greedo	200.00	400.00
NNO	Luke X-Wing Pilot	200.00	400.00
NNO	Power Droid	500.00	1000.00
NNO	Snaggletooth (red)	150.00	300.00
NNO	Walrus Man	200.00	400.00

1977-78 Kenner Star Wars 21-Backs D

NNO	Luke Skywalker (blond hair)	300.00	600.00

1977-78 Kenner Star Wars 21-Backs E4

NNO	Walrus Man	150.00	300.00

1977-78 Kenner Star Wars 21-Backs E5

NNO	Walrus Man	150.00	300.00

1977-78 Kenner Star Wars 21-Backs F

NNO	Walrus Man	150.00	300.00

1977-78 Kenner Star Wars (loose)

NNO	Ben Kenobi (grey hair)	30.00	60.00
NNO	Ben Kenobi (white hair)	30.00	60.00
NNO	Boba Fett	30.00	75.00
NNO	C-3PO	20.00	40.00
NNO	Chewbacca	20.00	40.00
NNO	Darth Vader	30.00	60.00
NNO	Death Squad Commander	20.00	40.00
NNO	Death Star Droid	15.00	30.00
NNO	Greedo	17.50	35.00
NNO	Hammerhead	15.00	30.00
NNO	Han Solo (large head)	30.00	60.00
NNO	Han Solo (small head)	30.00	60.00
NNO	Jawa	30.00	75.00
NNO	Luke Skywalker (blond hair)	40.00	80.00
NNO	Luke Skywalker (brown hair)	75.00	150.00
NNO	Luke Skywalker X-wing	25.00	50.00
NNO	Power Droid	17.50	35.00
NNO	Princess Leia	50.00	100.00
NNO	R2-D2	20.00	40.00
NNO	R5-D4	15.00	30.00
NNO	Snaggletooth blue	150.00	300.00
	(found in cantina playset)		
NNO	Snaggletooth (red)	20.00	40.00
NNO	Stormtrooper	17.50	35.00
NNO	Tusken Raider	20.00	40.00
NNO	Walrus Man	17.50	35.00

1978 Kenner Star Wars Accessories

NNO	1977 Early Bird Package	3500.00	6000.00
	w/figures Chewbacca, Leia, Luke, R2-D2		
NNO	Mini Collector's Case	200.00	400.00

1978 Kenner Star Wars Accessories (loose)

NNO	Mini Collector's Case	25.00	50.00

1978 Kenner Star Wars Playsets

NNO	Cantina Adventure Set/Greedo	500.00	1000.00
	Snaggletooth blue/Hammerhead		
	Walrusman		
NNO	Creature Cantina Action	300.00	600.00
NNO	Death Star Space Station	250.00	500.00
NNO	Droid Factory	200.00	400.00
NNO	Jawa Sandcrawler (radio controlled)	750.00	1500.00
NNO	Land of the Jawas	125.00	250.00

1978 Kenner Star Wars Playsets (loose)

NNO	Cantina Adventure Set/Greedo	100.00	200.00
	Snaggletooth blue/Hammerhead		
	Walrusman		
NNO	Creature Cantina Action	100.00	200.00
NNO	Death Star Space Station	150.00	300.00
NNO	Droid Factory	75.00	150.00
NNO	Jawa Sandcrawler (radio controlled)	300.00	600.00
NNO	Land of the Jawas	75.00	150.00

1978 Kenner Star Wars Vehicles

NNO	Imperial Troop Transporter	150.00	300.00
NNO	Land Speeder	125.00	250.00
NNO	Millenium Falcon	400.00	800.00
NNO	Patrol Dewback	100.00	200.00
NNO	Sonic Controlled Land Speeder	250.00	500.00
NNO	TIE Fighter	250.00	500.00
NNO	TIE Fighter Darth Vader	150.00	300.00
NNO	X-Wing Fighter	150.00	300.00

1978 Kenner Star Wars Vehicles (loose)

NNO	Imperial Troop Transporter	50.00	100.00
NNO	Land Speeder	30.00	60.00
NNO	Millenium Falcon	75.00	150.00
NNO	Patrol Dewback	30.00	60.00
NNO	Sonic Controlled Land Speeder	100.00	200.00
NNO	TIE Fighter	25.00	50.00
NNO	TIE Fighter Darth Vader	30.00	60.00
NNO	X-Wing Fighter	30.00	60.00

1979-80 Kenner Star Wars 12-Inch

NNO	Ben Kenobi	125.00	250.00
NNO	Boba Fett	400.00	800.00
NNO	C-3PO	100.00	200.00
NNO	Chewbacca	200.00	350.00
NNO	Darth Vader	200.00	400.00
NNO	Han Solo	250.00	500.00
NNO	IG-88	500.00	1000.00
NNO	Jawa	125.00	250.00
NNO	Luke Skywalker	225.00	450.00
NNO	Princess Leia	200.00	400.00
NNO	R2-D2	250.00	500.00
NNO	Stormtrooper	100.00	200.00

1979-80 Kenner Star Wars 12-Inch (loose)

NNO	Ben Kenobi	30.00	75.00
NNO	Boba Fett	150.00	300.00
NNO	C-3PO	25.00	50.00
NNO	Chewbacca	30.00	60.00
NNO	Darth Vader	30.00	60.00
NNO	Han Solo	100.00	200.00
NNO	IG-88	150.00	300.00
NNO	Jawa	50.00	100.00
NNO	Luke Skywalker	30.00	60.00
NNO	Princess Leia	30.00	60.00
NNO	R2-D2	30.00	75.00
NNO	Stormtrooper	25.00	50.00

1980-82 Kenner Star Wars Empire Strikes Back 21-Backs G

NNO	Ben Kenobi	125.00	200.00
NNO	Bespin Security Guard (White)	75.00	150.00
NNO	Boba Fett	1500.00	3000.00
NNO	Bossk	250.00	500.00
NNO	Chewbacca	150.00	300.00
NNO	FX-7	200.00	350.00
NNO	Greedo	125.00	250.00
NNO	Han Solo (Large Head)	150.00	300.00

NNO	Ben Kenobi	150.00	300.00
NNO	Boba Fett	750.00	1500.00
NNO	C-3PO	150.00	300.00
NNO	Chewbacca	125.00	250.00
NNO	Darth Vader	350.00	700.00
NNO	Death Squad Commander	300.00	600.00
NNO	Death Star Droid	125.00	250.00
NNO	Greedo	150.00	300.00
NNO	Hammerhead	150.00	300.00
NNO	Han Solo (Large Head)	150.00	300.00
NNO	Jawa	200.00	400.00
NNO	Luke Skywalker (Blond Hair)	500.00	1000.00
NNO	Luke X-Wing Pilot	150.00	300.00
NNO	Power Droid	200.00	350.00
NNO	Princess Leia	300.00	600.00
NNO	R2-D2	225.00	450.00
NNO	R5-D4	200.00	400.00
NNO	Sand People	150.00	300.00
NNO	Snaggletooth (Red)	150.00	300.00
NNO	Stormtrooper	1200.00	2000.00
NNO	Walrus Man	125.00	250.00

1980-82 Kenner Star Wars Empire Strikes Back 21-Backs H1

NNO	Ben Kenobi	125.00	250.00
NNO	Luke X-Wing Pilot		

1980-82 Kenner Star Wars Empire Strikes Back 21-Backs H2

NNO	Walrus Man	200.00	400.00

1980-82 Kenner Star Wars Empire Strikes Back 21-Backs I

NNO	Boba Fett	1250.00	2500.00
NNO	Greedo	150.00	300.00
NNO	Hammerhead	200.00	400.00

1980-82 Kenner Star Wars Empire Strikes Back 31-Backs A

NNO	Han Solo (Small Head)	125.00	250.00
NNO	Han Solo Hoth	125.00	250.00
NNO	IG-88	200.00	400.00
NNO	Imperial Stormtrooper Hoth	150.00	300.00
NNO	Jawa	125.00	250.00
NNO	Luke X-Wing Pilot	150.00	300.00
NNO	Power Droid	150.00	300.00
NNO	R2-D2		
NNO	R5-D4	250.00	500.00
NNO	Snaggletooth (Red)	100.00	200.00
NNO	Star Destroyer Commander	200.00	350.00
NNO	Stormtrooper	125.00	250.00

1980-82 Kenner Star Wars Empire Strikes Back 31-Backs B

NNO	C-3PO	150.00	300.00
NNO	Darth Vader	125.00	250.00
NNO	Death Star Droid	200.00	400.00
NNO	Hammerhead	125.00	250.00
NNO	Lando Calrissian (Without Teeth)	125.00	250.00
NNO	Luke Bespin (Blond Hair/Walking)	300.00	600.00
NNO	Luke Skywalker (Blond Hair)	350.00	700.00
NNO	Princess Leia	300.00	600.00
NNO	Princess Leia Bespin (Flesh Neck)	200.00	400.00
NNO	Rebel Soldier Hoth	100.00	200.00
NNO	Sand People	125.00	250.00
NNO	Star Destroyer Commander	150.00	300.00
NNO	Stormtrooper	150.00	300.00
NNO	Walrus Man	100.00	200.00

1980-82 Kenner Star Wars Empire Strikes Back 31-Backs C

NNO R5-D4

1980-82 Kenner Star Wars Empire Strikes Back 32-Backs A

NNO	Bespin Security Guard (White)	75.00	150.00
NNO	Boba Fett	1000.00	2000.00
NNO	C-3PO	100.00	200.00
NNO	Chewbacca	75.00	150.00
NNO	FX-7	100.00	200.00
NNO	Han Solo Hoth	100.00	200.00
NNO	IG-88	200.00	350.00
NNO	Luke Skywalker (Blond Hair)	275.00	550.00
NNO	Princess Leia	300.00	600.00
NNO	Rebel Soldier Hoth	75.00	150.00
NNO	Stormtrooper	150.00	300.00
NNO	Walrus Man	100.00	200.00

1980-82 Kenner Star Wars Empire Strikes Back 32-Backs B

NNO Ben Kenobi	100.00	200.00
NNO Bossk	100.00	200.00
NNO Darth Vader	100.00	200.00
NNO Greedo		
NNO Han Solo (Large Head)	225.00	450.00
NNO Imperial Stormtrooper Hoth	125.00	250.00
NNO Lando Calrissian (Without Teeth)		
NNO Luke Bespin (Blond Hair/Gun Drawn)	225.00	450.00
NNO Luke X-Wing Pilot	125.00	250.00
NNO Princess Leia Bespin (Flesh Neck)	125.00	250.00
NNO R2-D2	600.00	1200.00
NNO Star Destroyer Commander	100.00	200.00
NNO Yoda (Orange Snake)	125.00	250.00

1980-82 Kenner Star Wars Empire Strikes Back 32-Backs C

NNO Bespin Security Guard (White)	75.00	150.00
NNO Imperial Stormtrooper Hoth		

1980-82 Kenner Star Wars Empire Strikes Back 41-Backs A

NNO 2-1B	150.00	300.00
NNO 4-LOM		
NNO AT-AT Commander		
NNO AT-AT Driver	125.00	250.00
NNO Ben Kenobi	200.00	350.00
NNO Bespin Security Guard (Black)		
NNO Bespin Security Guard (White)	100.00	200.00

NNO Boba Fett	400.00	800.00
NNO Bossk	75.00	150.00
NNO C-3PO	125.00	250.00
NNO C-3PO (Removable Limbs)		
NNO Chewbacca	100.00	200.00
NNO Cloud Car Pilot		
NNO Darth Vader	250.00	500.00
NNO Death Star Droid	150.00	300.00
NNO Dengar	100.00	200.00
NNO FX-7	150.00	300.00
NNO Greedo	125.00	250.00
NNO Hammerhead	75.00	150.00
NNO Han Solo (Large Head)	250.00	500.00
NNO Han Solo Bespin	200.00	350.00
NNO Han Solo Hoth	100.00	200.00
NNO IG-88	75.00	150.00
NNO Imperial Commander	75.00	150.00
NNO Imperial Stormtrooper Hoth	60.00	120.00
NNO Imperial TIE Fighter Pilot		
NNO Jawa	100.00	200.00
NNO Lando Calrissian (With Teeth)		
NNO Lando Calrissian (Without Teeth)		
NNO Lobot	100.00	200.00
NNO Luke Bespin (Blond Hair/Gun Drawn)	225.00	450.00
NNO Luke Bespin (Brown Hair/Gun Drawn)	300.00	600.00
NNO Luke Hoth		
NNO Luke Skywalker (Blond Hair)	225.00	450.00
NNO Luke X-Wing Pilot	200.00	400.00
NNO Power Droid	100.00	200.00
NNO Princess Leia	200.00	400.00
NNO Princess Leia Hoth	225.00	450.00
NNO R2-D2	200.00	350.00
NNO R2-D2 (Sensorscope)		
NNO R5-D4	150.00	300.00
NNO Rebel Commander	125.00	250.00
NNO Rebel Soldier Hoth	100.00	200.00
NNO Sand People	125.00	250.00
NNO Snaggletooth (Red)	150.00	300.00
NNO Star Destroyer Commander	100.00	200.00
NNO Stormtrooper	250.00	500.00
NNO Walrus Man	125.00	250.00
NNO Yoda (Orange Snake)	125.00	250.00
NNO Zuckuss	125.00	250.00

1980-82 Kenner Star Wars Empire Strikes Back 41-Backs B

NNO 2-1B	125.00	250.00
NNO Boba Fett	500.00	1000.00
NNO Bossk	100.00	200.00
NNO C-3PO	100.00	200.00
NNO FX-7	125.00	250.00
NNO Han Solo (Large Head)	250.00	500.00
NNO Lobot	60.00	120.00
NNO Luke Bespin (Blond Hair/Gun Drawn)	250.00	500.00
NNO Luke X-Wing Pilot	100.00	200.00
NNO Rebel Soldier Hoth	75.00	150.00
NNO Stormtrooper	200.00	400.00
NNO Yoda (Brown Snake)		
NNO Yoda (Orange Snake)	150.00	300.00

1980-82 Kenner Star Wars Empire Strikes Back 41-Backs C

NNO AT-AT Driver	150.00	300.00
NNO Bespin Security Guard (White)	50.00	100.00
NNO Chewbacca	200.00	350.00
NNO Han Solo Hoth	75.00	150.00
NNO IG-88	125.00	250.00
NNO Imperial Commander	60.00	120.00
NNO Jawa	100.00	200.00
NNO Luke Skywalker (Blond Hair)		
NNO Princess Leia	300.00	600.00
NNO Rebel Commander	50.00	100.00
NNO Star Destroyer Commander	100.00	200.00
NNO Ugnaught	75.00	150.00
NNO Walrus Man	125.00	250.00

1980-82 Kenner Star Wars Empire Strikes Back 41-Backs D

NNO 2-1B	100.00	200.00
NNO Boba Fett	1000.00	2000.00
NNO FX-7	60.00	120.00
NNO Han Solo (Large Head)	200.00	350.00
NNO Han Solo Bespin	150.00	300.00
NNO Imperial Stormtrooper Hoth	100.00	200.00
NNO Lando Calrissian (With Teeth)	100.00	200.00
NNO Lobot	75.00	150.00
NNO Luke Bespin (Brown Hair/Gun Drawn)	225.00	450.00
NNO Luke X-Wing Pilot	200.00	400.00
NNO Princess Leia Bespin (Neck Painted/Front)	100.00	200.00
NNO Princess Leia Hoth	200.00	400.00

ACTION FIGURES AND FIGURINES

NNO Rebel Soldier Hoth	75.00	150.00
NNO Stormtrooper	125.00	250.00
NNO Yoda (Brown Snake)	200.00	400.00
NNO Yoda (Orange Snake)	125.00	250.00

1980-82 Kenner Star Wars Empire Strikes Back 41-Backs E

NNO AT-AT Driver	100.00	200.00
NNO Bespin Security Guard (White)	60.00	120.00
NNO C-3PO	200.00	350.00
NNO Chewbacca	200.00	350.00
NNO Dengar	75.00	150.00
NNO Greedo	100.00	200.00
NNO Han Solo Hoth	100.00	200.00
NNO IG-88	100.00	200.00
NNO Imperial Commander	75.00	150.00
NNO Imperial Stormtrooper Hoth	100.00	200.00
NNO Jawa	125.00	250.00
NNO Luke Skywalker (Blond Hair)		
NNO Luke Skywalker (Brown Hair)		
NNO Princess Leia	300.00	600.00
NNO Rebel Commander	75.00	150.00
NNO Rebel Soldier Hoth		
NNO Sand People	75.00	150.00
NNO Snaggletooth (Red)	100.00	200.00
NNO Star Destroyer Commander	150.00	300.00
NNO Ugnaught	60.00	120.00
NNO Walrus Man	125.00	250.00

1980-82 Kenner Star Wars Empire Strikes Back 45-Backs A

NNO 2-1B	75.00	150.00
NNO 4-LOM		
NNO AT-AT Commander	60.00	120.00
NNO Ben Kenobi	125.00	250.00
NNO Bespin Security Guard (Black)	50.00	100.00
NNO Bespin Security Guard (White)	50.00	100.00
NNO Bossk	125.00	250.00
NNO C-3PO		
NNO Chewbacca	125.00	250.00
NNO Cloud Car Pilot	75.00	150.00
NNO Darth Vader	200.00	400.00
NNO Death Star Droid	125.00	250.00
NNO Greedo	125.00	250.00
NNO Hammerhead	100.00	200.00
NNO Han Solo (Large Head)	200.00	350.00
NNO Han Solo Bespin	150.00	300.00
NNO Han Solo Hoth	100.00	200.00
NNO Imperial Commander	60.00	120.00
NNO Imperial Stormtrooper Hoth	125.00	250.00
NNO Imperial TIE Fighter Pilot		
NNO Jawa	150.00	300.00
NNO Lando Calrissian (With Teeth)	75.00	150.00
NNO Lobot	50.00	100.00

NNO Luke Bespin (Blond Hair/Walking)		
NNO Luke Bespin (Brown Hair/Gun Drawn)	225.00	450.00
NNO Luke Hoth	125.00	250.00
NNO Luke Skywalker (Brown Hair)		
NNO Luke X-Wing Pilot	200.00	400.00
NNO Princess Leia	250.00	500.00
NNO Princess Leia Bespin (Flesh Neck)		
NNO Princess Leia Bespin (Neck Painted/Front)	125.00	250.00
NNO Princess Leia Hoth	100.00	200.00
NNO R2-D2		
NNO R2-D2 (Sensorscope)	200.00	400.00
NNO R5-D4	100.00	200.00
NNO Rebel Commander	50.00	100.00
NNO Rebel Soldier Hoth	75.00	150.00
NNO Sand People	100.00	200.00
NNO Snaggletooth (Red)	100.00	200.00
NNO Star Destroyer Commander	125.00	250.00
NNO Stormtrooper	75.00	150.00
NNO Ugnaught	75.00	150.00
NNO Walrus Man	100.00	200.00
NNO Yoda (Brown Snake)	100.00	200.00
NNO Zuckuss		

1980-82 Kenner Star Wars Empire Strikes Back 45-Backs B

NNO AT-AT Commander		
NNO Bespin Security Guard (Black)	75.00	150.00
NNO Darth Vader		
NNO Imperial Stormtrooper Hoth		
NNO Rebel Soldier Hoth		

1980-82 Kenner Star Wars Empire Strikes Back 47-Backs A

NNO 2-1B	75.00	150.00
NNO 4-LOM		
NNO AT-AT Commander	60.00	120.00
NNO AT-AT Driver	75.00	150.00
NNO Ben Kenobi	125.00	250.00
NNO Bespin Security Guard (Black)	50.00	100.00
NNO Bespin Security Guard (White)	60.00	120.00
NNO Boba Fett	1000.00	2000.00
NNO Bossk	75.00	150.00
NNO C-3PO (Removable Limbs)	125.00	250.00
NNO Chewbacca	100.00	200.00
NNO Cloud Car Pilot	75.00	150.00
NNO Darth Vader	150.00	300.00
NNO Death Star Droid	100.00	200.00
NNO Dengar	75.00	150.00
NNO FX-7	100.00	200.00
NNO Greedo	150.00	300.00

NNO Hammerhead	125.00	250.00
NNO Han Solo (Large Head)	225.00	450.00
NNO Han Solo Bespin	200.00	400.00
NNO Han Solo Hoth	125.00	250.00
NNO IG-88	100.00	200.00
NNO Imperial Commander	50.00	100.00
NNO Imperial Stormtrooper Hoth	100.00	200.00
NNO Imperial TIE Fighter Pilot	100.00	200.00
NNO Jawa	75.00	150.00
NNO Lando Calrissian (With Teeth)	75.00	150.00
NNO Lobot	50.00	100.00
NNO Luke Bespin (Brown Hair/Gun Drawn)	225.00	450.00
NNO Luke Hoth	125.00	250.00
NNO Luke Skywalker (Blond Hair)		
NNO Luke Skywalker (Brown Hair)		
NNO Luke X-Wing Pilot	125.00	250.00
NNO Power Droid	75.00	150.00
NNO Princess Leia	250.00	500.00
NNO Princess Leia Bespin (Neck Painted/Front)	150.00	300.00
NNO Princess Leia Hoth	200.00	350.00
NNO R2-D2 (Sensorscope)	150.00	300.00
NNO R5-D4	125.00	250.00
NNO Rebel Commander	60.00	120.00
NNO Rebel Soldier Hoth	60.00	120.00
NNO Sand People	125.00	250.00
NNO Snaggletooth (Red)	125.00	250.00
NNO Star Destroyer Commander	150.00	300.00
NNO Stormtrooper	100.00	200.00
NNO Ugnaught	60.00	120.00
NNO Walrus Man	125.00	250.00
NNO Yoda (Brown Snake)	200.00	350.00
NNO Yoda (Orange Snake)	75.00	150.00

1980-82 Kenner Star Wars Empire Strikes Back 48-Backs A

NNO 2-1B	100.00	200.00
NNO AT-AT Commander	45.00	90.00
NNO Ben Kenobi	75.00	150.00
NNO Bespin Security Guard (Black)	45.00	90.00
NNO Bespin Security Guard (White)		
NNO C-3PO (Removable Limbs)	225.00	450.00
NNO Chewbacca	125.00	250.00
NNO Cloud Car Pilot	75.00	150.00
NNO Han Solo Hoth	100.00	200.00
NNO Imperial Commander	75.00	150.00
NNO Imperial Stormtrooper Hoth	200.00	350.00
NNO Imperial TIE Fighter Pilot	125.00	250.00
NNO Luke Hoth	200.00	350.00
NNO Luke X-Wing Pilot	150.00	300.00
NNO Princess Leia Hoth	125.00	250.00
NNO R2-D2 (Sensorscope)	200.00	350.00
NNO Rebel Commander	75.00	150.00
NNO Sand People	200.00	400.00
NNO Snaggletooth (Red)	100.00	200.00
NNO Stormtrooper	150.00	300.00
NNO Zuckuss	150.00	300.00

1980-82 Kenner Star Wars Empire Strikes Back 48-Backs B

NNO 4-LOM		
NNO Ben Kenobi	125.00	250.00
NNO Bespin Security Guard (Black)	50.00	100.00

NNO	Bespin Security Guard (White)	75.00	150.00
NNO	Bossk	125.00	250.00
NNO	C-3PO (Removable Limbs)	150.00	300.00
NNO	Darth Vader	200.00	400.00
NNO	Dengar	75.00	150.00
NNO	FX-7	75.00	150.00
NNO	Imperial Commander	60.00	120.00
NNO	Imperial Stormtrooper Hoth	100.00	200.00
NNO	Imperial TIE Fighter Pilot	75.00	150.00
NNO	Lando Calrissian (With Teeth)		
NNO	Luke Bespin (Blond Hair/Gun Drawn)		
NNO	Luke Bespin (Brown Hair/Gun Drawn)		
NNO	Luke X-Wing Pilot	125.00	250.00
NNO	Rebel Commander	50.00	100.00
NNO	Rebel Soldier Hoth	60.00	120.00
NNO	Star Destroyer Commander	100.00	200.00
NNO	Stormtrooper	125.00	250.00
NNO	Ugnaught	75.00	150.00
NNO	Yoda (Brown Snake)	200.00	400.00
NNO	Zuckuss	100.00	200.00

1980-82 Kenner Star Wars Empire Strikes Back 48-Backs C

NNO	2-1B	125.00	250.00
NNO	4-LOM	125.00	250.00
NNO	AT-AT Commander	60.00	120.00
NNO	AT-AT Driver	125.00	250.00
NNO	Ben Kenobi (grey hair)	150.00	300.00
NNO	Bespin Security Guard (Black)	50.00	100.00
NNO	Boba Fett	1250.00	2500.00
NNO	Bossk	100.00	200.00
NNO	C-3PO (Removable Limbs)	200.00	400.00
NNO	Chewbacca	150.00	300.00
NNO	Cloud Car Pilot	100.00	200.00
NNO	Darth Vader	125.00	250.00
NNO	FX-7	75.00	150.00
NNO	Han Solo Bespin	125.00	250.00
NNO	Han Solo Hoth	100.00	200.00
NNO	IG-88	150.00	300.00
NNO	Imperial Commander	60.00	120.00
NNO	Imperial TIE Fighter Pilot	125.00	250.00
NNO	Jawa	100.00	200.00
NNO	Lando Calrissian (With Teeth)	75.00	150.00
NNO	Lobot	60.00	120.00
NNO	Luke Bespin (Brown Hair/Gun Drawn)	250.00	500.00
NNO	Luke Hoth	150.00	300.00
NNO	Luke X-Wing Pilot	150.00	300.00
NNO	Rebel Commander	60.00	120.00
NNO	Rebel Soldier Hoth	75.00	150.00
NNO	Sand People	125.00	250.00
NNO	Snaggletooth (Red)	125.00	250.00
NNO	Star Destroyer Commander	150.00	300.00
NNO	Stormtrooper	150.00	300.00
NNO	Ugnaught	75.00	150.00
NNO	Yoda (Brown Snake)	300.00	600.00
NNO	Zuckuss	150.00	300.00

1980-82 Kenner Star Wars Empire Strikes Back (loose)

NNO	2-1B	15.00	30.00
NNO	4-LOM	15.00	30.00
NNO	AT-AT Commander	12.50	25.00

NNO	AT-AT Driver	12.50	25.00
NNO	Bespin guard (black)	15.00	30.00
NNO	Bespin guard (white)	12.50	25.00
NNO	Bossk	15.00	30.00
NNO	C-3PO (removable limbs)	15.00	30.00
NNO	Cloud Car Pilot	30.00	75.00
NNO	Dengar	10.00	20.00
NNO	FX-7	10.00	20.00
NNO	Han Solo (Bespin)	15.00	30.00
NNO	Han Solo (Hoth gear)	12.50	25.00
NNO	IG-88	20.00	40.00
NNO	Imperial Commander	12.50	25.00
NNO	Imperial Stormtrooper (Hoth)	20.00	40.00
NNO	Lando Calrissian	15.00	30.00
NNO	Lando Calrissian (no teeth)	12.50	25.00
NNO	Lobot	10.00	20.00
NNO	Luke Skywalker (Bespin yellow hair tan legs)	25.00	50.00
NNO	Luke Skywalker (Bespin yellow hair brown legs)	25.00	50.00
NNO	Luke Skywalker (Bespin brown hair)	30.00	75.00
NNO	Luke Skywalker (Bespin white shirt blond hair)	25.00	50.00
NNO	Luke Skywalker (Bespin white shirt brown hair)	30.00	75.00
NNO	Luke Skywalker (Hoth gear)	12.50	25.00
NNO	Princess Leia Organa (Bespin flesh neck)	30.00	60.00
NNO	Princess Leia Organa (Bespin turtle neck)	30.00	60.00
NNO	Princess Leia Organa (Bespin gold/green neck)	45.00	90.00
NNO	Leia Organa (Hoth gear)	30.00	60.00
NNO	R2-D2 (sensorscope)	17.50	35.00
NNO	Rebel Commander	10.00	20.00
NNO	Rebel Soldier (Hoth gear)	10.00	20.00
NNO	TIE Fighter Pilot	15.00	30.00
NNO	Ugnaught	15.00	30.00
NNO	Yoda (brown snake)	50.00	100.00
NNO	Yoda (orange snake)	40.00	80.00
NNO	Zuckuss	12.50	25.00

1980-82 Kenner Star Wars Empire Strikes Back Accessories

NNO	Darth Vader Case	100.00	200.00
NNO	Darth Vader Case/Boba Fett/IG88		
NNO	Mini Collector's Case	125.00	250.00

1980-82 Kenner Star Wars Empire Strikes Back Accessories (loose)

NNO	Darth Vader Case
NNO	Mini Collector's Case

1980-82 Kenner Star Wars Empire Strikes Back Playsets

NNO	Cloud City	400.00	800.00
NNO	Dagobah	100.00	200.00
NNO	Darth Vader/ Star Destroyer	250.00	500.00
NNO	Droid Factory	150.00	300.00
NNO	Hoth Ice Planet	100.00	200.00
NNO	Imperial Attack Base	300.00	600.00
NNO	Land of the Jawas	125.00	250.00
NNO	Rebel Command Center	350.00	700.00
NNO	Turret and Probot	100.00	200.00

1980-82 Kenner Star Wars Empire Strikes Back Playsets (loose)

NNO	Cloud City	75.00	150.00
NNO	Dagobah	30.00	60.00
NNO	Darth Vader/ Star Destroyer	60.00	120.00
NNO	Droid Factory	50.00	100.00
NNO	Hoth Ice Planet	30.00	75.00
NNO	Imperial Attack Base	30.00	60.00
NNO	Land of the Jawas	50.00	100.00
NNO	Rebel Command Center	40.00	80.00
NNO	Turret and Probot	30.00	60.00

1980-82 Kenner Star Wars Empire Strikes Back Vehicles

NNO	AT-AT	225.00	450.00
NNO	Imperial Cruiser	125.00	250.00
NNO	Imperial Transport	50.00	100.00
NNO	Millennium Falcon	125.00	250.00
NNO	Rebel Transport	100.00	200.00
NNO	Scout Walker	75.00	150.00
NNO	Slave 1	125.00	250.00
NNO	Snowspeeder (blue box)	75.00	150.00
NNO	Snowspeeder (pink box)	75.00	150.00

NNO Tauntaun	40.00	80.00
NNO Tauntaun (split belly)	75.00	150.00
NNO TIE Fighter	150.00	300.00
NNO Twin Pod Cloud Car	50.00	100.00
NNO Wampa	50.00	100.00
NNO X-Wing Fighter (battle damage red photo background box)	100.00	200.00
NNO X-Wing Fighter (battle damage landscape photo background box)	100.00	200.00

1980-82 Kenner Star Wars Empire Strikes Back Vehicles (loose)

NNO AT-AT	60.00	120.00
NNO Imperial Cruiser	30.00	75.00
NNO Rebel Transport	30.00	60.00
NNO Scout Walker	25.00	50.00
NNO Slave 1	40.00	80.00
NNO Snowspeeder	30.00	60.00
NNO Tauntaun	15.00	30.00
NNO Tauntaun split belly	20.00	40.00
NNO Twin Pod Cloud Car	20.00	40.00
NNO Wampa	15.00	30.00
NNO X-Wing Fighter	30.00	75.00

1980 Kenner Star Wars Empire Strikes Back Micro Set

NNO Bespin Control Room	25.00	50.00
NNO Bespin Freeze Chamber	100.00	200.00
NNO Bespin Gantry	30.00	75.00
NNO Bespin World	150.00	300.00
NNO Death Star Compactor	100.00	200.00
NNO Death Star Escape	50.00	100.00
NNO Death Star World	150.00	300.00
NNO Hoth Generator Attack	40.00	80.00
NNO Hoth Ion Cannon	125.00	250.00
NNO Hoth Turret Defense	75.00	150.00
NNO Hoth Wampa Cave	30.00	75.00
NNO Hoth World	150.00	300.00
NNO Imperial TIE Fighter	75.00	150.00
NNO Millenium Falcon	350.00	700.00
NNO Snowspeeder	200.00	400.00
NNO X-Wing	100.00	200.00

1980 Kenner Star Wars Empire Strikes Back Micro Set (loose)

NNO Bespin Control Room	7.50	15.00
NNO Bespin Freeze Chamber	12.50	25.00
NNO Bespin Gantry	7.50	15.00
NNO Bespin World	12.50	25.00
NNO Death Star Compactor	12.50	25.00
NNO Death Star Escape	7.50	15.00
NNO Death Star World	12.50	25.00
NNO Hoth Generator Attack	7.50	15.00
NNO Hoth Ion Cannon	10.00	20.00
NNO Hoth Turret Defense	6.00	12.00
NNO Hoth Wampa Cave	7.50	15.00
NNO Hoth World	12.50	25.00
NNO Imperial Tie Fighter	6.00	12.00
NNO Millenium Falcon	12.50	25.00
NNO Snowspeeder	6.00	12.00
NNO X-Wing	7.50	15.00
NNO AT-AT	6.00	12.00
NNO AT-AT Operator	.75	2.00
NNO Ben Kenobi	1.50	4.00
NNO Boba Fett	.75	2.00
NNO C-3PO	.75	2.00
NNO Chewbacca	.75	2.00
NNO Chewbacca (with wrench)	.75	2.00
NNO Darth Vader	1.25	3.00
NNO Darth Vader (lightsaber)	1.25	3.00
NNO Darth Vader (unpainted)	1.25	3.00
NNO Han Solo	1.25	3.00
NNO Han Solo (carbonite)	1.25	3.00
NNO Han Solo (in cuffs)	1.25	3.00
NNO Han Solo (stormtrooper)	1.25	3.00
NNO Lando Calrissian	.75	2.00
NNO Lobot	.75	2.00
NNO Luke Skywalker	1.25	3.00
NNO Luke Skywalker (hanging)	1.25	3.00
NNO Luke Skywalker (lightsaber)	1.25	3.00
NNO Luke Skywalker (stormtrooper)	1.25	3.00
NNO Princess Leia	1.25	3.00
NNO Princess Leia (holding gun)	1.25	3.00
NNO Probot	.75	2.00
NNO Rebel (crouching)	.75	2.00
NNO Rebel (gun at side/unpainted)	.75	2.00
NNO Rebel (gun on hip/unpainted)	.75	2.00
NNO Rebel (gun on sholder/unpainted)	.75	2.00
NNO Rebel (gun on shoulder)	.75	2.00
NNO Rebel (laying)	.75	2.00
NNO Rebel (laying unpainted)	.75	2.00
NNO Rebel (on Tauntaun)	.75	2.00
NNO Rebel (on Tauntaun w/blaster)	.75	2.00
NNO Rebel (w/blaster at side)	.75	2.00
NNO Rebel (w/blaster brown)	.75	2.00
NNO Rebel (w/blaster white)	.75	2.00
NNO Stormtrooper	.75	2.00
NNO Stormtrooper (firing)	.75	2.00
NNO Stormtrooper (kneeling)	.75	2.00
NNO Stormtrooper (on gun)	.75	2.00
NNO Stormtrooper (walking)	.75	2.00
NNO TIE Fighter Pilot	.75	2.00
NNO Turret Operator	.75	2.00
NNO Wampa	1.00	2.50
NNO X-Wing Pilot	.75	2.00
NNO X-Wing Pilot (crouching)	.75	2.00
NNO X-Wing Pilot (sitting)	.75	2.00

1980 Kenner Star Wars Empire Strikes Back Mini Rigs

NNO CAP-2	30.00	60.00
NNO INT-4	30.00	60.00
NNO MLC-3	30.00	75.00
NNO MTV-7	25.00	50.00
NNO PDT-8	50.00	100.00
NNO Tripod Laser Canon	20.00	40.00

1980 Kenner Star Wars Empire Strikes Back Mini Rigs (loose)

NNO CAP-2	7.50	15.00
NNO INT-4	10.00	20.00
NNO MLC-3	7.50	15.00
NNO MTV-7	7.50	15.00
NNO PDT-8	10.00	20.00
NNO Tripod Laser Canon	10.00	20.00

1983 Kenner Star Wars Return of the Jedi 48-Backs D

NNO 2-1B	100.00	200.00
NNO 4-LOM	75.00	150.00
NNO AT-AT Commander	50.00	100.00
NNO AT-AT Driver	125.00	250.00
NNO Ben Kenobi	60.00	120.00
NNO Bespin Security Guard (black)	75.00	150.00
NNO Bespin Security Guard (white)		
NNO Boba Fett	1250.00	2500.00
NNO Bossk	125.00	250.00
NNO C-3PO (removable limbs)	60.00	120.00
NNO Chewbacca	100.00	200.00
NNO Cloud Car Pilot	100.00	200.00
NNO Darth Vader	150.00	300.00
NNO Death Star Droid	100.00	200.00
NNO Dengar	30.00	80.00
NNO FX-7	75.00	150.00
NNO Greedo	125.00	250.00
NNO Hammerhead	100.00	200.00
NNO Han Solo (large head)		
NNO Han Solo (Bespin)	150.00	300.00
NNO Han Solo (Hoth gear)	150.00	300.00
NNO IG-88	125.00	250.00
NNO Imperial Commander	75.00	150.00
NNO Imperial Stormtrooper Hoth	150.00	300.00
NNO Imperial TIE Fighter Pilot	60.00	120.00
NNO Jawa	100.00	200.00
NNO Lando Calrissian (with teeth)	60.00	120.00
NNO Lobot	50.00	100.00
NNO Luke Bespin (brown hair gun drawn)	200.00	350.00
NNO Luke Hoth	200.00	400.00
NNO Luke Skywalker (brown hair)	250.00	500.00
NNO Luke X-Wing Pilot		
NNO Power Droid	225.00	450.00
NNO Princess Leia	600.00	1200.00
NNO Princess Leia (Bespin neck painted front)	125.00	250.00
NNO Princess Leia (Hoth)	400.00	800.00
NNO R2-D2 (sensorscope)		
NNO R5-D4	125.00	250.00
NNO Rebel Commander	75.00	150.00

NNO	Sand People	75.00	150.00
NNO	Snaggletooth (red)	75.00	150.00
NNO	Stormtrooper	60.00	120.00
NNO	Ugnaught	75.00	150.00
NNO	Walrus Man	100.00	200.00
NNO	Yoda (brown snake)	300.00	600.00
NNO	Zuckuss	60.00	120.00

1983 Kenner Star Wars Return of the Jedi 65-Backs A

NNO	4-LOM	75.00	150.00
NNO	Admiral Ackbar	50.00	100.00
NNO	AT-AT Driver	125.00	250.00
NNO	Ben Kenobi	100.00	200.00
NNO	Bespin Security Guard (black)	50.00	100.00
NNO	Bib Fortuna	75.00	150.00
NNO	Biker Scout	100.00	200.00
NNO	Boba Fett	1500.00	3000.00
NNO	C-3PO (removable limbs)	75.00	150.00
NNO	Chewbacca	100.00	200.00
NNO	Chief Chirpa	50.00	100.00
NNO	Cloud Car Pilot	75.00	150.00
NNO	Darth Vader	125.00	250.00
NNO	Death Star Droid		
NNO	Dengar		
NNO	Emperor's Royal Guard	60.00	120.00
NNO	Gamorrean Guard	30.00	75.00
NNO	General Madine	30.00	60.00
NNO	Han Solo (large head)	225.00	450.00
NNO	Imperial TIE Fighter Pilot		
NNO	Jawa	100.00	200.00
NNO	Klaatu	40.00	80.00
NNO	Lando Calrisian (skiff)	50.00	100.00
NNO	Logray	35.00	70.00
NNO	Luke Hoth	100.00	200.00
NNO	Luke Jedi Knight (blue lightsaber)	500.00	1000.00
NNO	Luke Jedi Knight (green lightsaber)	150.00	300.00
NNO	Luke X-Wing Pilot	125.00	250.00
NNO	Nien Nunb	50.00	100.00
NNO	Princess Leia (Boushh)	100.00	200.00
NNO	R2-D2 (sensorscope)	100.00	200.00
NNO	Rebel Commando	50.00	100.00
NNO	Ree-Yees	45.00	90.00

NNO	Squid Head	50.00	100.00
NNO	Stormtrooper	100.00	200.00
NNO	Weequay	30.00	60.00
NNO	Yoda (brown snake)	150.00	300.00
NNO	Yoda (brown snake/new image)	75.00	150.00
NNO	Zuckuss	20.00	40.00

1983 Kenner Star Wars Return of the Jedi 65-Backs B

NNO	2-1B	75.00	150.00
NNO	4-LOM	50.00	100.00
NNO	Admiral Ackbar	50.00	100.00
NNO	AT-AT Commander	30.00	75.00
NNO	AT-AT Driver	75.00	150.00
NNO	Ben Kenobi	100.00	200.00
NNO	Bespin Security Guard (black)	50.00	100.00
NNO	Bib Fortuna	30.00	60.00
NNO	Biker Scout	75.00	150.00
NNO	Bossk	100.00	200.00
NNO	C-3PO (removable limbs)	75.00	150.00
NNO	Chewbacca	75.00	150.00
NNO	Chief Chirpa	30.00	75.00
NNO	Cloud Car Pilot	40.00	80.00
NNO	Darth Vader (new image)	150.00	300.00
NNO	Death Star Droid	125.00	250.00
NNO	Emperor's Royal Guard	60.00	120.00
NNO	Gamorrean Guard	30.00	75.00
NNO	General Madine	30.00	75.00
NNO	Han Solo (large head)	200.00	350.00
NNO	Han Solo (Bespin)	100.00	200.00
NNO	Han Solo (Hoth gear)	125.00	250.00
NNO	IG-88	100.00	200.00
NNO	Imperial Commander	30.00	75.00
NNO	Imperial Stormtrooper Hoth	100.00	200.00
NNO	Imperial TIE Fighter Pilot	60.00	120.00
NNO	Jawa	75.00	150.00
NNO	Klaatu	30.00	60.00
NNO	Lando Calrisian (skiff)	50.00	100.00
NNO	Lando Calrissian (with teeth)	60.00	120.00
NNO	Logray	30.00	75.00
NNO	Luke Jedi Knight (blue lightsaber)	350.00	700.00
NNO	Luke Skywalker (blond hair)	300.00	600.00
NNO	Luke X-Wing Pilot	100.00	200.00
NNO	Nien Nunb	50.00	100.00
NNO	Power Droid	75.00	150.00
NNO	Princess Leia (Bespin neck painted/front picture)	125.00	250.00
NNO	Princess Leia (Boushh)	75.00	150.00
NNO	Princess Leia (Hoth gear)	125.00	250.00
NNO	R2-D2 (sensorscope)	100.00	200.00
NNO	R5-D4	100.00	200.00
NNO	Rebel Commander	30.00	75.00
NNO	Rebel Commando	40.00	90.00
NNO	Rebel Soldier Hoth		
NNO	Ree-Yees	30.00	75.00
NNO	Sand People	100.00	200.00
NNO	Squid Head	30.00	60.00
NNO	Star Destroyer Commander	100.00	200.00
NNO	Stormtrooper	100.00	200.00
NNO	Ugnaught	50.00	100.00

NNO	Weequay	30.00	60.00
NNO	Yoda (brown snake)	125.00	250.00
NNO	Zuckuss	60.00	120.00

1983 Kenner Star Wars Return of the Jedi 65-Backs C

NNO	4-LOM	60.00	120.00
NNO	Admiral Ackbar	30.00	75.00
NNO	Ben Kenobi (new image)	100.00	200.00
NNO	Bib Fortuna	40.00	80.00
NNO	Biker Scout	100.00	200.00
NNO	Boba Fett (new image)	1000.00	2000.00
NNO	C-3PO (removable limbs)	100.00	200.00
NNO	Chewbacca (new image)	100.00	200.00
NNO	Chief Chirpa	50.00	100.00
NNO	Darth Vader (new image)	100.00	200.00
NNO	Emperor's Royal Guard	75.00	150.00
NNO	Gamorrean Guard	30.00	75.00
NNO	General Madine	40.00	80.00
NNO	Han Solo (large head/new image)	200.00	400.00
NNO	Imperial TIE Fighter Pilot	75.00	150.00
NNO	Jawa	100.00	200.00
NNO	Klaatu	40.00	80.00
NNO	Klaatu (skiff)		
NNO	Lando Calrisian (skiff)	60.00	120.00
NNO	Logray	40.00	80.00
NNO	Luke Jedi Knight (blue lightsaber)	250.00	500.00
NNO	Luke Jedi Knight (green lightsaber)	125.00	250.00
NNO	Nien Nunb	60.00	120.00
NNO	Princess Leia (Boushh)	75.00	150.00
NNO	R2-D2 (sensorscope)	75.00	150.00
NNO	Rebel Commando	30.00	75.00
NNO	Ree-Yees	35.00	70.00
NNO	Squid Head	40.00	80.00
NNO	Stormtrooper	75.00	150.00
NNO	Weequay	30.00	60.00
NNO	Yoda (brown snake/new image)	200.00	350.00
NNO	Zuckuss	100.00	200.00

1983 Kenner Star Wars Return of the Jedi 65-Backs D

NNO	2-1B	60.00	120.00
NNO	Admiral Ackbar	40.00	80.00
NNO	Biker Scout	100.00	200.00

NNO Chewbacca	120.00	200.00
NNO Chief Chirpa	30.00	75.00
NNO Darth Vader (new image)	125.00	250.00
NNO Gamorrean Guard	30.00	60.00

1983 Kenner Star Wars Return of the Jedi 65-Backs E

NNO General Madine	30.00	60.00

1983 Kenner Star Wars Return of the Jedi 77-Backs A

NNO 2-1B	75.00	150.00
NNO 4-LOM	50.00	100.00
NNO 8D8	30.00	60.00
NNO Admiral Ackbar	30.00	75.00
NNO AT-AT Commander	50.00	100.00
NNO AT-AT Driver	100.00	200.00
NNO AT-ST Driver	30.00	75.00
NNO Ben Kenobi (new image)	100.00	200.00
NNO Bespin Security Guard (black)	50.00	100.00
NNO Bespin Security Guard (white)	60.00	120.00
NNO Bib Fortuna	40.00	80.00
NNO Biker Scout	75.00	150.00
NNO Boba Fett (new image)	1000.00	2000.00
NNO Bossk	100.00	200.00
NNO B-Wing Pilot	30.00	60.00
NNO C-3PO (removable limbs)	75.00	150.00
NNO Chewbacca (new image)	125.00	250.00
NNO Chief Chirpa	35.00	70.00
NNO Cloud Car Pilot	30.00	60.00
NNO Darth Vader (new image)	60.00	120.00
NNO Death Star Droid	30.00	60.00
NNO Dengar	30.00	60.00
NNO Emperor's Royal Guard	40.00	80.00
NNO FX-7	30.00	60.00
NNO Gamorrean Guard	25.00	50.00
NNO General Madine	20.00	40.00
NNO Greedo	40.00	80.00
NNO Hammerhead	25.00	50.00
NNO Han Solo (large head/new image)	100.00	200.00
NNO Han Solo (Bespin)	60.00	120.00
NNO Han Solo (Hoth gear)	60.00	120.00
NNO Han Solo (trench coat)	30.00	60.00
NNO IG-88	20.00	40.00
NNO Imperial Commander	40.00	80.00
NNO Imperial Stormtrooper Hoth	40.00	80.00
NNO Imperial TIE Fighter Pilot	50.00	100.00
NNO Jawa	50.00	100.00
NNO Klaatu	20.00	40.00
NNO Klaatu (skiff)	20.00	40.00
NNO Lando Calrisian (skiff)	25.00	50.00
NNO Lando Calrissian (with teeth)	30.00	60.00
NNO Lobot	30.00	60.00
NNO Logray	20.00	40.00
NNO Luke Bespin (brown hair gun drawn)	150.00	300.00
NNO Luke Hoth	60.00	120.00
NNO Luke Jedi Knight (green lightsaber)	75.00	150.00
NNO Luke Skywalker (blond hair gunner	350.00	600.00
NNO Luke X-Wing Pilot	100.00	200.00
NNO Nien Nunb	25.00	50.00
NNO Nikto	20.00	40.00
NNO Power Droid	50.00	100.00
NNO Princess Leia	450.00	800.00
NNO Princess Leia (Bespin neck painted/front picture)		
NNO Princess Leia (Boushh)	40.00	80.00
NNO Princess Leia (poncho)	40.00	80.00
NNO Princess Leia (Hoth gear)	125.00	250.00
NNO Prune Face	20.00	40.00
NNO R2-D2 (sensorscope)	40.00	80.00
NNO R5-D4	50.00	100.00
NNO Rancor Keeper	20.00	40.00
NNO Rebel Commander	30.00	60.00
NNO Rebel Commando	20.00	40.00
NNO Rebel Soldier Hoth	50.00	100.00
NNO Ree-Yees	20.00	40.00
NNO Sand People	40.00	80.00
NNO Snaggletooth (red)	50.00	100.00
NNO Squid Head	20.00	40.00
NNO Star Destroyer Commander	100.00	200.00
NNO Stormtrooper	50.00	100.00
NNO Teebo	20.00	40.00
NNO The Emperor	40.00	80.00
NNO Ugnaught	40.00	80.00
NNO Walrus Man	30.00	60.00
NNO Weequay	20.00	40.00
NNO Wicket	40.00	80.00
NNO Yoda (brown snake/new image)	60.00	120.00
NNO Zuckuss	20.00	40.00

1983 Kenner Star Wars Return of the Jedi 77-Backs B

NNO 2-1B		
NNO AT-AT Commander	75.00	150.00
NNO AT-ST Driver	40.00	80.00
NNO Bespin Security Guard (black)	30.00	60.00
NNO Bespin Security Guard (white)	60.00	120.00
NNO Biker Scout	75.00	150.00
NNO Chief Chirpa	30.00	75.00
NNO Darth Vader (new image)	125.00	250.00
NNO Dengar	100.00	200.00
NNO FX-7		
NNO Gamorrean Guard	40.00	80.00

NNO General Madine	30.00	75.00
NNO Hammerhead	75.00	150.00
NNO Han Solo (large head/new image)	300.00	600.00
NNO Han Solo (trench coat)	75.00	150.00
NNO Imperial TIE Fighter Pilot		
NNO Klaatu	30.00	60.00
NNO Luke Bespin (brown hair/gun drawn)	200.00	400.00
NNO Luke X-Wing Pilot	125.00	250.00
NNO Nikto	30.00	60.00
NNO Power Droid	100.00	200.00
NNO Princess Leia (poncho)	75.00	150.00
NNO Princess Leia (Hoth gear)	200.00	400.00
NNO Prune Face	30.00	75.00
NNO Rancor Keeper	30.00	75.00
NNO Rebel Soldier Hoth	60.00	120.00
NNO Ree-Yees	30.00	60.00
NNO Snaggletooth (red)	100.00	200.00
NNO Squid Head	40.00	80.00
NNO Stormtrooper	125.00	250.00
NNO Teebo	40.00	80.00
NNO Ugnaught	50.00	100.00
NNO Weequay	25.00	50.00

1983 Kenner Star Wars Return of the Jedi 79-Backs A

NNO 8D8	40.00	80.00
NNO AT-AT Driver	100.00	200.00
NNO AT-ST Driver	50.00	100.00
NNO Ben Kenobi (new image)	100.00	200.00
NNO Boba Fett (new image)	400.00	800.00
NNO B-Wing Pilot	50.00	100.00
NNO C-3PO (removable limbs)	75.00	150.00
NNO Darth Vader (new image)	125.00	250.00
NNO Emperor's Royal Guard	75.00	150.00
NNO Gamorrean Guard	50.00	100.00
NNO Greedo	75.00	150.00
NNO Han Solo Trench Coat	100.00	200.00
NNO Imperial TIE Fighter Pilot	100.00	200.00
NNO Jawa	125.00	250.00
NNO Klaatu	45.00	90.00
NNO Klaatu (skiff)	50.00	100.00
NNO Lando Calrisian (skiff)	60.00	120.00
NNO Lando Calrissian (with teeth)	60.00	120.00
NNO Luke Jedi Knight (green lightsaber)	150.00	300.00
NNO Nikto	40.00	80.00
NNO Princess Leia (Boushh)	60.00	120.00
NNO Princess Leia (poncho)	75.00	150.00
NNO Prune Face	50.00	100.00
NNO Rancor Keeper	25.00	50.00
NNO Ree-Yees	20.00	40.00
NNO Snaggletooth (red)	30.00	75.00
NNO Stormtrooper	75.00	150.00
NNO Teebo	50.00	100.00
NNO The Emperor	100.00	200.00
NNO Ugnaught	60.00	120.00
NNO Walrus Man		
NNO Wicket	100.00	200.00
NNO Yoda (brown snake/new image)	150.00	300.00
NNO Zuckuss	60.00	120.00

1983 Kenner Star Wars Return of the Jedi 79-Backs B

NNO 8D8	50.00	100.00
NNO AT-ST Driver	40.00	80.00
NNO Bib Fortuna	25.00	50.00
NNO B-Wing Pilot	40.00	80.00
NNO Chewbacca (new image)	125.00	250.00
NNO Chief Chirpa	30.00	60.00
NNO Darth Vader (new image)	125.00	250.00
NNO Emperor's Royal Guard	60.00	120.00
NNO Gamorrean Guard	50.00	100.00
NNO Han Solo Bespin		
NNO Klaatu	25.00	50.00
NNO Klaatu (skiff)	40.00	80.00
NNO Lando Calrisian (skiff)	60.00	120.00
NNO Logray	30.00	60.00
NNO Luke Jedi Knight (green lightsaber)	125.00	250.00
NNO Luke X-Wing Pilot	125.00	250.00
NNO Princess Leia (Boushh)	75.00	150.00
NNO Princess Leia (poncho)		
NNO R5-D4		
NNO Rancor Keeper	30.00	60.00
NNO Rebel Commando	45.00	90.00
NNO Ree-Yees	50.00	100.00
NNO Teebo	30.00	75.00
NNO The Emperor	125.00	250.00
NNO Weequay	25.00	50.00
NNO Wicket	60.00	120.00

1983 Kenner Star Wars Return of the Jedi 79-Backs C

NNO Lumat	100.00	200.00
NNO Paploo	75.00	150.00

1983 Kenner Star Wars Return of the Jedi (loose)

NNO 8D8	10.00	20.00
NNO Admiral Ackbar	12.50	25.00
NNO Amanaman	125.00	250.00
NNO Barada	75.00	150.00
NNO Ben Kenobi (blue saber)		
NNO Bib Fortuna	12.50	25.00

NNO Biker Scout (long mask)	25.00	50.00
NNO Biker Scout (short mask)	50.00	100.00
NNO B-Wing Pilot	25.00	50.00
NNO Chief Chirpa	10.00	20.00
NNO Dengar (white face)		
NNO Emperor	10.00	20.00
NNO Emperors Royal Guard	15.00	30.00
NNO Gamorrean Guard	10.00	20.00
NNO General Madine	12.50	25.00
NNO Han Solo (carbonite)	100.00	200.00
NNO Han Solo (trench coat)	20.00	40.00
NNO Imperial Dignitary	60.00	120.00
NNO Imperial Gunner	150.00	300.00
NNO Klaatu	10.00	20.00
NNO Klaatu (skiff)	12.50	25.00
NNO Lando Calrissian (skiff)	10.00	20.00
NNO Logray	10.00	20.00
NNO Luke Skywalker	150.00	300.00
NNO Luke Skywalker (stormtrooper)	60.00	120.00
NNO Luke Skywalker Jedi Knight (blue lightsaber)	40.00	80.00
NNO Luke Skywalker Jedi Knight(green lightsaber)	45.00	90.00
NNO Lumat	10.00	20.00
NNO Nien Nunb	12.50	25.00
NNO Nikto	45.00	90.00
NNO Paploo	20.00	40.00
NNO Princess Leia Organa (Boushh)	30.00	75.00
NNO Princess Leia Organa (poncho)	20.00	40.00
NNO Prune Face	20.00	40.00
NNO Rancor Keeper	10.00	20.00
NNO Rebel Commando	10.00	20.00
NNO Ree-Yees	75.00	150.00
NNO Romba	20.00	40.00
NNO Squid Head	12.50	25.00
NNO Teebo		
NNO Weequay		
NNO Wicket		

1983 Kenner Star Wars Return of the Jedi Accessories

NNO C-3PO Case	125.00	250.00
NNO Chewy Strap	30.00	75.00
NNO Darth Vader Case	125.00	250.00
NNO Jedi Vinyl Case	200.00	350.00
NNO Laser Rifle Case	125.00	250.00

1983 Kenner Star Wars Return of the Jedi Accessories (loose)

NNO C-3PO Case	25.00	50.00
NNO Chewy Strap	15.00	30.00
NNO Darth Vader Case	25.00	50.00
NNO Jedi Vinyl Case	50.00	100.00
NNO Laser Rifle Case	50.00	100.00

1983 Kenner Star Wars Return of the Jedi Playsets

NNO Ewok Village	150.00	300.00
NNO Jabba The Hutt	150.00	300.00
Salacious Crumb		
NNO Jabba The Hutt Dungeon	125.00	250.00
Klaatu/Nikto/8D8		
NNO Jabba The Hutt Dungeon	400.00	800.00
EV-9D9/Amanaman/Barada		

1983 Kenner Star Wars Return of the Jedi Playsets (loose)

NNO Ewok Village	50.00	100.00
NNO Jabba The Hutt	50.00	100.00
NNO Jabba The Hutt Dungeon	30.00	60.00

1983 Kenner Star Wars Return of the Jedi Vehicles

NNO AT-AT	400.00	800.00
NNO B-Wing Fighter	200.00	400.00
NNO Ewok Assault Catapult	50.00	100.00
NNO Ewok Glider	30.00	60.00

NNO Imperial Shuttle	300.00	600.00
NNO Millenium Falcon	150.00	300.00
NNO Rancor	100.00	200.00
NNO Scout Walker	100.00	200.00
NNO Speeder Bike	30.00	75.00
NNO Sy Snootles and the Rebo Band	125.00	250.00
(w/Sy Snootles/Droopy McCool/Max Rebo)		
NNO TIE Fighter (battle damage)	125.00	250.00
NNO TIE Interceptor	150.00	300.00
NNO X-Wing (battle damage)	125.00	250.00
NNO Y-Wing	125.00	250.00

1983 Kenner Star Wars Return of the Jedi Vehicles (loose)

NNO AT-AT	75.00	150.00
NNO B-Wing Fighter	60.00	120.00
NNO Droopy McCool	30.00	60.00
NNO Ewok Assault Catapult	15.00	30.00
NNO Ewok Glider	15.00	30.00
NNO Imperial Shuttle	125.00	250.00
NNO Max Rebo	25.00	50.00
NNO Millenium Falcon	75.00	150.00
NNO Rancor	50.00	100.00
NNO Scout Walker	30.00	60.00
NNO Speeder Bike	20.00	40.00
NNO Sy Snootles	30.00	75.00
NNO TIE Fighter (battle damage)	20.00	40.00
NNO TIE Interceptor	50.00	100.00
NNO X-Wing (battle damage)	30.00	75.00
NNO Y-Wing	50.00	100.00

1983 Kenner Star Wars Return of the Jedi Tri-Logo

NNO 2-1B	30.00	60.00
NNO 8D8	30.00	60.00
NNO A-Wing Pilot	40.00	80.00
NNO Admiral Ackbar	20.00	40.00
NNO Amanaman	100.00	200.00
NNO Anakin Skywalker	25.00	50.00
NNO AT-AT Commander	20.00	40.00
NNO AT-ST Driver	30.00	60.00
NNO B-Wing Pilot	20.00	40.00
NNO Barada	40.00	80.00
NNO Ben Kenobi (blue lightsaber)	60.00	120.00

NNO Bespin Guard (black/ tri-logo back only)	150.00	300.00
NNO Bespin Guard (white/ tri-logo back only)	250.00	500.00
NNO Bib Fortuna	15.00	30.00
NNO Biker Scout (long mask)	30.00	60.00
NNO Boba Fett	350.00	700.00
NNO Bossk	40.00	80.00
NNO C-3PO (removable limbs)	40.00	80.00
NNO Chewbacca	40.00	80.00
NNO Darth Vader	75.00	150.00
NNO Death Star Droid	40.00	80.00
NNO Dengar	25.00	50.00
NNO Emperor	30.00	60.00
NNO Emperors Royal Guard	150.00	300.00
NNO FX-7	30.00	60.00
NNO Gamorrean Guard	30.00	60.00
NNO General Madine	60.00	120.00
NNO Greedo (tri-logo back only)	60.00	120.00
NNO Hammerhead (tri-logo back only)	40.00	80.00
NNO Han Solo	75.00	150.00
NNO Han Solo (carbonite)	250.00	500.00
NNO IG-88	100.00	200.00
NNO Imperial Commander	50.00	100.00
NNO Imperial Dignitary	125.00	250.00
NNO Imperial Gunner	125.00	250.00
NNO Jawa	500.00	1000.00
NNO Klaatu	15.00	30.00
NNO Klaatu (skiff)	25.00	50.00
NNO Lando Calrissian	40.00	80.00
NNO Lando Calrissian (skiff)	30.00	60.00
NNO Lobot	30.00	60.00
NNO Luke Skywalker (Bespin)	200.00	400.00
NNO Luke Skywalker (gunner card)	125.00	250.00
NNO Luke Skywalker (Hoth gear)	200.00	400.00
NNO Luke Skywalker Jedi Knight	40.00	80.00
NNO Luke Skywalker (stormtrooper)	150.00	300.00
NNO Luke Skywalker (poncho)	30.00	60.00
NNO Luke Skywalker X-wing	100.00	200.00
NNO Lumat	30.00	60.00
NNO Nien Nunb	50.00	100.00
NNO Nikto	15.00	30.00
NNO Paploo	15.00	30.00
NNO Princess Leia Organa	60.00	120.00
NNO Princess Leia Organa (Bespin turtle neck)	60.00	120.00
NNO Princess Leia Organa (Boushh)	75.00	150.00
NNO Princess Leia Organa (poncho)	50.00	100.00
NNO Prune Face	25.00	50.00
NNO R2-D2 (sensorscope/blue background card)	20.00	40.00
NNO R2-D2 (sensorscope/sparks card)	75.00	120.00
NNO R5-D4	30.00	60.00
NNO Rancor	20.00	40.00
NNO Rebel Soldier (Hoth gear)	40.00	80.00
NNO Ree-Yees	20.00	40.00
NNO Romba	30.00	60.00
NNO Snowtrooper	30.00	60.00
NNO Squid Head	25.00	50.00
NNO Stormtrooper	100.00	200.00
NNO TIE Fighter Pilot	30.00	60.00
NNO Ugnaught	30.00	60.00

NNO Warok	50.00	100.00
NNO Wicket	40.00	80.00
NNO Yak Face	1200.00	2500.00
NNO Yoda (brown snake)	50.00	100.00
NNO Yoda (orange snake)	500.00	900.00

1985 Kenner Star Wars Droids Cartoon

NNO A-Wing Pilot	500.00	750.00
NNO Boba Fett	4000.00	8000.00
NNO C-3PO	750.00	1500.00
NNO Jann Tosh	125.00	250.00
NNO Jord Dusat	150.00	300.00
NNO Kea Moll	100.00	200.00
NNO Kez-Iban	200.00	400.00
NNO R2-D2	750.00	1500.00
NNO Sise Fromm	600.00	1200.00
NNO Thall Joben	150.00	300.00
NNO Tig Fromm	325.00	650.00
NNO Uncle Gundy	150.00	300.00

1985 Kenner Star Wars Droids Cartoon (loose)

NNO A-Wing Pilot	125.00	250.00
NNO Boba Fett	250.00	500.00
NNO C-3PO	250.00	500.00
NNO Jann Tosh	75.00	150.00
NNO Jord Dusat	60.00	120.00
NNO Kea Moll	60.00	120.00
NNO Kez-Iban	75.00	150.00
NNO R2-D2	300.00	600.00
NNO Sise Fromm	400.00	800.00
NNO Thall Joben	75.00	150.00
NNO Tig Fromm	150.00	300.00
NNO Uncle Gundy	75.00	150.00

1985 Kenner Star Wars Droids Cartoon Coins (loose)

NNO A-Wing Pilot	100.00	200.00
NNO Boba Fett	250.00	500.00
NNO C-3PO	75.00	150.00
NNO Jann Tosh	25.00	60.00
NNO Jord Dusat	20.00	50.00
NNO Kea Moll	20.00	50.00
NNO Kez-Iban	25.00	60.00
NNO R2-D2	75.00	150.00
NNO Sise Fromm	75.00	150.00
NNO Thall Joben	20.00	50.00

NNO Tig Fromm	60.00	120.00
NNO Uncle Gundy	20.00	50.00

1985 Kenner Star Wars Droids Cartoon Vehicles

NNO A-Wing Fighter	600.00	1200.00
NNO ATL Interceptor	300.00	600.00
NNO Sidegunner	200.00	400.00

1985 Kenner Star Wars Droids Cartoon Vehicles (loose)

NNO A-Wing Fighter	300.00	600.00
NNO ATL Interceptor	150.00	300.00
NNO Sidegunner	75.00	150.00

1985 Kenner Star Wars Ewoks Cartoons

NNO Dulok Scout	100.00	200.00
NNO Dulok Shaman	125.00	250.00
NNO King Gorneesh	75.00	150.00
NNO Lady Gorneesh	100.00	200.00
NNO Logray	200.00	350.00
NNO Wicket	300.00	500.00

1985 Kenner Star Wars Ewoks Cartoons (loose)

NNO Dulok Scout	30.00	75.00
NNO Dulok Shaman	60.00	120.00
NNO King Gorneesh	30.00	75.00
NNO Lady Gorneesh	50.00	100.00
NNO Logray	75.00	150.00
NNO Wicket	100.00	200.00

1985 Kenner Star Wars Ewoks Cartoons Coins (loose)

NNO Dulok Scout	10.00	25.00
NNO Dulok Shaman	12.00	30.00
NNO King Gorneesh	10.00	25.00
NNO Lady Gorneesh	10.00	25.00
NNO Logray	12.00	30.00
NNO Wicket	15.00	40.00

1985 Kenner Star Wars Power of the Force

NNO A-Wing Pilot	300.00	600.00
NNO Amanaman	250.00	500.00
NNO Anakin Skywalker	2500.00	5000.00
NNO AT-AT Driver	600.00	1200.00
NNO AT-ST Driver	100.00	200.00
NNO B-Wing Pilot	100.00	200.00
NNO Barada	125.00	250.00
NNO Ben Kenobi (blue saber)	150.00	300.00
NNO Biker Scout	200.00	400.00
NNO C-3PO (removable limbs)	125.00	250.00
NNO Chewbacca	200.00	400.00
NNO Darth Vader	300.00	600.00
NNO Emperor	150.00	300.00
NNO EV-9D9	225.00	450.00
NNO Gamorrean Guard	200.00	400.00
NNO Han Solo (carbonite)	350.00	700.00
NNO Han Solo (trench coat)	300.00	500.00
NNO Imperial Dignitary	125.00	250.00
NNO Imperial Gunner	200.00	400.00
NNO Jawa	125.00	250.00
NNO Lando Calrissian (general)	150.00	300.00
NNO Luke Skywalker (Hoth gear)		
NNO Luke Skywalker (Jedi)	300.00	500.00
NNO Luke Skywalker (poncho)	300.00	500.00
NNO Luke Skywalker (stormtrooper)	750.00	1500.00
NNO Luke Skywalker X-wing	225.00	450.00
NNO Lumat	125.00	250.00
NNO Nikto	1500.00	3000.00
NNO Paploo	150.00	300.00
NNO Princess Leia (poncho)	125.00	250.00
NNO R2-D2 (lightsaber)	750.00	1500.00
NNO Romba	125.00	250.00
NNO Stormtrooper	125.00	250.00
NNO Teebo	200.00	400.00
NNO TIE Fighter Pilot		
NNO Ugnaught		
NNO Warok	200.00	400.00
NNO Wicket	150.00	300.00
NNO Yak Face	3000.00	6000.00
NNO Yoda (brown snake)	1500.00	3000.00

1985 Kenner Star Wars Power of the Force (loose)

NNO A-Wing Pilot	100.00	200.00
NNO Amanaman	150.00	300.00
NNO Anakin Skywalker	30.00	60.00
NNO AT-AT Driver	15.00	30.00
NNO AT-ST Driver	30.00	60.00
NNO B-Wing Pilot	25.00	50.00
NNO Barada	75.00	150.00
NNO Ben Kenobi (blue saber)	20.00	40.00
NNO Biker Scout	15.00	30.00
NNO C-3PO (removable limbs)	25.00	50.00
NNO Chewbacca	15.00	30.00
NNO Darth Vader	25.00	50.00
NNO Emperor	20.00	40.00
NNO EV-9D9	125.00	250.00
NNO Gamorrean Guard	15.00	30.00
NNO Han Solo (carbonite)	150.00	300.00
NNO Han Solo (trench coat)	30.00	60.00
NNO Imperial Dignitary	75.00	150.00
NNO Imperial Gunner	125.00	250.00
NNO Jawa	20.00	40.00
NNO Lando Calrissian (general)	100.00	200.00
NNO Luke Skywalker (Hoth gear)	15.00	30.00
NNO Luke Skywalker (Jedi)	50.00	100.00
NNO Luke Skywalker (poncho)	150.00	300.00
NNO Luke Skywalker (stormtrooper)	250.00	500.00
NNO Luke Skywalker X-wing	20.00	40.00
NNO Lumat	60.00	120.00
NNO Nikto	20.00	40.00
NNO Paploo	60.00	120.00
NNO Princess Leia (poncho)	30.00	75.00
NNO R2-D2 (lightsaber)	300.00	600.00
NNO Romba	100.00	200.00
NNO Stormtrooper	25.00	50.00
NNO Teebo	20.00	40.00
NNO TIE Fighter Pilot	15.00	30.00
NNO Ugnaught	15.00	30.00
NNO Warok	100.00	200.00
NNO Wicket	25.00	50.00
NNO Yak Face	300.00	600.00
NNO Yoda (brown snake)	75.00	150.00

1985 Kenner Star Wars Power of the Force Coins (loose)

NNO A-Wing Pilot	12.00	30.00
NNO Amanaman	15.00	40.00
NNO Anakin Skywalker	200.00	400.00
NNO AT-AT Driver	150.00	300.00
NNO AT-ST Driver	20.00	50.00
NNO B-Wing Pilot	30.00	75.00
NNO Barada	15.00	40.00
NNO Ben Kenobi (blue saber)	75.00	150.00
NNO Biker Scout	30.00	75.00
NNO C-3PO (removable limbs)	25.00	60.00
NNO Chewbacca	30.00	75.00
NNO Darth Vader	50.00	100.00
NNO Emperor	60.00	120.00
NNO EV-9D9	15.00	40.00
NNO Gamorrean Guard	100.00	200.00
NNO Han Solo (carbonite)	30.00	75.00
NNO Han Solo (trench coat)	50.00	100.00
NNO Imperial Dignitary	15.00	40.00
NNO Imperial Gunner	20.00	50.00

NNO	Jawa	75.00	150.00
NNO	Lando Calrissian (general)	12.00	30.00
NNO	Luke Skywalker (Hoth gear)	10.00	20.00
NNO	Luke Skywalker (Jedi)	125.00	250.00
NNO	Luke Skywalker (poncho)	12.00	30.00
NNO	Luke Skywalker (stormtrooper)	15.00	40.00
NNO	Luke Skywalker X-wing	100.00	200.00
NNO	Lumat	30.00	75.00
NNO	Nikto		
NNO	Paploo	20.00	50.00
NNO	Princess Leia (poncho)	25.00	60.00
NNO	R2-D2 (lightsaber)	20.00	50.00
NNO	Romba	10.00	25.00
NNO	Stormtrooper	50.00	100.00

NNO	Teebo	50.00	100.00
NNO	TIE Fighter Pilot	50.00	100.00
NNO	Ugnaught		
NNO	Warok	12.00	30.00
NNO	Wicket	25.00	60.00
NNO	Yak Face	200.00	400.00
NNO	Yoda (brown snake)	75.00	150.00

1985 Kenner Star Wars Power of the Force Vehicles

NNO	Ewok Battle Wagon	300.00	600.00
NNO	Imperial Sniper Vehicle	200.00	400.00
NNO	Sand Skimmer	200.00	350.00
NNO	Security Scout	250.00	500.00
NNO	Tattoine Skiff	600.00	1200.00

1985 Kenner Star Wars Power of the Force Vehicles (loose)

NNO	Ewok Battle Wagon	150.00	300.00
NNO	Imperial Sniper Vehicle	125.00	200.00
NNO	Sand Skimmer	50.00	100.00
NNO	Security Scout	100.00	200.00
NNO	Tattoine Skiff	250.00	500.00

MODERN

2007 Disney Star Wars Disney Characters Series 1

NNO	Donald Duck as Han Solo	12.50	25.00
NNO	Goofy as Darth Vader	10.00	20.00
NNO	Mickey Mouse as Luke Skywalker	12.50	25.00
NNO	Minnie Mouse as Princess Leia	7.50	15.00
NNO	Stitch as Emperor Palpatine	12.50	25.00

2008 Disney Star Wars Disney Characters Series 2

NNO	Donald Duck as Darth Maul		
NNO	Goofy as Jar Jar Binks		
NNO	Mickey Mouse as Anakin Skywalker		
NNO	Minnie Mouse as Padme Amidala		
NNO	Stitch as Yoda		

2009 Disney Star Wars Disney Characters Series 3

NNO	Chip & Dale as Ewoks	20.00	40.00
NNO	Donald Duck as Stormtrooper	12.50	25.00
NNO	Goofy as Chewbacca	15.00	30.00
NNO	Mickey Mouse as Luke Skywalker (X-Wing Pilot)	12.50	25.00
NNO	Minnie Mouse as Slave Leia		

2010 Disney Star Wars Disney Characters Series 4

NNO	Bad Pete as Boba Fett	20.00	40.00
NNO	Donald Duck as Han in Carbonite	10.00	20.00
NNO	Goofy as C-3PO	20.00	40.00
NNO	Mickey Mouse as Jedi Knight Luke Skywalker		
NNO	Minnie Mouse as Princess Leia Boushh	15.00	30.00

2010-15 Disney Star Wars Disney Characters Exclusives

NNO	Bad Pete as Jango Fett	20.00	40.00
	(2015 Star Wars Weekends Exclusive)/2002		
NNO	Donald Duck as Darth Maul	25.00	50.00
	(2012 Star Wars Weekends Exclusive)		

NNO	Donald Duck as Savage Opress	25.00	50.00
	(2012 Star Wars Weekends Exclusive)/2012		
NNO	Donald Duck as Shadow Trooper	30.00	60.00
	(2010 Star Wars Celebration Exclusive)/5000		
NNO	Mickey Mouse and Donald Duck as X-Wing Luke and Han Solo	15.00	30.00
	(2014 Star Wars Weekends Exclusive)/1980		
NNO	Mickey Mouse/Chip & Dale as Luke Skywalker and Ewoks	20.00	40.00
	(2013 Star Wars Weekends Exclusive)/1983		
NNO	Pluto and Minnie Mouse as R2-D2 and Princess Leia	30.00	60.00
	(2015 Star Wars Weekends Exclusive)/1977		
NNO	Stitch as Emperor Palpatine	15.00	30.00
	(2010 Star Wars Weekends Exclusive)/1980		
NNO	Stitch as Hologram Yoda	15.00	30.00
	(2011 Star Tours Opening Exclusive)/2011		

2011 Disney Star Wars Disney Characters Series 5

NNO	Daisy Duck as Aurra Sing	15.00	30.00
NNO	Donald Duck as Commander Cody		
NNO	Goofy as Cad Bane		
NNO	Dewey/Huey/Louie as Jawas	20.00	40.00
NNO	Stitch as General Grievous	25.00	50.00

2012 Disney Star Wars Disney Characters Series 6

NNO	Donald Duck as Darth Maul	20.00	40.00
NNO	Goofy as TC-14	12.50	25.00
NNO	Mickey Mouse as Anakin Skywalker	25.00	50.00
NNO	Minnie Mouse as Queen Amidala	12.50	25.00
NNO	Pluto as R2-D2	20.00	40.00
NNO	Stitch as Yoda		

2015 Disney Star Wars Elite Series

NNO	Anakin Skywalker	25.00	50.00
NNO	Boba Fett (w/cape)	30.00	60.00
NNO	Boba Fett (w/o cape)	10.00	20.00
NNO	Darth Maul	20.00	40.00
NNO	Darth Vader	30.00	60.00

NNO	General Grievous	40.00	80.00
NNO	Prototype Boba Fett	25.00	50.00
NNO	Stormtrooper	15.00	30.00

2015-16 Disney Star Wars Elite Series

NNO	C-3PO	20.00	40.00
NNO	Captain Phasma	12.50	25.00
NNO	Finn	10.00	20.00
NNO	Finn (w/lightsaber)	10.00	20.00
NNO	Flametrooper	15.00	30.00
NNO	FN-2187 (Finn)	12.50	25.00
NNO	Han Solo	10.00	20.00
NNO	Kylo Ren	20.00	40.00
NNO	Kylo Ren (unmasked)	12.00	25.00
NNO	Poe Dameron	10.00	20.00
NNO	R2-D2	20.00	40.00
NNO	Rey and BB-8	12.00	25.00
NNO	Rey and BB-8 (w/lightsaber)	15.00	30.00
NNO	Stormtrooper	15.00	30.00
NNO	Stormtrooper (squad leader)	12.50	25.00
NNO	Stormtrooper (w/riot gear)	12.50	25.00
NNO	Stormtrooper Officer	15.00	30.00
NNO	TIE Fighter Pilot	12.50	25.00

2015-17 Disney Star Wars Elite Series Multipacks and Exclusives

NNO 8-Piece Gift Set	500.00	750.00
Darth Maul/Anakin/Grievous/Stormtrooper		
Vader/C-3PO/R2-D2/Boba Fett)		
(2016 D23 Exclusive)		
NNO Deluxe Gift Set	60.00	120.00
Stormtrooper/Phasma/Kylo Ren/Finn/Flametrooper		
NNO Droid Gift Pack	30.00	75.00
NNO Han Solo & Luke Skywalker w/blond hair		
(Stormtrooper Disguise)	50.00	100.00
NNO Han Solo & Luke Skywalker w/brown hair		
(Stormtrooper Disguise)	25.00	50.00
NNO Princess Leia & Darth Vader/1000*	75.00	150.00
(2017 D23 Exclusive)		

2018-19 Disney Star Wars Elite Series

NNO Gonk Droid	15.00	30.00
NNO R2-D2	25.00	50.00
NNO R4-G9	20.00	40.00
NNO R5-D4	20.00	40.00
NNO TC-14	25.00	50.00

2020 Disney Star Wars Elite Series

NNO Probe Droid		
NNO R5-P8		

2002-04 Hasbro Star Wars Saga 12-Inch

NNO Anakin Skywalker	12.50	25.00
NNO Anakin Skywalker (w/slashing lightsaber)	15.00	30.00
NNO AT-ST Driver	15.00	30.00
NNO Biker Scout	30.00	75.00
NNO Clone Commander	8.00	15.00
NNO Clone Trooper (black-and-white)	12.50	25.00
NNO Clone Trooper (red-and-white)	12.50	25.00
NNO Count Dooku	25.00	50.00
NNO Dengar	12.50	25.00
NNO Ewok 2-Pack (Logray & Keoulkeech)	20.00	40.00
NNO Gamorrean Guard	25.00	50.00
NNO Garindan	20.00	40.00
NNO Geonosian Warrior	12.50	25.00
NNO Han Solo		
NNO Imperial Officer	10.00	20.00
NNO Jango Fett	30.00	75.00
NNO Jango Fett (electronic battling)	20.00	40.00
NNO Jawas	25.00	50.00
NNO Ki-Adi-Mundi	20.00	40.00
NNO Lando Calrissian (Skiff disguise)	12.00	25.00
NNO Luke Skywalker & Tauntaun	50.00	100.00
NNO Luke Skywalker (w/slashing lightsaber)	25.00	50.00
NNO Mace Windu	15.00	30.00
NNO Obi-Wan Kenobi	12.00	25.00
NNO Obi-Wan Kenobi (electronic battling)	10.00	20.00
NNO Obi-Wan Kenobi (Tatooine encounter)	20.00	40.00
NNO Padme Amidala	15.00	30.00
NNO Plo Koon		
NNO Princess Leia (Boushh) & Han Solo (carbonite)	30.00	60.00
NNO Princess Leia (w/speeder bike)	30.00	75.00
NNO Super Battle Droid	12.00	25.00
NNO Yoda (w/hoverchair)	20.00	40.00
NNO Zam Wesell	12.00	25.00
NNO Zuckuss	20.00	40.00

2002-04 Hasbro Star Wars Saga 12-Inch Character Collectibles

NNO Anakin Skywalker		
NNO Darth Vader		
NNO Jango Fett	30.00	60.00
NNO Mace Windu	10.00	20.00

2002-04 Hasbro Star Wars Saga Accessory Sets

NNO Arena Conflict with/Battle Droid brown	12.00	25.00
NNO Death Star (w/Death Star trooper and droids)	10.00	20.00
NNO Endor Victory (w/scout trooper)	10.00	20.00
NNO Hoth Survival (w/Hoth Rebel soldier)	7.50	15.00

2002-04 Hasbro Star Wars Saga Arena Battle Beasts

NNO Acklay	25.00	50.00
NNO Reek	15.00	30.00

2002-04 Hasbro Star Wars Saga Cinema Scenes

NNO Death Star Trash Compactor	20.00	40.00
(Chewbacca & Princess Leia)		
NNO Death Star Trash Compactor (Luke Skywalker & Han Solo)	25.00	50.00
NNO Geonosian War Chamber	12.00	25.00
(Nute Gunray/Passel Argente/Shu Mai)		
NNO Geonosian War Chamber	12.00	25.00
(Poggle the Lesser/Count Dooku/San Hill)		
NNO Jedi High Council (Mace Windu	20.00	40.00
Oppo Rancisis/Even Piell)		
NNO Jedi High Council (Yarael Poof	10.00	20.00
Depa Billaba/Yaddle)		

2002-04 Hasbro Star Wars Saga Collectible Cup Figures

NNO Episode I/Darth Maul	10.00	20.00
NNO Episode II	10.00	20.00
Anakin Skywalker		
NNO Episode IV	10.00	20.00
Obi-Wan Kenobi		
NNO Episode V	10.00	20.00
Luke Skywalker		
NNO Episode VI	12.00	25.00
Princess Leia Organa		

2002-04 Hasbro Star Wars Saga Collection 1 (2002)

2002-04 Hasbro Star Wars Saga 12-Inch Character Collectibles

1 Anakin Skywalker (outland peasant disguise)	6.00	12.00
2 Padme Amidala (arena escape)	6.00	12.00
3 Obi-Wan Kenobi (Coruscant chase)	6.00	12.00
4 C-3PO (protocol droid)	5.00	10.00
5 Kit Fisto (Jedi Master)	5.00	10.00
6 Super Battle Droid	5.00	10.00
17 Clone Trooper	6.00	12.00
18 Zam Wesell (bounty hunter)	6.00	12.00
22 Anakin Skywalker (hangar duel)	12.00	25.00
23 Yoda (Jedi Master)		
27 Count Dooku (Dark Lord)	6.00	12.00
28 Mace Windu (Geonosian rescue)	8.00	15.00
29 Luke Skywalker (Bespin duel)	8.00	15.00
30 Darth Vader (Bespin duel)	6.00	12.00
31 Jango Fett (final battle)	5.00	10.00
36 Obi-Wan Kenobi (Jedi starfighter)	12.00	25.00
37 Han Solo (Endor bunker)		
38 Chewbacca (Cloud City capture w/C-3PO)	6.00	12.00
40 Djas Puhr (bounty hunter)	6.00	12.00
41 Padme Amidala (Coruscant attack)	6.00	12.00
43 Anakin Skywalker (Tatooine attack)	6.00	12.00
47 Jango Fett (Slave-1 pilot)	5.00	10.00
48 Destroyer Droid (Geonosis battle)		
49 Clone Trooper (Republic gunship pilot)	8.00	15.00
53 Yoda (Jedi High Council)		

2002-04 Hasbro Star Wars Saga Collection 1 (2003)

1 Obi-Wan Kenobi (acklay battle)	5.00	10.00
2 Mace Windu (arena confrontation)	5.00	10.00
3 Darth Tyranus (Geonosian escape)	8.00	15.00
7 Anakin Skywalker (secret ceremony)	8.00	15.00
8 Boba Fett (The Pit of Carkoon)	8.00	15.00
9 R2-D2 (droid factory)	6.00	12.00
13 Han Solo (Hoth rescue)		
14 Chewbacca (mynock hunt)	5.00	10.00
17 Luke Skywalker (throne room duel)	5.00	10.00
18 Darth Vader (throne room duel)	6.00	12.00
19 Snowtrooper (The Battle of Hoth)	8.00	15.00
20 Jango Fett (Kamino duel)		
21 C-3PO (Tatooine attack)		

2002-04 Hasbro Star Wars Saga Collection 2 (2002)

7 Boba Fett (Kamino escape)	8.00	15.00
8 Tusken Raider Female (w/Tusken child)	6.00	12.00
9 Captain Typho (Padme's head of security)	5.00	10.00
10 Shaak Ti (Jedi Master)	5.00	10.00
11a Battle Droid (arena battle tan)	5.00	10.00
11b Battle Droid (arena battle brown)	12.00	25.00
12 Plo Koon (arena battle)		
13 Jango Fett (Kamino escape)	8.00	15.00
14 R2-D2 (Coruscant sentry)	8.00	15.00
15 Geonosian Warrior	5.00	10.00
16 Dexter Jettster (Coruscant informant)	5.00	10.00
19 Royal Guard (Coruscant security)	6.00	12.00
20 Saesee Tin (Jedi Master)	5.00	10.00
21 Nikto (Jedi Knight)	6.00	12.00
24 Jar Jar Binks (Gungan Senator)	5.00	10.00
25 Taun We (Kamino cloner)	6.00	12.00
26 Luminara Unduli	5.00	10.00
32 Qui-Gon Jinn (Jedi Master)	6.00	12.00
33a Endor Rebel Soldier (facial hair)		
33a Endor Rebel Soldier (no facial hair)		
34 Massiff (w/Geonosian handler)	8.00	15.00
35 Orn Free Taa (senator)		
39 Supreme Chancellor Palpatine		
42 Darth Maul (Sith training)	5.00	10.00
44 Ki-Adi-Mundi (Jedi Master)	5.00	10.00
45 Ephant Man (Jabba's head of security)		
46 Teemto Pagalies (pod racer)		
50 Watto (Mos Espa junk dealer)	5.00	10.00
51 Lott Dod (Neimoidian Senator)		
52 Tusken Raider (w/massiff)	6.00	12.00
54 Rebel Trooper (Tantive IV defender)		
55 Imperial Officer		
56 Eeth Koth (Jedi Master)		
57 Teebo		

2002-04 Hasbro Star Wars Saga Collection 2 (2003)

4 Padme Amidala (droid factory chase)		
5 SP-4 & JN-66 (research droids)	6.00	12.00
6 Tusken Raider (Tatooine camp ambush)	5.00	10.00
10 Lama Su (w/clone child)	10.00	20.00
11 Aayla Secura (Battle of Geonosis)	8.00	15.00
12 Barriss Offee (Luminara Unduli's Padawan)	6.00	12.00
15 Yoda and Chian (Padawan lightsaber training)		
16 Ashla & Jempa (Jedi Padawans)	8.00	15.00
22 Padme Amidala (secret ceremony)	10.00	20.00
23 Wat Tambor (Geonosis war room)	10.00	20.00
24 Coleman Trebor (Battle of Geonosis)		
25 Darth Maul (Theed hangar duel)	8.00	15.00
26 Princess Leia Organa (Imperial captive)	5.00	10.00
27 Han Solo (fight to Alderaan)		
28 WA-7 (Dexter's diner)	8.00	15.00
29 Lt. Dannl Faytonni (Coruscant Outlander club)		
30 The Emperor (throne room)		
31 Luke Skywalker (Tatooine encounter)	5.00	10.00
32 Darth Vader (Death Star clash)	8.00	15.00
33 Bail Organa (Alderaan Senator)	6.00	12.00
34 Stormtrooper (McQuarrie concept)	8.00	15.00
35 Imperial Dignitary Janus Greejatus (Death Star procession)		
36 Padme Amidala (Lars' homestead)	15.00	30.00
37 Achk Med-Beq (Coruscant Outlander club)	6.00	12.00
38 Ayy Vida (Outlander nightclub patron)	10.00	20.00
39 Obi-Wan Kenobi (Outlander nightclub patron)	6.00	12.00
40 Elan Sleazebaggano (Outlander nightclub encounter)	8.00	15.00
41 Imperial Dignitary Kren Blista-Vanee (Death Star procession)		

2002-04 Hasbro Star Wars Saga Deluxe

NNO Anakin Skywalker (w/Force flipping attack)	4.00	8.00
NNO Anakin Skywalker (w/lightsaber slashing action)	6.00	12.00
NNO C-3PO (w/droid factory assembly line)	4.00	8.00
NNO Clone Trooper (w/speeder bike)	6.00	12.00
NNO Darth Tyranus (w/Force flipping attack)	4.00	8.00
NNO Flying Geonosian (w/sonic blaster and attack pod)	4.00	8.00
NNO Jango Fett (Kamino showdown)	4.00	8.00
NNO Jango Fett (w/electronic backpack and snap-on armor)	4.00	8.00
NNO Mace Windu (w/blast apart droid tan)	4.00	8.00
NNO Mace Windu (w/blast apart droid brown)	4.00	8.00
NNO Nexu (w/snapping jaw and attack roar)	12.00	25.00
NNO Obi-Wan Kenobi (Kamino showdown)	4.00	8.00
NNO Obi-Wan Kenobi (w/Force flipping attack)	4.00	8.00
NNO Spider Droid (w/rotating turret and firing cannon)	4.00	8.00
NNO Super Battle Droid Builder (w/droid factory assembly mold)	4.00	8.00
NNO Yoda (w/Force powers)	10.00	20.00

2002-04 Hasbro Star Wars Saga Exclusives

NNO Boba Fett (silver)	15.00	30.00
(2003 Convention Exclusive)		
NNO C-3PO (Santa) & R2-D2 (reindeer)	12.00	25.00
(2002 Holiday Edition Exclusive)		
NNO Clone Trooper (silver)	6.00	12.00
(2003 Toys R Us Exclusive)		
NNO Clone Trooper/Super Battle Droid	12.00	25.00
(2004 Jedi Con Exclusive)		
NNO Commander Jorg Sacul	20.00	40.00

(2002 Celebration 2 Exclusive)

NNO Darth Vader (silver)   30.00   60.00

(2002 New York Toy Fair Exclusive)

NNO R2-D2 (silver)   15.00   30.00

(2002 Toys R Us Silver Anniversary Exclusive)

NNO Sandtrooper (silver)

(2004 SDCC Exclusive)

NNO Yoda (Santa)

(2003 Holiday Edition Exclusive)

2002-04 Hasbro Star Wars Saga Mos Eisley Cantina Bar

NNO Dr. Evezan

NNO Greedo   8.00   15.00

NNO Kitik Keed'kak

NNO Momaw Nadon

NNO Ponda Baba

NNO Wuher

2002-04 Hasbro Star Wars Saga Multipacks

NNO Endor Soldiers (w/four soldiers paint may vary slightly)

NNO Imperial Forces (Darth Vader   15.00   30.00

Stormtrooper/AT-ST Driver/R4-I9)

NNO Jedi Warriors (Obi-Wan Kenobi   10.00   20.00

Saesee Tiin/Plo Koon/Fi-Ek Sirch)

NNO Light Saber Action Pack

(Anakin Skywalker/Count Dooku/Yoda)

NNO Rebel Troopers Builder Set

NNO Sandtroopers Builder Set

(orange, black, gray, & white shoulder pad)

NNO Skirmish at Karkoon   10.00   20.00

(Han Solo/Klaatu/Nikto/Barada)

NNO Stormtroopers Builder Set

NNO The Battle of Hoth (Luke   20.00   40.00

Leia/Chewbacca/R3-A2/Tauntaun)

NNO Ultimate Bounty (Boba Fett   12.00   25.00

Bossk/IG-88/Aurra Sing w/swoop vehicle)

NNO Value 4-Pack (Zam Wesell

Battle Droid/Kit Fisto/Super Battle Droid)

2002-04 Hasbro Star Wars Saga Playsets

NNO Geonosian Battle Arena   60.00   120.00

2002-04 Hasbro Star Wars Saga Playskool

NNO Arena Adventure   12.00   25.00

NNO Duel with Darth Maul   25.00   50.00

NNO Fast through the Forest   8.00   15.00

NNO Millennium Falcon Adventure   20.00   40.00

NNO The Stompin' Wampa

NNO X-Wing Adventure   25.00   50.00

2002-04 Hasbro Star Wars Saga Re-Issues

NNO Anakin Skywalker (hangar duel)   8.00   15.00

2002 Star Wars Saga Collection 1

NNO C-3PO (Death Star escape)

1997-98 Star Wars Power of the Force Green

NNO Chewbacca (escape from Hoth)

2000-01 Star Wars Power of the Jedi

NNO Darth Maul (Theed hangar duel)

2003 Star Wars Saga Collection 2

NNO Darth Vader (Death Star clash)

2003 Star Wars Saga Collection 2

NNO Han Solo (flight to Alderaan)

2003 Star Wars Saga Collection 2

NNO Luke Skywalker (Tatooine encounter)

2003 Star Wars Saga Collection 2

NNO Obi-Wan Kenobi (Coruscant chase)

2002 Star Wars Saga Collection 1

NNO Princess Leia Organa (Death Star captive)   10.00   20.00

2003 Star Wars Saga Collection 2

NNO R2-D2 (Tatooine mission)

2000-01 Star Wars Power of the Jedi

NNO Stormtrooper (Death Star chase)   8.00   15.00

1998-99 Star Wars Power of the Force

NNO Yoda (Battle of Geonosis)

2002 Star Wars Saga Collection 1

2002-04 Hasbro Star Wars Saga Ultra With Accessories

NNO C-3PO with Escape Pod   12.00   25.00

NNO Ewok (w/attack glider)

NNO General Rieekan (w/Hoth tactical screen)   20.00   40.00

NNO Jabba's Palace Court Denizens

NNO Jabba the Hutt (w/pipe stand)

NNO Jango Fett (Kamino confrontation)

NNO Obi-Wan Kenobi (Kamino confrontation)   15.00   30.00

NNO Wampa (w/Hoth cave)

2002-04 Hasbro Star Wars Saga Vehicles

NNO Anakin Skywalker's Speeder   10.00   20.00

NNO Anakin Skywalker's Swoop Bike (w/Anakin)   20.00   40.00

NNO A-Wing Fighter   20.00   40.00

NNO Darth Tyranus's Speeder Bike (w/Darth Tyranus)   15.00   30.00

NNO Imperial Dogfight TIE Fighter   20.00   40.00

NNO Imperial Shuttle   120.00   200.00

NNO Jango Fett's Slave 1   25.00   50.00

NNO Jedi Starfighter   15.00   30.00

NNO Jedi Starfighter (w/Obi-Wan Kenobi)   20.00   40.00

NNO Landspeeder (w/Luke Skywalker)   20.00   40.00

NNO Luke Skywalker's X-Wing Fighter (w/R2-D2)   60.00   120.00

NNO Red Leader's X-Wing Fighter (w/Red Leader)   30.00   60.00

NNO Republic Gunship   75.00   150.00

NNO TIE Bomber   30.00   75.00

NNO Zam Wesell's Speeder   10.00   20.00

2002-04 Hasbro Star Wars Saga Wave 1 Hoth

1 Hoth Trooper (Hoth evacuation)   8.00   15.00

2 R-3PM (Hoth evacuation)

3 Luke Skywalker (Hoth attack)

2002-04 Hasbro Star Wars Saga Wave 2 Tatooine

4 Luke Skywalker (Jabba's Palace)   6.00   12.00

5 R2-D2 (Jabba's sail barge)   8.00   15.00

6 R1-G4 (Tatooine transaction)

2002-04 Hasbro Star Wars Saga Wave 3 Jabba's Palace

7 Lando Calrissian (Jabba's sail barge)   5.00   10.00

8 Rappertunie (Jabba's Palace)

9 J'Quille (Jabba's sail barge)   12.00   25.00

10 Tanus Spojek

11 TIE Fighter Pildof

2002-04 Hasbro Star Wars Saga Wave 4 Battle of Yavin

12 General Jan Dodonna (Battle of Yavin)

13 Dutch Vander Gold Leader (Battle of Yavin)

14 TIE Fighter Pilot (Battle of Yavin)   6.00   12.00

15 Captain Antilles

2002-04 Hasbro Star Wars Saga Wave 5 Star Destroyer

16 Admiral Ozzel

17 Dengar (executor meeting)

18 Bossk (executor meeting)

2002-04 Hasbro Star Wars Saga Wave 6 Battle of Endor

19 Han Solo (Endor strike)
20 General Madine (Imperial shuttle capture)
21 Lando Calrissian (Death Star attack)   6.00   12.00

2002-07 Hasbro Star Wars Unleashed

NNO Aayla Secura	15.00	30.00
NNO Anakin Skywalker (2005)	15.00	30.00
NNO Anakin Skywalker (rage)	12.00	25.00
NNO Asajj Ventress	15.00	30.00
NNO Aurra Sing	15.00	30.00
NNO Boba Fett	25.00	50.00
NNO Bossk	15.00	30.00
NNO Chewbacca (2004)	10.00	20.00
NNO Chewbacca (2006)	15.00	30.00
NNO Clone Trooper (red)	15.00	30.00
NNO Clone Trooper (white)	12.00	25.00
NNO Count Dooku	15.00	30.00
NNO Darth Maul (fury)	15.00	30.00
NNO Darth Sidious	25.00	50.00
NNO Darth Tyranus (dissension)	6.00	12.00
NNO Darth Vader (2005)	15.00	30.00
NNO Darth Vader (power)	12.00	25.00
NNO Darth Vader (redemption)	30.00	75.00
NNO General Grievous	15.00	30.00
NNO General Grievous	20.00	40.00
(2006 Target Exclusive)		
NNO Han Solo	20.00	40.00
NNO Han Solo Stormtrooper	15.00	30.00
NNO IG-88	15.00	30.00
NNO Jango and Boba Fett (intensity)	15.00	30.00
NNO Luke Skywalker	20.00	40.00
NNO Luke Skywalker (snowspeeder pilot)	15.00	30.00
NNO Mace Windu (honor)	12.00	25.00
NNO Obi-Wan Kenobi (2003)	15.00	30.00
NNO Obi-Wan Kenobi (2005)	15.00	30.00
NNO Padme Amidala (courage)	30.00	60.00
NNO Palpatine vs. Yoda	20.00	40.00
NNO Princess Leia	30.00	75.00

NNO Shock Trooper	15.00	30.00
NNO Stormtrooper	20.00	40.00
NNO Tusken Raider	10.00	20.00
NNO Yoda	15.00	30.00

2003-05 Hasbro Star Wars Clone Wars

NNO Anakin Skywalker	6.00	12.00
NNO ARC Trooper (blue)	5.00	10.00
NNO ARC Trooper (blue w/gray shoulder pad and thick blue chin paint)	5.00	10.00
NNO ARC Trooper (red)	5.00	10.00
NNO Yoda	5.00	10.00
NNO Obi-Wan Kenobi (General of The Republic Army)	4.00	8.00
NNO Durge Commander of the Seperatist Forces	10.00	20.00
NNO Asajj Ventress (Sith Apprentice)	5.00	10.00
NNO Mace Windu (General of the Republic Army)	5.00	10.00
NNO Kit Fisto	8.00	15.00
NNO Clone Trooper (facing left)	8.00	15.00
NNO Clone Trooper (facing right)	30.00	60.00
NNO Saesee Tiin	8.00	15.00

2003-05 Hasbro Star Wars Clone Wars Animated Series

NNO Anakin Skywalker	12.50	25.00
NNO Anakin Skywalker (no sleeves torn pants)	5.00	12.00
NNO ARC Trooper		
NNO Asajj Ventress	12.50	25.00
NNO Clone Trooper	5.00	10.00
NNO Clone Trooper (blue)	12.00	30.00
NNO Clone Trooper (red)		
NNO Clone Trooper (yellow)	6.00	12.00
NNO Count Dooku	5.00	10.00
NNO Durge	5.00	10.00
NNO General Grievous		

NNO Mace Windu	5.00	10.00
NNO Obi-Wan Kenobi		
NNO Yoda		

2003-05 Hasbro Star Wars Clone Wars Animated Series Commemorative DVD Collection

NNO Volume 1 Jedi Force	15.00	30.00
(Anakin Skywalker/ARC Trooper/Obi-Wan Kenobi)		
NNO Volume 1 Sith Attack	12.00	25.00
(Asojj Ventress/Durge/General Grievous)		
NNO Volume 2 (Anakin Skywalker tattoo		
Clone Trooper/Saesee Tiin)		
NNO Volume 2 (Clone Commander Cody		
General Grievous/Obi-Wan Kenobi)		

2003-05 Hasbro Star Wars Clone Wars Animated Series Maquettes

NNO ARC Trooper Captain
NNO Anakin Skywalker
NNO Asajj Ventress
NNO Bariss Offee & Luminara Unduli
NNO General Grievous
NNO Obi-Wan Kenobi
NNO Padme Amidala
NNO Yoda

2003-05 Hasbro Star Wars Clone Wars Deluxe

1 Clone Trooper (w/speeder bike)	8.00	15.00
2 Spider Droid	6.00	12.00
3 Durge (w/swoop bike)	15.00	30.00

ACTION FIGURES AND FIGURINES

2003-05 Hasbro Star Wars Clone Wars Multipacks

NNO	Clone Trooper Army	8.00	15.00
NNO	Clone Trooper Army (w/blue lieutenant)	10.00	20.00
NNO	Clone Trooper Army (w/green sergeant)	8.00	15.00
NNO	Clone Trooper Army (w/red captain)	8.00	15.00
NNO	Clone Trooper Army (w/yellow commander)	8.00	15.00
NNO	Droid Army	6.00	12.00
NNO	Jedi Knight Army	6.00	12.00

2003-05 Hasbro Star Wars Clone Wars Value Packs

NNO	Anakin Skywalker/Clone Trooper (blue)	5.00	10.00
NNO	ARC Trooper/Clone Trooper	10.00	20.00
NNO	Yoda/Clone Trooper (yellow)	5.00	10.00

2003-05 Hasbro Star Wars Clone Wars Vehicles

NNO	Anakin Skywalker's Jedi Starfighter	25.00	50.00
NNO	Armored Assault/ Tank (AAT)	50.00	100.00
NNO	Command Gunship	30.00	75.00
NNO	Geonosian Starfighter	15.00	30.00
NNO	Hailfire Droid	12.00	25.00
NNO	Jedi Starfighter	15.00	30.00

2004-05 Hasbro Star Wars Jedi Force Blue

NNO	Anakin Skywalker (w/Jedi Pod)		
NNO	Anakin Skywalker (w/rescue glider)		
NNO	C-3PO/R2-D2		
NNO	Chewbacca (w/Wookiee Action Tool)		
NNO	Chewbacca (w/Wookiee Scout Flyer)		
NNO	Darth Vader (w/Imperial Claw Droid)		
NNO	Han Solo (w/Jet Bike)		
NNO	Luke Skywalker (w/Jedi Jet Pack)		
NNO	Luke Skywalker (w/Speeder Bike)		
NNO	Luke Skywalker (w/Speeder Board)		
NNO	Luke's X-Wing		
NNO	Mace Windu (w/Jedi Grappling Hook)		
NNO	Obi-Wan Kenobi (w/Boga)		
NNO	Yoda (w/Swamp Stomper)		

2004-05 Hasbro Star Wars Jedi Force White

NNO	Anakin Skywalker/Jar Jar Binks		
NNO	Anakin Skywalker's Jedi Starfighter (w/R2-D2)		
NNO	BARC Speeder Bike (w/Anakin Skywalker)	10.00	20.00
NNO	C-3PO/R2-D2		
NNO	Darth Vader/Stormtrooper		
NNO	Freeco Bike (w/Obi-Wan Kenobi)		
NNO	Han Solo/Chewbacca		
NNO	Landspeeder (w/Luke Skywalker)		
NNO	Millennium Falcon (w/Han Solo/Chewbacca)		
NNO	Obi-Wan Kenobi/Commander Cody		
NNO	Snowspeeder (w/Luke Skywalker/Han Solo)		
NNO	Yoda/Luke Skywalker		

2004-05 Hasbro Star Wars The Original Trilogy Collection

1	Luke Skywalker (Dagobah training)	6.00	12.00
2	Yoda (Dagobah training)	3.00	6.00
3	Spirit Obi-Wan Kenobi	8.00	15.00
4	R2-D2 (Dagobah training)	6.00	12.00
5	Luke Skywalker (X-Wing pilot)	8.00	15.00
6	Luke Skywalker (Jedi Knight)	8.00	15.00
7	Han Solo (Mos Eisley escape)	3.00	6.00
8	Chewbacca (Hoth escape)	6.00	12.00
9	Princess Leia	10.00	20.00
10	Darth Vader (throne room)	8.00	15.00
11	Scout Trooper	6.00	12.00
12	R2-D2	8.00	15.00
13	C-3PO	8.00	15.00
14	Boba Fett	12.00	25.00
15	Obi-Wan Kenobi	12.00	25.00
16	Stormtrooper (Death Star attack)	8.00	15.00
17	Wicket	3.00	6.00
18	Princess Leia (Cloud City)	8.00	15.00
19	Cloud Car Pilot	3.00	6.00
20	Lobot	3.00	6.00
21	TIE Fighter Pilot	8.00	15.00
22	Greedo	6.00	12.00
23	Tusken Raider	10.00	20.00
24	Jawas	3.00	6.00
25	Snowtrooper	6.00	12.00
26	Luke Skywalker (Bespin)	8.00	15.00
27	IG-88	12.00	25.00
28	Bossk	6.00	12.00
29	Darth Vader (Hoth)	10.00	20.00
30	Gamorrean Guard	10.00	20.00
31	Bib Fortuna	3.00	6.00
32	Darth Vader	3.00	6.00
33	Lando Calrissian (skiff guard)	6.00	12.00
34	Princess Leia (sail barge)	15.00	30.00
35	Han Solo (AT-ST driver uniform)	3.00	6.00
36	General Madine	3.00	6.00
37	Lando Calrissian (General)	8.00	15.00
38a	Imperial Trooper (white)	3.00	6.00
38b	Imperial Trooper (gray)	3.00	6.00

2004-05 Hasbro Star Wars The Original Trilogy Collection 12-Inch

1	Boba Fett	30.00	60.00
2	Chewbacca	20.00	40.00
3	Luke Skywalker	20.00	40.00
4	Stormtrooper	15.00	30.00

2004-05 Hasbro Star Wars The Original Trilogy Collection Cards

1 Pablo-Jill/ genosis arena
2 Yarua (Coruscant Senate)
3 Sly Moore (Coruscant Senate)
4 Queen Amidala (celebration ceremony)
5 Rabe (Queen's chambers)
6 Feltipern Trevagg (cantina encounter)
7 Myo (cantina encounter)
8 Dannik Jerrico (cantina encounter)
9 Luke Skywalker (Dagobah training)
10 Darth Vader (Death Star hangar)
11 Stormtrooper (Death Star attack)
12 Sandtrooper (Tatooine search)
13 Scout Trooper (Endor raid)
14 Han Solo (Mos Eisley escape)
15 Chewbacca (Hoth escape)
16 Yoda (Dagobah training)

2004-05 Hasbro Star Wars The Original Trilogy Collection DVD Collection

1 A New Hope		6.00	12.00
2 Empire Strikes Back		10.00	20.00
3 Return of the Jedi		8.00	15.00

2004-05 Hasbro Star Wars The Original Trilogy Collection Exclusives

1 Darth Vader (silver)		10.00	20.00
(2004 Toys R Us Exclusive)			
2 Emperor Palpatine (executor transmission)			
(2004 StarWarsShop.com Exclusive)			
3 Holiday Darth Vader		30.00	60.00
(2005 StarWarsShop.com Exclusive)			
4 Holographic Princess Leia		12.00	25.00
(2005 SDCC Exclusive)			
5 Holiday Edition Jawas		15.00	30.00
(2004 Entertainment Earth Exclusive)			
6 Luke Skywalker's Encounter with Yoda			
(2004 Encuentros Mexico Exclusive)			
7 Wedge Antilles			
(2005 Internet Exclusive)			

2004-05 Hasbro Star Wars The Original Trilogy Collection Multipacks

1 Clone Trooper/Troop Builder 4-Pack		25.00	50.00
Clone Trooper/Clone Trooper/Clone Tr			
2 Clone Trooper Builder 4-Pack (white w/battle damage)		30.00	60.00
3 Clone Trooper Builder 4-Pack (colored)			
4 Clone Trooper Builder 4-Pack (colored w/battle damage)		20.00	40.00
5 Endor Ambush (Han Solo/Logray/Rebel Trooper/Wicket/Speeder)		12.00	25.00
6 Naboo Final Combat (Battle Droid tan		20.00	40.00
Gungan Soldier/Captain Tarpals/Kaad)			

2004-05 Hasbro Star Wars The Original Trilogy Collection Screen Scenes

1 Mos Eisley Cantina I/Dr. Evanzan/Wuher/Kitik Keed'kak		30.00	60.00
2 Mos Eisley Cantina II (Obi-Wan Kenobi/Ponda Baba/Zutton)		30.00	60.00
3 Jedi High Council I (Qui-Gon Jinn/Ki-Adi Mundi/Yoda)			
4 Jedi High Council II (Plo Koon/Obi-Wan Kenobi/Eeth Koth)			
5 Jedi High Council III (Anakin Skywalker/Saesee Tiin/Adi Gallia)			
6 Jedi High Council IV (Shaak Ti/Agen Kolar/Stass Alli)			

2004-05 Hasbro Star Wars The Original Trilogy Collection Transitional

1 Pablo-Jill (Geonosis Arena)		6.00	12.00
2 Yarua (Wookiee Senator)		10.00	20.00
3 Sly Moore		5.00	10.00
4 Queen Amidala (Naboo Celebration)		5.00	10.00
5 Rabe (Royal Handmaiden)		4.00	10.00
6 Feltipern Trevagg (Cantina)		8.00	15.00
7 Myo (Cantina)		8.00	15.00
8 Dannik Jerriko (Cantina Encounter)		8.00	15.00
9 Luke Skywalker (Dagobah Training)			
10 Darth Vader (Death Star Hangar)		15.00	30.00
11 Stormtrooper (Death Star Attack)			
12 Sandtrooper (Tatooine Search)			
13 Scout Trooper (Endor Raid)			
14 Han Solo (Mos Eisley Escape)			
15 Chewbacca (Hoth Escape)		12.00	25.00
16 Yoda (Dagobah Training)			

2004-05 Hasbro Star Wars The Original Trilogy Collection Vehicles

1 Darth Vader's TIE Fighter		30.00	75.00
2 Millennium Falcon			
3 Millennium Falcon (w/Chewbacca/Han/Luke/Obi-Wan/C-3PO/R2-D2)			
(2004 Sam's Club Exclusive)			
4 Sandcrawler (w/RA-7 and Jawas)		100.00	200.00
5 Slave I (w/Boba Fett in tan cape)		75.00	150.00
6 TIE Fighter		30.00	75.00
7 TIE Fighter & X-Wing Fighter		30.00	75.00
8 X-Wing Fighter			
9 Y-Wing Fighter (w/pilot)			

2004-05 Hasbro Star Wars The Original Trilogy Collection Vintage

1 Boba Fett (ROTJ)		15.00	30.00
2 C-3PO (ESB)		6.00	12.00
3 Chewbacca (ROTJ)		12.00	25.00
4 Darth Vader (ESB)		8.00	15.00
5 Han Solo (SW)		6.00	12.00
6 Lando Calrissian (ESB)		12.00	25.00
7 Luke Skywalker (SW)		6.00	12.00
8 Obi-Wan Kenobi (SW)		5.00	10.00
9 Princess Leia Organa (SW)		5.00	10.00
10 R2-D2 (ROTJ)		15.00	30.00
11 Stormtrooper (ROTJ)		8.00	15.00
12 Yoda ESB		6.00	12.00

2004-10 Hasbro Star Wars Galactic Heroes

1 4-LOM/Bossk		8.00	15.00
2 Ahsoka Tano/Captain Rex		20.00	40.00
3 Ahsoka Tano/R3-S6 Goldie		20.00	40.00
4 Anakin Skywalker/Clone Trooper (white)		6.00	12.00
5 Anakin Skywalker/Clone Trooper (blue)		6.00	12.00
6 Anakin Skywalker/Count Dooku		6.00	12.00
7 Anakin Skywalker/STAP			

8 Asajj Ventress/Count Dooku	12.00	25.00
9 AT-AT Commander/AT-AT Driver	8.00	15.00
10 Battle Droid/Clone Trooper	6.00	12.00
11 C-3PO/Chewbacca	8.00	15.00
12 Chewbacca/Clone Trooper	6.00	12.00
13 Chewbacca/Death Star Droid/Mouse Droid	8.00	15.00
14 Chewbacca/Disassembled C-3PO	10.00	20.00
15 Clone Trooper/Dwarf Spider Droid	8.00	15.00
16 Clone Trooper/Mace Windu	12.50	25.00
17 Commander Bly/Aayla Secura	15.00	30.00
18 Dark Side Anakin/Clone Trooper	8.00	12.00
19 Darth Maul/Sith Speeder	8.00	15.00
20 Darth Vader/Holographic Emperor Palpatine		
21 Death Star Trooper/Imperial Officer	6.00	12.00
22 Dengar/Boba Fett	12.00	25.00
23 Duros/Garindan		
24 Emperor Palpatine/Shock Trooper		
25 Emperor Palpatine/Yoda	6.00	15.00
26 Figrin D'an/Hammerhead	6.00	12.00
27 Grand Moff Tarkin/Imperial Officer	5.00	10.00
28 Greedo/Han Solo	15.00	30.00
29 Han Solo/Logray	8.00	15.00
30 IG-86/Clone Commander Thire		
31 IG-88/Zuckuss	6.00	12.00
32 Jango Fett/Obi-Wan Kenobi	8.00	15.00
33 Jar Jar Binks/Destroyer Droid		
34 Jawa/Tusken Raider	6.00	12.00
35 Ki-Adi-Mundi/Commander Bacara		
36 Kit Fisto/General Grievous	8.00	15.00
37 Kit Fisto/Mace Windu	10.00	20.00
38 Luke Skywalker (w/Yoda)/Spirit of Obi-Wan	6.00	12.00
39 Luke Skywalker Stormtrooper/Han Solo Stormtrooper	10.00	20.00
40 Luke Skywalker/Darth Vader	8.00	15.00
41 Luke Skywalker/Gamorrean Guard	6.00	12.00
42 Luke Skywalker/Han Solo		
43 Luke Skywalker/Lando Calrissian	6.00	12.00
44 Luke Skywalker/R2-D2	6.00	12.00
45 Luke Skywalker/Speeder	15.00	30.00
46 Nien Nunb/Admiral Ackbar	10.00	20.00
47 Obi-Wan Kenobi/Clone Commander Cody	15.00	30.00
48 Obi-Wan Kenobi/Clone Trooper (blue Star Wars logo)		
49 Obi-Wan Kenobi/Clone Trooper (red Star Wars logo)		
50 Obi-Wan Kenobi/Darth Maul	8.00	15.00
51 Obi-Wan Kenobi/Darth Vader	6.00	12.00
52 Obi-Wan Kenobi/Durge	6.00	12.00
53 Obi-Wan Kenobi/General Grievous	15.00	30.00
54 Padme Amidala/Anakin Skywalker	12.00	25.00
55 Padme Amidala/Clone Trooper		
56 Padme Amidala/Jar Jar Binks		
57 Plo Koon/Captain Jag	8.00	15.00
58 Ponda Baba/Snaggletooth		
59 Princess Leia (Endor general)/Rebel Commando (Battle of Endor)		
60 Princess Leia Boushh/Han Solo		
61 Princess Leia/Darth Vader		
62 Princess Leia/Han Solo	12.00	25.00
63 R2-D2 (serving tray)/Princess Leia (slave)		
64 R2-D2/Jawas		
65 Royal Guard/Imperial Gunner		

66 Saesee Tiin/Agen Kolar		
67 Sandtrooper/Obi-Wan Kenobi		
68 Scout Trooper/Speeder Bike	6.00	12.00
69 Shaak Ti/Magna Guard	10.00	20.00
70 Skiff Guard/Lando Calrissian	8.00	15.00
71 Snowtrooper/Rebel Trooper		
72 Stormtrooper/Rebel Trooper		
73 Super Battle Droid/Luminara Unduli		
74 Super Battle Droid/R2-D2	8.00	15.00
75 Tarfful/Commander Gree		
76 Wedge/TIE Pilot		
77 Weequay/Barada		
78 Yoda/Clone Trooper		
79 Yoda/Kashyyyk Trooper		

2004-10 Hasbro Star Wars Galactic Heroes Backpack Heroes

1 Boba Fett
2 Darth Tater
3 Darth Vader
4 Han Solo
5 Luke Skywalker
6 Yoda

2004-10 Hasbro Star Wars Galactic Heroes Cinema Scenes

1 Assault on Ryloth	12.50	25.00
2 Assault on the Death Star	12.50	25.00
3 Assault on the Death Star 2	12.50	25.00
4 Battle of Geonosis	12.50	25.00
5 Battle of Hoth	12.50	25.00
6 Battle of Naboo	12.50	25.00
7 Battle of Kashyyyk	30.00	60.00
8 Battle of Mustafar	50.00	100.00
9 Cantina Band	12.50	25.00
10 Cantina Encounter	12.50	25.00
11 Death Star Escape	12.50	25.00
12 Endor Attack	12.50	25.00

13 Endor Celebration	12.50	25.00
14 Escape from Mos Eisley	12.50	25.00
15 Geonosis Battle Arena	12.50	25.00
16 Hoth Snowspeeder Assault	20.00	40.00
17 Jabba's Palace	12.50	25.00
18 Jabba's Sail Barge	12.50	25.00
19 Jabba's Skiff The Pit of Carkoon	30.00	60.00
20 Jedi Starfighter	20.00	40.00
21 Jedi vs. Sith	12.50	25.00
22 Kamino Showdown	12.50	25.00
23 Millennium Falcon	12.50	25.00
24 Purchase of the Droids	12.50	25.00
25 Rancor Pit	12.50	25.00
26 Shadow Squadron Y-Wing	12.50	25.00
27 Slave I and Boba Fett	25.00	50.00
28 Speeder Bike Chase	12.50	25.00
29 Vader's Bounty Hunters	12.50	25.00
30 Vader's TIE Fighter (w/Darth Vader)	12.50	25.00
31 X-Wing Dagobah Landing	12.50	25.00

2004-10 Hasbro Star Wars Galactic Heroes Exclusives

1 Scout Trooper
(2004 SDCC Exclusive)
2 Yoda/R2-D2
(2004 Burger King Exclusive)

2004-10 Hasbro Star Wars Galactic Heroes Singles

1 Anakin Skywalker	5.00	10.00
2 Battle Droid	5.00	10.00
3 Boba Fett	5.00	10.00
4 Bossk	5.00	10.00
5 C-3PO	5.00	10.00
6 Chewbacca	10.00	20.00
7 Clone Trooper	5.00	10.00
8 Darth Maul	8.00	15.00
9 Darth Vader	5.00	10.00
10 Han Solo	5.00	10.00
11 Luke Skywalker	12.50	25.00
12 Obi-Wan Kenobi	5.00	10.00
13 R2-D2	5.00	10.00

2004-10 Hasbro Star Wars Galactic Heroes Stocking Stuffers

1 Darth Vader/Boba Fett/Stormtrooper
2 Han Solo/Chewbacca/C-3PO
3 Luke Skywalker/Yoda/R2-D2
4 Obi-Wan Kenobi/Anakin Skywalker/Shock Trooper

2004-10 Hasbro Star Wars Galactic Heroes Vehicles

1 Anakin's Delta Starfighter	8.00	15.00
2 Landspeeder	8.00	15.00
3 Millennium Falcon	15.00	30.00
4 Obi-Wan's Starfighter	8.00	15.00
5 Snowspeeder	8.00	15.00
6 X-Wing Fighter	10.00	20.00
7 X-Wing Racer	8.00	15.00

2005 Hasbro Star Wars Force Battlers

1 Anakin Skywalker		
2 Chewbacca		
3 Clone Trooper		
4 Darth Vader/ slashing attack		
5 Darth Vader/ missle-launching/ glider cape		
6 Emperor Palpatine		
7 General Grievous		
8 Han Solo		
9 Luke Skywalker	12.00	25.00
10 Mace Windu	8.00	15.00
11 Obi-Wan Kenobi		
12 Yoda		

2005 Hasbro Star Wars M&M's Chocolate Mpire

1 Chewbacca/Mace Windu	6.00	12.00
2 Clone Trooper/Darth Vader	6.00	12.00
3 Count Dooku/Darth Maul	12.00	25.00
4 Emperor Palpatine/Anakin Skywalker	12.00	25.00
5 General Grievous/Obi-Wan Kenobi	8.00	15.00
6 Han Solo/Boba Fett	10.00	20.00
7 Luke Skywalker/Princess Leia	8.00	15.00
8 Queen Amidala/R2-D2/C-3PO	8.00	15.00

2005 Hasbro Star Wars Revenge of the Sith

III1 Obi-Wan Kenobi (slashing attack)	8.00	15.00
III2 Anakin Skywalker (slashing attack straight saber red)	6.00	12.00
III2a Anakin Skywalker (slashing attack bent saber red)	4.00	8.00
III2b Anakin Skywalker (slashing attack bent saber pink)	4.00	8.00
III3 Yoda (firing cannon)	4.00	8.00
III4 Super Battle Droid (firing arm blaster)	10.00	20.00
III5 Chewbacca (Wookiee rage)	8.00	15.00
III6a Clone Trooper (white - quick draw attack)	6.00	12.00
III6b Clone Trooper (red - quick draw attack)	6.00	12.00
III7 R2-D2 (droid attack)	5.00	10.00
III8 Grievous's Bodyguard (battle attack)	4.00	8.00
III9 General Grievous (four lightsaber attack)	4.00	8.00
III10 Mace Windu (Force combat)	6.00	12.00
III11 Darth Vader (lightsaber attack)	4.00	8.00
III12 Emperor Palpatine (firing Force lightning)	5.00	10.00
III13 Count Dooku (Sith Lord)	5.00	10.00
III14 Chancellor Palpatine (supreme chancellor)	4.00	8.00
III15 Bail Organa (Republic Senator)	5.00	10.00
III16 Plo Koon (Jedi Master)	4.00	8.00
III17 Battle Droid (separatist army)	5.00	10.00
III18 C-3PO (protocal droid)	4.00	8.00
III19 Padme republic senator	10.00	20.00
III20 Agen Kolar (Jedi Master)	6.00	12.00
III21 Shaak Ti (Jedi Master)	10.00	20.00
III22 Kit Fisto (Jedi Master)	6.00	12.00
III23a Royal Guard (blue - senate security)	6.00	12.00
III23b Royal Guard (red - senate security)	8.00	15.00
III24 Mon Mothma (Republic Senator)	6.00	12.00
III25 Tarfful (firing bowcaster)	4.00	8.00
III26 Yoda (spinning attack)	6.00	12.00
III27 Obi-Wan Kenobi (Jedi kick)	4.00	8.00
III28 Anakin Skywalker (slashing attack)	8.00	15.00
III29 Ki-Adi-Mundi (Jedi Master)	5.00	10.00
III30 Saesee Tiin (Jedi Master)	5.00	10.00
III31 Luminara Unduli (Jedi Master)	6.00	12.00
III32 Aayla Secura (Jedi Knight)	8.00	15.00
III33a Clone Commander (red - battle gear)	8.00	15.00
III33b Clone Commander (green - battle gear)	8.00	15.00
III34a Clone Pilot (firing cannon)	5.00	10.00
III34b Clone Pilot (black - firing cannon)	5.00	10.00
III35a Palpatine (red lightsaber - lightsaber attack)	6.00	12.00
III35b Palpatine (blue lightsaber - lightsaber attack)	6.00	12.00
III36 General Grievous (exploding body)	10.00	20.00
III37 Vader's Medical Droid (chopper droid)	4.00	8.00
III38 AT-TE Tank Gunner (clone army)	6.00	12.00
III39 Polis Massan (medic droid)	4.00	8.00
III40 Mas Amedda (Republic Senator)	5.00	10.00
III41 Clone Trooper (white - super articulation)	5.00	10.00
III42 Neimoidian Warrior (Neimoidian weapon attack)	4.00	8.00
III43a Warrior Wookie (dark - wookie battle bash)	4.00	8.00
III43b Warrior Wookie (light - wookie battle bash)	12.00	25.00
III44 Destroyer Droid (firing arm blaster)	8.00	15.00
III45 Tarkin (Governor)	4.00	8.00
III46 Ask Aak (Senator)	6.00	12.00
III47 Meena Tills (Senator)	4.00	8.00
III48 R2-D2 (try me electronic)	6.00	12.00
III49 Commander Bacara (quick-draw attack)	5.00	10.00
III50 Anakin Skywalker (battle damaged)	8.00	15.00
III51 Captain Antilles (Senate security)	4.00	8.00
III52 Jett Jukassa (Jedi Padawan)	4.00	8.00
III53 Utapaun Warrior (Utapaun security)	5.00	10.00
III54 AT-RT Driver (missile-firing blaster)	12.00	25.00
III55 Obi-Wan Kenobi (w/pilot gear)	8.00	15.00
III56 Mustafar Sentury (spinning energy bolt)	5.00	10.00
III57 Commander Bly (battle gear)	8.00	15.00
III58 Wookie Commando (Kashyyyk battle gear)	6.00	12.00
III59 Commander Gree (battle gear)	10.00	20.00
III60 Grievous's Bodyguard (battle attack)	6.00	12.00
III61 Passel Argente (separatist leader)	6.00	12.00
III62 Cat Miin (separatist)	4.00	8.00
III63 Neimoidian Commander (separatist bodyguard)	4.00	8.00
III64 R4-P17 (rolling action)	8.00	15.00
III65 Tactical Ops Trooper (Vader's legion)	6.00	12.00
III66 Plo Koon (Jedi hologram transmission)	8.00	15.00
III67 Aayla Secura (Jedi hologram transmission)	5.00	10.00
III68 Wookiee Heavy Gunner (blast attack)	5.00	10.00

2005 Hasbro Star Wars Revenge of the Sith 12-Inch

1	Anakin Skywalker/Darth Vader (ultimate villain)	30.00	60.00
2	Barriss Offee	15.00	30.00
3	Chewbacca	20.00	40.00
	(2005 KB Toys Exclusive)		
4	Clone Trooper	12.00	25.00
5	Darth Sidious		
6	General Grievous	30.00	60.00
7	Shaak Ti	15.00	30.00

2005 Hasbro Star Wars Revenge of the Sith
Accessories

10	Darth Vader Carrying Case (w/Clone Trooper & Anakin Skywalker)	
20	Darth Vader Carrying Case (w/Darth Vader & Obi-Wan Kenobi)	

2005 Hasbro Star Wars Revenge of the Sith
Battle Arena

1	Bodyguard vs. Obi-Wan (Utapau landing platform)	8.00	15.00
2	Dooku vs Anakin (Trade Federation cruiser)	8.00	15.00
3	Sidius vs. Mace (Chancellor's office)	8.00	15.00

2005 Hasbro Star Wars Revenge of the Sith
Battle Packs

NNO	Assault on Hoth (General Veers/Probot/3 Snowtroopers)		
NNO	Attack on Coruscant (5 Clone Troopers)	30.00	60.00
NNO	Imperial Throne Room (Emperor Palpatine		
	Imperial Dignitary/2 Royal Guards/Stormtrooper)		
NNO	Jedi Temple Assault (Anakin/Clone Pilot/3 Special Ops Troopers)		
NNO	Jedi vs. Sith (Anakin/Asajj Ventress	20.00	40.00
	General Grievous/Obi-Wan/Yoda)		

NNO	Jedi vs. Separatists (Anakin/Darth Maul	15.00	30.00
	Jango Fett/Obi-Wan/Mace Windu)		
NNO	Rebel vs. Empire (Chewbacca/Vader/Han/Luke/Stormtrooper)	20.00	40.00

2005 Hasbro Star Wars Revenge of the Sith
Collectible Cup Figures

1	Boba Fett	12.00	25.00
2	Clone Trooper		
3	Darth Vader	10.00	20.00
4	General Grievous		
5	Han Solo	10.00	20.00
6	Obi-Wan Kenobi	10.00	20.00
7	Princess Leia		
8	Stormtrooper	8.00	15.00
9	Yoda	8.00	15.00

2005 Hasbro Star Wars Revenge of the Sith
Commemorative Episode III DVD Collection

1	Jedi Knights (Anakin Skywalker/Mace Windu/Obi-Wan Kenobi)	10.00	20.00
2	Sith Lords (Emperor Palpatine/Darth Vader/Count Dooku)	10.00	20.00
3	Clone Troopers (3 Clone Troopers)	12.00	25.00

2005 Hasbro Star Wars Revenge of the Sith
Creatures

10	Boga (w/Obi-Wan Kenobi)	20.00	40.00

2005 Hasbro Star Wars Revenge of the Sith
Deluxe

1	Anakin Skywalker (changes to Darth Vader)	15.00	30.00
2	Clone Trooper (firing jet pack)	5.00	10.00
3	Clone Troopers (Build Your Army - 3 white)	8.00	15.00
4	Clone Troopers (Build Your Army - 2 white and 1 red)	10.00	20.00
5	Clone Troopers (Build Your Army - 2 white and 1 green)	8.00	15.00
6	Clone Troopers (Build Your Army - 2 white and 1 blue)	12.00	25.00
7	Crab Droid (moving legs/missile launcher)	12.00	25.00
8	Darth Vader (rebuild Darth Vader)	10.00	20.00
9	Emperor Palpatine (changes to Darth Sidious)	8.00	15.00
10	General Grievous (secret lightsaber attack)	15.00	30.00
11	Obi-Wan Kenobi (Force jump attack - w/super battle droid)	5.00	10.00
12	Spider Droid (firing laser action)	5.00	10.00
13	Stass Allie (exploding action - w/BARC speeder)	5.00	10.00
14	Vulture Droid (blue - firing missile launcher)	6.00	12.00
15	Vulture Droid (brown - firing missile launcher)	10.00	20.00
16	Yoda (fly into battle - w/can-cell)	8.00	15.00

2005 Hasbro Star Wars Revenge of the Sith
Evolutions

1	Anakin Skywalker to Darth Vader	12.00	25.00
2	Clone Trooper (Attack of the Clones	15.00	30.00
	Revenge of the Sith/A New Hope)		
3	Clone Trooper (Attack of the Clones	15.00	30.00
	Revenge of the Sith - gray/A New Hope - gray)		
4	Sith Lords (Darth Maul/Darth Tyranus/Darth Sidious)	15.00	30.00

2005 Hasbro Star Wars Revenge of the Sith Exclusives

1 Anakin Skywalker Paris-Mai		
(2005 Star Wars Reunion Convention Exclusive)		
2 Clone Trooper (Neyo logo)		
(2005 Target Exclusive)		
3 Clone Trooper (Sith logo)	12.00	25.00
(2005 Target Exclusive)		
4 Covert Ops Clone Trooper		
(2005 StarWarsShop.com Exclusive)		
5 Darth Vader (Duel at Mustafar)	8.00	15.00
(2005 Target Exclusive)		
6 Darth Vader (lava reflection)	8.00	15.00
(2005 Target Exclusive)		
7 Darth Vader	12.00	25.00
(2005 Celebration III Exclusive)		
8 Holographic Emperor	6.00	12.00
(2005 Toys R Us Exclusive)		
9 Holographic Yoda (Kashyyyk transmission)	6.00	12.00
(2005 Toys R Us Exclusive)		
10 Obi-Wan Kenobi (Duel at Mustafar)	12.00	25.00
(2005 Target Exclusive)		
11 R2-D2 (remote control)		
(2005 Japanese Exclusive)		
12 Utapau Shadow Trooper (super articulation)	10.00	20.00
(2005 Target Exclusive)		

2005 Hasbro Star Wars Revenge of the Sith Kay Bee Toys Collector Packs

1 Luminara Unduli/Count Dooku/Royal Guard/Kit Fisto	20.00	40.00
Darth Vader/Bail Organa/C-3PO/Ki-Adi-Mundi/Chancellor Palpatine		

2005 Hasbro Star Wars Revenge of the Sith Playsets

1 Mustafar Final Duel/Anakin		
Skywalker/Obi-Wan Kenobi		
2 Mustafar Final Duel (w/Obi-Wan	40.00	80.00
Darth Vader/4 Clone Troopers)		

2005 Hasbro Star Wars Revenge of the Sith Promos

1 Anakin Skywalker	
2 Darth Vader	

2005 Hasbro Star Wars Revenge of the Sith Sneak Preview

1 General Grievous	8.00	15.00
2 Tion Medon	4.00	8.00
3 Wookie Warrior	4.00	8.00
4 R4-G9	4.00	8.00
NNO Anakin's Jedi Starfighter (vehicle)	15.00	30.00

2005 Hasbro Star Wars Revenge of the Sith Super Deformed

1 Boba Fett	6.00	12.00
2 C-3PO	6.00	12.00
3 Chewbacca	6.00	12.00
4 Darth Maul	6.00	12.00
5 Darth Vader	6.00	12.00
6 R2-D2	6.00	12.00
7 Stormtrooper	6.00	12.00
8 Yoda	6.00	12.00

2005 Hasbro Star Wars Revenge of the Sith Vehicles

1 Anakin's Jedi Starfighter (w/Anakin)	20.00	40.00
(2005 Toys R Us Exclusive)		
2 ARC-170 Fighter	50.00	100.00
3 ARC-170 Fighter (w/4 Troopers)	75.00	150.00

4 AR-RT/AR-RT Driver		
5 AR-RT/AR-RT Driver (w/Clone Trooper white)		
6 Barc Speeder (w/Barc Trooper & Wookiee warrior)		
7 Barc Speeder (w/Barc Trooper)		
8 Droid Tri-Fighter		
9 Grievous's Wheel Bike (w/General Grievous)	25.00	50.00
10 Millennium Falcon		
11 Obi-Wan's Jedi Starfighter	20.00	40.00
12 Obi-Wan's Jedi Starfighter (w/Obi-Wan)	12.00	25.00
(2005 Toys R Us Exclusive)		
13 Plo Koon's Jedi Starfighter	15.00	30.00
(2005 Target Exclusive)		
14 Republic Gunship	100.00	200.00
15 Wookiee Flyer (w/Wookiee warrior)		

2005 Hasbro Star Wars Special Edition 500th Figure

1 Darth Vader/ meditation chamber	

2005-07 Hasbro Star Wars Unleashed Tubed Packs

NNO Anakin Skywalker	25.00	50.00
NNO ARC Heavy Gunner		
NNO Boba Fett	25.00	50.00
(2006 Target Exclusive)		
NNO Darth Vader	12.00	25.00
(2005 Best Buy Exclusive)		
NNO Darth Vader		
(2006 KB Toys Exclusive)		
NNO Darth Vader	10.00	20.00
(2006 Walmart Exclusive)		
NNO Luke Skywalker		
(2006 Walmart Exclusive)		
NNO Obi-Wan Kenobi	15.00	30.00
NNO Shadow Stormtrooper	8.00	15.00

2005-10 Hasbro Star Wars Transformers

NNO Anakin Skywalker/Jedi Starfighter	12.00	25.00
NNO Boba Fett/Slave One	15.00	30.00
NNO Clone Pilot/ARC-170 Fighter	15.00	30.00
NNO Clone Pilot/ARC-170 Fighter (repaint)	12.00	25.00
NNO Darth Maul/Sith Infiltrator	10.00	20.00
NNO Darth Vader/Death Star	30.00	60.00
NNO Darth Vader/Sith Starfighter	15.00	30.00
NNO Darth Vader/TIE Advanced	12.00	25.00
NNO Emperor Palpatine/Imperial Shuttle	10.00	20.00
NNO General Grievous/Wheel Bike	12.00	30.00
NNO Jango Fett/Slave One	12.00	25.00
NNO Luke Skywalker/Snowspeeder	15.00	30.00

NNO Luke Skywalker/X-Wing Fighter	25.00	50.00	
NNO Obi-Wan Kenobi/Jedi Starfighter	12.00	25.00	

2005-10 Hasbro Star Wars Transformers Deluxe

NNO Han Solo and Chewbacca/Millennium Falcon	30.00	75.00

2006 Hasbro Star Wars Force Battlers

NNO Chewbacca
NNO General Grievous
NNO Jango Fett
NNO Obi-Wan Kenobi

2006 Hasbro Star Wars Force Battlers International

NNO Darth Vader/ with missle-launching/ glider cape
NNO Emperor Palpatine

2006-07 Hasbro Star Wars The Saga Collection

SAGA1 Princess Leia boushh	7.50	15.00
SAGA2 Han Solo carbonite	7.50	15.00
SAGA3 Bib Fortuna	12.50	25.00
SAGA4 Barada skiff	4.00	8.00
SAGA5 Chewbacca/ boushh prisoner	6.00	12.00
SAGA6 Boba Fett	7.50	15.00
SAGA7 General Veers	12.50	25.00
SAGA8 Major Bren Derlin	6.00	12.00
SAGA9 AT-AT Driver	4.00	8.00
SAGA10 R2-D2	6.00	12.00
SAGA11 Snowtrooper	5.00	10.00
SAGA12 General Rieeken	4.00	8.00
SAGA13 Darth Vader	7.50	15.00
SAGA14 Power Droid	10.00	20.00
SAGA15 Sora Bulq	6.00	12.00
SAGA16 Sun Fac	10.00	20.00

SAGA17 C-3PO with/ battle droid head/ droid head on	4.00	8.00
SAGA18 Poggle the Lesser	4.00	8.00
SAGA19 Yoda	7.50	15.00
SAGA20 Jango Fett	5.00	10.00
SAGA21 Scorch	15.00	30.00
SAGA22 Firespeeder Pilot	4.00	8.00
SAGA23 Lushros Dofine	6.00	12.00
SAGA24 Clone Commander Cody/ orange highlights	7.50	15.00
SAGA25 Anakin Skywalker	5.00	10.00
SAGA26 Utapau Clone Trooper	7.50	15.00
SAGA27 Holographic Ki-Adi-Mundi	5.00	10.00
SAGA28 Obi-Wan Kenobi beard	4.00	8.00
SAGA29 Faul Maudama	6.00	12.00
SAGA30 General Grievous	7.50	15.00
SAGA31 Momaw Nadon/ clear cup	5.00	10.00
SAGA32 R5-D4	4.00	8.00
SAGA33 Hem Dazon blue cup	4.00	8.00
SAGA34 Garindan	10.00	20.00
SAGA35 Han Solo	6.00	12.00
SAGA36 Luke Skywalker	12.50	25.00
SAGA37 Sandtrooper	6.00	12.00
SAGA38 Darth Vader bespin/ saber fight	7.50	15.00
SAGA39 Chief Chirpa	10.00	20.00
SAGA40 Moff Jerjerrod	6.00	12.00
SAGA41 Death Star Gunner	7.50	15.00
SAGA42 C-3PO (with/ ewok throne/ unpainted knees)	10.00	20.00
SAGA43 Emperor Palpatine	6.00	12.00
SAGA44 Luke Skywalker	4.00	8.00
SAGA45 Darth Vader/ shocked by emperor	6.00	12.00
SAGA46 Rebel Trooper/ endor black	4.00	8.00
SAGA47 Obi-Wan Kenobi/ no beard	5.00	10.00
SAGA48 Holographic Darth Maul	4.00	8.00
SAGA49 Rep Been	5.00	10.00
SAGA50 Naboo Soldier yellow	6.00	12.00
SAGA51 Dud Bolt & Mars Guo	5.00	10.00
SAGA52 Gragra	7.50	15.00
SAGA53 Sith Training Darth Maul	7.50	15.00
SAGA54 Chewbacca with/ electronic C-3PO	10.00	20.00
SAGA55 Kit Fisto	4.00	8.00
SAGA56 Holographic Clone Commander Cody	5.00	10.00
SAGA57 Clone Trooper 442nd Siege Batallion	20.00	40.00
SAGA58 R5-J2	12.50	25.00
SAGA59 Clone Trooper Fifth Fleet Security/	15.00	30.00
SAGA60 Clone Trooper Sergeant	7.50	15.00
SAGA61 Super Battle Droid	6.00	12.00
SAGA62 Battle Droids (green and yellow)	4.00	8.00
SAGA63 Holographic Obi-Wan Kenobi	7.50	15.00
SAGA64 Commander Oppo (blue highlights/ blue shoulder)	5.00	10.00
SAGA65 Elite Corps Clone Commander	4.00	8.00
SAGA66 R4-K5 Darth Vader's Astromech Droid	4.00	8.00
SAGA67 Padme Amidala	4.00	8.00
SAGA68 Combat Engineer Clone Trooper (brown highlights)	4.00	8.00
SAGA69 Yarael Poof	4.00	8.00
SAGA70 Aurra Sing	4.00	8.00
SAGA71 Kitik Keed'Kak	4.00	8.00
SAGA72 Nabrun Leids & Kabe	4.00	8.00
SAGA73 Labria	4.00	8.00

SAGA74 R4-M6 Mace Windu's Astromech Droid	4.00	8.00
SAGA17a C-3PO with/ battle droid head/ C-3PO head on	4.00	8.00
SAGA31a Momaw Nadon/ blue cup	5.00	10.00
SAGA33a Hem Dazon white cup	4.00	8.00
SAGA42a C-3PO (with/ ewok throne/ painted knees)	10.00	20.00
SAGA46a Rebel Trooper/ endor white	4.00	8.00

2006-07 Hasbro Star Wars The Saga Collection Battle Packs

1 Battle Above the Sarlacc (Boba Fett	150.00	300.00	
2 Jedi vs. Darth Sidious (Darth Sidious	25.00	50.00	
Kit Fisto/Mace Windu/Saesee Tiin)			
3 Sith Lord Attack (Obi-Wan Kenobi	20.00	40.00	
Qui-Gon Jinn/Darth Maul/Battle Droid tan)			

2006-07 Hasbro Star Wars The Saga Collection Battle Packs Exclusives

1 Mace Windu's Attack Batallion (Mace Windu	50.00	100.00	
Clone Trooper purple/ with sk)			
2 Skirmish in the Senate (Emperor Palpatine	20.00	40.00	
Yoda/Clone Trooper red/Clone)			
3 The Hunt for Grievous (Clone Trooper red	30.00	75.00	
Clone Trooper blue/Clone Trooper)			

2006-07 Hasbro Star Wars The Saga Collection Commemorative DVD Collection

1 Luke Skywalker/Darth Vader/Obi-Wan Kenobi	10.00	20.00	
2 Han Solo/Chewbacca/Stormtrooper	10.00	20.00	
3 Luke Skywalker/Emperor Palpatine/R2-D2/C-3PO	15.00	30.00	

2006-07 Hasbro Star Wars The Saga Collection Episode III Greatest Battles Collection

1 501st Legion Trooper (blue with orange feet)	6.00	12.00
2 AT-TE Tank Gunner (gold helmet highlights)	6.00	12.00
3 C-3PO	4.00	8.00
4 Count Dooku	10.00	20.00
5 Royal Guard Blue	5.00	10.00
6 Padme	5.00	10.00

7 R4-G9		4.00	8.00
8 Kit Fisto		6.00	12.00
9 Wookiee Warrior		4.00	8.00
10 R2-D2		6.00	12.00
11 Shock Trooper		12.50	25.00
12 Obi-Wan Kenobi (flight helmet)		4.00	8.00
13 Emperor Palpatine		4.00	8.00
14a Clone Commander (green with skirt sash)		7.50	15.00
14b Clone Commander (red with skirt sash)		10.00	20.00

2006-07 Hasbro Star Wars The Saga Collection
Episode III Heroes & Villains Collection

1 Darth Vader		4.00	8.00
2 Anakin Skywalker		4.00	8.00
3 Yoda		4.00	8.00
4 Commander Bacara		4.00	8.00
5 Clone Trooper		4.00	8.00
6 Clone Pilot black		4.00	8.00
7 Chewbacca		4.00	8.00
8 Obi-Wan Kenobi		4.00	8.00
9 General Grievous cape		4.00	8.00
10 Mace Windu		4.00	8.00
11 R2-D2		4.00	8.00
12 Destroyer Droid		4.00	8.00
9a General Grievous/ no cape		4.00	8.00

2006-07 Hasbro Star Wars The Saga Collection
Exclusives

1 501st Stormtrooper		15.00	30.00
(2006 SDCC Exclusive)			
2 Clone Trooper (Saleucami)			
(2006 Toys R Us French Exclusive)			
3 Darth Vader		30.00	75.00
(2006 UK Woolworth's Exclusive)			
4 Demise of General Grievous		6.00	12.00
(2006 Target Exclusive)			
5 Early Bird Certificate Package			
(2005 Walmart Exclusive)			
6 Early Bird Kit (Luke Skywalker, Princess Leia, Chewbacca, and R2-D2)	30.00	75.00
(2005 Mailaway Exclusive)			
7 George Lucas Stormtrooper		30.00	75.00
(2006 Mailaway Exclusive)			
8 Separation of the Twins Leia Organa (w/Bail Organa)		15.00	30.00
(2005 Walmart Exclusive)			
9 Separation of the Twins Luke Skywalker (w/Obi-Wan Kenobi)		12.50	25.00
(2005 Walmart Exclusive)			

10 Shadow Stormtrooper		12.00	25.00
(2006 Starwarsshop.com Exclusive)			

2006-07 Hasbro Star Wars The Saga Collection
International

SAGA1 Princess Leia Boushh		
SAGA2 Han Solo (in carbonite)		
SAGA3 Bib Fortuna		
SAGA4 Barada Skiff Guard		
SAGA5 Chewbacca (Boushh Prisoner)		
SAGA6 Boba Fett		

2006-07 Hasbro Star Wars The Saga Collection
Multipacks

NNO Droid Pack I/R4-A22/R2-C4/R3-T2/R2-Q2/R3-T6		30.00	60.00
(2006 Entertainment Earth Exclusive)			
NNO Droid Pack II/R4-E1/R2-X2/R2-M5/R2-A6/R3-Y2		30.00	60.00
(2006 Entertainment Earth Exclusive)			
NNO Episode III Gift Pack/Darth Vader		20.00	40.00
General Grievous/Obi-Wan Kenobi/R2-D2			
(2006 UK Woolworth's Exclusive)			
NNO Jedi Knights/Anakin Skywalker			
Mace Windu/Obi-Wan Kenobi			
(2005 UK Argos Exclusive)			
NNO Lucas Collector's Set/Zett Jukassa		12.50	25.00
Baron Papanoida/Terr Taneel/Chi Eekway			
(2006 Starwarsshop.com Exclusive)			
NNO Revenge of the Sith Collector's Set			
(UK Exclusive)			

2006-07 Hasbro Star Wars The Saga Collection
Previews Exclusives

NNO Death Star Briefing (Darth Vader		60.00	125.00
NNO The Hunt For the Millenium Falcon		30.00	60.00
(Darth Vader/Dengar/IG-88/Boba Fett)			
NNO Republic Commando Delta Squad		150.00	300.00
(Delta Three-Eight orange/Scoarch blue)			

2006-07 Hasbro Star Wars The Saga Collection
Ultimate Galactic Hunt

SNOWTROOPER

NNO AT-AT Driver (ESB Stand)		6.00	12.00
NNO Anakin Skywalker (ROTS Stand)		4.00	8.00
NNO Boba Fett (ROTJ Stand)		30.00	60.00
NNO Commander Cody (ROTS Stand)		4.00	8.00
NNO Darth Vader (ESB Stand)		4.00	8.00
NNO General Grievous (ROTS Stand)		6.00	12.00
NNO Han Solo Carbonite (ROTJ Stand)		6.00	12.00
NNO Obi-Wan Kenobi (ROTS Stand)		10.00	20.00
NNO Scorch Republic Commando (SW Stand)		8.00	15.00
NNO Snowtrooper (ESB Stand)		15.00	30.00

2006-07 Hasbro Star Wars The Saga Collection
Ultimate Galactic Hunt Vehicles

NNO Republic Gunship		150.00	300.00
(Toys R Us Exclusive)			

2006-07 Hasbro Star Wars The Saga Collection
Ultimate Galactic Hunt Vintage

NNO Bossk		10.00	20.00
NNO IG-88		12.50	25.00
NNO Han Solo Hoth		15.00	30.00
NNO Luke Skywalker Bespin		15.00	30.00
NNO Princess Leia Organa (Endor combat poncho)		10.00	20.00
NNO Imperial Stormtrooper Hoth		12.50	25.00

2006-07 Hasbro Star Wars The Saga Collection
Vehicles

NNO Anakin's Jedi Starfighter		20.00	40.00
NNO Darth Vader's TIE Advanced X1 Starfighter			
NNO Droid Tri-Fighter			
NNO General Grievous's Wheel Bike			
NNO Obi-Wan's Jedi Starfighter			
NNO Mace Windu's Jedi Starfighter			

2006-07 Hasbro Star Wars The Saga Collection
Vehicles Exclusives

NNO Luke Skywalker's X-Wing w/Luke TRU		75.00	150.00
NNO TIE Fighter w/Pilot TRU			
NNO Imperial Shuttle w/Guard & Vader TAR		250.00	400.00
NNO Kit Fisto's Jedi Starfighter TAR		40.00	80.00
NNO Rogue Two Snowspeeder w/Zev TAR		50.00	100.00

2006-07 Hasbro Star Wars The Saga Collection
Vintage

NNO Biker Scout		8.00	15.00
NNO Greedo		6.00	12.00
NNO Han Solo (w/cape)		6.00	12.00
NNO Luke Skywalker X-Wing Pilot		10.00	20.00
NNO Sand People		6.00	12.00

ACTION FIGURES AND FIGURINES

2006-08 Hasbro Star Wars Unleashed Battle Packs

NNO	Attack on Tantive IV Commanders		
NNO	Attack on Tantive IV Rebel Blockade Troopers		
NNO	Attack on Tantive IV Stormtrooper Boarding Party		
NNO	Battle of Felucia Aayla Secura's 327th Star Corps		
NNO	Battle of Geonosis The Clone Wars		
NNO	Battle of Hoth Evacuation at Echo Base		
NNO	Battle of Hoth Imperial Encounter		
NNO	Battle of Hoth Imperial Invasion		
NNO	Battle of Hoth Imperial Stormtroopers		
NNO	Battle of Hoth Rebel Alliance Troopers		
NNO	Battle of Hoth Snowspeeder Assault		
NNO	Battle of Hoth Snowtrooper Battalion		
NNO	Battle of Hoth Wampa Assault		
NNO	Battle of Kashyyyk Droid Invasion		
NNO	Battle of Kashyyyk and Felucia Heroes	30.00	60.00
NNO	Battle of Kashyyyk Wookiee Warriors	15.00	30.00
NNO	Battle of Kashyyyk Yoda's Elite Clone Troopers		
NNO	Battle of Utapau Battle Droids		
NNO	Battle of Utapau Clone Trooper Attack Battalion	12.50	25.00
NNO	Battle of Utapau Commanders	12.00	25.00
NNO	Battle of Utapau Utapaun Warriors	10.00	20.00
NNO	Clone Wars 501st Legion		
NNO	Clone Wars ARC Troopers		
NNO	Clone Wars Battle of Mon Calamari		
NNO	Clone Wars Clone Pilots and AT-TE Gunners		
NNO	Clone Wars Clone Troopers		
NNO	Clone Wars Jedi Generals		
NNO	Clone Wars Jedi Heroes		
NNO	Clone Wars Jedi vs. Sith	15.00	30.00
NNO	Clone Wars Theed Battle Heroes		
NNO	Clone Wars Vader's Bounty Hunters		
NNO	Death Star Encounters Imperial and Rebel Commanders		
NNO	Death Star Encounters Imperial and Rebel Pilots		
NNO	Death Star Encounters Imperial Troops		
NNO	Order 66 A New Empire		
NNO	Order 66 Jedi Masters	7.50	15.00
NNO	Order 66 Shock Trooper Battalion		
NNO	Order 66 Vader's 501st Legion		
NNO	The Force Unleashed Empire		
NNO	The Force Unleashed Imperial Troopers	30.00	60.00
NNO	The Force Unleashed Unleashed Warriors	125.00	250.00
NNO	Trouble on Tatooine Cantina Encounter		
NNO	Trouble on Tatooine Jawas and Droids		
NNO	Trouble on Tatooine Sandtrooper Search		
NNO	Trouble on Tatooine The Streets of Mos Eisley		
NNO	Trouble on Tatooine Tusken Raiders		
NNO	Ultimate Battles 187th Legion Troopers		
NNO	Ultimate Battles Battle Droid Factory		
NNO	Ultimate Battles Mygeeto Clone Battalion		

2007 Hasbro Star Wars Order 66 Target Exclusives

1	Emperor Palpatine/Commander Thire	12.00	25.00
2	Mace Windu/Galactic Marine	15.00	30.00
3	Darth Vader/Commander Bow	12.00	25.00
4	Obi-Wan Kenobi/AT-RT Driver	10.00	20.00
5	Anakin Skywalker/Airborne Trooper	12.00	25.00
6	Yoda/Kashyyyk Trooper	10.00	20.00

2007 Hasbro Star Wars Unleashed Battle Packs Singles

1	Commander Bly
2	Darth Vader
3	Darth Vader (Anakin Skywalker)
4	Han Solo
5	Luke Skywalker
6	Mace Windu
7	Obi-Wan Kenobi
8	Shock Trooper
9	Stormtrooper

2007-08 Hasbro Star Wars 30th Anniversary Collection

1	Darth Vader (w/30th Anniversary coin album)	10.00	25.00
2	Galactic Marine	4.00	8.00
3	Mustafar Lava Miner	4.00	8.00
4	R2-D2	4.00	8.00
5	Obi-Wan Kenobi	4.00	8.00
6	Mace Windu	6.00	12.00
7	Airborne Trooper	12.50	25.00

8	Super Battle Droid	4.00	8.00
9	Concept Stormtrooper (McQuarrie Signature Series)	12.50	25.00
10	Rebel Honor Guard (Yavin)	4.00	8.00
11	Han Solo (smuggler)	6.00	12.00
12	Luke Skywalker (Yavin ceremony)	4.00	8.00
13	Death Star Trooper	5.00	10.00
14	Biggs Darklighter (Rebel pilot)	10.00	20.00
15	Concept Boba Fett (McQuarrie Signature Series)	12.00	25.00
16	Darth Vader (removable helmet)	10.00	20.00
17	Biggs Darklighter (academy gear)	4.00	8.00
18	Luke Skywalker (moisture farmer)	8.00	15.00
19	Jawa & LIN Droid (Tatooine scavenger)	4.00	8.00
20	Imperial Stormtrooper (Galactic Empire)	4.00	8.00
21	Concept Chewbacca (McQuarrie Signature Series)	7.50	15.00
22	M'liyoom Onith (Hementhe)	5.00	10.00
23	Elis Helrot (Givin)	5.00	10.00
24	Boba Fett (animated debut)	6.00	12.00
25	Luke Skywalker (Jedi Knight)	4.00	8.00
26	CZ-4 (CZ-Series droid)	4.00	8.00
27	Umpass-Stay (Klatooinian)	4.00	8.00
28	Concept Darth Vader (McQuarrie Signature Series)	8.00	15.00
29	Hermi Odle (Baragwin)	12.00	25.00
30	C-3PO & Salacious Crumb (Jabba's Servants)	10.00	20.00
31	Roron Corobb (Jedi Knight)	6.00	12.00
32	Yoda & Kybuck (Jedi Master)	4.00	8.00
33	Anakin Skywalker (Jedi Knight)	15.00	30.00
34	Darth Revan (Sith Lord)	30.00	60.00
35	Darth Malak (Sith Lord)	40.00	80.00
36	Pre-Cyborg Grievous	20.00	40.00
	(Kaleesh warlord Qymaen jai Sheelal)		
37	Concept Starkiller Hero (McQuarrie Signature Series)	4.00	8.00
38	Han Solo (w/torture rack)	10.00	20.00
39	Lando Calrissian (smuggler)	4.00	8.00
40	General McQuarrie (Rebel officer)	4.00	8.00
41	4-LOM (bounty hunter)	4.00	8.00
42	Concept Snowtrooper (McQuarrie Signature Series)	4.00	8.00
43	Romba & Graak (Ewok warriors)	12.00	25.00
44	Tycho Celchu (A-Wing pilot)	4.00	8.00
45	Anakin Skywalker (Jedi Spirit)	10.00	20.00
46	R2-D2 (w/cargo net)	4.00	8.00
47	Concept Han Solo (McQuarrie Signature Series)	12.00	25.00
48	Darth Vader (hologram)	7.50	15.00
49a	Clone Trooper (7th Legion Trooper)	4.00	8.00
49b	Clone Trooper (Revenge of the Sith stand/no coin)	4.00	8.00
50a	Clone Trooper (Hawkbat Batallion)	8.00	15.00
50b	Clone Trooper (Hawkbat Batallion)	4.00	8.00
	Revenge of the Sith stand/no coin)		
51a	R2-B1 (astromech droid)	4.00	8.00
51b	R2-B1 (Revenge of the Sith stand/no coin)	4.00	8.00
52	Naboo Soldier (Royal Naboo Army)	6.00	12.00
53a	Rebel Vanguard Trooper (Star Wars: Battlefront)	4.00	8.00
53b	Rebel Vanguard Trooper (Expanded Universe stand/no coin)	4.00	8.00
54	Pax Bonkik (Rodian podracer mechanic)	4.00	8.00
55	Clone Trooper (training fatigues)	8.00	15.00
56a	Padme Amidala (Naboo Senator)	4.00	8.00
56b	Padme Amidala (Attack of the Clones stand/no coin)	4.00	8.00
57a	Jango Fett (bounty hunter)	4.00	8.00
57b	Jango Fett (Attack of the Clones stand/no coin)	15.00	30.00

ACTION FIGURES AND FIGURINES

58a Voolvif Monn (Jedi Master)	4.00	8.00
58b Voolvif Monn (Expanded Universe stand/no coin)	4.00	8.00
59 Destroyer Droid (droideka)	4.00	8.00
60 Concept Rebel Trooper (McQuarrie Signature Series)	4.00	8.00

2007-08 Hasbro Star Wars 30th Anniversary Collection Battle Packs

1 Battle of Geonosis (Jango Fett/Obi-Wan Kenobi/Count Dooku/Aayla Secura)	20.00	40.00
2 Battle on Mygeeto (Galactic Marine/Ki-Adi Mundi Clone Commander Bacara/Super Battle Droid/Tri-Droid)	30.00	60.00
3 Betrayal at Bespin (Boba Fett/Chewbacca Darth Vader/Han Solo/Princess Leia)	20.00	40.00
4 Capture of Tantive IV (Darth Vader 2 Rebel Troopers/2 Stormtroopers)	20.00	40.00
5 Clone Attack on Coruscant (Clone Trooper Commander/4 Clone Troopers)	25.00	50.00
6 Droid Factory Capture (C-3PO with droid head R2-D2/Jango Fett/Anakin/Destroyer Droid)	20.00	40.00
7 Hoth Patrol (Luke Skywalker/Tauntaun/Wampa)	20.00	40.00
8 Jedi vs. Sith (Yoda/Anakin Skywalker Asajj Ventress/General Grievous/Obi-Wan)	10.00	20.00
9 Jedi vs. Sidious (Darth Sidious/Kit Fisto Mace Windu/Saesee-Tiin/Agen Kolar)	10.00	20.00
10 Jedi Training on Dagobah (Yoda/R2-D2 Luke Skywalker/Spirit of Obi-Wan/Darth Vader)	10.00	20.00
11 The Hunt for Grievous (Captain Fordo Clone Trooper Gunner/3 Clone Troopers)	30.00	60.00

2007-08 Hasbro Star Wars 30th Anniversary Collection Battle Packs Exclusives

1 Ambush on Ilum TAR	30.00	60.00
2 ARC-170 Elite Squad TAR	50.00	100.00
3 Arena Encounter TRU	100.00	200.00
4 AT-RT Assault Squad TAR	25.00	50.00
5 Attack on Kashyyyk TAR	20.00	40.00
6 Bantha with Tusken Raiders (brown) TRU	30.00	60.00
7 Bantha with Tusken Raiders (tan) TRU	50.00	100.00
8 Battle Rancor TAR	150.00	300.00
9 Betrayal on Felucia TAR	20.00	40.00
10 STAP Attack TRU	25.00	50.00
11 Treachery on Saleucami WM	30.00	60.00

2007-08 Hasbro Star Wars 30th Anniversary Collection Comic Packs

1 Carnor Jax & Kir Kanos (2006 Internet Exclusive)		
2 Darth Vader & Rebel Officer		
3 Governor Tarkin & Stormtrooper		
4 Chewbacca & Han Solo		
5 Quinlan Vos & Vilmarh Grahrk	25.00	50.00
6 Luke Skywalker & R2-D2		
7 Obi-Wan Kenobi & ARC Trooper		
8 A'sharad Hett & The Dark Woman	20.00	40.00
9 Leia Organa & Darth Vader		
10 Mara Jade & Luke Skywalker	20.00	40.00
11 Anakin Skywalker & Assassin Droid		
12 Baron Soontir Fel & Derek Hobbie Klivian		
13 Koffi Arana & Bultar Swan		
14 Lt. Jundland & Deena Shan		
15 Mouse & Basso		
16 Clone Commando & Super Battle Droid	50.00	100.00
NNO Obi-Wan Kenobi & Bail Organa (2007 Walmart Exclusive)		
NNO Boba Fett & RA-7 Droid (Wal-Mart Exclusive)	12.00	25.00
NNO Commander Keller & Galactic Marine (2007 Walmart Exclusive)	40.00	80.00
NNO Count Dooku & Anakin Skywalker	40.00	80.00
NNO Kashyyyk Trooper & Wookiee Warrior	30.00	60.00
NNO Lando Calrissian & Stormtrooper	25.00	50.00

2007-08 Hasbro Star Wars 30th Anniversary Collection Commemorative Tins

1 Episode I (Darth Maul/Anakin Skywalker Qui-Gon Ginn/R2-D9)	50.00	100.00
2 Episode II (Clone Trooper blue Anakin Skywalker/Count Dooku/Boba Fett)	20.00	40.00
3 Episode III (Yoda/Mace Windu Anakin Skywalker/Clone Trooper yellow shins)		
4 Episode IV (Stormtrooper black shoulders Princess Leia/Darth Vader/C-3PO)	20.00	40.00
5 Episode V (Snowtrooper/Luke Skywalker hoth Han Solo hoth/Chewbacca hoth)		
6 Episode VI (Bike Trooper/Darth Vader Princess Leia endor/Rebel Trooper)	20.00	40.00
7 The Modal Nodes Cantina Band	30.00	60.00
8 Episode II (Mace Windu/Sora Bulq/Oppo Rancisis/Zam Wesell) (2007 K-Mart Exclusive)		
9 Episode III (Commander Cody/Anakin/General Grievous/Clone Pilot) (2007 K-Mart Exclusive)		
10 Episode VI (Darth Vader/R5-J2/Biker Scout/Death Star Gunner) (2007 K-Mart Exclusive)		

2007-08 Hasbro Star Wars 30th Anniversary Collection Evolutions

1 Anakin Skywalker to Darth Vader	20.00	40.00
2 Clone Trooper to Stormtrooper	20.00	40.00
3 The Sith		
4 The Fett Legacy	60.00	125.00
5 The Jedi Legacy	40.00	80.00
6 The Sith Legacy	60.00	125.00
7 Vader's Secret Apprentice	30.00	75.00

2007-08 Hasbro Star Wars 30th Anniversary Collection Exclusives

1 Cantina Band Member (2007 Disney Weekends Exclusive)	20.00	40.00
2 Concept General Grievous (2007 SWS Exclusive)	15.00	30.00
3 Concept Luke Skywalker (McQuarrie Signature Series) (2007 C4 & CE Exclusive)	15.00	30.00
4 Concept Obi-Wan & Yoda (McQuarrie Signature Series) (2007 SDCC Exclusive)	20.00	40.00
5 Concept R2-D2 & C-3PO (McQuarrie Signature Series)	15.00	30.00
6 Darth Vader & Incinerator Troopers (The Force Unleashed) (2008 Walmart Exclusive)	25.00	50.00
7 Emperor Palpatine & Shadow Stormtroopers (The Force Unleashed) (2008 Walmart Exclusive)	30.00	75.00

8 R2-KT	30.00	60.00
(2007 Shared Exclusive)		
9 Shadow Scout Trooper & Speeder Bike	15.00	30.00
(2007 SDCC Exclusive)		
10 Shadow Troopers 2-Pack	50.00	100.00
(2008 Jedi-Con Exclusive)		
11 Star Wars Collector Coin	60.00	125.00
(2007 Toy Fair Exclusive)		
12 Stormtrooper Commander	25.00	50.00
(2008 GameStop Exclusive)		

2007-08 Hasbro Star Wars 30th Anniversary Collection Force Unleashed

9 Imperial EVO Trooper	12.50	25.00
10 Imperial Jumptrooper	12.50	25.00
11a Maris Brood (flesh)	25.00	50.00
11b Maris Brood (white)	10.00	20.00
12 Darth Vader (battle-damaged)	20.00	40.00
13 Rahm Kota	30.00	75.00
14 Emperor's Shadow Guard	25.00	50.00
15 Juno Eclipse	25.00	50.00

2007-08 Hasbro Star Wars 30th Anniversary Collection Multi-Packs

1 Clone Pack (Battlefront II)		
(2007 Shared Exclusive)		
2 Droid Pack (Battlefront II)	25.00	50.00
(2007 Shared Exclusive)		
3 Clones & Commanders Gift Pack	20.00	40.00
(Toys R Us Exclusive)		
4 I Am Your Father's Day Gift Pack (2007 Walmart Exclusive)		
5 The Max Rebo Band Jabba's Palace Entertainers	30.00	60.00
(2007 Walmart Exclusive)		
6 The Max Rebo Band Jabba's Palace Musicians	40.00	80.00
(2007 Walmart Exclusive)		
7 Republic Elite Forces Mandalorians & Clone Troopers		
(2007 Entertainment Earth Exclusive)		
8 Republic Elite Forces Mandalorians & Omega Squad	75.00	150.00
(2007 Entertainment Earth Exclusive)		

2007-08 Hasbro Star Wars 30th Anniversary Collection Revenge of the Sith

1 Obi-Wan Kenobi	6.00	12.00
2 Darth Vader	15.00	30.00
3 Clone Commander (green)	5.00	10.00
4 Kashyyyk Trooper	20.00	40.00
5 Tri-Droid	8.00	15.00
6 2-1B Surgical Droid	10.00	20.00
7 Po Nudo	8.00	15.00
8 Mustafar Panning Droid	10.00	20.00

2007-08 Hasbro Star Wars 30th Anniversary Collection Saga Legends

1 501st Legion Trooper	20.00	40.00
2 Boba Fett	15.00	30.00
3 C-3PO (w/battle droid head)	6.00	12.00
4 Chewbacca	6.00	12.00
5 Clone Trooper (AOTC)	8.00	15.00
6 Clone Trooper (ROTS)	6.00	12.00
7 Darth Maul	8.00	15.00
8 Darth Vader	8.00	15.00
9 Darth Vader (as Anakin Skywalker)	8.00	15.00
10 Destroyer Droid	6.00	12.00
11 General Grievous	12.00	25.00
12 Obi-Wan Kenobi	6.00	12.00
13 Princess Leia (Boushh disguise)	8.00	15.00
14 R2-D2 (electronic)	10.00	20.00
15 Saesee Tiin	8.00	15.00
16 Shock Trooper	10.00	20.00
17 Yoda	8.00	15.00

2007-08 Hasbro Star Wars 30th Anniversary Collection Saga Legends Battle Droid 2-Packs

1 Battle Droids 2-Pack I (tan infantry & commander)	15.00	30.00
2 Battle Droids 2-Pack II (maroon blaster and lightsaber damage)	8.00	15.00
3 Battle Droids 2-Pack III (tan blaster and lightsaber damage)	8.00	15.00
4 Battle Droids 2-Pack IV (tan dirty & clean)	8.00	15.00

2007-08 Hasbro Star Wars 30th Anniversary Collection Saga Legends Fan's Choice (2007)

1 Biker Scout	12.50	25.00
2 Biker Scout (w/Clone Wars sticker)		
3 Clone Commander (Coruscant)	12.00	25.00
4 Clone Trooper Officer (red)	8.00	15.00
5 Clone Trooper Officer (yellow)	8.00	15.00
6 Clone Trooper Officer (green)	15.00	30.00
7 Clone Trooper Officer (blue)	6.00	12.00
8 Dark Trooper (Fan's Choice Figure #1)	12.00	25.00
9 Imperial Officer (brown hair)	6.00	12.00
10 Imperial Officer (blonde hair)	8.00	15.00
11 Imperial Officer (red hair)		
12 Pit Droids 2-Pack (white)		
13 Pit Droids 2-Pack (brown)		
14 Pit Droids 2-Pack (orange)	12.00	25.00
15 R4-I9	10.00	20.00
16 RA-7	6.00	12.00
17 Sandtrooper (dirty; tan shoulder)	8.00	15.00
18 Sandtrooper (dirty; orange shoulder)	10.00	20.00
19 Sandtrooper (clean; black shoulder)	25.00	50.00
20 Sandtrooper (clean; white shoulder)	12.00	25.00
21 Sandtrooper (dirty; red shoulder)		
22 TC-14	10.00	20.00

2007-08 Hasbro Star Wars 30th Anniversary Collection Saga Legends Fan's Choice (2008)

1 501st Legion Trooper		
2 Commander Neyo	10.00	20.00
3 Covert Ops Clone Trooper (gold coin)	10.00	20.00
4 Pit Droids 2-Pack (white)	8.00	15.00
5 Pit Droids 2-Pack (maroon)	8.00	15.00
6 Pit Droids 2-Pack (orange)	8.00	15.00
7 Shadow Stormtrooper	12.00	25.00
8 Utapau Shadow Trooper	12.00	25.00
9 Zev Senesca	15.00	30.00

2007-08 Hasbro Star Wars 30th Anniversary Collection Silver Coins

1a Darth Vader
1b 30th Anniversary Coin Album
2 Galactic Marine
3 Mustafar Lava Miner
4 R2-D2
5 Obi-Wan Kenobi
6 Mace Windu
7 Airborne Trooper
8 Super Battle Droid
9 Concept Stormtrooper (McQuarrie Signature Series)
10 Rebel Honor Guard
11 Han Solo
12 Luke Skywalker ceremony
13 Death Star Trooper
14 Biggs Darklighter
15 Concept Boba Fett (McQuarrie Signature Series)
16 Darth Vader
17 Biggs Darklighter
18 Luke Skywalker tatooine
19 Jawa & Lin Droid
20 Imperial Stormtrooper
21 Concept Chewbacca (McQuarrie Signature Series)
22 M'liyoom Onith
23 Elis Helrot
24 Boba Fett
25 Luke Skywalker
26 CZ-4
27 Umpass-Stay
28 Concept Darth Vader (McQuarrie Signature Series)
29 Hermi Odle
30 C-3PO & Salacious Crumb
31 Roron Corobb
32 Yoda & Kybuck
33 Anakin Skywalker
34 Darth Revan
35 Darth Malak
36 Pre-Cyborg Grievous
37 Concept Starkiller Hero
38 Han Solo
39 Lando Calrissian
40 General McQuarrie
41 4-LOM
42 Concept Snowtrooper (McQuarrie Signature Series)
43 Romba & Graak
44 Tycho Celchu
45 Anakin Skywalker (Jedi Spirit)
46 R2-D2
47 Concept Han Solo (McQuarrie Signature Series)
48 Darth Vader (hologram)

49 Clone Trooper (7th Legion Trooper)
50 Clone Trooper (Hawkbat Batallion)
51 R2-B1
52 Naboo Soldier
53 Rebel Vanguard Trooper
54 Pax Bonkin
55 Clone Trooper (training fatigues)
56 Padme Amidala
57 Jango Fett
58 Voolvif Monn
59 Destroyer Droid
60 Concept Rebel Trooper (McQuarrie Signature Series)

2007-08 Hasbro Star Wars 30th Anniversary Collection Ultimate Galactic Hunt

1 Airborne Trooper	12.00	25.00
2 Biggs Darklighter (Rebel pilot)	7.50	15.00
3 Boba Fett (animated debut)	12.00	25.00
4 Concept Boba Fett (McQuarrie Signature Series)	20.00	40.00
5 Concept Chewbacca (McQuarrie Signature Series)	15.00	30.00
6 Concept Stormtrooper (McQuarrie Signature Series)	12.00	25.00
7 Darth Vader (Sith Lord)	10.00	20.00
8 Galactic Marine	10.00	20.00
9 Han Solo (smuggler)	7.50	15.00
10 Luke Skywalker (Yavin ceremony)	6.00	12.00
11 Mace Windu	7.50	15.00
12 R2-D2	6.00	12.00

2007-08 Hasbro Star Wars 30th Anniversary Collection Ultimate Galactic Hunt Gold Coins

1 Airborne Trooper	6.00	12.00
2 Biggs Darklighter	4.00	8.00
3 Boba Fett	6.00	12.00
4 Concept Boba Fett (McQuarrie Signature Series)	10.00	20.00
5 Concept Chewbacca (McQuarrie Signature Series)	7.50	15.00
6 Concept Stormtrooper (McQuarrie Signature Series)	6.00	12.00
7 Darth Vader	5.00	10.00
8 Galactic Marine	5.00	10.00
9 Han Solo	4.00	8.00
10 Luke Skywalker	3.00	6.00
11 Mace Windu	4.00	8.00
12 R2-D2	3.00	6.00

2007-08 Hasbro Star Wars 30th Anniversary Collection Vehicles

1 Aayla Secura's Jedi Starfighter	40.00	80.00
2 ARC-170 Fighter (Clone Wars)	50.00	100.00
3 AT-AP Walker	20.00	40.00
4 Anakin Skywalker's Jedi Starfighter (Coruscant)	20.00	40.00
5 Anakin Skywalker's Jedi Starfighter (Mustafar)	20.00	40.00
6 Darth Vader's Sith Starfighter	40.00	80.00
7 Darth Vader's TIE Advanced Starfighter	30.00	60.00
8 General Grievous' Starfighter	25.00	50.00
9 Hailfire Droid	30.00	60.00
10 Mace Windu's Jedi Starfighter	50.00	100.00
11 Obi-Wan's Jedi Starfighter (Coruscant)	25.00	50.00
12 Obi-Wan's Jedi Starfighter (Utapau)	25.00	50.00
13 Saesee Tiin's Jedi Starfighter	30.00	75.00
14 Sith Infiltrator	25.00	50.00
15 TIE Fighter	15.00	30.00
16 Trade Federation Armored Assault Tank (AAT)	30.00	75.00
17 V-Wing Starfighter/ spring-open wings	50.00	100.00

2007-08 Hasbro Star Wars 30th Anniversary Collection Vehicles Exclusives

1 Elite TIE Inteceptor TRU	75.00	150.00
2 Obi-Wan's Jedi Starfighter TRU	25.00	50.00
3 TIE Bomber TAR	75.00	150.00
4 TIE Fighter TRU	60.00	125.00
5 Y-Wing Fighter TRU	100.00	200.00

2008 Hasbro Star Wars Order 66 Target Exclusives

1 Obi-Wan Kenobi/ARC Trooper Commander	30.00	75.00
2 Anakin Skywalker/ARC Trooper	20.00	40.00
3 Tsui Choi/BARC Trooper	25.00	50.00
4 Emperor Palpatine/Commander Vill	25.00	50.00
5 Luminara Unduli/AT-RT Driver	15.00	30.00
6 Master Sev/ARC Trooper	25.00	50.00

2008-09 Hasbro Star Wars Mighty Muggs

NNO Anakin Skywalker		
NNO Asajj Ventress		
NNO Boba Fett	8.00	15.00
NNO C-3PO	8.00	15.00
NNO Captain Rex	6.00	12.00
NNO Chewbacca	8.00	15.00
NNO Commander Cody	12.00	25.00
NNO Count Dooku	6.00	12.00
NNO Darth Maul	6.00	12.00
NNO Darth Maul (shirtless)	6.00	12.00
NNO Darth Revan	10.00	20.00
NNO Darth Vader	8.00	15.00
NNO Darth Vader (unmasked)		
NNO Emperor	5.00	10.00
NNO Gamorrean Guard	5.00	10.00
NNO General Grievous	12.00	25.00
NNO Grand Moff Tarkin		
NNO Han Solo	8.00	15.00
NNO Han Solo (Hoth)	10.00	20.00
NNO Jango Fett	6.00	12.00
NNO Lando Calrissian	8.00	15.00
NNO Luke (Bespin)	8.00	15.00
NNO Luke Skywalker	8.00	15.00
NNO Luke Skywalker (Hoth)	8.00	15.00
NNO Mace Windu		
NNO Obi-Wan Kenobi (old)	6.00	12.00
NNO Obi-Wan Kenobi (young)		
NNO Plo Koon		
NNO Princess Leia		
NNO Qui-Gon Jinn	8.00	15.00
NNO Royal Guard		
NNO Stormtrooper	6.00	12.00
NNO Wampa	5.00	10.00
NNO Wicket	5.00	10.00
NNO Yoda	8.00	15.00

2008-09 Hasbro Star Wars Mighty Muggs Exclusives

1 Admiral Ackbar		
(2008 PX Previews Exclusive)		
2 Biggs Darklighter		
(2009 Target Exclusive)		
3 Bossk		
(2009 Target Exclusive)		
4 Commander Gree		
(2008 SDCC Exclusive)		
5 Shadow Trooper		
(2008 PX Previews Exclusive)		
6 Shock Trooper	8.00	15.00
(2009 Target Exclusive)		
7 Snowtrooper	8.00	15.00
(2009 Target Exclusive)		
8 Teebo		
(2009 Target Exclusive)		

2008-10 Hasbro Star Wars The Legacy Collection Battle Packs

NNO Battle at the Sarlaac Pit Ultimate TAR	150.00	300.00
NNO Battle of Endor		
NNO Birth of Darth Vader	30.00	60.00
NNO Clone Attack on Coruscant	20.00	40.00
NNO Disturbance at Lars Homestead TRU	60.00	125.00
NNO Duel on Mustafar	50.00	100.00
NNO Gelagrub Patrol	20.00	50.00
NNO Geonosis Assault	150.00	300.00
NNO Hoth Recon Patrol	25.00	50.00
NNO Hoth Speeder Bike Patrol	25.00	50.00
NNO Jedi Training on Dagobah		
NNO Jedi vs. Darth Sidious	15.00	30.00
NNO Kamino Conflict	30.00	60.00
NNO Resurgence of the Jedi	20.00	40.00
NNO Scramble on Yavin	125.00	250.00
NNO Shield Generator Assault	25.00	50.00
NNO Tatooine Desert Ambush	20.00	40.00
NNO Training on the Falcon	40.00	80.00

2008-10 Hasbro Star Wars The Legacy Collection Build-A-Droid Wave 1

BD1a Han Solo/ with R4-D6 left leg	10.00	20.00
BD1b Han Solo/ with R4-D6 left leg/ first day of issue sticker		
BD2a Luke Skywalker/ with R4-D6 right leg		
BD2b Luke Skywalker/ with R5-A2 head/ and center leg		
BD2c Luke Skywalker/ with R4-D6 right leg/ first day of issue sticker		
BD3a Chewbacca/ with R4-D6 head/ and center leg		
BD3b Chewbacca/ with R4-D6 head/ and center leg/ first day of issue sticker		
BD4a Leektar/Nippet/ with R4-D6 torso		
BD4b Leektar/Nippet/ with R4-D6 torso/ first day of issue sticker		
BD5a Ak-Rev/ with R7-Z0 left leg		
BD5b Ak-Rev/ with R7-Z0 left leg/ first day of issue sticker	6.00	12.00
BD6a Yarna D'Al'Gargan/ with R7-Z0 right leg	20.00	40.00
BD6b Yarna D'Al'Gargan/ with R7-Z0 right leg/ first day of issue sticker	20.00	40.00
BD7a Bane Malar/ with R7-Z0 torso	15.00	30.00
BD7b Bane Malar/ with R7-Z0 torso/ first day of issue sticker		
BD8a Darth Vader/ multi-piece helmet/ with R7-Z0 head	15.00	30.00
BD8b Darth Vader/ multi-piece helmet/ with R7-Z0 head/ first day of issue sti		
BD8c Darth Vader/ multi-piece helmet/ with MB-RA-7 head	20.00	40.00

2008-10 Hasbro Star Wars The Legacy Collection Build-A-Droid Wave 2

BD9 Obi-Wan Kenobi general/ with R4-J1 left leg	25.00	50.00
BD10 Clone Scuba Trooper/ with R4-J1 head/ and center leg	15.00	30.00
BD11 Saesee Tiin general/ with R7-T1 right leg	25.00	50.00
BD12 Padme Amidala snow/ with R7-T1 left leg	12.50	25.00
BD13 IG Lancer Droid/ with R4-J1 torso	30.00	60.00

BD14 Mon Calimari Warrior/ with R7-T1 Torso 12.50 25.00
BD15 Quarren Soldier/ with R7-T1 head/ and center leg 15.00 30.00
BD16 Clone Trooper blue/ with cannon/with R4-J1 right leg 20.00 40.00

2008-10 Hasbro Star Wars The Legacy Collection Build-A-Droid Wave 3

BD17a Clone Trooper coruscant/ landing platform/ with RD6-RA7 torso15.00 30.00
BD17b Clone Trooper coruscant/ landing platform/ with MB-RA-7 right arm
BD18a Jodo Kast/ with RD6-RA7 head 25.00 50.00
BD18b Jodo Kast/ with MB-RA-7 left leg 12.50 25.00
BD19 Yaddle/Evan Piell/ with RD6-RA7 right leg 15.00 30.00
BD20a Saleucami Trooper/ with 5D6-RA7 left leg 15.00 30.00
BD20b Saleucami Trooper/ with MB-RA-7 right arm
BD21 Count Dooku/ holographic transmission/ with RD6-RA7 right arm10.00 20.00
BD22 Imperial Engineer/ with RD6-RA7 left arm

2008-10 Hasbro Star Wars The Legacy Collection Build-A-Droid Wave 4

BD23 Stass Allie/ with MB-RA-7 left arm 20.00 40.00
BD24a Commander Faie/ with MB-RA-7 torso 25.00 50.00
BD24b Commander Faie/ with R5-A2 left leg 20.00 40.00
BD25a General Grievous/ with MB-RA-7 head 20.00 40.00
BD25b General Grievous/ with R5-A2 right leg
BD26a Bail Organa/ light skin/ with MB-RA-7 left arm 12.50 25.00
BD26b Bail Organa/ dark skin/ with MB-RA-7 left arm 10.00 20.00
BD27a Breha Organa/ light skin/ with MB-RA-7 left leg 7.50 15.00
BD27b Breha Organa/ dark skin/ with MB-RA-7 left leg 10.00 20.00
BD28 FX-6/ with MB-RA-7 right leg 10.00 20.00
BD29a Clone Trooper 327th Star
Corps yellow shoulder/ with R5-A2 torso 20.00 40.00
BD29b Clone Trooper 327th Star/ Corps yellow shoulder
with MB-RA-7 torso 15.00 30.00
BD29c Clone Trooper 327th Star/ Corps yellow shoulder/ with R5-A2 torso

2008-10 Hasbro Star Wars The Legacy Collection Comic Packs Blue and White

1 Asajj Ventress and Tol Skorr 50.00 100.00
2 Anakin Skywalker and Durge 30.00 75.00
3 Anakin Skywalker and Assassin Droid
4 Darth Talon and Cade Skywalker 75.00 150.00
5 Antares Draco and Ganner Krieg 40.00 80.00
6 Fenn Shysa and Dengar 50.00 100.00
7 Princess Leia and Tobbi Dala 30.00 60.00
8 Leia Organa and Prince Xizor 20.00 40.00
9 Grand Admiral Thrawn and Talon Karrde 60.00 125.00
10 Darth Vader and Grand Moff Trachta 30.00 60.00
11 Darth Vader and Princess Leia 40.00 80.00

12 Clone Emperor and Luke Skywalker 60.00 125.00
13 Quinlan Vos and Commander Faie 50.00 100.00
14 Wedge Antilles and Borsk Fey'lya
15 Luke Skywalker and Deena Shan
16 Ki-Adi-Mundi and Sharad Hett

2008-10 Hasbro Star Wars The Legacy Collection Comic Packs Blue and White Exclusives

NNO Ibtisam and Nrin Vakil WM 75.00 150.00
NNO Janek Sunber and Amanin WM 40.00 80.00
NNO Machook/Keoulkeech/Kettch WM 30.00 60.00

2008-10 Hasbro Star Wars The Legacy Collection Comic Packs Red and White

1 Darth Vader and Rebel Officer 15.00 30.00
2 Chewbacca and Han Solo
3 Yuuzhan Vong and Kyle Katarn 75.00 150.00
4 Wedge Antilles and Borsk Fey'lya 10.00 20.00
5 Luke Skywalker and Deena Shan 60.00 125.00
6 Ki-Adi-Mundi and Sharad Hett 60.00 125.00
7 Lumiya and Luke Skywalker
8 Darth Krayt and Sigel Dare 100.00 200.00
9 Clone Trooper and Clone Commander
10 Clone Trooper Lieutenant and Clone Trooper
11 Ulic Qel-Droma and Exar Kun 500.00 1000.00
12 T'ra Saa and Tholme
13 Stormtrooper and Blackhole Hologram 30.00 60.00

2008-10 Hasbro Star Wars The Legacy Collection Comic Packs Red and White Exclusives

NNO Baron Soontir Fel and Ysanne Isard EE 50.00 100.00
NNO Deliah Blue and Darth Nihl EE
NNO IG-97 and Rom Mohc WM
NNO Jarael and Rohlan Dyre EE
NNO Montross and Jaster Mareel EE
NNO Plourr Ilo and Dllr Nep OL
NNO Storm Commando and General Weir WM 30.00 75.00

2008-10 Hasbro Star Wars The Legacy Collection Creatures

NNO Dewback WM 30.00 60.00
NNO Jabba's Rancor TAR 125.00 250.00

2008-10 Hasbro Star Wars The Legacy Collection Evolutions

NNO Clone Commandos WM 50.00 100.00
NNO Imperial Pilot Legacy I 15.00 30.00
NNO Imperial Pilot Legacy II WM 30.00 60.00
NNO Rebel Pilot Legacy I 60.00 125.00
NNO Rebel Pilot Legacy II 25.00 50.00
NNO Rebel Pilot Legacy III WM 50.00 100.00
NNO The Fett Legacy 40.00 80.00
NNO The Jedi Legacy 25.00 50.00
NNO The Padme Amidala Legacy 40.00 80.00
NNO The Sith Legacy 60.00 125.00
NNO Vader's Secret Apprentice 40.00 80.00

2008-10 Hasbro Star Wars The Legacy Collection Geonosis Battle Arena 2009 Edition

1 Coleman Trebor Vs. Jango Fett
2 Kit Fisto Vs. Geonosis Warrior
3 Mace Windu Vs. Battle Droid Commander
4 Joclad Danva Vs. Battle Droid
5 Roth Del Masona Vs. Super Battle Droid
6 Yoda Vs. Destroyer Droid

2008-10 Hasbro Star Wars The Legacy Collection Geonosis Battle Arena 2010 Edition

1 Obi-Wan Kenobi & Super Battle Droid	15.00	30.00
2 Rodian Jedi & Battle Droid		
3 Anakin Skywalker & Droideka		
4 Shaak Ti & Geonosian Warrior		
5 Nicanas Tassu & Count Dooku		
6 C-3PO & R2-D2		

2008-10 Hasbro Star Wars The Legacy Collection Greatest Hits 2008

GH1 Commander Gree	15.00	30.00
GH2 Kashyyyk Trooper	15.00	30.00
GH3 Darth Vader (Battle Damage)	40.00	80.00
GH4 Imperial EVO Trooper	12.50	25.00

2008-10 Hasbro Star Wars The Legacy Collection Saga Legends Blue and White

SL1 R2-D2 (electronic)	10.00	20.00
SL2 Yoda and Kybuck		
SL3 Darth Vader (Anakin Skywalker)		
SL4 Obi-Wan Kenobi	12.50	25.00
SL5 Clone Trooper (AOTC)	15.00	30.00
SL6 C-3PO	15.00	30.00
SL7 General Grievous		
SL8 Mace Windu	7.50	15.00
SL9 Plo Koon	12.50	25.00
SL10 Super Battle Droid	10.00	20.00
SL11 Destroyer Droid	7.50	15.00
SL12a Clone Trooper Officer (red)		
SL12b Clone Trooper Officer (yellow)		
SL12c Clone Trooper Officer (blue)		
SL12d Clone Trooper Officer (green)		
SL13 Darth Vader	7.50	15.00
SL14 Darth Maul	10.00	20.00
SL15 Jango Fett	25.00	50.00
SL16 501st Legion Trooper	25.00	50.00
SL17 Shock Trooper	25.00	50.00

SL18 BARC Trooper		
SL19 ARC Trooper	20.00	40.00
SL20a Battle Droids (tan)		
SL20b Battle Droids (brown)		
SL21 Sandtrooper		
SL22 Luke Skywalker (X-Wing pilot)	10.00	20.00
SL23 ARC trooper Commander (red)		
SL24 Tri-Droid		
SL25 Snowtrooper	15.00	30.00
SL26 Saesee Tiin	12.50	25.00
SL27 Clone Trooper (ROTS)		

2008-10 Hasbro Star Wars The Legacy Collection Saga Legends Red and White

BIKER SCOUT

SL1 R2-D2 (electronic)	12.50	25.00
SL2 Darth Vader (Anakin Skywalker)	12.50	25.00
SL3 Obi-Wan Kenobi	10.00	20.00
SL4 Clone Trooper (Episode II)	20.00	40.00
SL5 Super Battle Droid	12.50	25.00
SL6 Darth Vader	12.50	25.00
SL7 Darth Maul	7.50	15.00
SL8 501st Legion Trooper	25.00	50.00
SL9 Yoda	12.50	25.00
SL10 Sandtrooper	15.00	30.00
SL11 Saesee Tiin	12.50	25.00
SL12 Clone Trooper (Episode III)	15.00	30.00
SL13 Plo Koon	12.50	25.00
SL14 Shocktrooper		
SL15a Chewbacca I		
SL15b Chewbacca II		
SL16 Han Solo		
SL17 Luke Skywalker		

2008-10 Hasbro Star Wars The Legacy Collection Vehicles

NNO AT-ST WM	30.00	75.00
NNO Dagger Squadron B-Wing Fighter TRU	75.00	150.00
NNO Darth Vader's TIE Advanced x1 Starfighter	60.00	125.00
NNO Green Leader's A-Wing Fighter WM	50.00	100.00
NNO Millennium Falcon	200.00	400.00
NNO Speeder Bike (w/biker scout) TRU	40.00	80.00
NNO TIE Fighter		
NNO TIE Fighter Pirate PX		

NNO TIE Fighter Shadows of the Empire TAR	150.00	300.00
NNO TIE Interceptor TRU	30.00	60.00
NNO Wedge Antilles' X-Wing Starfighter TAR	120.00	200.00

2008-13 Hasbro Star Wars The Clone Wars Battle Packs

NNO Ambush at Abregado	100.00	200.00
NNO Ambush on the Vulture's Claw	30.00	75.00
NNO Anti-Hailfire Droid Squad	30.00	60.00
NNO ARC Troopers	150.00	300.00
NNO Army of the Republic		
NNO Assault on Ryloth	125.00	250.00
NNO Assault on Geonosis	30.00	75.00
NNO AT-TE Assault Squad	20.00	40.00
NNO Battle of Orto Plutonia	30.00	75.00
NNO B'omarr Monastery Assault	30.00	60.00
NNO Cad Bane's Escape	75.00	150.00
NNO Capture of the Droids	30.00	75.00
NNO Clone Troopers & Droids	25.00	50.00
NNO Defend Kamino	100.00	200.00
NNO Holocron Heist	40.00	80.00
NNO Hunt for Grievous	30.00	75.00
NNO Jabba's Palace	15.00	30.00
NNO Jedi Showdown	50.00	100.00
NNO Mandalorian Warriors	75.00	150.00
NNO Republic Troopers	30.00	75.00
NNO Rishi Moon Outpost Attack	60.00	125.00
NNO Speeder Bike Recon	25.00	50.00
NNO Stop the Zillo Beast	30.00	75.00

2008-13 Hasbro Star Wars The Clone Wars Battle Packs Exclusives

NNO Assassin Spider Droid & Clones TRU	20.00	40.00
NNO Battle of Christophsis Ultimate TAR	150.00	300.00
NNO Darth Maul Returns TAR	30.00	75.00
NNO Hidden Enemy w/DVD TAR	30.00	60.00
NNO Hostage Crisis w/DVD TAR	30.00	75.00
NNO Obi-Wan & 212th Attack Battalion TAR	50.00	100.00
NNO Rise of Boba Fett Ultimate TRU	60.00	125.00
NNO Yoda & Coruscant Guard TAR	60.00	125.00

2008-13 Hasbro Star Wars The Clone Wars Blue and Black

CW1	Captain Rex	20.00	40.00
CW2	Obi-Wan Kenobi	15.00	30.00
CW3	Clone Commander Cody	20.00	40.00
CW4	Destroyer Droid	12.50	25.00
CW5	Yoda	20.00	40.00
CW6	Count Dooku	15.00	30.00
CW7	Anakin Skywalker	15.00	30.00
CW8	Pre Vizsla	30.00	75.00
CW9	Mandalorian Police Officer	10.00	20.00
CW10	General Grievous	20.00	40.00
CW11	Aurra Sing	25.00	50.00
CW12	Captain Rex (cold weather gear)	20.00	40.00
CW13	Cad Bane	30.00	60.00
CW14	Clone Pilot Odd Ball	15.00	30.00
CW15	Asajj Ventress	20.00	40.00
CW16	Super Battle Droid	12.50	25.00
CW17	Ahsoka Tano	20.00	40.00
CW18	ARF Trooper	15.00	30.00
CW19	Battle Droid	12.50	25.00
CW20	Mace Windu	12.50	25.00
CW21	Commander Gree	25.00	50.00
CW22	Battle Droid Commander	12.50	25.00
CW23	Kit Fisto	15.00	30.00
CW24	ARF Trooper (jungle deco)	20.00	40.00
CW25	Ki-Adi-Mundi	15.00	30.00
CW26	Clone Trooper (flamethrower)	20.00	40.00
CW27	R2-D2	12.50	25.00
CW28	Clone Pilot Goji	25.00	50.00
CW29	Mandalorian Warrior	30.00	60.00
CW30	R4-P17	15.00	30.00
CW31	Shaak Ti	25.00	50.00
CW32	Boba Fett	25.00	50.00
CW33	Embo	30.00	60.00
CW34	Undead Geonosian	15.00	30.00
CW35	Clone Trooper Draa	40.00	80.00
CW36	Quinlan Vos	20.00	40.00
CW37	Cato Parasiti	12.50	25.00
CW38	Clone Commander Jet	75.00	150.00
CW39	Hondo Ohnaka	25.00	50.00
CW40	Obi-Wan Kenobi (new outfit)	15.00	30.00
CW41	Clone Trooper Hevy (training armor)	15.00	30.00
CW42	Cad Bane (w/TODO-360)	30.00	75.00
CW43	R7-A7	25.00	50.00
CW44	Ahsoka (new outfit)	60.00	120.00
CW45	Anakin Skywalker (new outfit)	17.50	35.00
CW46	Aqua Battle Droid	12.50	25.00
CW47	El-Les	20.00	40.00
CW48	Clone Commander Wolffe	30.00	75.00
CW49	Riot Control Clone Trooper	60.00	125.00
CW50	Barriss Offee	50.00	100.00
CW51	Eeth Koth	40.00	80.00
CW52	Clone Commander Colt	75.00	150.00
CW53	Plo Koon (cold weather gear)	15.00	30.00
CW54	Saesee Tiin	50.00	100.00
CW55	Savage Opress (shirtless)	20.00	40.00
CW56	ARF Trooper (Kamino)	25.00	50.00
CW57	Stealth Ops Clone Trooper	25.00	50.00
CW58	Even Piell	30.00	75.00

CW59	Savage Opress (armored apprentice)	40.00	80.00
CW60	Kit Fisto (cold weather gear)	20.00	40.00
CW61	Seripas	30.00	60.00
CW62	Captain Rex (jet propulsion pack)	75.00	150.00
CW63	Chewbacca	10.00	20.00
CW64	R7-D4 (Plo Koon's astromech droid)	15.00	30.00
CW65	Jar Jar Binks	20.00	40.00

2008-13 Hasbro Star Wars The Clone Wars Blue and White

1	Anakin Skywalker	12.50	25.00
2	Obi-Wan Kenobi	15.00	30.00
3	Yoda	10.00	20.00
4	Captain Rex	15.00	30.00
5	Clone Trooper	12.50	25.00
6	General Grievous	20.00	40.00
7	Battle Droid	15.00	30.00
8	R2-D2	7.50	15.00
9	Ahsoka Tano	30.00	60.00
10	Clone Commander Cody	30.00	60.00
11	Clone Pilot Odd Ball	12.50	25.00
12	Super Battle Droid	12.50	25.00
13	Count Dooku	12.50	25.00
14	Plo Koon	15.00	30.00
15	Asajj Ventress	25.00	50.00
16	C-3PO	10.00	20.00
17	Destroyer Droid	15.00	30.00
18	IG-86 Assassin Droid	15.00	30.00
19	Clone Trooper (212th Attack Battalion)	20.00	40.00
20	Padme Amidala (diplomat)	20.00	40.00
21	Clone Trooper (space gear)	15.00	30.00
22	Magnaguard	20.00	40.00
23	R3-S6 (Goldie)	20.00	40.00
24	Jar Jar Binks	15.00	30.00
25	Rocket Battle Droid		
26	Clone Trooper (41st Elite Corps)	50.00	100.00
27	Kit Fisto	12.50	25.00

2008-13 Hasbro Star Wars The Clone Wars Darth Maul Pack

CW1	Anakin Skywalker (new sculpt)	12.50	25.00
CW2	Clone Trooper (Phase II armor)	40.00	80.00
CW3	Savage Opress (shirtless)	15.00	30.00
CW4	Cad Bane	30.00	60.00
CW5	Yoda	6.00	12.00
CW6	Plo Koon (cold weather gear)	15.00	30.00
CW7	Clone Commander Cody (jet propulsion pack)	30.00	60.00
CW8	Mace Windu	12.50	25.00
CW9	Chewbacca	12.50	25.00
CW10	Aqua Battle Droid	7.50	15.00
CW11	Republic Commando Boss	30.00	60.00
CW12	Obi-Wan Kenobi	12.50	25.00
CW13	Captain Rex (Phase II)	30.00	60.00
CW14	Aayla Secura	15.00	30.00
CW15	Ahsoka Tano (scuba gear)	60.00	125.00
CW16	Training Super Battle Droid	10.00	20.00
CW17	Clone Commander Wolffe (Phase II)	25.00	50.00
CW18	Clone Commander Fox (Phase II)	30.00	75.00

2008-13 Hasbro Star Wars The Clone Wars Deluxe Figures and Vehicles

NNO	212th Battalion Clone Troopers & Jet Backpacks	15.00	30.00
NNO	Armored Scout Tank (w/Battle Droid)	12.50	25.00
NNO	Armored Scout Tank (w/Tactical Droid)	15.00	30.00
NNO	AT-RT (w/ARF Trooper Boil)	25.00	50.00
NNO	Attack Cycle (w/General Grievous)	15.00	30.00
NNO	Attack Recon Fighter (w/Anakin Skywalker)	30.00	60.00
NNO	BARC Speeder (w/Commander Cody)	15.00	30.00
NNO	BARC Speeder (w/Clone Trooper)	25.00	50.00
NNO	BARC Speeder Bike (w/Clone Trooper Jesse)	75.00	150.00

NNO	BARC Speeder Bike (w/Obi-Wan Kenobi)	30.00	75.00
NNO	Can-Cell (w/Anakin Skywalker)	15.00	30.00
NNO	Crab Droid	25.00	50.00
NNO	Desert Skiff (w/Anakin Skywalker)	40.00	80.00
NNO	Freeco Speeder (w/Clone Trooper)	15.00	30.00
NNO	Freeco Speeder (w/Obi-Wan Kenobi)	20.00	40.00
NNO	Mandalorian Speeder (w/Mandalorian Warrior)	75.00	150.00
NNO	Naboo Star Skiff (w/Anakin Skywalker)	25.00	50.00
NNO	Pirate Speeder Bike (w/Cad Bane)	30.00	75.00
NNO	Republic Assault Submarine with Scuba Clone Trooper	25.00	50.00
NNO	Republic Attack Dropship with Clone Pilot	40.00	80.00
NNO	Republic Scout Speeder with ARF Trooper	15.00	30.00
NNO	Separatist Droid Speeder with Battle Droid	15.00	30.00
NNO	Speeder Bike with Castas	30.00	60.00
NNO	Speeder Bike with Count Dooku	30.00	60.00
NNO	Speeder Bike with Plo Koon	40.00	80.00
NNO	Turbo Tank Support Squad	75.00	150.00
NNO	Y-Wing Scout Bomber with Clone Trooper Pilot	60.00	125.00

2008-13 Hasbro Star Wars The Clone Wars Deluxe Figures and Vehicles Exclusives

1	AT-RT with ARF Trooper WM	25.00	50.00
2	BARC Speeder with Clone Trooper Buzz WM	30.00	60.00
3	Separatist Speeder with Geonosian Warrior TRU	25.00	50.00
4	STAP with Battle Droid TRU		

2008-13 Hasbro Star Wars The Clone Wars Exclusives

1	Captain Rex MAIL	25.00	50.00
2	Clone Captain Lock KM	30.00	60.00
3	Clone Trooper: 501st Legion WM	20.00	40.00
4	Clone Trooper: Senate Security SDCC	20.00	40.00
5	Commander Fox TAR	20.00	40.00
6	Commander Ponds TRU	30.00	75.00
7	General Grievous: Holographic TRU	20.00	40.00
8	Kul Teska TRU	15.00	30.00
9	Nahdar Vebb MAIL	25.00	50.00
10	Nikto Skiff Guard Puko Naga TRU	20.00	40.00
11	Sgt. Bric & Galactic Battle Mat MAIL	20.00	40.00
12	Stealth Operation Clone Trooper: Commander Blackout TRU	20.00	40.00

2008-13 Hasbro Star Wars The Clone Wars Red and White

KIT FISTO

CW1	General Grievous	25.00	50.00
CW2	Clone Trooper (space gear)	30.00	60.00
CW3	Rocket Battle Droid	10.00	20.00
CW4	Clone Trooper (41st Elite Corps)	20.00	40.00
CW5	Kit Fisto	12.50	25.00
CW6	Mace Windu	25.00	50.00
CW7	Admiral Yularen	20.00	40.00
CW8	Jawas	12.50	25.00
CW9	Commander Gree	25.00	50.00
CW10	ARF Trooper	12.50	25.00
CW11	Heavy Assault Super Battle Droid	15.00	30.00
CW12	Obi-Wan Kenobi (space suit)	12.50	25.00
CW13	4A-7	15.00	30.00
CW14	Yoda	15.00	30.00
CW15	Whorm Loathsom	12.50	25.00
CW16	Commando Droid	25.00	50.00
CW17	Clone Trooper Echo	20.00	40.00
CW18	Anakin Skywalker	12.50	25.00
CW19	Obi-Wan Kenobi	15.00	30.00
CW20	Clone Trooper Denal	30.00	60.00
CW21	Anakin Skywalker (space suit)	15.00	30.00
CW22	Cad Bane	15.00	30.00
CW23	Ahsoka Tano (space suit)	25.00	50.00
CW24	Captain Rex	30.00	60.00
CW25	R2-D2	12.50	25.00
CW26	Ahsoka Tano	15.00	30.00
CW27	Count Dooku	12.50	25.00
CW28	Commander Cody	12.50	25.00
CW29	Destroyer Droid	7.50	15.00
CW30	Luminara Unduli	20.00	40.00
CW31	Captain Argyus	20.00	40.00
CW32	Clone Commander Thire	30.00	75.00
CW33	Battle Droid (AAT Driver)	20.00	40.00
CW34	Matchstick	20.00	40.00
CW35	Padme Amidala (adventurer suit)	25.00	50.00
CW36	Clone Tank Gunner	20.00	40.00
CW37	Ziro's Assassin Droid	20.00	40.00
CW38	Clone Trooper Jek	30.00	60.00
CW39	Commander Bly	100.00	200.00
CW40	Aayla Secura	25.00	50.00

CW41	Hondo Ohnaka	30.00	75.00
CW42	Anakin Skywalker (cold weather gear)	7.50	15.00
CW43	Thi-Sen	20.00	40.00
CW44	Clone Commander Stone	30.00	75.00
CW45	Darth Sidious	100.00	200.00
CW46	Commander TX-20	50.00	100.00
CW47	Firefighter Droid	30.00	75.00
CW48	Obi-Wan Kenobi (cold weather gear)	12.50	25.00
CW49	Magnaguard (w/cape)	30.00	75.00
CW50	Captain Rex (cold assault gear)	25.00	50.00

2008-13 Hasbro Star Wars The Clone Wars Vehicles

NNO	Ahsoka Tano's Delta Starfighter		
NNO	Anakin's Delta Starfighter	8.00	15.00
NNO	Anakin's Modified Jedi Starfighter	15.00	40.00
NNO	ARC-170 Starfighter (Imperial Shadow Squadron)		
NNO	AT-AP Walker		
NNO	AT-TE (All Terrain Tactical Enforcer)		
NNO	Clone Turbo Tank	150.00	300.00
NNO	Corporate Alliance Tank Droid	30.00	60.00
NNO	Droid Tri-Fighter		
NNO	General Grievous' Starfighter	20.00	40.00
NNO	Hailfire Droid (Remote Control)	20.00	40.00
NNO	Homing Spider Droid	60.00	125.00
NNO	Hyena Bomber	30.00	75.00
NNO	Jedi Turbo Speeder	75.00	150.00
NNO	MagnaGuard Fighter	75.00	150.00
NNO	Mandalorian Assault Gunship	200.00	400.00
NNO	Obi-Wan Kenobi's Delta Starfighter	30.00	75.00
NNO	Obi-Wan's Jedi Starfighter (Utapau)	30.00	75.00
NNO	Plo Koon's Delta Starfighter	60.00	125.00
NNO	Republic Attack Shuttle	75.00	150.00
NNO	Republic AV-7 Mobile Cannon	75.00	150.00
NNO	Republic Fighter Tank	40.00	80.00
NNO	Republic Fighter Tank (blue deco)	40.00	80.00
NNO	Republic Fighter Tank (green deco)		
NNO	Republic Fighter Tank (Remote Control)	25.00	50.00
NNO	Republic Swamp Speeder	30.00	75.00
NNO	Separatist Droid Gunship	100.00	200.00
NNO	Trade Federation Armored Assault Tank (AAT - brown/blue)	20.00	40.00
NNO	Trade Federation Armored Assault Tank (AAT)	60.00	125.00
NNO	V-19 Torrent Starfighter	30.00	75.00
NNO	Vulture Droid	40.00	80.00
NNO	V-Wing Starfighter	40.00	80.00
NNO	Xanadu Blood	75.00	150.00
NNO	Y-Wing Bomber	60.00	125.00

2008-13 Hasbro Star Wars The Clone Wars Vehicles Exclusives

NNO	ARC-170 Starfighter TRU		
NNO	Hailfire Droid & General Grievous TRU		
NNO	Kit Fisto's Delta Starfighter WM		
NNO	Octuptarra Droid WM	60.00	125.00
NNO	Republic Gunship (crumb bomber) TRU	200.00	400.00
NNO	Republic Gunship (Lucky Lekku) WM	250.00	500.00
NNO	V-Wing Starfighter & V-Wing Pilot TRU		
NNO	V-Wing Starfighter (Imperial) TRU	200.00	400.00

2008-13 Hasbro Star Wars The Clone Wars Yoda Pack

CW1	Obi-Wan Kenobi	25.00	50.00
CW2	Savage Opress (armoured apprentice)	60.00	125.00
CW3	Anakin Skywalker		
CW4	Captain Rex	30.00	75.00
CW5	R2-D2	30.00	60.00
CW6	501st Legion Clone Trooper	100.00	200.00
CW7	Clone Commander Cody (jet propulsion pack)		
CW8	Darth Maul	30.00	60.00
CW9	Battle Droid	15.00	30.00

2010 Hasbro Star Wars Saga Legends

SL1	Bossk	25.00	50.00
SL2	IG-88	15.00	30.00
SL3	Zuckuss	20.00	40.00
SL4	Greedo	20.00	40.00

SL5	Jango Fett	20.00	40.00
SL6a	Darth Vader	12.50	25.00
SL6b	Darth Vader (unmasked)	8.00	15.00
SL7	Princess Leia Boushh	10.00	20.00
SL8	Darth Maul	6.00	12.00
SL9	General Grievous	12.50	25.00
SL10	Clone Trooper	15.00	30.00
SL11	Darth Vader (Anakin Skywalker)	10.00	20.00
SL12	Obi-Wan Kenobi	15.00	30.00
SL13	Yoda	8.00	15.00
SL14	R2-D2	10.00	20.00
SL15	Shocktrooper	15.00	30.00
SL16	Clone Trooper (Revenge of the Sith)	25.00	50.00
SL17	C-3PO	15.00	30.00
SL18	Chewbacca	8.00	15.00
SL19	501st Legion Trooper	20.00	40.00
SL20	Battle Droid 2-Pack	12.50	25.00
SL21	Luke Skywalker	10.00	20.00
SL22	Han Solo (Hoth)	8.00	15.00
SL23	Snowtrooper	10.00	20.00

2010-21 Hasbro Star Wars The Vintage Collection

VC1a	Dengar (age warning on left back)	60.00	125.00
VC1b	Dengar (age warning on bottom back)	75.00	150.00
VC2a	Leia (Hoth)(age warning on left back)	20.00	40.00
VC2b	Leia (Hoth)(age warning on bottom back)	30.00	60.00
VC3a	Han Solo (Echo Base)(age warning on left back)	25.00	50.00
VC3b	Han Solo (Echo Base)(age warning on bottom back)	12.50	25.00
VC3c	Han Solo (Echo Base)(FOIL card)	30.00	75.00
VC4a	Luke Skywalker (Bespin)(age warning on left back)	20.00	40.00
VC4b	Luke Skywalker (Bespin)(age warning on bottom back)	15.00	30.00
VC4c	Luke Skywalker (Bespin)(FOIL card)	60.00	125.00
VC5a	AT-AT Commander (age warning on left back)	125.00	250.00
VC5b	AT-AT Commander (age warning on bottom back)	50.00	100.00
VC6a	See-Threepio (C-3PO)(age warning on left back)	20.00	40.00
VC6b	See-Threepio (C-3PO)(age warning on bottom back)	30.00	60.00
VC7	Dack Ralter	50.00	100.00
VC8a	Darth Vader (age warning on left back)	30.00	75.00
VC8b	Darth Vader (age warning on bottom back)	25.00	50.00
VC8c	Darth Vader (Boba Fett sticker/plus shipping and handling)	20.00	40.00
VC8d	Darth Vader (barcode #54674 sticker)	20.00	40.00
VC8e	Darth Vader (barcode #54674 printed)	20.00	40.00
VC8f	Darth Vader (Revenge of the Jedi)	75.00	150.00
VC8g	Darth Vader (Return of the Jedi)	30.00	75.00
VC8h	Darth Vader (Wave 1 ESB figure back)	20.00	40.00
VC8i	Darth Vader (FOIL card)	100.00	200.00
VC9aa	Boba Fett (age warning on left back)	25.00	50.00
VC9ab	Boba Fett (age warning on bottom back)	20.00	40.00
VC9ac	Boba Fett (black gun barrel)	20.00	40.00
VC9ad	Boba Fett (no warning on card back)	60.00	120.00
VC9ae	Boba Fett (FOIL card)	200.00	400.00
VC9ba	Boba Fett (Revenge of the Jedi)	30.00	75.00
VC9bb	Boba Fett (Return of the Jedi)	15.00	30.00
VC10a	4-LOM (age warning on left back)	30.00	60.00
VC10b	4-LOM (age warning on bottom back)	30.00	75.00
VC11a	(Twin-Pod) Cloud Car Pilot (age warning on left back)	25.00	50.00
VC11b	(Twin-Pod) Cloud Car Pilot (age warning on bottom back)	25.00	50.00
VC12a	Darth Sidious	50.00	100.00
VC12b	Darth Sidious (FOIL card)	60.00	125.00
VC13a	Anakin Skywalker (Darth Vader)	75.00	150.00
VC13b	Anakin Skywalker (Darth Vader)	60.00	120.00
	(Darth Vader title on front and back)		
VC13c	Anakin Skywalker (Darth Vader)	60.00	120.00
	(Boba Fett sticker/shipping and handling)		
VC13d	Anakin Skywalker (Darth Vader)(barcode #54885)		

VC13e	Anakin Skywalker (Darth Vader)(FOIL card)	125.00	250.00
VC14a	Sandtrooper (dim photo front)	20.00	40.00
VC14b	Sandtrooper (bright photo front)	10.00	20.00
VC14c	Sandtrooper (Boba Fett sticker/shipping and handling)	17.50	35.00
VC14d	Sandtrooper (barcode #54573 sticker)	12.50	25.00
VC14e	Sandtrooper (barcode #54573 printed)	30.00	60.00
VC14e	Sandtrooper (FOIL card)	75.00	150.00
VC15a	Clone Trooper (dim photo front)	30.00	75.00
VC15b	Clone Trooper (bright photo front)	60.00	120.00
VC15c	Clone Trooper (Boba Fett sticker/shipping and handling)	25.00	50.00
VC15d	Clone Trooper (barcode #54888 sticker)	15.00	30.00
VC15e	Clone Trooper (barcode #54888 printed)	30.00	60.00
VC15f	Clone Trooper (FOIL card)	50.00	100.00
VC16a	Obi-Wan Kenobi	75.00	150.00
VC16b	Obi-Wan Kenobi (FOIL card)	100.00	200.00
VC17a	General Grievous (Boba Fett sticker on front)	60.00	125.00
VC17b	General Grievous (barcode #54572 sticker)	30.00	60.00
VC17c	General Grievous (barcode #54572 printed)	30.00	75.00
VC17d	General Grievous (FOIL card)	100.00	200.00
VC18a	MagnaGuard	50.00	100.00
VC18b	MagnaGuard (FOIL card)	60.00	125.00
VC19a	Clone Commander Cody (dim photo front)	75.00	150.00
VC19b	Clone Commander Cody (bright photo front)	75.00	150.00
VC19c	Clone Commander Cody (FOIL card)	75.00	150.00
VC20a	Yoda	60.00	125.00
VC20b	Yoda (Boba Fett sticker front)	60.00	120.00
VC20c	Yoda (Canadian art variant)	500.00	1000.00
VC21a	Gamorrean Guard (1st Boba Fett rocket sticker)	30.00	60.00
VC21b	Gamorrean Guard (2nd Boba Fett rocket sticker)	30.00	60.00
VC21c	Gamorrean Guard (barcode #54898 sticker)	30.00	60.00
VC21d	Gamorrean Guard (barcode #54898 printed)	20.00	40.00
VC21e	Gamorrean Guard (Darth Maul sticker front)	50.00	100.00
VC22a	Admiral Ackbar (1st Boba Fett rocket sticker)	25.00	50.00
VC22b	Admiral Ackbar (2nd Boba Fett rocket sticker)	25.00	50.00
VC22c	Admiral Ackbar (barcode #54900)	15.00	30.00
VC22d	Admiral Ackbar (barcode #52864)	15.00	30.00
VC23a	Luke Skywalker (Jedi Knight Outfit / Endor Captive)	20.00	50.00
VC23b	Luke Skywalker (Jedi Knight Outfit / Endor Captive)	15.00	30.00
	(2nd Boba Fett rocket sticker)		
VC23c	Luke Skywalker (Jedi Knight Outfit / Endor Captive)	30.00	75.00
VC23d	Luke Skywalker (Jedi Knight Outfit / Endor Captive)	20.00	40.00
	(barcode #54902)		
VC23e	Luke Skywalker (Jedi Knight Outfit / Endor Captive)		
	(portrait back)		
VC23f	Luke Skywalker (Jedi Knight Outfit / Endor Captive)		
	(no warning on back)		
VC23g	Luke Skywalker (Jedi Knight Outfit / Endor Captive)	30.00	60.00
VC23h	Luke Skywalker (Jedi Knight Outfit / Endor Captive)	20.00	40.00
	(barcode #52867)		
VC24a	Wooof (Klaatu)(1st Boba Fett rocket sticker)	50.00	100.00
VC24b	Wooof (Klaatu)(2nd Boba Fett rocket sticker)	30.00	75.00
VC24c	Wooof (Klaatu)(barcode #54905)	20.00	40.00
VC24d	Wooof (Klaatu)(figures left off backs)		
VC25a	R2-D2 (w/Pop-Up Lightsaber)	50.00	100.00
	(1st Boba Fett rocket sticker)		
VC25b	R2-D2 (w/Pop-Up Lightsaber)	17.50	35.00
	(2nd Boba Fett rocket sticker)		
VC25c	R2-D2 (w/Pop-Up Lightsaber)	20.00	40.00
	(R2-D2 back)		
VC25d	R2-D2 (w/Pop-Up Lightsaber)	75.00	150.00
	(Revenge of the Jedi)		
VC25e	R2-D2 (w/Pop-Up Lightsaber)		
	(no warning on back)		
VC26aa	Rebel Commando (1st Boba Fett rocket sticker)	50.00	100.00
VC26ab	Rebel Commando (2nd Boba Fett rocket sticker)	20.00	40.00
VC26ac	Rebel Commando (barcode #54907)	15.00	30.00
VC26ba	Rebel Commando (Version II)(Return of the Jedi logo)	30.00	75.00
VC26bb	Rebel Commando (Version II)(Revenge of the Jedi logo)	75.00	150.00
VC27a	Wicket (1st Boba Fett rocket sticker)	25.00	50.00
VC27b	Wicket (2nd Boba Fett rocket sticker)	25.00	50.00
VC27c	Wicket (barcode #54908)	20.00	40.00

ACTION FIGURES AND FIGURINES

Code	Item	Low	High
VC27d	Wicket (barcode #52900)	20.00	40.00
VC27e	Wicket (no warning on back)		
VC28a	Wedge Antilles (card image on back)	30.00	75.00
VC28b	Wedge Antilles (film image on back)	30.00	60.00
VC28ca	Wedge Antilles (light violet background)	30.00	60.00
VC28cb	Wedge Antilles (dark blue to violet background)	30.00	75.00
VC29	Kit Fisto	60.00	125.00
VC30	Zam Wesell	50.00	100.00
VC31a	Obi-Wan Kenobi (figures left of cardbacks)	20.00	40.00
VC31b	Obi-Wan Kenobi (Prototype Boba Fett sticker)	25.00	50.00
VC32a	Anakin Skywalker (Peasant Disguise)	20.00	40.00
VC32b	Anakin Skywalker (Peasant Disguise)(Boba Fett sticker front)	12.50	25.00
VC33	Padme Amidala (Peasant Disguise)	50.00	100.00
VC34a	Jango Fett (figures left of cardbacks)	100.00	200.00
VC34b	Jango Fett (no warning on back)	100.00	200.00
VC34c	Jango Fett (Prototype Boba Fett sticker)	100.00	200.00
VC35	Mace Windu	50.00	100.00
VC36a	Senate Guard (close-up photo front)	30.00	75.00
VC36b	Senate Guard (wide photo front)	25.00	50.00
VC37	Super Battle Droid	30.00	75.00
VC38	Clone Trooper (212th Battalion)	30.00	75.00
VC39	Luke Skywalker (Death Star Escape)	30.00	60.00
VC40	R5-D4	30.00	75.00
VC41a	Stormtrooper (barcode #62162 sticker)	60.00	125.00
VC41b	Stormtrooper (barcode #62162 printed)	30.00	75.00
VC41c	Stormtrooper (warning sticker on front)	30.00	75.00
VC41d	Stormtrooper (Revenge of the Jedi)	60.00	120.00
VC41e	Stormtrooper (Return of the Jedi)	30.00	60.00
VC42	Han Solo (Yavin Ceremony)	40.00	80.00
VC43	Commander Gree (Greatest Hits)	75.00	150.00
VC44	Luke Skywalker (Dagobah Landing)	75.00	150.00
VC45	Clone Trooper (Phase I)	30.00	60.00
VC46	AT-RT Driver	60.00	125.00
VC47	General Lando Calrissian	20.00	40.00
VC48	Weequay (Skiff Master)	50.00	100.00
VC49	Fi-Ek Sirch (Jedi Knight)	30.00	75.00
VC50	Han Solo (Bespin Outfit)	20.00	40.00
VC51	Barriss Offee (Jedi Padawan)	30.00	75.00
VC52	Rebel Fleet Trooper	30.00	60.00
VC53	Bom Vimdin (Cantina Patron)	25.00	50.00
VC54	ARC Trooper Commander (Captain Fordo)	75.00	150.00
VC55	Logray (Ewok Medicine Man)	30.00	75.00
VC56a	Kithaba (Skiff Guard)(black headband)	60.00	125.00
VC56b	Kithaba (Skiff Guard)(red headband)	50.00	100.00
VC57a	Dr. Cornelius Evazan (pink scar)	50.00	100.00
VC57b	Dr. Cornelius Evazan (no pink scar)	30.00	75.00
VC58	Aayla Secura	30.00	60.00
VC59	Nom Anor	30.00	75.00
VC60	Clone Trooper (501st Legion)	50.00	100.00
VC61	Prototype Armour Boba Fett	75.00	150.00
	(2011 Mailaway Exclusive)		
VC62	Han Solo (In Trench Coat)	15.00	30.00
VC63	B-Wing Pilot (Keyan Farlander)	30.00	60.00
VC64	Princess Leia (Slave Outfit)	250.00	500.00
VC65	TIE Fighter Pilot	20.00	40.00
VC66	Salacious Crumb	500.00	1000.00
VC67	Mouse Droid	500.00	1000.00
VC68	Rebel Soldier (Echo Base Battle Gear)	50.00	100.00
VC69	Bastila Shan	100.00	200.00
VC70	Ponda Baba (Walrus Man)	50.00	100.00
VC71	Mawhonic	30.00	60.00
VC72	Naboo Pilot	25.00	50.00
VC73	Aurra Sing	60.00	125.00
VC74	Gungan Warrior	30.00	75.00
VC75	Qui-Gon Jinn	30.00	60.00
VC76	Obi-Wan Kenobi (Jedi Padawan)	50.00	100.00
VC77	Ratts Tyerell & Pit Droid	25.00	50.00
VC78	Battle Droid	20.00	40.00
VC79	Darth Sidious	50.00	100.00
VC80	Anakin Skywalker (Jedi Padawan)	15.00	30.00
VC81	Ben Quadinaros & Pit Droid	30.00	60.00
VC82	Daultay Dofine	25.00	50.00
VC83	Naboo Royal Guard	20.00	40.00
VC84	Queen Amidala (Post-Senate)	20.00	40.00
VC85	Quinlan Vos (Mos Espa)	50.00	100.00
VC86	Darth Maul	25.00	50.00
VC87	Luke Skywalker (Lightsaber Construction)	30.00	60.00
VC88	Princess Leia (Sandstorm Outfit)	75.00	150.00
VC89	Lando Calrissian (Sandstorm Outfit)	30.00	75.00
VC90	Colonel Cracken (Millennium Falcon Crew)	30.00	75.00
VC91	Rebel Pilot (Mon Calamari)	40.00	80.00
VC92	Anakin Skywalker (The Clone Wars)	30.00	60.00
VC93	Darth Vader (A New Hope)	30.00	75.00
VC94	Imperial Navy Commander	30.00	75.00
VC95	Luke Skywalker (Hoth Outfit)	20.00	40.00
VC96	Darth Malgus (The Old Republic)	60.00	125.00
VC97	Clone Pilot Davijaan (Oddball)	100.00	200.00
VC98	Grand Moff Tarkin	125.00	250.00
VC99	Nikto (Vintage)	75.00	150.00
VC100	Galen Marek (The Force Unleashed II)	125.00	250.00
VC101	Shae Vizsla	200.00	400.00
VC102	Ahsoka Tano (The Clone Wars)	250.00	500.00
VC103	Obi-Wan Kenobi (The Clone Wars)	30.00	75.00
VC104	Lumat	100.00	200.00
VC105	Emperor's Royal Guard	30.00	75.00
VC106	Nien Nunb	75.00	150.00
VC107	Weequay (Hunter)	125.00	250.00
VC108a	Jar Jar Binks	60.00	125.00
VC108b	Jar Jar Binks (lost line)		
VC109a	Clone Trooper Lieutenant	75.00	150.00
VC109b	Clone Trooper Lieutenant (lost line)		
VC110a	Shock Trooper	60.00	125.00
VC110b	Shock Trooper (lost line)		
VC111a	Leia Organa (Bespin)	60.00	125.00
VC111b	Leia Organa (Bespin) (lost line)		
VC112a	Sandtrooper (with Patrol Droid)	100.00	200.00
VC112b	Sandtrooper (with Patrol Droid) (lost line)		
VC113	Republic Trooper	150.00	300.00
VC114	Orrimarko	60.00	120.00
VC115a	Darth Vader (Emperor's Wrath)	125.00	250.00
VC115b	Darth Vader (Emperor's Wrath) (lost line)		
VC116	Rey (Jakku)	15.00	30.00
VC117	Kylo Ren	15.00	30.00
VC118	First Order Stormtrooper	12.50	25.00
VC119	Jyn Erso	12.50	25.00
VC120	Rebel Soldier (Hoth)	15.00	30.00
VC121	Supreme Leader Snoke	10.00	20.00
VC122	Rey (Island Journey)	12.50	25.00
VC123	Stormtrooper (Mimban)	20.00	40.00
VC124	Han Solo	12.50	25.00
VC125	Enfys Nest	20.00	40.00
VC126	Imperial Assault Tank Driver	40.00	80.00
VC127	Imperial Death Trooper	12.50	25.00
VC128	Range Trooper	15.00	30.00
VC129	Doctor Aphra	25.00	50.00
VC130	Captain Cassian Andor	12.50	25.00
VC131	Luke Skywalker	12.50	25.00
VC132	Saelt-Marae	20.00	40.00
VC133	Scarif Stormtrooper	25.00	50.00
VC134	Princess Leia Organa (Boushh)	30.00	60.00
VC135	Klaatu (Skiff Guard)	15.00	30.00
VC136	Han Solo (Carbonite)	20.00	40.00
VC137	Ree Yees	15.00	30.00
VC138	Elite Praetorian Guard	15.00	30.00
VC139	Lando Calrissian	10.00	20.00
VC140	Imperial Stormtrooper	20.00	40.00
VC141	Chewbacca	15.00	30.00
VC142	Captain Phasma	20.00	40.00
VC143	Han Solo (Stormtrooper)	25.00	50.00
VC144	Lando Calrissian (Skiff Guard)	10.00	20.00
VC145	41st Elite Corps Clone Trooper	25.00	50.00
VC146	Luke Skywalker (Crait)	50.00	100.00
VC147	Death Star Gunner	30.00	60.00
VC148	Imperial Assault Tank Commander	100.00	200.00
VC149	Artoo-Detoo (R2-D2)	25.00	50.00
VC150	Princess Leia Organa (Yavin)	25.00	50.00
VC151	Luke Skywalker (Yavin)	15.00	30.00
	(Walmart Exclusive)		
VC152	Vedain	12.50	25.00
	(Skiff Guard 3-Pack)		
VC153	Vizam	12.50	25.00
	(Skiff Guard 3-Pack)		
VC154	Brock Starsher	12.50	25.00
	(Skiff Guard 3-Pack)		
VC155	Knight of Ren	20.00	40.00
VC156	Rey	50.00	100.00
VC157	Zorii Bliss	25.00	50.00
VC158	Luke Skywalker (X-Wing Pilot)	40.00	80.00
VC159	Sith Jet Trooper	20.00	40.00
VC160	Poe Dameron	25.00	50.00
VC161	Jawa	12.50	25.00
VC162A	Sith Trooper (w/armory pack)	25.00	50.00
VC163	Shadow Trooper	20.00	40.00
VC164	Cara Dune	25.00	50.00
VC165	Remnant Stormtrooper	12.50	25.00
VC166	The Mandalorian	20.00	40.00
VC167	Power Droid	12.50	25.00
VC168	Clone Commander Wolffe	12.50	25.00
VC169	Luke Skywalker (Stormtrooper)	20.00	40.00
VC170	K-2SO	15.00	30.00
VC171	Stormtrooper	25.00	50.00
VC172	Clone Trooper Fives	30.00	60.00
VC173	Hondo Ohnaka	15.00	30.00
VC174	Chirrut Imwe	12.50	25.00
VC175	Luke Skywalker	25.00	50.00
VC176	Clone Trooper Echo	25.00	50.00
VC177A	Incinerator Stormtrooper	15.00	30.00
VC177B	Din Djarin (w/Grogu)	25.00	50.00
VC178	Darth Vader	15.00	30.00
VC179	Armorer	12.50	25.00
VC180	Moff Gideon	12.50	25.00
VC181	Din Djarin	15.00	30.00
VC182	Captain Rex	15.00	30.00
VC183	Rebel Fleet Trooper	20.00	40.00
VC184	Grogu (w/Pram)	15.00	30.00
VC185	Greef Karga	12.50	25.00
VC186	Boba Fett	30.00	60.00
VC187	Princess Leia Organa	20.00	40.00
VC188	Magnaguard		
VC189	Zutton (Snaggletooth)	12.50	25.00
VC190	Papploo	15.00	30.00
	(2021 Walmart Exclusive)		
VC191	Princess Leia Organa (Endor)	15.00	30.00
	(2021 Walmart Exclusive)		
VC192	AT-ST Driver	15.00	30.00
VC193	Battle Droid	15.00	30.00
VC194	Shadow Stormtrooper	12.50	25.00
VC195	Purge Stormtrooper	20.00	40.00
	(2021 Entertainment Earth Exclusive)		
VC196	Biker Scout	15.00	30.00
VC197	Death Star Droid	15.00	30.00
VC198	Luke Skywalker (Endor)	20.00	40.00
VC199	Tusken Raider	15.00	30.00
VC200	The Emperor		
VC201	Darth Maul	12.50	25.00
VC202	Ahsoka Tano	20.00	40.00
VC203	Jawa	15.00	30.00
VC204	Antoc Merrick		
	(Target Exclusive)		
VC205	Lando Calrissian	12.50	25.00

VC206 IG-11		
VC207 Teebo		
VC208 Captain Rex	15.00	30.00
(Amazon Exclusive)		
VC209 Captain Grey		
(Amazon Exclusive)		
VC210 Captain Ballast		
(Amazon Exclusive)		
VC211a Elite Squad Trooper		
(Amazon Exclusive)		
VC211b The Mandalorian & Grogu (w/spider)	15.00	30.00
(Walmart Exclusive)		
VC212 ARC Trooper	12.50	25.00
(Walmart Exclusive)		
VC213 ARC Trooper Captain	12.50	25.00
(Walmart Exclusive)		
VC214 Barriss Offee	10.00	20.00
(Walmart Exclusive)		
VC215 Luminara Unduli	15.00	30.00
(Walmart Exclusive)		
VC216 Battle Droid	12.50	25.00
(Walmart Exclusive)		
VC217 Aayla Secura	12.50	25.00
(Walmart Exclusive)		
VC218 Yoda	10.00	20.00
VC219 Death Watch Mandalorian	12.50	25.00
VC220 Imperial Death Trooper (Nevarro)	15.00	30.00
VC221 Fennec Shand	12.50	25.00
VC222 Ahsoka Tano (Corvus)	20.00	40.00
VC223 Lobot	10.00	20.00
VC224 Bib Fortuna	10.00	20.00
VC225 The Mythrol	10.00	20.00
VC226 Bo-Katan Kryze	10.00	20.00
VC227 Kuiil	12.50	25.00
VC228 Axe Woves	20.00	40.00
(Target Exclusive)		
VC229 Migs Mayfield	15.00	30.00
(Target Exclusive)		
VC230 Koska Reeves	20.00	40.00
(Target Exclusive)		
VC231 Stormtrooper	15.00	30.00
(Walmart Exclusive)		
VC232 Imperial Gunner	20.00	40.00
(Walmart Exclusive)		
VC233 Bespin Security Guard		
(Walmart Exclusive)		
VC234 R2-D2		
(Walmart Exclusive)		
VC235 ARC Trooper (Star Wars: Battlefront II)	12.50	25.00
(Big Bad Toy Store Exclusive)		
VC236 ARC Trooper (Lambent Seeker)	12.50	25.00
(Entertainment Earth Exclusive)		
VC237 ARC Trooper (Umbra Operative)	12.50	25.00
(Entertainment Earth Exclusive)		
VC238 Lando Calrissian (Star Wars: Battlefront II)	15.00	30.00
(Fan Channel Exclusive)		
VC239 Bespin Security Guard	15.00	30.00
(Walmart Exclusive)		
VC240 Clone Trooper (501st Legion)	12.50	25.00
VC241 Darth Vader (The Dark Times)	12.50	25.00
VC242 Reva (Third Sister)	15.00	30.00
VC243 Mandalorian Super Commando	12.50	25.00
VC244 Anakin Skywalker (AOTC)	12.50	25.00
VC245 Obi-Wan Kenobi w/L0-LA59 (Wandering Jedi)	12.50	25.00
VC246 Mandalorian Super Commando Captain	15.00	30.00
VC247 Mandalorian Death Watch Airborne Trooper	15.00	30.00
VC248 332nd Ahsoka's Clone Trooper	15.00	30.00
VC249 Figrin D'an	15.00	30.00
VC250 ARC Trooper Jesse	12.50	25.00
VC251 Din Djarin (Morak)	10.00	20.00

VC252 Boba Fett (Morak)	15.00	30.00
(Target Exclusive)		
VC253 Heavy Assault Stormtrooper	12.50	25.00
(Fan Channel Exclusive)		
VC254 Stormtrooper Commander	12.50	25.00
(Fan Channel Exclusive)		
VC255 Biker Scout		
(Fan Channel Exclusive)		
VC256 KX Security Droid		
(Fan Channel Exclusive)		
VC257 Obi-Wan Kenobi (Tibidon Station)		
(Amazon Exclusive)		
VC258 Purge Stormtrooper		
(Amazon Exclusive)		
VC259 Jawa		
(Amazon Exclusive)		
VC260 R2-SHW		
(Fan Channel Exclusive)		
VC264 Luke Skywalker (The Mandalorian)		
VC265 Cal Kestis w/BD-1		
VC266 Klatooinian Raider		

2010-21 Hasbro Star Wars The Vintage Collection Creatures

NNO Luke Skywalker's Tauntaun	100.00	200.00
(Target Exclusive)		

2010-21 Hasbro Star Wars The Vintage Collection Exclusives

NNO Jocasta Nu	200.00	400.00
(Brian's Toys Exclusive)		
NNO Stewart Storm Trooper/1		
(2010 Jon Stewart One-of-a-Kind Exclusive)		
VCP3 Boba Fett (rocket-firing)	125.00	250.00
(Mailaway Exclusive)		
VCP12 4-LOM/Zuckuss 2-Pack	125.00	250.00
(TVC Convention Exclusive)		

2010-21 Hasbro Star Wars The Vintage Collection Multipacks

NNO 501st Legion Arc Troopers (Echo/Fives/Jesse)	100.00	200.00
NNO Android 3-Pack	125.00	250.00
C-3PO, R2-D2, Chewbacca		
(Target Exclusive)		
NNO Death Star Scanning Crew	60.00	125.00
NNO Doctor Aphra Comic Set	60.00	125.00
NNO Droid 3-Pack	60.00	120.00
R5-D4, Death Star Droid, Power Droid		
(Target Exclusive)		
NNO Endor AT-ST Crew 2-Pack	60.00	125.00
NNO Ewok Assault Catapult	60.00	125.00
NNO Ewok Scouts 2-Pack	50.00	100.00
NNO Hero 3-Pack	50.00	100.00
Luke Skywalker, Ben Kenobi, Han Solo		
(Target Exclusive)		
NNO Imperial 3-Pack	75.00	150.00
Imperial Commander, Dengar, AT-AT Driver		
(Target Exclusive)		
NNO Imperial Forces 3-Pack	125.00	250.00
Bossk, IG-88, Snowtrooper		
(Target Exclusive)		
NNO Imperial Scanning Crew	60.00	125.00

NNO Lost Line Carbon Freeze Chamber 7-Figure Set	100.00	200.00
(2012 SDCC Exclusive)		
NNO Rebel 3-Pack	60.00	120.00
2-1B, Leia (Hoth), Rebel Commander		
(Target Exclusive)		
NNO Revenge of the Jedi 14-Figure Death Star Set	750.00	1500.00
(2011 SDCC Exclusive)		
NNO Skiff Guard 3-Pack (Special)	30.00	60.00
NNO Special Action Figure Set	60.00	125.00
NNO Special Action Figure Set	30.00	75.00
NNO Villain 3-Pack 2012	30.00	60.00
NNO Villain 3-Pack	30.00	60.00

2010-21 Hasbro Star Wars The Vintage Collection Playsets

NNO Carbon-Freezing Chamber	30.00	75.00
NNO Jabba's Palace Adventure Set	60.00	125.00
NNO Tantive IV	75.00	150.00

2010-21 Hasbro Star Wars The Vintage Collection Vehicles

NNO AT-AP	100.00	200.00
NNO Biggs' Red 3 X-Wing Fighter	75.00	150.00
(Toys R Us Exclusive)		
NNO B-Wing Starfighter	125.00	250.00
(K-Mart Exclusive)		
NNO Imperial AT-AT (ESB)	250.00	400.00
(Toys R Us Exclusive)		
NNO Imperial AT-AT (ROTJ)	200.00	350.00
(Toys R Us Exclusive)		
NNO Imperial Combat Assault Tank (Rogue One)	60.00	120.00
NNO Imperial Combat Assault Tank	75.00	150.00
(2018)		
NNO Imperial TIE Fighter	75.00	150.00
(2018 Walmart Exclusive)		
NNO Imperial TIE Fighter	125.00	250.00
(Target Exclusive)		
NNO Imperial Troop Transport (The Mandalorian)	50.00	100.00
NNO Jabba's Sail Barge	1500.00	3000.00
(HasLab Exclusive)		
NNO Landspeeder	125.00	250.00
(Target Exclusive)		
NNO Luke Skywalker's X-Wing Fighter	100.00	200.00
NNO Millennium Falcon	600.00	1200.00
(Toys R Us Exclusive)		
NNO Obi-Wan Kenobi's Jedi Starfighter	100.00	200.00
NNO Rebel Armored Snowspeeder	125.00	250.00
(Target Exclusive)		
NNO Republic Gunship	600.00	1200.00
(Toys R Us Exclusive)		
NNO Scout Walker AT-ST	100.00	200.00
(K-Mart Exclusive)		
NNO Slave I	125.00	250.00
(Amazon Exclusive)		
NNO Tatooine Skiff	60.00	120.00
NNO TIE Interceptor	200.00	400.00
(Amazon Exclusive)		

NNO	V-19 Torrent Starfighter	75.00	150.00
NNO	Y-Wing Starfighter	100.00	200.00

(Toys R Us Exclusive)

2012 Hasbro Star Wars Movie Heroes

MH1	Shock Trooper	10.00	20.00
MH2	Super Battle Droid	7.50	15.00
MH3	R2-D2	20.00	40.00
MH4	Battle Droid (repaint)	15.00	30.00
MH4	Battle Droid (variant)	15.00	30.00
MH5	Darth Maul (repaint)	10.00	20.00
MH6	Darth Vader	7.50	15.00
MH7	General Grievous	15.00	30.00
MH8	Obi-Wan Kenobi	5.00	10.00
MH9	Yoda	6.00	12.00
MH10	Qui-Gon Jinn	5.00	10.00
MH11	Clone Trooper (with Jetpack)	6.00	12.00
MH12	Destroyer Droid	5.00	10.00
MH13	Jar Jar Binks	5.00	10.00
MH14	Anakin Skywalker	5.00	10.00
MH15	Darth Maul (Spinning Action)	10.00	20.00
MH16	Obi-Wan Kenobi (Light-Up Lightsaber)	15.00	30.00
MH17	Padme Amidala	6.00	12.00
MH18	Qui-Gon Jinn (Light-Up Lightsaber)	5.00	10.00
MH19	Anakin Skywalker (Light-Up Lightsaber)		
MH20	Darth Vader (Light-Up Lightsaber)	12.50	25.00
MH21	Luke Skywalker (zipline backpack)	7.50	15.00
MH22	Battle Droid (The Phantom Menace)(exploding action)		
MH23	Sandtrooper (Light-Up Weapon)		
MH24	Boba Fett (zipline jetpack)		

2012 Hasbro Star Wars Movie Heroes Battle Packs

NNO	Bespin Battle	20.00	40.00
NNO	Duel on Naboo	15.00	30.00
NNO	Ewok Pack		
NNO	Geonosis Arena Battle		
NNO	Rebel Heroes		
NNO	Rebel Pilots		
NNO	Republic Troopers		

2012 Hasbro Star Wars Movie Heroes Exclusives

NNO	Darth Maul Returns		
NNO	Podracer Pilots		

(Toys R Us Exclusive)

2012 Hasbro Star Wars Movie Heroes Vehicles

NNO	Anakin Skywalker's Jedi Starfighter (The Clone Wars)	60.00	125.00
NNO	Anakin Skywalker's Podracer	20.00	40.00
NNO	Attack Recon Fighter with Anakin Skywalker		
NNO	BARC Speeder with Clone Trooper		
NNO	Naboo Royal Fighter with Obi-Wan Kenobi		
NNO	Naboo Starfighter	60.00	120.00
NNO	Republic Assault Submarine with Scuba Clone Trooper		
NNO	Republic Attack Dropship with Clone Pilot		
NNO	Sebulba's Podracer		
NNO	Sith Infiltrator		
NNO	Sith Speeder with Darth Maul		
NNO	Speeder Bike with Scout and Cannon TRU		
NNO	STAP with Battle Droid		
NNO	Trade Federation AAT (Armored Assault Tank)	200.00	400.00

2012-13 Hasbro Star Wars Discover the Force

NNO	Aurra Sing	20.00	40.00
NNO	Darth Maul	20.00	40.00
NNO	Destroyer Droid	12.50	25.00
NNO	G8-R3	15.00	30.00
NNO	Gungan Warrior	15.00	30.00
NNO	Mawhonic	15.00	30.00
NNO	Obi-Wan Kenobi	12.50	25.00
NNO	Qui-Gon Jinn	12.50	25.00
NNO	Ric Olie	12.50	25.00
NNO	Naboo Pilot	15.00	30.00
NNO	Tusken Raider	5.00	10.00
NNO	Yoda	8.00	15.00

2012-13 Hasbro Star Wars Discover the Force Battle Packs

NNO	Mos Espa Arena	20.00	40.00

(C-3PO/Anakin/Sebulba/2 Pit Droids)

NNO	Royal Starship Droids

(R2-B1/R2-R9/R2-D2/R2-N3)

2012-13 Hasbro Star Wars Discover the Force Vehicles-Creatures

NNO	Dewback	20.00	40.00
NNO	Vulture Droid		

2013 Hasbro Star Wars Saga Legends

SL1	Mace Windu	12.50	25.00
SL2	Clone Trooper	15.00	30.00
SL3	Anakin Skywalker	10.00	20.00
SL4	Obi-Wan Kenobi (ROTS)	20.00	40.00
SL5	Super Battle Droid	12.50	25.00
SL6	R4-P17	20.00	40.00
SL7	Yoda	10.00	20.00
SL8	Shock Trooper	25.00	50.00
SL9	Boba Fett	20.00	40.00
SL10	Captain Rex	20.00	40.00
SL11	Stormtrooper	12.50	25.00
SL12	Clone Commander Cody	15.00	30.00
SL13	Obi-Wan Kenobi (Clone Wars)		
SL14	Luke Skywalker		
SL15	Darth Maul		
SL16	Snowtrooper	10.00	20.00

2013 Hasbro Star Wars Saga Legends Mission Series

MS1	Darth Vader/Seeker Droid (Star Destroyer)	10.00	20.00
MS2	Anakin/501st Legion Trooper (Coruscant)	6.00	12.00
MS3	Battle Droid/Jango Fett (Geonosis)	10.00	20.00
MS4	Battle Droid/212th Battalion Clone Trooper (Utapau)	20.00	40.00
MS5	R2-D2/C-3PO (Tantive IV)	12.50	25.00
MS6	Obi-Wan Kenobi/Darth Maul (Mandalore)	7.50	15.00
MS7	Han Solo/Chewbacca (Death Star)	10.00	20.00
MS8	Obi-Wan Kenobi/General Grievous (Utapau)	20.00	40.00
MS9	Luke Skywalker/Darth Vader (Bespin)	15.00	30.00
MS10	Darth Sidious/Yoda (Senate Duel)	12.50	25.00

2013 Hasbro Star Wars Saga Legends Multi-Packs

NNO	Battle of Geonosis I (Jedi Knights) TRU	60.00	125.00
NNO	Battle of Geonosis II (Jedi Knights) TRU	50.00	100.00

NNO The Evolution of Darth Vader		
NNO The Rise of Darth Vader TAR	60.00	125.00

2013 Hasbro Star Wars Saga Legends Vehicles

NNO Obi-Wan's Jedi Starfighter (red)		
NNO Obi-Wan's Jedi Starfighter (blue)		

2013 Hasbro Star Wars Titan Heroes 12-Inch

NNO Anakin Skywalker	15.00	30.00
NNO Clone Trooper	15.00	30.00
NNO Darth Vader	12.50	25.00
NNO Luke Skywalker	15.00	30.00
NNO Obi-Wan Kenobi	20.00	40.00

2013-14 Hasbro Star Wars Black Series 3.75-Inch Orange

1 Padme Amidala	25.00	50.00
2 Clone Trooper Sergeant	25.00	50.00
3A Anakin Skywalker	20.00	40.00
3B Anakin Skywalker	10.00	20.00
4 Biggs Darklighter	15.00	30.00
5A Luke Skywalker	7.50	15.00
5B Luke Skywalker	12.50	25.00
6 Darth Vader	15.00	30.00
7 Biker Scout	25.00	50.00
8 Clone Pilot	17.50	35.00
9 R2-D2	50.00	100.00
10 Pablo-Jill	30.00	60.00
11 Luminara Unduli	15.00	30.00
12A 41st Elite Corps Clone Trooper	15.00	30.00
12B 41st Elite Corps Clone Trooper	12.50	25.00
(correct markings)		
13 Stormtrooper	12.50	25.00
14 Mara Jade	30.00	75.00
15 Merumeru	17.50	35.00
16 Clone Commander Neyo	30.00	60.00
17 Vizam	17.50	35.00
18 Darth Plageuis	75.00	150.00
19 Mace Windu	30.00	75.00
20 Bastila Shan	40.00	80.00
21 Luke Skywalker	12.50	25.00
22 Yoda	15.00	30.00
23 Toryn Farr	25.00	50.00
24 Snowtrooper Commander	20.00	40.00

25 Dak Ralter	25.00	50.00
26 Darth Vader	25.00	50.00
27 Jabba's Skiff Guard	15.00	30.00
28 Ree-Yees	25.00	50.00
29 Wedge Antilles	15.00	30.00
31 Republic Trooper	75.00	150.00

2013-14 Hasbro Star Wars Black Series 3.75-Inch Orange Exclusives

1 Luke Skywalker Hoth Battle Gear	6.00	12.00
2 R5-D4		

2013-14 Hasbro Star Wars Black Series 6-Inch Orange

1 Luke Skywalker X-Wing Pilot	25.00	50.00
2 Darth Maul	30.00	75.00
3 Sandtrooper	30.00	60.00
4 R2-D2	45.00	90.00
5 Princess Leia Organa (Slave attire)	60.00	125.00
6 Boba Fett	30.00	60.00
7 Greedo	25.00	50.00
8 Han Solo	15.00	30.00
9 Stormtrooper	20.00	40.00
10 Obi-Wan Kenobi	15.00	30.00
11 Luke Skywalker Bespin Gear	20.00	40.00
12 Anakin Skywalker	60.00	125.00
13 Clone Trooper	20.00	40.00

2013-16 Hasbro Star Wars Black Series Titanium Series

1 Millennium Falcon	10.00	20.00
2 Resistance X-Wing	8.00	15.00
3A Kylo Ren's Command Shuttle	7.50	15.00
3B Kylo Ren Command Shuttle (black)	15.00	30.00
4 First Order Special Forces TIE Fighter	12.50	25.00
5 Rey's Speeder (Jakku)	7.50	15.00
6 First Order Star Destroyer	7.50	15.00
7 X-Wing	12.50	25.00
8 Y-Wing	6.00	12.00
9 Luke Skywalker Landspeeder	12.50	25.00
10 Slave I	15.00	30.00
11 First Order Snowspeeder	6.00	12.00
12 Poe's X-Wing Fighter	12.50	25.00
13 First Order TIE Fighter	10.00	20.00

14 First Order Transporter	10.00	20.00
15 TIE Advanced	10.00	20.00
16 B-Wing	12.00	25.00
17 Snowspeeder	15.00	30.00
18 AT-AT	30.00	60.00
19 Jakku Landspeeder	10.00	20.00
20 A-Wing	15.00	30.00
21 Sith Infiltrator	8.00	15.00
22 Anakin Skywalker's Jedi Starfighter	25.00	50.00
23 Republic Gunship	12.00	25.00
24 Star Destroyer	30.00	75.00
25 Imperial Shuttle	30.00	60.00
26 The Ghost	12.50	25.00
27 Jango Fett's Slave I	20.00	40.00
28 Inquisitor's TIE Advanced Prototype	10.00	20.00
29 Rebel U-Wing Fighter	10.00	20.00
30 TIE Striker	10.00	20.00
31 Imperial Cargo Shuttle SW-0608	10.00	20.00

2013-20 Hasbro Star Wars Black Series 6-Inch Exclusives

NNO Admiral Ackbar & First Order Officer 2-Pack	25.00	50.00
NNO Admiral Ackbar	15.00	30.00
(2017 Toys R Us Exclusive)		
NNO Admiral Piett	20.00	40.00
NNO Astromech 3-Pack	100.00	200.00
(2016 Toys R Us Exclusive)		
NNO Boba Fett (carbonized)	20.00	40.00
NNO Boba Fett (Prototype Armor)	50.00	100.00
NNO Boba Fett and Han Solo in Carbonite	200.00	400.00
NNO C-3PO & Babu Frik	25.00	50.00
NNO C-3PO	20.00	40.00
(2016 Walgreens Exclusive)		
NNO Cantina Showdown	75.00	150.00
(2014 Toys R Us Exclusive)		
NNO Captain Cardinal	50.00	100.00
(2020 Target Exclusive)		
NNO Captain Phasma (Quicksilver Baton)	15.00	30.00
(2018 Toys R Us Exclusive)		
NNO Captain Rex	100.00	200.00
NNO Chewbacca & C-3PO	40.00	80.00
(2019 Amazon Exclusive)		
NNO Chewbacca	20.00	40.00
(2018 Target Exclusive)		
NNO Clone Commander Obi-Wan Kenobi	75.00	150.00
NNO Commander Fox	50.00	100.00
NNO Commander Gree	20.00	40.00
NNO Commander Wolffe	17.50	35.00
NNO Darth Maul (Jedi Duel)	100.00	200.00
(2019 Celebration Exclusive)		
NNO Darth Vader (carbonized)	30.00	60.00
NNO Darth Vader Emperor's Wrath	30.00	60.00
NNO DJ R-3X	25.00	50.00
(2020 Target Exclusive)		
NNO Elite Praetorian Guard (w/heavy blade)	25.00	50.00
NNO Elite Snowtrooper (Collector Mystery Box)	12.50	25.00
NNO Emperor Palpatine and Throne	150.00	300.00
(2019 Amazon Exclusive)		

NNO First Order Jet Trooper (carbonized)	15.00	30.00
(2019 Walmart Exclusive)		
NNO First Order Officer	10.00	20.00
(2017 Toys R Us Exclusive)		
NNO First Order Snowtrooper Officer	12.50	25.00
NNO First Order Stormtrooper (w/extra gear)	15.00	30.00
NNO First Order Stormtrooper Executioner	15.00	30.00
NNO First Order Stormtrooper Officer	25.00	50.00
(2015 SDCC Exclusive)		
NNO Gamorrean Guard	25.00	50.00
NNO General Veers	30.00	60.00
NNO Grand Admiral Thrawn	150.00	300.00
(2017 SDCC Exclusive)		
NNO Guards 4-Pack	75.00	150.00
(2017 Barnes & Noble/GameStop Exclusive)		
NNO Han Solo & Princess Leia Organa	25.00	50.00
NNO Han Solo (Exogorth Escape)	30.00	75.00
NNO Heavy Battle Droid	30.00	60.00
NNO Hondo Ohnaka	25.00	50.00
(2020 Target Exclusive)		
NNO IG-11	20.00	40.00
NNO Imperial AT-ACT Driver	25.00	50.00
NNO Imperial Forces 4-Pack	60.00	125.00
NNO Imperial Hovertank Pilot	20.00	40.00
(2016 Toys R Us Exclusive)		
NNO Imperial Jumptrooper	30.00	60.00
(2019 GameStop Exclusive)		
NNO Imperial Shadow Squadron	100.00	200.00
NNO Imperial Shock Trooper	30.00	60.00
(2015 Walmart Exclusive)		
NNO Inferno Squad Agent	20.00	40.00
NNO Jabba's Throne Room	150.00	300.00
NNO Jango Fett (Gaming Greats)	30.00	60.00
NNO Jedi Knight Revan	30.00	60.00
NNO Kylo Ren (throne room)	20.00	40.00
NNO Kylo Ren (unmasked)	30.00	60.00
NNO Kylo Ren	15.00	30.00
(2015 K-Mart Exclusive)		
NNO Luke Skywalker (Ceremonial Outfit)	15.00	30.00
(2019 Convention Exclusive)		
NNO Luke Skywalker (Death Star Escape)	20.00	40.00
(2019 Target Exclusive)		
NNO Luke Skywalker (Jedi Knight)	30.00	75.00
NNO Luke Skywalker (Skywalker Strikes)	20.00	40.00
(2019 Fan Channel Exclusive)		
NNO Luke Skywalker (w/Ach-to base)	15.00	30.00
(2017 Target Exclusive)		
NNO Luke Skywalker X-Wing Pilot	125.00	250.00
(2017 Celebration Exclusive)		
NNO Mandalorian (carbonized)	20.00	40.00
NNO Moloch	12.50	25.00
NNO Mountain Trooper	20.00	40.00
NNO Obi-Wan Kenobi (Jedi Duel)	75.00	150.00
(2019 Celebration Exclusive)		
NNO Obi-Wan Kenobi	60.00	125.00
NNO Obi-Wan Kenobi (Force spirit)	20.00	40.00
(2017 Walgreens Exclusive)		

NNO Phase II Clone Trooper 4-Pack	60.00	125.00
NNO Poe Dameron and Riot Control Stormtrooper	20.00	40.00
(2015 Target Exclusive)		
NNO Princess Leia (Bespin Escape)	25.00	50.00
(2018 Target Exclusive)		
NNO Purge Stormtrooper	25.00	50.00
NNO Red Squadron 3-Pack	50.00	100.00
NNO Resistance Tech Rose	12.50	25.00
NNO Rey (Jedi Training) & Luke Skywalker (Jedi Master) 2-Pack	20.00	40.00
NNO Rey (Starkiller Base)	25.00	50.00
NNO Rey (w/Crait base)#[(2017 Toys R Us Exclusive)	15.00	30.00
NNO Rogue One 3-Pack	25.00	50.00
NNO Scarif Stormtrooper	17.50	35.00
NNO Second Sister Inquisitor (carbonized)	30.00	75.00
NNO Sergeant Jyn Erso (Eadu)	12.50	25.00
(2016 Kmart Exclusive)		
NNO Sergeant Jyn Erso	20.00	40.00
NNO Shadow Stormtrooper	25.00	50.00
NNO Sith Trooper (carbonized)	50.00	100.00
(2019 Amazon Exclusive)		
NNO Sith Trooper (multiple weapons)	30.00	75.00
NNO Stormtrooper (carbonized)	25.00	50.00
NNO Stormtrooper (Mimban)	25.00	50.00
(2018 Walmart Exclusive)		
NNO Stormtrooper (w/blast accessories)	25.00	50.00
NNO Stormtrooper Commander	15.00	30.00
NNO Stormtrooper Evolution 4-Pack	50.00	100.00
(2015 Amazon Exclusive)		
NNO Supreme Leader Snoke (Throne Room)	20.00	40.00
NNO X-34 Landspeeder (w/Luke Skywalker)	60.00	125.00
NNO Yoda (Force spirit)	12.50	25.00
NNO Zuckuss	20.00	40.00

2014-15 Hasbro Star Wars Black Series 3.75-Inch Blue

1 R5-G19	12.50	25.00
2A Luke Skywalker Hoth	25.00	50.00
2B Luke Skywalker Hoth	8.00	20.00
(correct elbow pegs)		
3 Darth Vader	30.00	75.00
(Revenge Of The Sith)		
4 Darth Malgus	30.00	75.00

5 Starkiller	50.00	100.00
(Galen Marek)		
6 Yoda	12.50	25.00
(pack forward)		
7 Darth Vader	10.00	20.00
8 Stormtrooper	20.00	40.00
9 Captain Rex	20.00	40.00
10 Jon Dutch Vander	10.00	20.00
11 Chewbacca	12.50	25.00
12 Clone Commander Wolffe	20.00	40.00
13 Clone Commander Doom	20.00	40.00
14 Imperial Navy Commander	15.00	30.00
15 Commander Thorn	25.00	50.00
16 C-3PO	15.00	30.00
17 Princess Leia Organa	20.00	40.00
18 Mosep Binneed	12.50	25.00
19 Han Solo	15.00	30.00
(with Carbonite Block)		
20 Jawas	15.00	30.00

2014-15 Hasbro Star Wars Black Series 3.75-Inch Blue Exclusives

1 Battle on Endor 8-Pack TRU	100.00	200.00
2 Jabba's Rancor Pit TRU	200.00	400.00

2014-15 Hasbro Star Wars Black Series 6-Inch Blue

1 Sandtrooper	30.00	60.00
2 Darth Vader	25.00	50.00
3 Luke Skywalker	30.00	75.00
Episode VI		
4 Chewbacca	20.00	40.00
5 TIE Pilot	15.00	30.00
6 Yoda	15.00	30.00
7 Clone Trooper Sergeant	30.00	75.00

8	Obi-Wan Kenobi	15.00	30.00
9	Han Solo Stormtrooper	20.00	40.00
10	Bossk	40.00	80.00
11	Luke Skywalker	20.00	40.00
12	Emperor Palpatine	25.00	50.00
13	Clone Trooper Captain	30.00	75.00
14	IG-88	25.00	50.00
15	Princess Leia	30.00	75.00
16	Clone Commander Cody	30.00	60.00

2014-15 Hasbro Star Wars Black Series 6-Inch Blue Deluxe

1	Han Solo (w/Tauntaun)	75.00	150.00
2	Jabba the Hutt	75.00	150.00
3	Luke Skywalker (w/Wampa)	60.00	125.00
4	Scout Trooper (w/Speeder Bike)	50.00	100.00

2015 Hasbro Star Wars Hero Mashers

NNO	Boba Fett	10.00	20.00
NNO	Bossk	12.50	25.00
NNO	Darth Vader	12.50	25.00
NNO	General Grievous	20.00	40.00
NNO	Jar Jar Binks	5.00	10.00
NNO	Kanan Jarrus	7.50	15.00
NNO	Zeb Orrelios		

2015 Hasbro Star Wars Hero Mashers Deluxe

NNO	Anakin Skywalker with Speeder Bike	12.50	25.00
NNO	Darth Maul with Sith Speeder Bike	10.00	20.00
NNO	Han Solo vs. Boba Fett	12.50	25.00
NNO	Luke Skywalker vs. Darth Vader	15.00	30.00
NNO	Yoda vs. Emperor Palpatine	15.00	30.00

2015-16 Hasbro Star Wars The Force Awakens 12-Inch

NNO	BB-8	10.00	20.00
NNO	Chewbacca	20.00	40.00
NNO	Darth Vader	12.00	25.00
NNO	Fifth Brother Inquisitor	7.50	15.00
NNO	Finn (Jakku)	10.00	20.00
NNO	First Order Flametrooper	10.00	20.00
NNO	First Order Stormtrooper	8.00	15.00
NNO	First Order TIE Fighter Pilot	7.50	15.00
NNO	Kylo Ren	7.50	15.00
NNO	R2-D2	10.00	20.00
NNO	Rey (Jakku)	10.00	20.00

2015-16 Hasbro Star Wars The Force Awakens 12-Inch Vehicles

NNO	Assault Walker (w/Riot Control Stormtrooper)	12.00	25.00
NNO	Speeder Bike (w/Poe Dameron)	12.00	25.00

2015-16 Hasbro Star Wars The Force Awakens 2-Packs

NNO	Anakin Skywalker & Yoda	12.00	25.00
NNO	Clone Commander Cody & Obi-Wan Kenobi	15.00	30.00
NNO	Darth Vader & Ahsoka Tano	20.00	40.00
NNO	First Order Snowtrooper Officer & Snap Wexley	12.50	25.00
NNO	Garazeb Orrelios & C1-10P Chopper	30.00	75.00
NNO	Han Solo & Princess Leia	12.50	25.00
NNO	R2-D2 & C-3PO	15.00	30.00
NNO	Sidon Ithano & First Mate Quiggold	6.00	12.00

2015-16 Hasbro Star Wars The Force Awakens Armor Up 1

NNO	Boba Fett	7.50	15.00
NNO	Captain Phasma (Epic Battles)	12.50	25.00
NNO	Chewbacca	7.50	15.00
NNO	Finn (Jakku)	7.50	15.00
NNO	Finn (Starkiller Base)	6.00	12.00
NNO	First Order Flametrooper	7.50	15.00
NNO	First Order Stormtrooper	10.00	20.00
NNO	First Order TIE Fighter Pilot	10.00	20.00
NNO	Kylo Ren	7.50	15.00
NNO	Luke Skywalker	10.00	20.00
NNO	Poe Dameron	7.50	15.00
NNO	Poe Dameron (Epic Battles)	6.00	12.00
(Toys R Us Exclusive)			

2015-16 Hasbro Star Wars The Force Awakens Build-a-Weapon Collection

NNO	Admiral Ackbar	10.00	20.00
NNO	Captain Phasma	7.50	15.00
NNO	Captain Rex	10.00	20.00
NNO	Constable Zuvio	6.00	12.00
NNO	Darth Maul		
NNO	Darth Vader	6.00	12.00
NNO	Ezra Bridger	10.00	20.00

NNO	Fifth Brother	25.00	50.00
NNO	Finn (FN-2187)	10.00	20.00
NNO	Finn (Jakku)	7.50	15.00
NNO	First Order Flametrooper	7.50	15.00
NNO	First Order Snowtrooper	5.00	10.00
NNO	First Order Stormtrooper (running image)	6.00	12.00
NNO	First Order Stormtrooper (shooting blaster image)	10.00	20.00
NNO	First Order Stormtrooper Squad Leader	10.00	20.00
NNO	First Order TIE Fighter Pilot	5.00	10.00
NNO	General Hux	7.50	15.00
NNO	Goss Toowers	6.00	12.00
NNO	Guavian Enforcer	7.50	15.00
NNO	Han Solo	7.50	15.00
NNO	Hassk Thug	6.00	12.00
NNO	Inquisitor	15.00	30.00
NNO	Kanan Jarrus	12.50	25.00
NNO	Kanan Jarrus (stormtrooper disguise)	6.00	12.00
NNO	Kylo Ren (Force grip image)	10.00	20.00
NNO	Kylo Ren (lightsaber image)	15.00	30.00
NNO	Kylo Ren Unmasked	12.50	25.00
NNO	Luke Skywalker (Episode V)	7.50	15.00
NNO	Nien Nunb	7.50	15.00
NNO	Poe Dameron	10.00	20.00
NNO	Princess Leia		
NNO	PZ-4CO	5.00	10.00
NNO	Resistance Trooper	7.50	15.00
NNO	Rey (Resistance fatigues)	7.50	15.00
NNO	Rey (Starkiller Base)	7.50	15.00
NNO	Sabine Wren	6.00	12.00
NNO	Särco Plank	7.50	15.00
NNO	Seventh Sister		
NNO	Tasu Leech	12.50	25.00
NNO	Unkar Plutt	10.00	20.00
NNO	X-Wing Pilot Asty	10.00	20.00

2015-16 Hasbro Star Wars The Force Awakens Multi-Packs

NNO	BB-8, Unkar's Thug, Jakku Scavenger 3-Pack	12.50	25.00
NNO	Forest Mission 5-Pack	20.00	40.00
	BB-8, Kylo Ren, Chewbacca, Stormtrooper, Resistance Trooper		
	(Amazon Exclusive)		
NNO	Takodana Encounter 4-Pack	12.00	25.00
	Maz Kanata, Rey, Finn, BB-8		
NNO	Troop Builder 7-Pack	30.00	60.00
	(Kohl's Exclusive)		

2015-16 Hasbro Star Wars The Force Awakens Vehicles

NNO	Assault Walker (w/Stormtrooper Sergeant)	12.50	25.00
NNO	Battle Action Millennium Falcon (w/Finn, BB-8, Chewbacca)	75.00	150.00
NNO	Desert Assault Walker (w/Stormtrooper Officer)	20.00	40.00
NNO	Desert Landspeeder (w/Jakku Finn)	15.00	30.00

NNO Elite Speeder Bike (w/Special Edition Stormtrooper)	10.00	20.00
NNO First Order Snowspeeder (w/Snowspeeder Officer)	15.00	30.00
NNO First Order Special Forces TIE Fighter (w/TIE Fighter Pilot)	10.00	20.00
NNO Poe Dameron's Black Squadron X-Wing (w/Poe Dameron)	30.00	75.00
NNO Rey's Speeder (w/Special Edition Rey)	12.50	25.00
NNO Slave I (w/Boba Fett)	25.00	50.00
NNO Y-Wing Scout Bomber (w/Kanan Jarrus)	12.50	25.00

2015-18 Hasbro Star Wars Black Series 3.75-Inch Red

NNO Admiral Ackbar	12.50	25.00
NNO Ahsoka Tano	20.00	40.00
NNO AT-ST Driver	25.00	50.00
NNO Boba Fett (prototype fatigues)	20.00	40.00
NNO Captain Cassian Andor	8.00	20.00
NNO Captain Phasma	12.50	25.00
NNO Chewbacca	15.00	30.00
NNO Darth Vader	12.50	25.00
NNO Elite Praetorian Guard	15.00	30.00
NNO Emperor's Royal Guard	12.50	25.00
NNO Finn (Jakku)	7.50	15.00
NNO First Order Stormtrooper	12.50	25.00
NNO First Order Stormtrooper Executioner	10.00	20.00
NNO Han Solo	7.50	15.00
NNO Han Solo (Starkiller Base)	7.50	15.00
NNO Imperial Death Trooper	12.50	25.00
NNO Kylo Ren	12.50	25.00
NNO Lando Calrissian	7.50	15.00
NNO Luke Skywalker	12.50	25.00
NNO Luke Skywalker (Jedi Master)	10.00	20.00
NNO Poe Dameron	10.00	20.00
NNO Ponda Baba	12.50	25.00
NNO Princess Leia Organa	10.00	20.00
NNO Princess Leia Organa (D'Qar Gown)	15.00	30.00
NNO Rey (Jakku)	12.50	25.00
NNO Rose Tico	7.50	15.00
NNO Sandtrooper	15.00	30.00
NNO Scarif Stormtrooper Squad Leader	12.50	25.00
NNO Sentry Droid Mark IV		
NNO Sergeant Jyn Erso	7.50	15.00
NNO Tusken Raider	15.00	30.00

2015-19 Hasbro Star Wars Black Series Red Vehicles

1 Special Forces TIE Fighter and Pilot Elite	125.00	250.00
2 X-34 Landspeeder (w/Luke Skywalker)	50.00	100.00
3 Rey's Speeder (Jakku)	30.00	60.00
4 Dewback & Sandtrooper	75.00	150.00
5 Enfys Nest's Swoop Bike	25.00	50.00
6 Snowspeeder (w/Dak Ralter)	100.00	200.00

2015-20 Hasbro Star Wars Black Series 6-Inch Red

1A Finn Jakku	10.00	20.00
1B Finn Jakku (Matte Head)	12.00	25.00
2A Rey and BB-8	15.00	30.00
2B Rey and BB-8	20.00	40.00
3 Kylo Ren	10.00	20.00
4 First Order Stormtrooper	12.50	25.00
5 Chewbacca	20.00	40.00
6 Captain Phasma	12.50	25.00
7 Poe Dameron	10.00	20.00
8 Guavian Enforcer	12.50	25.00

9A Constable Zuvio (green helmet)	10.00	20.00
9B Constable Zuvio (brown helmet)	10.00	20.00
10A Resistance Soldier (green helmet)	20.00	40.00
10B Resistance Soldier (brown helmet)	10.00	20.00
11 First Order TIE Fighter Pilot	12.50	25.00
12 First Order Snowtrooper	10.00	20.00
13 First Order General Hux	20.00	40.00
14 X-Wing Pilot Asty	25.00	50.00
15 Jango Fett	30.00	75.00
16 First Order Flametrooper	12.50	25.00
17 Finn (FN-2187)	15.00	30.00
18 Han Solo	12.00	25.00
19 Kanan Jarrus	15.00	30.00
20 Ahsoka Tano	25.00	50.00
21 Luke Skywalker	15.00	30.00
22 Sergeant Jyn Erso (Jedha)	10.00	20.00
23 Captain Cassian Andor (Eadu)	12.50	25.00
24 K-2SO	12.50	25.00
25 Imperial Death Trooper	15.00	30.00
26 Kylo Ren (unmasked)	12.50	25.00
27 Director Krennic	12.50	25.00
28 Scarif Stormtrooper Squad Leader	20.00	40.00
29 C-3PO (Resistance Base)	15.00	30.00
30 Princess Leia Organa	12.50	25.00
31 AT-AT Pilot/AT-AT Driver	20.00	40.00
32 Obi-Wan Kenobi	30.00	75.00
33 Sabine Wren	30.00	60.00
34 Darth Revan	30.00	60.00
35 Snowtrooper	20.00	40.00
36 Chirrut Imwe	12.50	25.00
37 Baze Malbus	20.00	40.00
38 Imperial Royal Guard	15.00	30.00
39 Lando Calrissian	12.50	25.00
40 Qui-Gon Jinn	40.00	80.00
41 Tusken Raider	30.00	75.00
42 Hera Syndulla	25.00	50.00
43 Darth Vader	25.00	50.00
44 Rey (Jedi Training)	12.50	25.00
45 Kylo Ren	12.50	25.00
46 Luke Skywalker (Jedi Master)	12.50	25.00
47 Grand Admiral Thrawn	30.00	75.00
48 Stormtrooper	25.00	50.00
49 Maz Kanata	10.00	20.00
50 Elite Praetorian Guard	12.50	25.00
51 Finn (First Order Disguise)	10.00	20.00
52 General Leia Organa	10.00	20.00
53 Poe Dameron	10.00	20.00
54 Supreme Leader Snoke	15.00	30.00
55 Rose Tico	15.00	30.00
56 Jaina Solo	30.00	60.00
57 DJ	10.00	20.00
58 Rey	12.50	25.00
59 Captain Rex	60.00	125.00
60 Death Squad Commander	15.00	30.00
61 Jawa	12.50	25.00
62 Han Solo	12.50	25.00
63 Grand Moff Tark (w/IT-O Droid)	20.00	40.00
64 Range Trooper	15.00	30.00
65 Lando Calrissian	12.50	25.00
66 Qi'Ra	15.00	30.00
67 4-LOM	15.00	30.00
68 Tobias Beckett	25.00	50.00
69 Rebel Fleet Trooper	20.00	40.00
70 Han Solo (Bespin)	20.00	40.00
71 Val (Vandor-1)	10.00	20.00
72 Imperial Patrol Trooper	20.00	40.00
73 L3-37	20.00	40.00

74 Dengar	30.00	60.00
75 Princess Leia Organa (Hoth)	12.50	25.00
76 Lando Calrissian (Skiff)	15.00	30.00
77 Rio Durant	20.00	40.00
78 Han Solo (Mimban)	20.00	40.00
79 Dryden Vos	10.00	20.00
80 Vice Admiral Holdo	10.00	20.00
81 Padme Amidala	15.00	30.00
82 Mace Windu	20.00	40.00
83 Battle Droid	20.00	40.00
84 Chopper (C1-10P)	30.00	75.00
85 Obi-Wan Kenobi (Padawan)	50.00	100.00
86 Ezra Bridger	30.00	75.00
87 Doctor Aphra	75.00	150.00
88 BT-1 (Beetee)	40.00	80.00
89 0-0-0 (Triple Zero)	60.00	125.00
90A Supreme Leader Kylo Ren	20.00	40.00
90B Supreme Leader Kylo Ren (Triple Force Friday First Edition)	25.00	50.00
91A Rey & D-0	20.00	40.00
91B Rey & D-0 (Triple Force Friday First Edition)	25.00	50.00
92A Sith Trooper	25.00	50.00
92B Sith Trooper (Triple Force Friday First Edition)	25.00	50.00
93A Cal Kestis (w/BD-1)	30.00	75.00
93B Cal Kestis (w/BD-1)	40.00	80.00
94A The Mandalorian	15.00	30.00
94B The Mandalorian	125.00	250.00
95A Second Sister Inquisitor	40.00	80.00
95B Second Sister Inquisitor	40.00	80.00
96A Offworld Jawa	20.00	40.00
96B Offworld Jawa	20.00	40.00
97A First Order Stormtrooper (w/riot gear)	15.00	30.00
97B First Order Stormtrooper (w/riot gear) (Triple Force Friday First Edition)	20.00	40.00
98 Jannah	8.00	20.00
99 First Order Jet Trooper	12.50	25.00
100A Luke Skywalker (Yavin Ceremony) ERR (misspelled last name)	12.50	25.00
100B Luke Skywalker (Yavin Ceremony)	10.00	20.00
101 Cara Dune	60.00	125.00
102 Wedge Antilles	20.00	40.00
103 Zorii Bliss	10.00	20.00
104 Commander Bly	15.00	30.00
105 Knight of Ren	15.00	30.00
106 Sith Jet Trooper	12.50	25.00
107 Count Dooku (AOTC)	20.00	40.00
108 Battle Droid (Geonosis)	20.00	40.00
109 Plo Koon	25.00	50.00
110 Anakin Skywalker (Padawan)	20.00	40.00
111 Obi-Wan Kenobi (Jedi Knight)	30.00	60.00
112 Kit Fisto	20.00	40.00

2015-21 Hasbro Star Wars Disney Parks Droid Factory

NNO 4-LOM (2020)		
NNO BB-19H (2019 Holiday Exclusive)		
NNO BB-8	12.50	25.00
NNO BB-BOO20 (2020 Halloween Exclusive)		
NNO BB-H20 (2020 Holiday Exclusive)		
NNO C1-10P Chopper (Disney Exclusive)	15.00	30.00
NNO CB-23 (SW Resistance Disney Exclusive)		

NNO Holographic R2-D2		
(Disney Exclusive)		
NNO R2-BOO	20.00	40.00
(2016 Halloween Exclusive)		
NNO R2-D60	25.00	50.00
(2015 Disneyland 60th Anniversary Exclusive)		
NNO R2-H15	30.00	75.00
(2015 Holiday Exclusive)		
NNO R2-H16	15.00	30.00
(2016 Holiday Exclusive)		
NNO R2-RN8W		
(2021 Disney Pride Month Exclusive)		
NNO R3-BOO17 (glow-in-the-dark)	60.00	120.00
(2017 Halloween Exclusive)		
NNO R-3DO	10.00	20.00
(Disney Exclusive)		
NNO R3-H17	12.50	25.00
NNO R4-BOO18	20.00	40.00
NNO R4-D23		
(2015 D23 Expo Exclusive)		
NNO R4-H18	25.00	50.00
(2018 Holiday Exclusive)		
NNO R5-BOO19	17.50	35.00
(2019 Halloween Exclusive)		
NNO R5-D23	20.00	40.00
(2017 D23 Expo Exclusive)		
NNO R5-M4	12.50	25.00
(2016 May 4th Exclusive)		
NNO R6-W1CH		
(2021 Halloween Exclusive)		

2015-21 Hasbro Star Wars Disney Parks Droid Factory Multipacks

NNO 3PO Droid/BB Unit/R4 Unit/CZ Droid		
NNO Artoo Detoo (R2-D2)/See-Threepio (C-3PO)	25.00	50.00
NNO BB-8/2BB-2/BB-4/BB-9E	30.00	60.00
NNO C2-B5/R2-BHD/R3-M2/R5-SK1	30.00	75.00
NNO D-0/R5-2JE/R6-LE5/R2-SHP		
NNO R0-4L0/R2-Q2/R4-M9/R5-X3		
NNO R1-J1/B-R72/L4-R6/C2-B9/EG-01		
NNO R4-X2/Y5-X2	15.00	30.00
NNO R5-013/R2-C2/R5-S9/R5-P8	25.00	50.00
NNO RA-7/BB Unit/R2 Unit/C1 Droid		
NNO RS-F1P/R5-232/R2-S8/R5-PHT		

2016 Hasbro Star Wars Rogue One 2-Packs

NNO Baze Malbus vs. Imperial Stormtrooper	10.00	20.00
NNO Captain Cassian Andor vs. Imperial Stormtrooper	12.50	25.00
NNO First Order Snowtrooper Officer vs. Poe Dameron	8.00	15.00
NNO Moroff vs. Scariff Stormtrooper Squad Leader	15.00	30.00
NNO Rebel Commander Pao vs. Imperial Death Trooper	15.00	30.00
NNO Seventh Sister Inquisitor vs. Darth Maul	15.00	30.00
NNO Captain Phasma vs. Finn	10.00	20.00

2016 Hasbro Star Wars Rogue One Build-A-Weapon

1 Admiral Raddus	12.50	25.00
2 Bodhi Rook	8.00	15.00
3 Captain Cassian Andor (Eadu)	8.00	15.00
4 Chirrut Imwe	5.00	10.00
5 Darth Vader	8.00	15.00
6 Director Krennic	10.00	20.00
7 Fenn Rau	25.00	50.00
8 Galen Erso	20.00	40.00
9 Grand Admiral Thrawn (admiral rank)	25.00	50.00
10 Grand Admiral Thrawn (director rank)	30.00	60.00
11 Imperial Death Trooper (Specialist Gear)	10.00	20.00
12 Imperial Ground Crew	8.00	15.00
13 Imperial Stormtrooper	8.00	15.00
14 K-2SO	10.00	20.00
15 Kanan Jarrus (stormtrooper disguise)(Star Wars Rebels)	10.00	20.00
16 Kylo Ren (The Force Awakens)	8.00	15.00
17 Lieutenant Sefla	6.00	12.00
18 Princess Leia Organa (Star Wars Rebels)	8.00	15.00
19 Rey (Jakku)(The Force Awakens)	6.00	12.00
20 Sabine Wren (Star Wars Rebels)	15.00	30.00
21 Sergeant Jyn Erso (Eadu)	8.00	15.00
22 Sergeant Jyn Erso (Imperial Ground Crew Disguise)	8.00	15.00
23 Sergeant Jyn Erso (Jedha)	6.00	12.00
24 Shoretrooper	10.00	20.00

2016 Hasbro Star Wars Rogue One Hero Series

NNO Captain Cassian Andor	8.00	15.00
NNO First Order Stormtrooper		
NNO Imperial Death Trooper	8.00	15.00
NNO Sergeant Jyn Erso	8.00	15.00
NNO Shoretrooper		

2016 Hasbro Star Wars Rogue One Multipacks

NNO Eadu 3-Pack	12.00	25.00
Sergeant Jyn Erso/Captain Cassian Andor/K-2SO		
(Walmart Exclusive)		
NNO Jedha Revolt 4-Pack	15.00	30.00
Edrio Two Tubes/Saw Gerrera/Sergeant Jyn Erso/Imperial Hovertank Pilot		
NNO Rey vs. Kylo Ren		
Poe Dameron vs. First Order TIE Fighter Pilot		
Finn vs. FN-2199		
NNO Scarif 4-Pack	12.00	25.00
Rebel Commando Pao/Moroff/Imperial Death Trooper/Imperial Stormtrooper		
(Kohl's Exclusive)		
NNO Star Wars 8-Pack	60.00	125.00

2016 Hasbro Star Wars Rogue One Vehicles

NNO Assault Walker (w/stormtrooper sergeant)(The Force Awakens)	20.00	40.00
NNO A-Wing (w/Hera Syndulla)(Star Wars Rebels)	20.00	40.00
NNO Ezra Bridger's Speeder (w/Ezra Bridger)(Star Wars Rebels)	10.00	20.00
NNO First Order Snowspeeder (w/stormtrooper)(The Force Awakens)	15.00	30.00
NNO Imperial AT-ACT Playset (w/Jyn Erso/astromech droid/driver)	75.00	150.00
NNO Imperial Speeder (w/AT-DP pilot)(Star Wars Rebels)	12.00	25.00
NNO Imperial TIE Striker (w/pilot)	20.00	40.00
NNO Imperial TIE Striker (w/pilot)	10.00	20.00
(Toys R Us Exclusive)		
NNO Rebel U-Wing Fighter (w/Cassian Andor)	30.00	60.00
NNO Y-Wing Scout Bomber (w/Kanan Jarrus)	20.00	40.00

2017 Hasbro Star Wars Black Series 40th Anniversary 6-Inch

NNO Artoo Detoo	40.00	80.00
NNO Ben (Obi-Wan) Kenobi	30.00	75.00
NNO Chewbacca	20.00	40.00
NNO Darth Vader Legacy Pack	20.00	40.00
NNO Death Squad Commander	17.50	35.00
NNO Han Solo	25.00	50.00
NNO Jawa	15.00	30.00
NNO Luke Skywalker	20.00	40.00
NNO Luke Skywalker X-Wing Pilot	125.00	250.00
NNO Princess Leia Organa	15.00	30.00
NNO R5-D4	25.00	50.00
(GameStop Exclusive)		
NNO Sand People	20.00	40.00
NNO See Threepio	30.00	75.00
NNO Stormtrooper	30.00	75.00

2017 Hasbro Star Wars Black Series 40th Anniversary Titanium Series 3.75-Inch

1 Darth Vader	15.00	30.00
2 Obi-Wan Kenobi	15.00	30.00
3 Luke Skywalker	8.00	15.00
4 Princess Leia Organa	10.00	20.00
5 Han Solo	15.00	30.00

2017 Hasbro Star Wars Forces of Destiny

NNO Ahsoka Tano	50.00	100.00
NNO Endor Adventure (Princess Leia Organa & Wicket)	12.50	25.00
NNO Jyn Erso		
NNO Luke Skywalker & Yoda		
NNO Padme Amidala	20.00	40.00
NNO Princess Leia & R2-D2	10.00	20.00
NNO Princess Leia & R2-D2 (Platinum Edition)	20.00	40.00
NNO Rey of Jakku	10.00	20.00
NNO Rey of Jakku & BB-8	12.50	25.00
NNO Rey of Jakku & Kylo Ren	20.00	40.00
NNO Roaring Chewbacca	20.00	40.00
NNO Sabine Wren	12.50	25.00

2017 Hasbro Star Wars The Last Jedi Force Link

1 C-3PO	6.00	12.00
2 C'Ai Threnalli	6.00	12.00
(Entertainment Earth Exclusive)		
3 Chewbacca (w/porg)	7.50	15.00
4 DJ (Canto Bight)	5.00	10.00
5 Emperor Palpatine		
6 Finn (Resistance Fighter)	6.00	12.00
7 First Order Flametrooper	7.50	15.00
(Entertainment Earth Exclusive)		
8 First Order Stormtrooper	7.50	15.00
9 General Hux (w/mouse droid)	5.00	10.00
10 General Leia Organa	7.50	15.00
11 Jyn Erso (Jedha)	6.00	12.00
12 Kylo Ren	7.50	15.00
13 Luke Skywalker (Jedi Exile)	7.50	15.00
14 Luke Skywalker (Jedi Master)	7.50	15.00
15 Obi-Wan Kenobi	7.50	15.00
16 Poe Dameron (Resistance Pilot)	5.00	10.00
17 R2-D2	6.00	12.00
18 Resistance Gunner Paige	6.00	12.00
19 Resistance Gunner Rose	6.00	12.00
20 Rey (Island Journey)	6.00	12.00
21 Rey (Jedi Training)	10.00	20.00
22 Yoda	10.00	20.00

2017 Hasbro Star Wars The Last Jedi Force Link 2-Packs

NNO Bala-Tik (w/Rathtar)	7.50	15.00
NNO Chirrut Imwe & Baze Malbus	10.00	20.00
NNO Darth Vader (w/Imperial probe droid)	20.00	40.00
NNO Finn & Captain Phasma	10.00	20.00
NNO Han Solo & Boba Fett	10.00	20.00
NNO Rey (Jedi Training) & Elite Praetorian Guard	7.50	15.00
NNO Rose Tico (w/BB-8 & BB-9E)	10.00	20.00

2017 Hasbro Star Wars The Last Jedi Force Link Multipacks

NNO Battle on Crait 4-Pack	15.00	30.00
Rey/First Order Walker Driver		
First Order Gunner/Rose		
NNO Emperor Palpatine/Luke Skywalker/Emperor's Royal Guard 3-Pack	10.00	20.00
(Target Exclusive)		
NNO Era of the Force 8-Pack		
Yoda/Luke/Kylo Ren/Rey		
Darth Maul/Mace Windu		
Obi-Wan Kenobi/Darth Vader		
(Target Exclusive)		
NNO Luke Skywalker/Resistance Tech Rose	20.00	40.00
Rey (Jedi Training)/First Order Stormtrooper 4-Pack		

2017 Hasbro Star Wars The Last Jedi Force Link Sets

NNO BB-8 2-in-1 Mega Playset	50.00	100.00
NNO Starter Set (w/Elite Praetorian Guard)	20.00	40.00
(Toys R Us Exclusive)		
NNO Starter Set (w/Kylo Ren)	7.50	15.00
NNO Starter Set (w/Stormtrooper Executioner)	15.00	30.00
(Toys R Us Exclusive)		

2017 Hasbro Star Wars The Last Jedi Force Link Vehicles

1 Canto Bight Police Speeder (w/Canto Bight Police)	12.50	25.00
2 Kylo Ren's TIE Silencer (w/Kylo Ren)	30.00	60.00
3 Resistance A-Wing Fighter (w/Resistance Pilot Tallie)	30.00	60.00
4 Ski Speeder (w/Poe Dameron)	12.50	25.00
5 TIE Fighter (w/TIE Fighter Pilot)	25.00	50.00
6 X-Wing Fighter (w/Poe Dameron)	50.00	100.00

2017-18 Hasbro Star Wars Black Series Centerpieces

NNO Rey vs. Kylo Ren	75.00	150.00
1 Darth Vader	30.00	60.00
2 Luke Skywalker	20.00	40.00
3 Kylo Ren	20.00	40.00
4 Rey	20.00	40.00

2017-21 Hasbro Star Wars Disney Store Toybox

1 Kylo Ren	10.00	20.00
2 Rey	10.00	20.00
3 Stormtrooper	7.50	15.00
4 Darth Vader	7.50	15.00
5 Luke Skywalker	12.50	25.00
6 Boba Fett	20.00	40.00
7 Princess Leia Organa	7.50	15.00
8 Han Solo	10.00	20.00
9 Chewbacca	7.50	15.00
10 Yoda/Force Ghost Yoda 2-Pack	25.00	50.00
11 Poe Dameron (w/BB-8)		
12 C-3PO (w/R2-D2)		
13 Kylo Ren	15.00	30.00
14 Rey	7.50	15.00
15 Sith Trooper		
16 Darth Maul		
17 Jango Fett		
18 Din Djarin (w/Grogu)		
19 Darth Vader		
20 Stormtrooper		
21 General Grievous	20.00	40.00
22 Ahsoka Tano (w/Captain Red)		
23 Wrecker		

2017-21 Hasbro Star Wars Disney Store Toybox Vehicles

NNO Millennium Falcon (w/Han Solo & Chewbacca)		
NNO Millennium Falcon (w/Rey/BB-8/D-0)		
NNO Slave 1 (w/Boba Fett)		
NNO TIE Fighter (w/Kylo Ren)		
NNO TIE Fighter (w/TIE Fighter Pilot)		

2018 Hasbro Solo A Star Wars Story Force Link 2.0

NNO	Chewbacca	7.50	15.00
NNO	Darth Vader	15.00	30.00
NNO	Emperor's Royal Guard	10.00	20.00
NNO	Han Solo		
NNO	K-2SO	10.00	20.00
NNO	Kylo Ren	7.50	15.00
NNO	L3-37	15.00	30.00
NNO	Luke Skywalker Jedi Knight	7.50	15.00
NNO	Luke Skywalker Jedi Master	7.50	15.00
NNO	Maz Kanata	15.00	30.00
NNO	Moloch	7.50	15.00
NNO	Princess Leia Organa	7.50	15.00
NNO	Qi'Ra	7.50	15.00
NNO	Quay Tolsite	20.00	40.00
NNO	Range Trooper	10.00	20.00
NNO	Rey	7.50	15.00
NNO	Rio Durant	10.00	20.00
NNO	Stormtrooper	15.00	30.00
NNO	Stormtrooper Officer	20.00	40.00
NNO	Supreme Leader Snoke	12.50	25.00
NNO	Tobias Beckett	10.00	20.00
NNO	Val	7.50	15.00

2018 Hasbro Solo A Star Wars Story Force Link 2.0 2-Packs

NNO	C-3PO & R2-D2	15.00	30.00
NNO	Han Solo/Chewbacca	10.00	20.00
NNO	Lando Calrissian/Kessel Guard	10.00	20.00
NNO	Qui-Gon Jinn/Darth Maul (w/probe droid)	15.00	30.00
NNO	Rebolt/Corellian Hound	10.00	20.00
NNO	Rose Tico (w/BB-8)/BB-9E	7.50	15.00

2018 Hasbro Solo A Star Wars Story Force Link 2.0 Creatures

NNO	Rathtar (w/Bala-Tik)	10.00	20.00
NNO	Wampa (w/Luke Skywalker)	20.00	40.00

2018 Hasbro Solo A Star Wars Story Force Link 2.0 Multi-Packs

NNO	Han Solo/Qi'Ra/Range Trooper/Weazel	20.00	40.00
NNO	Kylo Ren/Maz Kanata/Poe Dameron/Rey/Snowtrooper		

(Last Jedi 5-Pack Entertainment Earth Exclusive)

NNO	Starter Set (w/Han Solo)	10.00	20.00
NNO	Trooper 6-Pack		

(2018 Targe Exclusive)

2018 Hasbro Solo A Star Wars Story Force Link 2.0 Playsets

NNO	Kessel Mine Escape (w/Han Solo)	15.00	30.00
NNO	Vandor-1 Heist (w/Chewbacca)	20.00	40.00

2018 Hasbro Solo A Star Wars Story Force Link 2.0 Vehicles

NNO	A-Wing Fighter (w/Tallie)	20.00	40.00
NNO	Imperial AT-DT Walker (w/Stormtrooper)	50.00	10.00
NNO	Kessel Run Millennium Falcon (w/Han Solo)	50.00	100.00
NNO	M-68 Landspeeder (w/Han Solo)	15.00	30.00
NNO	Swoop Bike (w/Enfys Nest)	20.00	40.00
NNO	TIE Fighter (w/TIE Fighter Pilot)	30.00	60.00

2018 Hasbro Star Wars Resistance Collection

NNO	Commander Pyre
NNO	First Order Stormtrooper
NNO	Kaz Xiono
NNO	Major Vonreg
NNO	Synara San
NNO	Torra Doza

2018 Hasbro Star Wars Resistance Collection 1 2-Packs

NNO	Jarek Yeager & Bucket
NNO	Poe Dameron & BB-8

2018-20 Hasbro Star Wars Black Series 6-Inch Multi-Packs

NNO	The Child (w/frog and bowl)		
NNO	Porgs 2-Pack	10.00	20.00

2019 Hasbro Star Wars Black Series 6-Inch Multipacks

NNO	Droid Depot 4-Pack	50.00	100.00
NNO	First Order 4-Pack	60.00	120.00
NNO	Smuggler's Run 5-Pack	50.00	100.00

2019 Hasbro Star Wars Galaxy of Adventures 3.75-Inch

NNO	Boba Fett	10.00	20.00
NNO	Chewbacca	6.00	12.00
NNO	Darth Maul	7.50	15.00
NNO	Darth Vader	10.00	20.00
NNO	General Grievous	7.50	15.00
NNO	Han Solo	7.50	15.00
NNO	Kylo Ren	7.50	15.00
NNO	Luke Skywalker	7.50	15.00
NNO	Obi-Wan Kenobi	6.00	12.00
NNO	Princess Leia Organa	7.50	15.00
NNO	R2-D2	6.00	12.00
NNO	Rey	10.00	20.00
NNO	Stormtrooper	7.50	15.00
NNO	Yoda	7.50	15.00

2019 Hasbro Star Wars Galaxy of Adventures 5-Inch

NNO	Darth Vader	12.50	25.00
NNO	C-3PO	7.50	15.00
NNO	Han Solo	7.50	15.00
NNO	Chewbacca	7.50	15.00
NNO	Kylo Ren	10.00	20.00
NNO	Rey	12.50	25.00
NNO	Jet Trooper	7.50	15.00
NNO	Finn	7.50	15.00

2019 Hasbro Star Wars Galaxy of Adventures 5-Inch Multipacks

NNO	D-0/BB-8/R2-D2 3-Pack
NNO	Kylo Ren/Rey 2-Pack

2019 Hasbro Star Wars Galaxy of Adventures 5-Inch Vehicle

NNO	Treadspeeder (w/First Order Driver)	20.00	40.00

2019 Hasbro Star Wars Resistance

NNO	Commander Pyre		
NNO	First Order Stormtrooper		
NNO	Jarek Yeager & Bucket (R1-J5)	7.50	15.00
NNO	Kaz Xiono	7.50	15.00
NNO	Major Vonreg	6.00	12.00

NNO	Poe Dameron & BB-8		
NNO	Synara San	6.00	12.00
NNO	Torra Doza	7.50	15.00

2019 Hasbro Star Wars Retro Collection

NNO	Chewbacca	20.00	40.00
NNO	Darth Vader	30.00	60.00
NNO	Darth Vader (prototype edition)	100.00	200.00
NNO	Grand Moff Tarkin	20.00	40.00
NNO	Han Solo	20.00	40.00
NNO	Luke Skywalker	20.00	40.00
NNO	Princess Leia Organa	15.00	30.00
NNO	Stormtrooper	20.00	40.00

2019 Hasbro Star Wars Retro Collection Multipacks

NNO	Escape from Death Star Board Game (w/Grand Moff Tarkin)	25.00	50.00
NNO	Promotional Early Bird Certificate/Figure Six-Pack		

2019 Hasbro Star Wars Skywalker Saga Commemorative Edition 2-Packs

NNO	C-3PO/BB-8/R2-D2	10.00	20.00
NNO	Darth Maul/Yoda	7.50	15.00
NNO	Darth Vader/Stormtrooper	7.50	15.00
NNO	Finn/Poe Dameron	7.50	15.00
NNO	Han Solo/Princess Leia	10.00	20.00
NNO	Kylo Ren/Rey	10.00	20.00
NNO	Luke Skywalker/Chewbacca	10.00	20.00
NNO	Mace Windu/Jango Fett	10.00	20.00
NNO	Obi-Wan Kenobi/Anakin Skywalker	12.50	25.00

2019-20 Hasbro Star Wars Black Series Deluxe

D1	General Grievous	30.00	60.00
D2	Heavy Infantry Mandalorian	20.00	40.00
D3	Imperial Probe Droid	20.00	40.00
D4	Luke Skywalker & Yoda (Jedi Training)	20.00	40.00

2019-20 Hasbro Star Wars HyperReal

NNO	Darth Vader	40.00	80.00
NNO	Luke Skywalker	30.00	75.00

2019-21 Hasbro Star Wars Black Series Archive

NNO	501st Legion Clone Trooper	20.00	40.00
NNO	Anakin Skywalker	60.00	125.00
NNO	Boba Fett	25.00	50.00
NNO	Bossk	30.00	75.00
NNO	Clone Commander Cody	15.00	30.00
NNO	Darth Maul	30.00	75.00
NNO	Darth Revan	20.00	40.00
NNO	Grand Admiral Thrawn	20.00	40.00
NNO	Han Solo (Hoth)	12.50	25.00
NNO	IG-88	30.00	60.00
NNO	Imperial Death Trooper	12.50	25.00
NNO	Imperial Hovertank Driver	12.50	25.00
NNO	Luke Skywalker (Hoth)	12.50	25.00
NNO	Luke Skywalker (X-Wing)	12.50	25.00
NNO	Obi-Wan Kenobi	15.00	30.00
NNO	Princess Leia Organa	12.50	25.00
NNO	Scout Trooper	20.00	40.00
NNO	Shoretrooper	15.00	30.00
NNO	Tusken Raider	15.00	30.00
NNO	Yoda	20.00	40.00

2020 Hasbro Star Wars 9.5-Inch Series

NNO	Darth Vader	
NNO	First Order Stormtroooper	
NNO	Luke Skywalker	
NNO	Super Leader Kylo Ren	

2020 Hasbro Star Wars Battle Bobblers

NNO	Boba Fett vs. Han Solo	
NNO	Porgs vs. Chewie	
NNO	Stormtrooper vs. BB-8	
NNO	C-3PO vs. Trooper	
NNO	R2-D2 vs. Yoda	
NNO	Vader vs. Luke	

2020 Hasbro Star Wars Black Series Empire Strikes Back 40th Anniversary 6-Inch

NNO	4-LOM	20.00	40.00
NNO	Artoo-Detoo (R2-D2) (Dagobah)	25.00	50.00
NNO	AT-AT Driver	15.00	30.00
NNO	Boba Fett	20.00	40.00
NNO	Boba Fett	125.00	250.00
NNO	Chewbacca	25.00	50.00
NNO	Darth Vader	20.00	40.00
NNO	Han Solo (Bespin)	15.00	30.00
NNO	Han Solo (Carbonite)	25.00	50.00
NNO	Imperial Snowtrooper (Hoth)	25.00	50.00
NNO	Imperial TIE Fighter Pilot	12.50	25.00
NNO	Lando Calrissian	12.50	25.00
NNO	Luke Skywalker (Bespin)	15.00	30.00
NNO	Luke Skywalker (Dagobah)	12.50	25.00
NNO	Luke Skywalker (Snowspeeder)	15.00	30.00
NNO	Princess Leia Organa (Hoth)	15.00	30.00
NNO	Rebel Soldier (Hoth)	12.50	25.00
NNO	Yoda	15.00	30.00
NNO	Zuckuss	15.00	30.00

2020 Hasbro Star Wars Black Series Rebels 6-Inch

1	Garazeb "Zeb" Orrelios	20.00	40.00
2	C1-10P "Chopper"	30.00	75.00
3	Ezra Bridger	20.00	40.00
4	Kanan Jarrus	15.00	30.00
5	Hera Syndulla	30.00	60.00
6	Sabine Wren	30.00	75.00
7	Ahsoka Tano	25.00	50.00

2020 Hasbro Star Wars Black Series The Phantom Menace 6-Inch

1	Jar Jar Binks	12.50	25.00

2020 Hasbro Star Wars Black Series The Rise of Skywalker 6-Inch

1	Dark Rey	15.00	30.00

ACTION FIGURES AND FIGURINES

2020 Hasbro Star Wars Celebrate the Saga Multipacks

NNO	Bounty Hunter 5-Pack	12.50	25.00
NNO	First Order 6-Pack BB	20.00	40.00
NNO	Galactic Empire 5-Pack BB	30.00	60.00
NNO	Jedi Order 5-Pack	40.00	80.00
NNO	Rebel Alliance 5-Pack AMZ	20.00	40.00
NNO	Republic 5-Pack	35.00	70.00
NNO	Resistance 6-Pack AMZ	30.00	60.00
NNO	Sith 5-Pack FC	40.00	80.00

2020 Hasbro Star Wars The Mandalorian Bounty Collection 6-Inch

NNO	The Child		

2020 Hasbro Star Wars The Mandalorian Bounty Collection Series 1

NNO	The Child (eating frog)		
NNO	The Child (Force push)		
NNO	The Child (in blanket)		
NNO	The Child (sad face)		
NNO	The Child (w/ball)		
NNO	The Child (w/bowl)		

2020 Hasbro Star Wars The Mandalorian Bounty Collection Series 2

NNO	The Child (control panel)		
NNO	The Child (crib)		
NNO	The Child (helmet)		
NNO	The Child (in satchel)		
NNO	The Child (necklace)		
NNO	The Child (stopping fire)		

2020 Hasbro Star Wars The Mandalorian Bounty Collection Series 3

NNO	The Child (datapad)		
NNO	The Child (grabbing eggs)		
NNO	The Child (helmet)		
NNO	The Child (meditating)		
NNO	The Child (w/cup)		
NNO	The Child (w/spoon & soup)		

2020 Hasbro Star Wars The Mandalorian Talking Plush

NNO	The Child	15.00	30.00

2020 Hasbro Star Wars Retro Collection

NNO	Boba Fett	20.00	40.00
NNO	Han Solo (Hoth)	12.50	25.00
NNO	Lando Calrissian	10.00	20.00
NNO	Luke Skywalker (Bespin)	12.50	25.00
NNO	Luke Skywalker (snowspeeder gear)	25.00	50.00
	(Hoth Ice Planet Adventure Exclusive)		
NNO	Princess Leia Organa (Hoth)	15.00	30.00
NNO	Remnant Stormtrooper		
	(The Mandalorian Monopoly Exclusive)		
NNO	Yoda		

2020 Hasbro Star Wars Retro Collection Multipacks

NNO	Hoth Ice Planet Adventure Game (w/Luke Skywalker snowspeeder gear)		
NNO	The Mandalorian Monopoly (w/Remnant Stormtrooper)		

2020-21 Hasbro Star Wars Mission Fleet

NNO	Ahsoka Tano	12.50	25.00
NNO	Blurrg (w/Kuiil)	30.00	60.00
NNO	Boba Fett	20.00	40.00
NNO	Chewbacca	20.00	40.00
NNO	Clone Trooper	12.50	25.00
NNO	Darth Maul	12.50	25.00
NNO	Shock Trooper	12.50	25.00

2020-21 Hasbro Star Wars Mission Fleet Vehicles

NNO	AT-RT (w/Captain Rex)	12.50	25.00
NNO	Barc Speeder (w/Obi-Wan Kenobi)	10.00	20.00
NNO	Jedi Starfighter (w/Anakin Skywalker)	20.00	40.00
NNO	Jedi Starfighter (w/Obi-Wan Kenobi)		
NNO	Millennium Falcon (w/Han Solo)		
NNO	Razor Crest (w/Mandalorian)		
NNO	Speeder Bike (w/IG-11 and Child)	20.00	40.00
NNO	Speeder Bike (w/Mandalorian and Child)	12.50	25.00

NNO	Speeder Bike (w/Scout Trooper)		
NNO	TIE Advanced (w/Darth Vader)		
NNO	TIE Whisper (w/Kylo Ren)		
NNO	X-Wing Fighter (w/Luke Skywalker)	25.00	50.00

2020-22 Hasbro Star Wars Black Series The Bad Batch 6-Inch

1	Hunter	30.00	75.00
2	Crosshair	30.00	60.00
3	Elite Squad Trooper	15.00	30.00
4	Tech		
5	Wrecker	20.00	40.00
6	Captain Rex WM	25.00	50.00
7	Shock Trooper WM		
8	Vice Admiral Rampart w/MSE WM		
9	Crosshair (Imperial)		
10	Omega w/Ruby (Kamino)	15.00	30.00
11	Echo	15.00	30.00
12	Cad Bane (Bracca)	25.00	50.00
	(Amazon Exclusive)		

2020-22 Hasbro Star Wars Black Series Empire Strikes Back 6-Inch

1	Darth Vader	25.00	50.00
2	Luke Skywalker	20.00	40.00
3	Hoth Rebel Trooper	15.00	30.00
4	Boba Fett (prototype armor)		
	(Amazon Exclusive)		

2020-22 Hasbro Star Wars Black Series Exclusives 6-Inch

NNO	Anakin Skywalker	30.00	75.00
NNO	ARC Trooper Captain	30.00	75.00
	(Walmart Exclusive)		
NNO	Armorer	30.00	75.00
NNO	Battle Droid	15.00	30.00
	(Best Buy Exclusive)		
NNO	Boba Fett (Droids)	25.00	50.00
	(Target Exclusive)		
NNO	Cad Bane (w/Todo 360)	100.00	200.00
NNO	Cassian Andor w/B2EMO		
	(Hasbro Pulse Con Exclusive)		
NNO	Clone Pilot Hawk	15.00	30.00
NNO	Clone Trooper Echo	50.00	100.00
NNO	General Grievous	25.00	50.00
	(Walmart Exclusive)		
NNO	George Lucas (in stormtrooper disguise)	25.00	50.00
	(Fan Channel Exclusive)		
NNO	Greedo (classic)		
	(Amazon Exclusive)		
NNO	Greedo		
	(Hasbro Pulse Exclusive)		
NNO	Han Solo		
	(Hasbro Pulse Exclusive)		
NNO	Jar Jar Binks		
	(Best Buy Exclusive)		
NNO	Jawa		
	(Amazon Exclusive)		
NNO	Jon Favreau as Paz Vizsla		
	(Star Wars Celebration Exclusive)		
NNO	Luke Skywalker		
	(Hasbro Pulse Exclusive)		

NNO Mace Windu		
(Best Buy Exclusive)		
NNO Mace Windu	30.00	60.00
(Walmart Exclusive)		
NNO Obi-Wan Kenobi	20.00	40.00
(Amazon Exclusive)		
NNO Obi-Wan Kenobi	40.00	80.00
NNO Princess Leia Organa		
(Hasbro Pulse Exclusive)		
NNO Qui-Gon Jinn	25.00	50.00
(Best Buy Exclusive)		
NNO Trapper Wolf	30.00	75.00
(Hasbro Pulse Exclusive)		

2020-22 Hasbro Star Wars Black Series Holiday Edition 6-Inch

NNO Clone Trooper w/Porg GS	20.00	40.00
NNO Clone Trooper w/Porg Skeleton TAR		
NNO Imperial Stormtrooper w/Porg AMZ	20.00	40.00
NNO Range Trooper w/D-0 TAR	20.00	40.00
NNO Sith Trooper w/Babu Frik BB	15.00	30.00
NNO Snowtrooper w/Porg WM	15.00	30.00
NNO Wookiee w/Bogling Jack O Lantern WM		

2020-22 Hasbro Star Wars Black Series Multi-Packs 6-Inch

NNO Cantina Showdown 3PK HP		
NNO Concept Art Ed. 2PK SD		
NNO Droid Depot 5PK DIS		
NNO First Order 4PK DIS		
NNO Galactic Creatures 6PK DIS		
NNO Heroes of Endor 4PK HP		

2020-22 Hasbro Star Wars Black Series Return of the Jedi 6-Inch

1 Admiral Ackbar	15.00	30.00
2 Teebo	20.00	40.00
3 Princess Leia Organa (Endor)	15.00	30.00
4 Luke Skywalker (Endor)	30.00	60.00
5 Han Solo (Endor)	15.00	30.00
6 Boba Fett	25.00	50.00
7 Lando Calrissian	12.50	25.00
8 Bib Fortuna	20.00	40.00
9 Princess Leia (Ewok Village)		

2020-22 Hasbro Star Wars Black Series Rogue One 6-Inch

1 Jyn Erso	12.50	25.00
2 Cassian Andor	12.50	25.00
3 K-2SO	12.50	25.00
4 Chirrut Imwe	12.50	25.00
5 Baze Malbus	12.50	25.00
6 Bodhi Rook	12.50	25.00
7 Galen Erso	12.50	25.00
(Target Exclusive)		
8 Antoc Merrick	15.00	30.00
(Target Exclusive)		
9 Stormtrooper Jedha Patrol	12.50	25.00
10 Saw Gerrera	25.00	50.00

2020-23 Hasbro Star Wars Black Series Attack of the Clones 6-Inch

1 Clone Trooper Blue WG	25.00	50.00
2 Clone Trooper	20.00	40.00
3 Aayla Secura		

2020-23 Hasbro Star Wars Black Series The Clone Wars 6-Inch

1 Clone Trooper	25.00	50.00
2 Ahsoka Tano	30.00	75.00
3 332nd Ahsoka's Clone Trooper	25.00	50.00
4 Mandalorian Loyalist	30.00	60.00
5 Mandalorian Super Commando	30.00	60.00
6 Cad Bane	25.00	50.00
7 Asajj Ventress	20.00	40.00
8 Aurra Sing	12.50	25.00
9 212th Battalion Clone Trooper WG	30.00	60.00
10 187th Battalion Clone Trooper WG	20.00	40.00
11 Darth Maul		

2020-23 Hasbro Star Wars Black Series The Mandalorian 6-Inch

1 The Mandalorian	20.00	40.00
2 Stormtrooper	20.00	40.00
3 Incinerator Stormtrooper	15.00	30.00
4 The Armorer	15.00	30.00
5 Din Djarin w/Grogu TAR	30.00	75.00
6 Greef Karga	12.50	25.00
7 Kuiil	12.50	25.00
8 Moff Gideon	12.50	25.00
9 Stormtrooper TAR	20.00	40.00
10 Bo-Katan Kryze	12.50	25.00
11 Q9-0	15.00	30.00
12 Koska Reeves		
13 Artillery Stormtrooper AMZ		
14 The Mandalorian & Grogu (Arvala 7) TAR		
15 Migs Mayfield (Morak)	12.50	25.00
16 Boba Fett (Tython)		
17 The Mandalorian & Grogu w/Spider TAR		
18 Cobb Vanth	20.00	40.00
19 Ahsoka Tano	15.00	30.00
20 The Client	12.50	25.00
21 Death Watch Mandalorian	15.00	30.00
22 Boba Fett (Tython/Jedi Ruins) WM		
23 New Republic Security Droid	25.00	50.00
24 Greef Karga		

2020-23 Hasbro Star Wars Black Series The Mandalorian 6-Inch Vehicles

NNO Speeder Bike Scout Trooper & The Child	50.00	100.00

2020-23 Hasbro Star Wars Black Series The Mandalorian Credit Collection 6-Inch

NNO Ahsoka Tano TAR		
NNO Armorer GS		
NNO Boba Fett WM		
NNO Bo-Katan Kryze FC		
NNO Cara Dune TAR	30.00	75.00
NNO Dark Trooper HAS	30.00	75.00
NNO Din Djarin AMZ		
NNO Greef Karga FC	15.00	30.00
NNO Heavy Infantry Mandalorian BB	20.00	40.00

NNO IG-11 GS	15.00	30.00
NNO Imperial Death Trooper AMZ	15.00	30.00
NNO Kuiil AMZ	20.00	40.00
NNO The Mandalorian (Din Djarin w/thick credit) AMZ	20.00	40.00
NNO The Mandalorian (Din Djarin w/thin credit) AMZ		
NNO Moff Gideon BB	15.00	30.00
NNO Tusken Raider GS		

2021 Hasbro Star Wars Retro Collection

NNO Boba Fett (prototype edition)	25.00	50.00
(Target Exclusive)		
NNO Cara Dune	12.50	25.00
NNO Din Djarin	12.50	25.00
NNO Greef Karga	7.50	15.00
NNO Grogu		
NNO IG-11		
NNO Kuiil	7.50	15.00
NNO Moff Gideon	7.50	15.00
NNO Stormtrooper (prototype edition)	15.00	30.00
(Target Exclusive)		

2021-22 Hasbro Star Wars Black Series A New Hope 6-Inch

1 Princess Leia Organa (Yavin 4)	
2 Ponda Baba	
3 Dr. Evazan	
4 Figrin D'An	
5 Nalan Cheel (The Modal Nodes)	
(Hasbro Pulse/ShopDisney Exclusive)	

2021-22 Hasbro Star Wars Black Series Archive Collection 6-Inch

NNO Admiral Thrawn	
NNO C-3PO	
NNO Chewbacca	
NNO Clone Trooper	
NNO Commander Cody	
NNO Darth Revan	
NNO Death Trooper	
NNO Dengar	
NNO Grand Moff Tarkin w/IT-O	
NNO Han Solo	
NNO Han Solo (Hoth)	
NNO Imperial Assault Tank Driver	
NNO Lando Calrissian	
NNO Luke Skywalker	
NNO Obi-Wan Kenobi	
NNO Palpatine (Darth Sidious)	
NNO Princess Leia Organa	
NNO Princess Leia Organa (Boushh)	
NNO Shoretrooper	
NNO Tusken Raider	

2021-22 Hasbro Star Wars Black Series Carbonized Series 6-Inch

NNO Biker Scout	
(Target Exclusive)	
NNO Paz Vizsla	
(Target Exclusive)	
NNO Shoretrooper	
(Target Exclusive)	

2021-22 Hasbro Star Wars Black Series Comic Book and Novel 6-Inch

1	Black Krrsantan	20.00	40.00
2	Boba Fett (in disguise)	15.00	30.00
3	Carnor Jax	12.50	25.00
4	Darth Maul (Sith Apprentice)	20.00	40.00
5	Darth Vader		
6	Jaxxon	12.50	25.00
7	Luke Skywalker & Ysalamiri		
8	Princess Leia Organa		
9	Sergeant Kreel	20.00	40.00

2021-23 Hasbro Star Wars Black Series Gaming Greats 6-Inch

1 Imperial Rocket Trooper (Star Wars: Battlefront II)
2 Cal Kestis w/BD-1 & Bogling (Star Wars Jedi: Fallen Order)
3 Flametrooper (Star Wars Jedi: Fallen Order)
4 Zaalbar (Star Wars: Knights of the Old Republic)
5 Nightbrother Warrior (Star Wars Jedi: Fallen Order)
6 Jet Trooper (Star Wars: Battlefront II)
7 RC-1138 (Boss)(Star Wars: Republic Commando)
8 Imperial Senate Guard (Star Wars: The Force Unleashed)
9 Umbra Operative ARC Trooper (Star Wars: Battlefront II)
10 Nightbrother Archer (Star Wars Jedi: Fallen Order)
11 RC-1207 (SEV)(Star Wars: Republic Commando)
12 13th Battalion Clone Trooper
13 Fixer Republic Commando
14 Biker Scout (Star Wars Jedi: Survivor)

2021-23 Hasbro Star Wars Black Series The Book of Boba Fett 6-Inch

1 Fennec Shand
2 Boba Fett
3 Black Krrsantan

2022-23 Hasbro Star Wars Black Series Obi-Wan Kenobi 6-Inch

1 Obi-Wan Kenobi w/L0-La59 (Wandering Jedi)
2 Darth Vader
3 Reva (Third Sister)
4 Fifth Brother (Inquisitor)
5 Teeka (Jawa)
(Target Exclusive)
6 Obi-Wan Kenobi (Tibidon Station)
7 Purge Stormtrooper (Phase II Armor)
(Walmart Exclusive)
8 1-JAC
(Walmart Exclusive)
9 Grand Inquisitor
10 NED-B
11 Obi-Wan Kenobi (Jabiim)
12 Fourth Sister (Inquisitor)
13 Tala (Imperial Officer)

2023 Hasbro Star Wars Black Series Return of the Jedi 40th Anniversary 6-Inch

NNO Admiral Ackbar
NNO Bib Fortuna
NNO Biker Scout
NNO Boba Fett Deluxe

NNO Chewbacca
NNO Endor Rebel Soldier Commando
NNO Han Solo (Endor)
NNO Lando Calrissian (Skiff Guard)
NNO Palpatine (Darth Sidious)
NNO Paploo
NNO Princess Leia (Endor)
NNO Stormtrooper
NNO Wicket

2023 Hasbro Star Wars Black Series Revenge of the Sith 6-Inch

1 Ki-Adi Mundi

2023 Hasbro Star Wars Retro Collection

NNO Biker Scout
NNO Han Solo (Endor)
NNO Lando Calrissian (Skiff Guard)
NNO Luke Skywalker (Jedi Knight)
NNO Palpatine (Darth Sidious)
NNO Princess Leia Organa

2016 Jakks Pacific Star Wars Rogue One Big Figs

NNO	Imperial Death Trooper	20.00	40.00
NNO	Imperial Stormtrooper	30.00	60.00
NNO	K-2SO	25.00	50.00
NNO	Sergeant Jyn Erso	12.00	25.00

2017 Jakks Pacific Star Wars The Last Jedi Big Figs

NNO	Captain Phasma	15.00	30.00
NNO	Elite Praetorian Guard	12.50	25.00
NNO	First Order Executioner	25.00	50.00
NNO	First Order Stormtrooper	10.00	20.00
NNO	Kylo Ren	12.50	25.00
NNO	Poe Dameron	10.00	20.00
NNO	Rey	12.50	25.00

1993 JusToys Star Wars Bend Ems

1	Admiral Ackbar	7.50	15.00
2	Ben Kenobi	10.00	20.00
3	Bib Fortuna	7.50	15.00
4	Boba Fett	15.00	30.00
5	C-3PO	10.00	20.00

6	Chewbacca	7.50	15.00
7	Darth Vader	12.50	25.00
8	Emperor	10.00	20.00
9	Emperor's Royal Guard	7.50	15.00
10	Gamorrean Guard	7.50	15.00
11	Han Solo	10.00	20.00
12	Lando Calrissian	7.50	15.00
13	Leia Organa	10.00	20.00
14	Luke Skywalker	10.00	20.00
15	Luke Skywalker X-wing	10.00	20.00
16	R2-D2	7.50	15.00
17	Stormtrooper	7.50	15.00
18	Tusken Raider	7.50	15.00
19	Wicket	7.50	15.00
20	Yoda	7.50	15.00
21	4-Piece A New Hope	20.00	40.00
	(Chewbacca/Luke Skywalker/R2-D2/Tusken Raider)		
22	4-Piece Empire Strikes Back	20.00	40.00
	(Han Solo/Darth Vader/Yoda/Lando Calrissian)		
23	4-Piece Return of the Jedi	25.00	50.00
	(Admiral Ackbar/Boba Fett/Wicket/Bib Fortuna)		
24	4-Piece Gift Set 1	20.00	40.00
	(Ben Kenobi/Leia Organa/Han Solo/C-3PO)		
25	4-Piece Gift Set 2	20.00	40.00
	(Storm Trooper/Wicket/Yoda/Chewbacca)		
26	4-Piece Gift Set 3	20.00	40.00
	(Storm Trooper/R2-D2/C-3PO/Darth Vader)		
27	4-Piece Gift Set 4	20.00	40.00
	(Emperor/C-3PO/Luke Skywalker/Darth Vader)		
28	6-Piece Gift Set 1	25.00	50.00
	(Darth Vader/Stormtrooper/Luke Skywalker/R2-D2/C-3PO		
29	6-Piece Gift Set 2	25.00	50.00
	(Stormtrooper/Darth Vader/Emperor's Royal Guard		
	Admiral Ackbar/Lando Calrissian/Chewbacca)		
30	8-Piece Gift Set	25.00	50.00
	(Darth Vader/Luke Skywalker/C-3PO/Emperor		
	Stormtrooper/R2-D2/Princess Leia/Ewok)		
31	10-Piece Gift Set	30.00	60.00
	(R2-D2/Stormtrooper/Darth Vader/Admiral Ackbar		
	Chewbacca/Han Solo/Princess Leia/Luke Skywalker		
	Bib Fortuna/Emperor's Royal Guard)		

1995-00 Kenner Star Wars Power of the Force 3-Packs

NNO	Lando/Chewbacca/Han Solo	10.00	20.00
NNO	Lando/Luke Dagobah/TIE Fighter Pilot	10.00	20.00
NNO	Luke Jedi/AT-ST Driver/Leia Boushh	20.00	40.00
NNO	Luke Stormtrooper/Tusken Raider/Ben Kenobi	12.50	25.00
NNO	Luke/Ben Kenobi/Darth Vader	10.00	20.00
NNO	Stormtrooper/R2-D2/C-3PO	10.00	20.00

1995-00 Kenner Star Wars Power of the Force
Accessories

1 Escape the Death Star Action Figure Game	20.00	40.00
2 Millennium Falcon Carrying Case (w/Imperial Scanning Trooper)	20.00	40.00
3 Millennium Falcon Carrying Case (w/Wedge)	15.00	30.00
4 Power of the Force Carrying Case	6.00	12.00
5 Talking C-3PO Carrying Case	25.00	50.00

1995-00 Kenner Star Wars Power of the Force
Cinema Scenes

1 Cantina Aliens	10.00	20.00
2a Cantina Showdown (.00)	6.00	12.00
2b Cantina Showdown (.01)	6.00	12.00
3a Death Star Escape (.00)	12.00	25.00
3b Death Star Escape (.01)	12.00	25.00
4a Final Jedi Duel (.00)	10.00	20.00
4b Final Jedi Duel (.01)	12.50	25.00
5 Jabba the Hutt's Dancers	15.00	30.00
6 Jabba's Skiff Guards	12.50	25.00
7 Jedi Spirits	10.00	20.00
8 Mynock Hunt	12.50	25.00
9 Purchase of the Droids	10.00	20.00
10 Rebel Pilots	10.00	20.00

1995-00 Kenner Star Wars Power of the Force
Comm-Tech

1 Admiral Motti	20.00	40.00
2a Darth Vader (holographic chip)	8.00	15.00
2b Darth Vader (white chip)	8.00	15.00
3 Greedo	7.50	15.00
4 Han Solo	6.00	12.00
5a Jawa (w/Gonk Droid holographic chip)	8.00	15.00
5b Jawa (w/Gonk Droid white chip)	8.00	15.00
6 Luke Skywalker (w/T16 Skyhopper)	6.00	12.00
7 Princess Leia	8.00	15.00

8 R2-D2 (w/Princess Leia)	10.00	20.00
9 Stormtrooper	10.00	20.00
10a Wuher (no sticker)	8.00	15.00
(2000 Fan Club Exclusive)		
10b Wuher (sticker)	6.00	12.00
(2000 Fan Club Exclusive)		

1995-00 Kenner Star Wars Power of the Force
Complete Galaxy

1 Dagobah (w/Yoda)	8.00	15.00
2 Death Star (w/Darth Vader)	12.00	25.00
3a Endor (w/Ewok) (.00)	15.00	30.00
3b Endor (w/Ewok) (.01)	15.00	30.00
4 Tatooine (w/Luke)	10.00	20.00

1995-00 Kenner Star Wars Power of the Force
Creatures

1 Bantha & Tusken Raider	50.00	100.00
2 Dewback & Sandtrooper	30.00	75.00
3a Jabba the Hutt & Han Solo (Han on left)		
3b Jabba the Hutt & Han Solo (Han on right)	15.00	30.00
4 Rancor & Luke Skywalker	30.00	60.00
5 Ronto & Jawa	20.00	40.00
6 Tauntaun & Han Solo	25.00	50.00
7 Tauntaun & Luke Skywalker	25.00	50.00
8 Wampa & Luke Skywalker	20.00	40.00

1995-00 Kenner Star Wars Power of the Force
Deluxe

NNO Boba Fett (photon torpedo)	12.50	25.00
NNO Boba Fett (proton torpedo)	10.00	20.00
NNO Han Solo (Smuggler's Flight)	7.50	15.00
NNO Hoth Rebel Soldier	7.50	15.00
NNO Luke Skywalker (Desert Sport Skiff)	25.00	50.00
NNO Probe Droid (printed warning/green cardback)	12.50	25.00
NNO Probe Droid (printed warning/red cardback)	7.50	15.00
NNO Probe Droid (warning sticker/red cardback)	10.00	20.00

NNO Snowtrooper (Tripod Cannon)	12.50	25.00
NNO Stormtrooper (Crowd Control)(no sticker)	7.50	15.00
NNO Stormtrooper (Crowd Control)(warning sticker)	7.50	15.00

1995-00 Kenner Star Wars Power of the Force
Epic Force

1 Bespin Luke Skywalker	5.00	12.00
2 Boba Fett	20.00	40.00
3 C-3PO	8.00	15.00
4 Chewbacca	5.00	12.00
5 Darth Vader	15.00	30.00
6 Han Solo	5.00	12.00
7 Obi-Wan Kenobi	7.50	15.00
8 Princess Leia	4.00	8.00
9 Stormtrooper	6.00	12.00

1995-00 Kenner Star Wars Power of the Force
Exclusives

1a B-Omarr Monk (.00)	12.50	25.00
(1997 Online Exclusive)		
1b B-Omarr Monk (.01)	12.50	25.00
(1997 Online Exclusive)		
2 C-3PO (greenish tint)	15.00	30.00
(Japanese Exclusive)		
3 Cantina Band Member	6.00	15.00
(1997 Fan Club Exclusive)		
4 Han Solo (w/Tauntaun)	15.00	30.00
(1997 Toys R Us Exclusive)		
5 Han Solo Stormtrooper	8.00	15.00
(Kellogg's Mail Order Exclusive)		
6 Kabe and Muftak	15.00	30.00
(1998 Online Exclusive)		
7 Luke Skywalker Jedi Knight	10.00	20.00
(Theater Edition Exclusive)		
8 Oola & Salacious Crumb	20.00	40.00
(1998 Fan Club Exclusive)		
9 Spirit of Obi-Wan Kenobi	8.00	15.00
(Frito-Lay Mail Order Exclusive)		
10 Spirit of Obi-Wan Kenobi		
(UK Special Edition Exclusive)		

1995-00 Kenner Star Wars Power of the Force
Expanded Universe Vehicles

1 Airspeeder (w/pilot)	20.00	40.00
2 Cloud Car (w/pilot)	10.00	20.00
3 Rebel Speeder Bike (w/pilot)	12.00	25.00

ACTION FIGURES AND FIGURINES

1995-00 Kenner Star Wars Power of the Force
Flashback

1 Anakin Skywalker		5.00	10.00
2 Aunt Beru		7.50	15.00
3 C-3PO (removable arm)		10.00	20.00
4 Darth Vader		10.00	20.00
5 Emperor Palpatine		8.00	15.00
6 Hoth Chewbacca		6.00	12.00
7 Luke Skywalker		7.50	15.00
8 Obi-Wan Kenobi		6.00	12.00
9 Princess Leia (ceremonial dress)		7.50	15.00
10a R2-D2 (pop-up lightsaber)(forward position)		7.50	15.00
10b R2-D2 (pop-up lightsaber)(slanted)		7.50	15.00
11 Yoda		6.00	12.00

1995-00 Kenner Star Wars Power of the Force
Freeze Frame Collection 1

1 C-3PO (removable limbs)		7.50	15.00
2a Endor Rebel Commando (.00)		5.00	10.00
2b Endor Rebel Commando (.01)		5.00	10.00
3 Garindan (long snoot)		10.00	20.00
4 Han Solo		6.00	12.00
5 Han Solo (Bespin)		6.00	12.00
6a Han Solo (carbonite)(.04)		7.50	15.00
6b Han Solo (carbonite)(.05)		7.50	15.00
7a Han Solo (Endor)(.01)		5.00	10.00
7b Han Solo (Endor)(.02)		5.00	10.00
8a Hoth Rebel Soldier (.02)		5.00	10.00
8b Hoth Rebel Soldier (.03)		5.00	10.00

9a Lando Calrissian (General)(.00)		5.00	10.00
9b Lando Calrissian (General)(.01)		5.00	10.00
10a Lando Calrissian (Skiff guard)(.01)		5.00	10.00
10b Lando Calrissian (Skiff guard)(.02)		5.00	10.00
11 Lobot		5.00	10.00
12a Luke Skywalker (Bespin)(w/gold buckle)(.00)		6.00	12.00
12b Luke Skywalker (Bespin)(w/gold buckle)(.01)		6.00	12.00
12c Luke Skywalker (Bespin)(w/silver buckle)(.00)		6.00	12.00
12d Luke Skywalker (Bespin)(w/silver buckle)(.01)		6.00	12.00
13 Luke Skywalker (blast shield helmet)		7.50	15.00
14 Luke Skywalker (ceremonial)		5.00	10.00
15a Luke Skywalker (stormtrooper disguise)(.03)		7.50	15.00
15b Luke Skywalker (stormtrooper disguise)(.04)		5.00	10.00
16 Mon Mothma		6.00	12.00
17a Obi-Wan Kenobi (.03)		7.50	15.00
17b Obi-Wan Kenobi (.04)		7.50	15.00
18 Orrimaarko (Prune Face)		10.00	20.00
19 Princess Leia Organa (Ewok celebration)		5.00	10.00
20a Princess Leia Organa (Jabba's prisoner)(.01)		7.50	15.00
20b Princess Leia Organa (Jabba's prisoner)(.02)		7.50	15.00
21 Princess Leia Organa (new likeness)		5.00	10.00
22a R2-D2 (Death Star slide)		6.00	12.00
22b R2-D2 (Imperial slide)		6.00	12.00
23a Rebel Fleet Trooper (.01)		6.00	12.00
23b Rebel Fleet Trooper (.02)		6.00	12.00
23c Rebel Fleet Trooper (w/sticker)(.01)		5.00	10.00

1995-00 Kenner Star Wars Power of the Force
Freeze Frame Collection 2

1 8D8		7.50	15.00
2a Admiral Ackbar (comlink wrist blaster)		6.00	12.00
2b Admiral Ackbar (wrist blaster)		6.00	12.00
3 Biggs Darklighter		4.00	8.00
4 EV-9D9		5.00	10.00
5 Ewoks Wicket & Logray		12.50	25.00
6 Gamorrean Guard		6.00	12.00
7a Han Solo (Bespin)(.02)		7.50	15.00
7b Han Solo (Bespin)(.03)		7.50	15.00
8 Lak Sivrak		6.00	12.00
9 Malakili (Rancor Keeper)		5.00	10.00
10 Nien Nunb		5.00	10.00
11 Saelt-Marae (Yak Face)		5.00	10.00
12 Ugnaughts		7.50	15.00

1995-00 Kenner Star Wars Power of the Force
Freeze Frame Collection 3

1 AT-AT Driver		10.00	20.00
(1998 Fan Club Exclusive)			
2 Boba Fett		6.00	15.00
3a Captain Piett (baton sticker)		5.00	10.00
3b Captain Piett (pistol sticker)		5.00	10.00
4 Darth Vader		6.00	12.00
5 Darth Vader (removable helmet)		8.00	15.00
6 Death Star Droid (w/mouse droid)		8.00	15.00
7 Death Star Trooper		12.00	25.00
8 Emperor Palpatine		8.00	15.00
9 Emperor's Royal Guard		8.00	15.00
10 Grand Moff Tarkin		6.00	12.00
11a Ishi Tib (brown pouch)		5.00	10.00
11b Ishi Tib (gray pouch)		5.00	10.00
12 Pote Snitkin		12.00	25.00
(1999 Internet Exclusive)			
13 Princess Leia Organa (Hoth)		8.00	15.00
(1999 Fan Club Exclusive)			
14 Ree-Yees		6.00	12.00
15 Sandtrooper		25.00	50.00
16 Snowtrooper		5.00	10.00
17 Stormtrooper		5.00	10.00
18 TIE Fighter Pilot		5.00	10.00
19 Weequay		90.00	175.00
20 Zuckuss		4.00	8.00

1995-00 Kenner Star Wars Power of the Force
Green Collection 1

1a Bib Fortuna (hologram)	6.00	12.00
1b Bib Fortuna (photo)	6.00	12.00
2 Boba Fett (hologram)	15.00	30.00
3 C-3PO (hologram)	8.00	15.00
4a Chewbacca	10.00	20.00
4b Chewbacca (hologram)	4.00	8.00
5a Darth Vader	6.00	12.00
5b Darth Vader (hologram)	8.00	15.00
6a Death Star Gunner	6.00	12.00
6b Death Star Gunner (hologram)	6.00	12.00
7a Emperor Palpatine	6.00	12.00
7b Emperor Palpatine (hologram)	6.00	12.00
8 Garindan (long snoot)	4.00	8.00
9a Greedo	6.00	12.00
9b Greedo (hologram)	6.00	12.00
10a Han Solo	5.00	10.00
10b Han Solo (hologram)	6.00	12.00
11a Han Solo (Bespin)	6.00	12.00
11b Han Solo (Bespin)(hologram)	6.00	12.00
12a Han Solo (carbonite stand-up bubble)	8.00	15.00
12b Han Solo (carbonite stand-up bubble)(hologram)	8.00	15.00
13a Han Solo (Endor blue pants)	8.00	15.00
13b Han Solo (Endor blue pants)(hologram)	8.00	15.00
13c Han Solo (Endor brown pants)	10.00	20.00
14 Hoth Rebel Soldier (hologram)	5.00	10.00
15 Lando Calrissian	20.00	40.00
16 Lando Calrissian (Skiff guard)(hologram)	6.00	12.00
17a Luke Skywalker (ceremonial)	5.00	10.00
17b Luke Skywalker (ceremonial)(hologram)	5.00	10.00
18 Luke Skywalker (Hoth)(hologram)	5.00	10.00
19a Luke Skywalker (Jedi Knight)	6.00	12.00
19b Luke Skywalker (Jedi Knight)(hologram)	6.00	12.00
20 Luke Skywalker (stormtrooper disguise)(hologram)	6.00	12.00
21 Luke Skywalker (X-Wing pilot)(hologram)	8.00	15.00
22a Obi-Wan Kenobi (hologram)	5.00	10.00
22b Obi-Wan Kenobi (photo)	5.00	10.00
23a Princess Leia Organa (Jabba's prisoner)	5.00	10.00
23b Princess Leia Organa (Jabba's prisoner) (hologram)	5.00	10.00
24a Princess Leia Organa (photo)		
24b Princess Leia Organa (three-ring belt)	10.00	20.00
24c Princess Leia Organa (two-ring belt)(hologram)	8.00	15.00
25 R2-D2	10.00	20.00
26 Rebel Fleet Trooper (hologram)	5.00	10.00
27a Sandtrooper	8.00	15.00
27b Sandtrooper (hologram)	8.00	15.00
28a Yoda	6.00	12.00
28b Yoda (hologram)	6.00	12.00

1995-00 Kenner Star Wars Power of the Force Green Collection 2

1a 2-1B (.00)	5.00	10.00
1b 2-1B (.00)(hologram)	6.00	12.00
1c 2-1B (.01)	4.00	8.00
1d 2-1B (.01)(hologram)	6.00	12.00
2a 4-LOM	6.00	12.00
2b 4-LOM (hologram)	6.00	12.00
3 Admiral Ackbar	4.00	8.00
4a ASP-7 (hologram)	5.00	10.00
4b ASP-7 (photo)	5.00	10.00
5a AT-ST Driver	7.50	15.00
5b AT-ST Driver (hologram)	5.00	10.00
6a Bib Fortuna (hologram/stand-up bubble)	4.00	8.00
6b Bib Fortuna (hologram/straight bubble)	5.00	10.00
7a Bossk (.00)(hologram)	4.00	8.00
7b Bossk (.00)(photo)	4.00	8.00
7c Bossk (.01)(photo)	6.00	12.00
8 Clone Emperor Palpatine (Expanded Universe)	8.00	15.00
9 Darktrooper (Expanded Universe)	10.00	20.00
10a Dengar (hologram)	7.50	15.00
10b Dengar (photo)	6.00	12.00
11a EV-9D9 (hologram)	6.00	12.00
11b EV-9D9 (photo)	6.00	12.00
12 Gamorrean Guard (hologram)	5.00	10.00
13 Grand Admiral Thrawn (Expanded Universe)	20.00	40.00
14a Grand Moff Tarkin	5.00	10.00
14b Grand Moff Tarkin (hologram)	5.00	10.00
15a Han Solo (carbonite)	6.00	12.00
15b Han Solo (carbonite)(hologram)	7.50	15.00
16a Hoth Rebel Soldier	5.00	10.00
16b Hoth Rebel Soldier (hologram)	5.00	10.00
17 Imperial Sentinel (Expanded Universe)	10.00	20.00
18a Jawas	5.00	10.00
18b Jawas (hologram)	5.00	10.00
18c Jawas (new bubble)	6.00	12.00
18d Jawas (new bubble)(hologram)	6.00	12.00
19 Kyle Katarn (Expanded Universe)	10.00	20.00
20a Luke Skywalker (ceremonial)(hologram)	5.00	10.00
20b Luke Skywalker (ceremonial/different head)		
21 Luke Skywalker (Expanded Universe)	10.00	20.00

22a Luke Skywalker (Hoth)	5.00	10.00
22b Luke Skywalker (Hoth)(hologram)	5.00	10.00
23a Luke Skywalker (Jedi Knight)	6.00	12.00
23b Luke Skywalker (Jedi Knight)(hologram)	7.50	15.00
24a Luke Skywalker (stormtrooper disguise)	7.50	15.00
24b Luke Skywalker (stormtrooper disguise)(hologram)	6.00	12.00
25 Malakili (Rancor Keeper)(hologram)	4.00	8.00
26 Mara Jade (Expanded Universe)	15.00	30.00
27a Momaw Nadon (Hammerhead)	3.00	8.00
27b Momaw Nadon (Hammerhead)(hologram)	4.00	8.00
28 Nien Nunb (hologram)	4.00	8.00
29a Ponda Baba (black beard) (hologram)	5.00	10.00
29b Ponda Baba (gray beard) (hologram)	5.00	10.00
30 Princess Leia (Expanded Universe)	8.00	15.00
31a R5-D4 (no warning sticker/L-latch)	5.00	10.00
31b R5-D4 (no warning sticker/L-latch)(hologram)	5.00	10.00
31c R5-D4 (no warning sticker/straight latch)	5.00	10.00
31d R5-D4 (no warning sticker/straight latch)(hologram)	5.00	10.00
31e R5-D4 (warning sticker/L-latch)	5.00	10.00
31f R5-D4 (warning sticker/L-latch)(hologram)	5.00	10.00
31g R5-D4 (warning sticker/straight latch)	5.00	10.00
31h R5-D4 (warning sticker/straight latch)(hologram)	5.00	10.00
32a Rebel Fleet Trooper		
32b Rebel Fleet Trooper (hologram)		
33 Saelt-Marae (Yak Face)(hologram)		
34 Spacetrooper (Expanded Universe)	8.00	15.00
35 TIE Fighter Pilot (hologram)		
36 Tusken Raider (hologram)	4.00	8.00
37 Weequay		
38a Yoda		
38b Yoda (hologram)		

1995-00 Kenner Star Wars Power of the Force Green Collection 3

1 AT-ST Driver	5.00	10.00
2 AT-ST Driver (hologram)	5.00	10.00
3 Boba Fett (hologram)	12.00	25.00
4 Darth Vader (hologram)	4.00	8.00
5a Death Star Gunner	5.00	10.00
5b Death Star Gunner (hologram)	5.00	10.00
6 Emperor Palpatine (hologram)	4.00	8.00
7a Emperor's Royal Guard	6.00	12.00
7b Emperor's Royal Guard (hologram)	6.00	12.00
8a Garindan (long snoot)(hologram)	4.00	8.00

8b Garindan (long snoot)(photo)	4.00	8.00
9 Grand Moff Tarkin	4.00	8.00
10a Ponda Baba (black beard)	5.00	10.00
10b Ponda Baba (gray beard)	50.00	100.00
11a Sandtrooper	5.00	10.00
11b Sandtrooper (hologram)	5.00	10.00
12a Snowtrooper		
12b Snowtrooper (hologram)		
13a Stormtrooper	5.00	10.00
13b Stormtrooper (holosticker)	5.00	10.00
14 TIE Fighter Pilot (hologram)	6.00	12.00
15 Weequay (hologram)	4.00	8.00

1995-00 Kenner Star Wars Power of the Force Gunner Stations

1a Gunner Station (Millennium Falcon w/Han Solo)(.00)	6.00	12.00
1b Gunner Station (Millennium Falcon w/Han Solo)(.01)	6.00	12.00
2a Gunner Station (Millennium Falcon w/Luke Skywalker)(.00)	6.00	12.00
2b Gunner Station (Millennium Falcon w/Luke Skywalker)(.01)	6.00	12.00
3 Gunner Station (TIE Fighter w/Darth Vader)	8.00	15.00

1995-00 Kenner Star Wars Power of the Force Max Rebo Band Pairs

1a Droopy McCool & Barquin D'an (CGI Sy Snootles on back)	12.00	25.00
(1998 Walmart Exclusive)		
1b Droopy McCool & Barquin D'an (puppet Sy Snootles on back)	8.00	15.00
(1998 Walmart Exclusive)		
2 Max Rebo & Doda Bodonawieedo	15.00	30.00
3a Sy Snootles & Joh Yowza (CGI Sy Snootles on back)	12.00	25.00
(1998 Walmart Exclusive)		
3b Sy Snootles & Joh Yowza (puppet Sy Snootles on back)	8.00	15.00
(1998 Walmart Exclusive)		

1995-00 Kenner Star Wars Power of the Force Millennium Mint

1 C-3PO	5.00	12.00
2a Chewbacca (.00)	6.00	12.00
(1998 Toys R Us Exclusive)		
2b Chewbacca (.01/new insert)	6.00	12.00
(1998 Toys R Us Exclusive)		
3 Emperor Palpatine	5.00	12.00
(1998 Toys R Us Exclusive)		
4a Han Solo (Bespin)(.00)	6.00	12.00
(1998 Toys R Us Exclusive)		
4b Han Solo (Bespin)(.01/new insert)	12.00	25.00
(1998 Toys R Us Exclusive)		
5a Luke Skywalker (Endor gear)(.00)	10.00	20.00
(1998 Toys R Us Exclusive)		
5b Luke Skywalker (Endor gear)(.01)	8.00	15.00
(1998 Toys R Us Exclusive)		
6a Princess Leia (Endor gear)(.00)	12.00	25.00
(1998 Toys R Us Exclusive)		
6b Princess Leia (Endor gear)(.01)	10.00	20.00
(1998 Toys R Us Exclusive)		
7a Snowtrooper (.00)	6.00	12.00
(1998 Toys R Us Exclusive)		
7b Snowtrooper (.01)	8.00	15.00
(1998 Toys R Us Exclusive)		

1995-00 Kenner Star Wars Power of the Force Orange

1 Chewbacca	6.00	12.00
2a Darth Vader (long saber)	8.00	15.00
2b Darth Vader (short saber/long tray)	10.00	20.00
2c Darth Vader (short saber/short tray)	6.00	12.00
3 Han Solo	6.00	12.00
4a Stormtrooper	6.00	12.00
4b Stormtrooper (holosticker)	6.00	12.00

1995-00 Kenner Star Wars Power of the Force Playsets

1a Cantina Pop-Up Diorama (w/sandtrooper)	12.00	25.00
(Retail Store Version - 25" sticker correction)		
1b Cantina Pop-Up Diorama (w/sandtrooper)	15.00	30.00
(Retail Store Version - 25" wide description)		
1c Cantina Pop-Up Diorama (w/sandtrooper)		
(Retail Store Version - 26" wide description)		
2 Cantina Pop-Up Diorama		
(1997 Mail Order Exclusive)		
3 Death Star Escape	12.50	25.00
4 Detention Block Rescue	15.00	30.00
5a Endor Attack (no warning sticker)		
5b Endor Attack (warning sticker)	30.00	60.00
6a Hoth Battle (no warning sticker)	25.00	50.00
6b Hoth Battle (warning sticker)	20.00	40.00
7a Jabba's Palace (w/Han Solo)(podrace arena bio card)		
7b Jabba's Palace (w/Han Solo)(podracer bio card)	15.00	30.00
8 Millennium Falcon Cockpit	20.00	40.00
(PC Explorer Game)		

1995-00 Kenner Star Wars Power of the Force Power F/X

1 Ben (Obi-Wan) Kenobi	5.00	10.00
2 Darth Vader	5.00	10.00
3a Emperor Palpatine (.00)	6.00	12.00
3b Emperor Palpatine (.01)	4.00	8.00
4 Luke Skywalker	6.00	12.00
5a R2-D2 (.00)	4.00	8.00
5b R2-D2 (.01)	4.00	8.00
5c R2-D2 (.02)	4.00	8.00
5d R2-D2 (.103)	4.00	8.00

1995-00 Kenner Star Wars Power of the Force Princess Leia Collection

1a	Princess Leia & Han Solo (gold border)	4.00	8.00
1b	Princess Leia & Han Solo (gray border)	10.00	20.00
2a	Princess Leia & Luke Skywalker (gold border)	8.00	15.00
2b	Princess Leia & Luke Skywalker (gray border)	10.00	20.00
3a	Princess Leia & R2-D2 (gold border)	25.00	50.00
3b	Princess Leia & R2-D2 (gray border)	10.00	20.00
4a	Princess Leia & Wicket (gold border)	4.00	8.00
4b	Princess Leia & Wicket (gray border)	10.00	20.00

1995-00 Kenner Star Wars Power of the Force
Red

1a	Boba Fett (full circle)	7.50	15.00
1b	Boba Fett (half circle)	20.00	40.00
1c	Boba Fett (no circle)	12.00	25.00
2	C-3PO (.00)	6.00	12.00
3	Death Star Gunner	7.50	15.00
4	Greedo	5.00	10.00
5a	Han Solo (carbonite block)	7.50	15.00
5b	Han Solo (carbonite freezing chamber)	6.00	12.00
6a	Han Solo (Hoth - closed hand)	6.00	12.00
6b	Han Solo (Hoth - open hand)	6.00	12.00
7	Jawas	6.00	12.00
8	Lando Calrissian	3.00	6.00
9a	Luke Skywalker (Dagobah - long saber)	6.00	12.00
9b	Luke Skywalker (Dagobah - short saber/long tray)	10.00	20.00
9c	Luke Skywalker (Dagobah - short saber/short tray)		
10a	Luke Skywalker (Jedi Knight - black vest)	6.00	12.00
10b	Luke Skywalker (Jedi Knight - brown vest)	10.00	20.00
11a	Luke Skywalker (long saber)	8.00	15.00
11b	Luke Skywalker (short saber/long tray)	6.00	12.00
11c	Luke Skywalker (short saber/short tray)	6.00	12.00
12a	Luke Skywalker (stormtrooper disguise)	8.00	15.00
12b	Luke Skywalker (stormtrooper disguise)(hologram)	7.50	15.00
13a	Luke Skywalker (X-Wing pilot - long saber)	10.00	20.00
13b	Luke Skywalker (X-Wing pilot - short saber/long tray)	5.00	10.00
13c	Luke Skywalker (X-Wing pilot - short saber/short tray)		
14	Momaw Nadon (Hammerhead) (warning sticker)	4.00	8.00
15a	Obi-Wan Kenobi (hologram)	5.00	10.00
15b	Obi-Wan Kenobi (short saber/long tray)	5.00	10.00
15c	Obi-Wan Kenobi (short saber/short tray)	5.00	10.00
15d	Obi-Wan Kenobi (long saber)	15.00	30.00
15e	Obi-Wan Kenobi (photo)		
16a	Princess Leia Organa (2-band belt)	6.00	12.00
16b	Princess Leia Organa (3-band belt)	6.00	12.00
16c	Princess Leia Organa (hologram)		

17a	R2-D2	12.50	25.00
17b	R2-D2 (hologram)		
18a	R5-D4 (no warning sticker/straight latch)	6.00	12.00
18b	R5-D4 (warning sticker/straight latch)		
19	Sandtrooper		
20a	TIE Fighter Pilot (printed warning)	4.00	8.00
20b	TIE Fighter Pilot (SOTE)		
20c	TIE Fighter Pilot (warning sticker)		
21a	Tusken Raider (closed left hand)	6.00	12.00
21b	Tusken Raider (open left hand)		
22a	Yoda (.00)	6.00	12.00
22b	Yoda (.00)(hologram)		
22c	Yoda (.01)		

1995-00 Kenner Star Wars Power of the Force
Vehicles

NNO	AT-AT Walker (electronic)(no sticker)	60.00	120.00
NNO	AT-AT Walker (electronic)(sticker of figure's legs)		
NNO	AT-ST Scout Walker	30.00	60.00
NNO	A-Wing Fighter	25.00	50.00
NNO	Cruisemissile Trooper (.00)		
NNO	Cruisemissile Trooper (.01)		
NNO	Darth Vader's TIE Fighter	25.00	50.00
NNO	Landspeeder	12.00	25.00
NNO	Luke Skywalker's Red Five X-Wing Fighter	50.00	100.00
NNO	Millennium Falcon (electronic)	60.00	120.00
NNO	Power Racing Speeder Bike (w/scout)		
NNO	Rebel Snowspeeder (electronic)	30.00	75.00
NNO	Speeder Bike (w/Leia in Endor fatigues)(grassy background)		
NNO	Speeder Bike (w/Leia in Endor fatigues)(rocky background)	15.00	30.00
NNO	Speeder Bike (w/Luke in Endor fatigues glove)	30.00	60.00
NNO	Speeder Bike (w/Luke in Endor fatigues no glove)	12.50	25.00
NNO	Speeder Bike (w/scout)(aggressiveness removed)		
NNO	Speeder Bike (w/scout)(aggressiveness)		
NNO	Speeder Bike (w/scout)(Canadian windowless package)		
NNO	Speeder Bike (w/scout)(Topps Widevision card)	10.00	20.00
NNO	STAP and Battle Droid Sneak Preview (beige rod)	10.00	20.00
NNO	STAP and Battle Droid Sneak Preview (brown rod)	12.00	25.00
NNO	T-16 Skyhopper		
NNO	Tatooine Skiff	60.00	120.00
NNO	TIE Fighter	25.00	50.00
NNO	X-Wing Fighter (electronic green box)	15.00	30.00
NNO	X-Wing Fighter (electronic red box)	30.00	60.00
NNO	Y-Wing Fighter	40.00	80.00

1996 Kenner Star Wars Shadows of the Empire

1	Boba Fett vs IG-88/ with comic book	12.00	25.00
2	Chewbacca/ bounty hunter disguise	8.00	15.00

3	Darth Vader vs Prince Xizor	12.00	25.00
	with comic book		
4	Dash Rendar	10.00	20.00
5	Luke Skywalker/ imperial guard	10.00	20.00
6	Prince Xizor	6.00	12.00
7	Princess Leia / boushh disguise	10.00	20.00

1996 Kenner Star Wars Shadows of the Empire
European

1	Chewbacca bounty / hunter disguise	12.50	25.00
2	Dash Rendar	10.00	20.00
3	Luke Skywalker/ imperial guard	15.00	30.00
4	Princess Leia/ boushh disguise	10.00	20.00
5	Prince Xizor	15.00	30.00

1996 Kenner Star Wars Shadows of the Empire
Vehicles

1	Boba Fett's Slave I	40.00	80.00
2	Dash Rendar's Outrider	25.00	50.00
3	Swoop with Swoop Trooper	12.00	25.00
4	Speeder Bike/ with Endor Trooper	12.00	25.00

1996-99 Kenner Star Wars Collector Series

1	Admiral Ackbar	20.00	40.00
2	AT-AT Driver	15.00	30.00
3	Boba Fett	25.00	50.00
4	C-3PO	20.00	40.00
5	Cantina Band - Doikk Na'ts (w/Fizzz)	12.00	25.00
	(Walmart Exclusive)		
6	Cantina Band - Figrin D'an (w/Kloo Horn)	10.00	20.00
	(Walmart Exclusive)		
7	Cantina Band - Ickabel (w/fanfar)	12.00	25.00
	(Walmart Exclusive)		
8	Cantina Band - Nalan (w/Bandfill)	10.00	20.00
	(Walmart Exclusive)		
9	Cantina Band - Tech (w/Omni Box)	12.00	25.00
	(Walmart Exclusive)		
10	Cantina Band - Tedn (w/fanfar)	10.00	20.00

ACTION FIGURES AND FIGURINES

(Walmart Exclusive)

11 Chewbacca		20.00	40.00
12 Darth Vader		15.00	30.00
13 Greedo		15.00	30.00

(JC Penney Exclusive)

14 Han Solo		15.00	30.00
15 Lando Calrissian		12.00	25.00
16 Luke Skywalker		15.00	30.00
17 Luke Skywalker (Bespin)		12.00	25.00
18 Luke Skywalker (X-Wing Pilot)		20.00	40.00
19 Obi-Wan Kenobi		15.00	30.00
20 Princess Leia		15.00	30.00
21 Sandtrooper		15.00	30.00
22 Stormtrooper		15.00	30.00
23 TIE Fighter Pilot		20.00	40.00
24 Tusken Raider (blaster and binoculars)		12.00	25.00
25 Tusken Raider (gaderffii stick)		12.00	25.00

1996-99 Kenner Star Wars Collector Series 2-Packs

1 Grand Moff Tarkin and Imperial Gunner		25.00	50.00

(FAO Schwarz Exclusive)

2 Han Solo and Luke Skywalker (stormtrooper gear)		30.00	60.00

(KB Toys Exclusive)

3 Han Solo and Tauntaun		30.00	60.00
4 Luke Hoth and Wampa		25.00	50.00
5 Luke Jedi and Bib Fortuna		25.00	50.00

(FAO Schwarz Exclusive)

6 Obi-Wan Kenobi vs. Darth Vader (electronic)		25.00	50.00

(JC Penney/KB Toys Exclusive)

7 Princess Leia and R2-D2 (Jabba's prisoners)			

(FAO Schwarz/KB Toys Exclusive)

1996-99 Kenner Star Wars Collector Series European Exclusives

---

1 Han Solo (drawing action)		12.00	25.00
2 Luke Skywalker (drawing action)			

1996-99 Kenner Star Wars Collector Series Masterpiece Edition

1 Anakin Skywalker/Story of Darth Vader		10.00	20.00
2 Aurra Sing/Dawn of the Bounty Hunters		12.00	25.00
3 C-3PO/Tales of the Golden Droid		20.00	40.00

1998-99 Kenner Star Wars Action Collection

1 AT-AT Driver		15.00	30.00
2 Barquin D'an		10.00	20.00
3 Chewbacca in Chains		15.00	30.00
4 Emperor Palpatine		12.00	25.00
5 Grand Moff Tarkin		12.00	25.00
6 Greedo		15.00	30.00
7 Han Solo (carbonite)		15.00	30.00

(Target Exclusive)

8 Han Solo (Hoth)		15.00	30.00
9 Jawa		10.00	20.00
10 Luke Skywalker (ceremonial dress)			
11 Luke Skywalker (Hoth)		15.00	30.00
12 Luke Skywalker (Jedi Knight)		12.00	25.00
13 Princess Leia (Hoth)		12.00	25.00

(Service Merchandise Exclusive)

14 R2-D2		20.00	40.00
15 R2-D2 (detachable utility arms)		20.00	40.00
16 R5-D4		15.00	30.00

(Walmart Exclusive)

17 Sandtrooper (w/droid)		8.00	15.00
18 Snowtrooper		12.00	25.00
19 Snowtrooper (blue variant)			
20 Wicket		20.00	40.00

(Walmart Exclusive)

21 Yoda		20.00	40.00

1998-99 Kenner Star Wars Action Collection Electronic

1 Boba Fett		25.00	50.00

(KB Toys Exclusive)

2 Darth Vader		20.00	40.00

1998-99 Kenner Star Wars Action Collection Multi-Packs

1 C-3PO and R2-D2 2-Pack		40.00	80.00
2 Emperor Palpatine and Royal Guard 2-Pack		20.00	40.00
3 Wedge Antilles and Biggs Darklighter 2-Pack		25.00	50.00

(FAO Schwarz Exclusive)

4 Luke (Tatooine)/Leia (Boushh)/Han (Bespin) 3-Pack		40.00	80.00

(KB Toys Exclusive)

5 Luke/Han/Snowtrooper/AT-AT Driver Hoth 4-Pack		60.00	120.00

(JC Penney Exclusive)

1999-00 Kenner Star Wars Episode I 2-Packs

1 Darth Maul and Sith Infiltrator		8.00	15.00
2 Final Jedi Duel (Qui-Gon Jinn/Darth Maul break apart)		20.00	50.00

1999-00 Kenner Star Wars Episode I Accessory Sets

1	Flash Cannon	8.00	15.00
2	Gungan Catapult	10.00	20.00
3	Hyperdrive Repair Kit	25.00	50.00
4	Naboo Accessory Set	8.00	15.00
5	Pod Race Fuel Station	8.00	15.00
6	Rappel Line Attach	12.00	25.00
7	Sith Accessory Set	8.00	15.00
8	Tatooine Accessory Set	8.00	15.00
9	Tatooine Disguise Set	12.00	25.00
10	Underwater Accessory Set	8.00	15.00

1999-00 Kenner Star Wars Episode I Action Collection 12-Inch

1	Anakin Skywalker (fully poseable)	10.00	20.00
2	Anakin Skywalker (w/Theed Hangar Droid)	20.00	40.00
3	Battle Droid (w/blaster rifle)	15.00	30.00
4	Battle Droid Commander(#(w/electrobinoculars)	10.00	20.00
5	Boss Nass	15.00	30.00
6	Chancellor Valorum & Coruscant Guard	20.00	40.00
7	Darth Maul (w/lightsaber)	12.00	25.00
8	Darth Maul & Sith Speeder	20.00	40.00
	(Walmart Exclusive)		
9	Jar Jar Binks (fully poseable)	12.00	25.00
10	Mace Windu (w/lightsaber)	15.00	30.00
11	Obi-Wan Kenobi (w/lightsaber)	12.00	25.00

12	Pit Droids (fully poseable)	12.00	20.00
13	Qui-Gon Jinn (w/lightsaber)	15.00	30.00
14	Qui-Gon Jinn (Tatooine)	10.00	20.00
15	R2-A6 (metalized dome)	20.00	40.00
16	Sebulba (w/Chubas)	12.00	25.00
17	Watto (w/data pad)	10.00	20.00

1999-00 Kenner Star Wars Episode I Battle Bags

1	Sea Creatures I	6.00	12.00
2	Sea Creatures II	6.00	12.00
3	Swamp Creatures I	6.00	12.00
4	Swamp Creatures II	6.00	12.00

1999-00 Kenner Star Wars Episode I Bonus Battle Droid 2-Packs

NNO	Anakin Skywalker (Naboo)/Battle Droid (tan clean)		
NNO	Anakin Skywalker (Tatooine)/Battle Droid (tan clean)	10.00	20.00
NNO	Battle Droid (tan clean)/Battle Droid (tan clean)		
NNO	Battle Droid (tan clean)/Battle Droid (gold/dirty)		
NNO	Battle Droid (tan clean)/Battle Droid (tan/blast on chest)		
NNO	Battle Droid (tan clean)/Battle Droid (tan/slash on chest/burn marks)		
NNO	C-3PO/Battle Droid (tan clean)	15.00	30.00
NNO	Captain Panaka/Battle Droid (tan clean)		
NNO	Darth Maul (Jedi duel)/Battle Droid (tan clean)	7.50	15.00
NNO	Darth Maul (Tatooine)/Battle Droid (tan clean)	7.50	15.00
NNO	Darth Sidious/Battle Droid (tan clean)		
NNO	Destroyer Droid/Battle Droid (tan clean)	12.50	25.00
NNO	Jar Jar Binks/Battle Droid (tan clean)	12.50	25.00
NNO	Naboo Royal Security/Battle Droid (tan clean)		
NNO	Nute Gunray/Battle Droid (tan clean)	15.00	30.00
NNO	Obi-Wan Kenobi (Jedi duel)/Battle Droid (tan clean)	6.00	12.00
NNO	Obi-Wan Kenobi (Jedi Knight)/Battle Droid (tan clean)	6.00	12.00
NNO	Padme Naberrie/Battle Droid (tan clean)		
NNO	Queen Amidala (Naboo)/Battle Droid (tan clean)	6.00	12.00
NNO	Queen Amidala (red senate gown)/Battle Droid (tan clean)		
NNO	Qui-Gon Jinn/Battle Droid (tan clean)		
NNO	Qui-Gon Jinn (Jedi Master)/Battle Droid (tan clean)	12.50	25.00
NNO	R2-D2/Battle Droid (tan clean)	15.00	30.00
NNO	Ric Olie/Battle Droid (tan clean)		
NNO	Rune Haako/Battle Droid (tan clean)		

NNO	Senator Palpatine/Battle Droid (tan clean)		
NNO	Watto/Battle Droid (tan clean)	20.00	40.00
NNO	Yoda/Battle Droid (tan clean)	6.00	12.00

1999-00 Kenner Star Wars Episode I Bonus Pit Droid 2-Packs

NNO	Anakin Skywalker (Tatooine)/Pit Droid (maroon)		
NNO	Anakin Skywalker (Tatooine)/Pit Droid (orange)		
NNO	Anakin Skywalker (Tatooine)/Pit Droid (white)		
NNO	Darth Maul (Jedi duel)/Pit Droid (maroon)	25.00	50.00
NNO	Darth Maul (Jedi duel)/Pit Droid (orange)		
NNO	Darth Maul (Jedi duel)/Pit Droid (white)		
NNO	Darth Sidius (hologram)/Pit Droid (maroon)		
NNO	Darth Sidius (hologram)/Pit Droid (orange)		
NNO	Darth Sidius (hologram)/Pit Droid (white)		
NNO	Naboo Royal Guard/Pit Droid (maroon)	10.00	20.00
NNO	Naboo Royal Guard/Pit Drcid (orange)	20.00	40.00
NNO	Naboo Royal Guard/Pit Droid (white)	15.00	30.00
NNO	Obi-Wan Kenobi (Jedi Knight)/Pit Droid (maroon)		
NNO	Obi-Wan Kenobi (Jedi Knight)/Pit Droid (orange)		
NNO	Obi-Wan Kenobi (Jedi Knight)/Pit Droid (white)		

1999-00 Kenner Star Wars Episode I CommTech Cinema Scenes

1	Mos Espa Encounter (Sebulba/Jar Jar Binks/Anakin Skywalker)	12.00	25.00
2	Tatooine Showdown (Darth Maul/Qui-Gon Jinn Tatooine		
	Anakin Skywalker Tatooine)	8.00	20.00
3	Watto's Box (Watto/Graxol Kelvyyn/Shakka)	25.00	50.00

1999-00 Kenner Star Wars Episode I CommTech Collection 1

1a	Anakin Skywalker Naboo (new sticker)	6.00	12.00
1b	Anakin Skywalker Naboo (no new sticker)	12.00	25.00
2a	Anakin Skywalker Naboo pilot (new sticker)	6.00	12.00

2b Anakin Skywalker Naboo pilot (no new sticker)	3.00	6.00
3a Anakin Skywalker Tatooine (.00)	10.00	20.00
3b Anakin Skywalker Tatooine (.0100)	3.00	6.00
3c Anakin Skywalker Tatooine (.01 innovision back)	3.00	6.00
4a Battle Droid (tan clean .00)	5.00	10.00
4b Battle Droid (tan clean .01)	5.00	10.00
4c Battle Droid (tan clean .02 innovision back)	5.00	10.00
5a Battle Droid (tan slash on chest w/burn marks .00)	8.00	15.00
5b Battle Droid (tan slash on chest w/burn marks .01)	4.00	8.00
5c Battle Droid (tan slash on chest w/burn marks .02 innovision back)	3.00	6.00
6a Battle Droid (tan blast on chest .00)	4.00	8.00
6b Battle Droid (tan blast on chest .01)	3.00	6.00
6c Battle Droid (tan blast on chest .02 innovision back)	6.00	12.00
7a Battle Droid (gold/dirty .00)	3.00	6.00
7b Battle Droid (gold/dirty .01)	3.00	6.00
7c Battle Droid (gold/dirty .02 innovision back)	3.00	6.00
8a Darth Maul Jedi duel (.00)	8.00	15.00
8b Darth Maul Jedi duel (.01/ innovision back)	3.00	6.00
8c Darth Maul Jedi duel (.02)	5.00	10.00
8d Darth Maul Jedi duel (.0000 large eyes different face more red paint on)	4.00	8.00
8e Darth Maul Jedi duel (white strip on package card instead of yellow)	3.00	6.00
9a Darth Maul Sith Lord (new sticker)	5.00	10.00
9b Darth Maul Sith Lord (no new sticker)	5.00	10.00
10a Darth Maul Tatooine (new sticker)	4.00	8.00
10b Darth Maul Tatooine (new sticker/hologram chip sticker)	3.00	6.00
10c Darth Maul Tatooine (no new sticker)	3.00	6.00
10d Darth Maul Tatooine (no new sticker/hologram chip sticker)	3.00	6.00
10e Darth Maul Sith Lord (new sticker/white strip on package card)	3.00	6.00
11a Destroyer Droid battle damaged (new sticker)	5.00	10.00
11b Destroyer Droid battle damaged (no new sticker)	3.00	6.00
12a Jar Jar Binks (.00 large package photo)	12.00	25.00
12b Jar Jar Binks (.0100 small package photo)	3.00	6.00
12c Jar Jar Binks (.0200/ innovision back)	3.00	6.00
13 Jar Jar Binks (Naboo swamp)	4.00	8.00
14a Obi-Wan Kenobi Jedi duel (.00)	4.00	8.00
14b Obi-Wan Kenobi Jedi duel (.0100)	3.00	6.00
15a Obi-Wan Kenobi Jedi Knight (new sticker)	4.00	8.00
15b Obi-Wan Kenobi Jedi Knight (no new sticker)	3.00	6.00
16a Obi-Wan Kenobi Naboo (new sticker)	6.00	12.00
16b Obi-Wan Kenobi Naboo (no new sticker)	3.00	6.00
17a Padme Naberrie (.00)	10.00	20.00
17b Padme Naberrie (.0100 innovision back)	3.00	6.00
18a Queen Amidala Coruscant (new sticker)	4.00	8.00
18b Queen Amidala Coruscant (no new sticker)	4.00	8.00
19a Queen Amidala Naboo (.00)	3.00	6.00
19b Queen Amidala Naboo (.0100 innovision back)	6.00	12.00
20a Qui-Gon Jinn (.00)	6.00	12.00
20b Qui-Gon Jinn (.0100 innovision back)	4.00	8.00
21a Qui-Gon Jinn Jedi Master (new sticker)	3.00	6.00
21b Qui-Gon Jinn Jedi Master (no new sticker)	3.00	6.00

22a Qui-Gon Jinn Naboo (new sticker)	5.00	10.00
22b Qui-Gon Jinn Naboo (no new sticker)	3.00	6.00

1999-00 Kenner Star Wars Episode I CommTech Collection 2

1a C-3PO (.00)	5.00	10.00
1b C-3PO (.01 innovision back)	20.00	40.00
2a Captain Panaka (wrong chip line on back they need her to sign a treaty)	5.00	10.00
2b Captain Panaka (correct chip line on back this battle I do not think)	5.00	10.00
3a Darth Sidious (.00)	5.00	10.00
3b Darth Sidious (.01/innovision back)	3.00	6.00
4 Darth Sidious (holograph)	15.00	30.00
5a Destroyer Droid (new sticker)	6.00	12.00
5b Destroyer Droid (no new sticker)	4.00	8.00
6a Naboo Royal Guard	8.00	15.00
6b Naboo Royal Security	3.00	6.00
7a Nute Gunray (new sticker)	5.00	10.00
7b Nute Gunray (no new sticker)	8.00	15.00
8a R2-B1 (.0000/Astromech back/no space)	8.00	15.00
8b R2-B1 (.0100/Astromech back/space)	8.00	15.00
9a R2-D2 (large packing bubble/new sticker)	6.00	12.00
9b R2-D2 (small packing bubble)	6.00	12.00
10 Pit Droids	5.00	10.00
11 Queen Amidala (battle)	6.00	12.00
12a Ric Olie (.00)	3.00	6.00
12b Ric Olie (.0100/innovision back)	3.00	6.00
13a Rune Haako (new sticker)	4.00	8.00
13b Rune Haako (no new sticker)	3.00	6.00
14a Senator Palpatine (.00)	3.00	6.00
14b Senator Palpatine (.0100/innovision back)	3.00	6.00
15 Sio Bibble	10.00	20.00
16a Watto (.00)	3.00	6.00
16b Watto (.0100 innovision back)	3.00	6.00
17a Yoda (episode 1 on front)	3.00	6.00
17b Yoda (no episode 1 on front)	5.00	10.00

1999-00 Kenner Star Wars Episode I CommTech Collection 3

1 Adi Gallia	4.00	8.00
2a Boss Nass (.00)	3.00	6.00
2b Boss Nass (.01/innovision back)	3.00	6.00
3a Captain Tarpals (.00)	5.00	10.00
3b Captain Tarpals (.01)	3.00	6.00
4a Chancellor Valorum (.00/warning)	3.00	6.00
4b Chancellor Valorum (.00/no warning)	3.00	6.00
4c Chancellor Valorum (.01/no warning)	3.00	6.00
4d Chancellor Valorum (.02/no warning)	3.00	6.00
5a Gasgano with Pit Droid (.0100)	5.00	10.00
5b Gasgano with Pit Droid (.0200)	3.00	6.00
6a Ki-Adi-Mundi (.0000)	3.00	6.00
6b Ki-Adi-Mundi (.0100/innovision back)	3.00	6.00
7a Mace Windu (.0000)	3.00	6.00
7b Mace Windu (.0100/innovision back)	3.00	6.00
8a Ody Mandrell and Otoga (222 Pit Droid	3.00	6.00
8b Ody Mandrell and Otoga (222 Pit Droid/hologram chip sticker)	3.00	6.00
9a OOM-9 (binoculars in package)	3.00	6.00
9b OOM-9 (binoculars in package/hologram chip sticker)	3.00	6.00
9c OOM-9 (binoculars in right hand)	3.00	6.00
9d OOM-9 (binoculars in left hand/hologram chip sticker)	5.00	10.00
10 TC-14 Protocol Droid	8.00	15.00

1999-00 Kenner Star Wars Episode I CommTech Figure Collector 2-Packs

1 Anakin Skywalker naboo/Obi-Wan Kenobi naboo	12.00	25.00
2 Battle Droid (tan blast on chest)/Darth Maul Tatooine		
3 Battle Droid (tan slash on chest w/burn marks)/Darth Maul Tatooine		
4 Darth Maul Jedi duel/Anakin Skywalker Tatooine	10.00	20.00
5 Jar Jar Binks/Qui-Gon Jinn	6.00	12.00
6 Padme Naberrie/Obi-Wan Kenobi Jedi Knight		
7 Queen Amidala Naboo/Qui-Gon Jinn Jedi Knight		

1999-00 Kenner Star Wars Episode I Creature 2-Packs

1 Ammo Wagon and Falumpaset	20.00	40.00
2 Eopie (w/Qui-Gon Jinn)		
3 Fambaa (w/Gungan warrior)	50.00	100.00
4 Jabba the Hut (w/two-headed announcer)	10.00	20.00
5 Kaadu and Jar Jar Binks	10.00	20.00
6 Opee and Qui-Gon Jinn	10.00	20.00

1999-00 Kenner Star Wars Episode I Deluxe

1 Darth Maul	3.00	6.00
2 Obi-Wan Kenobi	3.00	6.00
3 Qui-Gon Jinn	5.00	10.00

1999-00 Kenner Star Wars Episode I Electronic Talking 12-Inch

1 C-3PO	15.00	30.00
2 Darth Maul	10.00	20.00
3 Jar Jar Binks	15.00	30.00
4 Qui-Gon Jinn	12.00	25.00
5 TC-14	20.00	40.00

1999-00 Kenner Star Wars Episode I Epic Force

1 Darth Maul	8.00	15.00
2 Obi-Wan Kenobi	10.00	20.00
3 Qui-Gon Jinn	8.00	15.00

1999-00 Kenner Star Wars Episode I Invasion Force

1 Armored Scout Tank (w/Battle Droid tan clean)	6.00	12.00
2 Gungan Assault Cannon (w/Jar Jar Binks)	6.00	12.00
3 Gungan Scout Sub (w/Obi-Wan Kenobi Naboo water)	8.00	15.00
4 Sith Attack Speeder (w/Darth Maul Tatooine)	10.00	20.00

1999-00 Kenner Star Wars Episode I Jabba Glob

1 Jabba the Hutt	10.00	20.00

1999-00 Kenner Star Wars Episode I Light-Up

1 Darth Maul hologram/ Wal-Mart exclusive		
2 Qui-Gon Jinn Hologram	10.00	20.00
(Walmart Exclusive)		

1999-00 Kenner Star Wars Episode I Playsets

1 R2-D2 Carryall	12.00	25.00
2 Theed Generator Complex (w/Battle Droid)	12.00	25.00
3 Theed Hangar Power Spin Qui-Gon Jinn/Battle Droid break up	25.00	50.00

1999-00 Kenner Star Wars Episode I Portrait Edition 12-Inch

1 Princess Leia (ceremonial dress)	20.00	40.00
2 Queen Amidala (black travel gown)	12.00	25.00
3 Queen Amidala (return to Naboo)	15.00	30.00
4 Queen Amidala (Senate gown)	15.00	30.00
5 Return to Naboo 2-Pack/Padme/Qui Gon Ginn		

1999-00 Kenner Star Wars Episode I Vehicles

1 Anakin's Podracer	20.00	40.00
2 Flash Speeder	15.00	30.00
3 Naboo Fighter	15.00	30.00
4 Naboo Royal Starship	100.00	200.00
5 Sith Speeder (w/Darth Maul Jedi duel)	8.00	15.00
6 Stap and Battle Droid (burn marks on arms and legs)	8.00	15.00
7 Sebulba's Podracer (w/Sebulba podrace gear)	15.00	30.00
8 Trade Federation Droid Fighters	15.00	30.00
9 Trade Federation Tank	20.00	40.00

2000-02 Kenner Star Wars Power of the Jedi Action Collection 12-Inch

1 4-LOM	12.00	25.00
2 Bossk	15.00	30.00

3 Captain Tarpals (w/Kaadu)	20.00	40.00
4 Death Star Droid	15.00	30.00
5 Death Star Trooper	20.00	40.00
6 Han Solo Stormtrooper	15.00	30.00
7 IG-88	8.00	15.00
8 Luke Skywalker & Yoda	20.00	40.00
9 Luke Skywalker (100th figure)	30.00	60.00
10 Luke Skywalker (w/speeder bike)	40.00	80.00

2000-02 Kenner Star Wars Power of the Jedi
Attack of the Clones Sneak Preview

1 Clone Trooper	4.00	8.00
2 Jango Fett	5.00	10.00
3 R3-T7	6.00	12.00
4 Zam Wesell	4.00	8.00

2000-02 Kenner Star Wars Power of the Jedi
Collection 1

1 Anakin Skywalker (mechanic)	8.00	15.00
2 Aurra Sing (bounty hunter)	6.00	12.00
3 Battle Droid (boomer damage)	4.00	8.00
4 Ben Obi Wan Kenobi (Jedi Knight)	5.00	10.00
5 Chewbacca (Millennium Falcon mechanic)	10.00	20.00
6 Darth Maul (final duel)	6.00	12.00
7 Darth Maul (Sith Apprentice)	5.00	10.00
8 Darth Vader (Dagobah)	8.00	15.00
9 Darth Vader (Emperor's wrath)	5.00	10.00
10 Han Solo (Bespin capture)	4.00	8.00
11 Han Solo (Death Star escape)	6.00	12.00

12 Leia Organa (general)	5.00	10.00
13 Luke Skywalker (X-Wing Pilot)	4.00	8.00
14 Obi-Wan Kenobi (cold weather gear)	4.00	8.00
15 Obi-Wan Kenobi (Jedi)	4.00	8.00
16 Qui-Gon Jinn (Jedi training gear)	8.00	15.00
17 Qui-Gon Jinn (Mos Espa disguise)	4.00	8.00
18 R2-D2 (Naboo escape)	5.00	10.00
19 Sandtrooper (Tatooine patrol)	6.00	12.00

2000-02 Kenner Star Wars Power of the Jedi
Collection 2

1 Battle Droid (security)	4.00	8.00
2 Bespin Guard (cloud city security)	4.00	8.00
3 BoShek	8.00	15.00
4 Boss Nass (Gungan sacred place)	4.00	8.00
5 Chewbacca (Dejarik Champion)	10.00	20.00
6 Coruscant Guard	5.00	10.00
7 Eeth Koth (Jedi Master)	6.00	12.00
8 Ellorrs Madak (Fan's Choice Figure #1)	5.00	10.00
9 Fode and Beed (pod race announcers)	5.00	10.00
10 FX-7 (medical droid)	10.00	20.00
11 Gungan Warrior	4.00	8.00
12 IG-88 (bounty hunter)	12.00	25.00
13 Imperial Officer	4.00	8.00
14 Jar Jar Binks (Tatooine)	4.00	8.00
15 Jek Porkins (X-Wing pilot)	10.00	20.00
16 K-3PO (Echo Base protocol droid)	6.00	12.00
17 Ketwol	4.00	8.00
18 Lando Calrissian (Bespin escape)	6.00	12.00
19 Leia Organa (Bespin escape)	8.00	15.00
20 Mas Amedda	5.00	10.00
21 Mon Calamari (officer)	8.00	15.00
22 Obi-Wan Kenobi (Jedi training gear)	4.00	8.00
23 Plo Koon (Jedi Master)	4.00	8.00
24 Queen Amidala (royal decoy)	6.00	12.00
25 Queen Amidala (Theed invasion)	6.00	12.00
26 R4-M9	8.00	15.00
27 R2-Q5 (Imperial astromech droid)	8.00	15.00
28 Rebel Trooper (Tantive IV defender)	4.00	8.00
29 Sabe (Queen's decoy)	5.00	10.00
30 Saesee Tiin (Jedi Master)	4.00	8.00
31 Scout Trooper (Imperial patrol)	6.00	12.00
32 Sebulba (Boonta Eve Challenge)	5.00	10.00
33 Shmi Skywalker	5.00	10.00

34 Teebo	6.00	12.00
35 Tessek	5.00	10.00
36 Tusken Raider (desert sniper)	6.00	12.00
37 Zutton (Snaggletooth)	5.00	10.00

2000-02 Kenner Star Wars Power of the Jedi
Deluxe

1 Amanaman (w/Salacious Crumb)	10.00	20.00
(Fan's Choice Figure #2)		
2 Darth Maul (w/Sith Attack Droid)	8.00	15.00
3 Luke Skywalker (in Echo Base Bacta Tank)	10.00	20.00
4 Princess Leia (Jabba's prisoner w/sail barge cannon)	8.00	15.00

2000-02 Kenner Star Wars Power of the Jedi
Masters of the Darkside

1 Darth Vader and Darth Maul	6.00	30.00

2000-02 Kenner Star Wars Power of the Jedi
Mega Action

1 Darth Maul	12.00	25.00
2 Destroyer Droid	20.00	40.00
3 Obi-Wan Kenobi	12.00	25.00

2000-02 Kenner Star Wars Power of the Jedi
Playsets

1 Carbon Freezing Chamber (w/Bespin guard)	40.00	80.00

2000-02 Kenner Star Wars Power of the Jedi
Special Edition

1 Boba Fett (300th figure)	15.00	30.00
2 Rorworr (Wookiee scout)	5.00	10.00

2000-02 Kenner Star Wars Power of the Jedi
Vehicles

1 B-Wing Fighter (w/Sullustan pilot)	40.00	80.00
2 Imperial AT-ST & Speeder Bike (w/Paploo)	25.00	50.00
3 Luke Skywalker's Snowspeeder (w/Dack Ralter)	40.00	80.00
4 TIE Bomber	25.00	50.00
5 TIE Interceptor (w/Imperial pilot)	30.00	60.00

ACTION FIGURES AND FIGURINES

FIGURINES

2005-18 Funko Mini Wacky Wobblers Star Wars

NNO	C-3PO	12.50	25.00
NNO	C-3PO/R2-D2 Ulta Mini	7.50	15.00
NNO	Chewbacca	20.00	40.00
NNO	Darth Vader	10.00	20.00
NNO	Darth Vader/Stormtrooper	7.50	15.00
NNO	Darth Vader Holiday	7.50	15.00
NNO	Jawa Holiday	12.50	25.00
NNO	R2-D2	7.50	15.00
NNO	R2-D2 Holiday	7.50	15.00
NNO	Star Wars 5Pk	15.00	30.00
NNO	Stormtrooper	7.50	15.00
NNO	Yoda	5.00	10.00
NNO	Yoda & Chewbacca (ultra mini)	7.50	15.00
NNO	Yoda (holiday)	6.00	12.00

2007-16 Funko Wacky Wobblers Star Wars

NNO	4-LOM	6.00	12.00
NNO	501st Clone Trooper	15.00	30.00
NNO	Admiral Ackbar	25.00	50.00
NNO	Ahsoka Tano	25.00	50.00
NNO	Anakin Skywalker Clone Wars	7.50	15.00
NNO	Battle Droid	10.00	20.00
NNO	Boba Fett	7.50	15.00
NNO	Boba Fett Chrome Base	15.00	30.00
NNO	Bossk	7.50	15.00
NNO	C-3PO	7.50	15.00
NNO	C-3PO TFA	7.50	15.00
NNO	Cantina Band	10.00	20.00
NNO	Captain Phasma	6.00	12.00
NNO	Captain Rex	10.00	20.00
NNO	Captain Red Chrome Base	12.50	25.00
NNO	Chewbacca	7.50	15.00
NNO	Chewbacca Chrome Base	25.00	50.00
NNO	Chewbacca TFA	5.00	10.00
NNO	Clone Trooper	25.00	50.00
NNO	Clone Trooper Utapau AFE	10.00	20.00
NNO	Clone Trooper (yellow)	15.00	30.00
(2008)			
NNO	Clone Trooper Denal Chrome Base WM	12.50	25.00
NNO	Clone Trooper Sinker	75.00	150.00
NNO	Clone Troooper Denal WM	7.50	15.00
NNO	Commander Gree/1500* DIAMOND	7.50	15.00
NNO	Darth Maul	15.00	30.00
NNO	Darth Maul HOLO Chrome Base/12* SDCC	90.00	175.00
NNO	Darth Maul HOLO/480* SDCC	60.00	120.00
NNO	Darth Vader	7.50	15.00
NNO	Darth Vader (chrome base)	25.00	50.00
NNO	Darth Vader Holiday EE	7.50	15.00
NNO	Darth Vader HOLO SDCC/WWC	20.00	40.00
NNO	Darth Vader HOLO Chrome Base SDCC/WWC	25.00	50.00
NNO	Emperor Palpatine	25.00	50.00
NNO	Emperor Palpatine (chrome base)	25.00	50.00
NNO	Finn	6.00	12.00

NNO	Finn/Kylo Ren HMV	15.00	30.00
NNO	Finn Stormtrooper	5.00	10.00
NNO	First Order Flametrooper	6.00	12.00
NNO	First Order Snowtrooper	5.00	10.00
NNO	First Order Stormtrooper	6.00	12.00
NNO	Gamorrean Guard	12.50	25.00
NNO	General Grievous	10.00	20.00
NNO	Greedo	7.50	15.00
NNO	Greedo Chrome Base	25.00	50.00
NNO	Han Solo	12.50	25.00
NNO	Han Solo Stormtrooper/1008* SDCC	20.00	40.00
NNO	Holiday C-3PO	7.50	15.00
NNO	Holiday Special Boba Fett	10.00	20.00
NNO	Holiday Yoda	7.50	15.00
NNO	Jango Fett	7.50	15.00
NNO	Jawa	10.00	20.00
NNO	K-3PO/1500*	6.00	12.00
NNO	Kylo Ren	5.00	10.00
NNO	Kylor Ren No Hood	6.00	12.00
NNO	Luke Skywalker	20.00	40.00
NNO	Luke Skywalker (stormtrooper)	25.00	50.00
(2008 Entertainment Earth Exclusive)			
NNO	Luke Skywalker X-Wing Pilot	20.00	40.00
NNO	Obi-Wan Kenobi	25.00	50.00
NNO	Obi-Wan Kenobi (Clone Wars)	12.50	25.00
NNO	Obi-Wan Kenobi Force Ghost NYCC	15.00	30.00
NNO	Obi-Wan Kenobi Force Ghost Chrome Base	25.00	50.00
NNO	Princess Leia	7.50	15.00
NNO	R2-D2	7.50	15.00
NNO	R2-Q2/756* EE		
NNO	R2-R9/756* EE	7.50	15.00
NNO	R2-X2/756* EE	20.00	40.00
NNO	Rey	6.00	12.00
NNO	Shadow Stormtrooper SDCC	12.50	25.00
NNO	Shock Trooper/1008* SDCC	30.00	75.00
NNO	Slave Leia	10.00	20.00
NNO	Stormtrooper	7.50	15.00
NNO	TC-14/480* SDCC	25.00	50.00
NNO	TIE Fighter Pilot	12.50	25.00
NNO	Tusken Raider	7.50	15.00
NNO	Wicket	7.50	15.00
NNO	Wicket Chrome Base	30.00	60.00
NNO	Yoda	6.00	12.00
NNO	Yoda Chrome Base	15.00	30.00
NNO	Yoda Force Ghost	6.00	12.00
NNO	Yoda Force Ghost/1500* DIAMOND SDCC	25.00	50.00
NNO	Yoda (holiday)	6.00	12.00

2009 Funko Force Star Wars

NNO	501st Clone Trooper/1008* SDCC	30.00	60.00
NNO	Boba Fett	7.50	15.00
NNO	Chewbacca	6.00	12.00
NNO	Darth Maul	15.00	30.00
NNO	Darth Vader	7.50	15.00

NNO	Emperor Palpatine	12.50	25.00
NNO	Shadow Trooper	12.50	25.00
NNO	Shocktrooper	20.00	40.00
NNO	Stormtrooper	12.50	25.00
NNO	Yoda	7.50	15.00

2010 Funko Wacky Wobblers Star Wars Monster Mash-Ups

NNO	Chewbacca	6.00	12.00
NNO	Darth Vader	6.00	12.00
NNO	Stormtrooper	7.50	15.00
NNO	Yoda	5.00	10.00

2011-12 Funko Blox

23	Darth Vader	10.00	20.00
24	Boba Fett	8.00	15.00
25	Stormtrooper	8.00	12.00

2011-22 Funko Pop Vinyl Freddy Funko

A9A	Clone Trooper/48* SDCC	750.00	1500.00
A9B	Cl.Trooper Blue Hair/12* SDCC	1500.00	3000.00
28A	Boba Fett/196* SDCC	2000.00	4000.00
28B	B.Fett Red Hair/24* SDCC	5000.00	10000.00
46	Kylo Ren/400* FD	500.00	1000.00
SE	Poe Dameron/200* FD	400.00	800.00
SE	Yoda/450* FD	600.00	1200.00
SE	C-3PO/520* FD	750.00	1500.00

2011-22 Funko Pop Vinyl Star Wars

1A	Darth Vader	10.00	20.00
1B	Darth Vader MET HT	20.00	40.00
2A	Yoda	7.50	15.00
2B	Yoda Spirit WG ERR	15.00	30.00
2C	Yoda Spirit WG COR	15.00	30.00
2C	Yoda Spirit WG COR Sticker	15.00	30.00
3A	Han Solo V	200.00	400.00
3B	Han Solo VAULT	30.00	75.00
4	Princess Leia	12.50	25.00
5A	Stormtrooper	12.50	25.00
5B	Stormtrooper Red TAR	7.50	15.00

#	Name	Low	High
6A	Chewbacca	10.00	20.00
6B	Chewbacca FLK/480* SDCC	2000.00	4000.00
6C	Chewbacca Hoth GS	12.50	25.00
6D	Chewbacca Hoth EB	20.00	40.00
6E	Chewbacca Hoth UT	30.00	60.00
7A	Greedo V	750.00	1500.00
7B	Greedo VAULT	30.00	60.00
8A	Boba Fett	12.50	25.00
8B	Boba Fett Prototype WG ERR	20.00	40.00
8D	Boba Fett Prototype WG COR Sticker	20.00	40.00
8C	Boba Fett Prototype WG COR	20.00	40.00
9A	Darth Maul	12.50	25.00
9B	Darth Maul Gold MET WM	10.00	20.00
10A	Obi-Wan Kenobi V	200.00	400.00
10B	Obi-Wan VAULT	60.00	125.00
10C	Obi-Wan Kenobi Tatooine AMZ	20.00	40.00
11A	Luke Skywalker Jedi Knight V	100.00	200.00
11B	Jedi Luke Skywalker VAULT	50.00	100.00
12A	Gamorrean Guard V	125.00	250.00
12B	Gamorrean Guard VAULT	7.50	15.00
13A	C-3PO	10.00	20.00
13B	C-3PO Gold Chrome SDCC	40.00	80.00
13C	C-3PO Gold Chrome SCE	40.00	80.00
14	Shadow Trooper/480* SDCC	1500.00	3000.00
15	H.Solo Stormtrooper/1000* ECCC	600.00	1200.00
16	L.Skywalker Stormtrooper/1000* ECCC	750.00	1500.00
17	Luke Skywalker X-Wing	25.00	50.00
18A	Slave Leia V	100.00	200.00
18B	Slave Leia VAULT	50.00	100.00
19A	Tusken Raider V	30.00	60.00
19B	Tusken Raider VAULT	40.00	80.00
20A	Jawa V	60.00	125.00
20B	Jawa VAULT	10.00	20.00
21A	Clone Trooper V	125.00	250.00
21B	Clone Trooper VAULT	30.00	75.00
22	Jabba the Hutt	15.00	30.00
23	Darth Maul HOLO/480* SDCC	4000.00	8000.00
24	Biggs Darklighter/480* SDCC	1250.00	2500.00
25	501st Clone Trooper/480* SDCC	1250.00	2500.00
26A	Wicket the Ewok	15.00	30.00
26B	Wicket the Ewok FLK FT	125.00	250.00
27	Jar Jar Binks V	100.00	200.00
28	Admiral Ackbar V	40.00	80.00
29	Queen Amidala V	150.00	300.00
30	Lando Calrissian V	60.00	125.00
31A	R2-D2	15.00	30.00
31B	R2-D2 Futura TAR	15.00	30.00
31C	R2-D2 Dagobah TAR	15.00	30.00
31D	R2-D2 Diamond Glitter SWC	150.00	300.00
31E	R2-D2 Diamond Glitter/3,000* GCE	150.00	300.00
31F	R2-D2 Diamond Glitter GCE	125.00	250.00
32	Boba Fett Droids/480* SDCC	1500.00	3000.00
33A	Darth Vader HOLO GITD DCC	500.00	1000.00
33B	Darth Vader HOLO GITD PE	500.00	1000.00
34A	Luke Skywalker Hoth V	12.50	25.00
34B	Luke Skywalker Hoth w/Pin AMZ	12.50	25.00
35	Bossk V	30.00	75.00
36A	The Emperor Pink Face V	50.00	100.00
36B	The Emperor White Face V	50.00	100.00
37	Hammerhead V	15.00	30.00
38	Biker Scout V	30.00	60.00
39A	6" Wampa V	15.00	30.00
39B	Wampa 6" FLK HT	15.00	30.00
40	Holographic Emperor TW	100.00	200.00
41A	R2-Q5 GCE	20.00	40.00
41B	R2-Q5 SWC	100.00	200.00
42A	Shock Trooper GCE	125.00	250.00
42B	Shock Trooper SWC	150.00	300.00
43A	Unmasked Vader GCE	12.50	25.00
43B	Unmasked Vader SWC	125.00	250.00
44A	R2-R9 GCE	25.00	50.00
44B	R2-R9 SWC	75.00	150.00
45A	R2-B1 GS	12.50	25.00
45B	R2-B1 EB	12.50	25.00
45C	R2-B1 UT	12.50	25.00
46A	E-3PO GCE	15.00	30.00
46B	E-3PO SWC	60.00	125.00
47A	Han Solo Hoth GS	12.50	25.00
47B	Han Solo Hoth EB	12.50	25.00
48A	Figrin D'an GS	10.00	20.00
48B	Figrin D'an EB	10.00	20.00
48C	Figrin D'an UT	12.50	25.00
49	Luke Skywalker Tatooine	15.00	30.00
50	Princess Leia Boussh	10.00	20.00
51A	TIE Fighter Pilot	6.00	12.00
51B	TIE Pilot MET	30.00	60.00
52	Nalan Cheel	10.00	20.00
53	Bib Fortuna	7.50	15.00
54A	Leia Boussh Unmasked SDCC	450.00	900.00
54B	Leia Boussh Unmasked SCE	250.00	500.00
55	K-3PO B&N	10.00	20.00
56A	Snowtrooper WG ERR	10.00	20.00
56B	Snowtrooper WG COR	10.00	20.00
56C	Snowtrooper WG COR Sticker	10.00	20.00
57A	Imperial Guard WG ERR	7.50	15.00
57B	Imperial Guard WG COR	7.50	15.00
57C	Imperial Guard WG COR Sticker	7.50	15.00
58A	Rey	7.50	15.00
59	Finn	7.50	15.00
60	Kylo Ren	10.00	20.00
61A	BB-8	6.00	12.00
61B	BB-8 Rainbow FS	7.50	15.00
62	Poe Dameron V	7.50	15.00
63A	Chewbacca	7.50	15.00
63B	Chewbacca FLK SB	12.50	25.00
63C	Chewbacca Blue Chrome SWC	40.00	80.00
63D	Chewbacca Gold Chrome GCE	6.00	12.00
63E	Chewbacca Gold MET WM	7.50	15.00
64A	C-3PO	6.00	12.00
64B	C-3PO MET B&N	10.00	20.00
64C	C-3PO Futura TAR	20.00	40.00
65A	Captain Phasma	6.00	12.00
65B	Captain Phasma Last Jedi Box	7.50	15.00
66	First Order Stormtrooper	10.00	20.00
67A	First Order Snowtrooper	6.00	12.00
67B	First Order Snowtrooper Last Jedi Box	6.00	12.00
68A	First Order Flametrooper	6.00	12.00
68B	First Order Flametrooper Last Jedi Box	7.50	15.00
69	Blue Snaggletooth CH SB	20.00	40.00
70	Red Snaggletooth SB	10.00	20.00
71	Shadow Guard WG	7.50	15.00
72	Poe Dameron No Helmet WM	7.50	15.00
73A	Rey w/Goggles HT	6.00	12.00
73B	Rey w/Goggles PA	12.50	25.00
73C	Rey w/Goggles UT	6.00	12.00
74	FO Stormtrooper w/Rifle AMZ	12.50	25.00
75	FO Stormtrooper w/Shield WG	7.50	15.00
76A	Finn Stormtrooper GS	7.50	15.00
76B	Finn Stormtrooper EB	7.50	15.00
76C	Finn Stormtrooper UT	7.50	15.00
77	Kylo Ren Unhooded TAR	7.50	15.00
78A	R2-L3 DST	25.00	50.00
78B	R2-L3 UT	25.00	50.00
79	Han Solo	7.50	15.00
80	Princess Leia	7.50	15.00
81	Admiral Ackbar	6.00	12.00
82	Nien Nunb	7.50	15.00
83	Sidon Ithano	7.50	15.00
84	Varmik	6.00	12.00
85A	Finn w/Lightsaber B&N	7.50	15.00
85B	Finn w/Lightsaber UT	7.50	15.00
86	Han Solo Snow Gear LC	7.50	15.00
87	Kylo Ren Unmasked WM	10.00	20.00
88	Nien Nunb w/Helmet GS	7.50	15.00
89	TIE Fighter Pilot SB	6.00	12.00
A90	TIE Fighter Pilot Red Stripe SB CH	10.00	20.00
B90A	Luke Ceremony SWC	50.00	100.00
B90B	Luke Ceremony GCE	12.50	25.00
A91	Captain Phasma MET SB	10.00	20.00
B91A	Han Ceremony SWC	7.50	15.00
B91B	Han Ceremony GCE	12.50	25.00
92A	AT-AT Driver WG	7.50	15.00
92B	AT-AT Driver UT	10.00	20.00
93A	Luke Skywalker Bespin	20.00	40.00
93B	Luke Skywalker Bespin Gold WM	7.50	15.00
94A	Luke Skywalker Bespin SWC	60.00	125.00
94B	Luke Skywalker Bespin GCE	15.00	30.00
95A	Ree Yees WG	7.50	15.00
95B	Ree Yees UT	10.00	20.00
96A	Kit Fisto WG	25.00	50.00

96B Kit Fisto UT		
97A Plo Koon WG	20.00	40.00
97B Plo Koon UT		
98A Blue Senate Guard SWC	25.00	50.00
98B Blue Senate Guard GCE		
99 Old Ben Kenobi SB	12.50	25.00
100A FN-2187 TAR	15.00	30.00
100B FN-2187 UT	20.00	40.00

101A 4-LOM SWC	45.00	90.00
101B 4-LOM GCE	20.00	40.00
102 Bobe Fett Action SB	50.00	100.00
103 IG-88 SB	7.50	15.00
104 Rey w/Lightsaber	7.50	15.00
105 Kylo Ren Unmasked Action	6.00	12.00
106 Luke Skywalker Force Awakens	10.00	20.00
107 General Leia	6.00	12.00
108 Maz Kanata	6.00	12.00
109 General Hux	6.00	12.00
110 Snap Wexley	7.50	15.00
111 FN-2199 V	7.50	15.00
112 Guavian	7.50	15.00
113 ME-809	7.50	15.00
114A Rey Jedi Temple WG	7.50	15.00
114B Rey Jedi Temple Gold MET WM	6.00	12.00
114C Rey Jedi Temple Gold MET SE	7.50	15.00
115A Han Solo w/Bowcaster SDCC	20.00	40.00
115B Han Solo w/Bowcaster SCE	10.00	20.00
116A BB-8 w/Lighter SDCC	30.00	60.00
116B BB-8 w/Lighter SCE	10.00	20.00
117 Poe Dameron Jacket/Blaster HT	7.50	15.00
118 Maz Kanata Goggles Up TAR	6.00	12.00
119 Rey X-Wing Helmet GS	7.50	15.00
120 Poe Dameron X-Wing Jumpsuit FYE	7.50	15.00
121 R2-D2 Jabba's Sail Barge SB	10.00	20.00
122 Zuckuss TW	7.50	15.00
123 Luke Skywalker (Endor)	7.50	15.00
124A Dagobah Yoda	7.50	15.00
124B Yoda Blue Chrome SWC	75.00	150.00
124C Yoda Gold Chrome GCE	7.50	15.00
124D Yoda Green Chrome SDCC	25.00	50.00
124E Yoda Green Chrome SCE	15.00	30.00
124F Yoda Gold MET WM	7.50	15.00
124G Yoda Green ECCC	25.00	50.00
124H Yoda Green SCE	15.00	30.00
A125 Hoth Han Solo w/Tauntaun SB	30.00	60.00
B125A Princess Leia Hoth SWC	50.00	100.00
B125B Princess Leia Hoth GCE	30.00	60.00
126A Luke Skywalker Hood SWC	75.00	150.00

126B Luke Skywalker Hood GCE	50.00	100.00
126C Luke Skywalker Hood SE	50.00	100.00
127A Garindan SWC	10.00	20.00
127B Garindan GCE	10.00	20.00
128A Qui Gon Jinn NYCC	500.00	1000.00
128B Qui Gon Jinn HOLO SWC	150.00	300.00
128C Qui Gon Jinn HOLO GCE	75.00	150.00
129A General Grievous WG	30.00	75.00
129B General Grievous SE	25.00	50.00
130A Ahsoka HT	30.00	75.00
130B Ahsoka SE	30.00	60.00
130C Ahsoka GITD Comikaze	50.00	100.00
131A Sabine Masked WG	40.00	80.00
131B Sabine Masked SE	30.00	60.00
132 Kanan	75.00	150.00
133A Chopper	50.00	100.00
133B Chopp ERR	75.00	150.00
133C Chopper Imperial SWC	30.00	60.00
133D Chopper Imperial GCE	25.00	50.00
134 Ezra	60.00	125.00
135 Sabine	30.00	75.00
136 Hera	20.00	40.00
137 Zeb	30.00	75.00
138 Jyn Erso	6.00	12.00
139 Captain Cassian Andor	10.00	20.00
140 Chirrut Imwe	10.00	20.00
141 Baze Malbus	7.50	15.00
142 Director Orson Krennic	6.00	12.00
143 Darth Vader	7.50	15.00
144 Imperial Death Trooper	7.50	15.00
145 Scarif Stormtrooper	12.50	25.00
146A K-2SO	7.50	15.00
146B K-2SO w/Pin AMZ	12.50	25.00
147 C2-B5	7.50	15.00
148 Jyn Erso Mountain Gear SB	6.00	12.00
149 Death Trooper Sniper SB	10.00	20.00
150 Jyn Erso Hooded HT	6.00	12.00
151 Capt. C.Andor Brown Jacket TAR	6.00	12.00
152 Jyn Erso Imperial Disguise TAR	7.50	15.00
153A Saw Gerrera WM	7.50	15.00
153B Saw Gerrera TSP	7.50	15.00
153C Saw Gerrera WT	7.50	15.00
154 Imp. Death Trooper Black MET WM	15.00	30.00
155A Bistan NYCC	7.50	15.00
155B Bistan TSP	30.00	60.00
156 Scarif Stormtrooper Striped WG	6.00	12.00
157A Vader Force Choke GS	20.00	40.00
157B D.Vader Force Choke Blue Chr. SWC	125.00	250.00
157C D.Vader Force Choke Gold Chr. GCE	12.50	25.00
157D Darth Vader Red Chrome TAR RC	7.50	15.00
157E Darth Vader Gold Chrome MCM	12.50	25.00
157F Darth Vader Black Chrome SB	15.00	30.00
157G Darth Vader Gold MET WM	7.50	15.00
157H Darth Vader Futura NYCC/TAR	60.00	125.00
157I Darth Vader Futura TAR	25.00	50.00
157J Darth Vader Futura SE	20.00	40.00
158 Darth Vader Bespin SB	15.00	30.00
159 Grand Moff Tarkin SB	12.50	25.00
160 Max Rebo SS	10.00	20.00
161 Rey w/Jacket TAR	7.50	15.00
162 Young Anakin	10.00	20.00

164 Captain Rex SB	40.00	80.00
165 Darth Maul Rebels SB	40.00	80.00
166 The Inquisitor WM	60.00	125.00
167 Seventh Sister WM	25.00	50.00
168 Fifth Brother WM	30.00	75.00
169A Han Solo SWC	40.00	80.00
169B Han Solo GCE	15.00	30.00
170A Grand Admiral Thrawn SWC	250.00	500.00
170B Grand Admiral Thrawn GCE	150.00	300.00
171A 442nd Clone Trooper SWC	75.00	150.00
171B 442nd Clone Trooper GCW	60.00	125.00
172A Mace Windu WG	25.00	50.00
172B Mace Windu SE	20.00	40.00
173A Muftak ECCC	25.00	50.00
173B Muftak SPCE	10.00	20.00
174A Rey w/Speeder SWC	25.00	50.00
174B Rey w/Speeder GCE	25.00	50.00
175 Luke w/Speeder SB	15.00	30.00
A176A Darth Vader w/TIE Fighter TAR	25.00	50.00
A176B Darth Vader w/TIE Fighter SE	25.00	50.00
B176A Commander Cody WG	75.00	150.00
B176B Commander Cody SE	60.00	125.00
177A Saw Gerrera w/Hair NYCC	15.00	30.00
177B Saw Gerrera w/Hair FCE	12.50	25.00
178A Jyn Erso w/Helmet NYCC	15.00	30.00
178B Jyn Erso w/Helmet FCE	10.00	20.00
179A K-2SO Action Pose NYCC	15.00	30.00
179B K-2SO Action Pose FCE	15.00	30.00
180 R5-D4 SB	7.50	15.00
181 C-3PO Unfinished SB	17.50	35.00
182A Snoke GITD SDCC	40.00	80.00
182B Supreme Leader Snoke GITD SCE	15.00	30.00
183A Bodhi Rook SDCC	30.00	60.00
183B Bodhi Rook SCE	7.50	15.00
184B Tank Trooper SDCC	50.00	100.00
184C Combat Assault Tank Trooper SCE	10.00	20.00
185 Young Jyn Erso	12.50	25.00
186 Galen Erso	7.50	15.00
187 Weeteef Cyubee	7.50	15.00
188A Death Star Droid Rogue One NYCC	10.00	20.00
188B Death Star Droid Rogue One FCE	15.00	30.00
189 Death Star Droid Black	6.00	12.00
190A Rey	7.50	15.00
190B Rey GITD COST	7.50	15.00
191 Finn	6.00	12.00
192 Poe Dameron	6.00	12.00
193 Luke Skywalker	6.00	12.00
194A Kylo Ren	6.00	12.00
194B Kylo Ren GITD COST	15.00	30.00
194C Kylo Ren HOLO TAR OL	40.00	80.00
194D Kylo Ren Gold MET WM	10.00	20.00
194E Kylo Ren Gold MET SE	6.00	12.00
195A Chewbacca w/Porg	10.00	20.00
195B Chewbacca w/Porg FLK FYE	12.50	25.00
195C Chewbacca w/Porg FLK FYE Blue Logo	12.50	25.00
196 BB-8	6.00	12.00
197 Rose	6.00	12.00
198A Porg	6.00	12.00
198B Porg Open Mouth CH	12.50	25.00
198C Porg FLK HT	10.00	20.00
198D Porg Open Mouth FLK HT	30.00	60.00

198E	Porg Wings Open TAR	6.00	12.00	239B	Chewbacca FLK BL	10.00	20.00	285C	Jango Fett Jet Pack Gold MET WM	15.00	30.00
198F	Porg 10" TAR	10.00	20.00	239C	Chewbacca FLK MCM	12.50	25.00	285D	Jango Fett Jet Pack Gold MET SE		
199	Supreme Leader Snoke	6.00	12.00	240	Lando Calrissian	6.00	12.00	286	Han Solo	7.50	15.00
200	Praetorian Guard	10.00	20.00	241	Qi'Ra	7.50	15.00	287A	Princess Leia	7.50	15.00
201	First Order Executioner	7.50	15.00	242	Tobias Beckett	6.00	12.00	287B	Princess Leia Gold MET WM	7.50	15.00
202A	BB-9E	7.50	15.00	243	Val	7.50	15.00	288A	Darth Vader	7.50	15.00
202B	BB-9E Chrome BL	7.50	15.00	244	Rio Durant	6.00	12.00	288B	Darth Vader GITD CH	10.00	20.00
203A	Kylo Ren w/Helmet TRU	7.50	15.00	245	L3-37	6.00	12.00	289	Emperor Palpatine Force Lightning	10.00	20.00
203B	Kylo Ren w/Helmet TSP	30.00	75.00	246	Range Trooper	7.50	15.00	290A	Wicket	12.50	25.00
205	Rose SS	7.50	15.00	247	Enfys Nest	6.00	12.00	290B	Wicket Endor AMZ	7.50	15.00
207	DJ GS	6.00	12.00	A248	Han Solo Goggles TAR	6.00	12.00	291	Lando Calrissian	6.00	12.00
208	Praetorian Guard w/Swords WG	7.50	15.00	B248	Mudtrooper FS	50.00	100.00	292	Baby Nippet FLK TAR	15.00	30.00
209A	Praetorian Guard w/Whip WG	7.50	15.00	250	Tobias Beckett w/Pistols WM	6.00	12.00	293	Wicket 10" TAR	30.00	60.00
209B	Praetorian Guard w/Whip SE	12.50	25.00	251	Lando Calrissian White Cape HT	10.00	20.00	294	Encounter on Endor	7.50	15.00
210	Resistance BB Unit Orange NBC	6.00	12.00	252A	Stormtrooper SDCC	75.00	150.00	295A	Princess Leia Blue Chrome SWC	60.00	125.00
211	Resistance BB Unit WM	6.00	12.00	252B	Stormtrooper SCE	30.00	75.00	295B	Princess Leia Gold Chrome GCE	6.00	12.00
212A	Medical Droid WG	7.50	15.00	252C	Stormtrooper PX	25.00	50.00	296A	Stormtrooper Blue Chrome SWC	50.00	100.00
212B	Medical Droid SE	15.00	30.00	253A	Dryden Voss Scars FYE	6.00	12.00	296B	Stormtrooper Gold Chrome GCE	10.00	20.00
213A	Boba Fett w/Slave I NYCC	125.00	250.00	253B	Dryden Voss No Scars FYE	6.00	12.00	296C	Stormtrooper Futura TAR	20.00	40.00
213B	Boba Fett w/Slave I FCE	75.00	150.00	254A	Dryden Gangster TAR	6.00	12.00	296D	Stormtrooper Rainbow	7.50	15.00
214	Obi-Wan Kenobi ROTS SB	60.00	125.00	254B	Dryden Gangster TRU	6.00	12.00	296E	Stormtrooper Empire Logo WC	15.00	30.00
215	Kylo Ren w/TIE Fighter	7.50	15.00	255A	Han Solo Vest WG	6.00	12.00	296F	Stormtrooper Empire Logo WCE	15.00	30.00
217	Aayla Secura SB	30.00	60.00	255B	Han Solo Vest SE	6.00	12.00	296G	Stormtrooper Silver MET P&T		
218	Princess Leia WM	6.00	12.00	256	Vulptex Crystal Fox	7.50	15.00	297A	Boba Fett Blue Chrome SWC	200.00	400.00
219	Wedge Antilles w/Snow Speeder WG	10.00	20.00	257	Rematch on the Supremacy	7.50	15.00	297B	Boba Fett Gold Chrome GCE	20.00	40.00
220	BB-8 Baseball and Bat Giants	25.00	50.00	258	Ewok w/Speeder Bike FS	25.00	50.00	297C	Boba Fett Green Chrome SDCC	60.00	125.00
221	TIE Fighter Pilot w/TIE Fighter	7.50	15.00	260	C'ai Threnalli	6.00	12.00	297D	Boba Fett Green Chrome SCE	20.00	40.00
A222	Escape Pod Landing WM	20.00	40.00	261	Porg Frowning	10.00	20.00	297E	Boba Fett Futura TAR	50.00	100.00
B222	Duel on Mustafar SB	150.00	300.00	262A	Cad Bane SDCC	75.00	150.00	297F	Boba Fett Futura Black TAR	40.00	80.00
223	Cantina Faceoff WM	25.00	50.00	262B	Cad Bane SCE	40.00	80.00	297G	Boba Fett Futura Red TAR	45.00	90.00
224	Trash Compactor Escape WM	10.00	20.00	263	Caretaker	6.00	12.00	297H	Boba Fett Futura Black ECCC	75.00	150.00
225	Death Star Duel WM	12.50	25.00	264	Clash on the Supremacy Rey	15.00	30.00	297I	Boba Fett Futura Black SCE	45.00	90.00
226A	Cloud City Duel WG	25.00	50.00	265	Clash on the Supremacy Kylo	17.50	35.00	297J	Boba Fett Futura Red WC	25.00	50.00
226B	Cloud City Duel SE	30.00	75.00	266A	Luke Skywalker	10.00	20.00	297K	Boba Fett Futura Red WCE	25.00	50.00
227	Poe Dameron w/X-Wing SB	7.50	15.00	266B	Luke Skywalker Gold/80* FD	1750.00	3500.00	297K	Boba Fett Camo/1000* NYCC	600.00	1200.00
228	Princess Leia w/Speeder Bike	7.50	15.00	267	Paige	6.00	12.00	297L	Boba Fett Camo/1000* FCE	500.00	1000.00
229	Luke Skywalker w/Speeder Bike CH	15.00	30.00	268	Ahsoka	10.00	20.00	297M	Boba Fett Retro BAIT	25.00	50.00
230A	Dengar NYCC	20.00	40.00	269	Yoda	17.50	35.00	297N	Boba Fett Retro/6* May 4th		
230B	Dengar FCE	7.50	15.00	270	Obi-Wan Kenobi	20.00	40.00	298A	Watto SWC	17.50	35.00
				271	Anakin Skywalker	20.00	40.00	298B	Watto GCE	12.50	25.00
				272A	Ahsoka Force Push HT	17.50	35.00	299A	Darth Maul SWC	75.00	150.00
				272B	Ahsoka Force Push SE	17.50	35.00	299B	Darth Maul GCE	30.00	75.00
				273A	Obi-Wan Kenobi Hooded WG	75.00	150.00	300	Chewbacca Oxygen Mask SB	15.00	30.00
				273B	Obi-Wan Kenobi Hooded SE	17.50	35.00	301	DJ R3X GE	20.00	40.00
				274A	Captain Rex NYCC	300.00	750.00	302	Hondo Ohnaka GE	20.00	40.00
				274B	Captain Rex FCE	250.00	500.00	303	Aurra Sing SB	12.50	25.00
				275	R2-D2 w/Antlers	15.00	30.00	304	Sebulba SB	10.00	20.00
				276	C-3PO w/Santa Hat	7.50	15.00	305A	Boba Fett Animated GSFIC	20.00	40.00
				277A	Yoda Santa Eyes Half Open	12.50	25.00	305B	Boba Fett Animated EB	12.50	25.00
				277B	Yoda Sant Eyes Fully Open	6.00	12.00	305C	Boba Fett Animated SE	20.00	40.00
				278	Chewbacca Christmas Lights	15.00	30.00	306	Sith Trooper SDCC	1000.00	2000.00
				279A	Darth Vader Candy Cane Lightsaber	7.50	15.00	307	Rey	7.50	15.00
				279B	Darth Vader GITD Candy Cane Lightsaber CH	15.00	30.00	308A	Kylo Ren	7.50	15.00
				280	Boba Gets His Bounty SB	40.00	80.00	308B	Kylo Ren Lights/Sound	17.50	35.00
				281A	Anakin Skywalker Dark Side Eyes WG	60.00	125.00	308C	Kylo Ren GITD TAR	10.00	20.00
				281B	Anakin Skywalker Dark Side Eyes SE	50.00	100.00	309	Finn	10.00	20.00
				282	Lando Calrissian Skiff SB	12.50	25.00	310	Poe Dameron	6.00	12.00
				283	Klaatu SB	7.50	15.00	311	Zorii Bliss	6.00	12.00
				284	Dagobah Face-Off SB	12.50	25.00	312	D-O	10.00	20.00

231A	Young Anakin Podracing WG	12.50	25.00	285A	Jango Fett Jet Pack WG	45.00	90.00	313	Lando Calrissian	6.00	12.00
231B	Young Anakin Podracing SE	12.50	25.00	285B	Jango Fett Jet Pack SE	30.00	75.00	314	BB-8	7.50	15.00
232A	Luke Skywalker w/X-Wing WM	40.00	80.00								
232B	Luke Skywalker w/X-Wing SE	40.00	80.00								
233	Count Dooku SB	45.00	90.00								
234	Scout Trooper w/Speeder SB	20.00	40.00								
235	Vice Admiral Holdo	7.50	15.00								
236	Chewbacca w/AT-ST	30.00	60.00								
237A	Padme Amidala ECCC	100.00	200.00								
237B	Padme Amidala SCE	60.00	125.00								
238	Han Solo	7.50	15.00								
239A	Chewbacca	7.50	15.00								

#	Name		
315	Jannah	7.50	15.00
316	Rose	6.00	12.00
317	First Order Jet Trooper	10.00	20.00
318	Sith Jet Trooper	7.50	15.00
319	Lieutenant Connix	6.00	12.00
320	First Order Tread Speeder	20.00	40.00
A321A	Han Solo/M.Falcon AMZ	75.00	150.00
A321B	Han Solo/M.Falcon SE	75.00	150.00
B321	Supreme Leader Kylo Ren/TIE Whisper	10.00	20.00
322A	Sandtrooper NYCC	50.00	100.00
322B	Sandtrooper FCE	25.00	50.00
322C	Sandtrooper WPLY		
324	Kylo Ren Supreme Leader Hooded SB	12.50	25.00
325A	Knight of Ren w/Long Axe SB	7.50	15.00
325B	Knight of Ren w/Long Axe Hematite AMZ	15.00	30.00
326A	The Mandalorian	7.50	15.00
326B	The Mandalorian D23	300.00	750.00
327	Cara Dune	20.00	40.00
328	IG-11	10.00	20.00
329	Kuiil	10.00	20.00
330A	The Mandalorian Pistol NYCC	300.00	500.00
330B	The Mandalorian Pistol FCE	150.00	300.00
331A	Knight of Ren w/Blaster GS	7.50	15.00
331B	Knight of Ren w/Blaster Hematite	6.00	12.00
332A	Knight of Ren w/Club HT	10.00	20.00
332B	Knight of Ren w/Club Hematite	10.00	20.00
333A	Knight of Ren w/Scythe FS	12.50	25.00
333B	Knight of Ren w/Scythe Hematite	6.00	12.00
334A	Knight of Ren w/Cannon WM	6.00	12.00
334B	Knight of Ren w/Cannon Hematite	7.50	15.00
335A	Knight of Ren w/Heavy Blade FYE	7.50	15.00
335B	Knight of Ren w/Heavy Blade Hematite	6.00	12.00
336	D-O 10" TAR	15.00	30.00
337	Cal Kestis with BD-1	30.00	75.00
338	Second Sister	17.50	35.00
339A	Purge Trooper GS	25.00	50.00
339B	Purge Trooper EB	12.50	25.00
339C	Purge Trooper SE	15.00	30.00
340	Babu Frik SB	20.00	40.00
341	C-3PO w/Bowcaster SB	7.50	15.00
342A	Jawa Futura TAR	15.00	30.00
342B	Jawa Futura SE	12.50	25.00
343	Darth Vader Electrical	15.00	30.00
344	Kylo Ren 10" GITD	20.00	40.00
345A	Mandalorian Full Chrome ERR	60.00	125.00
345B	Mandalorian	12.50	25.00
345C	Mandalorian Chrome Beskar Armor AMZ	12.50	25.00
345D	Mandalorian Chrome Beskar Armor SE	25.00	50.00
345E	Mandalorian Red Chrome Beskar Armor TAR	20.00	40.00
345F	Mandalorian Red Chrome Beskar Armor SE	15.00	30.00
345G	Mandalorian GITD EE	15.00	30.00
345H	Mandalorian GITD SE	15.00	30.00
346	The Client	7.50	15.00
347	Greef Karga	7.50	15.00
348	Heavy Infantryman Mandalorian	12.50	25.00
349	Q9-0	12.50	25.00
350	Incinerator Stormtrooper	12.50	25.00
351	Offworld Jawa	10.00	20.00
352	Covert Mandalorian	10.00	20.00
353	The Armorer	10.00	20.00
354A	Death Watch Mandalorian GS	15.00	30.00
354B	Death Watch Mandalorian EB	12.50	25.00
355	The Mandalorian Flame Gauntlet TAR	15.00	30.00
356A	Cara Dune FYE	30.00	75.00
356B	Cara Dune SE	20.00	40.00
357A	Trandoshan Thug WG	12.50	25.00
357B	Trandoshan Thug SE	12.50	25.00
358	The Mandalorian on Blurrg	30.00	60.00
359	Dark Side Rey	12.50	25.00
360A	C-3PO Red Eyes	7.50	15.00
360B	C-3PO Orange Chrome SF Giants/SW Day	50.00	100.00
360C	C-3PO Matte Black VIP/300* SF Giants/SW Day	250.00	500.00
361	Death Watch Mandalorian No Stripes GS	30.00	75.00
362	Princess Leia	7.50	15.00
363	Luke Skywalker/Yoda	10.00	20.00
364	Han Solo Carbonite	7.50	15.00
365	Darth Vader/Meditation	20.00	40.00
366	Luke w/Tauntaun	20.00	40.00
367A	Boba Fett 10" TAR	30.00	75.00
367B	Boba Fett 10" SE		
368	The Child	7.50	15.00
369	The Child 10"	30.00	60.00
370A	The Child w/Control Knob GS	12.50	25.00
370B	The Child w/Control Knob SE	20.00	40.00
371	Jawa Classic	6.00	12.00
372A	Echo Base Wampa AMZ	30.00	60.00
372B	Echo Base Wampa SE	25.00	50.00
373	Echo Base Han w/Tauntaun AMZ	20.00	40.00
374	Echo Base Chewbacca FLK AMZ	30.00	60.00
375	Echo Base Probe Droid AMZ	15.00	30.00
376	Echo Base Princess Leia AMZ	20.00	40.00
377	Echo Base Vader/Snowtrooper AMZ	20.00	40.00
378	The Child w/Cup	10.00	20.00
379	The Child w/Frog	7.50	15.00
A380A	Moff Gideon	12.50	25.00
A380B	Moff Gideon GITD TAR	15.00	30.00
B380	Mandalorian w/Child 10" Chrome	20.00	40.00
382A	Lesson in the Force SWC	60.00	125.00
382B	Lesson in the Force GCE	30.00	60.00
383A	Sith Jet Trooper Flying SDCCD	30.00	75.00
383B	Sith Jet Trooper Flying SCE	15.00	30.00
384A	The Child Concerned TAR	10.00	20.00
384B	The Child Concerned SE	12.50	25.00
385	The Child Force Push WM	7.50	15.00
386A	Concept Starkiller SWC	15.00	30.00
386B	Concept Starkiller GCE	12.50	25.00
387A	Concept Chewbacca SWC	20.00	40.00
387B	Concept Chewbacca GCE	20.00	40.00
388A	Concept Boba Fett SWC	75.00	150.00
388B	Concept Boba Fett GCE	60.00	125.00
389A	Concept Darth Vader SWC	20.00	40.00
389B	Concept Darth Vader GCE	10.00	20.00
390	Mandalorian and Child	25.00	50.00
391A	Stormtrooper 10" SWC	50.00	100.00
391B	Stormtrooper 10" GCE	45.00	90.00
391C	Stormtrooper 10" Art TARC	40.00	80.00
392	Obi-Wan Kenobi GITD SWC	400.00	800.00
393	Yoda Hooded GS	15.00	30.00
394A	Shadow Stormtrooper GS	15.00	30.00
394B	Shadow Stormtrooper EB	10.00	20.00
394C	Shadow Stormtrooper SE	20.00	40.00
395A	Darth Malak GS	7.50	15.00
395B	Darth Malak EB	12.50	25.00
395C	Darth Malak SE	20.00	40.00
396A	Darth Revan GS	25.00	50.00
396B	Darth Revan EB	30.00	60.00
396C	Darth Revan SE	25.00	50.00
397A	CB-6B TAR	12.50	25.00
397B	CB-6B SE	10.00	20.00
398A	The Child w/Pendant NYCC	25.00	50.00
398B	The Child w/Pendant FCE	15.00	30.00
398C	The Child w/Pendant PRM	20.00	40.00
399A	Luke Skywalker Jedi Training NYCC	30.00	75.00
399B	Luke Skywalker Jedi Training FCE	30.00	60.00
400A	Princess Leia Jedi Training NYCC	40.00	80.00
400B	Princess Leia Jedi Training FCE	30.00	60.00
401A	M5-R3 TAR	7.50	15.00
401B	M5-R3 SE	12.50	25.00
402A	The Mandalorian/Child w/Pin	15.00	30.00
402B	The Mandalorian/Child w/Pin AMZ	12.50	25.00
402C	The Mandalorian/Child w/Pin SE	25.00	50.00
403	Cara Dune	20.00	40.00
404	The Mythrol	10.00	20.00
405	The Child	25.00	50.00
406	Gamorrean Fighter	10.00	20.00
407	The Child with Egg Canister	25.00	50.00
408A	The Mandalorian Flying w/Blaster GS	12.50	25.00
408B	The Mandalorian Flying w/Blaster GITD GS	20.00	40.00
408C	The Mandalorian Flying w/Blaster EB	20.00	40.00
408D	The Mandalorian Flying w/Blaster GITD FIC	10.00	20.00
408E	The Mandalorian Flying w/Blaster SE	10.00	20.00
408F	The Mandalorian Flying w/Blaster GITD SE	17.50	35.00
409	Ahsoka	10.00	20.00
410	Darth Maul	7.50	15.00
411	Gar Saxon	7.50	15.00
412	Bo-Katan Kryze	10.00	20.00
413	Wrecker	12.50	25.00
414A	Ahsoka Mechanic GS	10.00	20.00
414B	Ahsoka Mechanic EB	15.00	30.00
414C	Ahsoka Mechanic SE	17.50	35.00
415	Mandalorian Super Commando FS	25.00	50.00
416	The Mandalorian & Child on Bantha	25.00	50.00
417	Darth Vader Pink	12.50	25.00
418	Stormtrooper Pink	10.00	20.00
419	Chewbacca Pink	10.00	20.00
420A	R2-D2 Pink FS	45.00	90.00
420B	R2-D2 Pink PC	40.00	80.00
421	Yoda Pink	10.00	20.00
422A	Qui-Gon Jinn Tatooine AMZ	10.00	20.00
422B	Qui-Gon Jinn Tatooine SE	12.50	25.00
423	Concept C-3PO	10.00	20.00
424	Concept R2-D2	7.50	15.00
425	Concept Yoda	12.50	25.00
426	Concept Darth Vader	10.00	20.00
427A	IG-11 w/Child GS	30.00	60.00
427B	IG-11 w/Child EB		
427C	IG-11 w/Child SE	20.00	40.00
428	Darth Vader Fist FS	20.00	40.00
429A	Bastilla Shan GS	17.50	35.00
429B	Bastilla Shan EB	12.50	25.00
429C	Bastilla Shan SE	20.00	40.00
430A	Jedi Revan GS	20.00	40.00
430B	Jedi Revan EB	20.00	40.00

No.	Name	Lo	Hi
430C	Jedi Revan SE	25.00	50.00
431	Ben Solo	7.50	15.00
432	Rey Yellow Lightsaber	7.50	15.00
433	Emperor Palpatine	10.00	20.00
434	Rey Two Lightsabers	7.50	15.00
435	Babu Frik 10"	12.50	25.00
436A	BHC Boba Fett GS	25.00	50.00
436B	BHC Boba Fett EB	25.00	50.00
436C	BHC Boba Fett SE	25.00	50.00
437A	BHC Bossk GS	25.00	50.00
437B	BHC Bossk EB	25.00	50.00
437C	BHC Bossk SE	25.00	50.00
438A	BHC IG-88 GS	25.00	50.00
438B	BHC IG-88 EB		
438C	BHC IG-88 SE		
439A	BHC 4-LOM GS	25.00	50.00
439B	BHC 4-LOM EB	25.00	50.00
439C	BHC 4-LOM SE	25.00	50.00
440A	BHC Dengar GS	25.00	50.00
440B	BHC Dengar EB	25.00	50.00
440C	BHC Dengar SE		
441A	BHC Zuckuss GS	25.00	50.00
441B	BHC Zuckuss EB		
441C	BHC Zuckuss SE		
442A	BHC Darth Vader GS	20.00	40.00
442B	BHC Darth Vader EB		
442C	BHC Darth Vader SE		
443	Wrecker	7.50	15.00
444A	Crosshair	12.50	25.00
444B	Crosshair Kamino with Pin AMZ	20.00	40.00
444C	Crosshair Kamino with Pin SE		
445	Tech	7.50	15.00
446A	Hunter	12.50	25.00
446B	Hunter Kamino AMZ	20.00	40.00
446C	Hunter Kamino SE		
447	Echo	20.00	40.00
448A	Omega TAR	15.00	30.00
448B	Omega SE	15.00	30.00
449A	General Grievous 4 Lightsabers HT	15.00	30.00
449B	General Grievous 4 Lightsabers SE	15.00	30.00
450A	Darth Maul w/Dark & Lightsaber CC	20.00	40.00
450B	Darth Maul w/Dark & Lightsaber SE	12.50	25.00
451A	Rey Jakku VF	15.00	30.00
451B	Rey Jakku SCE	10.00	20.00
452A	Imperial Super Commando VF	15.00	30.00
452B	Imperial Super Commando SCE	10.00	20.00
453A	Luke Skywalker Retro TAR	10.00	20.00
453B	Luke Skywalker Retro SE		
454A	C-3PO Retro TAR	12.50	25.00
454B	C-3PO Retro SE	15.00	30.00
455A	Stormtrooper Retro TAR	15.00	30.00
455B	Stormtrooper Retro SE	15.00	30.00
456A	Darth Vader Retro TAR	10.00	20.00
456B	Darth Vader Retro SE	30.00	60.00
457A	Nightbrother GS	15.00	30.00
457B	Nightbrother SE		
458A	Boss GITD GS	12.50	25.00
458B	Boss GITD SE		
459	Princess Leia Yavin AMZ	15.00	30.00
460A	Iden Versio GS	7.50	15.00
460B	Iden Versio SE		
460C	Iden Versio Armor GS CH	30.00	75.00
460D	Iden Versio Armor SE CH		
461	Mandalorian & Grogu w/o Helmet	12.50	25.00
462A	Boba Fett	10.00	20.00
462B	Boba Fett MET	12.50	25.00
462C	Boba Fett Red Chrome TAR	20.00	40.00
463A	Bo-Katan Kryze w/Helmet	7.50	15.00
463B	Bo-Katan Kryze w/o Helmet CH	17.50	35.00
464	Ahsoka	7.50	15.00
465	Grogu w/Cookies	12.50	25.00
466	Dark Trooper	7.50	15.00
467A	Ahsoka AMZ	12.50	25.00
467B	Ahsoka Hooded	12.50	25.00
468	Grogu w/Butterfly GS	15.00	30.00
468A	Grogu w/Butterfly PRM	17.50	35.00
468B	Grogu w/Butterfly SE	17.50	35.00
469A	Grogu w/Chowder Squid TAR	15.00	30.00
469B	Grogu w/Chowder Squid SE	12.50	25.00
470	CS Stormtrooper w/Lightsaber	7.50	15.00
471	CS Snowtrooper	7.50	15.00
472	CS Han Solo w/Lightsaber	12.50	25.00
473	CS Stormtrooper w/Saber & Shield FS	20.00	40.00
474	Grogu Macy's	15.00	30.00
475	Grogu 10" Macy's	30.00	75.00
476A	Cad Bane w/Todo 360 NYCC/ECCC FOF	50.00	100.00
476B	Cad Bane w/Todo 360 FCE	25.00	50.00
477A	Grogu Using the Force AMZ	15.00	30.00
477B	Grogu Using the Force SE	15.00	30.00
478A	Boba Fett Desert Gear NYCC	75.00	150.00
478B	Boba Fett Desert Gear FCE		
479	Mandalorian w/Beskar Staff FS	20.00	40.00
480	Boba Fett	6.00	12.00
481	Fennec Shand	10.00	20.00
482	Luke Skywalker w/Grogu	10.00	20.00
483	Fennec Shand	10.00	20.00
484A	Cobb Vanth w/Helmet	7.50	15.00
484B	Cobb Vanth w/o Helmet CH	17.50	35.00
488A	Dark Trooper w/Grogu GITD EE	10.00	20.00
488B	Dark Trooper w/Grogu GITD SE	12.50	25.00
490	Boba Fett WM	12.50	25.00
491	Mandalorian w/Darksaber GITD SE	25.00	50.00
492	Moroff Jedha AMZ	15.00	30.00
493	Grogu w/Cookies TAR	10.00	20.00
494	Luke Skywalker w/Grogu TAR	10.00	20.00
495	Mandalorian Pink TAR	12.50	25.00
496	Ahsoka Pink TAR	7.50	15.00
497	Bo-Katan Kryze Pink TAR	15.00	30.00
498	Mandalorian w/Grogu Pink TAR	10.00	20.00
500A	Jar Jar Binks GS	20.00	40.00
500B	Jar Jar Binks SE	15.00	30.00
501B	Luke Skywalker Hooded GITD SE	20.00	40.00
501A	Luke Skywalker Hooded GITD EE	12.50	25.00
502A	The Ronin and B5-56 TAR	30.00	60.00
502B	The Ronin and B5-56 GITD TAR	25.00	50.00
503A	Am TAR	12.50	25.00
503B	Am SE	25.00	50.00
504A	Karre TAR	15.00	30.00
504B	Karre SE	15.00	30.00
505	The Ronin TAR	12.50	25.00
506	DOTF Darth Maul AMZ	30.00	75.00
507	DOTF Obi-Wan Kenobi AMZ	40.00	80.00
508	DOTF Qui-Gon Jinn AMZ	30.00	75.00
509A	Darth Vader SWC	40.00	80.00
509B	Darth Vader GCE	25.00	50.00
510A	Stormtrooper SWC	40.00	80.00
510B	Stormtrooper GCE	25.00	50.00
511A	Luke Skywalker SWC	25.00	50.00
511B	Luke Skywalker GCE	17.50	35.00
512A	Princess Leia SWC	30.00	75.00
512B	Princess Leia GCE	15.00	30.00
513A	Chewbacca SWC	20.00	40.00
513B	Chewbacca GCE	17.50	35.00
514A	Lando in M.Falcon SWC	75.00	150.00
514B	Lando in M.Falcon GCE	60.00	125.00
519	RSSV1 Darth Sidious GS	20.00	40.00
520	RSSV1 Darth Maul GS	15.00	30.00
521	RSSV1 Savage Opress GS	30.00	75.00
522	RSSV1 Darth Tyranus GITD GS	15.00	30.00
524	CS Darth Vader DP	40.00	80.00
525	POTG Padme Amidala AMZ	20.00	40.00
533A	Purge Trooper SDCC	60.00	125.00
533B	Purge Trooper SCE	20.00	40.00
534A	Cassian Andor SDCC	50.00	100.00
534B	Cassian Andor SCE	15.00	30.00
535	Darth Vader Art Series TAR	25.00	50.00
536	Obi-Wan Kenobi Art Series TAR	15.00	30.00
538	Obi-Wan Kenobi	30.00	60.00
539	Darth Vader	7.50	15.00
540	Kawlan Roken	10.00	20.00
541	Tala Durith	10.00	20.00
542	Reva Third Sister	25.00	50.00
543	Darth Vader GS	20.00	40.00
544	Obi-Wan Kenobi FS	25.00	50.00
545A	Haja Estree TAR		
545B	Haja Estree SE		
546A	Reva Third Sister/Lightsaber WM	20.00	40.00
546B	Reva Third Sister/Lightsaber SE	12.50	25.00
547	POTG Sabine Wren AMZ	15.00	30.00
548A	Krrsantan SDCC	75.00	150.00
548A	Krrsantan SCE	20.00	40.00
550	ARC Umbra Trooper GS	17.50	35.00
551	Proxy GITD GS	12.50	25.00
552	Imperial Rocket Trooper GS	20.00	40.00
553	Merrin Nightsister GS	12.50	25.00
555	POTG Jyn Erso AMZ	12.50	25.00
556	Darth Vader Snowman	15.00	30.00
557	Stormtrooper Snowman	15.00	30.00
558	Boba Fett Snowman	12.50	25.00
559	C-3PO Snowman	20.00	40.00
560	R2-D2 Snowman	20.00	40.00
565	POTG Princess Leia AMZ	10.00	20.00
566A	B2EMO NYCC	75.00	150.00
566B	B2EMO FCE	25.00	50.00
567A	Anakin Skywalker w/Lightsabers NYCC	125.00	250.00
567B	Anakin Skywalker w/Lightsabers FCE	45.00	90.00
568	Yoda Snowman FS	10.00	20.00
570	Chewbacca Retro TAR		
571	R2-D2 Retro TAR		
572	Ben Kenobi Retro TAR		
573	Emperor Palpatine Retro TAR		
575	Grogu Macy's Thanksgiving Day Parade FS		
580	Cad Bane		

581	Krrsantan
582	Majordomo
583	Luke Skywalker & Grogu
584	Grogu with Armor
585	The Mandalorian
587	Grogu with Rancor EE
SE	BB-8 MAW
SE	Stormtrooper MAW

2011-22 Funko Pop Vinyl Star Wars Multi-Packs

NNO	Anakin/Yoda/Obi-Wan GITD AMZ	20.00	40.00
NNO	Anakin/Yoda/Obi-Wan GITD SE	40.00	80.00
NNO	BB-8/BB-9E BB	7.50	15.00
NNO	BB-8 Gold Dome HT BF	7.50	15.00
NNO	Biggs/Wedge/Porkins WM	15.00	30.00
NNO	CS Yoda/Vader/R2/C-3PO AMZ	25.00	50.00
NNO	Vader/STrooper/Fett/C-3PO/R2-D2 Snowmen AMZ	40.00	80.00
NNO	Vader/Trooper/Chewbacca/Yoda Valentine SE	50.00	100.00
NNO	D-0/BB-8 BAM!	12.50	25.00
NNO	D-0/BB-8 SE	12.50	25.00
NNO	Bad Batch 5PK EB	50.00	100.00
NNO	Bad Batch 5PK GS	25.00	50.00
NNO	Bad Batch 5PK PC	20.00	40.00
NNO	Bad Batch 5PK SE	40.00	80.00
NNO	Fighting Droids GS	10.00	20.00
NNO	First Order Kylo Ren/Snoke/BB-9E COSTCO	12.50	25.00
NNO	First Order Kylo Ren/Snoke/Executioner/BB-9E COSTCO	20.00	40.00
NNO	Greedo/Hammerhead/Walrus Man WM	7.50	15.00
NNO	Gunner/Officer/Trooper WM	20.00	40.00
NNO	Han Solo/Chewbacca SB	25.00	50.00
NNO	Han Solo/Princess Leia	20.00	40.00
NNO	Jabba/Slave Leia/Salacious Crumb WM	60.00	125.00
NNO	Jango Fett GITD/LEGO Star Wars III Bundle	40.00	80.00
NNO	Kylo Ren/Rey B&N	15.00	30.00
NNO	Lobot/Ugnaught/Bespin Guard WM	7.50	15.00
NNO	Luke Skywalker & Wampa SDCC	100.00	200.00
NNO	Luke Skywalker & Wampa B&N	75.00	150.00
NNO	Mandalorian/IG-11 B&N	60.00	125.00
NNO	Obi-Wan/Vader TAR	15.00	30.00
NNO	Obi-Wan/Vader/Roken/Durith/Reva WM	50.00	100.00
NNO	Praetorian Guards POPCULTCHA	25.00	50.00
NNO	Princess Leia/R2-D2 SDCC	60.00	125.00
NNO	Princess Leia/R2-D2 SCE	30.00	60.00
NNO	R2-D2 Gold Dome HT BF	10.00	20.00
NNO	Rancor/Luke/Slave Oola PX	50.00	100.00
NNO	Rebel Rey/Chewbacca/BB-8 COSTCO	12.50	25.00
NNO	Rebel Rey/Luke/Chewbacca/BB-8 COSTCO	30.00	60.00
NNO	Rogue One Jyn/Cassian/K-2SO/C2-B5/Krennic	100.00	200.00
NNO	Sandtrooper/Dewback WM	15.00	30.00
NNO	Tarfful/Unhooded Emperor/Clone Trooper WM	25.00	50.00
NNO	Tarfful/Unhooded Emperor/Clone Trooper SE	30.00	60.00
NNO	Teebo/Chirpa/Logray WM	20.00	40.00

2012 Funko Mini Wacky Wobblers Star Wars Monster Mash-Ups

NNO	Chewbacca	7.50	15.00
NNO	Darth Vader	7.50	15.00
NNO	Jawa	12.50	25.00
NNO	Stormtrooper	10.00	20.00
NNO	Tusken Raider	7.50	15.00
NNO	Yoda	7.50	15.00

2014-16 Funko Fabrikations

2	Yoda	8.00	15.00
3	Boba Fett	6.00	12.00
4	Greedo	6.00	12.00
5	Deadpool	8.00	15.00
12	Darth Vader	6.00	12.00
13	Chewbacca	6.00	12.00
26	Wicket Warrick	10.00	20.00
27	Princess Leia	12.00	25.00
29	Stormtrooper	6.00	12.00

2015-16 Funko Super Shogun

2	Shadowtrooper SWC	120.00	200.00
3	Boba Fett ROTJ SWC	120.00	200.00
4	Boba Fett ESB	60.00	120.00
5	Boba Fett Proto/400* FS	150.00	250.00

2015-18 Funko Hikari Star Wars

NNO	Boba Fett Clear Glitter/750* NYCC	25.00	50.00
NNO	Boba Fett Glitter/1200*	20.00	40.00
NNO	Boba Fett Infrared/1000* SDCC	25.00	50.00
NNO	Boba Fett Infrared/1000* SCE	25.00	50.00
NNO	Boba Fett Midnight/1000* SWC	60.00	120.00
NNO	Boba Fett Prism/750*	30.00	60.00
NNO	Boba Fett Proto/250* FS	30.00	75.00
NNO	Boba Fett/1500*	20.00	40.00
NNO	Bossk MET/1000*	25.00	50.00
NNO	Bossk Planet X/600*	20.00	40.00
NNO	Bossk Prism/500* EE	25.00	50.00
NNO	Bossk Rainbow/550* SLCC	30.00	75.00
NNO	Bossk Starfield/500* NYCC	30.00	75.00
NNO	Bossk/1000*	25.00	50.00
NNO	C-3PO Clear Glitter/750* SLCC	30.00	60.00
NNO	C-3PO Dirty Penny/500* TT	30.00	75.00
NNO	C-3PO Red/750* SLCC	25.00	50.00
NNO	C-3PO Rusty/500* Gemini	25.00	50.00
NNO	C-3PO/1500*	20.00	40.00
NNO	Captain Phasma Alloy/250*	30.00	60.00
NNO	Captain Phasma Blue Steel/400*	30.00	75.00
NNO	Captain Phasma Classic/500*	25.00	50.00

NNO	Captain Phasma Cold Steel/250*	30.00	60.00
NNO	Captain Phasma Meltdown/100* HT	100.00	175.00
NNO	Clone Trooper Dirty Penny/250* EE	25.00	50.00
NNO	Clone Trooper Rusty White/250* GS	20.00	40.00
NNO	Clone Trooper 442 Siege Glitter/100*	60.00	120.00
NNO	Clone Trooper 442 Siege/900*	20.00	40.00
NNO	Clone Trooper 501st Glitter/250*	30.00	75.00
NNO	Clone Trooper 501st/1500* SDCC	20.00	40.00
NNO	Clone Trooper Starfield/1000* SWC	25.00	50.00
NNO	Clone Trooper Utapau Glitter/100* EE	50.00	100.00
NNO	Clone Trooper Utapau/600* EE	25.00	50.00
NNO	Clone Trooper/1500*	15.00	30.00
NNO	Darth Vader Holographic GITD/300* Gemini	30.00	75.00
NNO	Darth Vader Holographic/750*	25.00	50.00
NNO	Darth Vader Infrared/500* EE	30.00	60.00
NNO	Darth Vader Lightning/1500*	20.00	40.00
NNO	Darth Vader Matte Back/1200* SDCC	25.00	50.00
NNO	Darth Vader Starfield/750*Gemini	30.00	75.00
NNO	Darth Vader/1500*	20.00	40.00
NNO	E-3PO/500*	20.00	40.00
NNO	FO Snowtrooper Ice Storm/500*	20.00	40.00
NNO	FO Snowtrooper Iron Age/250*	25.00	50.00
NNO	Stormtrooper Inferno/250*	30.00	75.00
NNO	FO Stormtrooper Kiln/400*	30.00	75.00
NNO	FO Stormtrooper Nocturne/400*	30.00	60.00
NNO	FO Stormtrooper Phantasm/250*	30.00	60.00
NNO	FO Stormtrooper/500*	15.00	30.00
NNO	Greedo Mystic Powers/750*	30.00	75.00
NNO	Greedo Platinum/600* NYCC	25.00	50.00
NNO	Greedo Sublime/750*	15.00	30.00
NNO	Greedo Verdigris/500* SWC	30.00	60.00
NNO	Greedo Original/2000*	20.00	40.00
NNO	K-3PO/750*	20.00	40.00
NNO	Kylo Ren Alchemy/300*	25.00	50.00
NNO	Kylo Ren Dark Side/500*	20.00	40.00
NNO	Kylo Ren Live Wire/250*	60.00	120.00
NNO	Kylo Ren Onyx/150* HT	75.00	150.00
NNO	Kylo Ren Rage/250* HT	60.00	120.00
NNO	Shadow Trooper/1000*	20.00	40.00
NNO	Snowtrooper Celsius/400*	30.00	60.00
NNO	Snowtrooper Galaxy/250*	20.00	40.00
NNO	Stormtrooper Blue MET/1000*	20.00	40.00
NNO	Stormtrooper Cosmic/2000* SDCC LC	15.00	30.00
NNO	Stormtrooper Green/100* ECCC	75.00	150.00
NNO	Stormtrooper Ice/750* SWC	60.00	120.00
NNO	Stormtrooper Prism/750* TT	30.00	75.00
NNO	Stormtrooper Relic/500*	20.00	40.00
NNO	Stormtrooper Rusty Silver/750*	25.00	50.00
NNO	Stormtrooper Starfied/750*	20.00	40.00
NNO	Stormtrooper/1500*	30.00	60.00
NNO	Wampa Bloody/750*	20.00	40.00
NNO	Wampa Glitter/750*	20.00	40.00
NNO	Wampa Grey Skull/250* EE	20.00	40.00
NNO	Wampa Ice/500* Gemini	30.00	60.00

2015-21 Funko Pop Vinyl Conan O'Brien

6	Stormtrooper Conan COCO SDCC	60.00	120.00
10	Jedi Conan COCO SDCC	60.00	120.00
14	Rebel Pilot Conan COCO SDCC	30.00	60.00

ACTION FIGURES AND FIGURINES

2016-18 Funko Pop Pens Star Wars

NNO BB-8
(2016)
NNO BB-9E
(2017)
NNO Boba Fett
(2016)
NNO C2-B5
(2017)
NNO Captain Phasma
(2016)
NNO Chewbacca
(2016 Smuggler's Bounty Exclusive)
NNO Darth Vader
(2016)
NNO Darth Vader (Rogue One)
(2017)
NNO Death Trooper
(2017)
NNO First Order Stormtrooper
(2016)
NNO Kylo Ren
(2016)
NNO Kylo Ren (unmasked)
(2017)
NNO Porg
(2017)
NNO Rey
(2017)
NNO Scarif Stormtrooper
(2017)
NNO Stormtrooper
(2016)
NNO Yoda
(2016)

2016-18 Funko Wobblers Star Wars

COMMON FIGURINE

NNO Boba Fett (prototype)	15.00	30.00
(2017 Galactic Convention Exclusive)		
NNO Boba Fett Proto SWC	15.00	30.00
NNO Boba Fett	6.00	12.00
NNO Captain Cassian Andor	4.00	8.00
NNO Chewbacca	6.00	12.00
NNO Darth Vader	7.50	15.00
NNO First Order Executioner	6.00	12.00
NNO Han Solo (Solo film)	7.50	15.00
(2018)		
NNO Imperial Death Trooper	6.00	12.00
NNO Jyn Erso	5.00	10.00
NNO Lando Calrissian	6.00	12.00
(2018)		
NNO Princess Leia	7.50	15.00
NNO Rey	7.50	15.00
NNO Scarif Stormtrooper	6.00	12.00

2017 Funko MyMoji Star Wars

COMMON MYMOJI	2.50	5.00
NNO Chewbacca (laughing)	4.00	8.00
NNO Chewbacca (smiling)	4.00	8.00
NNO Chewbacca (surprised)	2.50	5.00

NNO Darth Vader (angry)	4.00	8.00
NNO Darth Vader (sad)	2.50	5.00
NNO Darth Vader (staring)	2.50	5.00
NNO Jabba (bored)	2.50	5.00
NNO Jabba (closed eyes)	4.00	8.00
NNO Jabba (sad)	4.00	8.00
NNO Luke Skywalker (big smile)	2.50	5.00
NNO Luke Skywalker (closed eyes)	2.50	5.00
NNO Luke Skywalker (sad)	2.50	5.00
NNO Princess Leia (big smile)	3.00	6.00
NNO Princess Leia (closed eyes)	2.50	5.00
NNO Princess Leia (sad)	2.50	5.00
NNO Wampa (angry)	2.50	5.00
NNO Wampa (bored)	2.50	5.00
NNO Wampa (sad)	2.50	5.00
NNO Wicket (laughing)	2.50	5.00
NNO Wicket (sad)	2.50	5.00
NNO Wicket (smiling)	2.50	5.00
NNO Yoda (closed eyes)	2.50	5.00
NNO Yoda (curious)	2.50	5.00
NNO Yoda (smiling)	4.00	8.00

2017 Funko Mystery Minis Star Wars

NNO C-3PO	3.00	6.00
NNO Chewbacca	4.00	8.00
NNO Chewbacca (w/bowcaster)	10.00	20.00
(Walmart Exclusive)		
NNO Darth Vader (Force Choke)	75.00	150.00
(Hot Topic Exclusive)		
NNO Darth Vader (Force Lift)	15.00	30.00
NNO Darth Vader (lightsaber)	25.00	50.00
(GameStop Exclusive)		
NNO Grand Moff Tarkin	4.00	8.00
NNO Greedo	4.00	8.00
NNO Greedo (pistol up)	20.00	40.00
(Hot Topic Exclusive)		
NNO Hammerhead	4.00	8.00
NNO Han Solo	6.00	12.00
NNO Han Solo (stormtrooper)	12.00	25.00
(GameStop Exclusive)		
NNO Jawa	6.00	12.00
NNO Luke Skywalker	10.00	20.00
NNO Luke Skywalker (stormtrooper)	15.00	30.00
(GameStop Exclusive)		
NNO Obi Wan Kenobi	4.00	8.00
NNO Obi Wan Kenobi (Force Ghost)	30.00	75.00
(Walmart Exclusive)		
NNO Ponda Baba	3.00	6.00
NNO Princess Leia	2.50	5.00
NNO Shadow Trooper	5.00	10.00
NNO Snaggletooth	2.50	5.00

NNO Stormtrooper	4.00	8.00
NNO TIE Pilot	30.00	75.00
(Hot Topic Exclusive)		
NNO Tusken Raider	20.00	40.00
(Walmart Exclusive)		

2017 Funko Mystery Minis Star Wars The Last Jedi

COMPLETE SET (24)

NNO BB-8	2.50	5.00
NNO BB-9E	6.00	12.00
NNO C'ai Threnalli	50.00	100.00
(Walgreens Exclusive)		
NNO Captain Phasma	4.00	8.00
NNO Chewbacca (w/porg)	4.00	8.00
NNO DJ	4.00	8.00
NNO Finn	7.50	15.00
NNO Finn (First Order uniform)	3.00	6.00
NNO First Order Executioner	7.50	15.00
(GameStop Exclusive)		
NNO Kylo Ren	25.00	50.00
NNO Kylo Ren (unmasked)	60.00	120.00
(Walmart Exclusive)		
NNO Poe Dameron	3.00	6.00
NNO Porg	12.00	25.00
NNO Porg (wings open)	15.00	30.00
(GameStop Exclusive)		
NNO Praetorian Guard	5.00	10.00
NNO Praetorian Guard (w/staff)	6.00	12.00
(Walgreens Exclusive)		
NNO Praetorian Guard (w/whip)	12.50	25.00
(Walmart Exclusive)		
NNO Princess Leia	6.00	12.00
NNO Resistance BB Unit	6.00	12.00
NNO Rey	4.00	8.00
NNO Rey (cloaked)	8.00	15.00
(GameStop Exclusive)		
NNO Rose	3.00	6.00
NNO Supreme Leader Snoke	3.00	6.00
NNO Supreme Leader Snoke (holographic)	10.00	20.00
(Walgreens Exclusive)		

2017-18 Funko Hikari XS Star Wars

NNO Chopper (black)	7.50	15.00
(2017 Smuggler's Bounty Exclusive)		
NNO Chopper (clear)	4.00	8.00
(2017 Smuggler's Bounty Exclusive)		
NNO Chopper (gold)	5.00	10.00
(2017 Smuggler's Bounty Exclusive)		
NNO Chopper (orange)	4.00	8.00

ACTION FIGURES AND FIGURINES

(2017 Smuggler's Bounty Exclusive)

NNO	Chopper (red)	4.00	8.00

(2017 Smuggler's Bounty Exclusive)

NNO	Darth Vader (black)	6.00	12.00

(2017 Smuggler's Bounty Exclusive)

NNO	Darth Vader (blue)	4.00	8.00

(2017 Smuggler's Bounty Exclusive)

NNO	Darth Vader (gold)	15.00	30.00

(2017 Smuggler's Bounty Exclusive)

NNO	Darth Vader (red)	5.00	10.00

(2017 Smuggler's Bounty Exclusive)

NNO	Darth Vader (silver)	4.00	8.00

(2017 Smuggler's Bounty Exclusive)

NNO	Greedo 2-Pack (blue & clear)	10.00	20.00

(2017 Galactic Convention Exclusive)

NNO	Greedo 2-Pack (blue & clear)	10.00	20.00

(2017 Star Wars Celebration Exclusive)

NNO	Greedo 2-Pack (green & gold)	6.00	12.00

(2017 Galactic Convention Exclusive)

NNO	Greedo 2-Pack (green & gold)	12.50	25.00

(2017 Star Wars Celebration Exclusive)

2017-18 Funko Vynl Star Wars

NNO	Chewbacca + C-3PO	7.50	15.00
NNO	Darth Vader + Stormtrooper	7.50	15.00
NNO	Han Solo + Greedo	6.00	12.00
NNO	Han Solo + Lando Calrissian	6.00	12.00
NNO	Luke Skywalker + Darth Vader	7.50	15.00
NNO	Luke Skywalker + Princess Leia	10.00	20.00
NNO	Obi-Wan Kenobi + Darth Maul	5.00	10.00

2017-19 Funko Dorbz Star Wars

1	Luke Skywalker	7.50	15.00
2	Princess Leia	7.50	15.00
3A	Darth Vader	10.00	20.00

(2017)

3B	Darth Vader HOLO CH	10.00	20.00
4	Han Solo	6.00	12.00
5A	Chewbacca	10.00	20.00
5B	Chewbacca FLK CH	15.00	30.00
6	C-3PO	7.50	15.00
7	Stormtrooper	10.00	20.00
8	Jawa	7.50	15.00
9	Luke Skywalker w/Speeder	20.00	40.00
10	Tusken Raider w/Bantha	20.00	40.00
11	Han Solo	10.00	20.00

(2018)

12A	Chewbacca	7.50	15.00

(2018)

12B	Chewbacca FLK CH	15.00	30.00
13	Qi'Ra	6.00	12.00

(2018)

14A	Lando Calrissian		

(2018)

14B	Lando Calrissian White Cape CH	20.00	40.00

2017-19 Funko Dorbz Star Wars Multi-Pack

COMMON DORBZ

NNO	Greedo/Walrus Man/Snaggletooth D23	20.00	40.00

2017-19 Funko Mystery Minis Star Wars Smuggler's Bounty

NNO	Darth Maul	6.00	12.00
NNO	Darth Vader (hands on hips)		

(2019)

NNO	Emperor Palpatine	10.00	20.00
NNO	Lando Calrissian	7.50	15.00
NNO	Luke Skywalker TFA	7.50	15.00
NNO	Luke Skywalker TLJ	10.00	20.00

2017-22 Funko Pop Vinyl MLB

SE	Kevin Kiermaier Han Solo RAYS	10.00	20.00

2018 Funko Mystery Minis Solo A Star Wars Story

COMMON MYSTERY MINI		3.00	6.00
NNO	Chewbacca	4.00	8.00
NNO	Chewbacca (prisoner)	4.00	8.00

(Target Exclusive)

NNO	Dryden Voss	7.50	15.00
NNO	Enfys Nest	3.00	6.00
NNO	Han Solo	4.00	8.00
NNO	Han Solo (pilot)	125.00	250.00

(Target Exclusive)

NNO	Han Solo (prisoner)	7.50	15.00

(Target Exclusive)

NNO	L3-37	15.00	30.00
NNO	Lando Calrissian	4.00	8.00
NNO	Patrol Trooper	6.00	12.00
NNO	Qi'Ra	3.00	6.00
NNO	Qi'Ra (dress)	7.50	15.00

(Target Exclusive)

NNO	Range Trooper	10.00	20.00

(Target Exclusive)

NNO	Rio Durant	5.00	10.00
NNO	Tobias Beckett	4.00	8.00
NNO	Tobias Beckett (w/rifle)	15.00	30.00

(Target Exclusive)

NNO	Val	15.00	30.00
NNO	Weazel	5.00	10.00

2018 Funko Mystery Minis Star Wars Empire Strikes Back

COMMON MYSTERY MINI		3.00	6.00
NNO	4-LOM	25.00	50.00

(GameStop Exclusive)

NNO	Boba Fett	30.00	60.00
NNO	Bossk	75.00	150.00

(Hot Topic Exclusive)

NNO	Chewbacca	3.00	6.00
NNO	Darth Vader	3.00	6.00
NNO	Dengar	30.00	75.00
NNO	Han Solo (Bespin)	3.00	6.00
NNO	Han Solo (Hoth)	12.50	25.00

(Hot Topic Exclusive)

NNO	IG-88	12.50	25.00
NNO	Imperial AT-AT Driver	15.00	30.00

(GameStop Exclusive)

NNO	Lando Calrissian	6.00	12.00
NNO	Lobot	25.00	50.00

(Target Exclusive)

NNO	Luke Skywalker (Bespin)	12.50	25.00

(Target Exclusive)

NNO	Luke Skywalker (Hoth)	15.00	30.00
NNO	Princess Leia (Bespin)	7.50	15.00

(GameStop Exclusive)

NNO	Princess Leia (Hoth)	7.50	15.00
NNO	R2-D2	3.00	6.00
NNO	Snowtrooper	20.00	40.00

(Hot Topic Exclusive)

NNO	Wampa	7.50	15.00
NNO	Yoda	4.00	8.00
NNO	Zuckuss	60.00	120.00

(Target Exclusive)

2018-21 Funko Pop PEZ Star Wars

NNO	Boba Fett Prototype	7.50	15.00
NNO	Boba Fett	7.50	15.00
NNO	Bossk	6.00	12.00
NNO	Gamorrean Guard GCE	6.00	12.00
NNO	Gamorrean Guard SWC	5.00	10.00
NNO	Greedo	4.00	8.00
NNO	Jabba the Hutt GCE	6.00	12.00
NNO	Jabba the Hutt SWC	10.00	20.00
NNO	Jawa	6.00	12.00
NNO	Lando Calrissian Skiff	5.00	10.00
NNO	Logray	5.00	10.00
NNO	The Mandalorian/The Child	15.00	30.00
NNO	Ponda Boba Blue Stem CH	15.00	30.00
NNO	Ponda Boba	4.00	8.00
NNO	Salacious Crumb GCE	6.00	12.00
NNO	Salacious Crumb SWC	10.00	20.00
NNO	Snaggletooth Blue Stem CH	15.00	30.00
NNO	Snaggletooth	4.00	8.00
NNO	Tusken Raider	5.00	10.00

2021 Funko Pop Vinyl Pocket Pop Keychains Star Wars

NNO	Boba Fett	7.50	15.00
NNO	C-3PO	6.00	12.00
NNO	Chewbacca	7.50	15.00
NNO	The Child	7.50	15.00
NNO	The Child Using Force	7.50	15.00
NNO	The Child with Cup	6.00	12.00
NNO	Darth Vader	6.00	12.00
NNO	Grogu Macy's		
NNO	Han Solo	7.50	15.00
NNO	IG-11	7.50	15.00
NNO	Luke Skywalker	7.50	15.00
NNO	Mandalorian	6.00	12.00
NNO	Mandalorian Flying	7.50	15.00
NNO	Moff Gideon	6.00	12.00
NNO	Princess Leia	7.50	15.00
NNO	R2-D2	7.50	15.00
NNO	Stormtrooper	7.50	15.00
NNO	Yoda	6.00	12.00

2010 Mighty Beanz Star Wars

1	Luke Skywalker C	
2	Han Solo C	
3	Princess Leia C	
4	Darth Vader C	
5	R2-D2 C	

6 Obi-Wan Kenobi C
7 Yoda C
8 Chewbacca C
9 Jabba the Hutt C
10 Battle Droid C
11 C-3PO C
12 Clone Trooper C
13 501st Legion Trooper C
14 Commander Cody C
15 Stormtrooper C
16 Admiral Ackbar C
17 Gamorrean Guard C
18 Count Dooku C
19 Boba Fett C
20 Greedo C
21 Sandtrooper C
22 Anakin Skywalker (child) C
23 Mace Windu C
24 AT-AT Driver C
25 General Grievous C
26 TIE Pilot C
27 Snowtrooper C
28 Wicket C
29 Jawa C
30 Tusken Raider C
31 Padme Amidala R
32 Darth Maul R
33 Anakin Skywalker R
34 2-1B R
35 Han Solo (carbonite) R
36 Cantina Musician R
37 Bossk R
38 Lando Calrissian R
39 Biggs Darklighter R
40 Jango Fett R
41 Bib Fortuna R
42 IG-88 R
43 Emperor Palpatine R
44 Qui-Gon Jinn R
45 Rancor Keeper R
46 Max Rebo R
47 Luke Rebel Pilot R
48 Sebulba R
49 Rancor R
50 Ponda Baba R
51 Princess Leia UR
52 Jar Jar Binks UR
53 Dengar UR
54 Kit Fisto UR
55 Ki-Adi-Mundi UR
56 Jek Porkins UR
57 Nien Nunb UR
58 Salacious Crumb UR
59 Watto UR
60 Queen Amidala UR

2011 Vinylmation Star Wars Series 1

NNO	Boba Fett	12.00	25.00
NNO	C-3PO	8.00	15.00
NNO	Chewbacca	6.00	12.00
NNO	Darth Vader	10.00	20.00

NNO	Han Solo	12.00	25.00
NNO	Lando	10.00	20.00
NNO	Leia	6.00	12.00
NNO	Luke	6.00	12.00
NNO	Obi-Wan Kenobi Ghost (super chaser)	30.00	60.00
NNO	Obi-Wan Kenobi (chaser)	8.00	15.00
NNO	R2-D2	6.00	12.00
NNO	Stormtrooper	8.00	15.00
NNO	Yoda	8.00	15.00

2012 Vinylmation Star Wars Series 2

NNO	Darth Vader	20.00	40.00
NNO	Garindan (chaser)	25.00	50.00
NNO	Grand Moff Tarkin	6.00	12.00
NNO	Greedo	6.00	12.00
NNO	Han Solo	6.00	12.00
NNO	Hologram Princess Leia (LE 2500) Celebration VI Exclusive	30.00	60.00
NNO	Jawa (LE 2000)	15.00	30.00
NNO	Luke Skywalker	8.00	15.00
NNO	Muftak	6.00	12.00
NNO	Obi-Wan Kenobi	8.00	15.00
NNO	Ponda Baba	6.00	12.00
NNO	Princess Leia	8.00	15.00
NNO	R5-D4 (LE 2000)		
NNO	Tusken Raider	8.00	15.00
NNO	Wedge Antilles	6.00	12.00

2012-13 Vinylmation Star Wars Disney Characters

NNO	Boba Fett Pete	6.00	12.00
NNO	Chewbacca Goofy (LE 1500)	20.00	40.00
NNO	Darth Vader Goofy	8.00	15.00
NNO	Emperor Stitch (LE 2000)	25.00	50.00
NNO	Ewok Chip (LE 1500)	20.00	40.00
NNO	Ewok Dale (LE 1500)	20.00	40.00
NNO	Han Solo Donald (LE 1500)	30.00	60.00
NNO	Jedi Mickey (LE 2000)	20.00	40.00

NNO	Princess Leia Minnie	10.00	20.00
NNO	Stormtrooper Donald	6.00	12.00
NNO	X-Wing Pilot Luke Mickey	12.00	25.00
NNO	Yoda Stitch	20.00	40.00

2013 Vinylmation Star Wars Series 3

NNO	Admiral Ackbar	10.00	20.00
NNO	Bib Fortuna	6.00	12.00
NNO	Biker Scout	8.00	15.00
NNO	Emperor Palpatine (chaser)	30.00	60.00
NNO	Emperor's Royal Guard	10.00	20.00
NNO	Gamorrean Guard	6.00	12.00
NNO	Helmetless Princess Leia in Boushh Disguise (variant)		
NNO	Lando Calrissian Skiff Guard Disguise	8.00	15.00
NNO	Logray	10.00	20.00
NNO	Luke Skywalker Jedi	8.00	15.00
NNO	Nien Nunb	6.00	12.00
NNO	Princess Leia in Boushh Disguise	15.00	30.00
NNO	Wicket	10.00	20.00

2014 Vinylmation Star Wars Series 4

NNO	4-LOM	6.00	12.00
NNO	Bespin Princess Leia	6.00	12.00
NNO	Boba Fett Concept (combo topper)	20.00	40.00
NNO	Boba Fett Holiday Special (LE 1500)		
NNO	Boba Fett (combo topper)	15.00	30.00
NNO	Bossk	6.00	12.00
NNO	Dagobah Luke Skywalker 9-Inch (LE 2000)	30.00	60.00

NNO Dengar	6.00	12.00
NNO Han Solo Carbonite	50.00	100.00
(LE 2000)		
NNO Han Solo Hoth	6.00	12.00
NNO Holographic Emperor	12.00	25.00
(LE 2000)		
NNO Jabba the Hutt and Salacious Crumb 9-Inch	30.00	60.00
(LE 2000)		
NNO Luke Skywalker Hoth	6.00	12.00
NNO R2-D2 Dagobah	12.00	25.00
NNO R2-D2	15.00	30.00
(variant)		
NNO R2-MK	8.00	15.00
NNO Rancor and Malakili 9-and-3-Inch Combo	40.00	80.00
NNO Snowtrooper	10.00	20.00
NNO Tauntaun	6.00	12.00
NNO Ugnaught	6.00	12.00
NNO Wampa Attacked Luke		
(variant)		
NNO Wampa	15.00	30.00
(chaser)		
NNO Yoda 9-Inch		
(LE 2000)		
NNO Zuckuss	6.00	12.00

2015 Vinylmation Star Wars The Force Awakens Series 1

NNO BB-8	10.00	20.00
NNO C-3PO	4.00	8.00
NNO Finn (leather jacket)	5.00	10.00
NNO Finn (stormtrooper)		
NNO First Order Stormtrooper	12.00	25.00
NNO Han Solo (chaser)	15.00	30.00
NNO Kylo Ren	10.00	20.00
NNO Poe Dameron	4.00	8.00
NNO Rey		
NNO Rey (desert wear)	30.00	75.00

2015 Vinylmation Star Wars Rebels

NNO Chopper	
(LE 2500)	
NNO Inquisitor	
NNO Zeb	
(LE 2500)	

2015 Vinylmation Star Wars Series 5

NNO Death Star and Trooper 9-and-3-Inch Combo	40.00	80.00
(LE 1000)		
NNO Death Star Droid	8.00	15.00
NNO Dr. Evazan	6.00	12.00
NNO Duros		
NNO Figrin D'an	15.00	30.00
(instrument 1)		
NNO Figrin D'an	20.00	40.00
(instrument 2)		
NNO Figrin D'an	20.00	40.00
(instrument 3)		
NNO Figrin D'an	15.00	30.00
(instrument 4)		
NNO Figrin D'an	20.00	40.00
(instrument 5)		
NNO Han Solo Stormtrooper	12.00	25.00
NNO Heroes of Yavin Han		
(LE 2500)		
NNO Heroes of Yavin Luke	12.00	25.00
(LE 2500)		
NNO Jabba the Hutt	6.00	12.00
NNO Jawa	20.00	40.00
(LE 2500)		
NNO Labria	6.00	12.00
NNO Luke Skywalker Stormtrooper	50.00	100.00
(variant)		
NNO Luke Skywalker X-Wing Pilot	10.00	20.00
(combo topper)		
NNO Momaw Nadon	6.00	12.00
NNO Power Droid	10.00	25.00
(LE 2500)		
NNO Princess Leia	6.00	12.00
NNO Sandtrooper	8.00	15.00
NNO Snaggletooth	10.00	20.00
(chaser)		
NNO Tie Fighter Pilot	10.00	20.00

2016 Vinylmation Star Wars The Force Awakens Series 2

NNO Admiral Ackbar	5.00	10.00
NNO Captain Phasma		
NNO Ello Asty (w/ helmet)	6.00	12.00
NNO Ello Asty (helmetless)		
NNO First Mate Guiggold	4.00	8.00
NNO First Order Snowtrooper	6.00	12.00
NNO First Order TIE Fighter Pilot	8.00	15.00
NNO First Order TIE Fighter Pilot (red mark)		
NNO Princess Leia	12.00	25.00
NNO Sidon Ithano	5.00	10.00

2016 Vinylmation Star Wars Rogue One

NNO Admiral Raddus	8.00	15.00
NNO Baze Malbus	6.00	12.00
NNO Bistan	4.00	8.00
NNO C2-B5	6.00	12.00
NNO Cassian Andor	8.00	15.00
NNO Chirrut Imwe	8.00	15.00
NNO Director Orson Krennic	6.00	12.00

NNO Imperial Death Trooper (w/o shoulder pad)	8.00	15.00
NNO Imperial Death Trooper (w/ shoulder pad)	30.00	75.00
NNO Jyn Erso (w/o helm)	8.00	15.00
NNO Jyn Erso (w/ helm)	60.00	120.00
NNO K-2SO	10.00	20.00
NNO Rebel Commando Pao	8.00	15.00
NNO Saw Gererra	12.00	25.00

2016 Vinylmation Star Wars Series 6

NNO Anakin/Yoda/Obi-Wan Spirits		
(LE 2500)		
NNO Han Solo		
NNO Klaatu		
NNO Luke Skywalker		
NNO Luke Skywalker (w/o helmet)		
NNO Max Rebo		
NNO Oola		
NNO Princess Leia		
NNO Princess Leia (chaser)		
NNO Stormtrooper		
NNO Stormtrooper Battle Damaged (variant)		
NNO Teebo		
NNO Wicket 9"		
(LE 1000)		

2017 Vinylmation Star Wars The Last Jedi

NNO BB-9E	
NNO DJ	
NNO Finn	
NNO General Hux	
NNO General Leia Organa	
NNO Kylo Ren	
NNO Luke Skywalker	
NNO Luke Skywalker Island (variant)	
NNO Poe Dameron	
NNO Rey	
NNO Rey Island (variant)	
NNO Rose	
NNO Snoke (chaser)	
NNO Stormtrooper Executioner	

2017 Vinylmation Eachez Star Wars The Last Jedi

NNO Praetorian Guard Single Blade	30.00	75.00
NNO Praetorian Guard Double Blade (chaser)	50.00	100.00
NNO Praetorian Guard Whip	12.00	25.00

Trading Cards
PRICE GUIDE

STAR WARS FILMS

A NEW HOPE

1977 Star Wars

COMPLETE SET W/STICKERS (330)	500.00	1000.00
COMP.SER.1 SET W/STICKERS (66)	300.00	600.00
COMP.SER.2 SET W/STICKERS (66)	150.00	300.00
COMP.SER.3 SET W/STICKERS (66)	125.00	250.00
COMP.SER.4 SET W/STICKERS (66)	125.00	250.00
COMP.SER.5 SET W/STICKERS (66)	100.00	200.00
UNOPENED SER.1 BOX (36 PACKS)	8000.00	15000.00
UNOPENED SER.1 PACK (7 CARDS+1 STICKER)	150.00	300.00
UNOPENED SER.2 BOX (36 PACKS)	2000.00	3500.00
UNOPENED SER.2 PACK (7 CARDS+1 STICKER)	75.00	125.00
UNOPENED SER.3 BOX (36 PACKS)	1750.00	3000.00
UNOPENED SER.3 PACK (7 CARDS+1 STICKER)	60.00	100.00
UNOPENED SER.4 BOX (36 PACKS)	1750.00	3000.00
UNOPENED SER.4 PACK (7 CARDS+1 STICKER)	50.00	100.00
UNOPENED SER.5 BOX (36 PACKS)	1500.00	3000.00
UNOPENED SER.5 PACK (7 CARDS+1 STICKER)	50.00	100.00
COMMON BLUE (1-66)	1.25	3.00
COMMON RED (67-132)	.75	2.00
COMMON YELLOW (133-198)	.75	2.00
COMMON GREEN (199-264)	.75	2.00
COMMON ORANGE (265-330)	1.25	3.00
1 Luke Skywalker	25.00	60.00
2 C-3PO and R2-D2	4.00	10.00
3 The Little Droid R2-D2	6.00	15.00
4 Space pirate Han Solo	10.00	25.00

5 Princess Leia Organa	12.00	30.00
6 Ben Kenobi	4.00	10.00
7 The villainous Darth Vader	12.00	30.00
8 Grand Moff Tarkin	2.50	6.00
10 Princess Leia captured!	1.00	5.00
207A C-3PO A.Daniels ERR Obscene	75.00	150.00
207B C-3PO A.Daniels COR Airbrushed	15.00	40.00

1977 Star Wars Stickers

COMPLETE SET (55)	100.00	200.00
COMPLETE SERIES 1 (11)	50.00	100.00
COMPLETE SERIES 2 (11)	15.00	40.00
COMPLETE SERIES 3 (11)	15.00	40.00
COMPLETE SERIES 4 (11)	12.00	30.00
COMPLETE SERIES 5 (11)	12.00	30.00
COMMON STICKER (1-11)	3.00	8.00
COMMON STICKER (12-22)	2.00	5.00
COMMON STICKER (23-33)	1.50	4.00
COMMON STICKER (34-44)	1.25	3.00
COMMON STICKER (45-55)	1.25	3.00
1 Luke Skywalker	12.00	30.00
2 Princess Leia Organa	6.00	15.00
3 Han Solo	6.00	15.00
4 Chewbacca the Wookiee	5.00	12.00
5 See-Threepio	4.00	10.00
6 Artoo-Detoo	8.00	20.00
7 Lord Darth Vader	20.00	50.00
8 Grand Moff Tarkin	4.00	10.00
9 Ben (Obi-Wan) Kenobi	4.00	10.00
12 Han and Chewbacca	5.00	12.00

13 Alec Guinness as Ben	3.00	8.00
14 The Tusken Raider	2.50	6.00
15 See-Threepio	3.00	8.00
16 Chewbacca	3.00	8.00
18 The Rebel Fleet	2.50	6.00
19 The Wookiee Chewbacca	4.00	10.00
20 R2-D2 and C-3PO	2.50	6.00
23 Dave Prowse as Darth Vader	5.00	12.00
28 Peter Cushing as Grand Moff Tarkin	2.50	6.00
29 Han Solo Hero Or Mercenary?	4.00	10.00
30 Stormtroopers	3.00	8.00
31 Princess Leia Comforts Luke	3.00	8.00
32 Preparing for the Raid	2.00	5.00
34 The Star Warriors Aim for Action!	1.50	4.00
35 Han Solo (Harrison Ford)	5.00	12.00
36 Star Pilot Luke Skywalker	2.50	6.00
37 The Marvelous Droid See-Threepio!	2.00	5.00
38 R2-D2 (Kenny Baker)	2.50	6.00
40 Darth Vader (David Prowse)	12.00	30.00
42 Luke Poses with His Weapon	4.00	10.00
45 A Crucial Moment for Luke Skywalker	2.50	6.00
46 Chewie Aims for Danger!	1.50	4.00
48 Inside the Sandcrawler	1.50	4.00
50 George Lucas and Greedo	1.50	4.00
51 Technicians Ready C-3PO for the Cameras	1.50	4.00

1977 Star Wars Mexican

COMPLETE SET (66)	300.00	600.00
UNOPENED PACK (2 CARDS)	35.00	40.00
COMMON CARD (1-66)	5.00	12.00

1977 Star Wars OPC

COMPLETE SET (264)	200.00	400.00
COMPLETE SERIES 1 SET (66)	100.00	200.00
COMPLETE SERIES 2 SET (66)	60.00	120.00
COMPLETE SERIES 3 SET (132)	50.00	100.00
UNOPENED SERIES 1 BOX (36 PACKS)		
UNOPENED SERIES 1 PACK (7 CARDS+1 STICKER)		
UNOPENED SERIES 2 BOX (36 PACKS)		
UNOPENED SERIES 2 PACK (7 CARDS+1 STICKER)		
UNOPENED SERIES 3 BOX (36 PACKS)		
UNOPENED SERIES 3 PACK (7 CARDS+1 STICKER)		

COMMON BLUE (1-66)	2.50	5.00
COMMON RED (67-132)	1.25	3.00
COMMON ORANGE (133-264)	.50	1.25

1978 Star Wars General Mills

COMPLETE SET (18)	12.00	30.00
COMMON CARD (1-18)	1.00	2.50

1977 Star Wars Tip Top Ice Cream

COMPLETE SET (15)	150.00	300.00
COMMON CARD	15.00	40.00

UNNUMBERED SET LISTED ALPHABETICALLY

ALSO KNOWN AS R2-D2 SPACE ICE

1977 Star Wars Wonder Bread

COMPLETE SET (16)	100.00	200.00
COMMON CARD (1-16)	5.00	12.00
1 Luke Skywalker	10.00	25.00
3 Princess Leia Organa	8.00	20.00
4 Han Solo	10.00	25.00
5 Darth Vader	20.00	50.00
9 Chewbacca	6.00	15.00

10 Jawas	6.00	15.00
11 Tusken Raiders	6.00	15.00
13 Millenium Falcon	8.00	20.00
15 X-Wing	6.00	15.00
16 Tie-Vader's Ship	6.00	15.00

1995 Star Wars Widevision

COMPLETE SET (120)	15.00	40.00
UNOPENED BOX (36 PACKS)	60.00	100.00
UNOPENED PACK (10 CARDS)	2.50	3.00
COMMON CARD (1-120)	.20	.50

1995 Star Wars Widevision Finest

COMPLETE SET (10)	40.00	100.00
COMMON CARD (1-10)	5.00	12.00
STATED ODDS 1:11		

2007 Star Wars 30th Anniversary

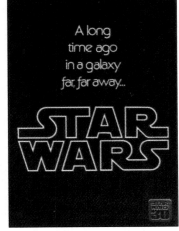

COMPLETE SET (120)	5.00	12.00
UNOPENED HOBBY BOX (24 PACKS)	500.00	800.00
UNOPENED HOBBY PACK (7 CARDS)	20.00	35.00
UNOPENED RETAIL BOX (24 PACKS)		
UNOPENED RETAIL PACK (7 CARDS)		
COMMON CARD (1-120)	.15	.40

*BLUE: 4X TO 10X BASIC CARDS

*RED: 8X TO 20X BASIC CARDS

*GOLD/30: 80X TO 150X BASIC CARDS

2007 Star Wars 30th Anniversary Animation Cels

COMPLETE SET (9)	6.00	15.00
COMMON CARD (1-9)	1.50	4.00
STATED ODDS 1:6 RETAIL		

2007 Star Wars 30th Anniversary Autographs

COMMON AUTO (UNNUMBERED)	10.00	20.00
STATED ODDS 1:43 HOBBY		
NNO Anthony Daniels	400.00	600.00
NNO Carrie Fisher	400.00	800.00
NNO Christine Hewett	25.00	60.00
NNO Colin Higgins	40.00	100.00
NNO David Prowse	200.00	400.00
NNO Gary Kurtz	30.00	75.00
NNO George Roubichek	12.00	30.00
NNO Harrison Ford	3000.00	5000.00
NNO Joe Viskocil	15.00	40.00
NNO John Dykstra	20.00	50.00
NNO John Williams	1000.00	2000.00
NNO Jon Berg	12.00	30.00
NNO Ken Ralston	15.00	40.00
NNO Kenny Baker	150.00	400.00
NNO Lorne Peterson	12.00	30.00
NNO Maria De Aragon	15.00	40.00
NNO Norman Reynolds	25.00	60.00
NNO Peter Mayhew	150.00	300.00
NNO Phil Tippet	30.00	75.00
NNO Richard Edlund	15.00	40.00
NNO Richard LeParmentier	8.00	20.00
NNO Rusty Goffe	20.00	50.00

2007 Star Wars 30th Anniversary Blister Bonus

COMPLETE SET (3)	3.00	8.00
COMMON CARD (1-3)	1.25	3.00
STATED ODDS 1:BLISTER PACK		

2007 Star Wars 30th Anniversary Magnets

The Tusken Raider

COMPLETE SET (9)	12.00	30.00
COMMON CARD (UNNUMBERED)	1.50	4.00
STATED ODDS 1:8 RETAIL		

2007 Star Wars 30th Anniversary Original Series Box-Toppers

Harrison Ford as Han Solo™

SERIES 1 (1-66) BLUE	12.00	30.00
SERIES 2 (67-132) RED	12.00	30.00
SERIES 3 (133-198) YELLOW	12.00	30.00
SERIES 4 (199-264) GREEN	12.00	30.00
SERIES 5 (265-330) ORANGE SP	30.00	80.00
STATED ODDS 1:BOX		

2007 Star Wars 30th Anniversary Triptych Puzzle

COMPLETE SET (27)	12.00	25.00
COMMON CARD (1-27)	.75	2.00
STATED ODDS 1:3		

2017 Star Wars 40th Anniversary

THE PHANTOM MENACE IS RELEASED
40 YEARS OF STAR WARS - 1999

COMPLETE SET (200)	10.00	25.00
UNOPENED BOX (24 PACKS)	120.00	150.00
UNOPENED PACK (8 CARDS)	5.00	6.50
COMMON CARD (1-200)	.20	.50
*GREEN: .5X TO 1.2X BASIC CARDS	.40	1.00
*BLUE: .6X TO 1.5X BASIC CARDS	.50	1.25
*PURPLE/100: 3X TO 8X BASIC CARDS	2.50	6.00
*GOLD/40: 6X TO 15X BASIC CARDS	5.00	12.00
*RED/1: UNPRICED DUE TO SCARCITY		

2017 Star Wars 40th Anniversary Autographed Medallions

COMMEMORATIVE MEDALLION

STATED PRINT RUN 10 SER.#'d SETS	
UNPRICED DUE TO SCARCITY	
AD Anthony Daniels	
CF Carrie Fisher	
HF Harrison Ford	
KB Kenny Baker	
MH Mark Hamill	

2017 Star Wars 40th Anniversary Autographs

COMMON AUTO	6.00	15.00
*PURPLE/40: .6X TO 1.5X BASIC AUTOS		
*GOLD/10: 1X TO 2.5X BASIC AUTOS		

*RED/1: UNPRICED DUE TO SCARCITY		
RANDOMLY INSERTED INTO PACKS		
AAAH Alan Harris	6.00	15.00
AAAL Al Lampert	10.00	20.00
AABF Barbara Frankland	10.00	25.00
AABL Bai Ling	8.00	20.00
AACR Clive Revill	10.00	25.00
AADL Denis Lawson	10.00	25.00
AADR Deep Roy	10.00	25.00
AAFF Femi Taylor	8.00	20.00
AAGB Glyn Baker	8.00	20.00
AAGH Garrick Hagon	8.00	20.00
AAGR George Roubicek	10.00	25.00
AAHQ Hugh Quarshie	10.00	25.00
AAIL Ian Liston	10.00	25.00
AAJB Jeremy Bulloch	15.00	40.00
AAJK Jack Klaff	10.00	25.00
AAKC Kenneth Colley	8.00	20.00
AAKR Kipsang Rotich	10.00	25.00
AAMC Michael Carter	12.00	30.00
AAMW Matthew Wood	10.00	25.00
AAPS Paul Springer	8.00	20.00
AARO Richard Oldfield	10.00	25.00
AASC Stephen Costantino	8.00	20.00
AATR Tim Rose	8.00	20.00
AACDW Corey Dee Williams	8.00	20.00
AAPBL Paul Blake	10.00	25.00
AAPBR Paul Brooke	8.00	20.00

2017 Star Wars 40th Anniversary Celebration Orlando Promos

40

Luke Skywalker

COMPLETE SET (4)	225.00	450.00
COMMON CARD (C1-C4)	50.00	100.00
C1 Luke Skywalker	80.00	150.00
C2 Princess Leia	80.00	150.00
C3 Han Solo	60.00	120.00

2017 Star Wars 40th Anniversary Classic Stickers

COMMON CARD	12.00	30.00
STATED PRINT RUN 100 SER.#'d SETS		

2017 Star Wars 40th Anniversary Dual Autographs

STATED PRINT RUN 3 SER.#'d SETS

UNPRICED DUE TO SCARCITY

NNO A.Daniels/K.Baker

NNO A.Daniels/P.Mayhew

NNO C.Fisher/W.Davis

NNO D.Barclay/M.Carter

NNO M.Hamill/K.Baker

2017 Star Wars 40th Anniversary Medallions

COMMON MEDALLION	6.00	15.00
MILLENNIUM FALCON (1-12)		
DEATH STAR (13-23)		
*BLUE/40: .5X TO 1.2X BASIC MEDALLIONS	8.00	20.00
*PURPLE/25: .6X TO 1.5X BASIC MEDALLIONS	10.00	25.00
*GOLD/10: 1.2X TO 3X BASIC MEDALLIONS	20.00	50.00
*RED/1: UNPRICED DUE TO SCARCITY		

2017 Star Wars 40th Anniversary Patches

COMMON CARD (1-20)	5.00	12.00
*BLUE/40: 6X TO 1.5X BASIC CARDS	8.00	20.00
*PURPLE/25: 1X TO 2.5X BASIC CARDS	12.00	30.00
*GOLD/10: 1.5X TO 4X BASIC CARDS	20.00	50.00
RANDOMLY INSERTED INTO PACKS		
TARGET EXCLUSIVE		

2017 Star Wars 40th Anniversary Quad Autographed Booklet

STATED PRINT RUN 2 SER.#'d SETS

UNPRICED DUE TO SCARCITY

NNO Hamill/Fisher/Daniels/Baker

2017 Star Wars 40th Anniversary Six-Person Autographed Booklet

STATED PRINT RUN 2 SER.#'d SETS

UNPRICED DUE TO SCARCITY

NNO Ford/Hamill/Fisher

Daniels/Baker/Mayhew

2017 Star Wars 40th Anniversary Triple Autographs

STATED PRINT RUN 3 SER.#'d SETS

UNPRICED DUE TO SCARCITY

TABDM Baker/Daniels/Mayhew

TAHBB Hamill/Barclay/Bauersfeld

TAHHK Hamill/Hagon/Klaff

TAPMW Park/McDiarmid/Wood

2017 Star Wars 1978 Sugar Free Wrappers Set

COMPLETE SET (49)	10.00	25.00
COMPLETE FACTORY SET (51)		
COMMON CARD (1-49)	.30	.75
*BLUE/75: 2X TO 5X BASIC CARDS	1.50	4.00
*GREEN/40: 4X TO 10X BASIC CARDS	3.00	8.00
*GOLD/10: 6X TO 15X BASIC CARDS	5.00	12.00

2017 Star Wars 1978 Sugar Free Wrappers Set Autographs

Carrie Fisher as Princess Leia Organa

STATED ODDS 2:SET		
NNO Alan Harris	10.00	25.00
NNO Angus MacInnes	10.00	25.00
NNO Anthony Daniels		
NNO Anthony Forrest		
NNO Barbara Frankland	15.00	40.00
NNO Billy Dee Williams	100.00	200.00
NNO Caroline Blakiston	20.00	50.00
NNO Carrie Fisher		
NNO Clive Revill	15.00	40.00

NNO Corey Dee Williams	10.00	25.00
NNO David Ankrum	25.00	60.00
NNO Deep Roy	12.00	30.00
NNO Denis Lawson	15.00	40.00
NNO Dermot Crowley	12.00	30.00
NNO Dickey Beer	12.00	30.00
Barada		
NNO Dickey Beer	15.00	40.00
Boba Fett		
NNO Dickey Beer	10.00	25.00
Scout Trooper		
NNO Erik Bauersfeld		
NNO Femi Taylor	10.00	25.00
NNO Garrick Hagon	10.00	25.00
NNO Harrison Ford		
NNO Ian McDiarmid		
NNO Jeremy Bulloch	20.00	50.00
NNO John Morton	10.00	25.00
NNO John Ratzenberger	10.00	25.00
NNO Julian Glover	12.00	30.00
NNO Kenneth Colley	8.00	20.00
NNO Kenny Baker		
NNO Mark Capri	8.00	20.00
NNO Mark Dodson	12.00	30.00
NNO Mark Hamill		
NNO Michael Carter	10.00	25.00
NNO Mike Quinn	12.00	30.00
Nien Nunb		
NNO Mike Quinn	15.00	40.00
Sy Snootles		
NNO Pam Rose	6.00	20.00
NNO Paul Blake	10.00	25.00
NNO Peter Mayhew		
NNO Rusty Goffe	8.00	20.00
NNO Sean Crawford	8.00	20.00
NNO Tim Dry	8.00	20.00
NNO Tim Rose	12.00	30.00
NNO Toby Philpott	10.00	25.00
NNO Warwick Davis	15.00	40.00

2013 Star Wars Illustrated A New Hope

COMPLETE SET (100)	8.00	20.00
COMMON CARD (1-100)	.20	.50
*PURPLE: 2.5X TO 6X BASIC CARDS		
*BRONZE: 5X TO 12X BASIC CARDS		
*GOLD/10: 50X TO 120X BASIC CARDS		

2013 Star Wars Illustrated A New Hope Film Cels

COMPLETE SET (20)	250.00	500.00
COMMON CARD (FR1-FR20)	12.00	30.00
FR8 Greedo's Bounty	15.00	40.00
FR14 The Final Encounter	60.00	120.00

2013 Star Wars Illustrated A New Hope Movie Poster Reinterpretations

COMPLETE SET (9)	5.00	12.00
COMMON CARD (MP1-MP9)	1.25	3.00
STATED ODDS 1:3		

2013 Star Wars Illustrated A New Hope One Year Earlier

COMPLETE SET (18)	5.00	12.00
COMMON CARD (OY1-OY18)	.60	1.50
STATED ODDS 1:2		

2013 Star Wars Illustrated A New Hope Radio Drama Puzzle

COMPLETE SET (6)	5.00	12.00
COMMON CARD (1-6)	1.50	4.00
STATED ODDS 1:8		

2013 Star Wars Illustrated A New Hope The Mission Destroy the Death Star

COMPLETE SET (12)	30.00	60.00
COMMON CARD (1-12)	3.00	8.00
STATED ODDS 1:12		

2013 Star Wars Illustrated A New Hope Promos

COMPLETE SET (4)	5.00	12.00

2018 Star Wars A New Hope Black and White

COMPLETE SET (140)	15.00	40.00
UNOPENED BOX (7 PACKS)		
UNOPENED PACK (8 CARDS)		
COMMON CARD (1-140)	.25	.60
*SEPIA: .75X TO 2X BASIC CARDS	.50	1.25
*BLUE: 1X TO 2.5X BASIC CARDS	.60	1.50
*GREEN/99: 3X TO 8X BASIC CARDS	2.00	5.00
*PURPLE/25: 8X TO 20X BASIC CARDS	5.00	12.00

2018 Star Wars A New Hope Black and White Autographs

COMMON AUTO	6.00	15.00
*BLUE/99: .5X TO 1.2X BASIC AUTOS		
*GREEN/25: .6X TO 1.5X BASIC AUTOS		
STATED ODDS 1:18		
NNO Al Lampert	8.00	20.00
NNO Annette Jones	8.00	20.00
NNO Barbara Frankland	8.00	20.00
NNO Denis Lawson	12.00	30.00
NNO Garrick Hagon	8.00	20.00
NNO Paul Blake	10.00	25.00

2018 Star Wars A New Hope Black and White Autographs Blue

*BLUE: .5X TO 1.2X BASIC AUTOS		
STATED ODDS 1:62		
STATED PRINT RUN 99 SER.#'d SETS		
NNO Peter Mayhew	30.00	75.00

2018 Star Wars A New Hope Black and White Autographs Green

*GREEN: .6X TO 1.5X BASIC AUTOS		
STATED ODDS 1:202		
STATED PRINT RUN 25 SER.#'d SETS		
NNO Anthony Daniels	75.00	150.00
NNO Kenny Baker	60.00	120.00

2018 Star Wars A New Hope Black and White Behind-the-Scenes

COMPLETE SET (41)	20.00	50.00
COMMON CARD (BTS1-BTS41)	2.00	5.00
STATED ODDS 1:2		

2018 Star Wars A New Hope Black and White Concept Art

COMPLETE SET (12)	10.00	25.00
COMMON CARD (CA1-CA12)	1.50	4.00
STATED ODDS 1:4		

2018 Star Wars A New Hope Black and White Dual Autographs

UNPRICED DUE TO SCARCITY

STATED ODDS 1:1,677

NNO A.Lampert/G.Roubicek

NNO A.MacInnes/G.Hagon

NNO D.Lawson/D.Ankrum

NNO H.Ford/P.Mayhew

NNO J.Klaff/A.MacInnes

NNO K.Baker/A.Daniels

2018 Star Wars A New Hope Black and White Iconic Characters

COMPLETE SET (12)	15.00	40.00
COMMON CARD (IC1-IC12)	2.00	5.00
STATED ODDS 1:12		
IC1 Luke Skywalker	4.00	10.00
IC2 Han Solo	5.00	12.00
IC3 Princess Leia Organa	4.00	10.00
IC4 Chewbacca	2.50	6.00
IC5 Ben (Obi-Wan) Kenobi	4.00	10.00
IC7 R2-D2	2.50	6.00
IC8 Darth Vader	5.00	12.00

2018 Star Wars A New Hope Black and White Posters

COMPLETE SET (12)	12.00	30.00
COMMON CARD (PO1-PO12)	1.50	4.00
STATED ODDS 1:6		

2018 Star Wars A New Hope Black and White Six-Person Autograph

STATED ODDS 1:88,844

STATED PRINT RUN 1 SER.#'d SET

UNPRICED DUE TO SCARCITY

NNO Ford/Hamill/Fisher/Mayhew/Baker/Daniels

2018 Star Wars A New Hope Black and White Triple Autographs

STATED ODDS 1:2,693

UNPRICED DUE TO SCARCITY

NNO Lampert/Forest/Roubicek

NNO Hagon/Klaff/MacInnes

NNO Baker/Goffe/Daniels

NNO Mayhew/Baker/Daniels

EMPIRE STRIKES BACK

1980 Star Wars Empire Strikes Back

"WELCOME, YOUNG LUKE!"

COMPLETE SET W/STICKERS (440)	125.00	250.00
COMPLETE SET (352)	100.00	200.00
COMPLETE SERIES 1 SET W/STICKERS (165)	75.00	150.00
COMPLETE SERIES 1 SET (132)	50.00	100.00
COMPLETE SERIES 2 SET W/STICKERS (165)	50.00	100.00
COMPLETE SERIES 2 SET (132)	30.00	75.00
COMPLETE SERIES 3 SET W/STICKERS (110)	30.00	75.00
COMPLETE SERIES 3 SET (88)	25.00	60.00
UNOPENED SERIES 1 BOX (36 PACKS)	1000.00	2000.00
UNOPENED SERIES 1 PACK (12 CARDS+1 STICKER)	30.00	60.00
UNOPENED SERIES 1 COL.BOX (80 CARDS+COL.BOX)	100.00	200.00
UNOPENED SERIES 1 RACK BOX (24 PACKS)		
UNOPENED SERIES 1 RACK PACK (51 CARDS)	75.00	150.00
UNOPENED SERIES 2 BOX (36 PACKS)	600.00	800.00
UNOPENED SERIES 2 PACK (12 CARDS+1 STICKER)	15.00	25.00
UNOPENED SERIES 3 BOX (36 PACKS)	500.00	1000.00
UNOPENED SERIES 3 PACK (12 CARDS+1 STICKER)	15.00	30.00
COMMON SERIES 1 CARD (1-132)	.60	1.50
COMMON SERIES 2 CARD (133-264)	.50	1.25
COMMON SERIES 3 CARD (265-352)	.60	1.50
210 The Captor, Boba Fett	2.00	5.00
220 Bounty Hunter Boba Fett	2.50	6.00
272 Boba Fett	8.00	20.00

1980 Star Wars Empire Strikes Back Stickers

COMPLETE SET (88)	60.00	150.00
COMPLETE SERIES 1 SET (33)	50.00	100.00
COMPLETE SERIES 2 SET (33)	15.00	40.00
COMPLETE SERIES 3 SET (22)	12.00	30.00
COMMON CARD (1-33)	2.50	6.00
COMMON CARD (34-66)	1.00	2.50
COMMON CARD (67-88)	1.50	4.00
27 Stormtrooper, Luke, Yoda	3.00	8.00
56 Darth Vader	3.00	8.00
57 Boba Fett	6.00	15.00
58 Probot	2.50	6.00
59 Luke Skywalker	2.50	6.00
60 Princess Leia	3.00	8.00
61 Han Solo	2.50	6.00
62 Lando Calrissian	3.00	8.00
63 Chewbacca	3.00	8.00
64 R2-D2	2.50	6.00
65 C-3PO	4.00	10.00
66 Yoda	2.00	5.00

1980 Star Wars Empire Strikes Back 5X7 Photos

COMPLETE SET (30)	25.00	50.00
UNOPENED BOX (36 PACKS)		
UNOPENED PACK (1 CARD)		
COMMON CARD (1-30)	1.50	4.00

1980 Star Wars Empire Strikes Back 5X7 Photos Test Issue

COMPLETE SET (30)	100.00	200.00
COMMON CARD (1-30)	3.00	8.00

1980 Star Wars Empire Strikes Back Hershey's

COMPLETE SET (5)	12.00	30.00
COMMON CARD	4.00	10.00
UNNUMBERED SET		
1 Boba Fett	5.00	12.00

1980 Star Wars Empire Strikes Back Twinkies New Zealand

COMPLETE SET (6)	15.00	40.00
COMMON CARD (UNNUMBERED)	4.00	10.00

1980 Star Wars Empire Strikes Back York Peanut Butter Discs

COMPLETE SET (6)	12.00	30.00
COMMON CARD (1-6)	3.00	8.00

1995 Star Wars Empire Strikes Back Widevision

COMPLETE SET (144)	12.00	30.00
UNOPENED BOX (36 PACKS)	50.00	75.00
UNOPENED PACK (9 CARDS)	2.00	3.00
COMMON CARD (1-144)	.25	.60

1995 Star Wars Empire Strikes Back Widevision Finest

COMPLETE SET (10)	40.00	100.00
COMMON CARD (C1-C10)	4.00	10.00
STATED ODDS 1:12		

1995 Star Wars Empire Strikes Back Widevision Mini Posters

COMPLETE SET (6)	40.00	80.00
COMMON CARD (1-6)	6.00	15.00
STATED ODDS 1:BOX		

1995 Star Wars Empire Strikes Back Widevision Promos

COMMON CARD	2.00	5.00
NNO 3-Card Sheet	5.00	12.00
P1-P3		

2010 Star Wars Empire Strikes Back 3-D Widevision

COMPLETE SET (48)	10.00	25.00
UNOPENED BOX (24 PACKS)		
UNOPENED PACK (3 CARDS)		
COMMON CARD (1-48)	.40	1.00
P1 Luke Skywalker PROMO	8.00	20.00

2010 Star Wars Empire Strikes Back 3-D Widevision Autographs

COMMON AUTO	125.00	250.00
STATED ODDS 1:1,055		
1 Irvin Kershner	500.00	1000.00
2 Ralph McQuarrie	2000.00	4000.00
4 David Prowse	250.00	400.00
6 Carrie Fisher	500.00	800.00
8 Mark Hamill	400.00	600.00

1996 Star Wars Empire Strikes Back 3-Di

P1 AT-ATs	2.00	5.00

2019 Star Wars Empire Strikes Back Black and White

COMPLETE SET (150)	20.00	50.00
UNOPENED BOX (7 PACKS)	200.00	300.00
UNOPENED PACK (8 CARDS)	30.00	40.00
COMMON CARD (1-150)	.30	.75
*SEPIA: 1X TO 2.5X BASIC CARDS		
*BLUE HUE: 2.5X TO 6X BASIC CARDS		
*GREEN HUE/99: 4X TO 10X BASIC CARDS		
*PURPLE HUE/25: 6X TO 15X BASIC CARDS		

2019 Star Wars Empire Strikes Back Black and White Autographs

COMMON AUTO		
*BLUE HUE/99: .5X TO 1.2X BASIC AUTOS		
*GREEN HUE/25: .6X TO 1.5X BASIC AUTOS		
STATED ODDS 1:22		
AAH Alan Harris	10.00	25.00
ACM Cathy Munro	8.00	20.00
ACP Chris Parsons	8.00	20.00
ACR Clive Revill	6.00	15.00
AHW Howie Weed	8.00	20.00
AJB Jeremy Bulloch	20.00	50.00
AJM John Morton/Dak'	8.00	20.00
AJR John Ratzenberger	15.00	40.00
AKC Kenneth Colley	8.00	20.00
AMC Mark Capri	6.00	15.00
AMJ Milton Johns	10.00	25.00
ARO Richard Oldfield	8.00	20.00
AJMB John Morton/Boba Fett's Double	10.00	25.00

2019 Star Wars Empire Strikes Back Black and White Behind-the-Scenes

COMPLETE SET (40)	25.00	60.00
COMMON CARD (BTS1-BTS40)	1.25	3.00
STATED ODDS 1:2		

2019 Star Wars Empire Strikes Back Black and White Color Short-Printed Autographs

STATED ODDS 1:3,947	
ACAD Anthony Daniels	
ACCF Carrie Fisher	
ACHF Harrison Ford	
ACKB Kenny Baker	
ACPM Peter Mayhew	

2019 Star Wars Empire Strikes Back Black and White Concept Art

COMPLETE SET (10)	12.00	30.00
COMMON CARD (CA1-CA10)	2.00	5.00
STATED ODDS 1:4		

2019 Star Wars Empire Strikes Back Black and White Dual Autographs

STATED ODDS 1:525	
UNPRICED DUE TO SCARCITY	
DABD K.Baker/A.Daniels	
DABH J.Bulloch/A.Harris	
DAWM B.Williams/P.Mayhew	
DAFF H.Ford/C.Fisher	

DAHM A.Harris/C.Munroe

DALM D.Lawson/J.Morton

DALO D.Lawson/R.Oldfield

DAPM C.Parsons/C.Munroe

2019 Star Wars Empire Strikes Back Black and White Iconic Characters

COMMON CARD (IC1-IC20)	5.00	12.00
STATED ODDS 1:12		

2019 Star Wars Empire Strikes Back Black and White Posters

COMPLETE SET (10)	12.00	30.00
COMMON CARD (PO1-PO10)	2.00	5.00
STATED ODDS 1:6		

2019 Star Wars Empire Strikes Back Black and White Six-Person Autograph

STATED ODDS 1:74,984

STATED PRINT RUN 1 SER.#'d SET

UNPRICED DUE TO SCARCITY

NNO H.Ford/C.Fisher/B.Williams

A.Daniels/K.Baker/P.Mayhew

2019 Star Wars Empire Strikes Back Black and White Triple Autographs

STATED ODDS 1:728

UNPRICED DUE TO SCARCITY

TABMP Bulloch/Munroe/Parsons

TAFFW Ford/Fisher/Williams

TALMO Lawson/Morton/Oldfield

TAMBD Mayhew/Baker/Daniels

TAMPH Munroe/Parsons/Harris

2015 Star Wars Illustrated Empire Strikes Back

COMPLETE SET (100)	10.00	25.00
UNOPENED BOX (24 PACKS)	200.00	300.00
UNOPENED PACK (6 CARDS)	8.00	12.00
COMMON CARD (1-100)	.20	.50
*PURPLE: 5X TO 12X BASIC CARDS	2.50	6.00
*BRONZE: 8X TO 20X BASIC CARDS	4.00	10.00
*GOLD/10: 20X TO 50X BASIC CARDS	10.00	25.00

2015 Star Wars Illustrated Empire Strikes Back Celebration VII Promos

COMPLETE SET (10)	10.00	25.00
COMMON CARD (1-10)	1.50	4.00

2015 Star Wars Illustrated Empire Strikes Back Artist Autographs

COMMON BUSCH (EVEN #'s)	5.00	12.00
COMMON MARTINEZ (ODD #'s)	5.00	12.00

2015 Star Wars Illustrated Empire Strikes Back Film Cel Relics

COMPLETE SET (25)	100.00	200.00
COMMON CARD (SKIP #'d)	6.00	15.00
FR2 Back at Echo Base	8.00	20.00
FR3 Monster in the Snow	8.00	20.00
FR6 The Imperial Walkers	10.00	25.00
FR7 Luke Vs. the AT-AT	8.00	20.00
FR8 Imperial Pursuit	10.00	25.00
FR9 Asteroid Field	8.00	20.00
FR10 Dagobah Landing	8.00	20.00
FR13 Message From the Emperor	12.00	30.00
FR15 Bounty Hunters Assemble	8.00	20.00

FR16 Failure at the Cave	10.00	25.00
FR20 A Most Gracious Host	10.00	25.00
FR25 You Are not a Jedi Yet	10.00	25.00
FR26 Lando's Redemption	8.00	20.00
FR27 Battle in the Gantry	10.00	25.00
FR28 The Truth Revealed	8.00	20.00
FR29 Rescuing Luke	15.00	40.00
FR30 Saying Farewell	8.00	20.00

2015 Star Wars Illustrated Empire Strikes Back Movie Poster Reinterpretations

COMPLETE SET (10)	8.00	20.00
COMMON CARD (MP1-MP10)	1.50	4.00
STATED ODDS 1:3		

2015 Star Wars Illustrated Empire Strikes Back One Year Earlier

COMPLETE SET (18)	15.00	40.00
COMMON CARD (OY1-OY18)	1.50	4.00
STATED ODDS 1:2		

2015 Star Wars Illustrated Empire Strikes Back The Force Awakens Inserts

COMPLETE SET (4)	20.00	50.00
COMMON CARD (SKIP #'d)	8.00	20.00

2015 Star Wars Illustrated Empire Strikes Back The Mission Capture Skywalker

COMPLETE SET (10)	12.00	30.00
COMMON CARD (1-10)	2.50	6.00
STATED ODDS 1:8		
3 Han Solo	3.00	8.00
9 Boba Fett	4.00	10.00

RETURN OF THE JEDI

1983 Star Wars Return of the Jedi

COMPLETE SET W/STICKERS (308)		
COMPLETE SET W/STICKERS (275)	75.00	150.00
COMPLETE SET (220)	60.00	120.00
COMPLETE SERIES 1 SET W/STICKERS (165)		
COMPLETE SERIES 1 SET (132)	30.00	75.00
COMPLETE SERIES 2 SET W/STICKERS (110)		
COMPLETE SERIES 2 SET (88)	20.00	50.00
UNOPENED SERIES 1 BOX (36 PACKS)	200.00	400.00
UNOPENED SERIES 1 PACK (12 CARDS+1 STICKER)	8.00	12.00
UNOPENED SERIES 2 BOX (36 PACKS)	150.00	300.00
UNOPENED SERIES 2 PACK (12 CARDS+1 STICKER)	6.00	10.00
COMMON SERIES 1 CARD (1-132)	.50	1.25
COMMON SERIES 2 CARD (133-264)	.50	1.25

1983 Star Wars Return of the Jedi Stickers

COMPLETE SET W/VARIANTS (88)	50.00	100.00
COMPLETE SET W/O VARIANTS (55)	30.00	75.00
COMPLETE S1 SET A&B (66)	25.00	60.00
COMPLETE S1 SET (33)	8.00	20.00
COMPLETE S2 SET (22)	25.00	60.00
COMMON S1 PURPLE (1-11)	.40	1.00
COMMON S1 YELLOW (1-11)	.60	1.50
COMMON S1 RED (12-22)	.75	2.00
COMMON S1 TURQUOISE (12-22)	.40	1.00
COMMON S1 GREEN (23-33)	.60	1.50
COMMON S1 ORANGE (23-33)	.40	1.00
COMMON S2 (34-55)	1.50	4.00
STATED ODDS 1:1		

2014 Star Wars Return of the Jedi 3-D Widevision

COMPLETE SET (44)	12.00	30.00
COMMON CARD (1-44)	.50	1.25
TOPPS WEBSITE EXCLUSIVE SET		

2014 Star Wars Return of the Jedi 3-D Widevision Autographs

COMMON AUTO (UNNUMBERED)	10.00	25.00
STATED ODDS 1:SET		
NNO Carrie Fisher	600.00	1000.00
NNO Femi Taylor	15.00	40.00
NNO Jeremy Bulloch	50.00	100.00
NNO Kenneth Colley	15.00	40.00
NNO Mark Hamill	500.00	800.00
NNO Mike Quinn	20.00	50.00
NNO Peter Mayhew	75.00	150.00
NNO Tim Rose	20.00	50.00

2014 Star Wars Return of the Jedi 3-D Widevision Manufactured Patches

COMPLETE SET (4)	50.00	100.00
COMMON CARD	10.00	25.00
STATED ODDS ONE PATCH/SKETCH PER SET		

2020 Star Wars Return of the Jedi Black and White

COMPLETE SET (133)	12.00	30.00
UNOPENED BOX (7 PACKS)	100.00	150.00
UNOPENED PACK (8 CARDS)	15.00	20.00
COMMON CARD (1-133)	.25	.60

*SEPIA: .5X TO 1.2X BASIC CARDS

*BLUE: .75X TO 2X BASIC CARDS

*GREEN/99: 2X TO 5X BASIC CARDS

*PURPLE/25: 3X TO 8X BASIC CARDS

2020 Star Wars Return of the Jedi Black and White Autographs

COMMON AUTO	5.00	12.00
RANDOMLY INSERTED INTO PACKS		
ACB Caroline Blakiston	6.00	15.00
ADR Deep Roy	8.00	20.00
AFT Femi Taylor	6.00	15.00
AJB Jeremy Bulloch	15.00	40.00
AMC Michael Carter	6.00	15.00
APB Paul Brooke	6.00	15.00
ATR Tim Rose	6.00	15.00
ADBB Dickey Beer	10.00	25.00
AMQS Mike Quinn	6.00	15.00

2020 Star Wars Return of the Jedi Black and White Behind-the-Scenes

COMPLETE SET (24)	12.00	30.00
COMMON CARD (BTS1-BTS24)	1.00	2.50
RANDOMLY INSERTED INTO PACKS		

2020 Star Wars Return of the Jedi Black and White Concept Art

COMPLETE SET (19)	15.00	40.00
COMMON CARD (CA1-CA19)	1.25	3.00
RANDOMLY INSERTED INTO PACKS		

2020 Star Wars Return of the Jedi Black and White Dual Autographs

UNPRICED DUE TO SCARCITY

DABC C.Blakiston/D.Crowley

DACC K.Colley/D.Crowley

DADE W.Davis/M.Edmonds

DADP M.Dodson/T.Philpott

DAFF H.Ford/C.Fisher

DAMP I.McDiarmid/M.Pennington

DARB T.Rose/C.Blakiston

DAWM B.Williams/P.Mayhew

DAWR S.Williamson/D.Roy

2020 Star Wars Return of the Jedi Black and White Iconic Characters

COMPLETE SET (15)	12.00	30.00
COMMON CARD (IC1-IC15)	1.50	4.00
RANDOMLY INSERTED INTO PACKS		

2020 Star Wars Return of the Jedi Black and White Posters

COMPLETE SET (6)	5.00	12.00
COMMON CARD (P1-P6)	1.00	2.50
RANDOMLY INSERTED INTO PACKS		

2020 Star Wars Return of the Jedi Black and White Six-Person Autograph

NNO Ford/Fisher/Williams/Daniels/Baker/Mayhew

2020 Star Wars Return of the Jedi Black and White Triple Autographs

UNPRICED DUE TO SCARCITY

NNO Williams/Rotich/Lawson

NNO Blakiston/Crowley/Rose

NNO Ford/Fishe /Williams

NNO Mayhew/Baker/Daniels

NNO Philpott/Carter/Taylor

1983 Star Wars Return of the Jedi Stick'R Kellogg's

COMPLETE SET (10)	12.00	30.00
COMMON CARD (1-10)	2.00	5.00

1983 Star Wars Return of the Jedi OPC

COMPLETE SET (132)	25.00	60.00
UNOPENED BOX (36 PACKS)	125.00	150.00
UNOPENED PACK	4.00	5.00
COMMON CARD (1-132)	.30	.75

1997 Star Wars Return of the Jedi Special Edition

NNO Crescent City Con XII

1996 Star Wars Return of the Jedi Widevision

COMPLETE SET (144)	10.00	25.00
UNOPENED BOX (24 PACKS)	50.00	100.00
UNOPENED PACK (9 CARDS)	2.50	4.00
COMMON CARD (1-144)	.20	.50

DIII Admiral Akbar

1996 Star Wars Return of the Jedi Widevision Finest

COMPLETE SET (10)	40.00	80.00
COMMON CARD (C1-C10)	4.00	10.00
STATED ODDS 1:12		

1996 Star Wars Return of the Jedi Widevision Mini Posters

COMPLETE SET (6)	40.00	80.00
COMMON CARD (1-6)	6.00	15.00
STATED ODDS 1:BOX		

1996 Star Wars Return of the Jedi Widevision Promos

COMMON CARD	2.00	5.00
P6 Luke, Han, & Chewbacca in Jabba's Palace	25.00	60.00
NNO 1-Card Sheet		
Complete the Trilogy		

THE PHANTOM MENACE

1999 Star Wars Episode One Widevision Series One

COMPLETE SET (80)	8.00	20.00
UNOPENED HOBBY BOX (36 PACKS)	50.00	75.00
UNOPENED HOBBY PACK (8 CARDS)	2.00	3.00
UNOPENED RETAIL BOX (11 PACKS)	30.00	45.00
UNOPENED RETAIL PACK (8 CARDS)	2.75	4.00
COMMON CARD (1-80)	.25	.60

1999 Star Wars Episode One Widevision Series One Chrome

COMPLETE SET (8)	30.00	60.00
COMMON CARD (C1-C8)	4.00	10.00
STATED ODDS 1:12		

1999 Star Wars Episode One Widevision Series One Expansion

COMPLETE SET (40)	30.00	60.00
COMMON CARD (X1-X40)	1.00	2.50
STATED ODDS 1:2		

1999 Star Wars Episode One Widevision Series One Foil

COMPLETE SET (10)	30.00	60.00
COMMON CARD (F1-F10)	3.00	8.00

1999 Star Wars Episode One Widevision Series One Stickers

COMPLETE SET (16)	8.00	20.00
COMMON CARD (S1-S16)	.60	1.50

1999 Star Wars Episode One Widevision Series One Tin Inserts

COMPLETE SET (5)	12.00	30.00
COMMON CARD (1-5)	4.00	10.00
STATED ODDS ONE PER RETAIL TIN		
2 Darth Maul	5.00	12.00

1999 Star Wars Episode One Widevision Series Two

COMPLETE SET (80)	8.00	20.00
UNOPENED HOBBY BOX (36 PACKS)	50.00	75.00
UNOPENED HOBBY PACK (8 CARDS)	2.00	3.00
UNOPENED RETAIL BOX (24 PACKS)	35.00	45.00
UNOPENED RETAIL PACK (8 CARDS)	1.50	1.75
COMMON CARD (1-80)	.25	.60

1999 Star Wars Episode One Widevision Series Two Box-Toppers

COMPLETE SET (3)	10.00	20.00
COMMON CARD (1-3)	4.00	10.00
STATED ODDS 1:HOBBY BOX		

1999 Star Wars Episode One Widevision Series Two Chrome Hobby

COMPLETE SET (4)	12.00	25.00
COMMON CARD (HC1-HC4)	4.00	10.00
STATED ODDS 1:18 HOBBY		

1999 Star Wars Episode One Widevision Series Two Chrome Retail

COMPLETE SET (4)	20.00	40.00
COMMON CARD (C1-C4)	6.00	15.00
STATED ODDS 1:18 RETAIL		

1999 Star Wars Episode One Widevision Series Two Embossed Hobby

COMPLETE SET (6)	8.00	20.00
COMMON CARD (HE1-HE6)	2.50	6.00
STATED ODDS 1:12 HOBBY		

1999 Star Wars Episode One Widevision Series Two Embossed Retail

COMPLETE SET (6)	20.00	40.00
COMMON CARD (E1-E6)	4.00	10.00
STATED ODDS 1:12 RETAIL		

1999 Star Wars Episode One Widevision Series Two Promos

COMPLETE SET (2)	3.00	8.00
COMMON CARD (P1-P2)	2.00	5.00

2000 Star Wars Episode One 3-D

COMPLETE SET (46)	20.00	40.00
UNOPENED BOX (36 PACKS)	45.00	60.00
UNOPENED PACK (2 CARDS)	1.50	2.00
COMMON CARD (1-46)	.50	1.25

2000 Star Wars Episode One 3-D Multi-Motion

COMPLETE SET (2)	10.00	25.00
COMMON CARD (1-2)	6.00	15.00

1999 Star Wars Episode I Bluebird Potato Chips New Zealand

COMPLETE SET (30)	10.00	25.00
COMMON CARD (1-30)	.60	1.50

1999 Star Wars Episode I Family Toy

COMPLETE SET (3)	8.00	20.00
COMMON CARD	4.00	10.00

1999 Star Wars Episode I Flip Images

COMPLETE SET (6)	5.00	12.00
COMMON CARD	1.25	3.00
UNNUMBERED SET		

1999 Star Wars Episode I Hallmark

H1 Anakin Skywalker and Obi-Wan Kenobi	2.00	5.00
H2 Obi-Wan Kenobi and Yoda	2.00	5.00
H3 Qui-Gon Jinn and Obi-Wan Kenobi	2.00	5.00

1999 Star Wars Episode I iKon

COMPLETE SET (60)	6.00	15.00
COMMON CARD (1-60)	.20	.50
*SILVER: 1.5X TO 4X BASIC CARDS		
*GOLD: 2.5X TO 6X BASIC CARDS		

1999 Star Wars Episode I KFC Australia

COMPLETE SET (10)	3.00	8.00
COMMON CARD (1-10)	.50	1.25

1999 Star Wars Episode I KFC UK

COMPLETE SET (20)	8.00	20.00
COMMON CARD (1-20)	.60	1.50
STATED ODDS 1:		

1999 Star Wars Episode I Lay's Minis

COMPLETE SET (12)	6.00	15.00
COMMON CARD (1-12)	.75	2.00

1999 Star Wars Episode I The Phantom Menace Harmony Foods

COMPLETE SET (24)	50.00	100.00
COMMON CARD (1-24)	2.00	5.00

1999 Star Wars Episode I The Phantom Menace Kentucky Fried Chicken Employee Stickers

COMPLETE SET (5)	6.00	15.00
COMMON CARD	2.00	5.00

1999 Star Wars Episode I The Phantom Menace Show Promo

NNO DLP Exclusive Presentation	5.00	12.00

2001 Star Wars Episode I The Phantom Menace Walmart DVD Promos

COMPLETE SET (4)	3.00	8.00
COMMON CARD	1.25	3.00

1999 Star Wars Episode I Star Mart

NNO Anakin Skywalker	2.00	5.00
NNO C-3PO	2.00	5.00
NNO Darth Maul	2.00	5.00
NNO R2-D2	2.00	5.00

2019 Star Wars On-Demand Phantom Menace 20th Anniversary

COMPLETE SET (25)	8.00	20.00
COMMON CARD (1-25)	.60	1.50
*SILVER: 1.2X TO 3X BASIC CARDS		

2019 Star Wars On-Demand Phantom Menace 20th Anniversary Autographs

COMMON AUTO	6.00	15.00
STATED OVERALL ODDS 1:SET		
1 Ian McDiarmid		
2 Samuel L. Jackson		
3 Ray Park	30.00	75.00
4 Oliver Ford Davies	6.00	15.00
5 Anthony Daniels		
6 Kenny Baker	75.00	150.00
7 Hugh Quarshie	6.00	15.00
8 Andy Secombe	6.00	15.00
9 Lewis MacLeod	6.00	15.00
10 Michonne Bourriague	6.00	15.00
11 Matthew Wood	6.00	15.00
12 Silas Carson	6.00	15.00
13 Jerome Blake	6.00	15.00
14 Ralph Brown	6.00	15.00

2019 Star Wars On-Demand Phantom Menace 20th Anniversary Dual Autographs

STATED PRINT RUN 5 SER.#'d SETS

UNPRICED DUE TO SCARCITY

1 I.McDiarmid/S.L.Jackson

2 I.McDiarmid/R.Park

3 A.Daniels/K.Baker

4 S.Carson/J.Blake

2019 Star Wars On-Demand Phantom Menace 20th Anniversary Jedi Council

COMPLETE SET (12)	150.00	300.00
COMMON CARD (1-12)	10.00	25.00
STATED ODDS 1:2		

2002 Star Wars Attack of the Clones

COMPLETE SET (100)	5.00	12.00
UNOPENED BOX (36 PACKS)	125.00	200.00
UNOPENED PACK (7 CARDS)	4.00	6.00
COMMON CARD (1-100)	.15	.40

2002 Star Wars Attack of the Clones Foil

COMPLETE SET (10)	6.00	15.00
COMMON CARD (1-10)	.75	2.00

2002 Star Wars Attack of the Clones Panoramic Fold-Outs

COMPLETE SET (5)	12.00	30.00
COMMON CARD (1-5)	3.00	8.00
STATED ODDS 1:12		

2002 Star Wars Attack of the Clones Prisms

COMPLETE SET (8)	8.00	20.00
COMMON CARD (1-8)	1.25	3.00

2002 Star Wars Attack of the Clones Promos

COMMON CARD	1.25	3.00
B1 UK Distribution	2.50	6.00
(Album Exclusive)		
P4 Star Wars Insider/Star Wars Gamer Exclusive	3.00	8.00
P6 Star Wars Celebration II Exclusive	3.00	8.00
NNO Best Buy Soundtrack Exclusive	3.00	8.00

2002 Star Wars Attack of the Clones Widevision

COMPLETE SET (80)	5.00	12.00
COMMON CARD (1-80)	.15	.40

2002 Star Wars Attack of the Clones Widevision Autographs

COMPLETE SET (24)		
COMMON AUTO	12.00	30.00
STATED ODDS 1:24		
NNO Ahmed Best	40.00	100.00
NNO Alethea McGrath	60.00	150.00
NNO Amy Allen	25.00	60.00
NNO Andrew Secombe	15.00	40.00
NNO Ayesha Dharker	50.00	125.00

NNO	Bodie Taylor	15.00	40.00
NNO	Bonnie Piesse	50.00	125.00
NNO	Daniel Logan	25.00	60.00
NNO	David Bowers	15.00	40.00
NNO	Frank Oz	800.00	1500.00
NNO	Jay Laga'aia	40.00	100.00
NNO	Joel Edgerton	75.00	200.00
NNO	Kenny Baker	150.00	300.00
NNO	Leeanna Walsman	15.00	40.00
NNO	Mary Oyaya	20.00	50.00
NNO	Matt Doran	15.00	40.00
NNO	Nalini Krishan	15.00	40.00
NNO	Rena Owen	15.00	40.00
NNO	Ronald Falk	50.00	100.00
NNO	Silas Carson/Ki-Adi-Mundi	40.00	100.00
NNO	Silas Carson/Nute Gunray	40.00	100.00

2002 Star Wars Attack of the Clones Widevision Promos

P1	Spider Droid	.60	1.50
	(Non-Sport Update Exclusive)		
S1	Spider Droid		
	(UK Exclusive)		

2002 Star Wars Attack of the Clones Widevision DVD Promos

COMPLETE SET (5)	3.00	8.00
COMMON CARD (W1-W5)	1.00	2.50

2016 Star Wars Attack of the Clones 3-D Widevision

COMPLETE SET (44)	12.00	30.00
COMMON CARD (1-44)	.50	1.25

2016 Star Wars Attack of the Clones 3-D Widevision Autographs

COMMON AUTO		12.00	30.00
STATED ODDS 1:SET			
NNO	Alan Ruscoe	15.00	40.00
NNO	Amy Allen	12.00	30.00
NNO	Daniel Logan	15.00	40.00
NNO	Jesse Jensen	15.00	40.00
NNO	Jett Lucas	15.00	40.00
NNO	Kenny Baker	80.00	150.00
NNO	Matthew Wood	25.00	60.00
	Magaloof		
NNO	Oliver Ford	15.00	40.00

2016 Star Wars Attack of the Clones 3-D Widevision Dual Autographs

UNPRICED DUE TO SCARCITY

1 A.Allen/N.Krishan

2 J.Jensen/H.Shapi

3 S.Carson/J.Jensen

2016 Star Wars Attack of the Clones 3-D Widevision Medallions

COMPLETE SET (10)	175.00	350.00
COMMON CARD (MC1-MC10)	15.00	40.00
STATED ODDS PATCH OR MEDALLION 1:1		

2016 Star Wars Attack of the Clones 3-D Widevision Patches

COMPLETE SET (12)	200.00	350.00
COMMON CARD (MP1-MP12)	15.00	40.00
STATED ODDS PATCH OR MEDALLION 1:1		

2002 Star Wars Episode II Instant Win

COMPLETE SET (5)	5.00	12.00
COMMON CARD (UNNUMBERED)	1.50	4.00

2002 Star Wars Episode II Jedi Fruit Rolls

COMPLETE SET (6)		5.00	12.00
UNNUMBERED SET			
1	Luke vs. Darth Vader	3.00	8.00
2	Luke vs. Darth Vader	3.00	8.00
3	Obi-Wan vs. Count Dooku	.75	2.00
4	Obi-Wan vs. Darth Vader	2.00	5.00
5	Obi-Wan vs. Jango Fett	.75	2.00
6	Qui-Gon Jinn vs. Darth Maul	1.25	3.00

REVENGE OF THE SITH

2005 Star Wars Revenge of the Sith

MACE VS. PALPATINE

COMPLETE SET (90)	5.00	12.00
UNOPENED HOBBY BOX (36 PACKS)	150.00	250.00
UNOPENED HOBBY PACK (7 CARDS)	5.00	8.00
UNOPENED RETAIL BOX (24 PACKS)	30.00	40.00
UNOPENED RETAIL PACK (7 CARDS)	1.50	1.75
COMMON CARD (1-90)	.15	.40

2005 Star Wars Revenge of the Sith Blister Bonus

COMPLETE SET (3)	6.00	15.00
COMMON CARD (B1-B3)	2.50	6.00
STATED ODDS ONE PER BLISTER PACK		

2005 Star Wars Revenge of the Sith Embossed Foil

COMPLETE SET (10)	20.00	50.00
COMMON CARD (1-10)	2.50	6.00
STATED ODDS 1:6 RETAIL		

2005 Star Wars Revenge of the Sith Etched Foil Puzzle

COMPLETE SET (6)	12.00	30.00
COMMON CARD (1-6)	2.50	6.00
STATED ODDS 1:6		

2005 Star Wars Revenge of the Sith Flix-Pix

COMPLETE SET (68)	50.00	100.00
UNOPENED BOX (36 PACKS)	100.00	150.00
UNOPENED PACK	3.00	5.00
COMMON CARD (1-68)	1.00	2.50
CL (TRI-FOLD INSERT)	.40	1.00

2005 Star Wars Revenge of the Sith Holograms

COMPLETE SET (3)	5.00	12.00
COMMON CARD (1-3)	2.00	5.00
STATED ODDS 1:14 RETAIL		

2005 Star Wars Revenge of the Sith Lenticular Morph Hobby

COMPLETE SET (2)	5.00	12.00
COMMON CARD (1-2)	3.00	8.00
STATED ODDS 1:24 HOBBY		

2005 Star Wars Revenge of the Sith Lenticular Morph Retail

COMPLETE SET (2)	5.00	12.00
COMMON CARD (1-2)	3.00	8.00
STATED ODDS 1:24 RETAIL		

2005 Star Wars Revenge of the Sith Stickers

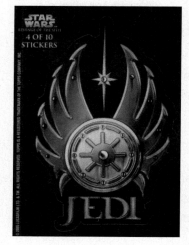

COMPLETE SET (10)	2.50	6.00
COMMON CARD (1-10)	.40	1.00
STATED ODDS 1:3 RETAIL		

2005 Star Wars Revenge of the Sith Tattoos

COMPLETE SET (10)	4.00	10.00
COMMON CARD (1-10)	1.00	2.50
STATED ODDS 1:3 RETAIL		

2005 Star Wars Revenge of the Sith Tin Gold

COMPLETE SET (6)	5.00	12.00
COMMON CARD (A-F)	1.00	2.50
STATED ODDS ONE PER TIN		

2005 Star Wars Revenge of the Sith Tin Story

COMPLETE SET (6)	5.00	12.00
COMMON CARD (1-6)	1.00	2.50
STATED ODDS ONE PER TIN		

2005 Star Wars Revenge of the Sith Promos

COMMON CARD (P1-P5)	1.00	2.50
P3 The Circle is Complete SW Shop	15.00	40.00

2005 Star Wars Revenge of the Sith Medalionz

COMPLETE SET (24)	15.00	40.00
COMMON CARD (1-24)	1.00	2.50
*GOLD: .8X TO 2X BASIC MED.		
CL Checklist	.20	.50

2005 Star Wars Revenge of the Sith Widevision

COMPLETE SET (80)	5.00	12.00
UNOPENED HOBBY BOX (24 PACKS)	150.00	250.00
UNOPENED HOBBY PACK (6 CARDS)	6.00	10.00
UNOPENED RETAIL BOX (24 PACKS)	25.00	40.00
UNOPENED RETAIL PACK (6 CARDS)	1.50	2.00
COMMON CARD (1-80)	.15	.40

2005 Star Wars Revenge of the Sith Widevision Autographs

COMMON CARD (UNNUMBERED)	12.00	30.00
STATED ODDS 1:48 HOBBY		
NNO Matthew Wood	75.00	150.00
NNO Peter Mayhew	100.00	200.00
NNO Samuel L. Jackson	750.00	1500.00

2005 Star Wars Revenge of the Sith Widevision Chrome Hobby

COMPLETE SET (10)	12.50	30.00
COMMON CARD (H1-H10)	1.50	4.00
STATED ODDS 1:6 HOBBY		

2005 Star Wars Revenge of the Sith Widevision Chrome Retail

COMPLETE SET (10)	15.00	40.00
COMMON CARD (R1-R10)	2.00	5.00
STATED ODDS 1:60 RETAIL		

2005 Star Wars Revenge of the Sith Widevision Flix-Pix

COMPLETE SET (10)	15.00	40.00
COMMON CARD (1-10)	2.00	5.00
STATED ODDS 1:6		

2015 Star Wars Revenge of the Sith 3-D Widevision

COMPLETE SET (44)	10.00	25.00
COMPLETE FACTORY SET (46)	60.00	120.00
COMMON CARD (1-44)	.40	1.00

2015 Star Wars Revenge of the Sith 3-D Widevision Autographs

COMMON AUTO	15.00	40.00
NNO Peter Mayhew	60.00	120.00
NNO Jeremy Bulloch	25.00	60.00
NNO Bai Ling	30.00	80.00

2015 Star Wars Revenge of the Sith 3-D Widevision Medallions

COMPLETE SET (8)	100.00	200.00
COMMON MEM	15.00	40.00
*SILVER/30: .6X TO 1.5X BASIC MEM		
STATED PRINT RUN 60 SER.#'d SETS		

2015 Star Wars Revenge of the Sith 3-D Widevision Patches

AUTHENTIC PATCH CARD

COMPLETE SET (4)	50.00	100.00
COMMON MEM	15.00	40.00
*SILVER/30: .6X TO 1.5X BASIC MEM		
STATED PRINT RUN 60 SER.#'d SETS		

THE FORCE AWAKENS

2017 Star Wars The Force Awakens 3-D Widevision

COMPLETE SET (44)	12.00	30.00
COMPLETE BOXED SET (46)		
COMMON CARD (1-44)	.40	1.00

2017 Star Wars The Force Awakens 3-D Widevision Autographs

COMMON AUTO	6.00	15.00
STATED ODDS 2:SET		
WVAAJ Andrew Jack	6.00	15.00
WVAASH Arti Shah	8.00	20.00
WVABH Brian Herring	10.00	25.00
WVABV Brian Vernel	6.00	15.00
WVACC Crystal Clarke	8.00	20.00
WVAEE Emun Elliott	6.00	15.00
WVAHW Harriet Walter	6.00	15.00
WVAIU Iko Uwais	10.00	25.00
WVAJH Jessica Henwick	10.00	25.00
WVAKF Kate Fleetwood	6.00	15.00
WVAPW Paul Warren	6.00	15.00
WVATC Tosin Cole	6.00	15.00
WVAYR Yayan Ruhian	6.00	15.00

2017 Star Wars The Force Awakens 3-D Widevision Dual Autographs

UNPRICED DUE TO SCARCITY

WVDAFG C.Fisher/G.Grunberg

WVDARB D.Ridley/J.Boyega

WVDARH D.Ridley/M.Hamill

WVDABM J.Boyega/P.Mayhew

WVDAAS M.Hamill/A.Serkis

2016 Star Wars The Force Awakens Chrome

COMPLETE SET (100)	8.00	20.00
UNOPENED BOX (24 PACKS)	50.00	70.00
UNOPENED PACK (6 CARDS)	3.00	3.50
COMMON CARD (1-100)	.25	.60
*REFRACTOR: 1.2X TO 3X BASIC CARDS	.60	1.50
*PRISM REF./99: 5X TO 12X BASIC CARDS	3.00	8.00
*SHIMMER REF./50: 10X TO 25X BASIC CARDS	6.00	15.00
*PULSAR REF./10: 15X TO 40X BASIC CARDS	10.00	25.00

2016 Star Wars The Force Awakens Chrome Autographs

TASU LEECH

COMMON CARD	5.00	12.00
*ATOMIC/99: .5X TO 1.2X BASIC CARDS		
*PRISM/50: .6X TO 1.5X BASIC CARDS		
*X-FRACTOR/25: .75X TO 2X BASIC CARDS		
OVERALL AUTO ODDS 1:24		
CAAB Anna Brewster	8.00	20.00
CABV Brian Vernel	10.00	25.00
CAGG Greg Grunberg	10.00	25.00
CAJS Joonas Suotamo	10.00	25.00
CAKS Kipsang Rotich	8.00	20.00
CAMD Mark Dodson	10.00	25.00
CAMQ Mike Quinn	8.00	20.00
CAPM Peter Mayhew	20.00	50.00
CASA Sebastian Armesto	8.00	20.00
CAYR Yayan Ruhian	10.00	25.00
CAMWG Matthew Wood	8.00	20.00

2016 Star Wars The Force Awakens Chrome Autographs Atomic Refractors

*ATOMIC/99: .5X TO 1.2X BASIC CARDS

CAJB	John Boyega	120.00	200.00
CAWD	Warwick Davis	12.00	30.00

2016 Star Wars The Force Awakens Chrome Autographs Prism Refractors

*PRISM/50: .6X TO 1.5X BASIC CARDS

CAAD	Anthony Daniels		
CAAS	Andy Serkis	120.00	200.00

2016 Star Wars The Force Awakens Chrome Autographs X-fractors

*X-FRACTORS: .75X TO 2X BASIC CARDS

CACF	Carrie Fisher	120.00	250.00
CADR	Daisy Ridley	600.00	1200.00
CAEB	Erik Bauersfeld		
CAKB	Kenny Baker	150.00	300.00
CAMWU	Matthew Wood		

2016 Star Wars The Force Awakens Chrome Behind-the-Scenes

COMPLETE SET (12)		10.00	25.00
COMMON CARD (1-12)		1.25	3.00

---

*SHIMMER REF./50: 1X TO 2.5X BASIC CARDS		3.00	8.00
STATED ODDS 1:4			

2016 Star Wars The Force Awakens Chrome Dual Autographs

STATED PRINT RUN 3 SER.#'d SETS

UNPRICED DUE TO SCARCITY

CDABF	C.Fisher/J.Boyega
CDAHF	M.Hamill/C.Fisher
CDAMA	R.Marshall/S.Armesto
CDAMS	J.Suotamo/P.Mayhew
CDAWB	P.Mayhew/H.Walker

2016 Star Wars The Force Awakens Chrome Heroes of the Resistance

COMPLETE SET (18)		10.00	25.00
COMMON CARD (1-18)		.75	2.00
*SHIMMER REF./50:1 X TO 2.5X BASIC CARDS		2.00	5.00
STATED ODDS 1:2			
1	Finn	1.25	3.00
2	Rey	1.25	3.00
3	Poe Dameron	1.00	2.50
9	BB-8	1.50	4.00
10	C-3PO	1.00	2.50
11	R2-D2	1.00	2.50
13	Han Solo	1.50	4.00
14	Chewbacca	1.00	2.50
18	General Leia Organa	1.00	2.50

2016 Star Wars The Force Awakens Chrome Medallions

COMPLETE SET (25)		200.00	400.00
COMMON CARD		3.00	8.00
*SILVER/25: .5X TO 1.2X BASIC CARDS			
M1	Han Solo	12.00	30.00
M2	General Leia Organa	12.00	30.00
M3	Admiral Ackbar	5.00	12.00
M4	Chewbacca	6.00	15.00
M5	Admiral Statura	5.00	12.00
M6	Snap Wexley	8.00	20.00
M7	Jess Testor Pava	8.00	20.00
M10	Poe Dameron	8.00	20.00
M11	Rey	20.00	50.00
M12	Finn	10.00	25.00
M13	BB-8	10.00	25.00
M14	Riot Control Stormtrooper	8.00	20.00
M16	Colonel Datoo	6.00	15.00
M17	Supreme Leader Snoke	6.00	15.00
M18	Flametrooper	5.00	12.00
M19	Kylo Ren	8.00	20.00
M20	Kylo Ren	8.00	20.00
M21	General Hux	5.00	12.00
M22	Captain Phasma	8.00	20.00
M23	FN-2187	10.00	25.00

2016 Star Wars The Force Awakens Chrome Patches

COMPLETE SET (27)		175.00	350.00
COMMON CARD (P1-P27)		5.00	12.00
*SHIMMER/199: .5X TO 1.2X BASIC CARDS			
*PULSAR/99: .6X TO 1.5X BASIC CARDS			
P1	Rey/686	15.00	40.00
P2	Han Solo/299	8.00	20.00
P4	Finn/686	8.00	20.00
P7	Kylo Ren/401	6.00	15.00
P11	General Leia Organa/755	8.00	20.00

P15 BB-8/686	6.00	15.00
P16 Poe Dameron & BB-8/686	6.00	15.00
P17 Rey & BB-8/686	12.00	30.00
P18 R2-D2/686	6.00	15.00
P19 Rey/299	10.00	25.00
P20 Rey/686	10.00	25.00
P23 Han Solo & Chewbacca/737	10.00	25.00

2016 Star Wars The Force Awakens Chrome Power of the First Order

COMPLETE SET (9)	6.00	15.00
COMMON CARD (1-9)	.75	2.00
*SHIMMER REF./50: 1X TO 2.5X BASIC CARDS		
STATED ODDS 1:12		
1 Supreme Leader Snoke	1.50	4.00
2 Kylo Ren	1.50	4.00
3 General Hux	1.25	3.00
4 Captain Phasma	1.25	3.00

2016 Star Wars The Force Awakens Chrome Ships and Vehicles

COMPLETE SET (11)	6.00	15.00
COMMON CARD (1-11)	1.00	2.50
*SHIMMER REF./50: 1X TO 2.5X BASIC CARDS	2.50	6.00
STATED ODDS 1:8		

2016 Star Wars The Force Awakens Chrome Triple Autographs

COMPLETE SET (4)		
STATED PRINT RUN 3 SER.#'d SETS		
UNPRICED DUE TO SCARCITY		
CTAFBR Boyega/Fisher/Rose		
CTAFGQ Fisher/Grunberg/Quinn		
CTAHFB Hamill/Fisher/Boyega		
CTASMA Serkis/Marshall/Armesto		

2015 Star Wars The Force Awakens Dog Tags

COMPLETE SET (16)	15.00	40.00
COMMON CARD (1-16)	1.25	3.00
*GOLD: 1X TO 2.5X BASIC TAGS		
1 Kylo Ren	2.00	5.00
2 Rey	2.00	5.00
3 Finn	1.50	4.00
5 Captain Phasma	1.50	4.00
10 BB-8	2.50	6.00
11 Rey	2.00	5.00
12 Finn	1.50	4.00
13 Kylo Ren	2.00	5.00

2015 Star Wars The Force Awakens Dog Tags Target Exclusives

COMPLETE SET (2)	10.00	25.00
COMMON CARD (T1-T2)	5.00	12.00
*GOLD: .75X TO 2X BASIC TAGS		
EXCLUSIVE TO TARGET		
T2 BB-8	8.00	20.00

2015 Star Wars The Force Awakens Dog Tags Toys 'R' Us Exclusives

COMPLETE SET (2)	10.00	25.00
COMMON CARD (TR1-TR2)	6.00	15.00
*GOLD: 1X TO 2.5X BASIC TAGS		
EXCLUSIVE TO TOYS 'R' US		

2015 Star Wars The Force Awakens Dog Tags Walmart Exclusives

COMPLETE SET (2)	6.00	15.00
COMMON CARD (W1-W2)	4.00	10.00
*GOLD: 1X TO 2.5X BASIC TAGS		
EXCLUSIVE TO WALMART		

2016 Star Wars The Force Awakens Factory Set

COMPLETE FACTORY SET (310)	40.00	80.00
COMMON CARD	.15	.40
JOURNEY TO TFA (1-110)		
TFA SERIES ONE (1-100)		
TFA SERIES TWO (1-100)		
*LIM.ED./100: 6X TO 15X BASIC CARDS	2.50	6.00

2015 Star Wars The Force Awakens Glow-in-the-Dark Decals

COMPLETE SET (7)	10.00	25.00
COMMON CARD	1.25	3.00
STATED ODDS 1:CEREAL BOX		
INSERTED IN BOXES OF GENERAL MILLS CEREAL		
MILLENNIUM FALCON IS KROGER EXCLUSIVE		
1 BB-8	2.50	6.00
2 C-3PO and R2-D2	1.50	4.00
3 Captain Phasma	2.00	5.00
5 Kylo Ren	2.00	5.00
6 Millennium Falcon SP	5.00	12.00
Kroger Exclusive		

2015 Star Wars The Force Awakens Series One

COMPLETE SET w/o SP (100)	10.00	25.00
COMMON CARD (1-100)	.20	.50
*LTSBR GREEN: .5X TO 1.2X BASIC CARDS		
*LTSBR BLUE: .6X TO 1.5X BASIC CARDS		
*LTSBR PURPLE: .75X TO 2X BASIC CARDS		
*FOIL/250: 4X TO 10X BASIC CARDS		
*GOLD/100: 6X TO 15X BASIC CARDS		
TARGET EXCLUSIVES SP 101-103		

100	Han Solo & Chewbacca return home	.75	2.00
101	Maz Kanata SP	3.00	8.00
102	Wollivan SP	3.00	8.00
103	Grummgar SP	3.00	8.00

2015 Star Wars The Force Awakens Series One
Autographs

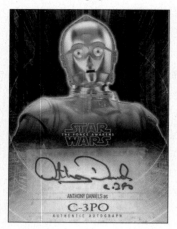

COMMON AUTO	15.00	40.00
STATED ODDS 1:106 H; 1:12,334 R		
NNO Anthony Daniels	100.00	200.00
NNO Carrie Fisher	200.00	350.00
NNO Daisy Ridley	750.00	1500.00
NNO John Boyega	100.00	200.00
NNO Peter Mayhew	50.00	100.00

2015 Star Wars The Force Awakens Series One
Behind-the-Scenes

COMPLETE SET (7)	5.00	12.00
COMMON CARD (1-7)	1.00	2.50
*LTSBR GREEN: .5X TO 1.2X BASIC CARDS		
*LTSBR BLUE: .6X TO 1.5X BASIC CARDS		
*LTSBR PURPLE: .75X TO 2X BASIC CARDS		
*FOIL/250: 4X TO 10X BASIC CARDS		
*GOLD/100: 6X TO 15X BASIC CARDS		
STATED ODDS 1:8 H; 1:5 R		

2015 Star Wars The Force Awakens Series One
Character Montages

COMPLETE SET (8)	4.00	10.00
COMMON CARD (1-8)	.75	2.00
*LTSBR GREEN: .5X TO 1.2X BASIC CARDS		
*LTSBR BLUE: .6X TO 1.5X BASIC CARDS		
*LTSBR PURPLE: .75X TO 2X BASIC CARDS		
*FOIL/250: 4X TO 10X BASIC CARDS		
*GOLD/100: 6X TO 15X BASIC CARDS		
STATED ODDS 1:7 H; 1:4 R		
1 Rey	1.50	4.00
5 Captain Phasma	1.25	3.00
7 BB-8	1.50	4.00

2015 Star Wars The Force Awakens Series One
Character Stickers

COMPLETE SET (18)	6.00	15.00
COMMON CARD (1-18)	.60	1.50
*LTSBR GREEN: .5X TO 1.2X BASIC CARDS		
*LTSBR BLUE: .6X TO 1.5X BASIC CARDS		
*LTSBR PURPLE: .75X TO 2X BASIC CARDS		
*FOIL/250: 4X TO 10X BASIC CARDS		
*GOLD/100: 6X TO 15X BASIC CARDS		
STATED ODDS 1:3 H; 1:2 R		
1 Rey	1.25	3.00
5 Captain Phasma	1.00	2.50
8 BB-8	1.25	3.00
12 Rey	1.25	3.00

2015 Star Wars The Force Awakens Series One
Concept Art

COMPLETE SET (20)	8.00	20.00
COMMON CARD (1-20)	.75	2.00
*LTSBR GREEN: .5X TO 1.2X BASIC CARDS		
*LTSBR BLUE: .6X TO 1.5X BASIC CARDS		
*LTSBR PURPLE: .75X TO 2X BASIC CARDS		
*FOIL/250: 4X TO 10X BASIC CARDS		
*GOLD/100: 6X TO 15X BASIC CARDS		
STATED ODDS 1:3 H; 1:2 R		

2015 Star Wars The Force Awakens Series One
Dual Autographs

UNPRICED DUE TO SCARCITY

1 A.Daniels/K.Baker

2 A.Daniels/P.Mayhew

3 C.Fisher/A.Daniels

4 M.Quinn/T.Rose

2015 Star Wars The Force Awakens Series One
First Order Rises

COMPLETE SET (9)	6.00	15.00
COMMON CARD (1-9)	1.25	3.00
*LTSBR GREEN: .5X TO 1.2X BASIC CARDS		
*LTSBR BLUE: .6X TO 1.5X BASIC CARDS		
*LTSBR PURPLE: .75X TO 2X BASIC CARDS		
*FOIL/250: 4X TO 10X BASIC CARDS		
*GOLD/100: 6X TO 15X BASIC CARDS		
STATED ODDS 1:6 H; 1:4 R		
2 Captain Phasma	1.50	4.00

2015 Star Wars The Force Awakens Series One
First Order Stormtrooper Costume Relics

COMMON CARD	12.00	30.00

*BRONZE/99: .75X TO 2X BASIC CARDS

*SILVER/50: 1.2X TO 3X BASIC CARDS

*GOLD/10: 2X TO 5X BASIC CARDS

2015 Star Wars The Force Awakens Series One
Locations

COMPLETE SET (9)	3.00	8.00
COMMON CARD (1-9)	.60	1.50

*LTSBR GREEN: .5X TO 1.2X BASIC CARDS

*LTSBR BLUE: .6X TO 1.5X BASIC CARDS

*LTSBR PURPLE: .75X TO 2X BASIC CARDS

*FOIL/250: 4X TO 10X BASIC CARDS

*GOLD/100: 6X TO 15X BASIC CARDS

STATED ODDS 1:6 H; 1:4 R

2015 Star Wars The Force Awakens Series One
Medallions

COMMON CARD (M1-M66)	8.00	20.00

STATED ODDS 1:BOX

2015 Star Wars The Force Awakens Series One
Movie Scenes

COMPLETE SET (20)	5.00	12.00
COMMON CARD (1-20)	.50	1.25

*LTSBR GREEN: .5X TO 1.2X BASIC CARDS

*LTSBR BLUE: .60X TO 1.5X BASIC CARDS

*LTSBR PURPLE: .75X TO 2X BASIC CARDS

*FOIL/250: 4X TO 10X BASIC CARDS

*GOLD/100: 6X TO 15X BASIC CARDS

STATED ODDS 1:3 H; 1:2 R

2015 Star Wars The Force Awakens Series One
Triple Autographs

UNPRICED DUE TO SCARCITY

NNO Fisher/Mayhew/Daniels

2015 Star Wars The Force Awakens Series One
Weapons

COMPLETE SET (10)	4.00	10.00
COMMON CARD (1-10)	.60	1.50

*LTSBR GREEN: .5X TO 1.2X BASIC CARDS

*LTSBR BLUE: .6X TO 1.5X BASIC CARDS

*LTSBR PURPLE: .75X TO 2X BASIC CARDS

*FOIL/250: 4X TO 10X BASIC CARDS

*GOLD/100: 6X TO 15X BASIC CARDS

STATED ODDS 1:6 H; 1:3 R

1 Kylo Ren's lightsaber	1.25	3.00
9 Han Solo's Blaster	.75	2.00

2016 Star Wars The Force Awakens Series Two

COMPLETE SET W/O SP (100)	10.00	25.00
COMPLETE SET W/SP (102)	20.00	50.00
UNOPENED HOBBY BOX (24 PACKS)	60.00	100.00
UNOPENED HOBBY PACK (8 CARDS)	2.50	4.00
COMMON CARD (1-100)	.20	.50

*LTSBR GREEN: .5X TO 1.2X BASIC CARDS

*LTSBR BLUE: .6X TO 1.5X BASIC CARDS

*LTSBR PURPLE: .75X TO 2X BASIC CARDS

*FOIL: 4X TO 10X BASIC CARDS

*GOLD/100: 6X TO 15X BASIC CARDS

101 Finding Luke Skywalker SP	6.00	15.00
102 The Lightsaber Returned SP	10.00	25.00

2016 Star Wars The Force Awakens Series Two
Autographs

COMMON CARD	8.00	20.00

*LTSBR PURPLE/50: .5X TO 1.2X BASIC AUTOS

*FOIL/25: .75X TO 2X BASIC AUTOS

1 David Acord	20.00	50.00
FN-2199		
2 David Acord	15.00	40.00
Teedo		
4 Kenny Baker	50.00	100.00
6 John Boyega	150.00	300.00
7 Anna Brewster	12.00	30.00
8 Dante Briggins	12.00	30.00
9 Thomas Brodie-Sangster	10.00	25.00
10 Aidan Cook	12.00	30.00
11 Anthony Daniels	50.00	100.00
12 Warrick Davis	10.00	25.00
13 Harrison Ford		
14 Greg Grunberg	15.00	40.00
17 Jessica Henwick	15.00	40.00
18 Brian Herring	60.00	120.00
19 Andrew Jack	10.00	25.00
20 Billie Lourd	15.00	40.00
21 Rocky Marshall	10.00	25.00
22 Peter Mayhew	25.00	60.00
25 Arti Shah	12.00	30.00
26 Kiran Shah	10.00	25.00
27 Joonas Suotamo	15.00	40.00
28 Brian Vernel	10.00	25.00
29 Dame Harriet Walter	12.00	30.00
30 Paul Warren	10.00	25.00

2016 Star Wars The Force Awakens Series Two
Card Trader Characters

COMPLETE SET (9)		
COMMON CARD (1-9)	50.00	100.00
STATED PRINT RUN 100 SER.#'d SETS		
1 BB-8	60.00	120.00
3 Finn	60.00	120.00
5 Kylo Ren	80.00	150.00
6 Captain Phasma	80.00	150.00
7 Poe Dameron	60.00	120.00
8 Rey	120.00	200.00

2016 Star Wars The Force Awakens Series Two
Character Poster Inserts

COMPLETE SET (5)	5.00	12.00
COMMON CARD (1-5)	1.50	4.00
STATED ODDS 1:24		
1 Rey	2.50	6.00
2 Finn	2.50	6.00
5 Han Solo	2.00	5.00

2016 Star Wars The Force Awakens Series Two
Character Stickers

COMPLETE SET (18)	6.00	15.00
COMMON CARD (1-18)	.50	1.25
1 Finn	.75	2.00
2 Rey	1.00	2.50

5 Han Solo	1.00	2.50
6 Leia Organa	.75	2.00
8 Poe Dameron	1.25	3.00
11 BB-8	1.25	3.00
12 Unkar Plutt	.60	1.50
13 General Hux	.75	2.00
15 Admiral Ackbar	.60	1.50
16 Stormtrooper	.75	2.00
18 Maz Kanata	.60	1.50

2016 Star Wars The Force Awakens Series Two
Concept Art

COMPLETE SET (9)	5.00	12.00
COMMON CARD (1-9)	1.00	2.50

2016 Star Wars The Force Awakens Series Two
Dual Autographs

STATED PRINT RUN 3 SER.#'d SETS

UNPRICED DUE TO SCARCITY

1 J.Boyega/C.Fisher

2 C.Fisher/T.Rose

3 A.Daniels/P.Mayhew

2016 Star Wars The Force Awakens Series Two
Dual Medallion Autographs

STATED PRINT RUN 5 SER.#'d SETS

UNPRICED DUE TO SCARCITY

1 J.Boyega/C.Fisher

2 C.Fisher/M.Quinn

3 M.Quinn/T.Rose

4 C.Fisher/A.Daniels

5 A.Daniels/P.Mayhew

2016 Star Wars The Force Awakens Series Two
Dual Medallions

STATED PRINT RUN 5 SER.#'d SETS

UNPRICED DUE TO SCARCITY

1 Kylo Ren, Captain Phasma

2 Rey, Finn

3 Stormtrooper, TIE Fighter Pilot

4 Finn, Poe Dameron

5 Han Solo, Rey

2016 Star Wars The Force Awakens Series Two
Galactic Connexions

COMPLETE SET (5)	120.00	250.00
COMMON CARD (1-5)	30.00	80.00
STATED PRINT RUN 100 ANNCD SETS		
WAL-MART EXCLUSIVE		
3 BB-8	50.00	100.00

2016 Star Wars The Force Awakens Series Two
Heroes of the Resistance

COMPLETE SET (16)	8.00	20.00
COMMON CARD (1-16)	.75	2.00
2 Poe Dameron	1.00	2.50
3 Finn	1.00	2.50
4 Rey	1.25	3.00
5 Han Solo	1.50	4.00
16 BB-8	1.50	4.00

2016 Star Wars The Force Awakens Series Two
Maz's Castle

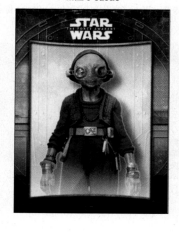

COMPLETE SET (9)	5.00	12.00
COMMON CARD (1-9)	.75	2.00

2016 Star Wars The Force Awakens Series Two Medallions

POE DAMERON

COMMON CARD	4.00	10.00

*SILVER p/r 244-399: .5X TO 1.2X BASIC CARDS

*SILVER p/r 120-199: .6X TO 1.5X BASIC CARDS

*SILVER p/r 50-99: 1X TO 2.5X BASIC CARDS

*GOLD p/r 120-199: .6X TO 1.5X BASIC CARDS

*GOLD p/r 74-100: .75X TO 2X BASIC CARDS

*GOLD p/r 25-50: 1.2X TO 3X BASIC CARDS

1 Kylo Ren	6.00	15.00
2 General Hux	5.00	12.00
3 Captain Phasma	5.00	12.00
4 FN-2187	5.00	12.00
6 Kylo Ren	6.00	15.00
12 Kylo Ren	6.00	15.00
13 Maz Kanata	5.00	12.00
14 Rey	6.00	15.00
15 BB-8	5.00	12.00
16 Han Solo	8.00	20.00
17 Chewbacca	5.00	12.00
18 Finn	6.00	15.00
19 Rey	6.00	15.00
22 Colonel Datoo	6.00	15.00
23 Captain Phasma	5.00	12.00
24 Finn	5.00	12.00
27 BB-8	5.00	12.00
28 Resistance X-Wing Fighter	5.00	12.00
29 Nien Nunb	6.00	15.00
30 C-3PO	6.00	15.00
31 R2-D2	8.00	20.00
32 Jess Testor Pava	10.00	25.00
33 Snap Wexley	6.00	15.00
34 Admiral Statura	6.00	15.00
35 Admiral Ackbar	6.00	15.00
36 Major Brance	5.00	12.00

2016 Star Wars The Force Awakens Series Two Power of the First Order

POWER OF THE FIRST ORDER

COMPLETE SET (11)	5.00	12.00
COMMON CARD (1-11)	.40	1.00
1 Kylo Ren	1.25	3.00
2 General Hux	1.00	2.50
3 Captain Phasma	1.25	3.00
11 Supreme Leader Snoke	1.00	2.50

2016 Star Wars The Force Awakens Series Two Quad Autographed Booklet

STATED PRINT RUN 1 SER.#'d SET

UNPRICED DUE TO SCARCITY

1 Boyega/Fisher/Rose/Quinn

2016 Star Wars The Force Awakens Series Two Triple Autographs

STATED PRINT RUN 3 SER.#'d SETS

UNPRICED DUE TO SCARCITY

1 Boyega/Fisher/Mayhew

2 Fisher/Rose/Quinn

2016 Star Wars Rogue One Series One

COMPLETE SET (90)	8.00	20.00
UNOPENED BOX (24 PACKS)	80.00	100.00
UNOPENED PACK (8 CARDS)	3.00	4.00
COMMON CARD (1-90)	.25	.60

*DEATH STAR BL.: .6X TO 1.5X BASIC CARDS

*GREEN SQ.: .75X TO 2X BASIC CARDS

*BLUE SQ.: 1X TO 2.5X BASIC CARDS

*GRAY SQ./100: 4X TO 10X BASIC CARDS

*GOLD SQ./50: 6X TO 15X BASIC CARDS

2016 Star Wars Rogue One Series One Autographs

COMMON CARD	10.00	25.00

*BLACK/50: .6X TO 1.5X BASIC CARDS

RANDOMLY INSERTED INTO PACKS

1 Donnie Yen	100.00	200.00
2 Felicity Jones	300.00	600.00
3 Forest Whitaker	100.00	200.00
4 Genevieve O'Reilly	15.00	40.00

2016 Star Wars Rogue One Series One Blueprints of Ships and Vehicles

COMPLETE SET (8)	5.00	12.00
COMMON CARD (BP1-BP8)	1.00	2.50

RANDOMLY INSERTED INTO PACKS

2016 Star Wars Rogue One Series One Character Icons

KRENNIC

COMPLETE SET (11)	8.00	20.00
COMMON CARD (CI1-CI11)	1.25	3.00
RANDOMLY INSERTED INTO PACKS		

2016 Star Wars Rogue One Series One Character Stickers

COMPLETE SET (18)	10.00	25.00
COMMON CARD (CS1-CS18)	.75	2.00
RANDOMLY INSERTED INTO PACKS		

2016 Star Wars Rogue One Series One Dual Autographs

UNPRICED DUE TO SCARCITY

1 F.Whitaker/D.Yen

2 G.O'Reilly/F.Whitaker

3 P.Kasey/N.Kellington

2016 Star Wars Rogue One Series One Gallery

COMPLETE SET (10)	4.00	10.00
COMMON CARD (G1-G10)	.50	1.25
RANDOMLY INSERTED INTO PACKS		

2016 Star Wars Rogue One Series One Heroes of the Rebel Alliance

COMPLETE SET (14)	8.00	20.00
COMMON CARD (HR1-HR14)	1.00	2.50
RANDOMLY INSERTED INTO PACKS		
HR1 Jyn Erso	1.50	4.00
HR4 Chirrut IMWE	1.25	3.00

2016 Star Wars Rogue One Series One Medallions

COMMON CARD	4.00	10.00
*BRONZE: SAME VALUE AS BASIC		
*SILVER/99: .5X TO 1.2X BASIC CARDS		
*GOLD/50: .6X TO 1.5X BASIC CARDS		
RANDOMLY INSERTED INTO PACKS		
5 Captain Cassian Andor with X-Wing	6.00	15.00
6 Captain Cassian Andor with U-Wing	6.00	15.00
7 Chirrut Imwe with Y-Wing	6.00	15.00
8 Darth Vader with Death Star	6.00	15.00
9 Darth Vader with Imperial Star Destroyer	6.00	15.00
10 Death Trooper with Imperial Star Destroyer	6.00	15.00
14 Edrio Two Tubes with U-Wing	6.00	15.00
15 Jyn Erso with X-Wing	8.00	20.00

16 Jyn Erso with U-Wing	8.00	20.00
17 Jyn Erso with Death Star	8.00	20.00
18 K-2SO with X-Wing	5.00	12.00
20 Moroff with U-Wing	5.00	12.00
24 Shoretrooper with AT-ACT	5.00	12.00
25 Stormtrooper with AT-ST	5.00	12.00
27 TIE Fighter Pilot with TIE Striker	5.00	12.00

2016 Star Wars Rogue One Series One Montages

COMPLETE SET (9)	5.00	12.00
COMMON CARD (M1-M9)	1.00	2.50

2016 Star Wars Rogue One Series One Triple Autographs

UNPRICED DUE TO SCARCITY

NNO Yen/Kellington/Kasey

NNO O'Reilly/Whitaker/Kasey

2016 Star Wars Rogue One Series One Villains of the Galactic Empire

COMPLETE SET (8)	6.00	15.00
COMMON CARD (VE1-VE8)	1.00	2.50

2017 Star Wars Rogue One Series Two

KRENNIC AND TARKIN CONFER

COMPLETE SET (100)	6.00	15.00
UNOPENED BOX (24 PACKS)	110.00	120.00
UNOPENED PACK (8 CARDS)	5.00	6.00
COMMON CARD (1-100)	.20	.50

*DTHSTR BLACK: .6X TO 1.5X BASIC CARDS

*GREEN SQ: .75X TO 2X BASIC CARDS

*BLUE SQ: 1X TO 2.5X BASIC CARDS

*GRAY SQ/100: 5X TO 12X BASIC CARDS

*GOLD SQ/50: 10X TO 25X BASIC CARDS

2017 Star Wars Rogue One Series Two Autographs

FELICITY JONES AS JYN ERSO

COMMON AUTO	10.00	25.00

*BLACK/50: .6X TO 1.5X BASIC AUTOS

*GOLD/10: 1.2X TO 3X BASIC AUTOS

STATED ODDS 1:36

DA	Derek Arnold	12.00	30.00
DY	Donnie Yen	80.00	150.00
GO	Genevieve O'Reilly	8.00	20.00
RA	Riz Ahmed	120.00	200.00
WD	Warwick Davis	12.00	30.00
AC1	Aidan Cook	10.00	25.00
	Benthic Two Tubes		
AC2	Aidan Cook	10.00	25.00
	Caitken		

2017 Star Wars Rogue One Series Two Autographs Black

*BLACK/50: .6X TO 1.5X BASIC AUTOS

STATED ODDS 1:163

STATED PRINT RUN 50 SER.#'d SETS

FJ	Felicity Jones	300.00	600.00
FW	Forest Whitaker	100.00	200.00
NK	Nick Kellington	20.00	50.00

2017 Star Wars Rogue One Series Two Character Stickers

BISTAN

COMPLETE SET (18)	30.00	80.00
COMMON CARD (CS1-CS18)	2.50	6.00
STATED ODDS 1:12		
CS1 Jyn Erso	5.00	12.00
CS8 Director Krennic	3.00	8.00
CS9 Darth Vader	4.00	10.00
CS10 K-2SO	3.00	8.00
CS14 Chirrut Imwe	4.00	10.00
CS18 Admiral Raddus	3.00	8.00

2017 Star Wars Rogue One Series Two Dual Autographs

GENEVIEVE O'REILLY AS MON MOTHMA

FELICITY JONES AS JYN ERSO

UNPRICED DUE TO SCARCITY

FJFW F.Jones/F.Whitaker

FJGO F.Jones/G.O'Reilly

GOAP G.O'Reilly/A.Petrie

2017 Star Wars Rogue One Series Two Heroes of the Rebel Alliance

BODHI ROOK

HEROES OF THE REBEL ALLIANCE

COMPLETE SET (10)	6.00	15.00
COMMON CARD (HR1-HR10)	1.00	2.50
STATED ODDS 1:7		

2017 Star Wars Rogue One Series Two Movie Posters

COMPLETE SET (10)	30.00	80.00
COMMON CARD (1-10)	3.00	8.00
STATED ODDS 1:24		
1 United States Theatrical Poster	6.00	15.00
5 Cassian Andor Character Poster	4.00	10.00
6 Bodhi Rook Character Poster	5.00	12.00
7 Chirrut Imwe Character Poster	6.00	15.00
9 K-2SO Character Poster	6.00	15.00

2017 Star Wars Rogue One Series Two Patches

RED SQUADRON

LT. ZAL DINNES (RED EIGHT)

COMMON CARD	5.00	12.00

*SILVER/100: .5X TO 1.2X BASIC CARDS

*GOLD/50: .6X TO 1.5X BASIC CARDS

*RED/10: 1.2X TO 3X BASIC CARDS

2017 Star Wars Rogue One Series Two Prime Forces

COMPLETE SET (10)	8.00	20.00
COMMON CARD (PF1-PF10)	1.50	4.00

STATED ODDS 1:2

2017 Star Wars Rogue One Series Two Triple Autographs

STATED ODDS 1:11,771

UNPRICED DUE TO SCARCITY

FJDYFW Jones/Yen/Whitaker

FJGOAP Jones/O'Reilly/Petrie

FWPKAC Whitaker/Kasey/Cook

2017 Star Wars Rogue One Series Two Troopers

COMPLETE SET (10)	8.00	20.00
COMMON CARD (TR1-TR10)	1.50	4.00

STATED ODDS 1:2

2017 Star Wars Rogue One Series Two Villains of the Galactic Empire

COMPLETE SET (10)	12.00	30.00
COMMON CARD (VG1-VG10)	2.50	6.00

STATED ODDS 1:7

2016-17 Star Wars Rogue One Darth Vader Continuity

COMPLETE SET (15)	20.00	50.00
COMMON CARD (1-15)	2.50	6.00

MISSION BRIEFING (1-5)

SERIES ONE (6-10)

SERIES TWO (11-15)

STATED ODDS 1:12

2017 Star Wars The Last Jedi Disney Movie Reward Oversized Theater Promos

COMPLETE SET (9)	15.00	40.00
COMMON CARD	2.00	5.00

THEATER PROMOTION EXCLUSIVE

2017 Star Wars The Last Jedi Series One

COMPLETE SET (100)	6.00	15.00
UNOPENED BOX (24 PACKS)	75.00	100.00
UNOPENED PACK (8 CARDS)	4.00	5.00
COMMON CARD (1-100)	.12	.30
*BLUE: 2X TO 5X BASIC CARDS	.60	1.50
*GREEN: 2.5X TO 6X BASIC CARDS	.75	2.00
*PURPLE: 3X TO 8X BASIC CARDS	1.00	2.50
*RED: 4X TO 10X BASIC CARDS	1.25	3.00
*SILVER/99: 10X TO 25X BASIC CARDS	3.00	8.00
*GOLD/25: 20X TO 50X BASIC CARDS	6.00	15.00

TRADING CARDS

2017 Star Wars The Last Jedi Series One Autographs

COMMON AUTO	6.00	15.00
*RED/99: .5X TO 1.2X BASIC AUTOS		
*SILVER/25: .6X TO 1.5X BASIC AUTOS		
RANDOMLY INSERTED INTO PACKS		
NNO Aidan Cook	8.00	20.00
NNO Andy Serkis TFA AU	60.00	120.00
NNO Billie Lourd	60.00	120.00
NNO Brian Herring	12.00	30.00
NNO Crystal Clarke	10.00	25.00
NNO Dave Chapman	12.00	30.00
NNO Ian Whyte	8.00	20.00
NNO Jimmy Vee	15.00	40.00
NNO Mike Quinn	8.00	20.00
NNO Paul Kasey	10.00	25.00
NNO Tom Kane	8.00	20.00
NNO Veronica Ngo	15.00	40.00

2017 Star Wars The Last Jedi Series One Autographs Red

*RED: .5X TO 1.2X BASIC AUTOS	
STATED PRINT RUN 99 SER.#'d SETS	
NNO John Boyega	120.00
NNO Joonas Suotamo	75.00

2017 Star Wars The Last Jedi Series One Autographs Silver

*SILVER: X TO X BASIC AUTOS		
STATED PRINT RUN 25 SER.#'d SETS		
NNO Gwendoline Christie	100.00	200.00

2017 Star Wars The Last Jedi Series One Blueprints and Schematics

COMPLETE SET (8)	6.00	15.00
COMMON CARD (BP1-BP8)	1.25	3.00
*PURPLE/250: .6X TO 1.5X BASIC CARDS	2.00	5.00
*RED/199: .75X TO 2X BASIC CARDS	2.50	6.00
*SILVER/99: 1X TO 2.5X BASIC CARDS	3.00	8.00
RANDOMLY INSERTED INTO PACKS		

2017 Star Wars The Last Jedi Series One Character Portraits

COMPLETE SET (16)	12.00	30.00
COMMON CARD (CP1-CP16)	1.50	4.00
*PURPLE/250: .6X TO 1.5X BASIC CARDS	2.50	6.00
*RED/199: .75X TO 2X BASIC CARDS	3.00	8.00
*SILVER/99: 1X TO 2.5X BASIC CARDS	4.00	10.00
RANDOMLY INSERTED INTO PACKS		

2017 Star Wars The Last Jedi Series One Character Stickers

COMPLETE SET (6)	8.00	20.00
COMMON CARD (DS1-DS6)	1.25	3.00
RANDOMLY INSERTED INTO PACKS		
DS1 Kylo Ren	1.50	4.00
DS4 Rey	3.00	8.00
DS5 Finn	2.50	6.00
DS6 Poe Dameron	2.00	5.00

2017 Star Wars The Last Jedi Series One Dual Autographs

STATED PRINT RUN 5 SER.#'d SETS

UNPRICED DUE TO SCARCITY

NNO A.Driver/A.Serkis

NNO A.Driver/G.Christie

NNO J.Boyega/G.Christie

NNO M.Hamill/D.Ridley

NNO M.Hamill/J.Vee

2017 Star Wars The Last Jedi Series One Illustrated

COMPLETE SET (11)	8.00	20.00
COMMON CARD (SWI1-SWI11)	1.25	3.00
*PURPLE/250: .6X TO 1.5X BASIC CARDS	2.00	5.00
*RED/199: .75X TO 2X BASIC CARDS	2.50	6.00
*SILVER/99: 1X TO 2.5X BASIC CARDS	3.00	8.00
RANDOMLY INSERTED INTO PACKS		

2017 Star Wars The Last Jedi Series One Medallions

COMMON MEDALLION	4.00	10.00
*PURPLE/99: .5X TO 1.2X BASIC MEDALLIONS	5.00	12.00
*RED/25: 1.2X TO 3X BASIC MEDALLIONS	12.00	30.00
RANDOMLY INSERTED INTO PACKS		
NNO BB-8 / BB-8	5.00	12.00
NNO BB-8 / Resistance	6.00	15.00
NNO C-3PO / R2-D2	5.00	12.00
NNO Chewbacca / R2-D2	8.00	20.00
NNO Executioner Stormtrooper / First Order	5.00	12.00
NNO Finn / BB-8	5.00	12.00
NNO Finn / Resistance	6.00	15.00
NNO General Hux / First Order	5.00	12.00
NNO General Leia Organa / Resistance	6.00	15.00
NNO Kylo Ren / First Order	6.00	15.00
NNO Luke Skywalker / Millennium Falcon	10.00	25.00
NNO Poe Dameron / BB-8	5.00	12.00
NNO Poe Dameron / Resistance	6.00	15.00
NNO Porg / Millennium Falcon	6.00	15.00
NNO Porg / R2-D2	6.00	15.00
NNO Praetorian Guard / First Order	5.00	12.00
NNO R2-D2 / Resistance	5.00	12.00
NNO Rey / BB-8	8.00	20.00
NNO Rey / Millennium Falcon	8.00	20.00
NNO Rey / Resistance	8.00	20.00
NNO Rose / Resistance	5.00	12.00

2017 Star Wars The Last Jedi Series One Red Character Illustrations

COMPLETE SET (8)	8.00	20.00
COMMON CARD (RL1-RL8)	1.50	4.00
*PURPLE/250: .6X TO 1.5X BASIC CARDS	2.50	6.00
*RED/199: .75X TO 2X BASIC CARDS	3.00	8.00
*SILVER/99: 1X TO 2.5X BASIC CARDS	4.00	10.00
RANDOMLY INSERTED INTO PACKS		

2017 Star Wars The Last Jedi Series One Resist!

COMPLETE SET (8)	5.00	12.00
COMMON CARD (R1-R8)	1.00	2.50
*PURPLE/250: .6X TO 1.5X BASIC CARDS	1.50	4.00
*RED/199: .75X TO 2X BASIC CARDS	2.00	5.00

*SILVER/99: 1X TO 2.5X BASIC CARDS	2.50	6.00
RANDOMLY INSERTED INTO PACKS		

2017 Star Wars The Last Jedi Series One Six-Person Autograph

NNO Hamill/Ridley/Boyega

Serkis/Driver/Christie

2017 Star Wars The Last Jedi Series One Source Material Fabric Relics

COMMON MEM	12.00	30.00
*SILVER/99: .5X TO 1.2X BASIC RELICS	15.00	40.00
RANDOMLY INSERTED INTO PACKS		

2017 Star Wars The Last Jedi Series One Triple Autographs

STATED PRINT RUN 3 SER.#'d SETS

UNPRICED DUE TO SCARCITY

NNO Driver/Serkis/Christie

NNO Herring/Daniels/Vee

NNO Hamill/Ridley/Vee

2018 Star Wars The Last Jedi Series Two

COMPLETE SET (100)	6.00	15.00
UNOPENED BOX (24 PACKS)		
UNOPENED PACK (8 CARDS)		
COMMON CARD (1-100)	.12	.30
*BLUE: 2X TO 5X BASIC CARDS	.60	1.50
*PURPLE: 3X TO 8X BASIC CARDS	1.00	2.50
*RED/199: 4X TO 10X BASIC CARDS	1.25	3.00
*BRONZE/99: 10X TO 25X BASIC CARDS	3.00	8.00
*SILVER/25: 20X TO 50X BASIC CARDS	6.00	15.00

2018 Star Wars The Last Jedi Series Two Autographs

COMMON AUTO	6.00	15.00
STATED ODDS 1:36		
AAD Adam Driver		
AAE Adrian Edmondson	10.00	25.00
AAL Amanda Lawrence	12.00	30.00
AAS Andy Serkis		
AADC Anthony Daniels		
ABL Billie Lourd		
ABH Brian Herring	8.00	20.00
ACC Crystal Clarke	8.00	20.00
ADR Daisy Ridley		
AGC Gwendoline Christie		
AHC Hermione Corfield	20.00	50.00
AJV Jimmy Vee	10.00	25.00
AJB John Boyega	50.00	100.00
AJS Joonas Suotamo		
AKS Kiran Shah	8.00	20.00
ALD Laura Dern		
AMQ Mike Quinn		
ATK Tom Kane		
AVN Veronica Ngo	15.00	40.00

2018 Star Wars The Last Jedi Series Two Autographs Red

*RED: .5X TO 1.2X BASIC AUTOS		
STATED ODDS 1:127		
STATED PRINT RUN 99 SER.#'d SETS		
ALD Laura Dern	75.00	150.00

2018 Star Wars The Last Jedi Series Two Autographs Silver

STATED ODDS 1:350		
STATED PRINT RUN 25 SER.#'d SETS		
NNO Adam Driver	300.00	500.00
AAS Andy Serkis	60.00	120.00
AADC Anthony Daniels	100.00	200.00
AJS Joonas Suotamo	50.00	100.00

2018 Star Wars The Last Jedi Series Two Character Stickers

POE DAMERON

COMPLETE SET (10)	15.00	40.00
COMMON STICKER (CS1-CS10)	1.25	3.00
STATED ODDS 1:16		
CS1 Rey	3.00	8.00
CS2 Kylo Ren	1.50	4.00
CS3 Finn	2.00	5.00
CS4 Poe Dameron	5.00	12.00
CS5 Supreme Leader Snoke	1.50	4.00
CS6 Captain Phasma	2.00	5.00
CS8 General Leia Organa	2.00	5.00
CS10 Luke Skywalker	2.50	6.00

2018 Star Wars The Last Jedi Series Two Commemorative Patches

C'AI THRENALLI

COMMON PATCH	3.00	8.00
STATED ODDS 1:67		
MEC Chewbacca	4.00	10.00
MEAH Vice Admiral Holdo	5.00	12.00
MEBB BB-8	5.00	12.00
MECB Chewbacca	4.00	10.00
MECP Captain Phasma	6.00	15.00
MECT C'ai Threnalli	5.00	12.00
MEDR Rey	6.00	15.00
MEFA Finn	6.00	15.00
MEFB Finn	6.00	15.00
MEGE General Ematt	5.00	12.00

MEJB Finn	6.00	15.00
MEKR Kylo Ren	6.00	15.00
MELO General Leia Organa	8.00	20.00
MELS Luke Skywalker	8.00	20.00
MENG Ensign Pamich Nerro Goode	5.00	12.00
MEPD Poe Dameron	5.00	12.00
MEPG Praetorian Guard	6.00	15.00
MEPT Resistance Gunner Paige Tico	5.00	12.00
MER2 R2-D2	5.00	12.00
MERA Rey	6.00	15.00
MERB Rey	6.00	15.00
MERT Rose Tico	5.00	12.00
MESE Stormtrooper Executioner	4.00	10.00
MEBB8 BB-8	5.00	12.00
MEBBR BB-8	5.00	12.00
MEC3B C-3PO	4.00	10.00
MEC3P C-3PO	4.00	10.00
MECPB Captain Phasma	6.00	15.00
MEGEA General Ematt	5.00	12.00
MEKCA Kaydel Ko Connix	6.00	15.00
MEKKC Kaydel Ko Connix	6.00	15.00
MEKRB Kylo Ren	6.00	15.00
MELOR General Leia Organa	8.00	20.00
MELSB Luke Skywalker	8.00	20.00
MENGA Ensign Pamich Nerro Goode	5.00	12.00
MEPDA Poe Dameron	5.00	12.00
MEPDB Poe Dameron	5.00	12.00
MEPDP Poe Dameron	5.00	12.00
MEPGB Praetorian Guard	6.00	15.00
MER2B R2-D2	5.00	12.00
MER2R R2-D2	5.00	12.00
MESLB Supreme Leader Snoke	5.00	12.00
MESLS Supreme Leader Snoke	5.00	12.00

2018 Star Wars The Last Jedi Series Two Dual Autographs

STATED ODDS 1:7,116		
STATED PRINT RUN 5 SER.#'d SETS		
UNPRICED DUE TO SCARCITY		
DARD D.Ridley/A.Driver		
DARS D.Ridley/A.Serkis		
DASV J.Suotamo/J.Vee		
DAQK M.Quinn/P.Kasey		
DARK T.Rose/T.Kane		

2018 Star Wars The Last Jedi Series Two Items and Artifacts

KYLO REN'S HELMET

COMPLETE SET (20)	10.00	25.00
COMMON CARD (IA1-IA20)	.75	2.00
*RED/99: .5X TO 1.2X BASIC CARDS		
*BRONZE/50: .75X TO 2X BASIC CARDS		
STATED ODDS 1:1		
IA1 Skywalker's Lightsaber	2.00	5.00
IA2 Luke Skywalker's Compass	2.00	5.00
IA4 Proton Bomb	1.25	3.00
IA14 Kylo Ren's Lightsaber	3.00	8.00

2018 Star Wars The Last Jedi Series Two Leaders of the Resistance

NIEN NUNB
THE RESISTANCE

COMPLETE SET (10)	5.00	12.00
COMMON CARD (RS1-RS10)	.75	2.00
*RED/99: .5X TO 1.2X BASIC CARDS		
*BRONZE/50: .75X TO 2X BASIC CARDS		
STATED ODDS 1:2		

2018 Star Wars The Last Jedi Series Two Leaders of the Resistance Autographs

STATED ODDS 1:5,024	
UNPRICED DUE TO SCARCITY	
RS3 Laura Dern	
RS4 Andrew Jack	
RS5 Tim Rose	
RS7 Mike Quinn	
RS8 Paul Kasey	

RS9 Anthony Daniels

RS10 Crystal Clarke

2018 Star Wars The Last Jedi Series Two Patrons of Canto Bight

COMPLETE SET (10)	6.00	15.00
COMMON CARD (CB1-CB10)	1.25	3.00
*RED/99: .5X TO 1.2X BASIC CARDS	1.50	4.00
*BRONZE/50: .75X TO 2X BASIC CARDS	2.50	6.00
STATED ODDS 1:6		

2018 Star Wars The Last Jedi Series Two Patrons of Canto Bight Autographs

COMMON AUTO

STATED ODDS 1:11,386

CB2 Kiran Shah

CB5 Warwick Davis

2018 Star Wars The Last Jedi Series Two Ships and Vehicles

COMPLETE SET (10)	8.00	20.00
COMMON CARD (SV1-SV10)	1.50	4.00
*RED/99: .5X TO 1.2X BASIC CARDS	2.00	5.00
*BRONZE/50: .75X TO 2X BASIC CARDS	3.00	8.00
STATED ODDS 1:8		

2018 Star Wars The Last Jedi Series Two Six-Person Autograph

STATED ODDS 1:85,344

STATED PRINT RUN 3 SER.#'d SETS

UNPRICED DUE TO SCARCITY

NNO Ridley/Boyega/Rose/Daniels/Vee/Suotamo

2018 Star Wars The Last Jedi Series Two Soldiers of the First Order

COMPLETE SET (10)	6.00	15.00
COMMON CARD (FO1-FO10)	1.25	3.00
*RED/99: .5X TO 1.2X BASIC CARDS	1.50	4.00
*BRONZE/50: .75X TO 2X BASIC CARDS	2.50	6.00
STATED ODDS 1:4		

2018 Star Wars The Last Jedi Series Two Soldiers of the First Order Autographs

FO1 Adam Driver

FO2 Gwendoline Christie

FO9 Adrian Edmondson

FO10 Andy Serkis

2018 Star Wars The Last Jedi Series Two Source Material Fabric Swatches

COMMON MEM	20.00	50.00
STATED ODDS 1:360		
STATED PRINT RUN 99 SER.#'d SETS		
MR1 Caretaker's Smock	60.00	120.00
MR3 Praetorian Guard's Ceremonial Battle Skirt	50.00	100.00
MR4 Captain Peavy's First Order Uniform	25.00	60.00

2018 Star Wars The Last Jedi Series Two Teaser Posters

COMPLETE SET (6)	8.00	20.00
COMMON CARD (TP1-TP6)	2.00	5.00
STATED ODDS 1:24		
TP1 Rey	2.50	6.00
TP5 General Leia Organa	2.50	6.00

2018 Star Wars The Last Jedi Series Two Triple Autographs

COMPLETE SET (4)

STATED ODDS 1:14,232

UNPRICED DUE TO SCARCITY

TADRV Daniels/Rose/Vee

TAKKQ Kasey/Kane/Quinn

TALCN Lourd/Clarke/Ngo

TARDB Ridley/Driver/Boyega

2018 Star Wars On-Demand The Last Jedi

COMPLETE SET (20)	15.00	40.00
COMMON CARD (1-20)	1.25	3.00
*PURPLE: .75X TO 2X BASIC CARDS	2.50	6.00

2018 Star Wars On-Demand The Last Jedi Autographs

STATED OVERALL ODDS 1:SET		
1A Daisy Ridley		
4A John Boyega	50.00	100.00
5A Adam Driver		

9A Gwendoline Christie		
11A Billie Lourd		
14AA Dave Chapman	8.00	20.00
14BA Brian Herring	8.00	20.00
15AA Tim Rose	15.00	40.00
15BA Tom Kane	8.00	20.00
16A Jimmy Vee	10.00	25.00
17A Anthony Daniels		
19A Andy Serkis		
21A Andrew Jack	10.00	25.00
22A Paul Kasey	8.00	20.00
23A Mike Quinn	15.00	40.00

SOLO

2018 Countdown to Solo A Star Wars Story

COMPLETE SET (25)	60.00	120.00
COMMON CARD (1-25)	4.00	10.00

2018 Solo A Star Wars Story

COMPLETE SET (100)	8.00	20.00
UNOPENED BOX (24 PACKS)	50.00	60.00
UNOPENED PACK (8 CARDS)	2.50	3.00
COMMON CARD (1-100)	.15	.40
*YELLOW: .6X TO 1.5X BASIC CARDS	.25	.60
*BLACK: .75X TO 2X BASIC CARDS	.30	.75
*SILVER: 1.5X TO 4X BASIC CARDS	.60	1.50
*PINK/99: 6X TO 15X BASIC CARDS	2.50	6.00
*ORANGE/25: 15X TO 40X BASIC CARDS	6.00	15.00

2018 Solo A Star Wars Story Autographs

COMMON AUTO	8.00	20.00
*PINK/99: .5X TO 1.2X BASIC AUTOS		
*ORANGE/25: .6X TO 1.5X BASIC AUTOS		
STATED ODDS 1:33		
AAF Anna Francolini	12.00	30.00
AAJ Andrew Jack	10.00	25.00
AAW Andrew Woodall	12.00	30.00
ADA Derek Arnold	12.00	30.00
ADT Dee Tails	10.00	25.00
AIK Ian Kenny	10.00	25.00

2018 Solo A Star Wars Story Autographs Pink

STATED ODDS 1:231		
STATED PRINT RUN 99 SER.#'d SETS		
AJS Joonas Suotamo	50.00	100.00
AWD Warwick Davis	20.00	50.00
AJSC Joonas Suotamo	50.00	100.00

2018 Solo A Star Wars Story Character Stickers

COMPLETE SET (7)	8.00	20.00
COMMON CARD (CS1-CS7)	2.00	5.00
STATED ODDS 1:12		

2018 Solo A Star Wars Story Dual Autographs

STATED PRINT RUN 10 SER.#'d SETS

UNPRICED DUE TO SCARCITY

DAJA Jack/Arnold

DAJS Jack/Suotamo

DASA Suotamo/Arnold

DASD Suotamo/Davis

2018 Solo A Star Wars Story Icons

COMPLETE SET (7)	5.00	12.00
COMMON CARD (I1-I7)	1.00	2.50
STATED ODDS 1:8		

2018 Solo A Star Wars Story Manufactured Patches

COMMON PATCH	3.00	8.00
*PINK/99: .5X TO 1.2X BASIC PATCHES		
*ORANGE/25: .6X TO 1.5X BASIC PATCHES		
STATED ODDS 1:32		
MPCC Chewbacca	5.00	12.00
MPCH Chewbacca	5.00	12.00
MPHM Han Solo	6.00	15.00
MPIS Imperial Fleet Trooper	4.00	10.00
MPLH L3-37	5.00	12.00
MPLM Lando Calrissian	6.00	15.00
MPME Enfys Nest	5.00	12.00
MPMS Mimban Stormtrooper	6.00	15.00
MPQC Qi'ra	8.00	20.00
MPQH Qi'ra	8.00	20.00
MPRS R5-PHT	4.00	10.00
MPSS Stormtrooper	4.00	10.00
MPTS TIE Fighter Pilot	6.00	15.00
MPENH Enfys Nest	5.00	12.00
MPHSC Han Solo	6.00	15.00
MPHSH Han Solo	6.00	15.00
MPLCH Lando Calrissian	6.00	15.00

2018 Solo A Star Wars Story Ships and Vehicles

COMPLETE SET (9)	4.00	10.00
COMMON CARD (SV1-SV9)	.60	1.50
STATED ODDS 1:4		

2018 Solo A Star Wars Story Silhouettes

COMPLETE SET (11)	6.00	15.00
COMMON CARD (SL1-SL11)	1.00	2.50
STATED ODDS 1:2		

2018 Solo A Star Wars Story Smooth Sayings

COMPLETE SET (8)	8.00	20.00
COMMON CARD (SS1-SS8)	1.50	4.00
STATED ODDS 1:6		
SS8 Double-Crossing No-Good Swindler	1.50	4.00

2018 Solo A Star Wars Story Target Exclusive Manufactured Patches

COMMON PATCH	5.00	12.00
*PINK/99: .5X TO 1.2X BASIC PATCHES	6.00	15.00
*ORANGE/25: .6X TO 1.5X BASIC PATCHES	8.00	20.00
STATED ODDS 1:TARGET BLASTER BOX		

2018 Solo A Star Wars Story Triple Autographs

STATED PRINT RUN 5 SER.#'d SETS

UNPRICED DUE TO SCARCITY

TASDA Suotamo/Davis/Arnold

TASJA Suotamo/Jack/Arnold

2018 Solo A Star Wars Story Promo

P1 Han Solo	4.00	10.00

2018 Solo A Star Wars Story Denny's

COMPLETE SET (12)	20.00	50.00
UNOPENED PACK (2 CARDS+1 COUPON)	3.00	8.00
COMMON CARD (UNNUMBERED)	2.00	5.00
*FOIL: 6X TO 15X BASIC CARDS	30.00	75.00

2018 Solo A Star Wars Story Odeon Cinemas

COMPLETE SET (4)	3.00	8.00
COMMON CARD (UNNUMBERED)	1.00	2.50

THE RISE OF SKYWALKER

2019 Star Wars The Rise of Skywalker Series One

COMPLETE SET (99)	10.00	25.00
UNOPENED BOX (24 PACKS)	60.00	100.00
UNOPENED PACK (8 CARDS)	2.50	4.00
COMMON CARD (1-99)	.20	.50
*RED: .75X TO 2X BASIC CARDS		
*BLUE: 1X TO 2.5X BASIC CARDS		
GREEN: 1.2X TO 3X BASIC CARDS		
*PURPLE: 1.5X TO 4X BASIC CARDS		
*ORANGE/99: 4X TO 10X BASIC CARDS		
*GOLD/25: 6X TO 15X BASIC CARDS		

2019 Star Wars The Rise of Skywalker Series One Autographed Commemorative Medallions

STATED PRINT RUN 10 SER.#'d SETS

UNPRICED DUE TO SCARCITY

MCAD Adam Driver
MCBF John Boyega
MCBH Brian Herring
MCDB Dave Chapman
MCDG Domhnall Gleeson
MCDR Daisy Ridley
MCJS Joonas Suotamo
MCBDW Billy Dee Williams
MCKMT Kelly Marie Tran
MCRC3 Anthony Daniels

2019 Star Wars The Rise of Skywalker Series One Autographs

COMMON AUTO	6.00	15.00
RANDOMLY INSERTED INTO PACKS		
AAH Amanda Hale	10.00	25.00
AAL Amanda Lawrence	8.00	20.00
ABB Brian Herring	6.00	15.00
ADB Dave Chapman	6.00	15.00
ADM Dominic Monaghan	50.00	100.00
AGF Geff Francis	10.00	25.00
AGG Greg Grunberg	12.00	30.00
AJA Josef Altin	10.00	25.00
AVR Vinette Robinson	12.00	30.00
ASPD Simon Paisley	10.00	25.00

2019 Star Wars The Rise of Skywalker Series One Autographs Blue

COMPLETE SET (20)

*BLUE: X TO X BASIC AUTOS

STATED PRINT RUN 99 SER.#'d SETS

AJB John Boyega	25.00	60.00
ANA Naomi Ackie	25.00	60.00

2019 Star Wars The Rise of Skywalker Series One Character Stickers

COMPLETE SET (19)	15.00	40.00
COMMON CARD (CS1-CS19)	1.25	3.00
RANDOMLY INSERTED INTO PACKS		
CS1 Rey	3.00	8.00
CS2 Kylo Ren	2.00	5.00

2019 Star Wars The Rise of Skywalker Series One Commemorative Medallions

KYLO REN

COMMON MEM	4.00	10.00
*PURPLE/99: .5X TO 1.2X BASIC MEM		
*ORANGE/50: .6X TO 1.5X BASIC MEM		
*GOLD/25: .75X TO 2X BASIC MEM		
RANDOMLY INSERTED INTO PACKS		
MCBD D-O	6.00	15.00
MCBF Finn	6.00	15.00
MCBP Poe Dameron	6.00	15.00
MCC3 C-3PO	5.00	12.00
MCCC Chewbacca	5.00	12.00
MCCL Lando Calrissian	6.00	15.00
MCCR R2-D2	5.00	12.00
MCD0 D-O	8.00	20.00
MCDB BB-8	5.00	12.00
MCDR R2-D2	5.00	12.00
MCKY Kylo Ren	8.00	20.00
MCR2 R2-D2	6.00	15.00
MCRP Poe Dameron	5.00	12.00
MCRR Rey	10.00	25.00
MCTK Kylo Ren	6.00	15.00

MCBB8 BB-8	6.00	15.00
MCDC3 C-3PO	6.00	15.00
MCRC3 C-3PO	5.00	12.00

2019 Star Wars The Rise of Skywalker Series One Crush the Resistance

COMPLETE SET (8)	5.00	12.00
COMMON CARD (CR1-CR8)	1.00	2.50
*GREEN/299: .6X TO 1.5X BASIC CARDS		
*PURPLE/199: 1X TO 2.5X BASIC CA		
*RED/149: 1.2X TO 3X BASIC CARDS		
*ORANGE/99: 1.5X TO 4X BASIC CARDS		
*GOLD/25: 2.5X TO 6X BASIC CARDS		
RANDOMLY INSERTED INTO PACKS		

2019 Star Wars The Rise of Skywalker Series One Dual Autographs

UNPRICED DUE TO SCARCITY

NNO A.Driver/D.Gleeson
NNO B.Lourd/G.Grunberg
NNO B.Williams/A.Daniels
NNO B.Williams/N.Ackie
NNO D.Ridley/A.Driver
NNO D.Ridley/J.Boyega
NNO D.Ridley/J.Suotamo
NNO J.Boyega/A.Daniels
NNO J.Boyega/K.Tran
NNO J.Boyega/N.Ackie
NNO J.Suotamo/B.Herring

2019 Star Wars The Rise of Skywalker Series One Illustrated Characters

COMMON CARD (IC1-IC19)	2.00	5.00
*GREEN/299: SAME VALUE AS BASIC		
*PURPLE/199: .5X TO 1.25X BASIC CARDS		
*RED/149: .6X TO 1.5X BASIC CARDS		
*ORANGE/99: 1X TO 2.5X BASIC CARDS		
*GOLD/25: 1.2X TO 3X BASIC CARDS		
RANDOMLY INSERTED INTO PACKS		

TRADING CARDS

2019 Star Wars The Rise of Skywalker Series One
Long Live the Resistance

COMPLETE SET (8)	4.00	10.00
COMMON CARD (RB1-RB8)	.75	2.00

*GREEN/299: .75X TO 2X BASIC CARDS
*PURPLE/199: 1X TO 2.5X BASIC CARDS
*RED/149: 1.2X TO 3X BASIC CARDS
*ORANGE/99: 2X TO 5X BASIC CARDS
*GOLD/25: 3X TO 8X BASIC CARDS
RANDOMLY INSERTED INTO PACKS

2019 Star Wars The Rise of Skywalker Series One
May the Force Be with You

COMPLETE SET (5)	5.00	12.00
COMMON CARD (FWY1-FWY5)	1.50	4.00

*GREEN/299: SAME VALUE AS BASIC
*PURPLE/199: .6X TO 1.5X BASIC CARDS
*RED/149: .75X TO 2X BASIC CARDS
*ORANGE/99: 1X TO 2.5X BASIC CARDS
*GOLD/25: 1.5X TO 4X BASIC CARDS

2019 Star Wars The Rise of Skywalker Series One
Millennium Falcon Relics

UNPRICED DUE TO SCARCITY
STATED PRINT RUN 15 SER.#'d SETS

MFCS Chewbacca
MFFS Finn
MFJS Jannah
MFLS Lando Calrissian
MF3FA C-3PO
MF3NH C-3PO
MFBFA BB-8
MFCHS Chewbacca
MFCNH Chewbacca
MFFFA Finn
MFHFA Han Solo
MFHHS Han Solo
MFLHS L3-37
MFLRJ Lando Calrissian
MFQHS Qi'Ra
MFRFA R2-D2
MFRFA Rey
MFRNH R2-D2
MFTHS Tobias Beckett
MFUFA Unkar Plutt

2019 Star Wars The Rise of Skywalker Series One
Ships and Vehicles

COMPLETE SET (7)	4.00	10.00
COMMON CARD (SV1-SV7)	1.00	2.50

*GREEN/299: .6X TO 1.5X BASIC CARDS
*PURPLE/199: .75X TO 2X BASIC CARDS
*RED/149: X TO X BASIC CARDS
*ORANGE/99: 1.2X TO 3X BASIC CARDS

2019 Star Wars The Rise of Skywalker Series One
Six-Person Autographs

NNO Ridley/Boyega/Tran/Williams/Daniels/Lourd
NNO Ridley/Boyega/Tran/Williams/Daniels/Suotamo

2019 Star Wars The Rise of Skywalker Series One
Triple Autographs

UNPRICED DUE TO SCARCITY

NNO Daniels/Suotamo/Herring
NNO Ridley/Driver/Boyega
NNO Ridley/Williams/Boyega
NNO Ridley/Boyega/Tran
NNO Ridley/Tran/Lourd
NNO Boyega/Grunberg/Chapman
NNO Boyega/Tran/Lourd
NNO Tran/Lourd/Grunberg

2019 Star Wars The Rise of Skywalker Series One
CineWorld UK Promos

COMPLETE SET (2)	2.00	5.00
COMMON CARD	1.25	3.00
CWD Be a Hero (Droids)	1.25	3.00
CWK Darkness Rises (Kylo Ren)	1.25	3.00

2020 Star Wars The Rise of Skywalker Series Two

COMPLETE SET (100)	6.00	15.00
UNOPENED BOX (24 PACKS)	100.00	150.00
UNOPENED PACK (8 CARDS)	4.00	6.00
COMMON CARD (1-100)	.12	.30

*BLUE: 1X TO 2.5X BASIC CARDS
*PURPLE: 2X TO 5X BASIC CARDS
*RED/199: 10X TO 25X BASIC CARDS
*BRONZE/99: 12X TO 30X BASIC CARDS
*SILVER/25: 20X TO 50X BASIC CARDS

2020 Star Wars The Rise of Skywalker Series Two
Autographed Commemorative Vehicle Medallions

UNPRICED DUE TO SCARCITY
RANDOMLY INSERTED INTO PACKS

MVMABF Brian Herring
MVMAFF John Boyega
MVMAJF Naomi Ackie
MVMAKF Billie Lourd
MVMAKT Adam Driver
MVMALF Billy Dee Williams
MVMARF Daisy Ridley
MVMASX Greg Grunberg
MVMABKF Dominic Monaghan

2020 Star Wars The Rise of Skywalker Series Two
Autographs

RANDOMLY INSERTED INTO PACKS

AAC	Aidan Cook	6.00	15.00
AAD	Adam Driver		
AAL	Amanda Lawrence	5.00	12.00
ABH	Brian Herring	10.00	25.00
ABL	Billie Lourd		
ADB	Dave Chapman	10.00	25.00
ADG	Domhnall Gleeson		
ADM	Dominic Monaghan		
ADR	Daisy Ridley		
ADW	Debra Wilson	6.00	15.00
AGF	Geff Francis	6.00	15.00
AGG	Greg Grunberg		
AJB	John Boyega		
AJS	Joonas Suotamo		
AKS	Kiran Shah	10.00	25.00
AMQ	Mike Quinn	8.00	20.00
AMW	Matthew Wood	6.00	15.00
ANA	Naomi Ackie		
ANK	Nick Kellington	8.00	20.00
APK	Paul Kasey	6.00	15.00
ATW	Tom Wilton	5.00	12.00
AWD	Warwick Davis		
ABDW	Billy Dee Williams		

TRADING CARDS

AKMT Kelly Marie Tran		
AKRN Kipsang Rotich	8.00	20.00
ASPD Simon Paisley Day	5.00	12.00

2020 Star Wars The Rise of Skywalker Series Two
Character Posters

COMPLETE SET (6)	12.00	30.00
COMMON CARD (TP1-TP6)	2.50	6.00
RANDOMLY INSERTED INTO PACKS		
TP1 Rey	4.00	10.00
TP2 Finn	2.50	6.00
TP3 Poe Dameron	2.50	6.00
TP4 Lando Calrissian	2.50	6.00
TP5 Chewbacca	2.50	6.00
TP6 Kylo Ren	3.00	8.00

2020 Star Wars The Rise of Skywalker Series Two
Commemorative Vehicle Medallions

*SILVER/50: .6X TO 1.5X BASIC MEM
RANDOMLY INSERTED INTO PACKS

MVMCF C-3PO	6.00	15.00
MVMCX C'ai Threnalli	6.00	15.00
MVMFF Finn	5.00	12.00
MVMJF Jannah	8.00	20.00
MVMKF Kaydel Ko Connix		20.00
MVMKT Kylo Ren	6.00	15.00
MVMLF Lando Calrissian	5.00	12.00
MVMPF Poe Dameron	6.00	15.00
MVMPX Poe Dameron	6.00	15.00
MVMRF Rey	15.00	40.00
MVMRX R2-D2	5.00	12.00
MVMWX Wedge Antilles	6.00	15.00

MVMBKF Beaumont Kin	5.00	12.00
MVMRDF R2-D2	6.00	15.00

2020 Star Wars The Rise of Skywalker Series Two
Costume Relics

RANDOMLY INSERTED INTO PACKS

CRAT Allegiant General Pryde/Tunic	30.00	75.00
CRFT Finn/Trousers	25.00	60.00
CRFW Finn/Waistcoat Lining	25.00	60.00
CRKC Kylo Ren/Cloak Hood Lining		
CRKU Kylo Ren/Undershirt		
CRLC Lando Calrissian/Cloak Lining	60.00	120.00
CRLS Lando Calrissian/Shirt	25.00	60.00
CRPT Poe Dameron/Trousers		
CRRH Rey/Hood		
CRRT Rey/Trousers		
CRZJ Zorii Bliss/Jumpsuit Sleeve		

2020 Star Wars The Rise of Skywalker Series Two
Dual Autographs

UNPRICED DUE TO SCARCITY
RANDOMLY INSERTED INTO PACKS

DAAD A.Driver/D.Gleeson
DAAJ A.Driver/J.Boyega
DAAV A.Lawrence/V.Robinson
DABG B.Lourd/G.Grunberg
DABN B.Williams/N.Ackie
DADA D.Ridley/A.Driver
DADJ D.Ridley/J.Boyega
DADK D.Ridley/K.Tran
DAGA G.Francis/A.Hale
DAGN G.Grunberg/N.Kellington
DAGS G.Francis/S.Day
DAJB J.Suotamo/B.Herring
DAJK J.Boyega/K.Tran
DAJN J.Boyega/N.Ackie
DAMP M.Quinn/P.Kasey
DASA S.Day/A.Hale
DAVJ V.Robinson/J.Altin

2020 Star Wars The Rise of Skywalker Series Two
Foil Puzzle

COMPLETE SET (9)	30.00	75.00
COMMON CARD (1-9)	5.00	12.00
RANDOMLY INSERTED INTO PACKS		

2020 Star Wars The Rise of Skywalker Series Two
Heroes of the Resistance

COMPLETE SET (11)	6.00	15.00
COMMON CARD (HR1-HR11)	1.00	2.50
*RED/99: .75X TO 2X BASIC CARDS		
*BRONZE/50: 1.2X TO 3X BASIC CARDS		
RANDOMLY INSERTED INTO PACKS		
HR1 Rey	4.00	10.00

2020 Star Wars The Rise of Skywalker Series Two
Heroes of the Resistance Autographs

UNPRICED DUE TO SCARCITY
RANDOMLY INSERTED INTO PACKS

HR1 Daisy Ridley
HR2 John Boyega
HR5 Naomi Ackie
HR8 Joonas Suotamo
HR10 Kelly Marie Tran

2020 Star Wars The Rise of Skywalker Series Two Image Variation Autographs

RANDOMLY INSERTED INTO PACKS

AAD2 Adam Driver		
ADG2 Domhnall Gleeson		
ADR2 Daisy Ridley		
AJB2 John Boyega		
ANA2 Naomi Ackie	25.00	60.00
ABDW2 Billy Dee Williams		

2020 Star Wars The Rise of Skywalker Series Two Millennium Falcon Relics

UNPRICED DUE TO SCARCITY

STATED PRINT RUN 15 SER.#'d SETS

MFE Chewbacca

MF2E R2-D2

MF2J R2-D2

MF2L R2-D2

MF2R R2-D2

MF3E C-3PO

MF3J C-3PO

MF3R C-3PO

MFCJ Chewbacca

MFCL Chewbacca

MFDL Poe Dameron

MFFL Finn

MFHE Han Solo

MFHJ Han Solo

MFLE Lando Calrissian

MFLJ Lando Calrissian

MFNJ Nien Nunb

MFPE Princess Leia Organa

MFPJ Princess Leia Organa

MFPL Porg

MFRJ Rey

MFRR Rey

MFSE Luke Skywalker

MFSJ Luke Skywalker

MFSL Luke Skywalker

2020 Star Wars The Rise of Skywalker Series Two Six-Person Autograph

SAAG Ridley/Boyega/Tran

Williams/Lourd/Monaghan

2020 Star Wars The Rise of Skywalker Series Two The Knights of Ren

COMPLETE SET (10)	5.00	12.00
COMMON CARD (KR1-KR10)	.75	2.00
*RED/99: .75X TO 2X BASIC CARDS		
*BRONZE/50: 1.2X TO 3X BASIC CARDS		
RANDOMLY INSERTED INTO PACKS		

2020 Star Wars The Rise of Skywalker Series Two Triple Autographs

UNPRICED DUE TO SCARCITY

RANDOMLY INSERTED INTO PACKS

TADAJ Ridley/Driver/Boyega

TADBJ Ridley/Williams/Boyega

TADJJ Ridley/Suotamo/Boyega

TADJK Ridley/Boyega/Tran

TADKB Ridley/Tran/Lourd

TAGPV Grunberg/Kasey/Robinson

TAKBG Tran/Lourd/Grunberg

2020 Star Wars The Rise of Skywalker Series Two Villains of the First Order

GENERAL HUX

2020 Star Wars The Rise of Skywalker Series Two

COMPLETE SET (9)		
COMMON CARD (VF1-VF9)	1.00	2.50
*RED/99: .6X TO 1.5X BASIC CARDS		
*BRONZE/50: 1X TO 2.5X BASIC CARDS		
RANDOMLY INSERTED INTO PACKS		
VF1 Kylo Ren	1.50	4.00

2020 Star Wars The Rise of Skywalker Series Two Villains of the First Order Autographs

UNPRICED DUE TO SCARCITY

RANDOMLY INSERTED INTO PACKS

VF1 Adam Driver

VF2 Domhnall Gleeson

VF6 Simon Paisley Day

VF7 Geff Francis

VF8 Amanda Hale

2020 Star Wars The Rise of Skywalker Series Two Weapons

COMPLETE SET (10)	5.00	12.00
COMMON CARD (W1-W10)	.75	2.00
*RED/99: .75X TO 2X BASIC CARDS		
*BRONZE/50: 1X TO 2.5X BASIC CARDS		
RANDOMLY INSERTED INTO PACKS		
W1 Skywalker Lightsaber	2.00	5.00

2019 Star Wars The Rise of Skywalker Trailer

COMPLETE SET (20)		
COMPLETE SET 1 (1-10)	10.00	25.00
COMPLETE SET 2 (11-20)		
COMMON CARD (1-10)	1.50	4.00
COMMON CARD (11-20)		
TOPPS ONLINE EXCLUSIVE		

STAR WARS GALAXY

2009 Art of Star Wars Comics Postcards

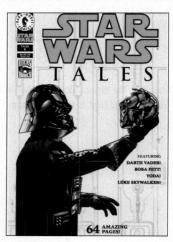

COMPLETE SET (100)	12.00	30.00
COMMON CARD (1-100)	.25	.60

2014 Disney Store Star Wars North America

COMPLETE SET (9)	10.00	25.00
COMMON CARD (1-10)	.75	2.00
US/CANADA EXCLUSIVE		
1 Luke Skywalker	2.00	5.00
4 Darth Vader	2.00	5.00
7 Princess Leia	2.00	5.00
9 Han Solo	2.00	5.00

2014 Disney Store Star Wars United Kingdom

COMPLETE SET (12)	15.00	.40.00
COMMON CARD (1-12)	1.00	2.50
UK EXCLUSIVE		
1 Chewbacca	1.25	3.00
2 Darth Vader	4.00	10.00
4 Han Solo	4.00	10.00
6 Luke Skywalker	3.00	8.00
8 Obi-Wan Kenobi	1.25	3.00
9 Princess Leia Organa	3.00	8.00
10 R2-D2 and C-3PO	1.25	3.00
11 Stormtrooper	1.25	3.00

2008 Family Guy Episode IV A New Hope

COMPLETE SET (50)	5.00	12.00
UNOPENED BOX (36 PACKS)		
UNOPENED PACK (6 CARDS)		
COMMON CARD (1-50)	.15	.40
CL1 ISSUED AS CASE EXCLUSIVE		
CL1 Evil Empire CI	12.00	25.00

2008 Family Guy Episode IV A New Hope Droid Chat

COMPLETE SET (3)	5.00	12.00
COMMON CARD (DC1-DC3)	2.00	5.00
STATED ODDS 1:23		

2008 Family Guy Episode IV A New Hope Promos

P1 Left half w/Han	1.00	2.50
Pi Right half w/Leia	1.00	2.50

2008 Family Guy Episode IV A New Hope Puzzle

COMPLETE SET (9)	4.00	10.00
COMMON CARD (NH1-NH9)	.75	2.00
STATED ODDS 1:7		

2008 Family Guy Episode IV A New Hope Scenes from Space

COMPLETE SET (6)	4.00	10.00
COMMON CARD (S1-S6)	1.25	3.00
STATED ODDS 1:11		

2008 Family Guy Episode IV A New Hope Spaceships and Transports

COMPLETE SET (9)	4.00	10.00
COMMON CARD (ST1-ST9)	1.00	2.50
STATED ODDS 1:9		

2008 Family Guy Episode IV A New Hope What Happens Next?

COMPLETE SET (6)	4.00	10.00
COMMON CARD (WN1-WN6)	1.25	3.00
STATED ODDS 1:11		

2017 Funko Pop Buttons Star Wars

NNO Boba Fett	2.00	5.00
NNO C-3PO	2.00	5.00
NNO Chewbacca	2.00	5.00
NNO Darth Maul	2.00	5.00
NNO Darth Vader	4.00	10.00
NNO Ewok (Wicket)	2.00	5.00
NNO Greedo	2.00	5.00
NNO Han Solo HT		
NNO Jabba	2.00	5.00
NNO Jabba (vaping) HT		
NNO Luke Skywalker HT		
NNO Luke/Han/Leia	2.00	5.00
NNO Princess Leia	6.00	15.00
NNO R2-D2	2.00	5.00
NNO Stormtroopers	2.00	5.00

2017 Funko Pop Buttons Star Wars The Force Awakens

COMPLETE SET (12)		
COMMON CARD (UNNUMBERED)		
NNO BB-8	2.00	5.00
NNO BB-8 (explosion)	2.00	5.00
NNO Captain Phasma	2.00	5.00
NNO Finn	2.00	5.00
NNO First Order Snowtrooper	2.00	5.00
NNO First Order Stormtrooper	2.00	5.00
NNO First Order Stormtrooper (w/riot gear)	2.00	5.00
NNO Kylo Ren	2.00	5.00
NNO Kylo Ren (Force push)	2.00	5.00
NNO Poe Dameron	2.00	5.00
NNO Poe Dameron (X-Wing pilot)	2.00	5.00
NNO Rey	2.00	5.00

2017 Funko Pop Flair Star Wars

NNO Chewbacca	1.50	4.00
NNO Darth Vader	2.50	6.00
NNO Greedo	1.25	3.00
NNO Han Solo	2.50	6.00
NNO Princess Leia	1.50	4.00
NNO Stormtrooper	1.25	3.00
NNO Yoda	1.50	4.00

2015-17 Funko Star Wars Smuggler's Bounty Patches

COMMON PATCH	2.00	5.00
SMUGGLER'S BOUNTY EXCLUSIVE		
NNO BB-8	2.50	6.00
NNO Darth Vader	2.50	6.00

2015 Star Wars Original Trilogy Series Bikkuriman Stickers

COMPLETE SET (24)	30.00	80.00
COMMON CARD	2.00	5.00

2015 Star Wars Prequel Trilogy Series Bikkuriman Stickers

COMPLETE SET (24)	25.00	60.00
COMMON CARD	1.25	3.00

1996 Star Wars 3-Di Widevision

COMPLETE SET (63)	30.00	60.00
COMMON CARD (1-63)	.60	1.50
1M STATED ODDS 1:24		
1M Death Star Explosion	6.00	15.00

1996 Star Wars 3-Di Widevision Promos

3Di1 Darth Vader	2.50	6.00
3Di2 Luke Skywalker	12.00	30.00
Darth Vader/1000*		

2015 Star Wars Abrams Promos

COMPLETE SET (4)	10.00	25.00
COMMON CARD (1-4)	3.00	8.00
STATED ODDS 1:SET PER BOOK		

1997 Star Wars Adventure Journal

NNO One of a Kind by Doug Shuler
NNO To Fight Another Day by Mike Vilardi
NNO Mist Encounter by Doug Shuler

2022 Star Wars Andor Trailer Set

COMPLETE SET (5)	15.00	40.00
COMMON CARD (1-5)	4.00	10.00
*BLUE/49: 1.2X TO 3X BASIC CARDS		
STATED PRINT RUN 1,075 ANNCD SETS		

2018 Star Wars Archives Signature Series Adam Driver

61 Adam Driver 2016 TFA Chrome/2
62 Adam Driver 2016 TFA Chrome/2
65 Adam Driver 2016 TFA Chrome/2
66 Adam Driver 2016 TFA Chrome/1
92 Adam Driver 2016 Evolution/4
P1 Adam Driver 2015 Journey TFA Patches/1

2018 Star Wars Archives Signature Series Adrian Edmonson

52 Adrian Edmonson 2017 TLJ S1/86
52 Adrian Edmonson 2017 TLJ S1 Red/1
52 Adrian Edmonson 2017 TLJ S1 Purple/35
52 Adrian Edmonson 2017 TLJ S1 Green/50
52 Adrian Edmonson 2017 TLJ S1 Blue/65

2018 Star Wars Archives Signature Series Aidan Cook

16 Aidan Cook 2015 TFA S1/9
44 Aidan Cook 2015 TFA S1/9
44 Aidan Cook 2015 TFA S1 Green/2
64 Aidan Cook 2016 Rogue One S1 Blue/4
64 Aidan Cook 2016 Rogue One S1/28

2018 Star Wars Archives Signature Series Al Lampert

10 Al Lampert 1977 SW/4
468 Al Lampert 2013 GF2 Blue/56

2018 Star Wars Archives Signature Series Alan Harris

13 Alan Harris 2001 Evolution/31
31 Alan Harris 2016 Card Trader/28
31 Alan Harris 2016 Card Trader Blue/7
53 Alan Harris 2015 Journey TFA/51
53 Alan Harris 2015 Journey TFA Green/7
73 Alan Harris 1980 ESB/8
74 Alan Harris 1980 ESB/18
B2 Alan Harris 2016 Card Trader Bounty/6
TC6 Alan Harris 2016 Card Trader Choice/17
ESB4 Alan Harris 2017 GF Reborn/35

2018 Star Wars Archives Signature Series Alan Ruscoe

60 Alan Ruscoe 2001 Evolution/35
82 Alan Ruscoe 2012 Galactic Files/35
8J Alan Ruscoe 2015 Chrome JvS/40
8S Alan Ruscoe 2015 Chrome JvS Refractors/13
8S Alan Ruscoe 2015 Chrome JvS/54
426 Alan Ruscoe 2013 GF2/42
TPM21 Alan Ruscoe 2017 GF Reborn/27

2018 Star Wars Archives Signature Series Alan Tudyk

18 Alan Tudyk 2017 Rogue One S2 Black/2
19 Alan Tudyk 2017 Rogue One S2/21
29 Alan Tudyk 2017 Rogue One S2/20
51 Alan Tudyk 2017 Rogue One S2/16
56 Alan Tudyk 2017 Rogue One S2/20
57 Alan Tudyk 2017 Rogue One S2/10
71 Alan Tudyk 2017 Rogue One S2/20
76 Alan Tudyk 2017 Rogue One S2/20
C18 Alan Tudyk 2016 Rogue One S1 Icons/13
HR3 Alan Tudyk 2016 Rogue One S1 Heroes/5
HR4 Alan Tudyk 2017 Rogue One S2 Heroes/4
MP2 Alan Tudyk 2016 Rogue One MB Patches/7
PF7 Alan Tudyk 2017 Rogue One S2 PF/15

2018 Star Wars Archives Signature Series Alistaire Petrie

10 Alistaire Petrie 2016 Rogue One S1 Green/16
10 Alistaire Petrie 2016 Rogue One S1 Black/19
10 Alistaire Petrie 2016 Rogue One S1/77

2018 Star Wars Archives Signature Series Amanda Lawrence

47 Amanda Lawrence 2017 TLJ S1 Purple/35
47 Amanda Lawrence 2017 TLJ S1 Green/50
47 Amanda Lawrence 2017 TLJ S1 Blue/65
47 Amanda Lawrence 2017 TLJ S1/85

2018 Star Wars Archives Signature Series Amy Allen

81 Amy Allen 2012 Galactic Files/14
424 Amy Allen 2013 GF2/22
AOTC18 Amy Allen 2017 GF Reborn Orange/2
AOTC18 Amy Allen 2017 GF Reborn/37

2018 Star Wars Archives Signature Series Andrew Jack

12 Andrew Jack 2016 TFA S2 Heroes/2
17 Andrew Jack 2015 TFA S1 Blue/1
31 Andrew Jack 2017 TLJ S1 Purple/35
31 Andrew Jack 2017 TLJ S1 Green/50
31 Andrew Jack 2017 TLJ S1 Blue/66
31 Andrew Jack 2017 TLJ S1/85
49 Andrew Jack 2016 Card Trader Blue/8
49 Andrew Jack 2016 Card Trader/22
TFA21 Andrew Jack 2017 GF Reborn/22

2018 Star Wars Archives Signature Series Andy Secombe

NNO Andy Secombe

2018 Star Wars Archives Signature Series Andy Serkis

1 Andy Serkis 2016 TFA Chrome Power of FO/11
10 Andy Serkis 2017 Journey TLJ/1
14 Andy Serkis 2017 Journey TLJ Characters/4
25 Andy Serkis 2017 TLJ S1/5
26 Andy Serkis 2016 Card Trader/26
30 Andy Serkis 2017 GF Reborn TFA10/30
60 Andy Serkis 2016 Card Trader Red/2
60 Andy Serkis 2016 Card Trader Blue/5
75 Andy Serkis 2016 TFA S2 Blue/4
75 Andy Serkis 2016 TFA S2 Green/5
75 Andy Serkis 2016 TFA Chrome Refractors/15
75 Andy Serkis 2016 TFA S2/16

2018 Star Wars Archives Signature Series Angus MacInnes

92 Angus MacInnes 2016 Rogue One MB Blue/1
92 Angus MacInnes 2016 Rogue One MB/47
476 Angus MacInnes 2013 GF 2/33
ANH28 Angus MacInnes 2017 GF Reborn/24

2018 Star Wars Archives Signature Series Anthony Forest

31 Anthony Forest 2016 Rogue One MB/36
94 Anthony Forest 1977 Star Wars/7
138 Anthony Forest 1977 Star Wars/9
223 Anthony Forest 2012 Galactic Files/45
WM1 Anthony Forest 2013 GF 2/17

2018 Star Wars Archives Signature Series Ashley Eckstein

AHSOKA TANO
STAR WARS REBELS

7 Ashley Eckstein 2010 CW ROTBH/3
8 Ashley Eckstein 2017 Journey TLJ Red/1
8 Ashley Eckstein 2017 Journey TLJ Green/1
8 Ashley Eckstein 2017 Journey TLJ/6
10 Ashley Eckstein 2016 Evolution/59
11 Ashley Eckstein 2016 Evolution/39
12 Ashley Eckstein 2016 Evolution/36
36 Ashley Eckstein 2008 CW/9
42 Ashley Eckstein 2010 CW ROTBH/5
44 Ashley Eckstein 2010 CW ROTBH/5
62 Ashley Eckstein 2017 Journey TLJ/9
70 Ashley Eckstein 2008 CW/6
82 Ashley Eckstein 2008 CW/15
88 Ashley Eckstein 2010 CW ROTBH/5
98 Ashley Eckstein 2016 Card Trader/30
I4 Ashley Eckstein 2013 Jedi Legacy Influencers/24
13J Ashley Eckstein 2015 Chrome JvS Refractors/16
13J Ashley Eckstein 2015 Chrome JvS/55
13S Ashley Eckstein 2015 Chrome JvS/56
231 Ashley Eckstein 2012 Galactic Files/12
ACW1 Ashley Eckstein 2017 GF Reborn/34

2018 Star Wars Archives Signature Series Ben Daniels

9 Ben Daniels 2016 Rogue One S1 Black/18
9 Ben Daniels 2016 Rogue One S1/72
9 Ben Daniels 2016 Rogue One S1 Green/15
49 Ben Daniels 2016 Rogue One S1 Blue/8
49 Ben Daniels 2016 Rogue One S1 Green/9
49 Ben Daniels 2016 Rogue One S1/37
63 Ben Daniels 2017 Rogue One S2/10

2018 Star Wars Archives Signature Series Ben Mendelsohn

5 Ben Mendelsohn 2016 Rogue One MB Patches/6
13 Ben Mendelsohn 2016 Rogue One S1 Blue/8
13 Ben Mendelsohn 2016 Rogue One S1 Black/9
13 Ben Mendelsohn 2016 Rogue One S1/38
37 Ben Mendelsohn 2017 Rogue One S2 Blue/1
37 Ben Mendelsohn 2017 Rogue One S2/11

52 Ben Mendelsohn 2016 Rogue One S1 Blue/7
52 Ben Mendelsohn 2016 Rogue One S1 Black/10
52 Ben Mendelsohn 2016 Rogue One S1/36
66 Ben Mendelsohn 2016 Rogue One S1 Green/8
66 Ben Mendelsohn 2016 Rogue One S1 Gray/8
66 Ben Mendelsohn 2016 Rogue One S1/37
83 Ben Mendelsohn 2016 Rogue One S1 Black/7
83 Ben Mendelsohn 2016 Rogue One S1 Green/8
83 Ben Mendelsohn 2016 Rogue One S1 Blue/8
83 Ben Mendelsohn 2016 Rogue One S1/39
CI2 Ben Mendelsohn 2016 Rogue One S1 Characters/14
RO6 Ben Mendelsohn 2017 GF Reborn/23
VE3 Ben Mendelsohn 2016 Rogue One S1 Villains/6

2018 Star Wars Archives Signature Series Billy Dee Williams

8 Billy Dee Williams 1980 ESB/9
64 Billy Dee Williams 2016 Evolution/1
189 Billy Dee Williams 1980 ESB/2
198 Billy Dee Williams 1980 ESB/2
IL4 Billy Dee Williams 2013 Jedi Legacy Influencers I14/7
ESB3 Billy Dee Williams 2017 GF Reborn/1

2018 Star Wars Archives Signature Series Brian Herring

6 Brian Herring 2015 TFA S1/3
6 Brian Herring 2015 TFA S1 Blue/3
7 Brian Herring 2017 40th Ann./3
10 Brian Herring 2016 TFA Chrome Refractors/1
16 Brian Herring 2016 TFA S2 Heroes/6
26 Brian Herring 2016 TFA S2/8
27 Brian Herring 2016 TFA Chrome Refractors/1
27 Brian Herring 2016 TFA S2 Green/1
28 Brian Herring 2016 TFA S2/1
28 Brian Herring 2016 TFA S2 Green/2
30 Brian Herring 2016 TFA Chrome Wave Ref./1
48 Brian Herring 2016 Card Trader/8
78 Brian Herring 2015 TFA S1 Green/1
78 Brian Herring 2015 TFA S1 Blue/1
78 Brian Herring 2015 TFA S1/3
81 Brian Herring 2015 TFA S1 Purple/1
81 Brian Herring 2015 TFA S1/11
82 Brian Herring 2015 TFA S1/5
82 Brian Herring 2015 Journey TFA Green/10
82 Brian Herring 2015 Journey TFA/19
97 Brian Herring 2016 Journey TLJ Green/1
104 Brian Herring 2015 Journey TFA Pink/1
104 Brian Herring 2015 Journey TFA Green/7
104 Brian Herring 2015 Journey TFA/20
TFA4 Brian Herring 2017 GF Reborn/10

2018 Star Wars Archives Signature Series Caroline Blakiston

9 Caroline Blakiston 2016 Rogue One MB Heroes/6
30 Caroline Blakiston 2016 Card Trader Red/2
30 Caroline Blakiston 2016 Card Trader Blue/4

30 Caroline Blakiston 2016 Card Trader/25
63 Caroline Blakiston 1983 ROTJ/11
64 Caroline Blakiston 1983 ROTJ/38
85 Caroline Blakiston 2016 Evolution/47
174 Caroline Blakiston 2012 Galactic Files/14
B15 Caroline Blakiston 2016 Card Trader Bounty/5
ROTJ8 Caroline Blakiston 2017 GF Reborn/25

2018 Star Wars Archives Signature Series Cathy Munroe

37 Cathy Munroe 2016 Card Trader/29
37 Cathy Munroe 2016 Card Trader Blue/3
89 Cathy Munroe 2001 Evolution/33
B8 Cathy Munroe 2016 Card Trader Bounty/5
ESB6 Cathy Munroe 2017 GF Reborn Orange/3
ESB6 Cathy Munroe 2017 GF Reborn/25

2018 Star Wars Archives Signature Series Chris Parsons

1 Chris Parsons 2001 Evolution/34
38 Chris Parsons 2016 Card Trader Blue/8
38 Chris Parsons 2016 Card Trader/28
53 Chris Parsons 2015 Journey TLA/13
B7 Chris Parsons 2016 Card Trader Bounty/6
136 Chris Parsons 2012 Galactic Files/38
ESB5 Chris Parsons 2017 GF Reborn/24

2018 Star Wars Archives Signature Series Corey Dee Williams

40 Corey Dee Williams 2001 Star Wars Evolution/34

2018 Star Wars Archives Signature Series Daisy Ridley

23 Daisy Ridley 2016 TFA S2/1
P6 Daisy Ridley 2015 Journey TFA Patches/1
R1 Daisy Ridley 2015 Journey TFA Heroes/1
P15 Daisy Ridley 2015 Journey TFA Patches/1

2018 Star Wars Archives Signature Series Daniel Logan

41 Daniel Logan 2012 Galactic Files/21
51 Daniel Logan 2016 Evolution Blue/4
51 Daniel Logan 2016 Evolution/48
78 Daniel Logan 2010 CW ROTBH/3
83 Daniel Logan 2010 CW ROTBH/4
408 Daniel Logan 2013 GF2/38
ACW7 Daniel Logan 2017 GF Reborn/24
AOTC5 Daniel Logan 2017 GF Reborn/28

2018 Star Wars Archives Signature Series Dave Chapman

6 Dave Chapman 2015 TFA S1/20
6 Dave Chapman 2015 TFA S1 Blue/3
9 Dave Chapman 2016 TFA Chrome Heroes/10
16 Dave Chapman 2016 TFA S2 Heroes/4
19 Dave Chapman 2015 TFA S1 Movie Scenes/6
26 Dave Chapman 2016 TFA Chrome Refractors/3
26 Dave Chapman 2016 TFA S2/16

27 Dave Chapman 2016 TFA S2 Blue/1

28 Dave Chapman 2016 TFA Chrome Refractors/1

28 Dave Chapman 2016 TFA S2/5

30 Dave Chapman 2016 TFA S2/4

30 Dave Chapman 2016 TFA Chrome/7

39 Dave Chapman 2016 TFA Chrome/9

39 Dave Chapman 2016 TFA S2/14

40 Dave Chapman 2016 TFA Chrome/3

48 Dave Chapman 2016 Card Trader Blue/4

48 Dave Chapman 2016 Card Trader/16

49 Dave Chapman 2016 TFA S2/3

49 Dave Chapman 2016 TFA Chrome/5

63 Dave Chapman 2016 TFA S2 Green/3

63 Dave Chapman 2016 TFA S2 Blue/3

63 Dave Chapman 2016 TFA S2/7

63 Dave Chapman 2016 TFA Chrome/23

73 Dave Chapman 2016 TFA S2 Blue/3

73 Dave Chapman 2016 TFA Chrome/7

73 Dave Chapman 2016 TFA S2/14

76 Dave Chapman 2015 TFA S1/25

77 Dave Chapman 2015 TFA S1/12

78 Dave Chapman 2015 TFA S1/6

79 Dave Chapman 2015 TFA S1/7

80 Dave Chapman 2015 TFA S1/6

81 Dave Chapman 2015 TFA S1 Green/3

81 Dave Chapman 2015 TFA S1/23

82 Dave Chapman 2015 Journey TFA Black/3

82 Dave Chapman 2015 Journey TFA/48

83 Dave Chapman 2015 TFA S1/5

97 Dave Chapman 2017 Journey TLJ/1

R4 Dave Chapman 2015 Journey TFA Heroes/7

104 Dave Chapman 2015 Journey TFA Black/3

104 Dave Chapman 2015 Journey to TFA Green/20

104 Dave Chapman 2015 Journey TFA/48

P18 Dave Chapman 2015 Journey TFA Patches/3

TFA4 Dave Chapman 2017 GF Reborn/16

2018 Star Wars Archives Signature Series David Acord

7 David Acord 2016 TFA S2 Maz's Castle/2

8 David Acord 2015 TFA S1/13

11 David Acord 2015 TFA S1/10

20 David Acord 2015 TFA S1 Blue/11

20 David Acord 2015 TFA S1 Green/11

20 David Acord 2015 TFA S1/28

25 David Acord 2016 TFA Chrome/4

29 David Acord 2015 TFA S1/26

43 David Acord 2016 TFA Chrome/4

52 David Acord 2016 TFA Chrome Refractors/2

52 David Acord 2015 TFA S1/6

58 David Acord 2016 Card Trader/23

61 David Acord 2016 Card Trader/23

68 David Acord 2016 TFA S2 Blue/5

68 David Acord 2016 TFA S2 Green/10

68 David Acord 2016 TFA S2/25

68 David Acord 2016 TFA Chrome Refractors/30

68 David Acord 2016 TFA Chrome/38

75 David Acord 2015 TFA S1/11

TFA29 David Acord 2017 GF Reborn/22

2018 Star Wars Archives Signature Series David Ankrum

19 David Ankrum 2016 Card Trader/13

88 David Ankrum 2016 Rogue One MB/16

88 David Ankrum 2016 Rogue One MB Black/1

9R David Ankrum 2014 Chrome 9R/11

118 David Ankrum 2012 Galactic Files/14

145 David Ankrum 2012 Galactic Files/13

175 David Ankrum 2012 Galactic Files/15

I12 David Ankrum 2013 Jedi Legacy Influencers/19

ANH23 David Ankrum 2017 GF Reborn/21

2018 Star Wars Archives Signature Series David Barclay

3 David Barclay 2017 40th Ann. Green/1

9 David Barclay 1980 ESB/10

9 David Barclay 2016 Card Trader/10

10 David Barclay 2016 Card Trader Blue/5

10 David Barclay 2016 Card Trader/19

13 David Barclay 1983 ROTJ/5

14 David Barclay 1983 ROTJ/18

15 David Barclay 1983 ROTJ/7

21 David Barclay 2012 Galactic Files/1

28 David Barclay 2017 40th Ann. Green/1

36 David Barclay 2001 Evolution/11

41 David Barclay 1999 Chrome Archives/1

46 David Barclay 1983 ROTJ/8

49 David Barclay 2015 Journey TFA Green/2

49 David Barclay 2015 Journey TFA/2

58 David Barclay 1980 ESB/7

63 David Barclay 1980 ESB/5

63 David Barclay Journey TFA/22

80 David Barclay 2015 Journey TFA Green/1

82 David Barclay 2016 Evolution/20

83 David Barclay 2016 Evolution Blue/19

83 David Barclay 2016 Evolution/19

163 David Barclay 2012 Galactic Files/11

172 David Barclay 1983 ROTJ/20

34L David Barclay Jedi Legacy/30

35J David Barclay 2015 Chrome JvS/19

35S David Barclay Chrome JvS/31

490 David Barclay 2013 GF2/1

50E David Barclay 2014 Chrome 50E/5

50R David Barclay 2014 Chrome 50R/5

519 David Barclay 2013 GF2/15

C15 David Barclay 2013 Jedi Legacy Connections/10

ESB2 David Barclay 2017 GF Reborn/22

2018 Star Wars Archives Signature Series Dee Bradley Baker

6 Dee Baker 2008 CW/6

8 Dee Baker 2010 CW ROTBH/5

94 Dee Baker 2016 Card Trader Blue/7

94 Dee Baker 2016 Card Trader/26

233 Dee Baker 2012 Galactic Files/19

475 Dee Baker 2015 Chrome JvS/8

ACW9 Dee Baker 2017 GF Reborn/1

ACW9 Dee Baker 2017 GF Reborn/27

2018 Star Wars Archives Signature Series Deep Roy

21 Deep Roy 1983 ROTJ/14

183 Deep Roy 2012 Galactic Files/32

ROTJ16 Deep Roy 2017 GF Reborn/42

2018 Star Wars Archives Signature Series Denis Lawson

19 Denis Lawson 2016 Card Trader Red/1

19 Denis Lawson 2016 Card Trader Blue/4

19 Denis Lawson 2016 Card Trader/11

83 Denis Lawson 2001 Evolution/16

88 Denis Lawson 2016 Rogue One MB/27

9R Denis Lawson 2014 Chrome Refractors/2

9R Denis Lawson 2014 Chrome 9R/12

127 Denis Lawson 1983 ROTJ/9

145 Denis Lawson 2012 Galactic Files/16

175 Denis Lawson 2012 Galactic Files/16

I12 Denis Lawson 2013 Jedi Legacy Influencers/16

ANH23 Denis Lawson 2017 GF Reborn/13

ESB13 Denis Lawson 2017 GF Reborn/15

2018 Star Wars Archives Signature Series Derek Arnold

19 Derek Arnold 2016 Rogue One S1 Blue/7
19 Derek Arnold 2016 Rogue One S1/38
34 Derek Arnold 2017 Rogue One S2 Blue/2
34 Derek Arnold 2016 Rogue One S1 Green/8
34 Derek Arnold 2016 Rogue One S1/34
58 Derek Arnold 2017 Rogue One S2 Black/2
58 Derek Arnold 2017 Rogue One S2/10
87 Derek Arnold 2016 Rogue One S1 Green/8
87 Derek Arnold 2016 Rogue One S1/39
HR10 Derek Arnold 2016 Rogue One S1 Heroes/2

2018 Star Wars Archives Signature Series Dermot Crowley

39 Dermot Crowley 2016 Card Trader Blue/6
39 Dermot Crowley 2016 Card Trader/24
ROTJ9 Dermot Crowley 2017 GF Reborn/24

2018 Star Wars Archives Signature Series Dickey Beer

47 Dickey Beer 1983 ROTJ/7
25L Dickey Beer 2013 Jedi Legacy/14
32L Dickey Beer 2013 Jedi Legacy/20
379 Dickey Beer GF2/44

2018 Star Wars Archives Signature Series Dual Autographs

18 Taylor Gray/Tiya Sircar 40th Ann./4
64 Tim Rose/Aidan Cook Rogue One S1/9
71 Tiya Sircar/Vanessa Marshall Rebels Foil/7
78 Tiya Sircar/Vanessa Marshall Rebels Foil/14
92 Tom Kane/James Taylor 40th Ann. Green/1
M5 Nick Kellington/Derek Arnold Rogue One S1 Montages/3
GM3 Taylor Gray/Tiya Sircar Card Trader GM/3
PF6 Nick Kellington/Derek Arnold Rogue One S2 PF/11
GM17 Kane/Taylor Card Trader GM/5

2018 Star Wars Archives Signature Series Felicity Jones

1 Felicity Jones 2016 Rogue One S1/6
21 Felicity Jones 2016 Rogue One S1/1
21 Felicity Jones 2016 Rogue One S1/4
24 Felicity Jones 2016 Rogue One S1/1
24 Felicity Jones 2016 Rogue One S1/6
46 Felicity Jones 2016 Rogue One S1/11
51 Felicity Jones 2016 Rogue One S1 Black/2
70 Felicity Jones 2016 Rogue One S1/1
70 Felicity Jones 2016 Rogue One S1/11
79 Felicity Jones 2016 Rogue One S1 Blue/1
79 Felicity Jones 2016 Rogue One S1/21
80 Felicity Jones 2016 Rogue One S1/11
84 Felicity Jones 2016 Rogue One S1/6
G1 Felicity Jones 2016 Rogue One S1 Gallery/1
RO1 Felicity Jones 2017 GF Reborn Blue/2

2018 Star Wars Archives Signature Series Femi Taylor

55 Femi Taylor 2001 Evolution/30
177 Femi Taylor 2012 Galactic Files/23
ROTJ5 Femi Taylor 2017 GF Reborn Blue/1
ROTJ5 Femi Taylor GF Reborn/30

2018 Star Wars Archives Signature Series Forest Whitaker

6 Forest Whitaker 2016 Rogue One S1 Green/16
6 Forest Whitaker 2016 Rogue One S1 Black/20
6 Forest Whitaker 2016 Rogue One S1/92
8 Forest Whitaker 2017 Rogue One S2 Posters/1
27 Forest Whitaker 2017 Rogue One S2/14
HR8 Forest Whitaker 2016 Rogue One S1 Heroes/4
RO7 Forest Whitaker 2017 GF Reborn/25

2018 Star Wars Archives Signature Series Garrick Hagon

10 Garrick Hagon 2001 Evolution/33
36 Garrick Hagon 2016 Card Trader Blue/4
36 Garrick Hagon 2016 Card Trader/25
89 Garrick Hagon 2016 Rogue One MB/32
111 Garrick Hagon 2007 30th Ann./10
119 Garrick Hagon 2012 Galactic Files/32
16E Garrick Hagon 2014 Chrome/5
16R Garrick Hagon 2014 Chrome/8
243 Garrick Hagon 1977 Star Wars/12
I10 Garrick Hagon 2013 Jedi Legacy Influencers I10/37
ANH25 Garrick Hagon 2017 GF Reborn/39

2018 Star Wars Archives Signature Series Genevieve O'Reilly

8 Genevieve O'Reilly 2016 Rogue One S1 Blue/15
8 Genevieve O'Reilly 2016 Rogue One S1 Black/19
8 Genevieve O'Reilly 2016 Rogue One S1/99
9 Genevieve O'Reilly 2016 Rogue One MB Heroes/4
10 Genevieve O'Reilly 2017 Rogue One S2 Black/3
10 Genevieve O'Reilly 2017 Rogue One S2/15
41 Genevieve O'Reilly 2017 Rogue One S2/16
60 Genevieve O'Reilly 2017 40th Ann./3
73 Genevieve O'Reilly 2016 Rogue One S1 Green/8
73 Genevieve O'Reilly 2016 Rogue One S1/57
84 Genevieve O'Reilly 2016 Evolution/37
91 Genevieve O'Reilly 2012 Galactic Files/15
102 Genevieve O'Reilly 2016 Rogue One MB/1
102 Genevieve O'Reilly 2016 Rogue One MB/19

2018 Star Wars Archives Signature Series Gerald Home

ROTJ15 Gerald Home 2017 GF Reborn/23

2018 Star Wars Archives Signature Series Harrison Ford

NNO Harrison Ford

2018 Star Wars Archives Signature Series Hayden Christensen

2 Hayden Christensen 2016 Evolution/8
3 Hayden Christensen 2017 Journey TLJ Red/1
3 Hayden Christensen 2016 Evolution/6
3 Hayden Christensen 2017 Journey TLJ/6
4 Hayden Christensen 2017 Journey TLJ/1
6 Hayden Christensen 2017 40th Ann./1
6 Hayden Christensen 2017 Journey TLJ/5
9 Hayden Christensen 2015 Journey TFA Black/1
9 Hayden Christensen 2015 Journey TFA Pink/1
9 Hayden Christensen 2017 Journey TLJ/4
12 Hayden Christensen 2017 Journey TLJ/3
13 Hayden Christensen 2010 CW ROTBH/8
14 Hayden Christensen 2016 Rogue One MB/4
15 Hayden Christensen 2016 Rogue One MB Black/1
17 Hayden Christensen 2015 Journey TFA Black/1
2J Hayden Christensen 2015 Chrome JvS Refractors/5
2J Hayden Christensen 2015 Chrome JvS/8
2S Hayden Christensen 2015 Chrome JvS/6
49 Hayden Christensen 2017 40th Ann. Blue/2
49 Hayden Christensen 2017 40th Ann./5
51 Hayden Christensen 2017 40th Ann./4
52 Hayden Christensen 2017 40th Ann./3
53 Hayden Christensen 2017 40th Ann./5
57 Hayden Christensen 2017 Journey TLJ Red/1
57 Hayden Christensen 2017 Journey TLJ/3
66 Hayden Christensen 2012 Galactic Files/10
71 Hayden Christensen 2016 Card Trader Blue/7
71 Hayden Christensen 2016 Card Trader/24
80 Hayden Christensen 2015 Journey TFA/6

89 Hayden Christensen 2017 40th Ann./1

93 Hayden Christensen 2004 Heritage/2

100 Hayden Christensen 2004 Heritage/1

17A Hayden Christensen 2013 Jedi Legacy/6

19A Hayden Christensen 2013 Jedi Legacy/8

21A Hayden Christensen 2013 Jedi Legacy/4

24A Hayden Christensen 2013 Jedi Legacy/6

27A Hayden Christensen 2013 Jedi Legacy/8

33A Hayden Christensen 2013 Jedi Legacy Blue/1

36A Hayden Christensen 2013 Jedi Legacy/8

38A Hayden Christensen 2013 Jedi Legacy/7

401 Hayden Christensen 2013 GF2/8

45A Hayden Christensen 2013 Jedi Legacy/5

CL7 Hayden Christensen 2012 Galactic Files Classic Lines/3

CL8 Hayden Christensen 2013 GF2/2

ROTS1 Hayden Christensen 2017 GF Reborn/24

2018 Star Wars Archives Signature Series Hermione Corfield

49 Hermione Corfield 2017 TLJ S1 Purple/36

49 Hermione Corfield 2017 TLJ S1 Green/50

49 Hermione Corfield 2017 TLJ S1 Blue/65

49 Hermione Corfield 2017 TLJ S1/85

2018 Star Wars Archives Signature Series Howie Weed

ESB15 Howie Weed 2017 GF Reborn/22

2018 Star Wars Archives Signature Series Ian McDiarmid

NNO Ian McDiarmid

2018 Star Wars Archives Signature Series Ian McElhinney

17 Ian McElhinney 2016 Rogue One S1 Green/6

17 Ian McElhinney 2016 Rogue One S1 Black/9

17 Ian McElhinney 2016 Rogue One S1/39

2018 Star Wars Archives Signature Series Jack Klaff

90 Jack Klaff 2016 Rogue One MB/48

122 Jack Klaff 2012 Galactic Files/21

2018 Star Wars Archives Signature Series James Arnold Taylor

3 James Arnold Taylor CW ROTBH/1

19 James Arnold Taylor CW ROTBH/3

26 James Arnold Taylor CW ROTBH/4

40 James Arnold Taylor CW ROTBH/3

2018 Star Wars Archives Signature Series Jason Isaacs

NNO Jason Isaacs

2018 Star Wars Archives Signature Series Jason Spisak

ACW15 Jason Spisak 2017 GF Reborn/24

2018 Star Wars Archives Signature Series Jeremy Bulloch

11 Jeremy Bulloch 2001 Evolution/19

12 Jeremy Bulloch 2016 Card Trader Blue/4

23 Jeremy Bulloch 1983 ROTJ/38

53 Jeremy Bulloch 2016 Evolution/14

53 Jeremy Bulloch 2016 Evolution/52

54 Jeremy Bulloch 2016 Evolution/48

73 Jeremy Bulloch 1980 ESB/13

75 Jeremy Bulloch 1980 ESB/22

162 Jeremy Bulloch 2012 Galactic Files/10

34J Jeremy Bulloch 2015 Chrome JvS/54

34S Jeremy Bulloch 2015 Chrome JvS/45

474 Jeremy Bulloch 2013 GF2/44

518 Jeremy Bulloch 2013 GF2/21

ESB1 Jeremy Bulloch GF Reborn/23

2018 Star Wars Archives Signature Series Jerome Blake

30 Jerome Blake 2012 Galactic Files/37

40 Jerome Blake 2006 Evolution Update/1

57 Jerome Blake 2001 Evolution/36

84 Jerome Blake 2016 Card Trader Blue/8

84 Jerome Blake 2016 Card Trader/25

382 Jerome Blake 2013 GF2/2

41J Jerome Blake 2015 Chrome JvS Refractors/6

41J Jerome Blake 2015 Chrome JvS/66

TPM15 Jerome Blake 2017 GF Reborn/23

2018 Star Wars Archives Signature Series Jesse Jensen

NNO Jesse Jensen

2018 Star Wars Archives Signature Series Jimmy Vee

13 Jimmy Vee 2017 TLJ S1 Red/1

13 Jimmy Vee 2017 TLJ S1 Purple/35

13 Jimmy Vee 2017 TLJ S1 Green/50

13 Jimmy Vee 2017 TLJ S1 Blue/66

13 Jimmy Vee 2017 TLJ S1/85

2018 Star Wars Archives Signature Series John Boyega

2 John Boyega 2015 TFA S1 Montages/1

2 John Boyega 2015 TFA S1 Green/2

4 John Boyega 2015 Journey TFA Silhouette/3

9 John Boyega 2017 Journey TLJ Green/1

9 John Boyega 2016 TFA S2/1

13 John Boyega 2016 Evolution Stained/1

21 John Boyega 2016 TFA S2/1

29 John Boyega 2016 TFA S2/1

29 John Boyega 2016 TFA S2 Blue/2

32 John Boyega 2016 TFA S2/3

38 John Boyega 2016 TFA S2/5

39 John Boyega 2016 TFA S2 Purple/1

40 John Boyega 2015 TFA S1/1

45 John Boyega 2016 TFA S2/1

67 John Boyega 2016 TFA S2/1

70 John Boyega 2016 TFA S2 Blue/1

73 John Boyega 2017 Journey TLJ/28

75 John Boyega 2017 Journey TLJ/29

82 John Boyega 2017 Journey TLJ/26

85 John Boyega 2016 TFA S2/1

89 John Boyega 2016 Evolution/1

90 John Boyega 2016 TFA S1/1

90 John Boyega 2016 TFA S2 Green/3

96 John Boyega 2017 Journey TLJ/25

97 John Boyega 2015 TFA S1/1

99 John Boyega 2015 TFA S1/1

R9 John Boyega 2015 Journey TFA Heroes/1

2018 Star Wars Archives Signature Series John Morton

11 John Morton 1980 ESB/12

20 John Morton 2016 Card Trader Blue/6

20 John Morton 2016 Card Trader/33

37 John Morton 2004 Heritage/2

38 John Morton 1980 ESB/14

50 John Morton 1999 Chrome Archives/1

91 John Morton 1980 ESB/23

98 John Morton 1980 ESB/7

C8 John Morton 2013 Jedi Legacy Connections/29

131 John Morton 2012 Galactic Files /11

146 John Morton 2012 Galactic Files/31

210 John Morton 1980 ESB/8

220 John Morton 1980 ESB/38

489 John Morton 2013 GF2/23

FQ3 John Morton 2016 Card Trader Film Quotes/8

CL10 John Morton 2012 Galactic Files Classic Lines/1

ESB14 John Morton 2017 GF Reborn Blue/1

ESB14 John Morton 2017 GF Reborn/25

2018 Star Wars Archives Signature Series Joonas Suotamo

10 Joonas Suotamo 2015 TFA S1 Movie Scenes/3

25 Joonas Suotamo 2015 TFA S1/20

41 Joonas Suotamo 2016 TFA Chrome/3

44 Joonas Suotamo 2016 TFA Chrome/1

44 Joonas Suotamo 2016 TFA Chrome/3

59 Joonas Suotamo 2016 Evolution/20

70 Joonas Suotamo 2016 TFA S2 Green/3

70 Joonas Suotamo 2016 TFA Chrome Ref./8

70 Joonas Suotamo 2016 TFA S2/9

70 Joonas Suotamo 2016 TFA S1/11

76 Joonas Suotamo 2016 TFA Chrome Ref./3

76 Joonas Suotamo 2016 TFA S2/5

76 Joonas Suotamo 2016 TFA Chrome/7

P5 Joonas Suotamo 2015 Journey TFA Patches/5

100 Joonas Suotamo 2016 TFA Factory/1

100 Joonas Suotamo 2015 TFA S1/7

109 Joonas Suotamo 2015 Journey TFA Black/2

P13 Joonas Suotamo 2015 Journey TFA Patches/4

TFA11 Joonas Suotamo 2017 GF Reborn/24

2018 Star Wars Archives Signature Series Julian Glover

29 Julian Glover 2016 Card Trader/31

31 Julian Glover 2001 Evolution/31

140 Julian Glover 2012 Galactic Files/23

30R Julian Glover 2014 Chrome/7

ESB11 Julian Glover 2017 GF Reborn/36

2018 Star Wars Archives Signature Series Ken Leung

5 Ken Leung 2016 TFA Chrome Heroes/2

15 Ken Leung 2015 TFA S1 Movie Scenes/2

27 Ken Leung 2015 TFA S1/8

51 Ken Leung 2016 Card Trader Blue/7

51 Ken Leung 2016 Card Trader/22

TFA22 Ken Leung 2017 GF Reborn/24

2018 Star Wars Archives Signature Series Kenneth Colley

4 Ken Colley 2001 Evolution/38

16 Ken Colley 2016 Card Trader Blue/8

16 Ken Colley 2016 Card Trader/28

141 Ken Colley 2012 Galactic Files/24

29E Ken Colley 2014 Chrome/1

ESB9 Ken Colley 2017 GF Reborn/26

ROTJ7 Ken Colley 2017 GF Reborn/38

2018 Star Wars Archives Signature Series Kiran Shah

35 Kiran Shah 2017 TLJ S1 Purple/35

35 Kiran Shah 2017 TLJ S1 Green/50

35 Kiran Shah 2017 TLJ S1 Blue/65

35 Kiran Shah 2017 TLJ S1/85

2018 Star Wars Archives Signature Series Lily Cole

34 Lily Cole 2017 TLJ S1 Red/1

34 Lily Cole 2017 TLJ S1 Purple/34

34 Lily Cole 2017 TLJ S1 Green/50

34 Lily Cole 2017 TLJ S1 Blue/65

34 Lily Cole 2017 TLJ S1/85

2018 Star Wars Archives Signature Series Mads Mikkelsen

2 Mads Mikkelsen Rogue One S2 Green/1

2 Mads Mikkelsen Rogue One S2/8

38 Mads Mikkelsen Rogue One S1 Blue/7

38 Mads Mikkelsen Rogue One Black/9

38 Mads Mikkelsen Rogue One S1/33

RO8 Mads Mikkelsen GF Reborn/23

2018 Star Wars Archives Signature Series Mark Dodson

16 Mark Dodson 1983 ROTJ/40

34 Mark Dodson 2016 Card Trader Red/1

34 Mark Dodson 2016 Card Trader Blue/7

34 Mark Dodson 2016 Card Trader/29

71 Mark Dodson 2001 Evolution/34

181 Mark Dodson 2012 GF Reborn/28

ROTJ14 Mark Dodson 2017 GF Reborn/42

2018 Star Wars Archives Signature Series Matt Lanter

2 Matt Lanter 2008 CW/13

9 Matt Lanter 2016 Rogue One MB/33

10 Matt Lanter 2017 40th Ann./2

10 Matt Lanter 2017 40th Ann./4

10 Matt Lanter 2016 Rogue One MB/5

23 Matt Lanter 2010 CW ROTBH/3

36 Matt Lanter 2010 CW ROTBH/3

71 Matt Lanter 2010 CW ROTBH/4

84 Matt Lanter 2008 CW/5

22A Matt Lanter 2013 Jedi Legacy/2

2018 Star Wars Archives Signature Series Matthew Wood

NNO Matthew Wood

2018 Star Wars Archives Signature Series Michaela Cottrell

25 Michaela Cottrell 2001 Evolution/39

28 Michaela Cottrell 2012 Galactic Files/29

17J Michaela Cottrell 2015 Chrome JvS Ref./24

17J Michaela Cottrell 2015 Chrome JvS/58

TPM22 Michaela Cottrell 2017 GF Reborn/31

2018 Star Wars Archives Signature Series Mike Edmonds

44 Mike Edmonds 2001 Evolution/34

82 Mike Edmonds 1983 ROTJ/8

84 Mike Edmonds 1983 ROTJ/16

85 Mike Edmonds 1983 ROTJ/33

92 Mike Edmonds 1983 ROTJ/14

103 Mike Edmonds 1983 ROTJ/4

171 Mike Edmonds 2012 Galactic Files/24

2018 Star Wars Archives Signature Series Mike Quinn

15 Mike Quinn 2016 Card Trader/29

16 Mike Quinn 2016 TFA Chrome Heroes/14

20 Mike Quinn 1983 ROTJ/41

22 Mike Quinn 1983 ROTJ/41

33 Mike Quinn 2016 Card Trader/25

39 Mike Quinn 2016 TFA Chrome Ref./4

39 Mike Quinn 2016 TFA Chrome/7

48 Mike Quinn 2016 TFA Factory/2

48 Mike Quinn 2016 TFA S1 Blue/4

48 Mike Quinn 2015 TFA S1 Green/7

48 Mike Quinn 2015 TFA S1/35

52 Mike Quinn 2001 Evolution/39

96 Mike Quinn 2016 TFA Green/4

96 Mike Quinn 2016 TFA Chrome/5

123 Mike Quinn 1983 ROTJ/28

182 Mike Quinn 2012 Galactic Files/12

184 Mike Quinn 1983 ROTJ/25

25R Mike Quinn 2014 Chrome Ref./1

25R Mike Quinn 2014 Chrome 25R/2

ROTJ12 Mike Quinn 2017 GF Reborn/25

ROTJ13 Mike Quinn 2017 GF Reborn/37

2018 Star Wars Archives Signature Series Nick Kellington

7 Nick Kellington 2016 Rogue One S1 Blue/15

7 Nick Kellington 2016 Rogue One S1 Black/17

7 Nick Kellington 2016 Rogue One S1/76

88 Nick Kellington 2016 Rogue One S1 Green/7

88 Nick Kellington 2016 Rogue One S1 Blue/8

88 Nick Kellington 2016 Rogue One S1/38

HR9 Nick Kellington 2016 Rogue One S1 Heroes/6

2018 Star Wars Archives Signature Series Nika Futterman

93 Nika Futterman 2016 Card Trader Blue/4

93 Nika Futterman 2016 Card Trader/21

30J Nika Futterman 2015 Chrome JvS/5
30S Nika Futterman 2015 Chrome JvS/4
ACW6 Nika Futterman 2017 GF Reborn/24

2018 Star Wars Archives Signature Series Oliver Ford Davies

AOTC8 Oliver Ford Davies 2017 GF Reborn/24
TPM10 Oliver Ford Davies 2017 GF Reborn/23

2018 Star Wars Archives Signature Series Orli Shoshan

65 Orli Shoshan 2012 Galactic Files/31
6J Orli Shoshan 2015 Chrome JvS/59
6S Orli Shoshan 2015 Chrome JvS/61

2018 Star Wars Archives Signature Series Paul Blake

21 Paul Blake 2016 Card Trader Blue/8
21 Paul Blake 2016 Card Trader/26
33 Paul Blake 2001 Evolution/30
73 Paul Blake 2007 30th Ann./11
B1 Paul Blake 2016 Card Trader Bounty/9
104 Paul Blake 2012 Galactic Files/28
ANH19 Paul Blake 2017 GF Reborn Orange/1
ANH19 Paul Blake 2017 GF Reborn/36

2018 Star Wars Archives Signature Series Paul Brooke

371 Paul Brooke 2013 GF2/41
ROTJ11 Paul Brooke 2013 GF Reborn Orange/1
ROTJ11 Paul Brooke 2013 GF Reborn/24

2018 Star Wars Archives Signature Series Paul Kasey

20 Paul Kasey 2017 TLJ S1 Red/1
20 Paul Kasey 2017 TLJ S1 Purple/40
20 Paul Kasey 2017 TLJ S1 Green/50
20 Paul Kasey 2017 TLJ S1 Blue/67
20 Paul Kasey 2017 TLJ S1/85

2018 Star Wars Archives Signature Series Peter Mayhew

Han Solo and Chewbacca

7 Peter Mayhew 1983 ROTJ/1
8 Peter Mayhew 2016 Card Trader Blue/7

8 Peter Mayhew 2016 Card Trader/22
33 Peter Mayhew 2015 Journey TFA Black/2
33 Peter Mayhew 2015 Journey TFA/3
40 Peter Mayhew Journey TFA/1
55 Peter Mayhew 2016 Evolution/25
56 Peter Mayhew 2016 Evolution/5
57 Peter Mayhew 2016 Evolution/4
58 Peter Mayhew 2016 Evolution/3
84 Peter Mayhew 1980 ESB/8
89 Peter Mayhew 1980 ESB/5
121 Peter Mayhew 1977 Star Wars/5
128 Peter Mayhew 1977 Star Wars/5
157 Peter Mayhew 2012 Galactic Files/3
217 Peter Mayhew 1980 ESB/2
24S Peter Mayhew 2015 Chrome JvS/8
24S Peter Mayhew 2015 Chrome JvS Ref./10
306 Peter Mayhew 1980 ESB/2
513 Peter Mayhew 2013 Galactic Files/2
FQ12 Peter Mayhew 2016 Card Trader Film Quotes/3
ROTS13 Peter Mayhew 2017 GF Reborn/24

2018 Star Wars Archives Signature Series Phil Eason

86 Phil Eason 2001 Evolution/35
393 Phil Eason 2013 GF2/48

2018 Star Wars Archives Signature Series Philip Anthony-Rodriguez

96 Philip Anthony-Rodriguez 2016 Card Trader Blue/4
96 Philip Anthony-Rodriguez 2016 Card Trader/22

2018 Star Wars Archives Signature Series Ralph Brown

TPM24 Ralph Brown 2017 GF Reborn/23

2018 Star Wars Archives Signature Series Ray Park

2 Ray Park 2016 Rogue One MB/6
4 Ray Park 2017 40th Ann./5
6 Ray Park 2012 Galactic Files/3
79 Ray Park 2004 Heritage/2
79 Ray Park 2016 Card Trader/22
94 Ray Park 2016 Evolution/30
B3 Ray Park 2016 Card Trader Bounty/5
285 Ray Park 2015 Chrome JvS/13
28J Ray Park 2015 Chrome JvS/4
FQ10 Ray Park 2016 Card Trader Film Quotes/7
TPM4 Ray Park 2017 GF Reborn/23

2018 Star Wars Archives Signature Series Riz Ahmed

NNO Riz Ahmed

2018 Star Wars Archives Signature Series Robin Atkin Downes

ACW17 Robin Atkin Downes 2017 GF Reborn/24

2018 Star Wars Archives Signature Series Rusty Goffe

11 Rusty Goffe 1977 Star Wars/9
13 Rusty Goffe 1977 Star Wars/16
19 Rusty Goffe 1983 ROTJ/23
24 Rusty Goffe 2015 Journey TFA Green/15
24 Rusty Goffe 2015 Journey TFA/38
27 Rusty Goffe 2016 Card Trader Red/2
27 Rusty Goffe 2016 Card Trader Blue/7
27 Rusty Goffe 2016 Card Trader/25
38 Rusty Goffe 2001 Evolution/36
186 Rusty Goffe 1977 Star Wars/12
203 Rusty Goffe 1977 Star Wars/6
257 Rusty Goffe 1977 Star Wars/12
304 Rusty Goffe 1977 Star Wars/1
314 Rusty Goffe 1977 Star Wars/1
ANH8 Rusty Goffe 2017 GF Reborn Orange/2
ANH8 Rusty Goffe 2017 GF Reborn/25

2018 Star Wars Archives Signature Series Sam Witwer

TPM4 Sam Witwer 2017 GF Reborn/23
ACW13 Sam Witwer 2017 GF Reborn/23

2018 Star Wars Archives Signature Series Silas Carson

82 Silas Carson 2016 Card Trader Red/1
82 Silas Carson 2016 Card Trader Blue/8
82 Silas Carson 2016 Card Trader/24
14J Silas Carson 2015 Chrome JvS Ref./7
14S Silas Carson 2015 Chrome JvS/7
TPM14 Silas Carson 2017 GF Reborn Orange/2
TPM14 Silas Carson 2017 GF Reborn/25
TPM19 Silas Carson 2017 GF Reborn/24

2018 Star Wars Archives Signature Series Simon Williamson

40 Simon Williamson 2016 Card Trader Blue/7
40 Simon Williamson 2016 Card Trader/23

2018 Star Wars Archives Signature Series Stephen Stanton

WHEN TARKIN MET ANAKIN

10 Stephen Stanton 2016 Rogue One MB/1
10 Stephen Stanton 2016 Rogue One MB/28
55 Stephen Stanton 2017 Journey TLJ Green/2
55 Stephen Stanton 2017 Journey TLJ/12
60 Stephen Stanton 2016 Evolution/34
42S Stephen Stanton 2015 Chrome JvS Ref./11

42S Stephen Stanton 2015 Chrome JvS/62

HR7 Stephen Stanton 2016 Rogue One S1 Heroes/8

MP4 Stephen Stanton 2016 Rogue One MB Patches/5

2018 Star Wars Archives Signature Series Steve Blum

4 Steve Blum 2015 Rebels Foil/7

57 Steve Blum 2015 Rebels/57

74 Steve Blum 2015 Rebels Foil/5

81 Steve Blum 2015 Rebels Foil/7

85 Steve Blum 2015 Rebels/5

90 Steve Blum 2016 Card Trader Red/1

90 Steve Blum 2016 Card Trader Blue/8

90 Steve Blum 2016 Card Trader/26

REB4 Steve Blum 2017 GF Reborn/38

2018 Star Wars Archives Signature Series Taylor Gray

1 Taylor Gray 2015 Rebels/5

1 Taylor Gray 2015 Rebels Foil/6

15 Taylor Gray 2017 Journey TLJ Red/1

15 Taylor Gray 2017 Journey TLJ/6

16 Taylor Gray 2017 40th Ann./2

39 Taylor Gray 2015 Rebels/3

50 Taylor Gray 2015 Rebels Foil/5

50 Taylor Gray 2015 Rebels/6

54 Taylor Gray 2015 Rebels/6

61 Taylor Gray 2017 Journey TLJ Green/1

61 Taylor Gray 2015 Rebels/5

61 Taylor Gray 2015 Rebels Foil/7

62 Taylor Gray 2015 Rebels Foil/4

66 Taylor Gray 2015 Rebels/6

67 Taylor Gray 2015 Rebels/5

67 Taylor Gray 2015 Rebels/6

69 Taylor Gray 2015 Rebels Foil/7

69 Taylor Gray 2015 Rebels/8

73 Taylor Gray 2015 Rebels Foil/3

82 Taylor Gray 2015 Rebels Foil/6

86 Taylor Gray 2018 Card Trader Blue/6

86 Taylor Gray 2016 Card Trader/28

96 Taylor Gray 2015 Rebels Foil/6

96 Taylor Gray 2015 Rebels/6

98 Taylor Gray 2017 40th Ann./17

99 Taylor Gray 2015 Rebels/5

EL7 Taylor Gray 2016 Evolution EOTL/8

REB6 Taylor Gray 2017 GF Reborn/37

2018 Star Wars Archives Signature Series Temuera Morrison

95 Temuera Morrison 2004 Heritage/4

25A Temuera Morrison 2013 Jedi Legacy/1

25A Temuera Morrison 2013 Jedi Legacy/12

33J Temuera Morrison 2015 Chrome JvS Ref./12

33J Temuera Morrison 2015 Chrome JvS/42

33S Temuera Morrison 2015 Chrome JvS/49

AOTC4 Temuera Morrison 2017 GF Reborn/23

2018 Star Wars Archives Signature Series Tim Dry

164 Tim Dry 1983 ROTJ/43

2018 Star Wars Archives Signature Series Tim Rose

2 Tim Rose 2016 TFA Chrome BTS/5

3 Tim Rose 2001 Evolution/37

7 Tim Rose 2016 TFA S2 Heroes/7

12 Tim Rose 2017 TLJ S1/35

14 Tim Rose 2016 Card Trader Blue/8

14 Tim Rose 2016 Card Trader/22

15 Tim Rose 2016 TFA Chrome Heroes/14

28 Tim Rose 2015 TFA S1 Blue/6

28 Tim Rose 2015 TFA S1 Green/12

28 Tim Rose 2015 TFA S1/28

35 Tim Rose 2017 Journey TLJ/6

37 Tim Rose 2017 Journey TLJ/7

10E Tim Rose 2015 Chrome/16

10R Tim Rose 2014 Chrome/24

124 Tim Rose 1983 ROTJ/33

167 Tim Rose 2012 Galactic Files/27

FQ16 Tim Rose 2016 Card Trader Film Quotes/8

ROTJ17 Tim Rose 2017 GF Reborn/24

2018 Star Wars Archives Signature Series Tiya Sircar

3 Tiya Sircar 2015 Rebels Foil/6

3 Tiya Sircar 2015 Rebels/7

56 Tiya Sircar 2015 Rebels/6

88 Tiya Sircar 2016 Card Trader/25

REB3 Tiya Sircar 2017 GF Reborn/34

2018 Star Wars Archives Signature Series Toby Philpott

3 Toby Philpott 2017 40th Ann. Green/2

3 Toby Philpott 2017 40th Ann./5

9 Toby Philpott 2016 Card Trader Blue/4

9 Toby Philpott 2016 Card Trader/18

14 Toby Philpott 1983 ROTJ/20

15 Toby Philpott 1983 ROTJ/6

36 Toby Philpott 2001 Evolution/20

46 Toby Philpott 1983 ROTJ/15

62 Toby Philpott 1999 Chrome Archives/2

63 Toby Philpott 2015 Journey TFA Green/2

63 Toby Philpott 2015 Journey TFA/25

82 Toby Philpott 2016 Evolution/26

83 Toby Philpott 2016 Evolution/36

83 Toby Philpott 2016 EvolutionBlue /36

86 Toby Philpott 2007 30th Ann./3

163 Toby Philpott Galactic Files/17

172 Toby Philpott 1983 ROTJ/19

34L Toby Philpott 2013 Jedi Legacy/44

35J Toby Philpott 2015 Chrome JvS/29

35S Toby Philpott 2015 Chrome JvS/32

50R Toby Philpott 2014 Chrome/6

519 Toby Philpott 2013 GF2/25

C15 Toby Philpott 2013 Jedi Legacy Connections/26

2018 Star Wars Archives Signature Series Tom Kane

9 Tom Kane 2017 40th Ann./6

12 Tom Kane 2017 TLJ S1 Purple/15

12 Tom Kane 2017 TLJ S1 Green/25

12 Tom Kane 2017 TLJ S1 Blue/35

12 Tom Kane 2017 TLJ S1/49

15 Tom Kane 2017 40th Ann. Green/2

15 Tom Kane 2017 40th Ann./10

35 Tom Kane 2010 CW ROTBH/3

61 Tom Kane 2010 CW ROTBH/10

76 Tom Kane 2017 TLJ S1 Red/1

76 Tom Kane 2017 TLJ S1 Purple/15

76 Tom Kane 2017 TLJ S1 Green/25

76 Tom Kane 2017 TLJ S1 Blue/35

76 Tom Kane 2017 TLJ S1/49

92 Tom Kane 2017 40th Ann./2

92 Tom Kane 2017 40th Ann. Green/3

2018 Star Wars Archives Signature Series Tom Wilton

14 Tom Wilton 2015 TFA S1 Purple/5

14 Tom Wilton 2015 TFA S1 Blue/12

14 Tom Wilton 2015 TFA S1 Green/13

14 Tom Wilton 2015 TFA S1/36

2018 Star Wars Archives Signature Series Vanessa Marshall

6 Vanessa Marshall 2015 Rebels/5

6 Vanessa Marshall 2015 Rebels Foil/6

17 Vanessa Marshall 2016 Rogue One MB Black/1

17 Vanessa Marshall 2016 Rogue One MB/29

53 Vanessa Marshall 2015 Rebels Foil/6

59 Vanessa Marshall 2015 Rebels Foil/5

80 Vanessa Marshall 2015 Rebels/6

84 Vanessa Marshall 2015 Rebels Foil/6

89 Vanessa Marshall 2016 Card Trader Red/2

89 Vanessa Marshall 2016 Card Trader Blue/6

89 Vanessa Marshall 2016 Card Trader/27

97 Vanessa Marshall 2015 Rebels Foil/6

REB2 Vanessa Marshall 2017 GF Reborn Orange/4

REB2 Vanessa Marshall 2017 GF Reborn/39

2018 Star Wars Archives Signature Series Warwick Davis

2 Warwick Davis 2016 TFA S2 Maz's Castle/9

24 Warwick Davis 2016 Card Trader Red/2		
24 Warwick Davis 2016 Card Trader Blue/5		
24 Warwick Davis 2016 Card Trader/24		
84 Warwick Davis 2001 Evolution/34		
138 Warwick Davis 1983 ROTJ/40		
142 Warwick Davis 1983 ROTJ/17		
169 Warwick Davis 2012 Galactic Files/12		
190 Warwick Davis 1983 ROTJ/22		
ROTJ3 Warwick Davis 2017 GF Reborn/24		

2018 Star Wars Archives Signature Series Zac Jensen

6 Zac Jensen 2015 Chrome JvS/11		
58 Zac Jensen 2012 Galactic Files/25		
59 Zac Jensen 2017 Journey TLJ/4		
78 Zac Jensen 2012 Galactic Files/23		
11J Zac Jensen 2015 Chrome JvS/53		
11S Zac Jensen 2015 Chrome JvS Ref./12		
11S Zac Jensen 2015 Chrome JvS/53		
AOTC17 Zac Jensen 2017 GF Reborn/24		

2019 Star Wars Authentics

COMPLETE SET (25)	150.00	300.00
UNOPENED BOX (1 CARD+1 AUTO'd 8X10)		
COMMON CARD (1-25)	4.00	10.00
*BLUE/25: .6X TO 1.5X BASIC CARDS		
*PURPLE/10: UNPRICED DUE TO SCARCITY		
*ORANGE/5: UNPRICED DUE TO SCARCITY		
*RED/1: UNPRICED DUE TO SCARCITY		
STATED PRINT RUN 75 SER.#'d SETS		
1 Ahsoka Tano	10.00	25.00
2 Anakin Skywalker	8.00	20.00
3 BB-8	12.00	30.00
5 Captain Tarkin	6.00	15.00
6 Chancellor Palpatine	10.00	25.00
7 Chirrut Œmwe	5.00	12.00
8 Darth Maul	10.00	25.00
9 Director Krennic	6.00	15.00
10 Dryden Vos	6.00	15.00
11 Finn	6.00	15.00
12 Han Solo	8.00	20.00
13 Jango Fett	5.00	12.00
14 Jyn Erso	6.00	15.00
15 K-2SO	5.00	12.00
16 Kanan Jarrus	6.00	15.00
17 Kylo Ren	10.00	25.00
18 Lando Calrissian	10.00	25.00
19 Maul (Sam Witwer)	8.00	20.00
20 Obi-Wan Kenobi	5.00	12.00
21 Rey	15.00	40.00
23 Seventh Sister	5.00	12.00
24 Vice Admiral Holdo	15.00	40.00

2019 Star Wars Authentics Series Two

COMPLETE SET (29)	100.00	200.00
UNOPENED BOX (1 CARD+1 AUTO'd 8X10)		
COMMON CARD (1-29)	3.00	8.00
*BLUE/25: .5X TO 1.2X BASIC CARDS		
STATED PRINT RUN 99 SER.#'d SETS		
1 Boba Fett	4.00	10.00
3 C'ai Threnalli	10.00	25.00
9 Han Solo	6.00	15.00
10 Hera Syndulla	6.00	15.00
16 Kazuda Xiono	10.00	25.00
19 Obi-Wan Kenobi	6.00	15.00
21 PadmÈ Amidala	5.00	12.00
23 Sabine Wren	5.00	12.00
25 Tallie Lintra	10.00	25.00
27 The Grand Inquisitor	5.00	12.00
29 Wicket	4.00	10.00

2020 Star Wars Authentics 8x10

UNOPENED BOX (1 AUTO+1 CARD)		
COMMON CARD	6.00	15.00
*BLUE/25: SAME VALUE AS BASIC CARDS		
ADRR Rey	10.00	25.00
AGCC Cara Dune	8.00	20.00
AHFH Han Solo	10.00	25.00

2020 Star Wars Authentics 11x14

UNOPENED BOX (1 AUTO+1 CARD)		
COMMON CARD	6.00	15.00
*BLUE/25: SAME VALUE AS BASIC CARDS		

AGC Cara Dune	8.00	20.00
ADRRS Rey	10.00	25.00
AHCRS Darth Vader	10.00	25.00

2018 Star Wars Authentics Funko Pop Vinyl Promos

NNO Kylo Ren (masked)/23	
NNO Kylo Ren (unmasked)/25	

2021 Star Wars The Bad Batch Exclusive Set

COMPLETE SET (10)	12.00	30.00
COMMON CARD (1-10)	2.00	5.00
STATED PRINT RUN 2,504 SETS		
EXCLUSIVE TO EBAY		
9 Omega	4.00	10.00

2021 Star Wars Battle Plans

COMPLETE SET (100)	10.00	25.00
UNOPENED BOX (24 PACKS)	100.00	150.00
UNOPENED PACK (8 CARDS)	5.00	6.00
COMMON CARD (1-100)	.20	.50
*FOILBOARD: .75X TO 2X BASIC CARDS		
*BLUE: 1.5X TO 4X BASIC CARDS		
*GREEN/99: 5X TO 12X BASIC CARDS		
*ORANGE/50: 6X TO 15X BASIC CARDS		
*PURPLE/25: 12X TO 30X BASIC CARDS		

2021 Star Wars Battle Plans Autographs

COMMON AUTO	6.00	15.00
*BLUE/149: .5X TO 1.2X BASIC AUTOS		
*GREEN/99: .6X TO 1.5X BASIC AUTOS		

*ORANGE/50: .75X TO 2X BASIC AUTOS

*PURPLE/25: 1X TO 2.5X BASIC AUTOS

STATED ODDS 1:45

AAE	Ashley Eckstein	75.00	150.00
AAH	Alan Harris	20.00	50.00
AAM	Angus MacInnes	8.00	20.00
ACL	Charlotte Louise	10.00	25.00
ACO	Candice Orwell	20.00	50.00
ADB	Dee Bradley Baker	25.00	60.00
ADM	Dominic Monaghan	12.00	30.00
ADY	Donnie Yen	150.00	300.00
AGH	Gerald Home	15.00	40.00
AJA	Jeremy Bulloch	60.00	120.00
AJK	Jaime King	8.00	20.00
AJM	John Morton	10.00	25.00
ALL	Lex Lang	10.00	25.00
AMJ	Mark Lewis Jones	8.00	20.00
AML	Matt Lanter	25.00	60.00
AMM	Mary Elizabeth McGlynn	10.00	25.00
ANA	Naomi Ackie	10.00	25.00
ANF	Nika Futterman	30.00	75.00
AOD	Oliver Ford Davies	8.00	20.00
ARA	Riz Ahmed	25.00	60.00
ARO	Rena Owen	8.00	20.00
ARP	Ray Park	60.00	120.00
ATG	Taylor Gray	12.00	30.00
ATR	Tim Rose	10.00	25.00

2021 Star Wars Battle Plans Autographs Blue

STATED PRINT RUN 149 SER.#'d SETS

AED	Adrian Edmondson	8.00	20.00

2021 Star Wars Battle Plans Dual Autographs

STATED ODDS 1:1,568

DABH J.Boyega/B.Herring

DACB J.Boyega/G.Christie

DAEL M.Lanter/A.Eckstein

DAGP T.Gray/F.Prinze Jr.

DAJM T.Morrison/S.L.Jackson

DAMA D.Monaghan/N.Ackie

DAMC H.Christensen/E.McGregor

DAMP I.McDiarmid/R.Park

DATL M.Lanter/J.A.Taylor

DAWJ F.Jones/F.Whitaker

2021 Star Wars Battle Plans Galactic Adversaries

COMMON CARD (GA1-GA30)		.75	2.00

*GREEN/99: .5X TO 1.2X BASIC CARDS

*ORANGE/50: .75X TO 2X BASIC CARDS

*PURPLE/25: 1.5X TO 4X BASIC CARDS

STATED ODDS 1:2

GA1	Princess Leia Organa	1.50	4.00
GA2	Luke Skywalker	1.50	4.00
GA3	Han Solo	1.50	4.00
GA4	Chewbacca	1.00	2.50
GA5	R2-D2	1.00	2.50
GA6	C-3PO	1.00	2.50
GA7	Jyn Erso	1.25	3.00
GA9	Yoda	1.50	4.00
GA10	Mace Windu	1.00	2.50
GA12	Obi-Wan Kenobi	1.00	3.00
GA13	Rey	2.50	6.00
GA14	Poe Dameron	1.00	2.50
GA15	Finn	1.00	2.50
GA16	Darth Vader	2.00	5.00
GA17	Kylo Ren	1.50	4.00
GA18	Emperor Palpatine	1.00	2.50
GA20	Boba Fett	2.00	5.00
GA26	Captain Phasma	1.00	2.50
GA29	Asajj Ventress	1.00	3.00
GA30	Aurra Sing	1.00	2.50

2021 Star Wars Battle Plans Manufactured Helmet Medallion Relics

COMMON MEM	4.00	10.00

*BLUE/149: .6X TO 1.2X BASIC MEM

*GREEN/99: .75X TO 2X BASIC MEM

*ORANGE/50: 1.2X TO 3X BASIC MEM

*PURPLE/25: 2X TO 5X BASIC MEM

HMAV	Anakin Skywalker	6.00	15.00
HMCS	Chewbacca	5.00	12.00
HMHS	Han Solo	15.00	40.00
HMKV	Kylo Ren	8.00	20.00
HMLS	Luke Skywalker	10.00	25.00
HMLV	Luke Skywalker	10.00	25.00
HMOV	Obi-Wan Kenobi	5.00	12.00
HMPV	Padmé Amidala	12.00	30.00
HMVS	Darth Vader	10.00	25.00
HMVT	Darth Vader	10.00	25.00
HMVV	Darth Vader	10.00	25.00
HMC3S	C-3PO	6.00	15.00
HMCST	Chewbacca	5.00	12.00
HMHST	Han Solo	15.00	40.00
HMLAT	Luke Skywalker	10.00	25.00
HMLST	Princess Leia Organa	8.00	20.00
HMMST	Luke Skywalker	10.00	25.00
HMOAT	Princess Leia Organa	8.00	20.00
HMPLS	Princess Leia Organa	8.00	20.00
HMPLV	Princess Leia Organa	8.00	20.00
HMWST	Wicket W. Warrick	5.00	12.00

2021 Star Wars Battle Plans Sourced Fabric Relics

COMMON MEM	15.00	40.00

*GREEN/99: SAME VALUE AS BASIC

*ORANGE/50: .5X TO 1.2X BASIC MEM

*PURPLE/25: .6X TO 1.5X BASIC MEM

STATED ODDS 1:87

STATED PRINT RUN 149 SER.#'d SETS

FRF	Finn/149	20.00	50.00
FRL	Luke Skywalker/149	75.00	150.00
FRP	Poe Dameron/149	25.00	60.00
FRQ	Qi'ra/149	75.00	150.00
FRR	Rey/149	75.00	150.00
FRDV	Dryden Vos/149	25.00	60.00
FREN	Enfys Nest/135	30.00	75.00
FRGE	Galen Erso/149	25.00	60.00

FRJE	Jyn Erso/149	50.00	100.00
FRLC	Lando Calrissian/85	50.00	100.00
FRLS	Luke Skywalker/149	50.00	100.00
FRPD	Poe Dameron/149	25.00	60.00
FRRT	Rose Tico/149	50.00	100.00
FRRY	Rey/149	100.00	200.00

2021 Star Wars Battle Plans Tools of Warfare

COMPLETE SET (10)	6.00	15.00
COMMON CARD (TW1-TW10)	1.00	2.50

*GREEN/99: .6X TO 1.5X BASIC CARDS

*ORANGE/50: .75X TO 2X BASIC CARDS

*PURPLE/25: 1.5X TO 4X BASIC CARDS

STATED ODDS 1:4

2021 Star Wars Battle Plans Triple Autographs

STATED PRINT RUN 10 SER.#'d SETS

UNPRICED DUE TO SCARCITY

TAFDT Dern/Fisher/Lourd

TALER Taylor/Lanter/Eckstein

TAMBB Logan/Morrison/McGregor

TARDS Ridley/Serkis/Driver

TATYA Yen/Tudyk/Ahmed

2021 Star Wars Battle Plans Ultimate Showdowns

COMPLETE SET (10)	8.00	20.00
COMMON CARD (US1-US10)	1.25	3.00

*GREEN/99: .6X TO 1.5X BASIC CARDS

*ORANGE/50: .75X TO 2X BASIC CARDS

*PURPLE/25: 1.5X TO 4X BASIC CARDS

STATED ODDS 1:4

US1	Luke Skywalker vs. Darth Vader	2.50	6.00
US2	Qui-Gon Jinn & Obi-Wan Kenobi vs. Darth Maul	2.00	5.00
US4	Luke Skywalker vs. Darth Vader	2.50	6.00
US6	Rey vs. Kylo Ren	3.00	8.00
US8	Yoda vs. Emperor Palpatine	1.50	4.00
US10	Kylo Ren & Rey vs. Praetorian Guards	2.50	6.00

2022 Star Wars The Book of Boba Fett

COMPLETE SET (35)	60.00	150.00
COMPLETE CH.1 SET (5)	10.00	25.00
COMPLETE CH.2 SET (5)	10.00	25.00
COMPLETE CH.3 SET (5)	10.00	25.00
COMPLETE CH.4 SET (5)	10.00	25.00
COMPLETE CH.5 SET (5)	10.00	25.00
COMPLETE CH.6 SET (5)	10.00	25.00
COMPLETE CH.7 SET (5)	10.00	25.00
CH.1 COMMON (1-5)	3.00	8.00
CH.2 COMMON (6-10)	3.00	8.00
CH.3 COMMON (11-15)	3.00	8.00
CH.4 COMMON (16-20)	3.00	8.00
CH.5 COMMON (21-25)	3.00	8.00
CH.6 COMMON (26-30)	3.00	8.00
CH.7 COMMON (31-35)	3.00	8.00
CH.1 PRINT RUN 2,623 SETS		
CH.2 PRINT RUN 1,630 SETS		
CH.3 PRINT RUN 1,510 SETS		
CH.4 PRINT RUN 1,453 SETS		
CH.5 PRINT RUN 1,769 SETS		
CH.6 PRINT RUN 2,005 SETS		
CH.7 PRINT RUN 1,920 SETS		
29 Cad Bane/2,005*	10.00	25.00

2021 Star Wars The Book of Boba Fett Trailer Set

COMPLETE SET (6)	12.00	30.00
COMMON CARD (1-6)	3.00	8.00

STATED PRINT RUN 1,279 ANNCD SETS

2021 Star Wars Bounty Hunters

COMPLETE SET (300)	100.00	250.00
COMPLETE L1 SET (100)	10.00	25.00
COMPLETE L2 SET (100)	20.00	50.00
COMPLETE L3 SET (100)	75.00	200.00
COMMON L1 (B11-B1100)	.20	.50
COMMON L2 (B21-B2100)	.40	1.00
COMMON L3 (B31-B3100)	1.50	4.00

*BLUE L1: .5X TO 1.2X BASIC CARDS

*BLUE L2: .75X TO 2X BASIC CARDS

*BLUE L3: 1.5X TO 4X BASIC CARDS

*GREEN L1/150: 3X TO 8X BASIC CARDS

*GREEN L2/99: 4X TO 10X BASIC CARDS

*GREEN L3/50: 5X TO 12X BASIC CARDS

*PURPLE L1/99: 5X TO 12X BASIC CARDS

*PURPLE L2/75: 6X TO 15X BASIC CARDS

*PURPLE L3/35: 8X TO 20X BASIC CARDS

*RED L1/75: 5X TO 12X BASIC CARDS

*RED L2/50: 6X TO 15X BASIC CARDS

*RED L3/25: 10X TO 25X BASIC CARDS

2021 Star Wars Bounty Hunters Autographs

*BLUE/99: .5X TO 1.2X BASIC AUTOS

*GREEN/75: .6X TO 1.5X BASIC AUTOS

*PURPLE/50: .75X TO 2X BASIC AUTOS

RANDOMLY INSERTED INTO PACKS

AAB	Anna Brewster	6.00	15.00
AAG	Anna Graves	8.00	20.00
ABW	Billy Dee Williams		
ACM	Cathy Munro		
ACP	Chris Parsons		
ACT	Catherine Taber	10.00	25.00

ACW	Carl Weathers		
ADB	Dee Bradley Baker	10.00	25.00
ADE	Dee Bradley Baker	20.00	50.00
ADL	Daniel Logan	20.00	50.00
AES	Emily Swallow		
AGE	Giancarlo Esposito		
AHC	Hayden Christensen		
AHF	Harrison Ford		
AIM	Ian McDiarmid		
AJB	Jeremy Bulloch		
AJD	Julie Dolan	10.00	25.00
AJT	James Arnold Taylor		
AKB	Kenny Baker		
ALM	Lars Mikkelsen		
ALW	Leanna Walsman	15.00	40.00
AMB	Michonne Bourriague	10.00	25.00
AME	Mike Edmonds	8.00	20.00
AML	Matt Lanter		
AMM	Mary Elizabeth McGlynn	6.00	15.00
ANF	Nika Futterman	12.00	30.00
ANN	Nick Nolte		
AOA	Omid Abtahi		
APB	Paul Blake	6.00	15.00
APM	Peter Mayhew		
ASK	Simon Kassianides	10.00	25.00
ATE	Temuera Morrison		
ATG	Taylor Gray	10.00	25.00
ATM	Temuera Morrison		
ATW	Taika Waititi		
AWH	Werner Herzog		

2021 Star Wars Bounty Hunters Dual Autographs

STATED PRINT RUN 25 SER.#'d SETS

DAFB J.Bulloch/H.Ford

DAML D.Logan/T.Morrison

DAMP C.Monroe/C.Parsons

DATF N.Futterman/A.Eckstein

DAWE C.Williams/M.Quinn

2021 Star Wars Bounty Hunters Feared Mercenaries Aurra Sing

COMPLETE SET (10)	5.00	12.00
COMMON CARD (IA1-IA10)	1.00	2.50
STATED ODDS 1:6		

2021 Star Wars Bounty Hunters Feared Mercenaries Boba Fett

COMPLETE SET (10)	5.00	12.00
COMMON CARD (IB1-IB10)	1.00	2.50
STATED ODDS 1:4		

2021 Star Wars Bounty Hunters Feared Mercenaries Cad Bane

COMPLETE SET (10)	8.00	20.00
COMMON CARD (IC1-IC10)	1.50	4.00
STATED ODDS 1:12		

2021 Star Wars Bounty Hunters Feared Mercenaries Die-Cuts

COMPLETE SET (5)	30.00	75.00
COMMON CARD	6.00	15.00
STATED ODDS 1:12		
DC4 Bossk	10.00	25.00
DCD Dengar	10.00	25.00
DCZ IG-88	8.00	20.00

2021 Star Wars Bounty Hunters Feared Mercenaries Jango Fett

COMPLETE SET (10)	5.00	12.00
COMMON CARD (IJ1-IJ10)	.75	2.00
STATED ODDS 1:4		

2021 Star Wars Bounty Hunters Feared Mercenaries The Mandalorian

COMPLETE SET (10)	6.00	15.00
COMMON CARD (IM1-IM10)	1.25	3.00
RANDOMLY INSERTED INTO PACKS		

2021 Star Wars Bounty Hunters Manufactured Bounty Hunter Patch Relics

COMMON MEM		10.00
*ORANGE/250: SAME VALUE AS BASIC		
*BLUE/199: .5X TO 1.2X BASIC MEM		
*GREEN/99: .6X TO 1.5X BASIC MEM		
*PURPLE/50: .75X TO 2X BASIC MEM		
*GOLD/25: 1X TO 2.5X BASIC MEM		
STATED ODDS 1:BLASTER BOX		
BLASTER BOX EXCLUSIVE		
PBHB Bossk	8.00	20.00
PBHD Dengar	6.00	15.00
PBHZ Zam Wesell	5.00	12.00
PBHAS Aurra Sing	6.00	15.00
PBHAV Asajj Ventress	6.00	15.00
PBHBF Boba Fett	12.00	30.00
PBHCB Cad Bane	12.00	30.00
PBHIG IG-88	8.00	20.00
PBHJF Jango Fett	8.00	20.00

2021 Star Wars Bounty Hunters Manufactured Bounty Patch Relics

COMMON MEM	4.00	10.00
*GREEN/99: .5X TO 1.2X BASIC MEM		
*PURPLE/50: .6X TO 1.5X BASIC MEM		
*GOLD/25: .75X TO 2X BASIC MEM		
STATED PRINT RUN 199 SER.#'d SETS		
PBHC Han Solo in Carbonite	12.00	30.00
PBHS Han Solo	10.00	25.00
PBPA Padme Amidala	8.00	20.00
PBSP Padme Amidala	6.00	15.00
PBZH Ziro the Hutt	8.00	20.00
PBSCP Supreme Chancellor Palpatine	5.00	12.00

2021 Star Wars Bounty Hunters Star Wars '77 Buybacks

COMMON CARD	150.00	400.00
STATED ODDS 1:1,122		

2021 Star Wars Bounty Hunters Triple Autographs

STATED PRINT RUN 5 SER.#'d SETS

UNPRICED DUE TO SCARCITY

TAFFW Billy Dee Williams/Carrie Fisher/Harrison Ford

TALBM Temuera Morrison/Jeremy Bulloch/Daniel Logan

TAMPB Jeremy Bulloch/Cathy Munroe/Chris Parsons

2021 Star Wars Bounty Hunters Ultimate Bounty Autographs

BABW Billy Dee Williams

BACW Carl Weathers

BAHC Hayden Christensen

BAHF Harrison Ford

BAJB Jeremy Bulloch

BAKB Kenny Baker

BAPM Peter Mayhew

BAPP Pedro Pascal

BATM Temuera Morrison

BAWH Werner Herzog

1984 Star Wars C-3PO's Cereal Masks

COMPLETE SET (6)	150.00	300.00
COMMON CARD	12.00	30.00
STATED ODDS 1:CEREAL BOX		
1 C-3PO	60.00	120.00
2 Chewbacca	25.00	60.00
5 Stormtrooper	15.00	40.00
6 Yoda	15.00	40.00

2016 Star Wars Card Trader

SAVAGE OPRESS
STAR WARS: THE CLONE WARS

COMPLETE SET (100)	6.00	15.00
UNOPENED BOX (24 PACKS)	35.00	50.00
UNOPENED PACK (6 CARDS)	2.00	3.00
COMMON CARD (1-100)	.12	.30
*BLUE: .6X TO 1.5X BASIC CARDS	.20	.50
*RED: 1.2X TO 3X BASIC CARDS	.40	1.00
*GREEN/99: 6X TO 15X BASIC CARDS	2.00	5.00
*ORANGE/50: 12X TO 30X BASIC CARDS	4.00	10.00
*BAT.DAM./10: 30X TO 80X BASIC CARDS	10.00	25.00
*SLAVE I/5: UNPRICED DUE TO SCARCITY		

2016 Star Wars Card Trader Actor Digital Autographs

COMPLETE SET (20)	150.00	300.00
COMMON CARD (DA1-DA20)	8.00	20.00
STATED ODDS 1:788		
STATED PRINT RUN 25 SER.#'d SETS		

2016 Star Wars Card Trader Bounty

COMPLETE SET (20)	15.00	40.00
COMMON CARD (B1-B20)	1.25	3.00
STATED ODDS 1:5		

2016 Star Wars Card Trader Classic Artwork

COMPLETE SET (20)	15.00	40.00
COMMON CARD (CA1-CA20))	1.25	3.00
STATED ODDS 1:5		

2016 Star Wars Card Trader Film Quotes

COMPLETE SET (20)	10.00	25.00
COMMON CARD (FQ1-FQ20)	1.00	2.50
STATED ODDS 1:4		

2016 Star Wars Card Trader Galactic Moments

GALACTIC MOMENTS
Lucas Begins
Filming Star Wars: A New Hope

COMPLETE SET (20)	15.00	40.00
COMMON CARD (GM1-GM20)	1.25	3.00
STATED ODDS 1:5		

2016 Star Wars Card Trader Reflections

REFLECTIONS
Darth Vader & Obi-Wan Kenobi

COMPLETE SET (7)	12.00	30.00
COMMON CARD (R1-R7)	2.50	6.00
STATED ODDS 1:8		

2016 Star Wars Card Trader Topps Choice

COMPLETE SET (13)	15.00	40.00
COMMON CARD (TC1-TC13)	2.00	5.00
STATED ODDS 1:16		
TC4 Kabe	8.00	20.00
TC7 Lak Sivrak	3.00	8.00
TC10 Bo-Katan Kryze	3.00	8.00
TC13 Todo 360	2.50	6.00

2015 Star Wars Celebration VII Oversized Vintage Wrappers

COMPLETE SET (16)	50.00	100.00
COMMON CARD	3.00	8.00

1999 Star Wars Chrome Archives

COMPLETE SET (90)	10.00	25.00
UNOPENED BOX (36 PACKS)	250.00	400.00
UNOPENED PACK (5 CARDS)	8.00	12.00
COMMON CARD (1-90)	.20	.50

1999 Star Wars Chrome Archives Clearzone

COMPLETE SET (4)	7.50	20.00
COMMON CARD (C1-C4)	2.50	6.00

1999 Star Wars Chrome Archives Double Sided

COMPLETE SET (9)	40.00	100.00
COMMON CARD (C1-C9)	6.00	15.00

1999 Star Wars Chrome Archives Promos

P1 Hate me, Luke! Destroy me!	1.00	2.50
P2 Welcome, young Luke	1.00	2.50

2019 Star Wars Chrome Legacy

COMPLETE SET (200)	75.00	150.00
COMMON CARD (1-200)	.60	1.50
*REFRACTOR: .75X TO 2X BASIC CARDS		
*BLUE/99: 1.2X TO 3X BASIC CARDS		
*GREEN/50: 1.5X TO 4X BASIC CARDS		
*ORANGE/25: 2X TO 5X BASIC CARDS		
*BLACK/10: 4X TO 10X BASIC CARDS		

2019 Star Wars Chrome Legacy Classic Trilogy Autographs

STATED ODDS 1:113		
CAAD Anthony Daniels		
CACB Caroline Blakiston	6.00	15.00
CACF Carrie Fisher		
CACR Clive Revill	6.00	15.00
CADB David Barclay	8.00	20.00
CAHF Harrison Ford		
CAJB Jeremy Bulloch		
CAKB Kenny Baker		
CAMQ Mike Quinn	5.00	12.00
CARG Rusty Goffe	5.00	12.00
CAWD Warwick Davis		
CABDW Billy Dee Williams		
CAIME Ian McDiarmid		

2019 Star Wars Chrome Legacy Concept Art

COMPLETE SET (20)	12.00	30.00
COMMON CARD (CA1-CA20)	1.00	2.50
*GREEN/50: .5X TO 1.2X BASIC CARDS		
*ORANGE/25: .6X TO 1.5X BASIC CARDS		
STATED ODDS 1:3		

2019 Star Wars Chrome Legacy Droid Medallions

COMMON MEM	5.00	12.00
*GREEN/50: .6X TO 1.5X BASIC MEM		
*ORANGE/25: .75X TO 2X BASIC MEM		
STATED ODDS 1:23		

TRADING CARDS

2019 Star Wars Chrome Legacy Dual Autographs

STATED ODDS 1:3,502

NNO A.Driver/D.Gleeson
NNO A.Daniels/D.Barclay
NNO A.Daniels/K.Baker
NNO D.Ridley/J.Boyega
NNO S.Jackson/H.Christensen

2019 Star Wars Chrome Legacy Marvel Comic Book Covers

COMPLETE SET (25)	15.00	40.00
COMMON CARD (MC1-MC25)	1.25	3.00

*GREEN/50: .6X TO 1.5X BASIC CARDS
*ORANGE/25: .75X TO 2X BASIC CARDS
STATED ODDS 1:3

2019 Star Wars Chrome Legacy New Trilogy Autographs

STATED ODDS 1:225

NAAD Adam Driver		
NAAL Amanda Lawrence	5.00	12.00
NAAS Andy Serkis		
NABH Brian Herring	6.00	15.00
NABL Billie Lourd		
NADG Domhnall Gleeson		
NADR Daisy Ridley		
NAJS Joonas Suotamo		
NALD Laura Dern		
NAJBF John Boyega		
NAKMT Kelly Marie Tran		

2019 Star Wars Chrome Legacy Posters

COMPLETE SET (25)	15.00	40.00
COMMON CARD (PC1-PC25)	1.25	3.00

*GREEN/50: .6X TO 1.5X BASIC CARDS
*ORANGE/25: .75X TO 2X BASIC CARDS
STATED ODDS 1:6

2019 Star Wars Chrome Legacy Prequel Trilogy Autographs

STATED ODDS 1:229

PAEM Ewan McGregor
PAGP Greg Proops
PAHC Hayden Christensen
PAHQ Hugh Quarshie

PAJB Jerome Blake	5.00	12.00
PALM Lewis MacLeod		
PAMW Matthew Wood	6.00	15.00
PARP Ray Park		
PATM Temuera Morrison		
PASLJ Samuel L. Jackson		

2021 Star Wars Chrome Legacy

COMPLETE SET (200)	100.00	200.00
UNOPENED BOX (12 PACKS)	250.00	400.00
UNOPENED PACK (5 CARDS)	20.00	35.00
COMMON CARD (1-200)	.60	1.50

*REFRACTORS: .5X TO 1.2X BASIC CARDS
*BLUE/99: .6X TO 1.5X BASIC CARDS
*GREEN/50: 1.2X TO 3X BASIC CARDS

2021 Star Wars Chrome Legacy Age of Rebellion Autographs

ARBAT Alan Tudyk	50.00	100.00
ARBBM Ben Mendelsohn	100.00	200.00
ARBDC Dermot Crowley	8.00	20.00
ARBDY Donnie Yen	75.00	150.00
ARBFJ Felicity Jones	500.00	1000.00
ARBFW Forest Whitaker	75.00	150.00
ARBGE Giancarlo Esposito	75.00	150.00
ARBHF Harrison Ford		
ARBIM Ian McDiarmid		
ARBJB Jeremy Bulloch		
ARBJM John Morton		
ARBKB Ben Burtt	20.00	50.00
ARBMB Mark Boone Jr.		
ARBMC Michael Carter		
ARBMM Mads Mikkelsen		

ARBMP Michael Pennington
ARBMQ Mike Quinn
ARBNN Nick Nolte
ARBPM Peter Mayhew
ARBPR Pam Rose
ARBRA Riz Ahmed
ARBRD Rosario Dawson
ARBTW Taika Waititi
ARBWH Werner Herzog
ARBBDW Billy Dee Williams

2021 Star Wars Chrome Legacy Age of Republic Autographs

ARPAB Ahmed Best	30.00	75.00
ARPAE Ashley Eckstein	60.00	150.00
ARPDL Daniel Logan	12.00	30.00
ARPDT David Tennant	15.00	40.00
ARPEM Ewan McGregor		
ARPHC Hayden Christensen		
ARPLM Lewis Macleod		
ARPRP Ron Perlman		
ARPJAT James Arnold Taylor		
ARPSLJ Samuel L. Jackson		

2021 Star Wars Chrome Legacy Age of Resistance Autographs

ARSAD Adam Driver	300.00	500.00
ARSAS Andy Serkis		
ARSCF Carrie Fisher		
ARSDC Dave Chapman	10.00	25.00
ARSDG Domhnall Gleeson		
ARSDM Dominic Monaghan	20.00	50.00
ARSDR Daisy Ridley		
ARSEE Emun Elliott	8.00	20.00
ARSGC Gwendoline Christie	125.00	250.00
ARSGG Greg Grunberg	10.00	25.00
ARSHF Harrison Ford		
ARSJB John Boyega		
ARSKB Kenny Baker		
ARSKL Ken Leung		
ARSMQ Mike Quinn		
ARSNA Naomi Ackie		
ARSTW Tom Wilton		
ARSBDW Billy Dee Williams		

2021 Star Wars Chrome Legacy Commemorative Ship Medallion Relics

GENERAL VEERS

COMMON MEM	3.00	8.00
*GREEN/50: .6X TO 1.5X BASIC MEM		
STATED PRINT RUN 99 SER.#'d SETS		
SMC Chewbacca	6.00	15.00
SMBM Baze Malbus	5.00	12.00
SMBR Bodhi Rook	4.00	10.00
SMC3 C-3PO	6.00	15.00
SMCA Captain Cassian Andor	5.00	12.00
SMCI Chirrut Imwe	6.00	15.00
SMDV Darth Vader	15.00	40.00
SMFT Finn	5.00	12.00
SMGE Galen Erso	6.00	15.00
SMHS Han Solo	12.00	30.00
SMJE Jyn Erso	15.00	40.00
SMK2 K-2SO	8.00	20.00
SMLC Lando Calrissian	5.00	12.00
SMLO Princess Leia Organa	12.00	30.00
SMLS Luke Skywalker	15.00	40.00
SMR2 R2-D2	5.00	12.00
SMRT Rey	10.00	25.00
SMSD Stormtrooper	6.00	15.00
SMSG Saw Gerrera	6.00	15.00
SMBBT BB-8	6.00	15.00
SMBKT Biggs Darklighter	8.00	20.00
SMDVD Darth Vader	15.00	40.00
SMDVT Darth Vader	15.00	40.00
SMEAX Ello Asty	4.00	10.00
SMKRT Kylo Ren	6.00	15.00
SMLST Luke Skywalker	15.00	40.00
SMLSX Luke Skywalker	15.00	40.00
SMPDT Poe Dameron	6.00	15.00
SMPDX Poe Dameron	6.00	15.00
SMTIE TIE Fighter Pilot	5.00	12.00
SMTLX Tallie Lintra	6.00	15.00

2021 Star Wars Chrome Legacy Dual Autographs

STATED PRINT RUN 25 SER.#'d SETS

DABA J.Boyega/N.Ackie
DAFM H.Ford/P.Mayhew
DAFR C.Fisher/D.Ridley
DAMJ E.McGregor/S.L.Jackson
DARQ D.Roy/M.Quinn

2021 Star Wars Chrome Legacy Mandalorian Concept Art

COMPLETE SET (15)	30.00	75.00
COMMON CARD (MCA1-MCA15)	3.00	8.00
*GREEN/50: .75X TO 2X BASIC CARDS		

2021 Star Wars Chrome Legacy Visions Concept Art

VISIONS

TATOOINE RHAPSODY

COMPLETE SET (15)	20.00	50.00
COMMON CARD (MCA1-MCA15)	2.50	6.00
*GREEN/50: .75X TO 2X BASIC CARDS		

2021 Star Wars Chrome Legacy Wielders of the Lightsaber

STAR WARS — COUNT DOOKU

COMPLETE SET (15)	50.00	100.00
COMMON CARD (MCA1-MCA15)	2.00	5.00
RANDOMLY INSERTED INTO PACKS		
WL1 Luke Skywalker	6.00	15.00
WL2 Anakin Skywalker	3.00	8.00
WL3 Darth Vader	4.00	10.00
WL4 Darth Sidious	2.50	6.00
WL7 Kylo Ren	4.00	10.00
WL8 Rey	4.00	10.00
WL10 Ahsoka Tano	8.00	20.00
WL13 Yoda	5.00	12.00
WL14 Mace Windu	3.00	8.00
WL15 Obi-Wan Kenobi	3.00	8.00
WL16 Qui-Gon Jinn	2.50	6.00
WL19 The Grand Inquisitor	2.50	6.00
WL20 Seventh Sister	2.50	6.00

2014 Star Wars Chrome Perspectives

COMPLETE SET (100)	30.00	60.00
UNOPENED BOX (24 PACKS)	300.00	500.00
UNOPENED PACK (6 CARDS)	12.00	20.00
COMMON CARD (1E-50E)	.40	1.00
COMMON CARD (1R-50R)	.40	1.00

*REFRACTOR: 1.2X TO 3X BASIC CARDS

*PRISM: 1.5X TO 4X BASIC CARDS

*X-FRACTOR/99: 3X TO 8X BASIC CARDS

*GOLD REF./50: 6X TO 15X BASIC CARDS

2014 Star Wars Chrome Perspectives Autographs

COMMON AUTO	6.00	15.00
STATED ODDS 1 PER BOX W/SKETCHES		
NNO Angus MacInnes	12.00	30.00
NNO Anthony Daniels	125.00	250.00
NNO Billy Dee Williams	60.00	120.00
NNO Carrie Fisher	400.00	800.00
NNO Harrison Ford	1500.00	3000.00
NNO James Earl Jones	200.00	400.00
NNO Jeremy Bulloch	30.00	75.00
NNO John Ratzenberger	10.00	20.00
NNO Kenneth Colley	12.00	25.00
NNO Mark Capri	12.00	25.00
NNO Mark Hamill	800.00	1500.00
NNO Paul Blake	12.00	30.00

2014 Star Wars Chrome Perspectives Empire Priority Targets

COMPLETE SET (10)	8.00	20.00
COMMON CARD (1-10)	1.25	3.00
STATED ODDS 1:4		

2014 Star Wars Chrome Perspectives Empire Propaganda

COMPLETE SET (10)	15.00	40.00
COMMON CARD (1-10)	3.00	8.00
STATED ODDS 1:24		

2014 Star Wars Chrome Perspectives Helmet Medallions

COMPLETE SET (30)	75.00	200.00
COMMON CARD (1-30)	5.00	12.00
*GOLD/50: 1.2X TO 3X BASIC MEDALLIONS		
STATED ODDS 1:24		

2014 Star Wars Chrome Perspectives Rebel Propaganda

COMPLETE SET (10)	12.00	30.00
COMMON CARD (1-10)	2.00	5.00
STATED ODDS 1:12		

2014 Star Wars Chrome Perspectives Rebel Training

COMPLETE SET (10)	6.00	15.00
COMMON CARD (1-10)	1.25	3.00
STATED ODDS 1:8		

2014 Star Wars Chrome Perspectives Triple Autograph

1 H. Ford/M. Hamill/C. Fisher EXCH

2014 Star Wars Chrome Perspectives Wanted Posters Rebellion

COMPLETE SET (10)	5.00	12.00
COMMON CARD (1-10)	.75	2.00
STATED ODDS 1:2		

2015 Star Wars Chrome Perspectives Jedi vs. Sith

COMPLETE SET (100)	25.00	60.00
UNOPENED BOX (24 PACKS)	200.00	400.00
UNOPENED PACK (6 CARDS)	8.00	15.00
COMMON CARD	.40	1.00
*REFRACTOR: 1.2X TO 3X BASIC CARDS		
*PRISM REF/199: 1.5X TO 4X BASIC CARDS		
*X-FRACTOR/99: 3X TO 8X BASIC CARDS		
*GOLD REF/50: 6X TO 15X BASIC CARDS		

2015 Star Wars Chrome Perspectives Jedi vs. Sith Autographs

COMMON AUTO	6.00	15.00
*PRISM REF./50: .5X TO 1.2X BASIC AUTOS		
* X-FRACTORS/25: .6X TO 1.5X BASIC AUTOS		
NNO Ashley Eckstein	40.00	100.00
NNO Barbara Goodson	10.00	25.00
NNO Carrie Fisher	400.00	600.00
NNO David Prowse	50.00	100.00
NNO Jerome Blake	10.00	25.00
NNO Matthew Wood	10.00	25.00
NNO Michaela Cottrell	10.00	25.00
NNO Nalini Krishan	12.00	30.00
NNO Olivia D'Abo	10.00	25.00
NNO Peter Mayhew	25.00	60.00
NNO Ray Park	20.00	50.00
NNO Sam Witwer	10.00	25.00

2015 Star Wars Chrome Perspectives Jedi vs. Sith Jedi Hunt

COMPLETE SET (10)	10.00	25.00
COMMON CARD (1-10)	2.00	5.00
STATED ODDS 1:4		

2015 Star Wars Chrome Perspectives Jedi vs. Sith Jedi Information Guide

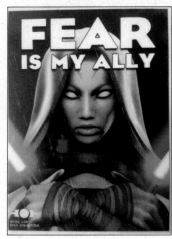

COMPLETE SET (10)	20.00	50.00
COMMON CARD (1-10)	4.00	10.00
STATED ODDS 1:12		

2015 Star Wars Chrome Perspectives Jedi vs. Sith Jedi Training

COMPLETE SET (10)	12.00	30.00
COMMON CARD (1-10)	2.50	6.00
STATED ODDS 1:24		

2015 Star Wars Chrome Perspectives Jedi vs. Sith Medallions

COMPLETE SET (36)	120.00	250.00
COMMON MEDALLION (1-36)	5.00	10.00
*SILVER/150: .6X TO 1.5X BASIC MEDALLIONS	6.00	15.00
*GOLD/50: .75X TO 2X BASIC MEDALLIONS	8.00	20.00
OVERALL MEDALLION ODDS 1:BOX		

2015 Star Wars Chrome Perspectives Jedi vs. Sith Rare Dual Autographs

COMMON AUTO	25.00	60.00
STATED PRINT RUN 200 SER.#'d SETS		
NNO A.Allen/O.Shoshan	50.00	100.00
NNO A.Eckstein/N.Futterman	30.00	75.00
NNO A.Eckstein/O.D'Abo	50.00	100.00
NNO M.Cottrell/Z.Jensen	50.00	100.00

2015 Star Wars Chrome Perspectives Jedi vs. Sith Sith Fugitives

COMPLETE SET (10)	8.00	20.00
COMMON CARD (1-10)	1.50	4.00
STATED ODDS 1:2		

2015 Star Wars Chrome Perspectives Jedi vs. Sith Sith Propaganda

COMPLETE SET (10)	12.00	30.00
COMMON CARD (1-10)	2.50	6.00
STATED ODDS 1:8		

2015 Star Wars Chrome Perspectives Jedi vs. Sith The Force Awakens

COMPLETE SET (8)	20.00	50.00
COMMON CARD	4.00	10.00
*MATTE BACK: .6X TO1.5X BASIC CARDS		
STATED ODDS 1:24		

2015 Star Wars Chrome Perspectives Jedi vs. Sith Ultra Rare Dual Autographs

STATED PRINT RUN 3 SER.#'d SETS

UNPRICED DUE TO SCARCITY

1 I.McDiarmid/D.Prowse

2 I.McDiarmid/R.Park

3 M.Hamill/C.Fisher

2015 Star Wars Chrome Perspectives Jedi vs. Sith Ultra Rare Triple Autographs

UNPRICED DUE TO SCARCITY

1 M.Hamill/D.Prowse/I.McDiarmid

2 M.Hamill/D.Prowse/R.Park

2020 Star Wars Chrome Perspectives Resistance vs. First Order

COMPLETE SET (100)	15.00	40.00
UNOPENED BOX (18 PACKS)	100.00	150.00
UNOPENED PACK (6 CARDS)	6.00	8.00
COMMON CARD	.40	1.00
*REFRACTOR: .75X TO 2X BASIC CARDS		
*PRISM REF/299: 1.2X TO 3X BASIC CARDS		
*BLUE REF/150: 2X TO 5X BASIC CARDS		
*XFRAC/99: 3X TO 8X BASIC CARDS		
*GOLD REF/50: 4X TO 10X BASIC CARDS		

2020 Star Wars Chrome Perspectives Resistance vs. First Order Choose Your Allegiance First Order

COMPLETE SET (15)	8.00	20.00
COMMON CARD (CF1-CF15)	1.00	2.50
RANDOMLY INSERTED INTO PACKS		

2020 Star Wars Chrome Perspectives Resistance vs. First Order Choose Your Allegiance Resistance

COMPLETE SET (15)	8.00	20.00
COMMON CARD (CR1-CR15)	1.00	2.50
RANDOMLY INSERTED INTO PACKS		

2020 Star Wars Chrome Perspectives Resistance vs. First Order Dual Autographs

STATED PRINT RUN 5 SER.#'d SETS

UNPRICED DUE TO SCARCITY

DABF T.Brodie-Sangster/K.Fleetwood

DABT J.Boyega/K.Tran

DAKH P.Kasey/J.Henwick

DALC A.Lawrence/C.Clarke

DALR K.Leung/T.Rose

DAQK M.Quinn/P.Kasey

DAWA B.Williams/N.Ackie

2020 Star Wars Chrome Perspectives Resistance vs. First Order Duel Dual Autographs

STATED PRINT RUN 5 SER.#'d SETS

UNPRICED DUE TO SCARCITY

DDABA J.Boyega/D.Accord
DDABH A.Brewster/B.Herring
DDACB G.Christie/J.Boyega
DDADB A.Driver/J.Boyega
DDAFD H.Ford/A.Driver
DDAHS B.Herring/K.Shah
DDARD D.Ridley/A.Driver
DDASD A.Serkis/A.Driver

2020 Star Wars Chrome Perspectives Resistance vs. First Order Empire at War

THE FOREST DUEL

COMPLETE SET (20)	10.00	25.00
COMMON CARD (EW1-EW20)	1.25	3.00
RANDOMLY INSERTED INTO PACKS		

2020 Star Wars Chrome Perspectives Resistance vs. First Order First Order Autographs

COMMON AUTO	8.00	12.00
RANDOMLY INSERTED INTO PACKS		
AAE Adrian Edmondson	6.00	15.00
AMJ Michael Jibson	6.00	15.00
AMLJ Mark Lewis Jones	8.00	20.00

2020 Star Wars Chrome Perspectives Resistance vs. First Order Resistance Autographs

COMMON AUTO	5.00	12.00
RANDOMLY INSERTED INTO PACKS		
ABH Brian Herring	10.00	25.00
ACC Crystal Clarke	6.00	15.00
ADB Dave Chapman	6.00	15.00
AIW Ian Whyte	8.00	20.00
ANC Nathalie Cuzner	8.00	20.00
ATK Tom Kane	6.00	15.00

2020 Star Wars Chrome Perspectives Resistance vs. First Order Triple Autographs

STATED PRINT RUN 5 SER.#'d SETS

UNPRICED DUE TO SCARCITY

TARAL Ridley/Ackie/Lourd
TARBH Ridley/Boyega/Herring
TARDS Ridley/Driver/Serkis

2022 Star Wars Chrome Sapphire Edition

COMPLETE SET (132)	500.00	1200.00
UNOPENED BOX (8 PACKS)	600.00	800.00
UNOPENED PACK (4 CARDS)	75.00	100.00
COMMON CARD (1-132)	5.00	12.00
*AQUA/99: 1.5X TO 4X BASIC CARDS		
*PERIDOT/75: 2X TO 5X BASIC CARDS		
*GREEN/50: 2.5X TO 6X BASIC CARDS		
*ORANGE/25: 6X TO 15X BASIC CARDS		
1 Luke Skywalker	150.00	400.00
2 See-Threepio and Artoo-Detoo	15.00	40.00
3 The Little Droid, Artoo-Detoo	15.00	40.00
4 Space Pirate Han Solo	20.00	50.00
5 Princess Leia Organa	40.00	100.00
6 Ben (Obi-Wan) Kenobi	15.00	40.00
7 The Villainous Darth Vader	60.00	150.00
8 Grand Moff Tarkin	10.00	25.00
10 Princess Leia - Captured!	12.00	30.00
13 A Sale on Droids	8.00	20.00
17 Lord Vader Threatens Princess Leia!	8.00	20.00
20 Hunted by the Sandpeople!	8.00	20.00
24 Stormtroopers Seek the Droids!	12.00	30.00
26 A Horrified Luke Sees His Family Killed	10.00	25.00
27 Some Repairs for See-Threepio	8.00	20.00

31 Sighting the Death Star	12.00	30.00
34 See-Threepio Diverts the Guards	8.00	20.00
43 Luke Prepares to Swing Across the Chasm	10.00	25.00
44 Han and Chewie Shoot it Out!	12.00	30.00
45 The Lightsaber	15.00	40.00
46 A Desperate Moment for Ben	8.00	20.00
47 Luke Prepares for the Battle	10.00	25.00
53 Battle in Outer Space!	8.00	20.00
54 The Victors Receive Their Reward	12.00	30.00
55 Han, Chewie and Luke	10.00	25.00
57 Mark Hamill as Luke Skywalker	20.00	50.00
58 Harrison Ford as Han Solo	30.00	75.00
59 Alec Guinness as Ben Kenobi	10.00	25.00
60 Peter Cushing as Grand Moff Tarkin	8.00	20.00
62 Lord Vader's Stormtroopers	8.00	20.00
63 May the Force be With You!	12.00	30.00
65 Carrie Fisher and Mark Hamill	10.00	25.00
66 Amazing Robot See-Threepio	8.00	20.00
68 The Millennium Falcon	8.00	20.00
71 The Incredible See-Threepio	12.00	30.00
76 Artoo-Detoo on the Rebel Starship!	8.00	20.00
86 A Mighty Explosion!	8.00	20.00
87 The Droids Try to Rescue Luke!	10.00	25.00
89 The Imprisoned Princess Leia	15.00	40.00
96 The Droids on Tatooine	8.00	20.00
98 See-Threepio	10.00	25.00
99 Ben with the Lightsaber!	15.00	40.00
100 Our Heroes at the Spaceport	8.00	20.00
101 The Wookiee Chewbacca	12.00	30.00
106 A Message From Princess Leia!	8.00	20.00
108 Princess Leia Observes the Battle	10.00	25.00
111 Chewie and Han Solo!	15.00	40.00
118 R2-D2 and C-3PO	8.00	20.00
121 Han Solo and Chewbacca	12.00	30.00
122 The Millennium Falcon Speeds Through Space!	8.00	20.00
124 Threepio Searches for R2-D2	8.00	20.00
125 Luke in Disguise!	15.00	40.00
129 May the Force be With You!	8.00	20.00
132 Lord Vader and a Soldier	10.00	25.00

2022 Star Wars Chrome Sapphire Edition Aqua

*AQUA: 1.5X TO 4X BASIC CARDS

STATED PRINT RUN 99 SER.#'d SETS

1 Luke Skywalker	750.00	2000.00
2 See-Threepio and Artoo-Detoo	50.00	125.00
4 Space Pirate Han Solo	125.00	300.00
5 Princess Leia Organa	200.00	500.00
6 Ben (Obi-Wan) Kenobi	75.00	200.00
7 The Villainous Darth Vader	200.00	500.00
8 Grand Moff Tarkin	40.00	100.00
10 Princess Leia - Captured!	50.00	120.00
19 Searching for the Little Droid	30.00	75.00
20 Hunted by the Sandpeople!	30.00	75.00

TRADING CARDS

2022 Star Wars Chrome Sapphire Edition Green

*GREEN: 2.5X TO 6X BASIC CARDS

STATED PRINT RUN 50 SER.#'d SETS

1 Luke Skywalker	2000.00	5000.00
3 The Little Droid, Artoo-Detoo	75.00	200.00
4 Space Pirate Han Solo	200.00	500.00
5 Princess Leia Organa	300.00	800.00
6 Ben (Obi-Wan) Kenobi	250.00	600.00
7 The Villainous Darth Vader	300.00	800.00

2022 Star Wars Chrome Sapphire Edition Orange

*ORANGE: 6X TO 15X BASIC CARDS

STATED PRINT RUN 25 SER.#'d SETS

1 Luke Skywalker	3000.00	8000.00
4 Space Pirate Han Solo	250.00	600.00
5 Princess Leia Organa	500.00	1200.00
6 Ben (Obi-Wan) Kenobi	300.00	750.00
7 The Villainous Darth Vader	600.00	1500.00

2022 Star Wars Chrome Sapphire Edition Peridot

*PERIDOT: 2X TO 5X BASIC CARDS

STATED PRINT RUN 75 SER.#'d SETS

1 Luke Skywalker	1200.00	3000.00
2 See-Threepio and Artoo-Detoo	50.00	125.00
3 The Little Droid, Artoo-Detoo	150.00	400.00
4 Space Pirate Han Solo	150.00	400.00
5 Princess Leia Organa	250.00	600.00
6 Ben (Obi-Wan) Kenobi	150.00	400.00
7 The Villainous Darth Vader	250.00	600.00

2004 Star Wars Clone Wars Cartoon

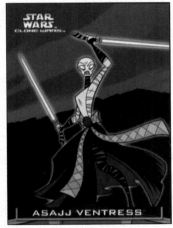

ASAJJ VENTRESS

COMPLETE SET (90)	5.00	12.00
UNOPENED HOBBY BOX (36 PACKS)	50.00	60.00
UNOPENED HOBBY PACK (7 CARDS)	1.50	2.00
UNOPENED RETAIL BOX (36 PACKS)	55.00	65.00
UNOPENED RETAIL PACK (7 CARDS)	1.75	2.25
COMMON CARD (1-90)	.15	.40

2004 Star Wars Clone Wars Cartoon Autographs

COMMON AUTO	12.00	30.00

2004 Star Wars Clone Wars Cartoon Battle Motion

COMPLETE SET (10)	15.00	40.00
COMMON CARD (B1-B10)	2.00	5.00

2004 Star Wars Clone Wars Cartoon Stickers

COUNT DOOKU

COMPLETE SET (10)	3.00	8.00
COMMON CARD (1-10)	.40	1.00

2008 Star Wars Clone Wars

ROTTA THE HUTTLET

COMPLETE SET (90)	5.00	12.00
UNOPENED BOX (36 PACKS)	100.00	150.00
UNOPENED PACK (7 CARDS)	2.50	4.00
COMMON CARD (1-90)	.15	.40
*GOLD: 8X TO 20X BASIC CARD		

2008 Star Wars Clone Wars Foil

COMPLETE SET (10)	12.00	25.00
COMMON CARD (1-10)	2.00	5.00
STATED ODDS 1:3 RETAIL		

2008 Star Wars Clone Wars Animation Cels

COMPLETE SET (10)	7.50	15.00
COMMON CARD (1-10)	1.25	3.00
STATED ODDS 1:6		
ALSO KNOWN AS THE WHITE CELS		

2008 Star Wars Clone Wars Blue Animation Cels

COMPLETE SET (5)	15.00	40.00
COMMON CARD	4.00	10.00
STATED ODDS 1:6 WALMART PACKS		

2008 Star Wars Clone Wars Red Animation Cels

COMPLETE SET (5)	20.00	50.00
COMMON CARD	5.00	12.00
STATED ODDS 1:6 TARGET PACKS		

2008 Star Wars Clone Wars Coins Purple

COMPLETE SET (12)	15.00	40.00
COMMON CARD (1-12)	2.50	6.00
*RED: SAME VALUE		
*YELLOW: SAME VALUE		
PURPLE ODDS 2:WALMART/MEIER BONUS BOX		
RED ODDS 2:TARGET BONUS BOX		
YELLOW ODDS 2:TRU BONUS BOX		

2008 Star Wars Clone Wars Motion

COMPLETE SET (5)	4.00	8.00
COMMON CARD (1-5)	1.25	3.00
STATED ODDS 1:8 RETAIL		

2008 Star Wars Clone Wars Promos

COMPLETE SET (2)	2.50	6.00
COMMON CARD (P1-P2)	1.50	4.00

2008 Star Wars Clone Wars Stickers

COMPLETE SET (90)	15.00	40.00
COMMON CARD (1-90)	.40	1.00

2008 Star Wars Clone Wars Stickers Die-Cut Magnets

COMPLETE SET (9)	10.00	25.00
COMMON CARD (1-9)	2.00	5.00
STATED ODDS 1:12		

2008 Star Wars Clone Wars Stickers Die-Cut Pop-Ups

COMPLETE SET (10)	3.00	8.00
COMMON CARD (1-10)	.60	1.50
STATED ODDS 1:3		

2008 Star Wars Clone Wars Stickers Foil

COMPLETE SET (10)	5.00	12.00
COMMON CARD (1-10)	.75	2.00
STATED ODDS 1:3		

2008 Star Wars Clone Wars Stickers Temporary Tattoos

COMPLETE SET (10)	6.00	15.00
COMMON CARD (1-10)	1.00	2.50
STATED ODDS 1:4		

2008 Star Wars Clone Wars Stickers Tin Lid Stickers

COMPLETE SET (6)	12.00	30.00
STATED ODDS 1 PER TIN		
1 Anakin	3.00	8.00
2 Obi-Wan	3.00	8.00
3 Anakin and Obi-Wan	3.00	8.00
4 Clone Troopers	3.00	8.00
5 Yoda	3.00	8.00
6 Anakin and Ahsoka	3.00	8.00

2010 Star Wars Clone Wars Rise of the Bounty Hunters

COMPLETE SET (90)	4.00	10.00
UNOPENED BOX (24 PACKS)	100.00	200.00
UNOPENED PACK (7 CARDS)	4.00	8.00
COMMON CARD (1-90)	.10	.30
*SILVER/100: 20X TO 50X BASIC CARDS		

2010 Star Wars Clone Wars Rise of the Bounty Hunters Cels Red

COMPLETE SET (5)	8.00	20.00
COMMON CARD (1-5)	3.00	8.00

2010 Star Wars Clone Wars Rise of the Bounty Hunters Cels Yellow

COMPLETE SET (5)	6.00	15.00
COMMON CARD (1-5)	2.50	6.00

2010 Star Wars Clone Wars Rise of the Bounty Hunters Foil

COMPLETE SET (20)	8.00	20.00
COMMON CARD (1-20)	.60	1.50
STATED ODDS 1:3		

2010 Star Wars Clone Wars Rise of the Bounty Hunters Motion

COMPLETE SET (5)	6.00	15.00
COMMON CARD (1-5)	1.50	4.00
STATED ODDS 1:6		

2010 Star Wars Clone Wars Rise of the Bounty Hunters Promos

P1	Cad Bane and Others	1.25	3.00
P3	Pre Vizsla and Mandalorian Death Watch	1.25	3.00

2018 Star Wars Clone Wars 10th Anniversary

COMPLETE SET (25)	15.00	40.00
COMMON CARD (1-25)	1.00	2.50
*PURPLE: .75X TO 2X BASIC CARDS		

2018 Star Wars Clone Wars 10th Anniversary Autographs

STATED OVERALL ODDS 1:SET

1A	Matt Lanter		
2A	Ashley Eckstein		
3A	James Arnold Taylor	8.00	20.00
4A	Tom Kane		
6A	Tim Curry		
7A	Catherine Taber		
8A	Phil Lamarr		
9A	Nika Futterman		
10A	Meredith Salenger		
12A	Stephen Stanton		
13A	Daniel Logan		
14A	Sam Witwer		
15A	Anna Graves		
16A	Anthony Daniels		
18A	Dee Bradley Baker		
20A	Matthew Wood		
21A	David Tennant		
22A	Blair Bess		
23A	Cas Anvar		
24A	Kathleen Gati		
25A	George Takei		

2018 Star Wars Clone Wars 10th Anniversary Dual Autographs

UNPRICED DUE TO SCARCITY

NNO J.Taylor/M.Lanter

NNO J.Taylor/S.Witwer

NNO J.Taylor/T.Kane

NNO M.Lanter/A.Eckstein

NNO S.Stanton/A.Eckstein

2009 Star Wars Clone Wars Widevision

COMPLETE SET (80)	5.00	12.00
UNOPENED BOX (24 PACKS)	60.00	70.00
UNOPENED PACK (7 CARDS)	2.50	3.00
COMMON CARD (1-80)	.15	.40
*SILVER: .5X TO 12X BASIC CARDS		

2009 Star Wars Clone Wars Widevision Animation Cels

THREEPIO AND JAR JAR

COMPLETE SET (10)	6.00	15.00
COMMON CARD (1-10)	.75	2.00
STATED ODDS 1:4		

2009 Star Wars Clone Wars Widevision Autographs

MATT LANTER
AS ANAKIN SKYWALKER

COMMON AUTO	8.00	20.00
STATED ODDS 1:67 HOBBY; 1:174 RETAIL		
NNO Ian Abercrombie	75.00	200.00
NNO James Arnold Taylor	40.00	100.00
NNO Matt Lanter	15.00	40.00
NNO Matthew Wood/Droids	15.00	40.00
NNO Matthew Wood/Grievous	15.00	40.00
NNO Nika Futterman	12.00	30.00
NNO Tom Kane	12.00	30.00

2009 Star Wars Clone Wars Widevision Foil Characters

GENERAL GRIEVOUS

COMPLETE SET (20)	15.00	40.00
COMMON CARD (1-20)	1.00	2.50
STATED ODDS 1:3		

2009 Star Wars Clone Wars Widevision Motion

COMPLETE SET (5)	6.00	15.00
COMMON CARD (1-5)	1.50	4.00
STATED ODDS 1:8		

2009 Star Wars Clone Wars Widevision Season Two Previews

COMPLETE SET (8)	3.00	8.00
COMMON CARD (PV1-PV8)	.50	1.25
STATED ODDS 1:2		

2019 Star Wars Comic Convention Exclusives

1	Darth Vader SWC	75.00	150.00
2	Luke Skywalker SWC		
3	Princess Leia Organa SWC	25.00	60.00
4	Han Solo SWC	30.00	75.00
5	Chewbacca SWC	30.00	75.00
6	Anakin Skywalker SDCC	12.00	30.00
7	Obi-Wan Kenobi SDCC	12.00	30.00
8	Padme Amidala SDCC	10.00	25.00
9	Qui-Gon Jinn SDCC	10.00	25.00
10	Darth Maul SDCC	20.00	50.00
11	Rey NYCC	60.00	120.00
12	Kylo Ren NYCC	20.00	50.00
13	Finn NYCC	15.00	40.00
14	Poe Dameron NYCC	25.00	60.00
15	General Hux NYCC	20.00	50.00

2017 Star Wars Countdown to The Last Jedi

COMPLETE SET (20)		75.00	150.00
COMMON CARD (1-20)		5.00	12.00
1	Rey Encounters Luke Skywalker/775*	8.00	20.00

1994 Star Wars Day

COMPLETE SET (2)	6.00	15.00
COMMON CARD (SD1-SD2)	4.00	10.00

1995 Star Wars Day

NNO Millennium Falcon w/X-Wings and TIE Fighters	5.00	12.00

1999 Star Wars Defeat the Dark Side and Win Medallions

COMPLETE SET W/O SP (16)	12.00	30.00
COMMON MEDALLION	1.00	2.50
2 Daultay Dofine/50*		
4 Yoda/1500*		
10 Shmi Skywalker/1*		
13 Battle Droid/1*		
20 Chancellor Valorum/1*		

2015 Star Wars Disney Pixar Cars Promos

COMPLETE SET (5)	30.00	80.00
COMMON CARD	10.00	25.00

TRADING CARDS

2015 Star Wars Disney Store The Force Awakens Promos

Finn on the run!

COMPLETE SET (8)	20.00	50.00
COMMON CARD (SKIP #'d)	4.00	10.00
11 BB-8 on the move!	6.00	15.00
67 Kylo Ren ignites his Lightsaber!	5.00	12.00
96 The Millennium Falcon	5.00	12.00

2011 Star Wars Dog Tags

COMPLETE SET (24)	25.00	60.00
UNOPENED BOX (PACKS)		
UNOPENED PACK (1 TAG+1 CARD)		
COMMON TAG (1-24)	2.00	5.00
*SILVER: .5X TO 1.2X BASIC TAGS	2.50	6.00
*RAINBOW: 1.2X TO 3X BASIC TAGS	6.00	15.00

2001 Star Wars Evolution

COMPLETE SET (93)	5.00	12.00
UNOPENED BOX (36 PACKS)		
UNOPENED PACK (8 CARDS)		
COMMON CARD (1-93)	.15	.40

2001 Star Wars Evolution Autographs

COMMON AUTO	15.00	40.00
GROUP A/1000* STATED ODDS 1:37		
GROUP B/400* STATED ODDS 1:919		
GROUP C/300* STATED ODDS 1:2450		
GROUP D/100* STATED ODDS 1:3677		
NNO Anthony Daniels/100*	1000.00	1500.00
NNO Billy Dee Williams/300*	150.00	300.00
NNO Carrie Fisher/100*	1000.00	1500.00
NNO Dalyn Chew/1000*	50.00	100.00
NNO Dermot Crowley/1000*	20.00	50.00
NNO Ian McDiarmid/400*	200.00	400.00
NNO James Earl Jones/1000*	600.00	1500.00
NNO Jeremy Bulloch/1000*	150.00	400.00
NNO Kenneth Colley/1000*	30.00	75.00
NNO Kenny Baker/1000*	150.00	300.00
NNO Lewis MacLeod	25.00	60.00
NNO Michael Culver/1000*	50.00	100.00
NNO Michael Pennington/1000*	25.00	60.00
NNO Michael Sheard/1000*	20.00	50.00
NNO Michonne Bourriague/1000*	20.00	50.00
NNO Peter Mayhew/400*	125.00	250.00
NNO Phil Brown/1000*	50.00	100.00
NNO Tim Rose/1000*	25.00	60.00
NNO Warwick Davis/1000*	30.00	75.00

2001 Star Wars Evolution Insert A

COMPLETE SET (12)	15.00	30.00
COMMON CARD (1A-12A)	1.50	4.00
STATED ODDS 1:6		

2001 Star Wars Evolution Insert B

COMPLETE SET (8)	20.00	40.00
COMMON CARD (1B-8B)	2.50	6.00
STATED ODDS 1:12		

2001 Star Wars Evolution Promos

COMMON CARD	1.00	2.50
P3 Nien Nunb ALPHA CON	3.00	8.00
P4 Anakin Skywalker SDCC	2.00	5.00

2006 Star Wars Evolution Update

COMPLETE SET (90)	5.00	12.00
UNOPENED BOX (24 PACKS)	150.00	250.00
UNOPENED PACK (6 CARDS)	8.00	12.00
COMMON CARD (1-90)	.15	.40
1D ISSUED AS DAMAGED AUTO REPLACEMENT		
CL1 Luke Connections CL	.40	1.00
CL2 Leia Connections CL	.40	1.00
1D Luke Skywalker SP	2.00	5.00
P1 Obi-Wan Kenobi PROMO	1.00	2.50
P2 Darth Vader PROMO	1.00	2.50

2006 Star Wars Evolution Update Autographs

COMMON AUTO (UNNUMBERED)	6.00	15.00
STATED ODDS 1:24 HOBBY		
GROUP A ODDS 1:2,005		
GROUP B ODDS 1:231		
GROUP C ODDS 1:81		
GROUP D ODDS 1:259		
GROUP E ODDS 1:48		
NNO Alec Guinness		
NNO Bob Keen B	20.00	50.00
NNO David Barclay B	20.00	50.00
NNO Garrick Hagon E	10.00	25.00
NNO George Lucas		
NNO Hayden Christensen A	800.00	1200.00
NNO James Earl Jones A	200.00	400.00
NNO John Coppinger B	15.00	40.00
NNO Maria De Aragon C	10.00	25.00

NNO	Matt Sloan E	8.00	20.00
NNO	Michonne Bourriague C	10.00	25.00
NNO	Mike Edmonds B	15.00	40.00
NNO	Mike Quinn B	20.00	50.00
NNO	Nalini Krishan D	8.00	20.00
NNO	Peter Cushing		
NNO	Richard LeParmentier C	10.00	25.00
NNO	Sandi Finlay C	8.00	20.00
NNO	Toby Philpott B	20.00	50.00
NNO	Wayne Pygram B	50.00	100.00

2006 Star Wars Evolution Update Etched Foil Puzzle

COMPLETE SET (6)	6.00	15.00
COMMON CARD (1-6)	1.25	3.00
STATED ODDS 1:6		

2006 Star Wars Evolution Update Galaxy Crystals

COMPLETE SET (10)	12.50	30.00
COMMON CARD (G1-G10)	1.50	4.00
STATED ODDS 1:4 RETAIL		

2006 Star Wars Evolution Update Insert A

COMPLETE SET (20)	20.00	40.00
COMMON CARD (1A-20A)	1.50	4.00
STATED ODDS 1:6		

2006 Star Wars Evolution Update Insert B

COMPLETE SET (15)	20.00	40.00
COMMON CARD (1B-15B)	2.00	5.00
STATED ODDS 1:12		

2006 Star Wars Evolution Update Luke and Leia

COMPLETE SET (2)	1000.00	2000.00
COMMON CARD (1-2)	600.00	1200.00
STATED ODDS 1:1975 HOBBY		
STATED PRINT RUN 100 SER. #'d SETS		

2016 Star Wars Evolution

COMPLETE SET (100)	8.00	20.00
UNOPENED BOX (24 PACKS)	60.00	75.00
UNOPENED PACK (8 CARDS)	2.50	3.00
COMMON CARD (1-100)	.15	.40
*LTSBR BLUE: 4X TO 10X BASIC CARDS		
*LTSBR PURPLE: 8X TO 20X BASIC CARDS		
*GOLD/50: 15X TO 40X BASIC CARDS		

2016 Star Wars Evolution Autographs

COMMON AUTO	6.00	15.00
*PURPLE/25: .6X TO 1.5X BASIC AUTOS		
RANDOMLY INSERTED INTO PACKS		
NNO Alan Harris	8.00	20.00
NNO Amy Allen	10.00	25.00
NNO Andy Serkis	100.00	200.00
NNO Angus MacInnes	12.00	30.00
NNO Ashley Eckstein	40.00	100.00
NNO Clive Revill	25.00	60.00
NNO Dee Bradley Baker	8.00	20.00
NNO Deep Roy	10.00	25.00
NNO Denis Lawson	15.00	40.00
NNO Dickey Beer	12.00	30.00
NNO Freddie Prinze Jr.	60.00	120.00
NNO George Takei	15.00	40.00
NNO Greg Grunberg	15.00	40.00
NNO Harriet Walter	12.00	30.00
NNO Hugh Quarshie	20.00	50.00
NNO Jeremy Bulloch	15.00	40.00
NNO Jerome Blake	10.00	25.00
NNO John Boyega	75.00	150.00
NNO John Ratzenberger	8.00	20.00
NNO Keisha Castle-Hughes	10.00	25.00
NNO Kenneth Colley	12.00	30.00
NNO Matthew Wood	12.00	30.00
NNO Mercedes Ngoh	20.00	50.00
NNO Michael Carter	20.00	50.00
NNO Mike Quinn	8.00	20.00
NNO Orli Shoshan	8.00	20.00
NNO Paul Blake	8.00	20.00
NNO Phil Lamarr	15.00	40.00
NNO Ray Park	25.00	60.00
NNO Sam Witwer	8.00	20.00
NNO Stephen Stanton	10.00	25.00
NNO Taylor Gray	10.00	25.00
NNO Tim Dry	12.00	30.00
NNO Tiya Sircar	8.00	20.00

NNO Tom Kane	10.00	25.00
NNO Vanessa Marshall	8.00	20.00
NNO Warwick Davis	12.00	30.00

2016 Star Wars Evolution Dual Autographs

STATED PRINT RUN 3 SER.#'d SETS

UNPRICED DUE TO SCARCITY

NNO A.Eckstein/D.Baker
NNO I.McDiarmid/C.Revill
NNO I.McDiarmid/M.Wood
NNO J.Bulloch/D.Logan
NNO M.Hamill/D.Roy
NNO M.Carter/M.Wood
NNO R.Park/S.Witwer

2016 Star Wars Evolution Dual Patch Banner Books

COMPLETE SET (8)

STATED PRINT RUN 5 SER.#'d SETS

UNPRICED DUE TO SCARCITY

NNO Bail Organa
Padme Amidala
NNO Count Dooku
General Grievous
NNO Emperor Palpatine
Darth Vader
NNO Finn
Rey
NNO Kanan Jarrus
Ezra Bridger
NNO Kylo Ren
Captain Phasma
NNO Luke Skywalker
Princess Leia
NNO Yoda
Mace Windu

2016 Star Wars Evolution Evolution of the Lightsaber

COMPLETE SET (9)	12.00	30.00
COMMON CARD (EL1-EL9)	2.00	5.00
STATED ODDS 1:8		

2016 Star Wars Evolution Evolution of Vehicles and Ships

COMPLETE SET (18)	8.00	20.00
COMMON CARD (EV1-EV18)	.75	2.00
STATED ODDS 1:2		

2016 Star Wars Evolution Lenticular Morph

COMPLETE SET (9)	60.00	120.00
COMMON CARD (1-9)	6.00	15.00
STATED ODDS 1:72		
1 Darth Vader	10.00	25.00
2 Luke Skywalker	10.00	25.00

3 Leia Organa	8.00	20.00
4 Han Solo	10.00	25.00
9 Chewbacca	8.00	20.00

2016 Star Wars Evolution Marvel Star Wars Comics

COMPLETE SET (17)	12.00	30.00
COMMON CARD (EC1-EC17)	1.50	4.00
STATED ODDS 1:4		

2016 Star Wars Evolution Patches

COMMON CARD	5.00	12.00
*SILVER/50: 5X TO 1.2X BASIC CARDS		
*GOLD/25: .6X TO 1.5X BASIC CARDS		
NNO Admiral Ackbar	6.00	15.00
NNO Ahsoka Tano	6.00	15.00
NNO BB-8	8.00	20.00
NNO Chancellor Palpatine	6.00	15.00
NNO Clone Trooper	6.00	15.00
NNO Darth Vader	6.00	15.00
NNO Ezra Bridger	6.00	15.00
NNO General Hux	6.00	15.00
NNO Grand Moff Tarkin	8.00	20.00
NNO Han Solo	8.00	20.00
NNO Kylo Ren	8.00	20.00
NNO Luke Skywalker	6.00	15.00
NNO Mon Mothma	6.00	15.00
NNO Poe Dameron	6.00	15.00
NNO Princess Leia Organa	6.00	15.00
NNO Qui-Gon Jinn	6.00	15.00
NNO Rey	10.00	25.00
NNO Senator Amidala	6.00	15.00
NNO Supreme Leader Snoke	6.00	15.00

2016 Star Wars Evolution Quad Autograph

STATED PRINT RUN 1 SER.#'d SET

UNPRICED DUE TO SCARCITY

1 Bulloch

Morton

Beers

Logan

2016 Star Wars Evolution SP Inserts

COMPLETE SET (9)	250.00	500.00
COMMON CARD (1-9)	25.00	60.00
STATED PRINT RUN 100 SER.#'d SETS		
1 Luke	30.00	80.00
Stormtrooper Disguise		
2 Leia	30.00	80.00
Boussh Disguise		
5 Vader	50.00	100.00
Birth of the Dark Lord		
6 Boba Fett	30.00	80.00
Skiff Battle		

2016 Star Wars Evolution Stained Glass Pairings

COMPLETE SET (9)	20.00	50.00
COMMON CARD (1-9)	2.50	6.00
STATED ODDS 1:24		
1 Luke Skywalker	5.00	12.00
Princess Leia		
2 Han Solo	4.00	10.00
Lando Calrissian		
4 Darth Sidious	4.00	10.00
Darth Maul		
5 Darth Vader	3.00	8.00
Grand Moff Tarkin		
6 Kylo Ren	3.00	8.00
Captain Phasma		
7 Chewbacca	3.00	8.00
C-3PO		
9 Rey	6.00	15.00
Finn		

2016 Star Wars Evolution Triple Autographs

STATED PRINT RUN 3 SER.#'d SETS

UNPRICED DUE TO SCARCITY

1 Blakinston

Crowley

Rose

---

2 McDiarmid

Wood

Blake

3 Bulloch

Morton

Beer

4 Gray

Eckstein

Baker

2007 Star Wars Family Guy Blue Harvest DVD Promos

COMPLETE SET (12)	3.00	8.00
COMMON CARD	.60	1.50
*GERMAN: SAME VALUE AS ENGLISH		
*ITALIAN: SAME VALUE AS ENGLISH		
*SPANISH: SAME VALUE AS ENGLISH		

1996 Star Wars Finest

COMPLETE SET (90)	10.00	25.00
UNOPENED BOX (36 PACKS)	300.00	500.00
UNOPENED PACK (5 CARDS)	10.00	15.00
COMMON CARD (1-90)	.20	.50
*REF.: 5X TO 12X BASIC CARDS		

1996 Star Wars Finest Embossed

COMPLETE SET (6)	10.00	25.00
COMMON CARD (F1-F6)	2.00	5.00

1996 Star Wars Finest Matrix

COMPLETE SET (4)	6.00	15.00
COMMON CARD (M1-M4)	2.00	5.00

NNO Exchange Card

1996 Star Wars Finest Promos

COMPLETE SET (3)	2.50	6.00
COMMON CARD (SWF1-SWF3)	1.00	2.50
B1 Han Solo & Chewbacca	3.00	8.00
(Album Exclusive)		
NNO 1-Card Sheet		
NNO 1-Card Sheet Refractor		
NNO Star Wars Goes Split Level	200.00	400.00

2018 Star Wars Finest

COMPLETE SET W/SP (120)	75.00	150.00
COMPLETE SET W/O SP (100)	20.00	50.00
UNOPENED BOX (12 PACKS)		
UNOPENED PACK (5 CARDS)		
COMMON CARD (1-100)	.40	1.00
COMMON SP (101-120)	3.00	8.00
*REF.: 1.25X TO 3X BASIC CARDS		
*BLUE/150: 2X TO 5X BASIC CARDS		
*GREEN/99: 3X TO 8X BASIC CARDS		
*GOLD/50: 4X TO 10X BASIC CARDS		
*GOLD SP/50: .5X TO 1.2X BASIC CARDS		

2018 Star Wars Finest Autographs

FAAL Amanda Lawrence		
FADBB Dee Bradley Baker	8.00	20.00
FAHCT Hermione Corfield	10.00	25.00
FAJAT James Arnold Taylor		
FAJBM Jerome Blake	5.00	12.00
FAMEM Mary Elizabeth McGlynn	6.00	15.00
FAJZ Zac Jensen		

2018 Star Wars Finest Droids and Vehicles

COMPLETE SET (20)	12.00	30.00
COMMON CARD (DV1-DV20)	1.50	4.00
*GOLD/50: .75X TO 2X BASIC CARDS		

2018 Star Wars Finest Lightsaber Hilt Medallions

COMMON MEM	5.00	12.00
*GOLD/50: .5X TO 1.2X BASIC MEM		
LMAV Asajj Ventress	6.00	15.00
LMBO Barriss Offee	6.00	15.00
LMSF Finn	6.00	15.00
LMSR Rey	15.00	40.00
LMST Shaak Ti	6.00	15.00
LMY2 Yoda	8.00	20.00
LMYC Yoda	6.00	15.00
LMA22 Anakin Skywalker	12.00	30.00
LMAS1 Anakin Skywalker	6.00	15.00
LMAS2 Ahsoka Tano	6.00	15.00
LMAS3 Ahsoka Tano	6.00	15.00

LMASC Ahsoka Tano	6.00	15.00
LMDM1 Darth Maul	10.00	25.00
LMDS3 Darth Sidious	6.00	15.00
LMDV4 Darth Vader	8.00	20.00
LMDV5 Darth Vader	10.00	25.00
LMDVR Darth Vader	10.00	25.00
LMGIR The Grand Inquisitor	8.00	20.00
LMKR7 Kylo Ren	12.00	30.00
LMKR8 Kylo Ren	12.00	30.00
LML24 Luke Skywalker	10.00	25.00
LML25 Luke Skywalker	8.00	20.00
LML28 Luke Skywalker	10.00	25.00
LMLS6 Luke Skywalker	10.00	25.00
LMLS8 Luke Skywalker	10.00	25.00
LMMW2 Mace Windu	8.00	20.00
LMO22 Obi-Wan Kenobi	6.00	15.00
LMR27 Rey	15.00	40.00
LMSAS Anakin Skywalker	10.00	25.00
LMSLS Luke Skywalker	10.00	25.00

2018 Star Wars Finest Prime Autographs

STATED PRINT RUN 10 SER.#'d SETS		
UNPRICED DUE TO SCARCITY		
PAAD Adam Driver		
PAAS Andy Serkis		
PAADC Anthony Daniels		
PACF Carrie Fisher		
PADR Daisy Ridley		
PAHF Harrison Ford		
PAKB Kenny Baker		
PAPM Peter Mayhew		

2018 Star Wars Finest Rogue One

COMPLETE SET (20)	20.00	50.00
COMMON CARD (RO1-RO20)	2.00	5.00
*GOLD/50: .6X TO 1.5X BASIC CARDS		

2018 Star Wars Finest Rogue One Autographs

RAAP Alistair Petrie		
RAAT Alan Tudyk		
RABD Ben Daniels		
RABM Ben Mendelsohn		
RADA Derek Arnold		
RADY Donnie Yen		
RAFJ Felicity Jones		
RAFW Forest Whitaker		
RAGO Genevieve O'Reilly		
RAIM Ian McElhinney	6.00	15.00
RAMM Mads Mikkelsen		
RARA Riz Ahmed		

2018 Star Wars Finest Solo A Star Wars Story

COMPLETE SET (20)	15.00	40.00
COMMON CARD (SO1-SO20)	1.25	3.00
*GOLD/50: .75X TO 2X BASIC CARDS		

TRADING CARDS

2022 Star Wars Finest

GALEN ERSO
STAR WARS

COMPLETE SET W/O SP (100)		30.00	75.00
COMMON CARD (1-100)		.60	1.50
COMMON SP (101-120)		4.00	12.00

*REF.: .6X TO 1.5X BASIC CARDS
*BLUE:/150: 1.2X TO 3X BASIC CARDS
*GREEN/99: 2X TO 5X BASIC CARDS
*GOLD/50: 3X TO 8X BASIC CARDS

101	Ahsoka Tano SP	25.00	60.00
102	Anakin Skywalker SP	10.00	25.00
104	C-3PO SP	6.00	15.00
108	Maul SP	10.00	25.00
109	Darth Vader SP	15.00	40.00
110	Fennec Shand SP	6.00	15.00
111	Grogu SP	30.00	75.00
112	Han Solo SP	10.00	25.00
113	Kylo Ren SP	10.00	25.00
114	General Leia Organa SP	8.00	20.00
115	Obi-Wan Kenobi SP	10.00	25.00
116	R2-D2 SP	8.00	20.00
117	Rey SP	12.00	30.00
118	The Mandalorian SP	12.00	30.00
119	Finn SP	6.00	15.00
120	Yoda SP	15.00	40.00

2022 Star Wars Finest Autographs

AUTHENTIC AUTOGRAPH
KORSO
STAR WARS

COMMON AUTO		5.00	12.00

*PURPLE/299: .5X TO 1.2X BASIC AUTOS
*BLUE/199: .6X TO 1.5X BASIC AUTOS
*AQUA/199: .6X TO 1.5X BASIC AUTOS
*GREEN/99: .75X TO 2X BASIC AUTOS
*GOLD/50: 1.2X TO 3X BASIC AUTOS
STATED ODDS 1 AUTO OR SKETCH PER BOX

FAAP	Angelique Perrin	6.00	15.00
FACB	Caroline Blakiston	6.00	15.00
FAJD	Julie Dolan	10.00	25.00
FAJS	Jason Spisak	8.00	20.00
FAMC	Michaela Cottrell	6.00	15.00
FAPW	Paul Warren	6.00	15.00
FARB	Richard Brake	12.00	30.00
FATR	Tim Rose	12.00	30.00
FAVK	Valene Kane	10.00	25.00
FAAPE	Alistair Petrie	6.00	15.00

2022 Star Wars Finest The Bad Batch

BAD BATCH
OMEGA

COMPLETE SET (20)		20.00	50.00
COMMON CARD (BB1-BB20)		2.50	6.00

*GOLD/50: 2X TO 5X BASIC CARDS
RANDOMLY INSERTED INTO PACKS

2022 Star Wars Finest The Book of Boba Fett

FENNEC SHAND
THE BOOK OF BOBA FETT

COMPLETE SET (2)		5.00	12.00
COMMON CARD (BF1-BF2)		3.00	8.00

*GOLD/50: 6X TO 15X BASIC CARDS
RANDOMLY INSERTED INTO PACKS

2022 Star Wars Finest The Book of Boba Fett Autographs

UNPRICED DUE TO SCARCITY

BATM Temuera Morrison

2022 Star Wars Finest Galaxy's Finest Heroes Die-Cut Autographs

UNPRICED DUE TO SCARCITY

GFAE Ashley Eckstein
GFAT Alan Tudyk
GFBL Billie Lourd
GFDY Donnie Yen
GFHQ Hugh Quarshie
GFJB John Boyega
GFJH Jessica Henwick
GFLD Laura Dern
GFNA Naomi Ackie
GFOD Olivia d'Abo
GFPL Phil Lamarr
GFRA Riz Ahmed
GFRD Rosario Dawson
GFTG Taylor Gray
GFBDW Billy Dee Williams
GFFPJ Freddie Prinze Jr.
GFJAT James Arnold Taylor
GFKMT Kelly Marie Tran
GFPSL Paul Sun-Hyung Lee
GFRAD Robin Atkin Downes

2022 Star Wars Finest Galaxy's Finest Heroes Die-Cuts

COMMON CARD (GF1-GF20)		10.00	25.00

RANDOMLY INSERTED INTO PACKS

GF1	Luke Skywalker	15.00	40.00
GF2	Han Solo	30.00	75.00
GF3	Yoda	25.00	60.00
GF4	Leia Organa	15.00	40.00
GF5	The Mandalorian	20.00	50.00
GF6	Chewbacca	15.00	40.00
GF7	Rey	50.00	125.00
GF9	R2-D2		30.00
GF10	Obi-Wan Kenobi		50.00
GF11	Lando Calrissian	25.00	60.00
GF13	Poe Dameron	30.00	75.00
GF14	Chirrut Imwe		40.00
GF15	Ahsoka Tano	50.00	125.00
GF17	Qui-Gon Jinn	20.00	50.00
GF18	Mace Windu	30.00	75.00
GF20	Padme Amidala	40.00	100.00

2022 Star Wars Finest The High Republic Concept Art

COMPLETE SET (20)	15.00	40.00
COMMON CARD (HR1-HR20)	2.00	5.00

*GOLD/50: 3X TO 8X BASIC CARDS

RANDOMLY INSERTED INTO PACKS

2022 Star Wars Finest The Mandalorian

COMPLETE SET (20)	40.00	100.00
COMMON CARD (MD1-MD20)	2.50	6.00

*GOLD/50: .75X TO 2X BASIC CARDS

RANDOMLY INSERTED INTO PACKS

MD1 Grogu	8.00	20.00
MD2 The Mandalorian	6.00	15.00
MD3 Koska Reeves	3.00	8.00
MD5 IG-11	4.00	10.00
MD6 Boba Fett	3.00	8.00
MD7 Fennec Shand	3.00	8.00
MD9 Ahsoka Tano	6.00	15.00
MD10 Moff Gideon	4.00	10.00
MD12 Mayfeld	3.00	8.00
MD13 Cobb Vanth	3.00	8.00
MD14 Peli Motto	5.00	12.00
MD15 Bo-Katan Kryze	5.00	12.00
MD17 The Client	3.00	8.00
MD19 Valin Hess	3.00	8.00
MD20 Luke Skywalker	5.00	12.00

2022 Star Wars Finest The Mandalorian Autographs

UNPRICED DUE TO SCARCITY

MACW Carl Weathers

MAGE Giancarlo Esposito

MAMV Mercedes Varnado

MANN Nick Nolte

MAOA Omid Abtahi

MASK Simon Kassianides

MATM Temuera Morrison

MATW Taika Waititi

MAWH Werner Herzog

MADLI Diana Lee Inosanto

2022 Star Wars Finest Prime Autographs

UNPRICED DUE TO SCARCITY

PAAD Adam Driver

PACF Carrie Fisher

PADR Daisy Ridley

PAEM Ewan McGregor

PAFJ Felicity Jones

PAHC Hayden Christensen

PAHF Harrison Ford

PANP Natalie Portman

PASJ Samuel L. Jackson

2022 Star Wars Finest Promo

NNO Grogu NYCC	12.00	30.00

2015 Star Wars Galactic Connexions

COMPLETE SET (75)	8.00	20.00
COMMON DISC	.20	.50

*FOIL: .6X TO 1.5X BASIC DISCS

*BLK: .75X TO 2X BASIC DISCS

*HOLOFOIL: .75X TO 2X BASIC DISCS

*BLK FOIL: 1.5X TO 4X BASIC DISCS

*CLR: 1.5X TO 4X BASIC DISCS

*PATTERN FOIL: 2X TO 5X BASIC DISCS

*BLK PATTERN FOIL: 2.5X TO 6X BASIC DISCS

*JABBA SLIME GREEN: 3X TO 8X BASIC DISCS

*CLR FOIL: 4X TO 10X BASIC DISCS

*LTSABER RED: 4X TO 10X BASIC DISCS

*CLR PATTERN FOIL: 8X TO 20X BASIC DISCS

*C-3PO GOLD: 10X TO 25X BASIC DISCS

*DEATH STAR SILVER: 12X TO 30X BASIC DISCS

*SOLID GOLD: 20X TO 50X BASIC DISCS

2015 Star Wars Galactic Connexions Battle Damaged Border

RANDOMLY INSERTED INTO PACKS

1 Darth Vader	250.00	500.00
Red		
2 Han Solo	150.00	300.00
Red		
3 Luke Skywalker	120.00	250.00
Red		
4 Obi-Wan Kenobi		
Red		
5 Princess Leia Organa		
Red		

2015 Star Wars Galactic Connexions Blue Starfield Exclusives

COMPLETE SET (10)	10.00	25.00
COMMON DISC	1.50	4.00

2015 Star Wars Galactic Connexions SDCC Promos

COMPLETE SET (6)	100.00	200.00
COMMON DISC	12.00	30.00
4 Stormtrooper	30.00	80.00
Red		
5 Stormtrooper	20.00	50.00
Gold		

2015 Star Wars Galactic Connexions Series 2

COMPLETE SET (75)	8.00	20.00
COMMON DISC	.20	.50

*GRAY FOIL: .6X TO 1.5X BASIC DISCS

*BLK: .75X TO 2X BASIC DISCS

*GRAY: .75X TO 2X BASIC DISCS

*BLK FOIL: 1.5X TO 4X BASIC DISCS

*CLR: 1.5X TO 4X BASIC DISCS

*GRAY PATTERN FOIL: 2X TO 5X BASIC DISCS

*BLK PATTERN FOIL: 2.5X TO 6X BASIC DISCS

*JABBA SLIME GREEN: 3X TO 8X BASIC DISCS

*CLR FOIL: 4X TO 10X BASIC DISCS

*LTSABER PURPLE: 4X TO 10X BASIC DISCS

*LTSABER RED: 4X TO 10X BASIC DISCS

*CLR PATTERN FOIL: 8X TO 20X BASIC DISCS

*C-3PO GOLD: 10X TO 25X BASIC DISCS

*DEATH STAR SILVER: 12X TO 30X BASIC DISCS

*SOLID GOLD: 20X TO 50X BASIC DISCS

2012 Star Wars Galactic Files

COMPLETE SET (350)	25.00	50.00
UNOPENED BOX (24 PACKS)	250.00	400.00
UNOPENED PACK (12 CARDS)	10.00	15.00
COMMON CARD (1-350)	.15	.40

*BLUE: 8X TO 20X BASIC CARDS

*RED: 20X TO 50X BASIC CARDS

76 Darth Vader (Jedi Purge) SP	12.00	30.00
96 Luke Skywalker (Stormtrooper) SP	12.00	30.00
125B Princess Leia (Despair) SP	12.00	30.00

2012 Star Wars Galactic Files Autographs

COMMON AUTO	8.00	20.00

STATED ODDS ONE AUTO OR PATCH PER HOBBY BOX

NNO	Amy Allen	12.00	30.00
NNO	Carrie Fisher	500.00	1000.00
NNO	Felix Silla	25.00	60.00
NNO	Harrison Ford	2000.00	3000.00
NNO	Irvin Kershner	600.00	1000.00
NNO	Jake Lloyd	100.00	200.00
NNO	James Earl Jones	200.00	400.00
NNO	Jeremy Bulloch	20.00	50.00
NNO	Mark Hamill	500.00	1000.00
NNO	Matthew Wood	15.00	40.00
NNO	Peter Mayhew	125.00	250.00
NNO	Ray Park	30.00	75.00
NNO	Richard LeParmentier	15.00	40.00

2012 Star Wars Galactic Files Classic Lines

COMPLETE SET (10)	3.00	8.00
COMMON CARD (CL1-CL10)	.75	2.00

STATED ODDS 1:4

2012 Star Wars Galactic Files Duels of Fate

COMPLETE SET (10)	4.00	10.00
COMMON CARD (DF1-DF10)	1.00	2.50

STATED ODDS 1:6

2012 Star Wars Galactic Files Galactic Moments

COMPLETE SET (20)	20.00	40.00
COMMON CARD (GM1-GM20)	1.50	4.00

STATED ODDS 1:6

2012 Star Wars Galactic Files Heroes on Both Sides

COMPLETE SET (10)	4.00	10.00
COMMON CARD (HB1-HB10)	1.00	2.50

STATED ODDS 1:6

2012 Star Wars Galactic Files I Have a Bad Feeling About This

COMPLETE SET (8)	3.00	8.00
COMMON CARD (BF1-BF8)	.75	2.00

STATED ODDS 1:4

2012 Star Wars Galactic Files Patches

COMMON CARD	8.00	20.00

STATED ODDS ONE AUTO OR PATCH PER HOBBY BOX

PR1	X-Wing Fighter Pilots: Red Leader	50.00	100.00
	Garven Dreis		
PR2	X-Wing Fighter Pilots: Red Two	50.00	100.00
	Wedge Antilles		
PR3	X-Wing Fighter Pilots: Red Three	50.00	100.00
	Biggs Darklighter		
PR4	X-Wing Fighter Pilots: Red Four	50.00	100.00
	John D. Branon		
PR5	X-Wing Fighter Pilots: Red Five	100.00	200.00
	Luke Skywalker		
PR6	X-Wing Fighter Pilots: Red Six	50.00	100.00
	Jek Porkins		
PR12	Jedi Starfighter Pilots	12.00	30.00
	Obi-Wan Kenobi		
PR13	Jedi Starfighter Pilots	15.00	40.00
	Anakin Skywalker		
PR14	Jedi Starfighter Pilots	12.00	30.00
	Plo Koon		
PR17	Snowspeeder Pilots: Rogue Leader	75.00	150.00
	Luke Skywalker		
PR18	Snowspeeder Pilots: Rogue Two	40.00	80.00
	Zev Senesca		
PR19	Snowspeeder Pilots: Rogue Three	40.00	80.00
	Wedge Antilles		
PR20	Snowspeeder Pilots: Rogue Four	30.00	60.00
	Derek Hobbie Kuvian		
PR21	Snowspeeder Pilots: Rogue Leader	30.00	60.00
	(Gunner) Dak Ralter		
PR23	Death Star Command	15.00	40.00
	Grand Moff Tarkin		
PR24	Death Star Command	15.00	40.00
	Darth Vader		
PR25	Millennium Falcon Pilots	35.00	70.00
	Han Solo		
PR26	Millennium Falcon Pilots	15.00	40.00
	Chewbacca		
PR27	Millennium Falcon Pilots: Gold Leader	25.00	50.00
	Lando Calrissian		
PR28	Millennium Falcon Pilots: Gold Leader	15.00	40.00
	Nien Numb		

2013 Star Wars Galactic Files 2

COMPLETE SET (353)	20.00	50.00
COMP.SET W/O SP (350)	12.00	30.00
UNOPENED BOX (24 PACKS)	200.00	300.00
UNOPENED PACK (12 CARDS)	8.00	12.00
COMMON CARD (351-699)	.15	.40
COMMON SP	4.00	10.00

*BLUE/350: 2X TO 5X BASIC CARDS

*RED/35: 15X TO 40X BASIC CARDS

*GOLD/10: 50X TO 120X BASIC CARDS

463b	Han Solo Stormtrooper SP	4.00	10.00
481b	Luke Skywalker Bacta Tank SP	4.00	10.00
510b	Princess Leia Slave Girl SP	4.00	10.00

2013 Star Wars Galactic Files 2 Autographs

COMMON AUTO	12.00	30.00

STATED ODDS 1:55

NNO	Ashley Eckstein	40.00	100.00
NNO	Billy Dee Williams	50.00	100.00
NNO	Carrie Fisher	200.00	350.00
NNO	Ian McDiarmid	400.00	600.00
NNO	James Earl Jones	200.00	350.00
NNO	Jeremy Bulloch	15.00	40.00
NNO	Mark Hamill	350.00	500.00
NNO	Peter Mayhew	30.00	75.00

2013 Star Wars Galactic Files 2 Dual Autographs

ANNOUNCED COMBINED PRINT RUN 200

NNO A.Eckstein/T.Kane	100.00	200.00
NNO J.Bulloch/A.Harris	100.00	200.00
NNO J.Jones/I.McDiarmid		
NNO C.Fisher/M.Hamill		
NNO H.Ford/P.Mayhew		

2013 Star Wars Galactic Files 2 Classic Lines

COMPLETE SET (10)	3.00	8.00
COMMON CARD (CL1-CL10)	.60	1.50
STATED ODDS 1:4		

2013 Star Wars Galactic Files 2 Galactic Moments

COMPLETE SET (20)	30.00	60.00
COMMON CARD (GM1-GM20)	2.00	5.00
STATED ODDS 1:12		

2013 Star Wars Galactic Files 2 Honor the Fallen

COMPLETE SET (10)	4.00	10.00
COMMON CARD (HF1-HF10)	.75	2.00
STATED ODDS 1:6		

2013 Star Wars Galactic Files 2 Medallions

COMMON MEDALLION (MD1-MD30)	8.00	20.00
STATED ODDS 1:55		
MD1 Luke Skywalker	12.00	30.00
MD3 Han Solo	20.00	50.00
MD5 Lando Calrissian	12.00	30.00
MD6 Han Solo	150.00	250.00
MD7 Boba Fett	30.00	75.00
MD9 Princess Leia Organa	15.00	40.00
MD10 Bail Organa	10.00	25.00
MD12 General Veers	20.00	50.00
MD13 Jawa	20.00	50.00
MD14 C-3PO	30.00	75.00
MD15 R2-D2	15.00	40.00
MD16 R5-D4	12.00	30.00
MD19 Luke Skywalker	30.00	75.00
MD20 Obi-Wan Kenobi	12.00	30.00
MD21 C-3PO & R2-D2	30.00	75.00
MD22 TIE Fighter Pilot	10.00	25.00
MD23 Darth Vader	15.00	40.00
MD24 Stormtrooper	12.00	30.00
MD25 Obi-Wan Kenobi	12.00	30.00
MD26 Plo Koon	12.00	30.00
MD27 Captain Panaka	12.00	30.00
MD28 Qui-Gon Jinn	12.00	30.00
MD29 Obi-Wan Kenobi	15.00	40.00
MD30 Queen Amidala	50.00	100.00

2013 Star Wars Galactic Files 2 Ripples in the Galaxy

COMPLETE SET (10)	4.00	10.00
COMMON CARD (RG1-RG10)	.75	2.00
STATED ODDS 1:6		

2013 Star Wars Galactic Files 2 The Weak Minded

COMPLETE SET (7)	2.50	6.00
COMMON CARD (WM1-WM7)	.60	1.50
STATED ODDS 1:3		

2017 Star Wars Galactic Files Reborn

KANAN JARRUS

COMPLETE SET (200)	10.00	25.00
UNOPENED BOX (24 PACKS)	80.00	100.00
UNOPENED PACK (6 CARDS)	4.00	5.00
COMMON CARD	.15	.40

*ORANGE: .75X TO 2X BASIC CARDS
*BLUE: 1.2X TO 3X BASIC CARDS
*GREEN/199: 4X TO 10X BASIC CARDS
*PURPLE/99: 8X TO 20X BASIC CARDS
*GOLD/10: 20X TO 50X BASIC CARDS

2017 Star Wars Galactic Files Reborn Autographs

COMMON AUTO	5.00	12.00
NNO Adrienne Wilkinson	6.00	15.00
NNO Alan Tudyk	100.00	200.00
NNO Anna Graves	8.00	20.00
NNO Ashley Eckstein	50.00	125.00
NNO Bruce Spence	5.00	12.00
NNO Catherine Taber	15.00	40.00
NNO Dave Barclay	10.00	25.00
NNO David Bowers	6.00	15.00
NNO Dee Bradley	12.00	30.00
NNO Denis Lawson	10.00	25.00
NNO Freddie Prinze		
NNO George Takei	12.00	30.00
NNO Hassani Shapi	8.00	20.00
NNO Jeremy Bulloch	20.00	50.00
NNO Jerome Blake	6.00	15.00
NNO Jesse Jensen	6.00	15.00
NNO Jim Cummings	6.00	15.00
NNO Julian Glover	6.00	15.00
NNO Kath Soucie	8.00	20.00
NNO Keone Young	20.00	50.00
NNO Lewis MacLeod	5.00	12.00
NNO Mary Oyaya	12.00	30.00
NNO Megan Udall	6.00	15.00
NNO Michael Carter	8.00	20.00
NNO Michonne Bourriague	6.00	15.00
NNO Nika Futterman	12.00	30.00
NNO Oliver Ford	8.00	20.00
NNO Oliver Walpole	10.00	25.00
NNO Olivia D'Abo	8.00	20.00
NNO Phil Eason	6.00	15.00
NNO Phil LaMarr	10.00	25.00
NNO Rajia Baroudi	8.00	20.00
NNO Rena Owen	6.00	15.00
NNO Rohan Nichol	10.00	25.00
NNO Sam Witwer	15.00	40.00
NNO Stephen Stanton	25.00	60.00
NNO Tom Kenny	6.00	15.00
NNO Wayne Pygram	8.00	20.00
NNO Zac Jensen	8.00	20.00

2017 Star Wars Galactic Files Reborn Dual Autographs

COMMON CARD	15.00	40.00
STATED PRINT RUN 5-50 SER.#'d SETS		
NNO Blakiston/Rose/50	20.00	50.00
NNO Fisher/Blakiston/5		
NNO McDiarmid/Carson/5		

2017 Star Wars Galactic Files Reborn Famous Quotes

COMPLETE SET (15)	8.00	20.00
COMMON CARD (MQ1-MQ15)	1.00	2.50

2017 Star Wars Galactic Files Reborn Galactic Moments

VADER STRIKES DOWN KENOBI

COMPLETE SET (9)	8.00	20.00
COMMON CARD (GM1-GM9)	1.25	3.00

2017 Star Wars Galactic Files Reborn Locations

COMPLETE SET (10)	6.00	15.00
COMMON CARD (L1-L10)	1.00	2.50

TRADING CARDS

2017 Star Wars Galactic Files Reborn Six-Person Autograph

UNPRICED DUE TO SCARCITY

NNO McDiarmid/Wood/Carson/Pygram/Colley/Glover

2017 Star Wars Galactic Files Reborn Triple Autographs

UNPRICED DUE TO SCARCITY

NNO Fisher/Barclay/Carter
NNO Revill/Colley/Glover
NNO Prinze Jr./Gray/Eckstein
NNO Grunberg/Rotich/Rose
NNO McDiarmid/Park/Blake
NNO Hamill/Baker/Daniels
NNO Wood/Carson/Blake
NNO Witwer/Goodson/Futterman

2017 Star Wars Galactic Files Reborn Vehicle Medallions

COMMON MEM	5.00	12.00
*SILVER/99: .6X TO 1.5X BASIC MEM		
*GOLD/25: 1.2X TO 3X BASIC MEM		

2017 Star Wars Galactic Files Reborn Vehicles

COMPLETE SET (20)	10.00	25.00
COMMON CARD (V1-V20)	.75	2.00
*PURPLE/99: 1.5X TO 4X BASIC CARDS		

2017 Star Wars Galactic Files Reborn Weapons

CHEWBACCA'S BOWCASTER

COMPLETE SET (10)	6.00	15.00
COMMON CARD (W1-W10)	1.00	2.50
*PURPLE/99: 1.2X TO 3X BASIC CARDS		

2018 Star Wars Galactic Files

COMPLETE SET (200)	12.00	30.00
UNOPENED BOX (24 PACKS)	60.00	90.00
UNOPENED PACK (8 CARDS)	3.00	4.00
COMMON CARD (RO9-ROTS23)	.20	.50
*ORANGE: .6X TO 1.5X BASIC CARDS		
*BLUE: .75X TO 2X BASIC CARDS		
*GREEN/199: 4X TO 10X BASIC CARDS		
*PURPLE/99: 6X TO 15X BASIC CARDS		

2018 Star Wars Galactic Files Autographs

AAB Ariyon Bakare	6.00	15.00
AAD Adam Driver		
AAG Anna Graves	5.00	12.00
AAP Alistair Petrie		

AAT Alan Tudyk		
ABG Barbara Goodson		
ABP Bonnie Piesse	5.00	12.00
ACA Cas Anvar	10.00	25.00
ACF Carrie Fisher		
ACR Clive Revill		
ADM Daniel Mays	6.00	15.00
ADR Daisy Ridley		
ADT David Tennant		
ADY Donnie Yen		
AFJ Felicity Jones		
AFW Forest Whitaker		
AGC Gwendoline Christie		
AGG Greg Grunberg		
AGT George Takei		
AHC Hayden Christensen		
AHF Harrison Ford		
AHS Hugh Skinner	8.00	20.00
AIM Ian McDiarmid		
AJB John Boyega		
AJL Jett Lucas	6.00	15.00
AKB Kenny Baker		
AKF Kate Fleetwood	5.00	12.00
AKR Kipsang Rotich	5.00	12.00
ALD Laura Dern		
AMS Meredith Salenger	6.00	15.00
ARA Riz Ahmed		
ARD Robbie Daymond	5.00	12.00
ARN Robert Nairne	10.00	25.00
ARP Ray Park		
ATM Temuera Morrison		
AVK Valene Kane	6.00	15.00
AADT Andy De La Tour	12.00	30.00
AAEK Ashley Eckstein		
AAND Anthony Daniels		
ABDW Billy Dee Williams		
AFPJ Freddie Prinze Jr.		
AJSC Jordan Stephens	5.00	12.00
AMSA Marc Silk	5.00	12.00
ASMG Sarah Michelle Gellar		

2018 Star Wars Galactic Files Band of Heroes

THE RESISTANCE

COMPLETE SET (7)	5.00	12.00
COMMON CARD (BH1-BH7)	1.25	3.00
*PURPLE/99: .6X TO 1.5X BASIC CARDS		

2018 Star Wars Galactic Files Dual Autographs

UNPRICED DUE TO SCARCITY

DAAT R.Ahmed/A.Tudyk
DAFF H.Ford/C.Fisher
DAGB T.Gray/S.Blum
DAJW F.Jones/F.Whitaker
DAKL T.Kenny/P.LaMarr
DARB D.Ridley/J.Boyega
DARQ T.Rose/M.Quinn
DATB G.Takei/D.Baker
DATL J.A.Taylor/M.Lanter

2018 Star Wars Galactic Files Galactic Moments

COMPLETE SET (10)	6.00	15.00
COMMON CARD (GM1-GM10)	1.00	2.50
*PURPLE/99: .75X TO 2X BASIC CARDS		

2018 Star Wars Galactic Files Locations

CLOUD CITY GANTRY

COMPLETE SET (10)	8.00	20.00
COMMON CARD (L1-L10)	1.25	3.00
*PURPLE/99: .75X TO 2X BASIC CARDS		

2018 Star Wars Galactic Files Manufactured Movie Poster Patches

DARTH MAUL

COMMON PATCH	6.00	15.00
*BLUE/99: .5X TO 1.2X BASIC PATCHES		
*GREEN/50: .6X TO 1.5X BASIC PATCHES		
*PURPLE/25: .75X TO 2X BASIC PATCHES		
MAF Finn		
MAR Rey	10.00	25.00
MAY Yoda		
MAAA Admiral Ackbar		

MAAS Anakin Skywalker	8.00	20.00
MABF Boba Fett	10.00	25.00
MABM Baze Malbus		
MABR Bodhi Rook	15.00	40.00
MACA Cassian Andor		
MACD Count Dooku		
MACI Chirrut Imwe	10.00	25.00
MACP Captain Phasma		
MADK Director Krennic	8.00	20.00
MADM Darth Maul	10.00	25.00
MADS Darth Sidious		
MADV Darth Vader		
MAFJ Finn		
MAGH General Hux	6.00	15.00
MAHS Han Solo	12.00	30.00
MAJE Jyn Erso		
MAJF Jango Fett	6.00	15.00
MAKR Kylo Ren		
MALC Lando Calrissian	8.00	20.00
MALO Princess Leia Organa	10.00	25.00
MALS Luke Skywalker	10.00	25.00
MAPA Queen Amidala	12.00	30.00
MAPD Poe Dameron		
MARD R2-D2	8.00	20.00
MARJ Rey	15.00	40.00
MASG Saw Gerrera	15.00	40.00
MATE The Emperor	15.00	40.00
MAASM Anakin Skywalker	8.00	20.00
MAASR Anakin Skywalker	8.00	20.00
MACPO C-3PO	10.00	25.00
MADVS Darth Vader		
MAGGS General Grievous	6.00	15.00
MAGMT Grand Moff Tarkin	8.00	20.00
MAHSE Han Solo	12.00	30.00
MAHSF Han Solo	12.00	30.00
MAHSH Han Solo	12.00	30.00
MAJTH Jabba The Hutt	6.00	15.00
MAKRF Kylo Ren		
MALOF General Leia Organa	12.00	30.00
MALOJ Princess Leia Organa	10.00	25.00
MALSH Luke Skywalker	10.00	25.00
MALSJ Luke Skywalker	10.00	25.00
MALSR Luke Skywalker	10.00	25.00
MAOKC Obi-Wan Kenobi	6.00	15.00
MAOKH Obi-Wan Kenobi	6.00	15.00
MAOKS Obi-Wan Kenobi	12.00	30.00
MAOWK Obi-Wan Kenobi	6.00	15.00
MAPAC Padme Amidala	12.00	30.00
MAPDJ Poe Dameron		
MAPLO Princess Leia Organa	15.00	40.00
MAQGJ Qui-Gon Jinn	15.00	40.00
MASLS Supreme Leader Snoke		

2018 Star Wars Galactic Files Memorable Quotes

COMPLETE SET (10)	6.00	15.00

COMMON CARD (MQ1-MQ10)	1.00	2.50
*PURPLE/99: .75X TO 2X BASIC CARDS		

2018 Star Wars Galactic Files Sinister Syndicates

COMPLETE SET (15)	10.00	25.00
COMMON CARD (SS1-SS15)	1.25	3.00
*PURPLE/99: .75X TO 2X BASIC CARDS		

2018 Star Wars Galactic Files Six-Person Autograph

UNPRICED DUE TO SCARCITY

NNO Jones/Whitaker/Ahmed

Yen/Tudyk/O'Reilly

2018 Star Wars Galactic Files Source Material Fabric Swatches

COMMON SWATCH	20.00	50.00
CRGE Galen Erso's Jacket	25.00	60.00
CRJE Jyn Erso's Poncho	50.00	100.00
CRPD Poe Dameron's Shirt	25.00	60.00
CRPG Praetorian Guard's Uniform	30.00	75.00
CRRH Rey's Head Wrap	60.00	120.00
CRRJ Rey's Jacket	100.00	200.00

2018 Star Wars Galactic Files Triple Autographs

STATED PRINT RUN 5 SER.#'d SETS

UNPRICED DUE TO SCARCITY

NNO Williams/Quinn/Mayhew

NNO Mikkelsen/McGlynn/Baker

2018 Star Wars Galactic Files Vehicles

COMPLETE SET (10)	6.00	15.00
COMMON CARD (V1-V10)	1.00	2.50
*NO FOIL: .5X TO 1.2X BASIC CARDS		
*PURPLE/99: .75X TO 2X BASIC CARDS		

2018 Star Wars Galactic Files Weapons

CHIRRUT IMWE'S STAFF

COMPLETE SET (10)	6.00	15.00
COMMON CARD (W1-W10)	1.00	2.50
*PURPLE/99: .75X TO 2X BASIC CARDS		

2018-19 Star Wars Galactic Moments Countdown to Episode 9

DARTH VADER

STAR WARS: A NEW HOPE

COMMON CARD	5.00	12.00

1993-95 Star Wars Galaxy

COMPLETE SET (365)	15.00	40.00
COMP.SER 1 SET (140)	6.00	15.00
COMP.SER 2 SET (135)	6.00	15.00
COMP.SER 3 SET (90)	6.00	15.00
UNOPENED SER.1 BOX (36 PACKS)	30.00	40.00
UNOPENED SER.1 PACK (8 CARDS)	1.00	1.25
UNOPENED SER.2 BOX (36 PACKS)	20.00	30.00
UNOPENED SER.2 PACK (8 CARDS)	.75	1.00
UNOPENED SER.3 BOX (36 PACKS)	20.00	30.00
UNOPENED SER.3 PACK (7 CARDS)	.75	1.00
COMMON CARD (1-365)	.15	.40
*MIL.FALCON FOIL: .8X TO 2X BASIC CARDS		
*FIRST DAY: 1X TO 2.5X BASIC CARDS		
DARTH VADER FOIL UNNUMBERED	4.00	10.00

1993-95 Star Wars Galaxy Clearzone

COMPLETE SET (6)	15.00	40.00
COMMON CARD (E1-E6)	3.00	8.00

1993-95 Star Wars Galaxy Etched Foil

COMPLETE SET (18)	60.00	120.00
COMMON CARD (1-18)	3.00	8.00

1993-95 Star Wars Galaxy LucasArts

COMPLETE SET (12)	6.00	15.00
COMMON CARD (L1-L12)	.60	1.50

1993-95 Star Wars Galaxy Promos

0 Ralph McQuarrie (Darth Vader)	2.50	6.00
0 Drew Sturzan artwork (SW Galaxy Magazine)	1.25	3.00
0 Ken Steacy Art		
P1 Jae Lee/Rancor Monster(dealer cello pack)	1.25	4.00
P1 Jae Lee/Rancor Monster/AT-AT		
P1 Rancor Card		
AT-AT/Yoda 5X7		
P2 Chris Sprouse/Luke building lightsaber (NSU)	2.00	5.00
P2 Snowtrooper (Convention exclusive)	1.50	4.00

P3 Yoda Shrine SP	250.00	400.00
P3 Darth Vader on Hoth (NSU)	1.25	3.00
P4 Dave Gibbons/C-3PO and Jawas (SW Galaxy 1 Tin Set)		
P4 Luke on Dagobah/Art Suydam	.60	1.50
P5 Joe Phillips/Han and Chewbacca (Cards Illustrated)	2.00	5.00
P5 AT-AT	.75	2.00
P6 Tom Taggart/Boba Fett (Hero)	2.50	6.00
P6 Luke with lightsaber (SW Galaxy Magazine)		
P7 Leia with Jacen and Jania (Wizard Magazine)	2.00	5.00
P8 Boba Fett and Darth Vader (Cards Illustrated)	4.00	10.00
140 Look for Series Two (Bend Ems Toys)		
DH2 Cam Kennedy artwork/BobaFett	2.00	5.00
DH3 Cam Kennedy artwork/Millennium Falcon	2.00	5.00
NNO Jim Starlin/Stormtrooper and Ewoks (Triton #3)	1.50	4.00
NNO Tim Truman/Tuskan Raiders	3.00	8.00
NNO Boba Fett	3.00	8.00
NNO AT-AT 5 x 7 (Previews)		
NNO Boba Fett/Dengar (Classic Star Wars)	2.00	5.00
NNO Jabba the Hutt (NSU/Starlog/Wizard)	1.25	3.00
NNO Princess Leia (NSU)	1.50	4.00
NNO Sandtrooper (Wizard Magazine)	1.50	4.00
NNO Truce at Bakura (Bantam exclusive)	4.00	10.00
NNO Princess Leia/Sandtrooper 2-Card Panel (Advance exclusive)		
NNO Jabba the Hutt, Obi-Wan/Darth Vader 5X7 (Previews exclusive)		
DH1A Cam Kennedy artwork/Battling Robots		
(Dark Lords of the Sith comic)	2.00	5.00
Series at line 8		
DH1B Cam Kennedy artwork/Battling Robots		
(Dark Lords of the Sith comic)	2.00	5.00
Series at line 9		
SWB1 Grand Moff Tarkin (album exclusive)	4.00	10.00

2021 Star Wars Galaxy Chrome

COMPLETE SET (100)	20.00	50.00
UNOPENED BOX (24 PACKS)	350.00	500.00
UNOPENED PACK (8 CARDS)	15.00	20.00
COMMON CARD (1-100)	.40	1.00
*REF./: .75X TO 2X BASIC CARDS		

---

*ATOMIC/150: 3X TO 8X BASIC CARDS

*WAVE/99: 4X TO 10X BASIC CARDS

*PRISM/75: 5X TO 12X BASIC CARDS

*MOJO/50: 6X TO 15X BASIC CARDS

*PURPLE/25: 8X TO 20X BASIC CARDS

2021 Star Wars Galaxy Chrome Dual Autographs

UNPRICED DUE TO SCARCITY

DACB J.Boyega/G.Christie

DACC H.Corfield/C.Clarke

DAEB P.Bettany/A.Ehrenreich

DAFB B.Blessed/O.Davies

DAFM P.Mayhew/H.Ford

DAJM M.Mikkelsen/F.Jones

DAKE A.Eckstein/J.King

DAMB E.McGregor/A.Best

DAML T.Morrison/D.Logan

DANE G.Esposito/W.Herzog

DARS J.Suotamo/D.Ridley

DASL C.Louise/S.Smart

DATE G.Takei/A.Eckstein

2021 Star Wars Galaxy Chrome Mandalorian Visions

COMPLETE SET (10)	20.00	50.00
COMMON CARD (MN1-MN10)	3.00	8.00
*GREEN/99: .6X TO 1.5X BASIC CARDS		
*PURPLE/50: .75X TO 2X BASIC CARDS		
*ORANGE/25: 2X TO 5X BASIC CARDS		
STATED ODDS 1:9		

2021 Star Wars Galaxy Chrome Star Wars Global Posters

COMPLETE SET (20)	15.00	40.00
COMMON CARD (GP1-GP20)	2.00	5.00
*GREEN/99: .5X TO 1.2X BASIC CARDS		
*PURPLE/50: .6X TO 1.5X BASIC CARDS		
*ORANGE/25: .75X TO 2X BASIC CARDS		
STATED ODDS 1:9		

2021 Star Wars Galaxy Chrome Triple Autographs

STATED PRINT RUN SER.#'d SETS

UNPRICED DUE TO SCARCITY

TADSC Driver/Serkis/Christie

TAEKD Ehrenreich/Davis/Kellyman

TAFET Bulloch/Morrison/Logan

TAFWM Ford/Mayhew/Williams

TAHFP Hale/Paisley Day/Francis

TALHK Lawson/Klaff/Hagon

TAMAC Rose/Blakiston/Crowley

TARBT Ridley/Boyega/Tran

TAWRQ Williamson/Quinn/Roy

TAYKK Kasey/Kellington/Yen

2021 Star Wars Galaxy Chrome Vintage Star Wars Posters

COMPLETE SET (15)	15.00	40.00
COMMON CARD (V1-V15)	2.50	6.00
*GREEN/99: .5X TO 1.2X BASIC CARDS		
*PURPLE/50: .6X TO 1.5X BASIC CARDS		
*ORANGE/25: .75X TO 2X BASIC CARDS		
STATED ODDS 1:9		

1999 Star Wars Galaxy Collector

COMPLETE SET W/O SP (9)	6.00	15.00
COMMON CARD (SW0-SW9)	1.25	3.00
SW0 Episode I	30.00	75.00
(Non-Sport Update Gummie Award Exclusive)		

1996 Star Wars Galaxy Magazine Cover Gallery

COMPLETE SET (4)	3.00	8.00
COMMON CARD (C1-C4)	1.00	2.50

1995 Star Wars Galaxy Magazine Finest Promos

COMPLETE SET (4)	3.00	8.00
COMMON CARD (SWGM1-SWGM4)	1.50	4.00

2009 Star Wars Galaxy Series 4

COMPLETE SET (120)	5.00	12.00
UNOPENED BOX (24 PACKS)	75.00	125.00
UNOPENED PACK (7 CARDS)	3.00	5.00
COMMON CARD (1-120)	.15	.40

2009 Star Wars Galaxy Series 4 Silver Foil

COMPLETE SET (15)	5.00	12.00
COMMON CARD (1-15)	.60	1.50
*BRONZE: 2X TO 5X BASIC CARDS		
*GOLD: .8X TO 2X BASIC CARDS		
STATED ODDS 1:3		

2009 Star Wars Galaxy Series 4 Etched Foil

COMPLETE SET (6)	6.00	12.00
COMMON CARD (1-6)	1.50	4.00
STATED ODDS 1:6		

2009 Star Wars Galaxy Series 4 Galaxy Evolutions

COMPLETE SET (6)	30.00	80.00
COMMON CARD (1-6)	8.00	20.00
STATED ODDS 1:24 RETAIL		

2009 Star Wars Galaxy Series 4 Lost Galaxy

COMPLETE SET (5)	12.00	25.00
COMMON CARD (1-5)	3.00	8.00
STATED ODDS 1:24		
YODA'S WORLD/999 STATED ODDS 1:277		
JOHN RHEAUME AUTO STATED ODDS 1:2,789		
NNO Yoda's World/999	15.00	30.00
NNOAU Yoda's World		
Rheaume AU		

2009 Star Wars Galaxy Series 4 Promos

COMPLETE SET (4)	8.00	20.00
COMMON CARD (P1A-P3)	.75	2.00
P1A Ventress	1.50	4.00
Dooku GEN		
P1B Starcruiser crash/ (Fan Club Excl.)	6.00	15.00
P3 Group shot WW	2.00	5.00

2010 Star Wars Galaxy Series 5

COMPLETE SET (120)	8.00	20.00
UNOPENED BOX (24 PACKS)		
UNOPENED PACK (7 CARDS)		
COMMON CARD (1-120)	.15	.40

2010 Star Wars Galaxy Series 5 Etched Foil

COMPLETE SET (6)	4.00	10.00
COMMON CARD (1-6)	1.25	3.00
STATED ODDS 1:6 H/R		

2010 Star Wars Galaxy Series 5 Silver Foil

COMPLETE SET (15)	6.00	15.00
COMMON CARD (1-15)	.60	1.50
*BRONZE FOIL: 1.2X TO 3X BASIC CARDS		
*GOLD FOIL/770: 6X TO 15X BASIC CARDS		
STATED ODDS 1:3 H/R		

2010 Star Wars Galaxy Series 5 Autographs

COMMON AUTO	75.00	150.00
STATED ODDS 1:274 HOBBY		
DP David Prowse	100.00	200.00
JJ James Earl Jones	150.00	300.00
MH Mark Hamill	600.00	1200.00
PM Peter Mayhew	100.00	200.00

2010 Star Wars Galaxy Series 5 Lost Galaxy

COMPLETE SET (5)	10.00	25.00
COMMON CARD (1-5)	3.00	8.00
STATED ODDS 1:24 HOBBY		

2011 Star Wars Galaxy Series 6

COMPLETE SET (120)	8.00	20.00
UNOPENED BOX (24 PACKS)	225.00	350.00
UNOPENED PACK (7 CARDS)	10.00	15.00
COMMON CARD (1-120)	.15	.40

2011 Star Wars Galaxy Series 6 Silver Foil

COMPLETE SET (10)	6.00	15.00
COMMON CARD (1-10)	1.00	2.50
*BRONZE: 1.2X TO 3X BASIC CARDS		
*GOLD/600: 4X TO 10X BASIC CARDS		
STATED ODDS 1:3		

2011 Star Wars Galaxy Series 6 Animation Cels

COMPLETE SET (9)	20.00	40.00
COMMON CARD (1-9)	3.00	8.00
STATED ODDS 1:4 RETAIL		

2011 Star Wars Galaxy Series 6 Etched Foil

COMPLETE SET (6)	5.00	12.00
COMMON CARD (1-6)	1.25	3.00
STATED ODDS 1:6		

2012 Star Wars Galaxy Series 7

COMPLETE SET (110)	8.00	20.00
UNOPENED BOX (24 PACKS)	250.00	400.00
UNOPENED PACK (7 CARDS)	10.00	15.00
COMMON CARD (1-110)	.15	.40

2012 Star Wars Galaxy Series 7 Silver Foil

COMPLETE SET (15)	6.00	15.00
COMMON CARD (1-15)	.75	2.00
*BRONZE: 1.5X TO 4X SILVER		
*GOLD: 3X TO 8X SILVER		
STATED ODDS 1:3		

2012 Star Wars Galaxy Series 7 Cels

COMPLETE SET (9)	35.00	70.00
COMMON CARD (1-9)	4.00	10.00

2012 Star Wars Galaxy Series 7 Etched Foil

COMPLETE SET (6)	5.00	12.00
COMMON CARD (1-6)	1.50	4.00
STATED ODDS 1:6		

2018 Star Wars Galaxy

COMPLETE SET (100)	15.00	40.00
UNOPENED BOX (24 PACKS)	65.00	80.00
UNOPENED PACK (8 CARDS)	3.00	4.00
COMMON CARD (1-100)	.40	1.00
*BLUE: .6X TO 1.5X BASIC CARDS		
*GREEN: 1.2X TO 3X BASIC CARDS		
*PURPLE/99: 2.5X TO 6X BASIC CARDS		
*ORANGE/25: 6X TO 15X BASIC CARDS		

2018 Star Wars Galaxy Art Patches

COMMON MEM		
*BLUE/199: SAME VALUE AS BASIC		
*GREEN/150: .5X TO 1.2X BASIC MEM		
*PURPLE/99: .6X TO 1.5X BASIC MEM		
*ORANGE/25: .75X TO 2X BASIC MEM		
MD Droids	8.00	20.00
MDV Darth Vader	8.00	20.00
MHL Han and Leia	10.00	25.00
MJW Jawas	6.00	15.00
MLL Luke and Leia	10.00	25.00
MLS Luke Skywalker	8.00	20.00
MPL Princess Leia	8.00	20.00
MSC Salacious B. Crumb	6.00	15.00
MTR Tusken Raider	8.00	20.00
MWT Wilhuff Tarkin	6.00	15.00
MWW Wicket W. Warrick	6.00	15.00
MXW X-Wings	8.00	20.00

2018 Star Wars Galaxy Autographs

ANAKIN SKYWALKER
AUTHENTIC AUTOGRAPH

RANDOMLY INSERTED INTO PACKS

GAAA Amy Allen	8.00	20.00
GAAD Anthony Daniels		
GAAE Ashley Eckstein		
GAAS Andrew Secombe		
GAAT Alan Tudyk		
GABL Bai Ling	6.00	15.00
GACF Carrie Fisher		
GACR Clive Revill		
GADL Daniel Logan	12.00	30.00
GADR Daisy Ridley		
GADT David Tennant		
GADY Donnie Yen		
GAEL Eric Lopez	6.00	15.00
GAFJ Felicity Jones		
GAFP Freddie Prinze Jr.		
GAFW Forest Whitaker		
GAGC Gwendoline Christie		
GAGT George Takei		
GAHC Hayden Christensen		
GAHF Harrison Ford		
GAHQ Hugh Quarshie		
GAIM Ian McDiarmid		
GAJB John Boyega		
GAJC Jim Cummings	6.00	15.00
GAJI Jason Isaacs		
GAKB Kenny Baker		
GALS Lloyd Sherr		
GAMC Michaela Cottrell	6.00	15.00
GAMK Michael Kingma		
GAMO Mary Oyaya	5.00	12.00
GANF Nika Futterman		
GANK Nalini Krishan	6.00	15.00
GAOD Olivia d'Abo		
GAPM Peter Mayhew		
GAPW Paul Warren	5.00	12.00
GARA Riz Ahmed		
GARB Raija Baroudi	6.00	15.00
GARN Rohan Nichol	5.00	12.00

GARP Ray Park		
GASB Steven Blum	5.00	12.00
GASS Stephen Stanton		
GASW Sam Witwer		
GATB Tom Baker		
GATK Tom Kenny		
GAADK Adam Driver		
GABDW Billy Dee Williams		
GADRY Deep Roy		
GAGAT James Arnold Taylor		
GAJCW John Coppinger	8.00	20.00
GAKCH Keisha Castle-Hughes		
GAPAR Philip Anthony-Rodriguez	5.00	12.00
GARWB Ralph Brown	8.00	20.00
GASMG Sarah Michelle Gellar		
GATCB Tosin Cole	5.00	12.00

2018 Star Wars Galaxy Dual Autographs

KYLO REN
AUTHENTIC AUTOGRAPHS
SUPREME LEADER SNOKE

STATED PRINT RUN 25 SER.#'d SETS

DABD J.Boyega/A.Driver		
DABH D.Barclay/G.Home	15.00	40.00
DABW J.Boyega/M.Wood		
DADS A.Driver/A.Serkis		
DAFD N.Futterman/A.Ventress		
DAGR G.Grunberg/K.Rotich		
DAJA F.Jones/R.Ahmed		
DATE G.Takei/A.Eckstein		
DAVR B.Vernel/Y.Ruhian	15.00	40.00
DAWU O.Walpole/M.Udall	12.00	30.00

2018 Star Wars Galaxy Etched Foil Galaxy Puzzle

COMPLETE SET (6)	15.00	40.00
COMMON CARD (GP1-GP6)	4.00	10.00
RANDOMLY INSERTED INTO PACKS		

2018 Star Wars Galaxy Ghost Crew Wanted Posters

COMPLETE SET (6)	5.00	12.00
COMMON CARD (P1-P6)	1.25	3.00
RANDOMLY INSERTED INTO PACKS		

2018 Star Wars Galaxy Journey of Ahsoka

COMPLETE SET (10)	6.00	15.00
COMMON CARD (1-10)	1.00	2.50
*PURPLE/99: .6X TO 1.5X BASIC CARDS		
*ORANGE/25: 1.2X TO 3X BASIC CARDS		
RANDOMLY INSERTED INTO PACKS		

2018 Star Wars Galaxy Legends

COMPLETE SET (5)	10.00	25.00
COMMON CARD (C1-C5)	3.00	8.00

*PURPLE/99: .6X TO 1.5X BASIC CARDS

RANDOMLY INSERTED INTO PACKS

2018 Star Wars Galaxy New Trilogy Propaganda

COMPLETE SET (6)	5.00	10.00
COMMON CARD (TP1-TP6)	1.00	2.50

RANDOMLY INSERTED INTO PACKS

2018 Star Wars Galaxy Rogue One Propaganda

COMPLETE SET (9)	6.00	15.00
COMMON CARD (RP1-RP9)	1.25	3.00

RANDOMLY INSERTED INTO PACKS

2018 Star Wars Galaxy Six-Person Autograph

UNPRICED DUE TO SCARCITY

NNO Ridley/Boyega/Dern
Serkis/Driver/Christie

2018 Star Wars Galaxy Triple Autographs

UNPRICED DUE TO SCARCITY

TACMW Christensen/McDiarmid/Wood
TAESF Eckstein/Salenger/Futterman
TAFFD Ford/Fisher/Daniels
TAYKK Yen/Kellington/Kasey

2022 Star Wars Galaxy Promo

NNO Vader vs. Obi-Wan NYCC	10.00	25.00

2022 Star Wars The Galaxy's Most Powerful Women

COMPLETE SET (12)	12.00	30.00
COMMON CARD (1-12)	1.50	4.00

*RED/25: 8X TO 20X BASIC CARDS

ANNCD PRINT RUN SER.#'d SETS

1 Leia Organa	2.50	6.00
2 Rey	3.00	8.00
4 Padme Amidala	3.00	8.00
5 Ahsoka Tano	2.00	5.00
9 Jyn Erso	2.00	5.00
11 Omega	2.50	6.00
12 Fennec Shand	3.00	8.00

2004 Star Wars Heritage

COMPLETE SET (120)	8.00	20.00
UNOPENED BOX (36 PACKS)	300.00	600.00
UNOPENED PACK (5 CARDS)	2.00	2.50
COMMON CARD (1-120)	.15	.40

2004 Star Wars Heritage Alphabet Stickers

COMPLETE SET (30)	12.00	30.00

STATED ODDS 1:3 RETAIL

2004 Star Wars Heritage Autographs

STATED ODDS 1:578

NNO Carrie Fisher	1000.00	2000.00
NNO James Earl Jones	600.00	1200.00
NNO Mark Hamill	1000.00	2000.00

2004 Star Wars Heritage Etched Wave One

COMPLETE SET (6)	6.00	15.00
COMMON CARD (1-6)	1.25	3.00

STATED ODDS 1:9

2004 Star Wars Heritage Etched Wave Two

COMPLETE SET (6)	6.00	15.00
COMMON CARD (1-6)	1.25	3.00

STATED ODDS 1:9

2004 Star Wars Heritage Promos

COMMON CARD (P1-P6, S1)	.75	2.00
P1 The Phantom Menace	2.00	5.00
P2 Attack of the Clones	6.00	15.00
P6 Return of the Jedi	2.00	5.00
S1 Empire Strikes Back CT UK	2.50	6.00

2015 Star Wars High Tek

COMPLETE SET w/o SP (112)	60.00	120.00
COMPLETE SET w/SP (127)	250.00	500.00
UNOPENED BOX (8 CARDS)	150.00	250.00
COMMON CARD (1-112)	.40	1.00

*DS CORE: .5X TO 1.2X BASIC CARDS

*HOTH TAC.: .5X TO 1.2X BASIC CARDS

*TIE FRONT: .6X TO 1.5X BASIC CARDS

*VADER TIE: .6X TO 1.5X BASIC CARDS

*MIL.FALCON: .75X TO 2X BASIC CARDS

*STAR DEST.: .75X TO 2X BASIC CARDS
*CARBON: 1X TO 2.5X BASIC CARDS
*EMP.THRONE: 1X TO 2.5X BASIC CARDS
*DS EXT.: 2X TO 5X BASIC CARDS
*TIE WING: 2X TO 5X BASIC CARDS
TIDAL/99: 1.2X TO 3X BASIC CARDS
GOLD RAINBOW/50: 1.5X TO 4X BASIC CARDS
CLOUDS/25: 2X TO 5X BASIC CARDS

1A Luke lightsaber	3.00	8.00
1B Luke blaster SP	10.00	25.00
1C Luke Jedi Knight SP	12.00	30.00
2A Leia A New Hope	3.00	8.00
2B Leia Bespin uniform SP	15.00	40.00
2C Leia Slave SP	120.00	200.00
3A Han Solo blaster	4.00	10.00
3B Han Solo Bespin SP	20.00	50.00
3C Han Solo Endor SP	12.00	30.00
4 Darth Vader	5.00	12.00
5A The Emperor	2.00	5.00
5B Sheev Palpatine SP	4.00	10.00
5C Darth Sidious SP	12.00	30.00
6 Yoda	1.25	3.00
7A C-3PO shiny chrome	4.00	10.00
7B C-3PO dirty chrome SP	8.00	20.00
8 R2-D2	1.25	3.00
9 Chewbacca	1.25	3.00
10A Lando cape	2.00	5.00
10B Lando blaster SP	8.00	20.00
11 Boba Fett	2.00	5.00
36A Anakin Skywalker	1.25	3.00
36B Anakin two lightsabers SP	6.00	15.00
37A Obi-Wan Kenobi	1.25	3.00
37B Obi-Wan young SP	12.00	30.00
37C Obi-Wan old SP	8.00	20.00
40A Padme dark dress	1.25	3.00
40B Padme Amidala white outfit SP	10.00	25.00
42 Darth Maul	1.25	3.00
44B Boba Fett armor SP	25.00	60.00
88 Anakin Skywalker	1.25	3.00
94 The Inquisitor	.75	2.00
106 Finn	3.00	8.00
107 Kylo Ren	3.00	8.00
108 Rey	5.00	12.00
109 Poe Dameron	3.00	8.00
110 BB-8	4.00	10.00
111 Captain Phasma	3.00	8.00
112 Flametrooper	2.00	5.00

2015 Star Wars High Tek Armor Tek

COMPLETE SET (10)	120.00	250.00
COMMON CARD (AT1-AT10)	8.00	20.00
STATED PRINT RUN 50 SER.#'d SETS		
AT1 Boba Fett	15.00	40.00
AT3 Commander Cody	15.00	40.00
AT4 Darth Vader	20.00	50.00
AT5 Jango Fett	12.00	30.00
AT7 Luke Skywalker	12.00	30.00
AT8 Sabine Wren	10.00	25.00
AT9 Poe Dameron	15.00	40.00
AT10 Kylo Ren	15.00	40.00

2015 Star Wars High Tek Autographs

COMMON AUTO	6.00	15.00
*TIDAL/75: .5X TO 1.2X BASIC AUTOS		
*GOLD RAINBOW/50: .6X TO 1.5X BASIC AUTOS		
*CLOUDS/25: .75X TO 2X BASIC AUTOS		
2 Carrie Fisher	200.00	400.00
4 David Prowse	120.00	250.00
6 Deep Roy	20.00	50.00
7 Anthony Daniels	80.00	150.00
9 Peter Mayhew	25.00	60.00
11 Jeremy Bulloch	15.00	40.00
12 Paul Blake	10.00	25.00
14 Alan Harris	8.00	20.00
16 Tim Rose	10.00	25.00
20 Warwick Davis	12.00	30.00
23 Dickey Beer	10.00	25.00
27 John Ratzenberger	10.00	25.00
28 Pam Rose	30.00	80.00
29 Dickey Beer	15.00	40.00
30 Paul Brooke	10.00	25.00
42 Ray Park	20.00	50.00
49 Bai Ling	8.00	20.00
57 Amy Allen	10.00	25.00
61 Silas Carson	10.00	25.00
78 Bruce Spence	8.00	20.00
79 Wayne Pygram	10.00	25.00
80 Silas Carson	10.00	25.00
90 Andy Secombe	8.00	20.00
96 Taylor Gray	10.00	25.00
97 Vanessa Marshall	8.00	20.00
100 Tiya Sircar	12.00	30.00
102 Ashley Eckstein	40.00	100.00
104 George Takei	20.00	50.00
105 Dee Bradley Baker	12.00	30.00

2015 Star Wars High Tek Moments of Power

COMPLETE SET (15)	175.00	350.00
COMMON CARD (MP1-MP15)	8.00	20.00
STATED PRINT RUN 50 SER.#'d SETS		
MP1 Anakin Skywalker	10.00	25.00
MP2 Darth Maul	12.00	30.00
MP3 Obi-Wan Kenobi	15.00	40.00
MP4 Padme Amidala	12.00	30.00
MP6 Yoda	12.00	30.00
MP7 The Emperor	10.00	25.00
MP8 Han Solo	20.00	50.00
MP9 Luke Skywalker	15.00	40.00

MP10	Boba Fett	15.00	40.00
MP11	Chewbacca	10.00	25.00
MP13	Princess Leia Organa	15.00	40.00
MP15	Darth Vader	20.00	50.00

2015 Star Wars High Tek Tek Heads

COMPLETE SET (15)		150.00	275.00
COMMON CARD (TH1-TH15)		6.00	15.00
STATED PRINT RUN 50 SER.#'d SETS			
TH1	Darth Vader	20.00	50.00
TH2	C-3PO	10.00	25.00
TH3	Luke Skywalker	10.00	25.00
TH4	R2-D2	8.00	20.00
TH5	IG-88	8.00	20.00
TH7	BB-8	12.00	30.00
TH8	FX-7	8.00	20.00
TH10	2-1B	10.00	25.00
TH12	R7-A7	10.00	25.00
TH13	General Grievous	8.00	20.00
TH14	Chopper	10.00	25.00

2016 Star Wars High Tek

COMPLETE SET W/O SP (112)		100.00	200.00
COMPLETE SET W/SP (127)		300.00	600.00
UNOPENED BOX (1 PACK/8 CARDS)		50.00	60.00
COMMON CARD (SW1-SW112)		1.25	3.00
*F1P1: SAME VALUE AS BASIC			

*F1P2: SAME VALUE AS BASIC			
*F1P3: .75X TO 2X BASIC CARDS			
*F1P4: .75X TO 2X BASIC CARDS			
*F1P5: 1.5X TO 4X BASIC CARDS			
*F2P1: SAME VALUE AS BASIC			
*F2P2: SAME VALUE AS BASIC			
*F2P3: .75X TO 2X BASIC CARDS			
*F2P4: 1X TO 2.5X BASIC CARDS			
*F2P5: 1.50X TO 4X BASIC CARDS			
*BLUE RAIN/99: .75X TO 2X BASIC CARDS			
*GOLD RAIN/50: 1.5X TO 4X BASIC CARDS			
*ORANGE MAGMA/25: 3X TO 6X BASIC CARDS			
*GREEN CUBE/10: 4X TO 10X BASIC CARDS			
*RED ORBIT/5: 6X TO 15X BASIC CARDS			
SW60A Kylo Ren		15.00	40.00
Dark Side Disciple SP			
SW72A General Leia Organa		25.00	60.00
Resistance Leader SP			
SW75A Rey		15.00	40.00
Jakku Scavenger SP			
SW75B Rey		80.00	150.00
Force Sensitive SP			
SW75C Rey		60.00	120.00
Starkiller Base Duel SP			
SW76A FN-2187		30.00	80.00
First Order Stormtrooper SP			
SW76B Flametrooper		12.00	30.00
First Order Infantry SP			
SW76C Snowtrooper		12.00	30.00
First Order Infantry SP			
SW76D TIE Pilot		12.00	30.00
First Order Pilot SP			
SW84A Han Solo		50.00	100.00
Smuggler SP			
SW87A Finn		30.00	80.00
Resistance Warrior SP			
SW87B Finn		20.00	50.00
Resistance Fighter SP			
SW88A Chewbacca		30.00	80.00
Millennium Falcon Co-Pilot SP			
SW100A Poe Dameron		25.00	60.00
Resistance Messenger SP			
SW100B Poe Dameron		15.00	40.00
Resistance Pilot SP			

2016 Star Wars High Tek Armor Tek

COMMON CARD (AT1-AT11)		8.00	20.00
STATED PRINT RUN 50 SER.#'d SETS			
AT1	Kylo Ren	15.00	40.00
AT2	Captain Phasma	12.00	30.00
AT3	Poe Dameron	10.00	25.00
AT6	First Order Tie Fighter Pilot	12.00	30.00
AT7	First Order Stormtrooper	12.00	30.00
AT8	Rey	20.00	50.00
AT9	Stormtrooper (Heavy Gunner)	10.00	25.00
AT11	Sidon Ithano	12.00	30.00

2016 Star Wars High Tek Autographs

COMMON CARD		5.00	12.00
*BLUE RAIN/75: .5X TO 1.2X BASIC CARDS			
*GOLD RAIN/50: .6X TO 1.5X BASIC CARDS			
*ORANGE MAGMA/25: .75X TO 2X BASIC CARDS			
RANDOMLY INSERTED INTO PACKS			
3	Aidan Cook/Cookie Tuggs	8.00	20.00
4	Alan Ruscoe/Bib Fortuna	6.00	15.00
6	Amy Allen	8.00	20.00
8	Anna Brewster	8.00	20.00
10	Ashley Eckstein	50.00	120.00
13	Brian Vernel	6.00	15.00
15	Catherine Taber	6.00	15.00
17	Cristina da Silva	8.00	20.00
20	Dave Barclay	8.00	20.00
21	David Acord/Med.Droid	6.00	15.00
22	David Acord/Voiceover	6.00	15.00
23	David Bowers	6.00	15.00
24	Dee Bradley Baker	6.00	15.00
26	Dickey Beer		
30	Harriet Walter	6.00	15.00
33	Jeremy Bulloch	12.00	30.00
38	Julie Dolan	8.00	20.00
39	Kiran Shah	6.00	15.00
40	Marc Silk	6.00	15.00
42	Mark Dodson/S.Crumb	6.00	15.00
45	Michael Kingma	6.00	15.00
47	Mike Edmonds	6.00	15.00
48	Mike Quinn	8.00	20.00
50	Paul Blake	6.00	15.00
51	Paul Springer	6.00	15.00
57	Sam Witwer	8.00	20.00
59	Sebastian Armesto	6.00	15.00
60	Silas Carson	8.00	20.00
62	Taylor Gray	6.00	15.00
63	Tim Rose	6.00	15.00
64	Tiya Sircar	6.00	15.00
66	Tosin Cole	10.00	25.00

2016 Star Wars High Tek Autographs Gold Rainbow

*GOLD RAINBOW/50: .6X TO 1.5X BASIC CARDS

12	Brian Herring	25.00	60.00
25	Denis Lawson	15.00	40.00
67	Warwick Davis	12.00	30.00

2016 Star Wars High Tek Autographs Orange Magma Diffractor

*ORANGE MAGMA/25: .75X TO 2X BASIC CARDS

14	Carrie Fisher	250.00	500.00
28	Freddie Prinze Jr.	30.00	80.00
37	John Boyega	120.00	250.00

2016 Star Wars High Tek Living Tek

COMMON CARD (LT1-LT13)	6.00	15.00
STATED PRINT RUN 50 SER.#'d SETS		
LT1 Crusher Roodown	10.00	25.00
LT2 Luke Skywalker	15.00	40.00
LT3 C-3PO	8.00	20.00
LT4 BB-8	12.00	30.00
LT5 GA-97	8.00	20.00
LT6 Luggabeast	8.00	20.00
LT7 PZ-4CO	8.00	20.00
LT9 B-U4D	12.00	30.00
LT11 Sidon Ithano	12.00	30.00
LT12 HURID-327	8.00	20.00
LT13 R2-D2	8.00	20.00

2017 Star Wars High Tek

UNOPENED BOX (1 PACK OF 8 CARDS)	50.00	80.00
COMMON FORM 1 (1-56)	1.00	2.50

COMMON FORM 2 (57-112)	1.50	4.00
*F1P1: .75X TO 2X BASIC CARDS	2.00	5.00
*F1P2: .75X TO 2X BASIC CARDS	2.00	5.00
*F1P3: 1X TO 2.5X BASIC CARDS	2.50	6.00
*F2P1: .6X TO 1.5X BASIC CARDS	2.50	6.00
*F2P3: .6X TO 1.5X BASIC CARDS	2.50	6.00
*TIDAL DIFF./99: 1X TO 2.5X BASIC CARDS	2.50	6.00
*F2P2: .75X TO 2X BASIC CARDS	3.00	8.00
*GOLD R.F./50: 1.2X TO 3X BASIC CARDS	3.00	8.00
*F1P4: 2X TO 5X BASIC CARDS	5.00	12.00
*F2P4: 1.2X TO 3X BASIC CARDS	5.00	12.00
*F1P5: 3X TO 8X BASIC CARDS	8.00	20.00
7 Rey	2.50	6.00
14 Han Solo	1.50	4.00
15 Luke Skywalker	1.50	4.00
16 Princess Leia Organa	3.00	8.00
20 Jango Fett	2.00	5.00
36 Boba Fett	1.50	4.00
53 Kylo Ren	1.25	3.00
56 Yoda	1.25	3.00
57 Jyn Erso	4.00	10.00
62 Chirrut Imwe	2.00	5.00
68 Darth Vader	2.00	5.00

2017 Star Wars High Tek Autographs

RANDOMLY INSERTED INTO PACKS

NNO	Adrienne Wilkinson	6.00	15.00
NNO	Alistair Petrie	6.00	15.00
NNO	Angus MacInnes	6.00	15.00
NNO	Anthony Forest	6.00	15.00
NNO	Ariyon Bakare	10.00	25.00
NNO	Ashley Eckstein	40.00	100.00
NNO	Ben Daniels	6.00	15.00
NNO	Brian Herring	15.00	40.00
NNO	Cathy Munroe	12.00	30.00
NNO	Chris Parsons	8.00	20.00
NNO	Daniel Mays	15.00	40.00
NNO	David Acord	6.00	15.00
NNO	Derek Arnold	6.00	15.00
NNO	Duncan Pow	6.00	15.00
NNO	Guy Henry	20.00	50.00

NNO	Ian McElhinney	6.00	15.00
NNO	Ian Whyte	6.00	15.00
NNO	Jeremy Bulloch	15.00	40.00
NNO	Jordan Stephens	10.00	25.00
NNO	Lars Mikkelsen	10.00	25.00
NNO	Lloyd Sherr	6.00	15.00
NNO	Matthew Wood	6.00	15.00
NNO	Olivia d'Abo	6.00	15.00
NNO	Stephen Stanton		
NNO	Valene Kane	10.00	25.00
NNO	Zarene Dallas	6.00	15.00

2017 Star Wars High Tek Dual Autographs

UNPRICED DUE TO SCARCITY

NNO	A.Graves/P.LaMarr
NNO	B.Lourd/C.Clarke
NNO	G.Takei/A.Eckstein/25
NNO	H.Quarshie/R.Brown
NNO	I.Uwais/Y.Ruhian
NNO	J.Isaacs/K.Soucie
NNO	J.Cummings/T.Gray
NNO	J.Coppinger/M.Kingma
NNO	J.Morton/A.Harris
NNO	J.Ratzenberger/A.MacInnes
NNO	M.Wood/J.Henwick
NNO	S.Witwer/A.Wilkinson
NNO	T.Rose/K.Rotich
NNO	T.Kane/C.Taber
NNO	T.Cole/M.Quinn

2017 Star Wars High Tek Heroes and Villains of The Force Awakens

COMPLETE SET (20)	150.00	300.00
COMMON CARD (HV1-HV20)	6.00	15.00
STATED PRINT RUN 50 SER.#'d SETS		
HV1 Han Solo	10.00	25.00
HV2 Luke Skywalker	10.00	25.00
HV4 Kylo Ren	8.00	20.00
HV5 Rey	20.00	50.00
HV6 Finn	12.00	30.00
HV8 Supreme Leader Snoke	8.00	20.00
HV9 R2-D2	10.00	25.00
HV12 Snap Wexley	10.00	25.00
HV13 Captain Phasma	8.00	20.00
HV14 General Hux	8.00	20.00
HV17 Ello Asty	8.00	20.00
HV18 Unkar Plutt	8.00	20.00
HV19 Chewbacca	10.00	25.00
HV20 Riot Control Stormtrooper	12.00	30.00

2017 Star Wars High Tek A More Elegant Weapon

COMMON CARD (MW1-MW10)	10.00	25.00
STATED PRINT RUN 50 SER.#'d SETS		
MW1 Yoda	15.00	40.00
MW2 Ahsoka Tano	12.00	30.00

TRADING CARDS

MW3	Anakin Skywalker	12.00	30.00
MW5	Rey	30.00	75.00
MW6	Luke Skywalker	15.00	40.00
MW7	Darth Vader	15.00	40.00
MW8	Obi-Wan Kenobi	12.00	30.00
MW10	Mace Windu	12.00	30.00

2017 Star Wars High Tek Rogue One Vehicles

STATED PRINT RUN 50 SER.#'d SETS

RV1	Jyn Erso/U-wing	10.00	25.00
RV2	Gunner/Death Star	6.00	15.00
RV3	Krennic/Krennic's Shuttle	12.00	30.00
RV4	Tank Commander/Combat Assault Tank	6.00	15.00
RV5	Tarkin/Imperial Star Destroyer	8.00	20.00
RV6	Merrick/X-wing	12.00	30.00
RV7	TIE Striker Pilot/TIE Striker		
RV8	Cassian Andor/U-wing		
RV9	K-2SO/U-wing		
RV10	Bodhi Rook/Imperial Zeta-Class Transport	6.00	15.00

2017 Star Wars High Tek Troopers

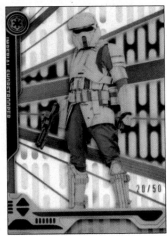

| COMMON CARD (TR1-TR16) | 6.00 | 15.00 |

STATED PRINT RUN 50 SER.#'d SETS

TR1	First Order TIE Fighter Pilot	10.00	25.00
TR2	First Order Stormtrooper	8.00	20.00
TR3	First Order Riot Control Stormtrooper	10.00	25.00
TR9	Imperial Death Trooper	15.00	40.00
TR12	Imperial Sandtrooper	10.00	25.00
TR14	Imperial TIE Fighter Pilot	8.00	20.00
TR15	Galactic Republic Clone Trooper	8.00	20.00
TR16	Galactic Marine	10.00	25.00

2020 Star Wars Holocron

IG-88

COMPLETE SET W/SP (225)	200.00	400.00
COMPLETE SET W/O SP (200)	15.00	40.00
UNOPENED BOX (18 PACKS)	100.00	200.00
UNOPENED PACK (8 CARDS)	6.00	10.00
COMMON CARD	.20	.50
COMMON SP	10.00	25.00

*FOILBOARD: .75X TO 2X BASIC CARDS

*GREEN: 1.5X TO 4X BASIC CARDS

*ORANGE/99: 3X TO 8X BASIC CARDS

N21	The Child	4.00	10.00
PX7	Ahsoka Tano	2.00	5.00
BH14	Boba Fett	1.25	3.00
BH15	The Mandalorian	2.00	5.00
BH2S	Boba Fett SP	20.00	50.00
CD1S	Qi'Ra SP	25.00	60.00
FO1S	Kylo Ren SP	15.00	40.00
N21S	The Child SP	50.00	100.00
BH15S	The Mandalorian SP	15.00	40.00
EMP1S	Darth Vader SP	15.00	40.00
REB1S	Luke Skywalker SP	12.00	30.00
REB2S	Princess Leia Organa SP	12.00	30.00
REB33	Cara Dune	6.00	15.00
REB3S	Han Solo SP	12.00	30.00
REP6S	Padme Amidala SP	20.00	50.00
REP8S	C-3PO SP	12.00	30.00
REP9S	R2-D2 SP	12.00	30.00
RES1S	Rey SP	15.00	40.00
JEDI15	Ahsoka Tano	2.00	5.00
JEDI1S	Obi-Wan Kenobi SP	12.00	30.00
JEDI3S	Yoda SP	15.00	40.00
REB23S	Jyn Erso SP	15.00	40.00
SITH1S	Darth Maul SP	12.00	30.00
JEDI15S	Ahsoka Tano SP	20.00	50.00

2020 Star Wars Holocron The Adventures of Han Solo

| COMPLETE SET (20) | 10.00 | 25.00 |
| COMMON CARD (AH1-AH20) | 1.25 | 3.00 |

*ORANGE/99: .6X TO 1.5X BASIC CARDS

STATED ODDS 1:3

2020 Star Wars Holocron Autographs

KANAN JARRUS
AUTHENTIC AUTOGRAPH

| COMMON AUTO | 6.00 | 15.00 |

*GREEN/99: .5X TO 1.2X BASIC AUTOS

*BLUE/50: .6X TO 1.5X BASIC AUTOS

STATED ODDS 1:859

AAV	Attila Vajda	8.00	20.00
ADA	David Ankrum	8.00	20.00
AHD	Harley Durst	8.00	20.00

2020 Star Wars Holocron Autographs Green

STATED ODDS 1:3,258

STATED PRINT RUN 99 SER.#'d SETS

| ACR | Clive Revill | 12.00 | 30.00 |

2020 Star Wars Holocron Charting the Galaxy

| COMPLETE SET (20) | 12.00 | 30.00 |
| COMMON CARD (CG1-CG20) | 1.00 | 2.50 |

*ORANGE/99: .5X TO 1.2X BASIC CARDS

STATED ODDS 1:3

2020 Star Wars Holocron Commemorative Creature Patches

| COMMON MEM | 3.00 | 8.00 |

*GREEN/99: .5X TO 1.2X BASIC MEM

STATED ODDS 1:RETAIL BOX

PCB	The Child	10.00	25.00
PCE	Chewbacca	5.00	12.00
PCJ	The Child	10.00	25.00
PCP	Chewbacca	5.00	12.00
PHE	Han Solo	8.00	20.00
PHT	Han Solo	8.00	20.00
PKB	Kuiil	4.00	10.00
PKJ	Kuiil	4.00	10.00
PLJ	Luke Skywalker	6.00	15.00
PLP	Luke Skywalker	6.00	15.00
PLT	Luke Skywalker	6.00	15.00
PMJ	Mudhorn	4.00	10.00
PPP	Paploo	5.00	12.00
PRP	Rey	8.00	20.00
PSJ	Stormtrooper	4.00	10.00
PTE	Teebo	4.00	10.00
PTT	Tauntaun	5.00	12.00
PLOE	Princess Leia Organa	6.00	15.00
POWJ	Obi-Wan Kenobi	4.00	10.00
PPGP	Porg	4.00	10.00
PTKE	Tokkat	5.00	12.00
PTMB	The Mandalorian	6.00	15.00
PTMJ	The Mandalorian	6.00	15.00

2020 Star Wars Holocron Dual Autographs

STATED ODDS 1:43,158

STATED PRINT RUN 25 SER.#'d SETS

UNPRICED DUE TO SCARCITY

DACM H.Christensen/E.McGregor

DAES A.Ehrenreich/J.Suotamo

DAET A.Eckstein/J.Taylor

DAFS F.Prinze Jr./S.Blum

DAJT F.Jones/A.Tudyk

DAKD I.Kenny/H.Durst

DAMB P.Mayhew/K.Baker

DAPB F.Prinze Jr./T.Baker

DAPJ P.Anthony-Rodriguez/J.Isaacs

DARD D.Ridley/A.Driver

2020 Star Wars Holocron Lightsabers of the Jedi

COMPLETE SET (10)	6.00	15.00
COMMON CARD (LJ1-LJ10)	1.00	2.50

*ORANGE/99: 1.5X TO 4X BASIC CARDS

STATED ODDS 1:3

2020 Star Wars Holocron Six-Person Autographs

COMPLETE SET (5)

STATED ODDS 1:172,080

UNPRICED DUE TO SCARCITY

NNO Ridley/Boyega/Tran/Williams/Lourd/Ackie

NNO McGregor/Jackson/Christensen/Morrison/McDiarmid/Park

NNO Jones/Whitaker/Ahmed/Yen/Mendelsohn/Mikkelsen

NNO Prinze Jr./Anthony-Rodriguez/Gellar/Gray/Witwer/Eckstein

NNO Ford/Fisher/Mayhew/Baker/Williams/Revill

2020 Star Wars Holocron Triple Autographs

UNPRICED DUE TO SCARCITY

STATED ODDS 1:86,315

TAEBW Ehrenreich/Bettany/Sam Witwer

TARBT Ridley/Boyega/Tran

TAMJC McGregor/Jackson/Christensen

TAJAT Jones/Ahmed/Tudyk

TATPB Prinze Jr./Blum/Reubens

2015 Star Wars Honey Maid

COMPLETE SET (12)	3.00	8.00
COMMON CARD	.40	1.00
PAN1 Obi-Wan Kenobi	2.00	5.00
Darth Vader		
Han Solo		
Chewbacca		
Storm Trooper		
C-3PO		
PAN2 R2-D2	2.00	5.00
The Emperor		
Yoda		
Luke Skywalker		
Boba Fett		
Princess Leia Organa		

2020 Star Wars I Am Your Father's Day

COMPLETE SET (10)	12.00	30.00
COMMON CARD (1-10)	2.50	6.00

STATED PRINT RUN 896 SETS

2021 Star Wars I Am Your Father's Day

COMPLETE SET (10)	15.00	40.00
COMMON CARD (1-10)	2.00	5.00

STATED PRINT RUN 896 SETS

1	The Mandalorian / Grogu	6.00	15.00
2	Darth Vader / Luke Skywalker	3.00	8.00

2013 Star Wars Jedi Legacy

COMPLETE SET (90)	6.00	15.00
UNOPENED BOX (24 PACKS)	250.00	400.00
UNOPENED PACK (8 CARDS)	12.00	20.00
COMMON CARD (1A-45L)	.20	.50

*BLUE: 1.2X TO 3X BASIC CARDS

*MAGENTA: 4X TO 10X BASIC CARDS

*GREEN: 5X TO 12X BASIC CARDS

*GOLD/10: 50X TO 120X BASIC CARDS

2013 Star Wars Jedi Legacy Autographs

COMMON AUTO	8.00	20.00

STATED ODDS 1:72

NNO	Alan Harris	20.00	50.00
NNO	Amy Allen	10.00	25.00
NNO	Anthony Daniels	150.00	300.00
NNO	Anthony Forrest	10.00	25.00
NNO	Billy Dee Williams	100.00	200.00
NNO	Carrie Fisher	500.00	1000.00
NNO	Harrison Ford	1200.00	2000.00
NNO	Ian McDiarmid	150.00	300.00
NNO	James Earl Jones	250.00	400.00
NNO	Jeremy Bulloch	60.00	120.00
NNO	Kenny Baker	125.00	250.00
NNO	Mark Hamill	500.00	800.00

2013 Star Wars Jedi Legacy Chewbacca Fur Relics

COMMON MEM (CR1-CR4)	125.00	250.00
STATED ODDS 1:720		

2013 Star Wars Jedi Legacy Connections

COMPLETE SET (15)	5.00	12.00
COMMON CARD (C1-C15)	.60	1.50
STATED ODDS 1:2		

2013 Star Wars Jedi Legacy Ewok Fur Relics

COMMON CARD (ER1-ER4)	20.00	50.00
STATED ODDS 1:120		
ER1 Wicket W. Warrick	125.00	250.00
ER4 Widdle Warrick	100.00	200.00

2013 Star Wars Jedi Legacy Film Cels

COMMON CARD (FR1-FR30)	10.00	25.00
STATED ODDS 1:BOX		
FR6 Darth Vader	20.00	50.00

2013 Star Wars Jedi Legacy Dual Film Cels

COMPLETE SET (6)	120.00	250.00
COMMON CARD (DFR1-DFR6)	20.00	50.00
STATED ODDS 1:144		
DFR1 Darth Vader/Luke Skywalker	30.00	60.00

2013 Star Wars Jedi Legacy Triple Film Cels

COMPLETE SET (10)	250.00	500.00
COMMON CARD (TFR1-TFR10)	30.00	60.00
STATED ODDS 1:144		

2013 Star Wars Jedi Legacy Influencers

COMPLETE SET (18)	5.00	12.00
COMMON CARD (I1-I18)	.50	1.25
STATED ODDS 1:2		

2013 Star Wars Jedi Legacy Jabba's Sail Barge Relics

COMPLETE SET (5)	300.00	600.00
COMMON CARD (JR1-JR5)	50.00	100.00
STATED ODDS 1:336		
JR1 Luke Skywalker	100.00	200.00
JR2 Leia Organa	100.00	200.00
JR3 Boba Fett	75.00	150.00

2013 Star Wars Jedi Legacy The Circle is Now Complete

COMPLETE SET (12)	35.00	70.00
COMMON CARD (CC1-CC12)	4.00	10.00

STATED ODDS 1:12

NNO1 Luke Skywalker PROMO

2013 Star Wars Jedi Legacy Promos

COMMON CARD	3.00	8.00
P1 Battle Through Blood	8.00	20.00
(Darth Vader)		
P2 Battle Through Blood	8.00	20.00
(Luke Skywalker)		
P3 Challenge of a Fallen Jedi	8.00	20.00
(Anakin vs. Count Dooku)		
P4 Challenge of a Fallen Jedi	8.00	20.00
(Luke vs. Vader)		
P5 Death of a Mentor	3.00	8.00
(Qui Gon vs. Darth Maul)		
(Philly Non-Sports Show Exclusive)		
NNO Darth Vader Disc	1.50	4.00
NNO Luke Skywalker Disc	1.50	4.00
NNO Two Paths. Two Journeys. One Destiny		
(5 X 7 Jumbo)		

2015 Star Wars Journey to The Force Awakens

COMPLETE SET (110)	10.00	25.00
UNOPENED HOBBY BOX (24 PACKS)		
UNOPENED HOBBY PACK (6 CARDS)		
UNOPENED RETAIL BOX (24 PACKS)		
UNOPENED RETAIL PACK (6 CARDS)		

UNOPENED BLASTER BOX (10 PACKS)		
UNOPENED BLASTER PACK (6 CARDS)		
UNOPENED JUMBO PACK (14 CARDS)		
COMMON CARD (1-110)	.20	.50

*JABBA SLIME GREEN: .5X TO 1.2X BASIC CARDS

*BLACK: .6X TO 1.5X BASIC CARDS

*DEATH STAR SILVER: .75X TO 2X BASIC CARDS

*LTSBR. NEON PINK: 1.5X TO 4X BASIC CARDS

*PURPLE: 4X TO 10X BASIC CARDS

*HOTH ICE/150: 6X TO 15X BASIC CARDS

*GOLD/50: 10X TO 25X BASIC CARDS

*HOLOGRAM/25: 15X TO 40X BASIC CARDS

2015 Star Wars Journey to The Force Awakens Autographs

ALAN HARRIS

COMMON AUTO	8.00	20.00
*SILVER/50: .75X TO 2X BASIC AUTOS		
NNO Alan Harris	10.00	25.00
NNO Amy Allen	12.00	30.00
NNO Angus MacInnes	8.00	20.00
NNO Anthony Daniels	200.00	400.00
NNO Ashley Eckstein	40.00	100.00
NNO Bai Ling	15.00	40.00
NNO Billy Dee Williams	50.00	100.00
NNO Caroline Blakiston	10.00	25.00
NNO Carrie Fisher	120.00	250.00
NNO David Prowse	80.00	150.00
NNO Dickey Beer	10.00	25.00
NNO Femi Taylor	12.00	30.00
NNO Hassani Shapi	12.00	30.00
NNO Jeremy Bulloch	25.00	60.00
NNO Jerome Blake	10.00	25.00
NNO John Ratzenberger	12.00	30.00
NNO Kenji Oates	10.00	25.00
NNO Kenneth Colley	10.00	25.00
NNO Kenny Baker	100.00	200.00
NNO Mark Hamill	225.00	350.00
NNO Michonne Bourriague	12.00	30.00

NNO Mike Quinn	25.00	60.00
NNO Nika Futterman	10.00	25.00
NNO Olivia d'Abo	80.00	150.00
NNO Orli Shoshan	10.00	25.00
NNO Pam Rose	10.00	25.00
NNO Peter Mayhew	50.00	100.00
NNO Ray Park	25.00	60.00
NNO Rohan Nichol	12.00	30.00
NNO Steven Blum	10.00	25.00
NNO Taylor Gray	12.00	30.00
NNO Tiya Sircar	25.00	60.00
NNO Vanessa Marshall	15.00	40.00
NNO Wayne Pygram	12.00	30.00

2015 Star Wars Journey to The Force Awakens Behind-the-Scenes

The Birth of 2-1B

COMPLETE SET (9)	5.00	12.00
COMMON CARD (BTS1-BTS9)	1.00	2.50

2015 Star Wars Journey to The Force Awakens Blueprints

COMPLETE SET (8)	15.00	40.00
COMMON CARD (BP1-BP8)	3.00	8.00
BP1 BB-8	6.00	15.00
BP3 Millennium Falcon	5.00	12.00
BP4 X-Wing Fighter	4.00	10.00

2015 Star Wars Journey to The Force Awakens Character Stickers

COMPLETE SET (18)	15.00	40.00
COMMON CARD (S1-S18)	1.25	3.00
S1 Luke Skywalker	1.50	4.00
S2 Han Solo	2.00	5.00
S9 BB-8	2.50	6.00
S10 Captain Phasma	1.50	4.00
S11 Kylo Ren	2.00	5.00
S14 Darth Vader	2.00	5.00
S15 Boba Fett	1.50	4.00
S17 Kylo Ren	2.00	5.00
S18 Yoda	1.50	4.00

2015 Star Wars Journey to The Force Awakens Choose Your Destiny

COMPLETE SET (9)	12.00	30.00
COMMON CARD (CD1-CD9)	2.50	6.00

2015 Star Wars Journey to The Force Awakens Classic Captions

COMPLETE SET (8)	15.00	40.00
COMMON CARD (CC1-CC8)	4.00	10.00

2015 Star Wars Journey to The Force Awakens Cloth Stickers

COMPLETE SET (9)	8.00	20.00
COMMON CARD (CS1-CS9)	1.50	4.00
CS6 Kylo Ren	2.00	5.00
CS9 Kylo Ren (w/TIE Fighters)	2.00	5.00

2015 Star Wars Journey to The Force Awakens Concept Art

COMPLETE SET (9)	5.00	12.00
COMMON CARD (CA1-CA9)	1.00	2.50

2015 Star Wars Journey to The Force Awakens Dual Autographs

STATED PRINT RUN 3 SER.#'d SETS

UNPRICED DUE TO SCARCITY

1 Mark Hamill/Kenny Baker
2 Ian McDiarmid/Wayne Pygram
3 Peter Mayhew/Anthony Daniels
4 Mark Hamill/David Prowse

2015 Star Wars Journey to The Force Awakens Family Legacy Matte Backs

COMPLETE SET (8)	10.00	25.00
COMMON CARD (FL1-FL8)	1.50	4.00
*GLOSSY: .5X TO 1.2X BASIC CARDS		
FL1 Boba Fett and Jango Fett	2.00	5.00
FL2 Anakin Skywalker and Luke Skywalker	2.00	5.00
FL3 Padme Amidala and Leia Organa	2.00	5.00

2015 Star Wars Journey to The Force Awakens Heroes of the Resistance

COMPLETE SET (9)	6.00	15.00
COMMON CARD (R1-R9)	1.25	3.00
R4 BB-8	2.00	5.00
R8 The Millennium Falcon	1.50	4.00

2015 Star Wars Journey to The Force Awakens Patches

COMPLETE SET (20)	150.00	300.00
COMMON CARD (P1-P20)	8.00	20.00
P1 Kylo Ren	12.00	30.00
P3 Captain Phasma	12.00	30.00
P9 BB-8	12.00	30.00
P18 BB-8	12.00	30.00

2015 Star Wars Journey to The Force Awakens Power of the First Order

COMPLETE SET (8)	6.00	15.00
COMMON CARD (FD1-FD8)	1.25	3.00
FD1 Kylo Ren	2.00	5.00
FD2 Captain Phasma	1.50	4.00

2015 Star Wars Journey to The Force Awakens Silhouette Foil

COMPLETE SET (8)	4.00	10.00
COMMON CARD (1-8)	.75	2.00
ERRONEOUSLY LISTED AS A 9-CARD SET		
ON THE CARD BACKS		
5 Kylo Ren	1.50	4.00
7 Captain Phasma	1.25	3.00

2015 Star Wars Journey to The Force Awakens Triple Autographs

STATED PRINT RUN 5 SER.#'d SETS

UNPRICED DUE TO SCARCITY

1 McDiarmid/Park/Pygram

2 Prowse/Park/Pygram

2015 Star Wars Journey to The Force Awakens Promos

COMPLETE SET (6)	10.00	25.00
COMMON CARD (P1-P6)	2.00	5.00
P1 Luke Skywalker	6.00	15.00
(SDCC Marvel Star Wars Lando exclusive)		
P6 Kanan Jarrus	5.00	12.00
(NYCC exclusive)		

2015 Star Wars Journey to The Force Awakens UK

COMPLETE SET (208)	30.00	80.00
COMMON CARD	.30	.75

LEY Yoda	
LEBF Boba Fett	
LECH Chewbacca	
LEHS Han Solo	
LELC Lando Calrissian	
LELS Luke Skywalker	
LEPL Princess Leia	
LER2 R2-D2	
LEST Stormtrooper	
LETE The Emperor	

2017 Star Wars Journey to The Last Jedi

Heroes United

COMPLETE SET (110)	12.00	30.00
UNOPENED BOX (24 PACKS)	85.00	100.00
UNOPENED PACK (8 CARDS)	3.00	4.00
COMMON CARD (1-110)	.20	.50
*GREEN STAR.: .5X TO 1.2X BASIC CARDS	.25	.60
*PINK STAR.: .6X TO 1.5X BASIC CARDS	.30	.75
*BLACK STAR.: .75X TO 2X BASIC CARDS	.40	1.00
*SILVER STAR.: 1.2X TO 3X BASIC CARDS	.60	1.50
*PURPLE STAR.: 2X TO 5X BASIC CARDS	1.00	2.50
*WHITE STAR./199: 12X TO 30X BASIC CARDS	6.00	15.00
*ORANGE STAR./50: 15X TO 40X BASIC CARDS	8.00	20.00
*GOLD STAR./25: 25X TO 60X BASIC CARDS	12.00	30.00

2017 Star Wars Journey to The Last Jedi Allies

HAN SOLO   CHEWBACCA

COMPLETE SET (5)	50.00	100.00
COMMON CARD (1-5)	10.00	25.00
RANDOMLY INSERTED INTO PACKS		
GAMESTOP EXCLUSIVE		

2017 Star Wars Journey to The Last Jedi Autographs

LANDO CALRISSIAN

AAD	Adam Driver		
AAE	Ashley Eckstein		
AAP	Alistair Petrie		
AAS	Andy Serkis		
AAT	Alan Tudyk		
ABD	Ben Daniels	20.00	50.00
ABH	Brian Herring	12.00	30.00
ABL	Billie Lourd		
ABW	Billy Dee Williams		
ACD	Cristina da Silva	12.00	30.00
ACF	Carrie Fisher		
ACR	Clive Revill		
ACT	Catherine Taber	15.00	40.00
ADB	Dee Bradley Baker	12.00	30.00
ADC	Dave Champman	20.00	50.00
ADL	Daniel Logan	12.00	30.00
ADP	Duncan Pow	8.00	20.00
ADR	Daisy Ridley		
ADY	Donnie Yen		
AFJ	Felicity Jones		
AFP	Freddie Prinze Jr.		
AFW	Forest Whitaker		
AGC	Gwendoline Christie		
AGT	George Takei		
AHC	Hayden Christensen		
AHF	Harrison Ford		
AIU	Iko Uwais		
AIW	Ian Whyte	10.00	25.00
AJB	John Boyega		
AJC	Jim Cummings	10.00	25.00
AJD	Julie Dolan	10.00	25.00
AJI	Jason Isaacs		
AKB	Kenny Baker		
AKF	Kate Fleetwood		
AKY	Keone Young	15.00	40.00
AMH	Mark Hamill		

APB	Paul Blake	15.00	40.00
APM	Peter Mayhew		
APW	Paul Warren	10.00	25.00
ARA	Riz Ahmed		
ARC	Richard Cunningham	12.00	30.00
ARP	Ray Park		
ASG	Stefan Grube	12.00	30.00
ASR	Scott Richardson	15.00	40.00
ASW	Sam Witwer		
ATB	Thomas Brodie-Sangster		
ATC	Tosin Cole		
ATK	Tom Kane		
ATW	Tom Wilton	12.00	30.00
AWP	Wayne Pygram	10.00	25.00
AYR	Yayan Ruhian		
AZD	Zarene Dallas	12.00	30.00
AADA	Anthony Daniels		
AADX	Adam Driver Unmasked		
ACAR	Cecp Arif Rahman	15.00	40.00
ADAR	Derek Arnold		
ADBA	Dave Barclay	10.00	25.00
ADRX	Daisy Ridley Scavenger		
AGGA	Gloria Garcia	12.00	30.00
AGGA	Greg Grunberg		
AIMD	Ian McDiarmid		
AIME	Ian McElhinney	12.00	30.00
AJBL	Jerome Blake	10.00	25.00
AJBU	Jeremy Bulloch		
ASDB	Sharon Duncan-Brewster	15.00	40.00

2017 Star Wars Journey to The Last Jedi Blueprints

COMPLETE SET (7)	8.00	20.00
COMMON CARD (1-7)	2.00	5.00
RANDOMLY INSERTED INTO PACKS		

2017 Star Wars Journey to The Last Jedi Character Retro Stickers

BB-8

COMPLETE SET (18)	100.00	200.00
COMMON CARD (1-18)	6.00	15.00
RANDOMLY INSERTED INTO PACKS		

2017 Star Wars Journey to The Last Jedi Characters

COMPLETE SET (16)	12.00	30.00
COMMON CARD (1-16)	1.25	3.00
RANDOMLY INSERTED INTO PACKS		

2017 Star Wars Journey to The Last Jedi Choose Your Destiny

GENERAL LEIA ORGANA

COMPLETE SET (10)	8.00	20.00
COMMON CARD (1-10)	1.25	3.00

RANDOMLY INSERTED INTO PACKS

2017 Star Wars Journey to The Last Jedi Darkness Rises

COMPLETE SET (6)	6.00	15.00
COMMON CARD (1-6)	1.50	4.00

2017 Star Wars Journey to The Last Jedi Dual Autographs

UNPRICED DUE TO SCARCITY

NNO Serkis/Driver

NNO Ridley/Driver

NNO Ridley/Herring

NNO Grunberg/Lourd

2017 Star Wars Journey to The Last Jedi Family Legacy

COMPLETE SET (6)	5.00	12.00
COMMON CARD (1-6)	1.25	3.00

RANDOMLY INSERTED INTO PACKS

2017 Star Wars Journey to The Last Jedi Illustrated Characters

COMPLETE SET (14)	10.00	25.00
COMMON CARD (1-14)	1.00	2.50

RANDOMLY INSERTED INTO PACKS

2017 Star Wars Journey to The Last Jedi Patches

COMMON CARD	5.00	12.00
*ORANGE/99: .75X TO 2X BASIC CARDS	10.00	25.00
*GOLD/25: 1.2X TO 3X BASIC CARDS	15.00	40.00

RANDOMLY INSERTED INTO PACKS

2017 Star Wars Journey to The Last Jedi Rey Continuity

COMPLETE SET (10)	12.00	30.00
COMMON CARD (1-5)	1.25	3.00
COMMON CARD (6-10)	2.00	5.00

RANDOMLY INSERTED INTO PACKS

1-5 JOURNEY TO THE LAST JEDI EXCLUSIVE

6-10 THE LAST JEDI SER.1 EXCLUSIVE

11-15 THE LAST JEDI SER.2 EXCLUSIVE

2017 Star Wars Journey to The Last Jedi Six-Person Autographed Booklet

UNPRICED DUE TO SCARCITY

NNO Ford/Hamill/Fisher/Ridley/Boyega/Herring

2017 Star Wars Journey to The Last Jedi Triple Autographs

UNPRICED DUE TO SCARCITY

NNO Serkis/Driver/Christie

NNO Ridley/Driver/Boyega

2019 Star Wars Journey to The Rise of Skywalker

COMPLETE SET (110)	10.00	25.00
UNOPENED BOX (24 PACKS)	60.00	100.00
UNOPENED PACK (8 CARDS)	2.50	4.00
COMMON CARD (1-110)	.20	.50

*RED: .6X TO 1.5X BASIC CARDS

*GREEN: .75X TO 2X BASIC CARDS

*SILVER: 1.2X TO 3X BASIC CARDS

*BLACK/199: 3X TO 8X BASIC CARDS

*ORANGE/50: 6X TO 15X BASIC CARDS

*GOLD/25: 12X TO 30X BASIC CARDS

2019 Star Wars Journey to The Rise of Skywalker Six-Person Autographs

UNPRICED DUE TO SCARCITY

NNO Ridley/Boyega/Tran/Serkis/Driver/Gleeson

SAGG Ford/Fisher/Ridley/Boyega/Baker/Daniels

2019 Star Wars Journey to The Rise of Skywalker Autographed Commemorative Patches

*RED/1: UNPRICED DUE TO SCARCITY

UNPRICED DUE TO SCARCITY

NNO Adam Driver

NNO Andy Serkis

NNO Daisy Ridley

NNO Domhnall Gleeson

NNO Greg Grunberg

NNO John Boyega

NNO Joonas Suotamo

NNO Matthew Wood

NNO Mike Quinn

NNO Paul Kasey

2019 Star Wars Journey to The Rise of Skywalker Autographs

COMMON AUTO	5.00	12.00
AAD Adam Driver		
AAD Anthony Daniels		
AAE Adrian Edmondson	5.00	12.00
AAJ Andrew Jack	5.00	12.00
AAL Amanda Lawrence	5.00	12.00
AAS Andy Serkis 1		

AAS Andy Serkis 2		
AAS Arti Shah	6.00	15.00
ABL Billie Lourd		
ABV Brian Vernel		
ACC Cavin Cornwall	8.00	20.00
ACC Crystal Clarke		
ACF Carrie Fisher		
ADA David Acord		
ADC Dave Chapman		
ADG Domhnall Gleeson		
ADR Daisy Ridley		
AEE Emun Elliott		
AGG Greg Grunberg		
AHC Hermione Corfield	12.00	30.00
AHF Harrison Ford		
AHS Hugh Skinner	6.00	15.00
AIU Iko Uwais	5.00	12.00
AIW Ian Whyte	6.00	15.00
AJB John Boyega 1		
AJB John Boyega 2		
AJS Joonas Suotamo		
AJV Jimmy Vee	8.00	20.00
AKB Kenny Baker		
AKS Kiran Shah	5.00	12.00
ALC Lily Cole	6.00	15.00
ALD Laura Dern		
AMQ Mike Quinn	6.00	15.00
ANC Nathalie Cuzner	5.00	12.00
APK Paul Kasey	5.00	12.00
APW Paul Warren	5.00	12.00
ARM Rocky Marshall		
ASA Sebastian Armesto		
ASG Stefan Grube	5.00	12.00
ATK Tom Kane	6.00	15.00
ATR Tim Rose		
ATW Tom Wilton	6.00	15.00
AWD Warwick Davis		
ACAR Cecep Arif Rahman		
ADAV Derek Arnold		
AGGJ Gloria Garcia	6.00	15.00
AKMT Kelly Marie Tran		
ATBS Thomas Brodie-Sangster		

2019 Star Wars Journey to The Rise of Skywalker Battle Lines

COMPLETE SET (10)	25.00	60.00
COMMON CARD (BL1-BL10)	4.00	10.00
RANDOMLY INSERTED IN PACKS		

2019 Star Wars Journey to The Rise of Skywalker Character Foil

COMPLETE SET (8)	6.00	15.00
COMMON CARD (FC1-FC8)	1.00	2.50
RANDOMLY INSERTED INTO PACKS		

2019 Star Wars Journey to The Rise of Skywalker Character Stickers

COMPLETE SET (19)	10.00	25.00
COMMON CARD (CS1-CS19)	1.25	3.00
RANDOMLY INSERTED INTO PACKS		

2019 Star Wars Journey to The Rise of Skywalker Choose Your Destiny

COMPLETE SET (10)	12.00	30.00
COMMON CARD (CD1-CD10)	2.00	5.00
RANDOMLY INSERTED INTO PACKS		

2019 Star Wars Journey to The Rise of Skywalker Commemorative Jumbo Patches

COMMON MEM	3.00	8.00
*BLACK/99: .5X TO 1.2X BASIC MEM		
*ORANGE/50: .6X TO 1.5X BASIC MEM		
RANDOMLY INSERTED INTO PACKS		
JPC Chewbacca	3.00	8.00
JPF Finn	5.00	12.00
JPR Rey	6.00	15.00
JPAA Admiral Ackbar	3.00	8.00
JPAH Vice Admiral Holdo	4.00	10.00
JPBB BB-8	4.00	10.00
JPBO Bail Organa	3.00	8.00
JPC3 C-3PO	4.00	10.00
JPCT C'ai Threnalli	4.00	10.00
JPHS Han Solo	6.00	15.00
JPKC Lieutenant Connix	5.00	12.00
JPLC Lando Calrissian	4.00	10.00
JPLO General Leia Organa	5.00	12.00
JPLS Luke Skywalker	5.00	12.00
JPME Major Ematt	3.00	8.00
JPMM Mon Mothma	3.00	8.00
JPPA PadmÈ Amidala	5.00	12.00
JPPD Poe Dameron	4.00	10.00
JPR2 R2-D2	4.00	10.00
JPRT Rose Tico	3.00	8.00

2019 Star Wars Journey to The Rise of Skywalker Commemorative Patches

*BLACK/99: .5X TO 1.2X BASIC MEM		
*ORANGE/50: .6X TO 1.5X BASIC MEM		
RANDOMLY INSERTED INTO PACKS		
PCCR Chewbacca	5.00	12.00
PCFR Finn	4.00	10.00
PCRR Rey	6.00	15.00
PCCCT Captain Canady	3.00	8.00
PCCPK Captain Phasma	4.00	10.00
PCCPT Captain Peavey	3.00	8.00
PCCTX C'ai Threnalli	3.00	8.00
PCCXP C'ai Threnalli	3.00	8.00
PCEAX Ello Asty	3.00	8.00
PCEXP Ello Asty	3.00	8.00
PCGHK General Hux	3.00	8.00
PCHFO General Hux	3.00	8.00
PCHSR Han Solo	8.00	20.00
PCKFO Kylo Ren	5.00	12.00
PCKRK Kylo Ren	5.00	12.00
PCKRT Kylo Ren	6.00	15.00
PCLOR General Leia Organa	5.00	12.00
PCLSR Luke Skywalker	5.00	12.00
PCNNX Nien Nunb	3.00	8.00
PCNXP Nien Nunb	3.00	8.00
PCPDX Poe Dameron	5.00	12.00
PCPFO Captain Phasma	4.00	10.00
PCPGK Praetorian Guard	3.00	8.00
PCPXP Poe Dameron	5.00	12.00
PCSFO Supreme Leader Snoke	4.00	10.00
PCSLK Supreme Leader Snoke	4.00	10.00
PCSWX Snap Wexley	3.00	8.00
PCSXP Snap Wexley	3.00	8.00
PCTFO Stormtrooper	3.00	8.00
PCTFP Tie Fighter Pilot	3.00	8.00

2019 Star Wars Journey to The Rise of Skywalker Dual Autographs

UNPRICED DUE TO SCARCITY

DASD A.Serkis/A.Driver
DASG A.Serkis/D.Gleeson
DADB A.Daniels/K.Baker
DARD D.Ridley/A.Driver
DAGC G.Grunberg/H.Corfield
DATN K.Tran/V.Ngo
DADS L.Dern/Hugh Skinner
DAKR P.Kasey/T.Rose

2019 Star Wars Journey to The Rise of Skywalker Illustrated Characters

COMPLETE SET (16)	12.00	30.00
COMMON CARD (IC1-IC16)	1.25	3.00
RANDOMLY INSERTED INTO PACKS		

TRADING CARDS

2019 Star Wars Journey to The Rise of Skywalker Schematics

COMPLETE SET (10)	5.00	12.00
COMMON CARD (S1-S10)	.75	2.00
RANDOMLY INSERTED INTO PACKS		

2019 Star Wars Journey to The Rise of Skywalker Triple Autographs

STATED PRINT RUN SER.#'d SETS

UNPRICED DUE TO SCARCITY

TASRD Serkis/Ridley/Driver

TADBM Daniels/Baker/Mayhew

TADCS Davis/Cole/Shah

TADSL Dern/Skinner/Lawrence

1996 Star Wars Laser

0 Star Wars 20th Anniversary Commemorative Magazine	3.00	8.00

2016 Star Wars LEGO Droid Tales

COMPLETE SET (9)	15.00	40.00
UNOPENED PACK (3 CARDS)	6.00	8.00
COMMON CARD (DT1-DT9)		
ONE PACK INSERTED INTO		
STAR WARS LEGO DROID TALES DVD		

2019-22 Star Wars Living Set

COMMON CARD	3.00	8.00
TOPPS ONLINE EXCLUSIVE		
1 Darth Vader/3,909*	25.00	60.00
2 Nien Nunb/2,888*	10.00	25.00
3 R2-D2/2,710*	10.00	20.00
4 Stormtrooper/2,601*	15.00	30.00
5 Bossk/2,205*	10.00	20.00
6 Val/2,161*	6.00	15.00
7 Queen Amidala/2,038*	10.00	20.00
8 Death Star Gunner/1,922*	5.00	12.00
9 Grand Admiral Thrawn/1,760*	40.00	100.00
10 Uncle Owen Lars/1,721*	10.00	20.00
11 Wedge Antilles/1,662*	6.00	15.00
12 Dengar/1,641*	6.00	15.00
13 Jar Jar Binks/1,692*	12.00	30.00
14 Moloch/1,565*	8.00	20.00
15 Orson Krennic/1,385*	15.00	40.00
16 Jawa/1,441*	15.00	40.00
17 Lando Calrissian/1,427*	20.00	50.00
18 Rancor/1,405*	12.00	30.00
19 Ezra Bridger/1,375*	15.00	40.00
20 Admiral Piett/1,378*	10.00	25.00

21 Han Solo/2,376*	15.00	40.00
22 Tasu Leech/1,501*	8.00	20.00
23 Mon Mothma/1,435*	10.00	25.00
24 Wampa/1,454*	8.00	20.00
25 Darth Maul/1,739*	25.00	60.00
26 Tallie Lintra/1,493*	12.00	30.00
27 Shaak Ti/1,311*	20.00	50.00
28 Quay Tolsite/1,307*	12.00	30.00
29 4-LOM/1,356*	15.00	40.00
30 BB-8/1,502*	12.00	30.00
31 Aurra Sing/1,343*	10.00	25.00
32 Tobias Beckett/1,395*	10.00	25.00
33 Wicket W. Warrick/1,390*	40.00	100.00
34 Scout Trooper/1,283*	12.00	30.00
35 General Hux/1,170*	30.00	75.00
36 Dak Ralter/1,164*	20.00	50.00
37 Bail Organa/1,124	15.00	40.00
38 Gamorrean Guard/1,161*	25.00	60.00
39 Sebulba/1,101*	12.00	30.00
40 Kanan Jarrus/1,086*	30.00	75.00
41 K-2SO/1,151*	30.00	75.00
42 Echo Base Trooper/1,136*	15.00	40.00
43 Maz Kanata/1,122*	10.00	25.00
44 Captain Needa/1,108*	10.00	25.00
45 Salacious B. Crumb/1,090*	20.00	50.00
46 Chirrut Imwe/1,102*	25.00	60.00
47 Rey/1,503*	40.00	100.00
48 Savage Opress/1,114*	30.00	75.00
49 Captain Phasma/1,011	20.00	50.00
50 Cliegg Lars/938*	25.00	60.00
51 L3-37/902*	60.00	150.00
52 Nute Gunray/985*	60.00	150.00
53 General Grievous/1,007*	50.00	125.00
54 Saw Gerrera/967*	60.00	150.00
55 Finn/1,079*	25.00	60.00
56 Imperial Pilots/1,021*	30.00	75.00
57 Dorme/2,021*	8.00	20.00
58 The Child/9,663*	20.00	50.00
59 Supreme Leader Snoke/942*	60.00	150.00
60 Plo Koon/887*	100.00	250.00
61 Greedo/1,178*	15.00	40.00
62 Young Anakin Skywalker/1,207*	10.00	25.00
63 Poe Dameron/1,301	12.00	30.00
64 Mother Talzin/1,203	25.00	60.00
65 Watto/1,259*	15.00	40.00
66 Darth Sidious/1,422*	15.00	40.00
67 Jyn Erso/1,425*	20.00	50.00
68 BB-9E/1,068*	12.00	30.00
69 Max Rebo/956*	25.00	60.00
70 Count Dooku/946*	25.00	50.00
71 Admiral Ackbar/1,041*	25.00	60.00
72 Young Boba Fett/1,158*	50.00	125.00
73 C-3PO/1,156*	20.00	50.00
74 Lady Proxima/959*	40.00	100.00
75 Kylo Ren/1,187*	20.00	50.00

76 Kit Fisto/960*	20.00	50.00
77 Princess Leia/2,093*	15.00	40.00
78 Lieutenant Connix/1,351*	12.00	30.00
79 Emperor Palpatine/1,103*	15.00	40.00
80 Porg/1,130*	15.00	40.00
81 Ahsoka Tano/1,293*	60.00	150.00
82 Bala Tik/992*	15.00	40.00
83 Boba Fett/1,913*	60.00	120.00
84 Tauntaun/1,190*	12.00	30.00
85 Kuiil/1,068*	20.00	50.00
86 Elite Praetorian Guard/1,038*	12.00	30.00
87 Dryden Vos/1,003*	30.00	75.00
88 Bistan/996*	30.00	75.00
89 Paige Tico/996*	15.00	40.00
90 Rose Tico/901*	50.00	100.00
91 Grand Moff Tarkin/1,042*	30.00	75.00
92 Galen Erso/1,005*	20.00	50.00
93 Vice Admiral Holdo/1,079*	15.00	40.00
94 General Veers/979*	25.00	60.00
95 Jango Fett/1,252*	12.00	30.00
96 Jannah/1,074*	8.00	20.00
97 Hera Syndulla/1,131*	25.00	60.00
98 Jabba the Hutt/1,395*	10.00	20.00
99 Obi-Wan Kenobi/2,656*	6.00	15.00
100 Luke Skywalker/2,833*	8.00	20.00
101 Royal Guard/1,255*	10.00	25.00
102 Captain Rex/1,259*	12.00	30.00
103 Babu Frik/1,279*	6.00	15.00
104 Mas Amedda/1,105*	6.00	15.00
105 Fennec Shand/1,217*	30.00	75.00
106 Zorri Bliss/1,244*	6.00	15.00
107 Cassian Andor/1,246*	8.00	20.00
108 Clone Trooper/1,257*	8.00	20.00
109 Kazuda "Kaz" Xiono/1,241*	6.00	15.00
110 Aayla Secura/1,286*	10.00	25.00
111 Peli Motto/1,305*	12.00	30.00
112 Yaddle/1,328*	6.00	15.00
113 Sabine Wren/1,480*	15.00	40.00
114 Allegiant General Pryde/1,222*	6.00	15.00
115 Baze Malbus/1,268*	6.00	15.00
116 The Grand Inquisitor/1,228*	10.00	25.00
117 Ben Solo/2,304*	12.00	30.00
118 Rio Durant/1,325*	6.00	15.00
119 Bodhi Rook/1,277*	10.00	25.00
120 Mythrol/1,265*	8.00	20.00
121 Logray/1,303*	6.00	15.00
122 Chancellor Valorum/*	5.00	12.00
123 Qi'Ra/1,737*	8.00	20.00
124 Battle Droid/1,376*	10.00	25.00
125 Snap Wexley/1,191*	6.00	15.00
126 Bendu/1,114*	8.00	20.00
127 Cara Dune/2,316*	20.00	50.00
128 Klaud/1,421*	6.00	15.00
129 Rebolt/1,259*	6.00	15.00
130 Zam Wesell/1,293*	6.00	15.00

#	Name	Low	High
131	Moff Gideon/1,411*	15.00	40.00
132	Torra Doza/1,184*	5.00	12.00
133	Jan Dodonna/1,209*	5.00	12.00
134	Zuckuss/1,227*	6.00	15.00
135	Beaumont Kin/1,184*	6.00	15.00
136	Pre Vizsla/1,317*	8.00	20.00
137	Cal Kestis/1,278*	6.00	15.00
138	Lobot/1,252*	5.00	12.00
139	Ello Asty/1,242*	6.00	15.00
140	First Order TIE Fighter Pilot/1,319*	5.00	12.00
141	D-O/1,283*	6.00	15.00
142	Bazine Netal/1,023*	8.00	20.00
143	Tam Ryvora/1,130*	6.00	15.00
144	Second Sister/1,215*	6.00	15.00
145	The Mandalorian/4,283*	20.00	50.00
146	Bo-Katan Kryze/1,352*	10.00	25.00
147	WG-22/1,186*	6.00	15.00
148	The Client/1,291*	8.00	20.00
149	Gardulla the Hutt/1,240*	4.00	10.00
150	Master Codebreaker/1,215*	6.00	15.00
151	Bo Keevil/1,139*	6.00	15.00
152	Blurrg/1,250*	5.00	12.00
153	Vulptex/1,142*	8.00	20.00
154	IG-88/1,298*	6.00	15.00
155	Stass Allie/1,192*	8.00	20.00
156	Xi'an/1,296*	5.00	12.00
157	General Leia Organa/1,740*	6.00	15.00
158	Queen Breha Organa/1,328*	6.00	15.00
159	Chopper/1,332*	6.00	15.00
160	Toro Calican/1,269*	6.00	15.00
161	Even Piell/1,131*	4.00	10.00
162	2-1B Droid/1,148*	6.00	15.00
163	Iden Versio/1,286*	6.00	15.00
164	Ap'lek/1,251*	5.00	12.00
165	Bo-Katan Kryze/2,171*	8.00	20.00
166	Commander Cody/1,541*	6.00	15.00
167	Yoda/5,157*	8.00	20.00
168	Mace Windu/2,985*	5.00	12.00
169	Shmi Skywalker/1,236*	4.00	10.00
170	Gasgano/1,217*	4.00	10.00
171	Han Solo/1,838*	5.00	12.00
172	Dark Trooper/1,945*	5.00	12.00
173	DJ/1,334*	4.00	10.00
174	Greez/1,309*	4.00	10.00
175	Bantha/1,667*	4.00	10.00
176	Tusken Raider/1,811*	6.00	15.00
177	The Armorer/2,277*	8.00	20.00
178	Slowen Lo/1,388*	5.00	12.00
179	Loth-cat/1,544*	8.00	20.00
180	Beru Lars/1,435*	5.00	12.00
181	Therm Scissorpunch/1,519*	6.00	15.00
182	Seventh Sister/1,586*	8.00	20.00
183	Greef Karga/2,112*	4.00	10.00
184	Aftab Ackbar/1,576*	4.00	10.00
185	Aurodia Ventafoli/1,731*	8.00	20.00
186	Darth Bane/2,548*	6.00	15.00
187	Alexsandr Kallus/1,504*	6.00	15.00
188	Malakili/1,466*	6.00	15.00
189	Lando Calrissian/1,786*	4.00	10.00
190	Neeku Vozo/1,416*	5.00	12.00
191	Cobb Vanth/2,048*	5.00	12.00
192	Sagwa/1,504*	5.00	12.00
193	Lyra Erso/1,441*	4.00	10.00
194	Admiral Motti/1,428*	4.00	10.00
195	Axe Woves/2,155*	6.00	15.00
196	General Quinn/1,372*	4.00	10.00
197	Wes Janson/1,437*	5.00	12.00
198	Emir Wat Tambor/1,376*	5.00	12.00
199	Zeb Orrelios/2,153*	4.00	10.00
200	Chewbacca/4,903*	4.00	10.00
201	Zero/1,589*	4.00	10.00
202	Hunter/1,873*	8.00	20.00
203	Caretakers/1,303*	5.00	12.00
204	Sidon Ithano/1,363*	6.00	15.00
205	Boolio/1,296*	5.00	12.00
206	Dr. Pershing/1,440*	4.00	10.00
207	Barriss Offee/1,363*	6.00	15.00
208	FN-2199/1,430*	8.00	20.00
209	General Rieekan/1,252*	4.00	10.00
210	Boussh/1,435*	4.00	10.00
211	Pamich Nerro Goode/1,160*	5.00	12.00
212	Tion Medon/1,210*	4.00	10.00
213	Chief Chirpa/1,505*	4.00	10.00
214	Luminara Unduli/1,340*	6.00	15.00
215	Koska Reeves/2,637*	12.00	30.00
216	Sith Jet Troopers/1,519*	4.00	10.00
217	Mon Mothma/1,154*	4.00	10.00
218	EV-9D9/1,162*	4.00	10.00
219	Dexster Jettster/1,102	6.00	15.00
220	Sarlacc/1,146*	6.00	15.00
221	C-3PO/2,676*	4.00	10.00
222	Mouse Droid/1,412*	4.00	10.00
223	Commander Pyre/1,345*	6.00	15.00
224	Padme Amidala/3,356*	5.00	12.00
225	Captain Panaka/1,246*	4.00	10.00
226	Clone Commander Bly/1,343*	4.00	10.00
227	Enfys Nest/1,514*	6.00	15.00
228	Tank Trooper/1,443*	6.00	15.00
229	Sy Snootles/1,299*	6.00	15.00
230	GA-97/1,290*	5.00	12.00
231	Biggs Darklighter/1,266*	5.00	12.00
232	Lor San Tekka/1,211*	6.00	15.00
233	Bib Fortuna/1,621*	4.00	10.00
234	Boba Fett/3,700*	5.00	12.00
243	Crosshair/2,137*	4.00	10.00
246	Derek "Hobbie" Klivia/1,173*	4.00	10.00
248	Qui-Gonn Jinn/2,470*	5.00	12.00
255	Echo/1,487*	6.00	15.00
256	Omega/1,606*	8.00	20.00
261	Major Bren Derlin/1,192*	5.00	12.00
263	Momaw Nadon/1,321*	5.00	12.00
268	R5-D4/1,363*	4.00	10.00
270	Obi-Wan Kenobi/2,813*	4.00	10.00
275	Migs Mayfield/1,797*	5.00	12.00
278	Darth Vader/3,449*	4.00	10.00
280	Weeteef Cyu-Bee/1,244*	10.00	25.00
282	Garsa Fwip/1,811*	5.00	12.00
285	Rancor/2,044*	4.00	10.00
286	Krrsantan/2,625*	5.00	12.00
290	Cad Bane/2,975*	6.00	15.00
294	Jek Lawquane/1,189*	4.00	10.00
300	Ahsoka Tano/4,649*	6.00	15.00
303	Fennec Shand/1,863*	4.00	10.00
309	Tarfful/1,346*	5.00	12.00
312	Tiplee/1,296*	4.00	10.00
345	Klaatu/		
346	Daultey Dofine/		
347	Ilco Munica/		
348	AZI-3/		
349	R3-S1/		
350	Clone Commander Jet/		
351	Luke Skywalker/		
352	Owen Lars/		
353	DT-F16/		
354	Gor Koresh/		
355	Haja Estree/		
356	Darth Vader/		
357	BD-1/		
358	Temiri Blagg/		
NNO	Checklist 1-100/1,667*		
NNO	Checklist 101-200/1,582*		
NNO	Checklist 201-300/		

2021 Star Wars Lucasfilm 50th Anniversary

		Low	High
COMPLETE SET (25)		60.00	150.00
COMMON CARD (1-25)		3.00	8.00

2020 Star Wars The Mandalorian Art eBay Exclusive Set

		Low	High
COMPLETE SET (10)		20.00	50.00
COMMON CARD (1-10)		3.00	8.00
EBAY EXCLUSIVE			

2022 Star Wars The Mandalorian Chrome Beskar Edition

		Low	High
COMPLETE SET (100)		15.00	40.00
UNOPENED BOX (18 PACKS)		100.00	125.00
UNOPENED PACK (4 CARDS)		6.00	8.00
COMMON CARD		.40	1.00

*REF: 1.2X TO 3X BASIC CARDS
*BLUE/99: 1.5X TO 4X BASIC CARDS
*PURPLE/75: 2X TO 5X BASIC CARDS
*GREEN/50: 2.5X TO 6X BASIC CARDS

2022 Star Wars The Mandalorian Chrome Beskar Edition Armored and Ready

COMPLETE SET (10)	10.00	25.00
COMMON CARD (AR1-AR10)	1.50	4.00
*BLUE/99: .6X TO 1.5X BASIC CARDS		
*GREEN/50: .75X TO 2X BASIC CARDS		
STATED ODDS 1:6		
AR1 The Mandalorian	1.50	4.00
AR2 Boba Fett	1.50	4.00
AR3 The Armorer	1.50	4.00
AR4 Clan Kryze	1.50	4.00
AR5 Cobb Vanth	1.50	4.00
AR6 Dark Trooper	1.50	4.00
AR7 Paz Vizsla	1.50	4.00
AR8 IG-11	1.50	4.00
AR9 The Mandalorian	1.50	4.00
AR10 Fennec Shand	1.50	4.00

2022 Star Wars The Mandalorian Chrome Beskar Edition Autographs

COMMON AUTO	5.00	12.00
*BLUE/150: .5X TO 1.2X BASIC AUTOS		
*GREEN/99: .6X TO 1.5X BASIC AUTOS		
*PURPLE/50: .75X TO 2X BASIC AUTOS		
STATED ODDS 1:33		
AAW Alexander Wraith	6.00	15.00
ACB Chris Bartlett	10.00	25.00
ADB Dmitrious Bistrevsky	8.00	20.00
AIS Isaac Singleton Jr.	15.00	40.00
AJJ Julia Jones	12.00	30.00
ALS Leilani Shiu	8.00	20.00
AMR Misty Rosas	10.00	25.00
AMV Mercedes Varnado	30.00	75.00
AMW Matthew Wood	12.00	30.00
AOA Omid Abtahi	8.00	20.00
APL Paul Sun-Hyung Lee	10.00	25.00
ARB Richard Brake	6.00	15.00
ASK Simon Kassianides	15.00	40.00
ATF Tait Fletcher	6.00	15.00
ACBT Chris Bartlett	10.00	25.00
ACHB Chris Bartlett	10.00	25.00
ADLI Diana Lee Inosanto	8.00	20.00
AISF Isla Farris	10.00	25.00
AJKC Jake Cannavale	15.00	40.00
AMBJ Mark Boone Jr.	12.00	30.00
AMRK Misty Rosas	10.00	25.00
AWEB W. Earl Brown	15.00	40.00

2022 Star Wars The Mandalorian Chrome Beskar Edition Comic Covers

COMPLETE SET (5)	6.00	15.00
COMMON CARD (CC1-CC5)	2.00	5.00
*BLUE/99: .5X TO 1.2X BASIC CARDS		
*GREEN/50: .75X TO 2X BASIC CARDS		
STATED ODDS 1:3		

2022 Star Wars The Mandalorian Chrome Beskar Edition Die-Cut Autographs

STATED ODDS 1:12,751		
UNPRICED DUE TO SCARCITY		
MLA1 Pedro Pascal		
MLA2 Carl Weathers		
MLA3 Rosario Dawson		
MLA4 Nick Nolte		
MLA5 Taika Waititi		
MLA6 Ming-Na Wen		
MLA7 Temuera Morrison		
MLA8 Katee Sackhoff		

2022 Star Wars The Mandalorian Chrome Beskar Edition Dual Autographs

STATED ODDS 1:2,082		
STATED PRINT RUN 25 SER.#'d SETS		
UNPRICED DUE TO SCARCITY		
DAEH G.Esposito/W.Herzog		
DAHA W.Herzog/O.Abtahi		
DAMW T.Morrison/M.Wen		
DANW N.Nolte/T.Waititi		
DAPD P.Pascal/R.Dawson		
DAPG P.Pascal/G.Esposito		
DAPW P.Pascal/C.Weathers		
DASP K.Sackhoff/P.Pascal		
DASV K.Sackhoff/M.Varnado		

2022 Star Wars The Mandalorian Chrome Beskar Edition Illustrated Characters

COMPLETE SET (25)	25.00	60.00
COMMON CARD (IC1-IC25)	1.00	4.00
*BLUE/99: .5X TO 1.2X BASIC CARDS		
*GREEN/50: .75X TO 2X BASIC CARDS		
STATED ODDS 1:6		

2022 Star Wars The Mandalorian Chrome Beskar Edition Legends Die-Cuts

COMMON CARD (ML1-ML10)	20.00	50.00
RANDOMLY INSERTED INTO PACKS		
ML1 Grogu	40.00	100.00
ML2 The Mandalorian	30.00	75.00
ML4 IG-11	25.00	60.00
ML5 Boba Fett	40.00	100.00
ML7 Ahsoka Tano	50.00	125.00
ML8 Fennec Shand	25.00	60.00

2022 Star Wars The Mandalorian Chrome Beskar Edition Triple Autographs

*SUPER/1: UNPRICED DUE TO SCARCITY		
STATED PRINT RUN 5 SER.#'d SETS		
TAMWW Morrison/Wen/Wood		
TAPNW Pascal/Nolte/Waititi		
TAPWE Pascal/Weathers/Esposito		
TASKV Sackhoff/Kassianides/Varnado		

2020 Star Wars The Mandalorian Journey of the Child

COMPLETE SET (25)	5.00	12.00
UNOPENED BOX (32 CARDS)	15.00	25.00
COMMON CARD (1-25)	.20	.50
*GREEN: .6X TO 1.5X BASIC CARDS		
*RED/99: 1X TO 2.5X BASIC CARDS		
*BLUE/50: 1.5X TO 4X BASIC CARDS		

2020 Star Wars The Mandalorian Journey of the Child Illustrated

COMPLETE SET (5)	2.50	6.00
COMMON CARD (1-5)	.75	2.00
*GREEN: .6X TO 1.5X BASIC CARDS		
*RED/99: 1X TO 2.5X BASIC CARDS		
*BLUE/50: 1.5X TO 4X BASIC CARDS		
STATED ODDS 1 SET PER BOX		

2019 Star Wars The Mandalorian Season 1 Trailer Set

COMPLETE SET (10)	10.00	25.00
COMMON CARD (1-10)	2.00	5.00
STATED PRINT RUN 1,425 SER.#'d SETS		

2020 Star Wars The Mandalorian Season 1

COMPLETE SET (100)	15.00	40.00
UNOPENED BOX (7 PACKS)	125.00	250.00
UNOPENED PACK (8 CARDS)	15.00	40.00
COMMON CARD (1-100)	.40	1.00
*BLUE: .5X TO 1.2X BASIC CARDS		
*PURPLE: .75X TO 2X BASIC CARDS		
*BRONZE/50: 3X TO 8X BASIC CARDS		
*SILVER/25: 5X TO 12X BASIC CARDS		

2020 Star Wars The Mandalorian Season 1 Aliens and Creatures

COMPLETE SET (10)	8.00	20.00
COMMON CARD (AC1-AC10)	1.25	3.00
*RED/99: .5X TO 1.2X BASIC CARDS		

*BRONZE/50: .75X TO 2X BASIC CARDS

STATED ODDS 1:7

2020 Star Wars The Mandalorian Season 1 Autographs

COMMON AUTO	8.00	20.00
*RED/99: .5X TO 1.2X BASIC AUTOS		
*BRONZE/50: .6X TO 1.5X BASIC AUTOS		
STATED ODDS 1:19 HOBBY		
STATED ODDS 1:372 RETAIL BLASTER		
ADB Dmitrious Bistrevsky	10.00	25.00
AGC Gina Carano	100.00	200.00
AGE Giancarlo Esposito	50.00	100.00
AML Matt Lanter	10.00	25.00
AMR Misty Rosas	15.00	40.00
AOA Omid Abtahi	12.00	30.00
ATF Tait Fletcher	12.00	30.00
ACBF Chris Bartlett as Ferryman	10.00	25.00
ACBZ Chris Bartlett as Zero	12.00	30.00

2020 Star Wars The Mandalorian Season 1 Autographs Bronze

STATED PRINT RUN 50 SER.#'d SETS		
ACW Carl Weathers EXCH	125.00	250.00

2020 Star Wars The Mandalorian Season 1 Autographs Red

AES Emily Swallow	100.00	200.00
AHS Horatio Sanz	25.00	60.00

2020 Star Wars The Mandalorian Season 1 Characters

COMPLETE SET (18)	10.00	25.00
COMMON CARD (C1-C18)	1.25	3.00
*RED/99: .75X TO 2X BASIC CARDS		
*BRONZE/50: 1X TO 2.5X BASIC CARDS		
STATED ODDS 1:2 HOBBY & RETAIL BLASTER		

2020 Star Wars The Mandalorian Season 1 Commemorative Medallions

COMMON MEM	6.00	15.00
*RED/99: .5X TO 1.2X BASIC MEM		
*BRONZE/50: .6X TO 1.5X BASIC MEM		
STATED ODDS 1:98 HOBBY		
STATED ODDS 1:1 RET.BLASTER BOXES		
MAH The Armorer	12.00	30.00
MBM Blurrg	10.00	25.00
MCC The Child	15.00	40.00
MCH The Child	15.00	40.00
MCM The Child	15.00	40.00
MGC Greef Karga	8.00	20.00
MMC The Mandalorian	12.00	30.00
MMH The Mandalorian	12.00	30.00
MMM The Mandalorian	12.00	30.00
MOH Omera	8.00	20.00
MTC Toro Calican	10.00	25.00
MCDC Cara Dune	10.00	25.00

MCDH Cara Dune	10.00	25.00
MIGC IG-11	12.00	30.00
MMGC Moff Gideon	8.00	20.00

2020 Star Wars The Mandalorian Season 1 Concept Art

COMPLETE SET (10)	8.00	20.00
COMMON CARD (CA1-CA10)	1.25	3.00
*RED/99: .75X TO 2X BASIC CARDS		
*BRONZE/50: 1X TO 2.5X BASIC CARDS		
STATED ODDS 1:7 HOBBY & RETAIL BLASTER		

2020 Star Wars The Mandalorian Season 1 Dual Autographs

STATED ODDS 1:1,258 HOBBY		
STATED ODDS 1:25,176 RETAIL BLASTER		
STATED PRINT RUN 25 SER.#'d SETS		
UNPRICED DUE TO SCARCITY		
DACW G.Carano/C.Weathers		
DAFW T.Fletcher/R.Watson		
DAHA W.Herzog/O.Abtahi		
DAHC W.Herzog/G.Carano		
DANC N.Nolte/G.Carano		
DANW N.Nolte/T.Waititi		
DAPC P.Pascal/G.Carano		
DAPE P.Pascal/G.Esposito		
DAPH P.Pascal/W.Herzog		
DAPN P.Pascal/N.Nolte		
DAPW P.Pascal/T.Waititi		
DAPCW P.Pascal/C.Weathers		

2020 Star Wars The Mandalorian Season 1 Sourced Fabric Relics

COMMON MEM	30.00	75.00
*BRONZE/50: .5X TO 1.2X BASIC MEM		
STATED ODDS 1:175 HOBBY EXCLUSIVE		

2020 Star Wars The Mandalorian Season 1 Tools of the Bounty Hunter

COMPLETE SET (10)	10.00	25.00
COMMON CARD (TB1-TB10)	1.50	4.00
*RED/99: .5X TO 1.2X BASIC CARDS		
*BRONZE/50: .6X TO 1.5X BASIC CARDS		
STATED ODDS 1:7 HOBBY & RETAIL BLASTER		

2020 Star Wars The Mandalorian Season 1 Triple Autographs

STATED ODDS 1:3,774 HOBBY		
STATED ODDS 1:88,115 RETAIL BLASTER		
STATED PRINT RUN 5 SER.#'d SETS		
UNPRICED DUE TO SCARCITY		
TACWN Carano/Weathers/Nolte		
TAFWB Fletcher/Watson/Bistrevsky		
TAHAC Herzog/Abtahi/Carano		
TANCW Nolte/Carano/Waititi		
TAPCN Pascal/Carano/Nolte		
TAPCW Pascal/Carano/Waititi		

2021 Star Wars The Mandalorian Season 2

COMPLETE SET (100)	12.00	30.00
UNOPENED BOX (7 PACKS)	100.00	150.00
UNOPENED PACK (8 CARDS)	15.00	20.00
COMMON CARD (1-100)	.25	.60
*BLUE: 1.2X TO 3X BASIC CARDS		
*PURPLE: 2.5X TO 6X BASIC CARDS		
*BRONZE/50: 8X TO 20X BASIC CARDS		
*SILVER/25: 15X TO 40X BASIC CARDS		

2021 Star Wars The Mandalorian Season 2 Autographed Commemorative Metal Buttons

UNPRICED DUE TO SCARCITY		
AMCW Carl Weathers		
AMPP Pedro Pascal		
AMSK Simon Kassianides		

2021 Star Wars The Mandalorian Season 2 Autographs

COMMON AUTO	10.00	25.00
*RED/99: SAME VALUE AS BASIC		
*BRONZE/50: .5X TO 1.2X BASIC AUTOS		
*SILVER/25: .6X TO 1.5X BASIC AUTOS		
RANDOMLY INSERTED INTO PACKS		
ACB Chris Bartlett	12.00	30.00
ACW Carl Weathers	150.00	300.00
AGE Giancarlo Esposito	60.00	120.00
AHS Horatio Sanz	30.00	75.00
ALS Leilani Shiu	15.00	40.00
AMR Misty Rosas	20.00	50.00
APA Philip Alexander	12.00	30.00
APL Paul Sun-Hyung Lee	30.00	75.00

APP Pedro Pascal	600.00	1200.00
ASK Simon Kassianides	30.00	75.00
ATM Temuera Morrison	150.00	300.00
ADLI Diana Lee Inosanto	20.00	50.00

2021 Star Wars The Mandalorian Season 2 Characters

COMPLETE SET (14)		
COMMON CARD (C1-C14)	.75	2.00
*BRONZE/50: 3X TO 8X BASIC CARDS		
*SILVER/25: 2X TO 5X BASIC CARDS		
RANDOMLY INSERTED INTO PACKS		
C1 The Mandalorian	1.50	4.00
C2 The Child	2.00	5.00
C4 Moff Gideon	1.25	3.00
C8 Cobb Vanth	1.50	4.00
C9 Dark Trooper	1.25	3.00
C11 Bo-Katan Kryze	1.50	4.00
C12 Koska Reeves	1.50	4.00
C13 Ahsoka Tano	3.00	8.00
C14 Boba Fett	1.50	4.00

2021 Star Wars The Mandalorian Season 2 The Child

COMPLETE SET (12)	15.00	40.00
COMMON CARD (TC1-TC12)	2.00	5.00
*BRONZE/50: 2X TO 5X BASIC CARDS		
*SILVER/25: 5X TO 12X BASIC CARDS		
RANDOMLY INSERTED INTO PACKS		

2021 Star Wars The Mandalorian Season 2 Comic Covers

COMPLETE SET (7)	15.00	40.00
COMMON CARD (CC1-CC7)	3.00	8.00
*BRONZE/50: 2X TO 5X BASIC CARDS		
*SILVER/25: 3X TO 8X BASIC CARDS		
RANDOMLY INSERTED INTO PACKS		

2021 Star Wars The Mandalorian Season 2 Commemorative Metal Buttons

COMMON MEM	5.00	12.00
*RED/99: SAME VALUE AS BASIC		
*BRONZE/50: .5X TO 1.2X BASIC CARDS		
*SILVER/25: .6X TO 1.5X BASIC CARDS		
RANDOMLY INSERTED INTO PACKS		
MCCB The Child	10.00	25.00
MCCF The Child	10.00	25.00
MCMB The Mandalorian	12.00	30.00
MCMC The Mandalorian	12.00	30.00
MCMF The Mandalorian	12.00	30.00
MCBHW Bo-Katan Kryze	8.00	20.00
MCBMF Bo-Katan Kryze	8.00	20.00
MCBTW Bo-Katan Kryze	8.00	20.00
MCCCC The Child	10.00	25.00
MCCGC The Child	10.00	25.00
MCCMC The Child	10.00	25.00
MCCMF The Child	10.00	25.00

MCKHW Koska Reeves	10.00	25.00
MCKTW Koska Reeves	10.00	25.00
MCMGC The Mandalorian	12.00	30.00
MCMHW The Mandalorian	12.00	30.00
MCMMC The Mandalorian	12.00	30.00
MCMMF The Mandalorian	12.00	30.00
MCMTW The Mandalorian	12.00	30.00
MCPMF Ahsoka Tano	15.00	40.00

2021 Star Wars The Mandalorian Season 2 Concept Art

COMPLETE SET (16)	20.00	50.00
COMMON CARD (CA1-CA16)	2.50	6.00
*BRONZE/50: .6X TO 1.5X BASIC CARDS		
*SILVER/25: 2X TO 5X BASIC CARDS		
RANDOMLY INSERTED INTO PACKS		

2021 Star Wars The Mandalorian Season 2 Dual Autographs

UNPRICED DUE TO SCARCITY

DAPG G.Esposito/P.Pascal	
DAPW C.Weathers/P.Pascal	
DAWA P.Alexander/A.Wraith	
DAWS H.Sanz/C.Weathers	

2021 Star Wars The Mandalorian Season 2 Prop Relics

STATED PRINT RUN 50 SER.#'d SETS

PRAF The Armorer/Razor Crest	200.00	400.00
PRCR The Child/Razor Crest	350.00	700.00
PRKR Kuiil/Razor Crest		
PRMF The Mandalorian/Chimney	250.00	500.00
PRMR The Mandalorian/Chimney	250.00	500.00

2021 Star Wars The Mandalorian Season 2 Sourced Fabric Relics

COMMON MEM	50.00	100.00
*BRONZE/50: .5X TO 1.2X BASIC MEM		
*SILVER/25: .6X TO 1.5 BASIC MEM		
STATED PRINT RUN 99 SER.#'d SETS		
FRM Mythrol/Jacket	50.00	100.00
FRAA Ahsoka Tano/Pants	100.00	200.00
FRAB Ahsoka Tano/Arm Wraps	125.00	250.00
FRAC Ahsoka Tano/Body Suit	125.00	250.00
FRGG Gamorrean Guard/Shirt	50.00	100.00
FRMG Magistrate Morgan Elsbeth/Body Suit	60.00	120.00

2021 Star Wars The Mandalorian Season 2 Triple Autographs

UNPRICED DUE TO SCARCITY

TAPWE Pascal/Esposito/Weathers	
TAPWS Sanz/Pascal/Weathers	

2020 Star Wars The Mandalorian Season 2 Trailer Set

COMPLETE SET (7)	15.00	40.00
COMMON CARD (1-7)	4.00	10.00

STATED PRINT RUN 1,482 SETS		
NNO A Curious Figure Watches	4.00	10.00
NNO A Tusken Raider Spots the Razor Crest	4.00	10.00
NNO Landing on a Mysterious Planet	4.00	10.00
NNO Scout Trooper in Pursuit	4.00	10.00
NNO So I've Heard	4.00	10.00
NNO The Child Surveys the Situation	4.00	10.00
NNO The Mandalorian and The Child Inspect the Location	4.00	10.00

1995 Star Wars Mastervisions

COMPLETE BOXED SET (36)	10.00	25.00
COMMON CARD (1-36)	.30	.75

1995 Star Wars Mastervisions Promos

COMMON CARD	.75	2.00
P2 Luke on Hoth	1.25	3.00
(Star Wars Galaxy Magazine Exclusive)		

2015 Star Wars Masterwork

COMPLETE SET w/o SP (50)	60.00	120.00
UNOPENED BOX (4 MINIBOXES)		
UNOPENED MINIBOX (5 CARDS)		
COMMON CARD (1-50)	2.00	5.00
COMMON CARD (51-75)	5.00	12.00
*BLUE/299: .5X TO 1.2X BASIC CARDS		
*BLUE SP/299: .2X TO .50X BASIC CARDS		
*SILVER/99: .75X TO 2X BASIC CARDS		
*SILVER SP/99: .3X TO .80X BASIC CARDS		
*GREEN/50: 1.2X TO 3X BASIC CARDS		
*GREEN SP/50: .5X TO 1.2X BASIC CARDS		

2015 Star Wars Masterwork Autographs

COMMON AUTO	8.00	20.00
STATED ODDS 1:4		
NNO Alan Harris	10.00	25.00
NNO Amy Allen	12.00	30.00
NNO Angus MacInnes	10.00	25.00
NNO Anthony Daniels	120.00	250.00
NNO Ashley Eckstein	50.00	125.00
NNO Billy Dee Williams	100.00	200.00
NNO Carrie Fisher	600.00	1000.00
NNO Chris Parsons	10.00	25.00
NNO Dermot Crowley	10.00	25.00
NNO Dickey Beer	8.00	20.00
NNO Gerald Home	10.00	25.00
NNO Harrison Ford	1800.00	3000.00
NNO James Earl Jones	300.00	450.00
NNO Jeremy Bulloch	20.00	50.00
NNO Jesse Jensen	10.00	25.00
NNO John Morton	15.00	40.00
NNO John Ratzenberger	12.00	30.00
NNO Julian Glover	12.00	30.00
NNO Kenneth Colley	10.00	25.00
NNO Kenny Baker	150.00	300.00
NNO Mark Hamill	400.00	750.00
NNO Michonne Bourriague	10.00	25.00

NNO Mike Quinn	12.00	30.00
NNO Oliver Ford Davies	10.00	25.00
NNO Orli Shoshan	10.00	25.00
NNO Pam Rose	10.00	25.00
NNO Paul Brooke	12.00	30.00
NNO Peter Mayhew	75.00	150.00
NNO Phil Eason	10.00	25.00
NNO Rusty Goffe	12.00	30.00
NNO Tim Rose	15.00	40.00
NNO Wayne Pygram	10.00	25.00

2015 Star Wars Masterwork Companions

COMPLETE SET (10)	25.00	60.00
COMMON CARD (C1-C10)	10.00	10.00
*RAINBOW/299: .6X TO 1.5X BASIC CARDS		
*CANVAS/99: 1X TO 2.5X BASIC CARDS		
*WOOD/50: 1.2X TO 3X BASIC CARDS		
*CLEAR ACE./25: 1.5X TO 4X BASIC CARDS		
C1 Han Solo and Chewbacca	6.00	15.00
C2 Luke and Leia	6.00	15.00
C3 Vader and Palpatine	5.00	12.00
C5 C-3PO and R2-D2	5.00	12.00
C8 R2-D2 and Luke Skywalker	5.00	12.00
C10 Boba Fett and Jango Fett	5.00	12.00

2015 Star Wars Masterwork Defining Moments

COMPLETE SET (10)	25.00	60.00
COMMON CARD (DM1-DM10)	4.00	10.00
*RAINBOW/299: .6X TO 1.5X BASIC CARDS		
*CANVAS/99: 1X TO 2.5X BASIC CARDS		
*WOOD/50: 1.2X TO 3X BASIC CARDS		
*CLEAR ACE./25: 1.5X TO 4X BASIC CARDS		
DM1 Darth Vader	5.00	12.00
DM2 Luke Skywalker	5.00	12.00
DM3 Han Solo	8.00	20.00
DM4 Princess Leia Organa	5.00	12.00
DM7 Anakin Skywalker	5.00	12.00
DM8 Obi-Wan Kenobi	5.00	12.00
DM10 Chewbacca	5.00	12.00

2015 Star Wars Masterwork Dual Autograph Booklets

STATED PRINT RUN 5 SER. #'d SETS

UNPRICED DUE TO SCARCITY

1 Anthony Daniels/Kenny Baker

2 Billy Dee Williams/Mike Quinn	
3 Jeremy Bulloch/Chris Parsons	
4 Mark Hamill/James Earl Jones	

2015 Star Wars Masterwork Return of the Jedi Bunker Relics Bronze

COMMON CARD	12.00	30.00
*SILVER/77: .75X TO 2X BASIC CARDS		
CARDS 1, 2, 3, 4, 10, 12 SER.#'d TO 155		
CARDS 5, 6, 7, 8, 9, 11 SER.#'d TO 255		
1 Han Solo/155	20.00	50.00
2 Princess Leia Organa/155	20.00	50.00
3 Chewbacca/155	15.00	40.00
4 Luke Skywalker/155	25.00	60.00
10 Ewok (frame)/155	15.00	40.00
12 Han, Leia & Luke/155	20.00	50.00

2015 Star Wars Masterwork Scum and Villainy

COMPLETE SET (10)	25.00	60.00
COMMON CARD (SV1-SV10)	4.00	10.00
*RAINBOW/299: 1.5X TO 6X BASIC CARDS		
*CANVAS/99: 1X TO 2.5X BASIC CARDS		
*WOOD/50: 1.2X TO 3X BASIC CARDS		
*CLEAR ACE./25: 1.5X TO 4X BASIC CARDS		
SV1 Boba Fett	6.00	15.00
SV2 Jabba the Hutt	5.00	12.00
SV4 General Grievous	6.00	15.00
SV5 Jango Fett	5.00	12.00
SV8 Ponda Baba	6.00	15.00
SV9 Bossk	5.00	12.00
SV10 Tusken Raider	6.00	15.00

2015 Star Wars Masterwork Autographed Pen Relics

STATED PRINT RUN 1 SER. #'d SET

UNPRICED DUE TO SCARCITY

NNO Alan Harris
NNO Amy Allen
NNO Angus MacInnes
NNO Anthony Daniels
NNO Ashley Eckstein
NNO Billy Dee Williams
NNO Bonnie Piesse
NNO Bruce Spence
NNO Caroline Blakiston
NNO Carrie Fisher
NNO Chris Parsons
NNO Dermot Crowley
NNO Dickey Beer
NNO Gerald Home
NNO Harrison Ford
NNO Ian Liston
NNO James Earl Jones
NNO Jeremy Bulloch
NNO Jerome Blake
NNO Jesse Jensen

NNO John Morton
NNO John Ratzenberger
NNO Julian Glover
NNO Kenneth Colley
NNO Kenny Baker
NNO Mark Hamill
NNO Matt Sloan
NNO Michonne Bourriague
NNO Mike Quinn
NNO Oliver Ford Davies
NNO Orli Shoshan
NNO Pam Rose
NNO Paul Brooke
NNO Peter Mayhew
NNO Phil Eason
NNO Ralph Brown
NNO Rusty Goffe
NNO Tim Rose
NNO Wayne Pygram
NNO Zachariah Jensen

2015 Star Wars Masterwork Stamp Relics

COMMON CARD	20.00	50.00
STATED ODDS 1:CASE		
NNO Anakin vs. Obi-Wan	50.00	100.00
NNO Ben (Obi-Wan) Kenobi	30.00	80.00
NNO Boba Fett	60.00	120.00
NNO C-3PO	25.00	60.00
NNO Darth Maul	50.00	100.00
NNO Darth Vader	30.00	80.00
NNO Emperor Palpatine	30.00	80.00
NNO Han Solo and Chewbacca	50.00	100.00
NNO Luke Skywalker	30.00	80.00
NNO The Millennium Falcon	50.00	100.00
NNO X-Wing Fighter	30.00	80.00

2015 Star Wars Masterwork Triple Autograph

STATED PRINT RUN 2 SER. #'d SETS

UNPRICED DUE TO SCARCITY

1 Mark Hamill

Harrison Ford

Carrie Fisher

2015 Star Wars Masterwork Weapons Lineage Medallions

COMPLETE SET (30)	250.00	500.00
COMMON CARD	8.00	20.00
*SILVER/50: 1.2X TO 3X BASIC CARDS		
STATED ODDS 1:6		
NNO Anakin Skywalker	10.00	25.00
Mace Windu's Lightsaber		
NNO Anakin Skywalker	12.00	30.00
Anakin Skywalker's Lightsaber		
NNO B. Fett's Blaster	10.00	25.00
NNO B. Fett's Blaster	12.00	30.00
NNO Darth Maul's Lightsaber	10.00	25.00
NNO Vader	10.00	25.00
Vader's Lightsaber		
NNO Vader	10.00	25.00
Vader's Lightsaber		
NNO Vader	10.00	25.00
Vader's Lightsaber		
NNO Vader Solo's Blaster	12.00	30.00
NNO Darth Vader	15.00	40.00
Luke Skywalker's Lightsaber		
NNO Han Solo	12.00	30.00
Han Solo's Blaster		
NNO Han Solo	12.00	30.00
Han Solo's Blaster		
NNO Han Solo	15.00	40.00
Luke Skywalker's Lightsaber		
NNO Luke Skywalker	10.00	25.00
Luke Skywalker's Lightsaber		
NNO Luke Skywalker	10.00	25.00
Luke Skywalker's Lightsaber		
NNO Mace Windu	10.00	25.00
Mace Windu's Lightsaber		
NNO Princess Leia Organa	10.00	25.00
Stormtrooper Blaster Rifle		
NNO Leia	12.00	30.00
Leia's Blaster		
NNO R2-D2	10.00	25.00
Luke's Lightsaber		
NNO Stormtrooper	12.00	30.00
Stormtrooper Blaster Rifle		
NNO Yoda	15.00	40.00
Yoda's Lightsaber		

2016 Star Wars Masterwork

GREEDO

COMPLETE SET W/SP (75)	200.00	400.00
COMPLETE SET W/O SP (50)	30.00	80.00
UNOPENED BOX (4 PACKS)	150.00	200.00
UNOPENED PACK (5 CARDS)	50.00	60.00
COMMON CARD (1-75)	2.00	5.00
COMMON SP (51-75)	4.00	10.00
*BLUE MET.: SAME VALUE	2.00	5.00
*BLUE MET.SP: SAME VALUE	4.00	10.00
*SILVER MET./99: .75X TO 1.5X BASIC CARDS	3.00	8.00
*SILVER MET.SP/99: .30X TO .75X BASIC CARDS	3.00	8.00
*GREEN MET./50: 1.2X TO 3X BASIC CARDS	6.00	15.00
*GREEN MET.SP/50: .6X TO 1.5X BASIC CARDS	6.00	15.00
*LTSBR PURP./25: 1.5X TO 4X BASIC CARDS	8.00	20.00
*LTSBR PURP.SP/25: .75X TO 2X BASIC CARDS	8.00	20.00
66 Han Solo SP	6.00	15.00
71 Rey SP	8.00	20.00

2016 Star Wars Masterwork Alien Identification Guide

COMPLETE SET (10)	20.00	50.00
COMMON CARD (AI1-AI10)	2.50	6.00
*FOIL/299: .6X TO 1.5X BASIC CARDS	3.00	8.00
*CANVAS/99: .75X TO 2X BASIC CARDS	5.00	12.00
*WOOD/50: 1X TO 2.5X BASIC CARDS	6.00	15.00
STATED ODDS 1:4		

2016 Star Wars Masterwork Autographs

CARRIE FISHER AS
Princess Leia
AUTHENTIC AUTOGRAPH

COMMON AUTO	6.00	15.00
*FOIL/50: .6X TO 1.5X BASIC CARDS		
*CANVAS/25: .75X TO 2X BASIC CARDS		
5 Andy Serkis	80.00	150.00
8 Ashley Eckstein	75.00	200.00
11 Caroline Blakiston	8.00	20.00
14 Clive Revill	12.00	30.00
15 Corey Dee Williams	8.00	20.00
19 David Ankrum	8.00	20.00
20 David Barclay	8.00	20.00
24 Dickey Beer	10.00	25.00
34 Jeremy Bulloch	15.00	40.00
39 John Coppinger	8.00	20.00
47 Mark Dodson	10.00	25.00
50 Matthew Wood	8.00	20.00
55 Mike Edmonds	8.00	20.00
56 Mike Quinn	8.00	20.00
65 Sam Witwer	8.00	20.00
73 Tim Dry	8.00	20.00
74 Tim Rose	8.00	20.00
75 Tiya Sircar	8.00	20.00

2016 Star Wars Masterwork Autographs Canvas

*CANVAS/25: .75X TO 2X BASIC CARDS		
STATED ODDS 1:25		
STATED PRINT RUN 25 SER.#'d SETS		
1 Adam Driver	400.00	800.00
5 Andy Serkis	150.00	300.00
7 Anthony Daniels	80.00	150.00
10 Billy Dee Williams		
12 Carrie Fisher	300.00	600.00
16 Daisy Ridley	1200.00	2000.00
23 Denis Lawson	25.00	60.00
26 Freddie Prinze Jr.	30.00	80.00
29 Greg Grunberg	12.00	30.00
31 Harrison Ford/1		
32 Hugh Quarshie		
38 John Boyega		
42 Julian Glover		
43 Keisha Castle-Hughes		
48 Mark Hamill	250.00	500.00
52 Michael Carter	12.00	30.00
60 Peter Mayhew		
61 Ray Park		
79 Warwick Davis	15.00	40.00

2016 Star Wars Masterwork Autographs Foil

*FOIL/50: .6X TO 1.5X BASIC CARDS		
STATED ODDS 1:30		
STATED PRINT RUN 50 SER.#'d SETS		
3 Alan Harris		
7 Anthony Daniels	50.00	100.00
12 Carrie Fisher		
14 Clive Revill		
15 Corey Dee Williams		

19 David Ankrum		
20 David Barclay		
23 Denis Lawson		
25 Femi Taylor		
26 Freddie Prinze Jr.		
27 Garrick Hagon		
28 George Takei	15.00	40.00
29 Greg Grunberg	10.00	25.00
32 Hugh Quarshie	10.00	25.00
33 Jack Klaff		
38 John Boyega	120.00	250.00
40 John Morton		
41 John Ratzenberger		
43 Keisha Castle-Hughes		
44 Kenneth Colley		
47 Mark Dodson		
51 Mercedes Ngoh		
52 Michael Carter		
59 Paul Blake		
60 Peter Mayhew	30.00	80.00
61 Ray Park		
67 Sean Crawford		
76 Toby Philpott		
79 Warwick Davis		

2016 Star Wars Masterwork Dual Autographs

STATED ODDS 1:4,658

NNO Fisher/Baker		
NNO Barclay/Philpott	25.00	60.00
NNO McDiarmid/Revil		
NNO Blake/Bowers	20.00	50.00
NNO Hamill/Ridley		
NNO Hamill/Baker		
NNO Pygram/Stanton	15.00	40.00

2016 Star Wars Masterwork Great Rivalries

COMPLETE SET (10)	15.00	40.00
COMMON CARD (GR1-GR10)	2.50	6.00
*FOIL/299: .6X TO 1.5X BASIC CARDS		

---

*CANVAS/99: .75X TO 2X BASIC CARDS

*WOOD/50: 1X TO 2.5X BASIC CARDS

STATED ODDS 1:2

2016 Star Wars Masterwork Medallion Relics

COMMON CARD	5.00	12.00
*SILVER/99: .6X TO 1.5X BASIC CARDS	8.00	20.00
*GOLD/10: 1.5X TO 4X BASIC CARDS	20.00	50.00
STATED ODDS 1:7		
NNO Han Solo	6.00	15.00
Hoth		
NNO Han Solo	6.00	15.00
Starkiller Base		
NNO Han Solo	6.00	15.00
Yavin		
NNO Kylo Ren		
Starkiller Base		
NNO Rey	6.00	15.00
Starkiller Base		

2016 Star Wars Masterwork Quad Autographed Booklet

STATED ODDS 1:20,960

UNPRICED DUE TO SCARCITY

1 McDiarmid/Jones/Glover/Colley

2016 Star Wars Masterwork Show of Force

COMPLETE SET (10)	25.00	60.00
COMMON CARD (SF1-SF10)	3.00	8.00
*FOIL/299: .6X TO 1.5X BASIC CARDS	5.00	12.00
*CANVAS/99: .75X TO 2X BASIC CARDS	6.00	15.00

---

*WOOD/50: 1X TO 2.5X BASIC CARDS	8.00	20.00
STATED ODDS 1:4		
SF10 Rey	4.00	10.00

2016 Star Wars Masterwork Stamp Relics

COMPLETE SET (12)	100.00	200.00
COMMON CARD	8.00	20.00
*BRONZE/99: .6X TO 1.5X BASIC CARDS	12.00	30.00
*SILVER/50: .75X TO 2X BASIC CARDS	15.00	40.00
STATED ODDS 1:13		
STATED PRINT RUN 249 SER.#'d SETS		
NNO Han Solo	10.00	25.00
NNO Rey	12.00	30.00

2016 Star Wars Masterwork Triple Autographs

STATED ODDS 1:4,658

UNPRICED DUE TO SCARCITY

1 McDiarmid/Colley/Glover

2 Hamill/Boyega/Ridley

3 Hamill/Fisher/Baker

2017 Star Wars Masterwork

COMMON CARD (1-75)	2.50	6.00
COMMON SP (76-100)	5.00	12.00
*BLUE: .5X TO 1.25X BASIC CARDS	3.00	8.00
*GREEN/99: .6X TO 1.5X BASIC CARDS	4.00	10.00
*PURPLE/50: .75X TO 2X BASIC CARDS	5.00	12.00
*GOLD/25: 1X TO 2.5X BASIC CARDS	6.00	15.00
*RED/1: UNPRICED DUE TO SCARCITY		

TRADING CARDS

2017 Star Wars Masterwork Adventures of R2-D2

COMMON CARD (AR1-AR10)	2.50	6.00
*RAINBOW FOIL: .5X TO 1.25X BASIC CARDS	3.00	8.00
*CANVAS: .6X TO 1.5X BASIC CARDS	4.00	10.00
*WOOD/50: .75X TO 2X BASIC CARDS	5.00	12.00

2017 Star Wars Masterwork Autographed Pen Relics

STATED PRINT RUN 1 SER.#'d SET

UNPRICED DUE TO SCARCITY

NNO Adam Driver
NNO Alan Ruscoe
NNO Alan Tudyk
NNO Andy Serkis
NNO Ashley Eckstein
NNO Ben Daniels
NNO Billy Dee Williams
NNO Brian Herring
NNO Clive Revill
NNO Daisy Ridley
NNO Daniel Logan
NNO David Acord
NNO David Bowers
NNO Derek Arnold
NNO Donnie Yen
NNO Felicity Jones
NNO Forest Whitaker
NNO Freddie Prinze Jr.
NNO Garrick Hagon
NNO Genevieve O'Reilly
NNO Gwendoline Christie
NNO Hayden Christensen
NNO Ian McDiarmid
NNO Ian McElhinney
NNO Ian Whyte
NNO Jeremy Bulloch
NNO Jerome Blake
NNO John Boyega
NNO Julian Glover
NNO Julie Dolan
NNO Kath Soucie
NNO Lars Mikkelson
NNO Lloyd Sherr
NNO Marc Silk
NNO Mary Elizabeth McGlynn
NNO Matthew Wood

NNO Nick Kellington
NNO Paul Kasey
Admiral Raddus
NNO Paul Kasey
Edrio Two Tubes
NNO Philip Anthony-Rodriguez
NNO Ray Park
NNO Richard Oldfield
NNO Riz Ahmed
NNO Robbie Daymond
NNO Sam Witwer
NNO Sarah Michelle Gellar
NNO Shardon Duncan-Brewster
NNO Stephen Stanton
NNO Taylor Gray
NNO Temuera Morrison
NNO Tim Rose
NNO Tiya Sircar
NNO Tom Baker
NNO Valene Kane
NNO Warwick Davis
NNO Zarene Dallas

2017 Star Wars Masterwork Autographs

COMMON CARD	6.00	15.00
NNO Adam Driver (horizontal)		
NNO Adam Driver (vertical)		
NNO Alan Tudyk	50.00	100.00
NNO Andy Serkis		
NNO Ashley Eckstein	40.00	100.00
NNO Ben Daniels	8.00	20.00
NNO Billy Dee Williams		
NNO Brian Herring	15.00	40.00
NNO Clive Revill	8.00	20.00
NNO Daisy Ridley		
NNO Dee Bradley Baker	10.00	25.00
NNO Derek Arnold	8.00	20.00
NNO Donnie Yen	60.00	120.00
NNO Felicity Jones (horizontal)		
NNO Felicity Jones (vertical)		
NNO Forest Whitaker (horizontal)		
NNO Forest Whitaker (vertical)		

NNO Freddie Prinze Jr.		
NNO Gwendoline Christie		
NNO Harrison Ford		
NNO Hayden Christensen	150.00	300.00
NNO Ian McDiarmid		
NNO Ian Whyte	10.00	25.00
NNO Jeremy Bulloch	15.00	40.00
NNO John Boyega (horizontal)		
NNO John Boyega (vertical)	60.00	120.00
NNO Julian Glover	12.00	30.00
NNO Lars Mikkelsen	25.00	60.00
NNO Mark Hamill		
NNO Mary Elizabeth McGlynn	12.00	30.00
NNO Matt Lanter	15.00	40.00
NNO Matthew Wood		
NNO Phil LaMarr	8.00	20.00
NNO Ray Park		
NNO Riz Ahmed		
NNO Robbie Daymond	10.00	25.00
NNO Sam Witwer	10.00	25.00
NNO Sarah Michelle Gellar		
NNO Temuera Morrison	25.00	60.00
NNO Tiya Sircar	8.00	20.00
NNO Tom Baker		
NNO Valene Kane	25.00	60.00
NNO Warwick Davis	10.00	25.00
NNO Zarene Dallas	8.00	20.00

2017 Star Wars Masterwork Droid Medallion Relics

COMMON CARD	5.00	12.00
*SILVER/40: .5X TO 1.2X BASIC RELICS	6.00	15.00
*GOLD/25: .6X TO 1.5X BASIC RELICS	8.00	20.00
*BLACK/1: UNPRICED DUE TO SCARCITY		
STATED PRINT RUN 150 SER.#'d SETS		

2017 Star Wars Masterwork Dual Autographs

NNO Graves/Taber		20.00	50.00
NNO Daniels/Baker			
NNO Herring/Baker			
NNO Fisher/Baker			
NNO Barclay/Taylor		15.00	40.00
NNO Jones/Tudyk			
NNO Whitaker/Ahmed			
NNO Prinze Jr./Gellar			
NNO Christie/Boyega			
NNO Christensen/Baker			
NNO Christensen/Wood			
NNO McDiarmid/Christensen			
NNO Uwais/Qin-Fee		12.00	30.00
NNO Isaccs/Gray		20.00	50.00
NNO Ratzenberger/MacInnes		12.00	30.00
NNO Hamill/Christensen			
NNO Hamill/Baker			
NNO Salenger/Futterman		12.00	30.00
NNO Kasey/Stanton		12.00	30.00
NNO Marshall/Fleetwood			
NNO Witwer/Wilkinson		15.00	40.00
NNO Morrison/Logan		20.00	50.00
NNO Cole/Grube			

2017 Star Wars Masterwork Evolution of the Rebel Alliance

COMMON CARD (LP1-LP10)	2.50	6.00
*RAINBOW FOIL/249: .5X TO 1.25X BASIC CARDS	3.00	8.00
*CANVAS/99: .6X TO 1.5X BASIC CARDS	4.00	10.00
*WOOD/50: .75X TO 2X BASIC CARDS	5.00	12.00

2017 Star Wars Masterwork Film Strips

COMMON CARD (FCR1-FCR40)	10.00	25.00

2017 Star Wars Masterwork Hall of Heroes

COMPLETE SET (10)	12.00	30.00
COMMON CARD (HH1-HH10)	3.00	8.00
*RAINBOW FOIL: .5X TO 1.2X BASIC CARDS	4.00	10.00
*CANVAS: .6X TO 1.5X BASIC CARDS	5.00	12.00

2017 Star Wars Masterwork Quad Autographed Booklets

UNPRICED DUE TO SCARCITY

NNO McDiarmid/Christensen/Park/Wood

NNO Hamill/Fisher/Daniels/Baker

2017 Star Wars Masterwork Source Material Jumbo Swatch Relics

COMMON CARD	25.00	60.00
JRCAR Admiral Ackbar Resistance Uniform	30.00	75.00
JRCGE Galen Erso Farmer Disguise	60.00	120.00
JRCGF General Hux First Order Uniform	50.00	100.00
JRCRD Rey Desert Tunic	200.00	400.00
JRCRO Rey Outer Garment	150.00	300.00

2017 Star Wars Masterwork Triple Autographs

NNO Daniels/Herring/Baker

NNO Williams/Mayhew/Baker

NNO Jones/Tudyk/Ahmed

NNO Prinze Jr./Gray/Isaacs

NNO Ford/Fisher/Driver

NNO McDiarmid/Christensen/Baker

NNO McDiarmid/Christensen/Wood

NNO Bulloch/Morrison/Logan

NNO Hamill/Fisher/Baker

NNO Mayhew/Daniels/Baker

2018 Star Wars Masterwork

COMPLETE SET W/SP (125)		
COMPLETE SET W/O SP (100)		
UNOPENED BOX (4 PACKS)	150.00	200.00
UNOPENED PACK (5 CARDS)	40.00	50.00
COMMON CARD (1-100)	2.50	6.00
COMMON SP (101-125)	6.00	15.00
*BLUE: .5X TO 1.2X BASIC CARDS		
*GREEN/99: .6X TO 1.5X BASIC CARDS		
*PURPLE/50: .75X TO 2X BASIC CARDS		
101 Luke Skywalker SP	8.00	20.00
102 Princess Leia Organa SP	12.00	30.00
103 Rey SP	15.00	40.00
104 Finn SP	10.00	25.00
105 Obi-Wan Kenobi SP	10.00	25.00
106 Anakin Skywalker SP	10.00	25.00
108 Darth Vader SP	8.00	20.00
109 Darth Maul SP	8.00	20.00
110 Boba Fett SP	12.00	30.00
111 Han Solo SP	12.00	30.00
113 Lando Calrissian SP	10.00	25.00
114 Saw Gerrera SP	10.00	25.00
115 Jyn Erso SP	12.00	30.00
116 Captain Cassian Andor SP	10.00	25.00
119 Kylo Ren SP	10.00	25.00
121 Ahsoka Tano SP	8.00	20.00
124 Bo-Katan Kryze SP	8.00	20.00

2018 Star Wars Masterwork Autographed Commemorative Vehicle Patches

UNPRICED DUE TO SCARCITY

MPAAD Anthony Daniels

MPABH Brian Herring

MPABM Ben Mendelsohn

MPAFJ Felicity Jones

MPAGO Genevieve O'Reilly

MPAHC Hayden Christensen

MPAHQ Hugh Quarshie

MPAIM Ian McDiarmid

MPAJB John Boyega

MPALM Lars Mikkelsen

MPAMQ Mike Quinn

MPARA Riz Ahmed
MPASB Steve Blum
MPATG Taylor Gray
MPATS Tiya Sircar
MPAVM Vanessa Marshall
MPADBB Dee Bradley Baker
MPAFPJ Freddie Prinze Jr.
MPAGMT Guy Henry
MPAMEM Mary Elizabeth McGlynn

2018 Star Wars Masterwork Autographed Pen Relics

PRAD Adam Driver
PRAE Ashley Eckstein
PRAJ Andrew Jack
PRAK Andrew Kishino
PRAS Andy Serkis
PRAT Alan Tudyk
PRBD Ben Daniels
PRBH Brian Herring
PRBM Ben Mendelsohn
PRCB Caroline Blakiston
PRCR Clive Revill
PRDB David Barclay
PRDC Dave Chapman
PRDL Denis Lawson
PRDR Daisy Ridley
PRFW Forest Whitaker
PRGH Guy Henry
PRHC Hayden Christensen
PRHF Harrison Ford
PRHW Howie Weed
PRIM Ian McDiarmid
PRJB Jeremy Bulloch
PRJV Jimmy Vee
PRKL Ken Leung
PRLD Laura Dern
PRLM Lars Mikkelsen
PRML Matt Lanter
PRMM Mads Mikkelsen
PRNC Nathalie Cuzner
PRPK Paul Kasey
PRRP Ray Park
PRSW Sam Witwer
PRSW Simon Williamson
PRTW Tom Wilton
PRBDW Billy Dee Williams
PRCCK Crystal Clarke
PRCCS Cavin Cornwall
PRJAT James Arnold Taylor
PRJSL Jason Spisak
PRSLJ Samuel L. Jackson

2018 Star Wars Masterwork Autographs

COMMON AUTO	6.00	15.00
*BLUE FOIL/99: .5X TO 1.2X BASIC AUTOS		
AAE Ashley Eckstein	40.00	100.00
AAK Andrew Kishino	8.00	20.00
ABS Brent Spiner	12.00	30.00
ACC Cavin Cornwall	12.00	30.00
ADB David Barclay	10.00	25.00
ADL Denis Lawson	8.00	20.00
ADM Daniel Mays	8.00	20.00
AGH Guy Henry	8.00	20.00
AHW Howie Weed	12.00	30.00
AJB Jeremy Bulloch	15.00	40.00
AJV Jimmy Vee	10.00	25.00
ALD Laura Dern	100.00	200.00
ALM Lars Mikkelsen	10.00	25.00
AML Matt Lanter	8.00	20.00
AMW Matthew Wood	10.00	25.00
ANC Nathalie Cuzner	8.00	20.00
ARN Robert Nairne	8.00	20.00
ASW Simon Williamson	12.00	30.00
ATW Tom Wilton	8.00	20.00
AJAT James Arnold Taylor	10.00	25.00
AJSP Jason Spisak	8.00	20.00
ASWT Sam Witwer	12.00	30.00

2018 Star Wars Masterwork Commemorative Vehicle Patches

COMMON PATCH	4.00	10.00
*PURPLE/50: .6X TO 1.5X BASIC PATCHES		
STATED PRINT RUN 175 SER.#'d SETS		
MPBHF Slave I/Boba Fett	8.00	20.00

MPGEA Chimaera/Grand Admiral Thrawn	6.00	15.00
MPGEK Chimaera/Kassius Konstantine	6.00	15.00
MPGEM Krennic's Shuttle/Grand Moff Tarkin	6.00	15.00
MPGEP Chimaera/Governor Arihnda Pryce	5.00	12.00
MPGEV Star Destroyer/Darth Vader	5.00	12.00
MPGRB Radiant VII/Bail Organa	6.00	15.00
MPGRP Radiant VII/PadmÈ Amidala	8.00	20.00
MPJOA Anakin's Fighter/Anakin Skywalker	5.00	12.00
MPJOO Anakin's Fighter/Obi-Wan Kenobi	6.00	15.00
MPJOQ Anakin's Fighter/Qui-Gon Jinn	5.00	12.00
MPPSA The Ghost/Ahsoka Tano	5.00	12.00
MPPSE The Ghost/Ezra Bridger	5.00	12.00
MPPSH The Ghost/Hera Syndulla	5.00	12.00
MPPSZ The Ghost/Zeb Orrelios	6.00	15.00
MPRAB U-Wing/Bodhi Rook	5.00	12.00
MPRAH Y-Wing/Han Solo	12.00	30.00
MPRAJ U-Wing/Jyn Erso	5.00	12.00
MPRAK U-Wing/K-2SO	5.00	12.00
MPRAM U-Wing/Baze Malbus	6.00	15.00
MPRAP Y-Wing/Princess Leia Organa	8.00	20.00
MPRAR Y-Wing/R2-D2	5.00	12.00
MPRAS Y-Wing/Luke Skywalker	6.00	15.00
MPRMH The Millennium Falcon/Han Solo	10.00	25.00
MPRML The Millennium Falcon/Lando Calrissian	5.00	12.00
MPRMN The Millennium Falcon/Nien Nunb	5.00	12.00
MPRMP The Millennium Falcon/Princess Leia Organa	8.00	20.00
MPRMS The Millennium Falcon/Luke Skywalker	6.00	15.00
MPTRF Black One/Finn	6.00	15.00
MPTRL Black One/General Leia Organa	8.00	20.00
MPTRR Black One/Rey	8.00	20.00

2018 Star Wars Masterwork Dual Autographs

DAAT R.Ahmed/A.Tudyk		
DABB K.Baker/D.Barclay		
DABH J.Boyega/B.Herring	75.00	150.00
DABO C.Blakiston/G.O'Reilly		
DABR E.Bauersfeld/K.Rotich	20.00	50.00
DABS J.Boyega/J.Suotamo	75.00	150.00
DACP H.Christensen/R.Park		
DACW A.Cook/I.Whyte		
DAGA S.Gellar/P.Anthony-Rodriguez		
DAGM G.Takei/M.Lanter		
DAJM F.Jones/B.Mendelsohn		
DALG K.Leung/G.Grunberg	15.00	40.00
DAMH B.Mendelsohn/G.Henry		
DAMM L.Mikkelsen/M.McGlynn	20.00	50.00

DAPW R.Park/M.Wood		
DARB D.Ridley/J.Boyega		
DASD M.Salenger/O.D'Abo	30.00	75.00
DATF J.Taylor/N.Futterman		
DAWQ B.Williams/M.Quinn		
DAWS S.Witwer/S.Stanton		

2018 Star Wars Masterwork History of the Jedi

COMPLETE SET (10)	10.00	25.00
COMMON CARD (HJ1-HJ10)	1.50	4.00
*RAINBOW/299: SAME VALUE AS BASIC		
*CANVAS/25: 1.2X TO 3X BASIC CARDS		
HJ1 Yoda	2.50	6.00
HJ2 Mace Windu	2.50	6.00
HJ4 Qui-Gon Jinn	2.00	5.00
HJ5 Obi-Wan Kenobi	2.00	5.00
HJ6 Anakin Skywalker	2.00	5.00
HJ9 Luke Skywalker	2.00	5.00
HJ10 Rey	3.00	8.00

2018 Star Wars Masterwork Powerful Partners

COMPLETE SET (8)	10.00	25.00
COMMON CARD (PP1-PP8)	1.50	4.00
*RAINBOW/299: SAME VALUE AS BASIC		
PP1 Han Solo & Chewbacca	2.50	6.00
PP3 Luke Skywalker & Princess Leia Organa	2.50	6.00
PP4 Darth Vader & Grand Moff Tarkin	2.50	6.00
PP6 Jyn Erso & Captain Cassian Andor	3.00	8.00
PP7 Rey & Finn	3.00	8.00
PP8 Finn & Rose Tico	2.00	5.00

2018 Star Wars Masterwork Quad Autographed Booklets

UNPRICED DUE TO SCARCITY	
NNO C.Fisher/F.Jones	
D.Ridley/L.Dern	
NNO D.Ridley/A.Driver	
J.Boyega/G.Christie	
NNO F.Jones/D.Yen	
R.Ahmed/A.Tudyk	
NNO H.Ford/C.Fisher	
B.Williams/P.Mayhew	

2018 Star Wars Masterwork Source Material Fabric Swatches

RANDOMLY INSERTED INTO PACKS		
JRGH General Hux Jacket Lining		
JRLP Luke Skywalker Pants		
JRLT Luke Skywalker Tunic	75.00	150.00
JRPD Poe Dameron Jacket Lining	100.00	200.00
JRRG Poe Dameron Shirt	50.00	100.00
JRRS Jyn Erso Poncho		
JRRT Rey Desert Tunic Sleeves	150.00	300.00
JRCRT Rose Tico Ground Crew Flightsuit Lining	100.00	200.00

2018 Star Wars Masterwork Stamp Relics

COMMON MEM	6.00	15.00
RANDOMLY INSERTED INTO PACKS		
SBF Finn	8.00	20.00
BB-8!		
SBP Poe Dameron	8.00	20.00
BB-8!		
SBR Rey	10.00	25.00
BB-8!		
SCC Chewbacca	8.00	20.00
Chewbacca!		
SCH Han Solo	8.00	20.00
Chewbacca!		

SCL Lando Calrissian	6.00	15.00
Chewbacca!		
SCP Princess Leia Organa	12.00	30.00
C-3PO and Jabba the Hutt's Palace		
SCR R2-D2	6.00	15.00
C-3PO and Jabba the Hutt's Palace		
SCS Luke Skywalker	6.00	15.00
C-3PO and Jabba the Hutt's Palace		
SKC Captain Cassian Andor	6.00	15.00
K-2SO on Scarif!		
SKJ Jyn Erso	10.00	25.00
K-2SO on Scarif!		
SKK K-2SO	12.00	30.00
K-2SO on Scarif!		
SMF Finn	6.00	15.00
Maz Kanata's Castle!		
SMH Han Solo	8.00	20.00
Maz Kanata's Castle!		
SMR Rey	8.00	20.00
Maz Kanata's Castle!		
SPC Chewbacca	6.00	15.00
Ahch-To Island Porgs!		
SPL Luke Skywalker	6.00	15.00
Ahch-To Island Porgs!		
SPR Rey	12.00	30.00
Ahch-To Island Porgs!		
SRA Anakin Skywalker	6.00	15.00
R2-D2!		
SRO Obi-Wan Kenobi	8.00	20.00
R2-D2!		
SRP PadmÈ Amidala	8.00	20.00
R2-D2!		
SSH General Hux	6.00	15.00
Supreme Leader Snoke and the First Order		
SSK Kylo Ren	10.00	25.00
Supreme Leader Snoke and the First Order		
SSP Captain Phasma	6.00	15.00
Supreme Leader Snoke and the First Order		

2018 Star Wars Masterwork Super Weapons

COMPLETE SET (7)	8.00	20.00
COMMON CARD (SW1-SW7)	2.00	5.00
*RAINBOW/299: .5X TO 1.2X BASIC CARDS		
*CANVAS/25: 1.2X TO 3X BASIC CARDS		

2018 Star Wars Masterwork Triple Autographs

TABPG T.Baker/F.Prinze Jr./T.Gray
TACML H.Christensen/T.Morrison/D.Logan
TAIES A.Eckstein/M.Salenger/N.Futterman
TAJMW F.Jones/B.Mendelsohn/F.Whitaker
TALGR K.Leung/G.Grunberg/T.Rose
TARBD D.Ridley/J.Boyega/L.Dern
TASDR A.Serkis/A.Driver/D.Ridley
TATLE J.Taylor/M.Lanter/A.Eckstein
TAVDC J.Vee/A.Daniels/D.Chapman
TAWMD B.Williams/P.Mayhew/A.Daniels

2019 Star Wars Masterwork Promo

NYCC2019 Darth Maul	6.00	15.00

2019 Star Wars Masterwork

COMPLETE SET (100)	15.00	40.00
UNOPENED BOX (4 MINI BOXES)	300.00	450.00
UNOPENED MINI BOX (5 CARDS)	75.00	125.00
COMMON CARD (1-100)	.60	1.50

*BLUE: .75X TO 2X BASIC CARDS
*GREEN/99: 1.5X TO 4X BASIC CARDS
*PURPLE/50: 2.5X TO 6X BASIC CARDS

2019 Star Wars Masterwork Autographed Commemorative Artifact Medallions

RANDOMLY INSERTED INTO PACKS

AMCDRC Daisy Ridley
Luke's Compass
AMCDRR Daisy Ridley
Snoke's Ring
AMCFJK Felicity Jones
Jyn's Kyber Pendant
AMCGHI Guy Henry
Imperial Rank Badge
AMCHCB Hayden Christensen
Amidala's Belt Buckle
AMCHFD Harrison Ford
Han Solo's Dice
AMCJBM John Boyega
Rose Tico's Medallion

AMCJGI Julian Glover
Imperial Rank Badge
AMCKBL Kenny Baker
Yoda's Necklace
AMCKCI Kenneth Colley
Imperial Rank Badge
AMCMMK Mads Mikkelsen
Jyn's Kyber Pendant
AMCMPI Michael Pennington
Imperial Rank Badge
AMCRPC Ray Park
Sith Chalice
AMCVKK Valene Kane
Jyn's Kyber Pendant
AMCADRR Adam Driver
Snoke's Ring
AMCKMTM Kelly Marie Tran
Rose Tico's Medallion

2019 Star Wars Masterwork Autographed Pen Relics

PRAB Ahmed Best
PRAE Ashley Eckstein
PRAS Andy Serkis
PRAT Alan Tudyk
PRCL Charlotte Louise
PRCS Christopher Sean
PRDG Domhnall Gleeson
PRDL Denis Lawson
PRDR Daisy Ridley
PRDT David Tennant
PRDY Donald Faison
PRDY Donnie Yen
PREM Ewan McGregor
PRFW Forest Whitaker
PRGC Billie Lourd
PRHC Hayden Christensen
PRHF Harrison Ford
PRIM Ian McDiarmid
PRJB Jeremy Bulloch
PRJI Jason Isaacs

PRJS Joonas Suotamo
PRJV Gwendoline Christie
PRKK Katy Kartwheel
PRLD Laura Dern
PRLL Lex Lang
PRLM Lars Mikkelsen
PRMA Mark Austin
PRML Matt Lanter
PRMM Mads Mikkelsen
PRMP Michael Pennington
PRMV Myrna Velasco
PRMW Matthew Wood
PRPB Paul Bettany
PRPR Paul Reubens
PRRA Riz Ahmed
PRRP Ray Park
PRSL Scott Lawrence
PRSM Suzie McGrath
PRTC Tim Curry
PRTF Tovah Feldshuh
PRTM Temuera Morrison
PRADR Adam Driver
PRAEH Alden Ehrenreich
PRBDW Billy Dee Williams
PRBMR Bobby Moynihan
PRDBB Dee Bradley Baker
PRFPJ Freddie Prinze Jr.
PRJAT James Arnold Taylor
PRKMT Kelly Marie Tran
PRMEM Mary Elizabeth McGlynn
PRRPG Ron Perlman
PRSWM Sam Witwer

2019 Star Wars Masterwork Autographs

COMMON AUTO	6.00	15.00

*BLUE/99: .5X TO 1.2X BASIC AUTOS
*RAINBOW/50: .6X TO 1.5X BASIC AUTOS
RANDOMLY INSERTED INTO PACKS

AAE Ashley Eckstein	15.00	40.00
ACR Clive Revill	8.00	20.00
ACS Christopher Sean	10.00	25.00

ADT David Tennant	20.00	50.00
AFT Fred Tatasciore	8.00	20.00
AKK Katy Kartwheel	10.00	25.00
AKS Katee Sackhoff	15.00	40.00
ALL Lex Lang	10.00	25.00
ALM Lars Mikkelsen	8.00	20.00
AMA Mark Austin	20.00	50.00
AMP Michael Pennington	10.00	25.00
AMV Myrna Velasco	10.00	25.00
ANC Nazneen Contractor	8.00	20.00
ASL Scott Lawrence	12.00	30.00
AJAT James Arnold Taylor	8.00	20.00
AJBR Josh Brener	8.00	20.00
AJVM Jimmy Vee	8.00	20.00
ASIL Stephanie Silva	8.00	20.00

2019 Star Wars Masterwork Commemorative Artifact Medallions

COMMON MEM	3.00	8.00
*PURPLE/50: .5X TO 1.2X BASIC MEM		
RANDOMLY INSERTED INTO PACKS		
MCFR Finn	5.00	12.00
MCJK Jyn Erso	6.00	15.00
MCPR Paige Tico	4.00	10.00
MCRR Rose Tico	4.00	10.00
MCSD Han Solo	6.00	15.00
MCYN Yoda	6.00	15.00
MCASB Anakin Skywalker	5.00	12.00
MCGJK Galen Erso	5.00	12.00
MCHBH Han Solo	6.00	15.00
MCKSR Kylo Ren	6.00	15.00
MCLBH Luke Skywalker	8.00	20.00
MCLJK Lyra Erso	4.00	10.00
MCLSC Luke Skywalker	10.00	25.00
MCLSY Luke Skywalker	8.00	20.00
MCMRB Grand Moff Tarkin	4.00	10.00
MCMSC Darth Maul	5.00	12.00
MCOBH Obi-Wan Kenobi	5.00	12.00
MCPDN Poe Dameron	4.00	10.00
MCQAB Queen Amidala	6.00	15.00
MCR2C R2-D2	5.00	12.00
MCR2Y R2-D2	5.00	12.00
MCRLC Rey	8.00	20.00

MCRSR Rey	8.00	20.00
MCSSB Sabe	5.00	12.00
MCVSC Darth Vader	6.00	15.00

2019 Star Wars Masterwork The Dark Side

COUNT DOOKU

COMPLETE SET (10)	8.00	20.00
COMMON CARD (DS1-DS10)	1.25	3.00
*RAINBOW/299: .6X TO 1.5X BASIC CARDS		
*CANVAS/25: 1X TO 2.5X BASIC CARDS		
RANDOMLY INSERTED INTO PACKS		

2019 Star Wars Masterwork Defining Moments

COMPLETE SET (25)	12.00	30.00
COMMON CARD (DM1-DM25))	1.00	2.50
*RAINBOW/299: 1X TO 2.5X BASIC CARDS		
*CANVAS/25: 2.5X TO 6X BASIC CARDS		
RANDOMLY INSERTED INTO PACKS		

2019 Star Wars Masterwork Dual Autographs

STATED PRINT RUN 50 SER.#'d SETS

DAAK D.Arnold/N.Kellington
DAAW R.Ahmed/F.Whitaker
DABT J.Boyega/K.Tran
DACJ H.Christensen/S. Jackson
DACS L.Cole/K.Shah
DACW T.Curry/S.Witwer
DADQ O.Davies/H.Quarshie
DAEB A.Ehrenreich/P.Bettany
DAES A.Ehrenreich/J.Suotamo
DAGW S.Gellar/S.Witwer
DAHF G.Hagon/A.Forrest
DAIG J.Isaacs/T.Gray
DAJK A.Jack/J.Kenny

DAJM F.Jones/B.Mendelsohn
DALM S.Lawrence/S.McGrath
DALS M.Lanter/L.Sherr
DAMC E.McGregor/H.Christensen
DAMM B.Mendelsohn/M.Mikkelsen
DAMS M.Glynn/S.Stanton
DAMY L.Mikkelsen/K.Young
DAPC G.Proops/S.Capurro
DAPG M.Pennington/J.Glover
DARD D.Ridley/A.Driver
DASC A.Shah/A.Cook
DASG A.Serkis/D.Gleeson
DASL C.Sean/L.Lang
DASM C.Sean/S.McGrath
DASS J.Spisak/K.Soucie
DAVF M.Velasco/D.Faison
DAWM B.Williams/P.Mayhew
DAWR S.Williamson/D.Roy

2019 Star Wars Masterwork Film Cel Relics

FCB6 Bib Fortuna
FCC4 Chewbacca
FCC5 Chewbacca
FCC6 Chewbacca
FCO6 Oola
FCY5 Yoda
FCAA6 Admiral Ackbar
FCAP5 Admiral Piett
FCBF5 Boba Fett
FCBF6 Boba Fett
FCCP5 C-3PO
FCCP6 C-3PO
FCDV5 Darth Vader
FCDV6 Darth Vader
FCEP5 Emperor Palpatine
FCEP6 Emperor Palpatine
FCHS4 Han Solo
FCHS5 Han Solo
FCHS6 Han Solo
FCJH6 Jabba The Hutt
FCLB6 Boushh
FCLC5 Lando Calrissian
FCLC6 Lando Calrissian
FCLS4 Luke Skywalker
FCLS5 Luke Skywalker
FCLS6 Luke Skywalker
FCMJ6 Moff Jerjerrod
FCMR6 Sy Snootles
FCNN6 Nien Nunb
FCOK4 Obi-Wan Kenobi
FCOK6 Obi-Wan Kenobi
FCPL4 Princess Leia Organa
FCPL5 Princess Leia Organa
FCPL6 Princess Leia Organa
FCR25 R2-D2

FCR26 R2-D2

FCRC4 R2-D2 & C-3PO

FCSC6 Salacious Crumb

FCTL6 Logray

FCWW6 Wicket

2019 Star Wars Masterwork Heroes of the Rebellion

COMPLETE SET (15)	8.00	20.00
COMMON CARD (HR1-HR15)	1.00	2.50

*RAINBOW/299: .75X TO 2X BASIC CARDS

*CANVAS/25: 1.5X TO 4X BASIC CARDS

RANDOMLY INSERTED INTO PACKS

2019 Star Wars Masterwork Jumbo Costume Relics

RANDOMLY INSERTED INTO PACKS

CRAC Air Traffic Controller

CRBB Beckett

CRBC Beckett

CRBT Beckett

CREN Enfys Nest

CRKJ Korso

CRKO Korso

CRQB Qi'Ra

CRQD Qi'Ra

CRWW Rebolt

CRENC Enfys Nest

CRENL Enfys Nest

CRHSC Han Solo

CRHSJ Han Solo

CRHSL Han Solo

2019 Star Wars Masterwork Quad Autograph Booklets

STATED PRINT RUN 2 SER.#'d SETS

UNPRICED DUE TO SCARCITY

QAESKD Ehrenreich/Suotamo/Kellyman/Davis

QAFFRD Ford/Fisher/Ridley/Driver

QAJWYT Jones/Whitaker/Yen/Tudyk

QAPGIG Prinze/Taylor/Jason/Gellar

2019 Star Wars Masterwork The Ultimate Autograph Booklet

NNO Ford/Fisher/Williams/Mayhew/Baker/Daniels

Christensen/Jackson/McGregor/Best/McDiarmid

Park/Jones/Mikkelsen/Whitaker/Yen

Ahmed/Tudyk/Mendelsohn/O'Reilly/Prinze

Isaacs/Lanter/Taylor/Eckstein/Baker

Ridley/Driver/Boyega/Tran/Gleeson

Christie/Lourd/Dern/

2019 Star Wars Masterwork Triple Autographs

STATED PRINT RUN 25 SER.#'d SETS

TADGS Driver/Gleeson/Serkis

TAEBS Ehrenreich/Bettany/Suotamo

TAFWM Ford/Williams/Mayhew

TAGSE Gray/Sircar/Eckstein

TAJMM Jones/Mendelsohn/Mikkelsen

TAJTA Jones/Tudyk/Ahmed

TAMDB Mayhew/Daniels/Baker

TAMJC McGregor/Jackson/Christensen

TARBD Ridley/Boyega/Dern

TASML Sean/McGrath/Lawrence

2020 Star Wars Masterwork

COMPLETE SET (100)	15.00	40.00
UNOPENED BOX (4 MINIBOXES)	300.00	450.00
UNOPENED MINIBOX (5 CARDS)	75.00	110.00
COMMON CARD (1-100)	.60	1.50

*BLUE: .75X TO 2X BASIC CARDS

*GREEN/99: 1.5X TO 4X BASIC CARDS

*PURPLE/50: 2.5X TO 6X BASIC CARDS

2020 Star Wars Masterwork Autographed Commemorative Dog Tag Medallions

UNPRICED DUE TO SCARCITY

ADKBW Kenny Baker

ADDLW Denis Lawson 3

NNO Harrison Ford

ADBFS Barbara Frankland

NNO Carrie Fisher

ADAFS Anthony Forrest

ADAMS Angus MacInnes

ADDLF Denis Lawson 1

ADDLX Denis Lawson 2

ADGHF Garrick Hagon 1

ADGHR Garrick Hagon 2

ADJGI Julian Glover

ADJKF Jack Klaff 1

ADJKR Jack Klaff 2

ADKCI Kenneth Colley

ADPBS Paul Blake

ADPMW Peter Mayhew

ADRGS Rusty Goffe

2020 Star Wars Masterwork Autographed Pen Relics

STATED PRINT RUN 1 SER.#'d SET

UNPRICED DUE TO SCARCITY

NNO Adam Driver

NNO Ahmed Best

NNO Alden Ehrenreich

NNO Andy Serkis

NNO Annabelle Davis

NNO Ashley Eckstein

NNO Ben Daniels

NNO Billie Lourd

NNO Billy Dee Williams

NNO Cameron Monaghan

NNO Carl Weathers

NNO Daisy Ridley

NNO Debra Wilson

NNO Dee Bradley Baker

NNO Denis Lawson

NNO Dominic Monaghan

NNO Donnie Yen

NNO Emily Swallow

NNO Erin Kellyman

NNO Ewan McGregor

NNO Giancarlo Esposito

NNO Gina Carano

NNO Greg Grunberg

NNO Harrison Ford

NNO Hayden Christensen

NNO Hermione Corfield

NNO Ian McDiarmid

NNO Janina Gavankar

NNO John Tui

NNO Joonas Suotamo

NNO Leeanna Walsman

NNO Mads Mikkelsen
NNO Michael Pennington
NNO Naomi Ackie
NNO Nick Kellington
NNO Nick Nolte
NNO Omid Abtahi
NNO Paul Blake
NNO Pedro Pascal
NNO Sam Witwer
NNO Taika Waititi
NNO Valene Kane
NNO Werner Herzog

2020 Star Wars Masterwork Autographs

COMMON AUTO	6.00	15.00

*BLUE/99: .5X TO 1.2X BASIC AUTOS
*RAINBOW/50: .6X TO 1.5X BASIC AUTOS
RANDOMLY INSERTED INTO PACKS

AAB Ahmed Best	20.00	50.00
AAH Amanda Hale	8.00	20.00
ACM Cameron Monaghan	20.00	50.00
ADL Denis Lawson	10.00	25.00
ADW Debra Wilson	8.00	20.00
AEK Erin Kellyman	20.00	50.00
AES Emily Swallow	50.00	100.00
AGE Giancarlo Esposito	75.00	150.00
AGG Greg Grunberg	10.00	25.00
AJG Janina Gavankar	15.00	40.00
AJT John Tui	8.00	20.00
ALW Leeanna Walsman	12.00	30.00
AML Misty Lee	10.00	25.00
AMW Matthew Wood	20.00	50.00
ANA Naomi Ackie	15.00	40.00
AOA Omid Abtahi	12.00	30.00
APB Paul Blake	10.00	25.00
AVK Valene Kane	10.00	25.00
AADW Annabelle Davis EXCH	10.00	25.00
AAEA Ashley Eckstein	50.00	125.00
ADBB Dee Bradley Baker	12.00	30.00
AHCT Hermione Corfield	15.00	40.00
ALRB Lynn Robertson Bruce	10.00	25.00

2020 Star Wars Masterwork Autographs Blue Foil

STATED PRINT RUN 99 SER.#'d SETS

ADY Donnie Yen	60.00	120.00
ASW Sam Witwer	20.00	50.00
ADMB Dominic Monaghan	15.00	40.00

2020 Star Wars Masterwork Autographs Rainbow Foil

STATED PRINT RUN 50 SER.#'d SETS

AWH Werner Herzog	100.00	200.00

2020 Star Wars Masterwork Behind-the-Scenes Autographed Pen Relics

NNO Ben Burtt
NNO Jake Lunt Davies
NNO Neal Scanlan
NNO Lee Towersey

2020 Star Wars Masterwork Behind-the-Scenes Autographs

COMMON AUTO	15.00	40.00

*RAINBOW/50: .5X TO 1.2X BASIC AUTOS
STATED PRINT RUN 99 SER.#'d SETS

BSABB Ben Burtt	30.00	75.00
BSALT Lee Towersey	25.00	60.00
BSANS Neal Scanlan	25.00	60.00

2020 Star Wars Masterwork Commemorative Dog Tag Medallions

COMMON MEM	4.00	10.00

*PURPLE/50: .5X TO 1.2X BASIC MEM
STATED PRINT RUN 99 SER.#'d SETS

DTEB Sandtrooper	5.00	12.00
DTED Commander Daine Jir	5.00	12.00
DTES Stormtrooper	6.00	15.00
DTET Grand Moff Tarkin	6.00	15.00
DTEV Darth Vader	10.00	25.00
DTEX Death Star Trooper	8.00	20.00
DTFB Biggs Darklighter	5.00	12.00
DTFD Biggs Darklighter	5.00	12.00
DTFW Wedge Antilles	8.00	20.00
DTJC Chewbacca	6.00	15.00
DTJH Han Solo		25.00
DTJL Luke Skywalker	12.00	30.00
DTJP Princess Leia Organa	10.00	25.00
DTJR R2-D2	6.00	15.00
DTRD Garven Dreis	6.00	15.00
DTRJ John D. Branon	5.00	12.00
DTRW Wedge Antilles	8.00	20.00
DTSD Darth Vader	10.00	25.00
DTSG Greedo	5.00	12.00
DTST Stormtrooper	6.00	15.00
DTSV Jon "Dutch" Vander	5.00	12.00
DTXL Luke Skywalker	12.00	30.00
DTXW Wedge Antilles	8.00	20.00

2020 Star Wars Masterwork Dual Autographs

STATED PRINT RUN 50 SER.#'d SETS

DADA H.Durst/D.Arnold	15.00	40.00
DADK H.Durst/I.Kenny	15.00	40.00
DADM R.Downes/V.Marshall	30.00	75.00
DAHP A.Harris/C.Parsons	60.00	120.00
DAMW T.Morrison/L.Walsman	150.00	400.00
DASL S.Smart/C.Louise	12.00	30.00

2020 Star Wars Masterwork Empire Strikes Back 40th Anniversary

COMPLETE SET (25)	30.00	75.00
COMMON CARD (ESB1-ESB25)	2.00	5.00

*RAINBOW/299: .5X TO 1.2X BASIC CARDS
RANDOMLY INSERTED INTO PACKS

2020 Star Wars Masterwork Quad Autographs

STATED PRINT RUN 2 SER.#'d SETS
UNPRICED DUE TO SCARCITY

NNO Ford/Fisher/Baker/Mayhew
NNO Ridley/Williams/Driver/Boyega
NNO Pascal/Carano/Nolte/Waititi
QAMN Nolte/Carano/Herzog/Esposito

2020 Star Wars Masterwork Sourced Fabric Dual Relics

COMMON MEM	30.00	75.00

RANDOMLY INSERTED INTO PACKS

DCBD Beckett/Dryden Vos	100.00	200.00
DCBQ Beckett/Qi'ra	100.00	200.00
DCDQ Dryden Vos/Qi'ra	125.00	250.00
DCFR Finn/Rose Tico	50.00	100.00
DCJB Jyn Erso/Bodhi Rook	75.00	150.00
DCJG Jyn Erso/Galen Erso	100.00	200.00
DCJM Jyn Erso/General Merrick	75.00	150.00
DCLF Luke Skywalker/Finn	50.00	100.00
DCLP Luke Skywalker/Poe Dameron	100.00	200.00
DCPG Poe Dameron/General Hux	60.00	120.00
DCRP Rey/Poe Dameron	125.00	250.00
DCRPJ Rey/Poe Dameron	125.00	250.00
DCRPW Rey/Poe Dameron	125.00	250.00

2020 Star Wars Masterwork Stamps

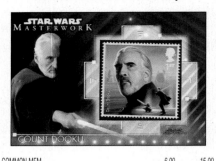

COMMON MEM	6.00	15.00

*GREEN/99: .5X TO 1.2X BASIC MEM

*PURPLE/50: .6X TO 1.5X BASIC MEM

RANDOMLY INSERTED INTO PACKS

SCAA	Anakin Skywalker/Queen Amidala	8.00	20.00
SCCD	Count Dooku/Count Dooku	10.00	25.00
SCCJ	Chewbacca/Jannah	8.00	20.00
SCDM	Darth Maul/Darth Maul	10.00	25.00
SCFP	Finn/Poe Dameron	8.00	20.00
SCKS	Kylo Ren/Sith Trooper	8.00	20.00
SCLC	Lando Calrissian/Lando Calrissian	10.00	25.00
SCLL	Lobot/Lando Calrissian	8.00	20.00
SCLW	Logray/Wicket W. Warrick	8.00	20.00
SCOM	Obi-Wan Kenobi/Darth Maul	10.00	25.00
SCPZ	Poe Dameron/Zorii Bliss	10.00	25.00
SCQA	Queen Amidala/Queen Amidala	8.00	20.00
SCQM	Qui-Gon Jinn/Darth Maul	10.00	25.00
SCSS	Sith Trooper/Sith Trooper	8.00	20.00
SCVM	Darth Vader/Grand Moff Tarkin	10.00	25.00
SCYD	Yoda/Count Dooku	8.00	20.00
SCPLW	Princess Leia Organa/Wicket W. Warrick	10.00	25.00

2020 Star Wars Masterwork Triple Autographs

STATED PRINT RUN 25 SER.#'d SETS

UNPRICED DUE TO SCARCITY

TABPG Baker/Prinze Jr./Gray

TABTL Boyega/Tran/Lourd

TACLE Curry/Lanter/Eckstein

TADGC Driver/Gleeson/Christie

TAFFM Ford/Fisher/Mayhew

TAFWB Ford/Williams/Bulloch

TAGFG Goodson/Futterman/Gati

TAJWY Jones/Whitaker/Yen

TAMJC McGregor/Jackson/Christensen

TAPNW Pascal/Nolte/Waititi

TASMF Sean/McGrath/Faison

2020 Star Wars Masterwork Troopers of the Galactic Empire

COMPLETE SET (15)	15.00	40.00
COMMON CARD (TE1-TE15)	2.00	5.00

*RAINBOW/299: .5X TO 1.2X BASIC CARDS

RANDOMLY INSERTED INTO PACKS

2020 Star Wars Masterwork Ultra Autographs

NNO Ford/Fisher/Williams/Mayhew/Baker

McDiarmid/Blakiston/Bulloch/Lawson/Davis

NNO Ridley/Driver/Boyega/Tran/Williams

Suotamo/Gleeson/McDiarmid/Monaghan/Lourd

UARO Jones/Mendelsohn/Whitaker/Yen/Ahmed

Tudyk/OiReilly/Mikkelsen/Henry/Daniels

2020 Star Wars Masterwork The Wisdom of Yoda

"Impossible to see, the future is."

COMPLETE SET (10)	20.00	50.00
COMMON CARD (WY1-WY10)	3.00	8.00

*RAINBOW/299: .5X TO 1.2X BASIC CARDS

RANDOMLY INSERTED INTO PACKS

2021 Star Wars Masterwork

SUPREME LEADER SNOKE

COMPLETE SET (100)	100.00	250.00
UNOPENED BOX (4 MINIBOXES)	300.00	500.00
UNOPENED MINIBOX (5 CARDS)	75.00	125.00
COMMON CARD (1-100)	1.50	4.00

*BLUE: .5X TO 1.2X BASIC CARDS

*GREEN/99: .6X TO 1.5X BASIC CARDS

*PURPLE/50: .75X TO 2X BASIC CARDS

4	Ahsoka Tano	6.00	15.00
11	BB-8	2.00	5.00
15	Boba Fett	5.00	12.00
17	Bo-Katan Kryze	2.50	6.00
21	Cad Bane	2.50	6.00
28	Darth Maul	3.00	8.00
41	Grand Admiral Thrawn	4.00	10.00
45	Grogu	10.00	25.00
46	Han Solo	4.00	10.00
55	Jedi Master Yoda	3.00	8.00
64	Kylo Ren	2.50	6.00
69	Luke Skywalker	3.00	8.00
70	Mandalorian	4.00	10.00
74	Koska Reeves	2.50	6.00
84	Rey	6.00	15.00

2021 Star Wars Masterwork Autographed Pen Relics

STATED PRINT RUN 1 SER.#'d SET

UNPRICED DUE TO SCARCITY

PRAAB Ahmed Best

PRAAD Adam Driver

PRAAE Ashley Eckstein

PRAAL Amanda Lawrence

PRABD Ben Daniels

PRABH Brian Herring

PRABL Billie Lourd

PRACW Carl Weather

PRADI Diana Lee Inosanto

PRADL Daniel Logan

PRADR Daisy Ridley

PRAEC Emilia Clarke

PRAES Emily Swallow

PRAGE Giancarlo Esposito

PRAGG Greg Grunberg

PRAHC Hayden Christensen

PRAIM Ian McDiarmid

PRAJL John Leguizamo

PRAJT James Arnold Taylor

PRAKO Katy O'Brian

PRALM Lars Mikkelsen

PRAMM Mary Elizabeth McGlynn

PRAMW Matthew Wood

PRANP Natalie Portman

PRAOA Omid Abtahi

PRAPK Paul Kasey

PRAPL Paul Sun-Hyung Lee

PRARB Richard Brake

PRARD Rosario Dawson

PRARO Rena Owen

PRASK Simon Kassianides

PRASS Stephen Stanton

PRATG Taylor Gray

PRATM Temuera Morrison

PRAABR Anna Brewster

PRAADA Annabelle Davis

PRADBC Dee Bradley Baker

PRADBE Dee Bradley Baker

PRADBH Dee Bradley Baker
PRADBR Dee Bradley Baker
PRADBT Dee Bradley Baker
PRADBW Dee Bradley Baker
PRAMBO Mark Boone Junior

2021 Star Wars Masterwork Autographs

COMMON AUTO	6.00	15.00
*BLUE/99: SAME VALUE AS BASIC		
*RAINBOW/50: .75X TO 2X BASIC AUTOS		
*CANVAS/25: 1.2X TO 3X BASIC AUTOS		
RANDOMLY INSERTED INTO PACKS		
MWAAB Ahmed Best	30.00	75.00
MWAAE Ashley Eckstein	60.00	150.00
MWAAL Amanda Lawrence	8.00	20.00
MWAAS Amy Sedaris	30.00	75.00
MWAAW Alexander Wraith	10.00	25.00
MWABH Brian Herring	10.00	25.00
MWACG Clare Grant	15.00	40.00
MWADI Diana Lee Inosanto	12.00	30.00
MWAES Emily Swallow	25.00	60.00
MWAGE Giancarlo Esposito	60.00	150.00
MWAGG Greg Grunberg	8.00	20.00
MWAIM Ian McDiarmid	125.00	300.00
MWAJG Janina Gavankar	10.00	25.00
MWAJL John Leguizamo	75.00	200.00
MWAKO Katy O'Brian	10.00	25.00
MWALM Lars Mikkelsen	40.00	100.00
MWALS Leilani Shiu	12.00	30.00
MWAMM Mary Elizabeth McGlynn	10.00	25.00
MWAMV Mercedes Varnado	75.00	200.00
MWANF Nika Futterman	12.00	30.00
MWAOA Omid Abtahi	10.00	25.00
MWAPA Philip Anthony-Rodriguez	10.00	25.00
MWAPL Paul Sun-Hyung Lee	25.00	60.00
MWARB Richard Brake	12.00	30.00
MWARG Richard Grant	40.00	100.00
MWASK Simon Kassianides	12.00	30.00
MWASS Stephen Stanton	10.00	25.00
MWASW Sam Witwer	40.00	100.00
MWATG Taylor Gray	20.00	50.00
MWATR Tim Rose	20.00	50.00
MWAADA Annabelle Davis	10.00	25.00
MWADBC Dee Bradley Baker	30.00	75.00
MWADBE Dee Bradley Baker	30.00	75.00
MWADBH Dee Bradley Baker	30.00	75.00
MWADBR Dee Bradley Baker	30.00	75.00
MWADBT Dee Bradley Baker	30.00	75.00
MWADBW Dee Bradley Baker	30.00	75.00
MWAMBO Mark Boone Junior	12.00	30.00
MWAMIB Michonne Bourriague	10.00	25.00
MWAPAL Philip Alexander	10.00	25.00

2021 Star Wars Masterwork Commemorative Character Medallion Relics

COMMON MEM	5.00	12.00
*GREEN/99: .6X TO 1.5X BASIC MEM		
*PURPLE/50: .75X TO 2X BASIC MEM		
RANDOMLY INSERTED INTO PACKS		
CMCC Chewbacca	6.00	15.00
CMCR Chewbacca	6.00	15.00
CMLC Luke Skywalker	10.00	25.00
CMLR Luke Skywalker	10.00	25.00
CMLS Luke Skywalker	10.00	25.00
CMLV Luke Skywalker	10.00	25.00
CMRC R2-D2	8.00	20.00
CMRR R2-D2	8.00	20.00
CMVS Darth Vader	12.00	30.00
CMVV Darth Vader	12.00	30.00
CMC3C C-3PO	6.00	15.00
CMC3R C-3PO	6.00	15.00
CMLOR Princess Leia Organa	12.00	30.00
CMPLC Princess Leia Organa	12.00	30.00
CMPLV Princess Leia Organa	12.00	30.00

2021 Star Wars Masterwork Dual Autographs

STATED PRINT RUN 50 SER.#'d SETS	
UNPRICED DUE TO SCARCITY	
MWDBM M.E.McGlynn/S.Blum	
MWDCE A.Ehrenreich/E.Clarke	
MWDCP N.Portman/H.Christensen	
MWDDC A.Driver/G.Christie	
MWDDI D.L.Inosanto/R.Dawson	
MWDHA W.Herzog/O.Abtahi	
MWDHR R.Brown/H.Quarshie	
MWDJM B.Mendelsohn/F.Jones	
MWDMB T.Morrison/J.Bulloch	
MWDMC E.McGregor/H.Christensen	
MWDMG T.Gray/L.Mikkelsen	
MWDRM D.Ridley/I.McDiarmid	
MWDSW N.Nolte/C.Weathers	
MWDWB D.Beer/C.D.Williams	
MWDWG M.Wood/K.Gati	

2021 Star Wars Masterwork Galactic Autograph Book

GAB2021 Serkis/Weathers/Pascal/Williams/Christie
Boyega/McDiarmid/Driver/Ridley/Ford
Prowse/McGregor/Jackson/Christensen/Mikkelsen
Jones/Fisher/Ehrenreich/Clarke/Portman

2021 Star Wars Masterwork Jumbo Sourced Fabric Costume Relics

COMMON MEM	30.00	75.00
RANDOMLY INSERTED INTO PACKS		
JCRAT Ahsoka Tano	100.00	250.00
Shirt Lining		
JCRBE Tobias Beckett	40.00	100.00
Trench Coat		
JCRBF Boba Fett	150.00	400.00
Pants		
JCRBR Bodhi Rook	40.00	100.00
Imperial Jumpsuit		
JCRFN Finn	40.00	100.00
Imperial Disguise Tunic		
JCRGE Galen Erso	40.00	100.00
Farmer Disguise Jacket		
JCRJE Jyn Erso	60.00	150.00
Poncho		
JCRLS Luke Skywalker	150.00	400.00
Battle Tunic		
JCRLU Luke Skywalker	150.00	400.00
Pants		
JCRMC The Mandalorian	60.00	150.00
Cloak		
JCRPO Poe Dameron	40.00	100.00
Shirt		
JCRQI Qi'ra	100.00	250.00
Leggings		
JCRRE Rey	125.00	300.00
Jacket		

JCRTMA The Mandalorian Vest	60.00	150.00

2021 Star Wars Masterwork Lucasfilm 50th Anniversary

COMPLETE SET (14)	20.00	50.00
COMMON CARD (LFA1-LFA14)	2.50	6.00

*RAINBOW/299: 1.5X TO 4X BASIC CARDS
RANDOMLY INSERTED INTO PACKS

2021 Star Wars Masterwork Out of the Box

COMPLETE SET (25)	12.00	30.00
COMMON CARD (OTB1-OTB25)	1.25	3.00

*RAINBOW/299: .75X TO 2X BASIC CARDS
RANDOMLY INSERTED INTO PACKS

2021 Star Wars Masterwork Postage Stamp Relics

COMMON MEM	3.00	8.00

*GREEN/99: .6X TO 1.5X BASIC MEM
*PURPLE/50: .75X TO 2X BASIC MEM
RANDOMLY INSERTED INTO PACKS

SCAN Anakin Skywalker	8.00	20.00
SCAS Anakin Skywalker	8.00	20.00
SCBB BB-8	5.00	12.00
SCFB Fode and Beed	4.00	10.00
SCFN Finn	6.00	15.00
SCKR Kylo Ren	8.00	20.00
SCLO Leia Organa	10.00	25.00
SCLS Luke Skywalker	10.00	25.00
SCPD Poe Dameron	6.00	15.00
SCQG Qui Gon Jin	4.00	10.00
SCR2 R2-D2	6.00	15.00
SCCHW Chewbacca	8.00	20.00
SCPDA Poe Dameron	6.00	15.00

2021 Star Wars Masterwork Quad Autographs

MWQMBSP Ahmed/Yen/Tudyk/Jones
MWQMPCD Christensen/Park/McDiarmid/Driver
MWQMWWN Barclay/Carter/Dodson/Bulloch
MWQPJFR Portman/Jones/Fisher/Ridley

2021 Star Wars Masterwork Triple Autographs

STATED PRINT RUN 25 SER.#'d SETS

MWTBMT Boyega/Tran/Monaghan
MWTCFD Ford/Driver/Serkis
MWTCPF Portman/Christensen/McDiarmid
MWTEBC Clarke/Bettany/Ehrenreich
MWTGBS Blum/Gray/Sircar
MWTMPC Park/McDiarmid/Christensen

2021 Star Wars Masterwork Welcome to the Dark Side

"The Force is strong in this one."

COMPLETE SET (10)	10.00	25.00
COMMON CARD (WDS1-WDS10)	.75	2.00

*RAINBOW/299: 1.2X TO 3X BASIC CARDS
RANDOMLY INSERTED INTO PACKS

2017 Star Wars May the 4th Be with You

COMPLETE SET (20)	12.00	30.00
COMPLETE FACTORY SET (21)	40.00	80.00
COMMON CARD (1-20)	1.00	2.50
*SILVER/10: 6X TO 15X BASIC CARDS	15.00	40.00

RELEASED 5/4/2017

2017 Star Wars May the 4th Be with You Autographs

COMMON CARD	10.00	25.00

*SILVER/10: .6X TO 1.5X BASIC AUTOS
STATED ODDS 1:SET

1A Harrison Ford		
2A Mark Hamill	400.00	600.00
3A Carrie Fisher		
4A Kenny Baker		
5A Anthony Daniels	175.00	300.00
7A Jeremy Bulloch	25.00	60.00
8A Ian McDiarmid	250.00	400.00
10A Billy Dee Williams		
14A Kenneth Colley	12.00	30.00
16A Erik Bauersfeld	25.00	60.00
16A Tim Rose	15.00	40.00
19A Paul Blake		

2022 Star Wars May the 4th Wrapper Art

COMPLETE SET (8)	75.00	200.00
COMMON CARD (1-8)	12.00	30.00

*RAINBOW/99: 1.5X TO 4X BASIC CARDS
*SILVER/49: 2.5X TO 6X BASIC CARDS

4 Boba Fett by Blake Jamieson/1,378*	15.00	40.00
6 The Mandalorian by Blake Jamieson/1,302*	15.00	40.00
7 Obi-Wan & Luke Skywalker by Blake Jamieson/1,102*	15.00	40.00

1997-98 Star Wars Men Behind the Masks

COMPLETE SET (4)		
COMMON CARD (P1-P4)		
P1 Darth Vader & Boba Fett	10.00	25.00
(Given to Auction Seat Holders)		
P2 Darth Vader & Boba Fett	10.00	25.00
(Given as Admission Ticket)		
P3 Peter Mayhew as Chewbacca	8.00	20.00
(Given to Auction Reserve Seat Holders)/1000*		
P4 Maria de Aragon as Greedo	10.00	25.00
(Show Exclusive)/800*		

1997-98 Star Wars Men Behind the Masks Test Issue

COMPLETE SET (7)		
COMMON CARD		
NNO Chewbacca	125.00	250.00
(prismatic foil/triangles)		
NNO Chewbacca	125.00	250.00
(prismatic foil/vertical lines)		
NNO Chewbacca	125.00	250.00
(refractor foil)		
NNO Greedo	125.00	250.00
(prismatic foil/spotted)		
NNO Greedo	125.00	250.00
(prismatic foil/triangles)		
NNO Greedo	125.00	250.00
(prismatic foil/vertical lines)		
NNO Greedo	125.00	250.00
(refractor foil)		

1994-96 Star Wars Metal

COMPLETE SET (60)	30.00	75.00
COMMON CARD (1-60)	1.00	2.50

1994-96 Star Wars Metal Promos

COMPLETE SET (3)	12.00	30.00
COMMON CARD (P1-P3)	6.00	15.00
P1 Star Wars Episode IV	6.00	15.00
P2 The Empire Strikes Back	6.00	15.00
P3 Return of the Jedi	6.00	15.00

1996 Star Wars Metal Art of Ralph McQuarrie

COMPLETE SET (20)	10.00	25.00
COMMON CARD (1-20)	1.00	2.50
COA Certificate of Authenticity		

1998 Star Wars Metal Bounty Hunters

COMPLETE SET (5)	2.50	6.00
COMMON CARD (1-5)	1.00	2.50
HSJH Han Solo and Jabba the Hutt SE		

1995 Star Wars Metal Dark Empire I

COMPLETE SET (6)	3.00	8.00
COMMON CARD (1-6)	1.00	2.50

1996 Star Wars Metal Dark Empire II

COMPLETE SET (6)	3.00	8.00
COMMON CARD (1-6)	1.00	2.50

1998 Star Wars Metal Jedi Knights

COMPLETE SET (5)	3.00	8.00
COMMON CARD (1-5)	1.00	2.50
MES Mos Eisley Spaceport SE	1.50	4.00

1998 Star Wars Metal Jedi Knights Avon

COMPLETE SET (4)	3.00	8.00
COMMON CARD (1-4)	1.00	2.50
WIC Wampa Ice Creature SE	1.50	4.00

1997 Star Wars Metal Shadows of the Empire

COMPLETE SET (6)	4.00	10.00
COMMON CARD (1-6)	1.00	2.50

2015 Star Wars Micro Collector Packs

COMPLETE SET (36)	60.00	120.00
COMMON CARD (1-36)	1.50	4.00
NNO 3-D Glasses	.40	1.00

2015 Star Wars Micro Collector Packs 3-D Posters

COMPLETE SET (6)	3.00	8.00
COMMON CARD	.60	1.50
STATED ODDS 1:1		

2015 Star Wars Micro Collector Packs Micro-Comics

COMPLETE SET (6)	4.00	10.00
COMMON CARD	.75	2.00
STATED ODDS 1:1		

1996 Star Wars Multimotion

2M Star Wars 20th Anniversary Commemorative Magazine	2.50	6.00

1999 Star Wars The New Jedi Order

NNO SDCC Exclusive	2.00	5.00

2018 Star Wars Nickel City Con Promos

COMPLETE SET (3)	3.00	8.00
COMMON CARD (P1-P3)	1.25	3.00
NNO Darth Vader	2.00	5.00
NNO Luke Skywalker	1.50	4.00

2015 Star Wars NYCC Oversized Exclusives

COMPLETE SET (70)	75.00	150.00
COMMON CARD (1-70)	2.00	5.00

2022 Star Wars Obi-Wan Kenobi Set

COMPLETE SET (30)	50.00	125.00
COMPLETE EP.I SET (5)	10.00	25.00
COMPLETE EP.II SET (5)	10.00	25.00
COMPLETE EP.III SET (5)	10.00	25.00
COMPLETE EP.IV SET (5)	10.00	25.00
COMPLETE EP.V SET (5)	10.00	25.00
COMPLETE EP.VI SET (5)	10.00	25.00
COMMON EP.I (1-5)	3.00	8.00
COMMON EP.II (6-10)	3.00	8.00
COMMON EP.III (11-15)	3.00	8.00
COMMON EP.IV (16-20)	3.00	8.00
COMMON EP.V (21-25)	3.00	8.00
COMMON EP.VI (26-30)	3.00	8.00
*BLUE/49: 1X TO 2.5X BASIC CARDS		
EP.I SET PRINT RUN 1,221 SETS		
EP.II SET PRINT RUN 1,161 SETS		
EP.III SET PRINT RUN 1,330 SETS		
EP.IV SET PRINT RUN 1,019 SETS		
EP.V SET PRINT RUN		
EP.VI SET PRINT RUN		

2021 Star Wars On-Demand The High Republic

COMPLETE SET (20)	15.00	40.00
*BLACK/25: 4X TO 10X BASIC CARDS		
ANNCD PRINT RUN 1,180 SETS		

2021 Star Wars On-Demand The High Republic Cover Art

COMPLETE SET (5)	200.00	350.00
COMMON CARD (1-5)	50.00	100.00
STATED ODDS 1:1 W/ PARALLELS		
3 A Test of Courage	75.00	150.00
5 Marvel #1	60.00	120.00

2019 Star Wars On-Demand The Power of the Dark Side

COMPLETE SET W/EXCL. (26)	15.00	40.00
COMPLETE SET W/O EXCL. (25)	10.00	25.00
COMMON CARD (1-26)	1.25	3.00
*BLUE: 1X TO 2.5X BASIC CARDS		
STATED PRINT RUN 700 SETS		
SDCC SITH TROOPER PRINT RUN 300 CARDS		
26 Sith Trooper/300*	8.00	20.00
(SDCC Exclusive)		

2019 Star Wars On-Demand The Power of the Dark Side Autographs

STATED OVERALL ODDS 1:SET	
2A Ian McDiarmid	
3A Hayden Christensen	
4A Guy Henry	
5A Nika Futterman	
7A Barbara Goodson	
8A Matthew Wood	
9A Ray Park	
10A Sam Witwer	
11A Adam Driver	
12A Domhnall Gleeson	
13A Andy Serkis	
15A Jeremy Bulloch	
17A Ben Mendelsohn	
18A Paul Bettany	
20A Lars Mikkelson	
21A Jason Isaacs	
22A Sarah Michelle Gellar	
23A Phillip Anthony Rodriguez	
24A Kathleen Gati	

2019 Star Wars On-Demand The Power of the Dark Side Galactic Battles

COMPLETE SET (6)	15.00	40.00
COMMON CARD (G1-G6)	4.00	10.00
STATED ODDS 1:SET		

2019 Star Wars On-Demand The Power of the Light Side

COMPLETE SET W/EXCL. (26)	15.00	40.00
COMPLETE SET W/O EXCL.(25)	10.00	25.00

COMMON CARD (1-25)	1.25	3.00

*BLUE: 1X TO 2.5X BASIC CARDS

26 Luke Skywalker	12.00	30.00

(NYCC Exclusive)

2019 Star Wars On-Demand The Power of the Light Side Autographs

STATED ODDS 1:SET

2A Carrie Fisher
3A Harrison Ford
4A Peter Mayhew
5A Billy Dee Williams
6A Kenny Baker
7A Anthony Daniels
8A Caroline Blakiston
11A Tim Rose
12A Hayden Christensen
13A Samuel L. Jackson
14A Ewan McGregor
17A Daisy Ridley
19A John Boyega
20A Felicity Jones
21A Hermione Corfield
22A Matt Lanter
23A James Arnold Taylor
24A Ashley Eckstein
25A Taylor Gray

2019 Star Wars On-Demand The Power of the Light Side Galactic Battles

COMPLETE SET (6)	25.00	60.00
COMMON CARD (G1-G6)	4.00	10.00

STATED ODDS 1:SET

2019 Star Wars On-Demand Women of Star Wars

COMPLETE SET (25)	12.00	30.00
COMMON CARD (1-25)	.75	2.00

*PURPLE: 2X TO 5X BASIC CARDS

2019 Star Wars On-Demand Women of Star Wars Autographs

Amy Allen as
Aayla Secura

COMMON AUTO	8.00	20.00

STATED OVERALL ODDS 1:SET

1 Carrie Fisher		
2 Daisy Ridley	300.00	500.00
3 Felicity Jones	125.00	250.00
4 Genevieve O'Reilly	10.00	25.00
5 Ashley Eckstein	15.00	40.00
6 Sarah Michelle Gellar	75.00	150.00
7 Vanessa Marshall	12.00	30.00
8 Tiya Sircar	10.00	25.00
9 Nika Futterman	10.00	25.00
10 Laura Dern		
12 Tovah Feldshuh	15.00	40.00
13 Orli Shoshan	12.00	30.00
15 Billie Lourd	60.00	120.00
16 Gwendoline Christie		

2019 Star Wars On-Demand Women of Star Wars Evolution of Leia

PRINCESS LEIA
STAR WARS: RETURN OF THE JEDI

COMPLETE SET (8)	75.00	150.00
COMMON CARD (EL1-EL8)	12.00	30.00

2019 Star Wars On-Demand Women of Star Wars Women of the Galaxy

COMPLETE SET (10)	75.00	150.00

COMMON CARD (WG1-WG10)	10.00	25.00

RANDOMLY INSERTED INTO SETS

1995 Star Wars The Power of the Force

NNO Luke Skywalker	2.00	5.00

2011 Star Wars Power Plates

COMPLETE SET W/SP (30)	75.00	150.00
COMP.SET W/O SP (24)	50.00	100.00
UNOPENED BOX (48 PACKS)	120.00	150.00
UNOPENED PACK (1 PLATE)	2.50	3.00
COMMON PLATE	3.00	8.00
COMMON PLATE SP	5.00	12.00

SP STATED ODDS 1:8

1999 Star Wars Preview Guide

NNO Pod Racers		5.00

(Orange County Register Exclusive)

1997 Star Wars Quality Bakers

COMPLETE SET (10)	12.00	30.00
COMMON CARD (1-10)	2.00	5.00

2016 Star Wars Rancho Obi-Wan Little Debbie

COMPLETE SET (12)	20.00	50.00
COMMON CARD (1-12)	2.50	6.00

STATED ODDS 1:1 BOXES OF STAR CRUNCH

2018 Star Wars On-Demand Rebels Series Finale

COMPLETE SET (20)	15.00	40.00
COMMON CARD (1-20)	1.25	3.00

*BLUE: 1X TO 2.5X BASIC CARDS
STATED PRINT RUN 461 SETS

2018 Star Wars On-Demand Rebels Series Finale Autographs

STATED OVERALL ODDS 1:SET

NNO Ashley Eckstein		
NNO Dee Bradley Baker	12.00	30.00
NNO Forest Whitaker		
NNO Freddie Prinze Jr.		
NNO Genevieve O'Reilly	10.00	25.00
NNO Ian McDiarmid	60.00	120.00
NNO Lars Mikkelsen	30.00	75.00
NNO Mary Elizabeth McGlynn	15.00	40.00
NNO Stephen Stanton	12.00	30.00
NNO Steve Blum	15.00	40.00
NNO Taylor Gray		
NNO Tom Baker		
NNO Vanessa Marshall		
NNO Warwick Davis		

2015 Star Wars Rebels

COMPLETE SET (100)	6.00	15.00
UNOPENED BOX (24 PACKS)	50.00	75.00
UNOPENED PACK (6 CARDS)	2.00	3.00
COMMON CARD (1-100)	.12	.30
*FOIL: 2X TO 5X BASIC CARDS		

2015 Star Wars Rebels Stickers

COMPLETE SET (20)	5.00	12.00
COMMON CARD (1-20)	.40	1.00

2015 Star Wars Rebels Tattoos

COMPLETE SET (10)	6.00	15.00
COMMON CARD (1-10)	1.00	2.50
STATED ODDS 1:8		

2017 Star Wars Rebels Season 4 Preview Set

COMPLETE SET (25)	30.00	80.00
UNOPENED BOXED SET (27 CARDS)		
COMMON CARD	2.00	5.00
*PURPLE/25: 1.2X TO 3X BASIC CARDS	6.00	15.00
RELEASED 10/17/2017		

2017 Star Wars Rebels Season 4 Preview Set Autographs

STATED ODDS 1:1 PER BOX SET

NNO Freddie Prinze Jr.		
NNO Taylor Gray		
NNO Vanessa Marshall		
NNO Tiya Sircar		
NNO Steve Blum		
NNO Ashley Eckstein		
NNO Sam Witwer		
NNO Jason Isaacs		
NNO Philip Anthony Rodriguez		
NNO Sarah Michelle Gellar		
NNO Stephen Stanton	12.00	30.00
NNO Billy Dee Williams		
NNO Forest Whitaker		
NNO Stephen Stanton		
NNO Genevieve OiReilly		
NNO Mary Elizabeth McGlynn	12.00	30.00
NNO Phil Lamarr		
NNO Tom Baker		
NNO Jim Cummings		

2014 Star Wars Rebels Subway Promos

COMPLETE SET (6)	6.00	15.00
COMMON CARD	1.50	4.00

2019 Star Wars Resistance Surprise Packs

COMPLETE SET (100)	12.00	30.00
UNOPENED BOX (24 PACKS)		
UNOPENED PACK (6 CARDS)		
COMMON CARD (1-100)	.25	.60
*BRONZE/50: 4X TO 10X BASIC CARDS		
*SILVER/25: 6X TO 15X BASIC CARDS		

2019 Star Wars Resistance Surprise Packs Character Foil

COMPLETE SET (25)	12.00	30.00
COMMON CARD (1-25)	.75	2.00

2019 Star Wars Resistance Surprise Packs Danglers

COMPLETE SET (12)	12.00	30.00
COMMON CARD (1-12)	2.50	6.00

2019 Star Wars Resistance Surprise Packs Mini Albums

COMPLETE SET (4)	12.00	30.00
COMMON ALBUM	4.00	10.00

2019 Star Wars Resistance Surprise Packs Pop-Ups

COMPLETE SET (10)	6.00	15.00
COMMON CARD (1-10)	1.00	2.50

2019 Star Wars Resistance Surprise Packs Temporary Tattoos

COMPLETE SET (10)	8.00	20.00
COMMON CARD (1-10)	1.25	3.00

2016 Star Wars Rogue One Mission Briefing

COMPLETE SET (110)	8.00	20.00
UNOPENED BOX (24 PACKS)	85.00	100.00
UNOPENED PACK (8 CARDS)	4.00	5.00
COMMON CARD (1-110)	.20	.50
*BLACK: .75X TO 2X BASIC CARDS	.40	1.00
*GREEN: 1.2X TO 3X BASIC CARDS	.60	1.50
*BLUE: 1.5X TO 4X BASIC CARDS	.75	2.00
*GRAY/100: 8X TO 20X BASIC CARDS	4.00	10.00
*GOLD/50: 12X TO 30X BASIC CARDS	6.00	15.00

2016 Star Wars Rogue One Mission Briefing Autographs

JASON ISAACS
AUTHENTIC AUTOGRAPH
AS THE GRAND INQUISITOR

COMMON CARD	6.00	15.00
*BLACK/50: .6X TO 1.5X BASIC AUTOS		
*BLUE/25: 1.2X TO 3X BASIC AUTOS		
RANDOMLY INSERTED INTO PACKS		
NNO Adrienne Wilkinson	12.00	30.00
NNO Al Lampert	10.00	25.00
NNO Anna Graves	15.00	40.00
NNO Barbara Frankland	10.00	25.00
NNO Brian Blessed	8.00	20.00
NNO Candice Orwell	12.00	30.00
NNO Catherine Taber		
NNO Clive Revill	12.00	30.00
NNO Corey Dee Williams	10.00	25.00
NNO Dave Barclay		
NNO David Ankrum	10.00	25.00
NNO Eric Lopez	10.00	25.00
NNO Femi Taylor	8.00	20.00
NNO Garrick Hagon	10.00	25.00
NNO George Roubicek	10.00	25.00
NNO Glyn Baker	10.00	25.00
NNO Ian Liston	10.00	25.00
NNO Jack Klaff	8.00	20.00
NNO Jim Cummings	12.00	30.00

NNO John Coppinger	15.00	40.00
NNO Kenneth Colley	8.00	20.00
NNO Lloyd Sherr	10.00	25.00
NNO Megan Udall	10.00	25.00
NNO Mercedes Ngoh	8.00	20.00
NNO Michaela Cottrell	8.00	20.00
NNO Mike Edmonds	12.00	30.00
NNO Oliver Walpole	10.00	25.00
NNO Paul Springer	12.00	30.00
NNO Rajia Baroudi	12.00	30.00
NNO Rich Oldfield	15.00	40.00
NNO Rusty Goffe	10.00	25.00
NNO Sam Witwer	15.00	40.00
NNO Scott Capurro	12.00	30.00
NNO Sean Crawford	10.00	25.00
NNO Stephen Stanton	8.00	20.00
NNO Tom Kane	8.00	20.00
NNO Wayne Pygram	10.00	25.00

2016 Star Wars Rogue One Mission Briefing Character Foil

COMPLETE SET (9)	12.00	20.00
COMMON CARD (1-9)	2.00	5.00
STATED ODDS 1:8		

2016 Star Wars Rogue One Mission Briefing Comic Strips Inserts

2016 Star Wars Rogue One Mission Briefing The Death Star

COMPLETE SET (12)	8.00	20.00
COMMON CARD (1-12)	1.25	3.00

COMPLETE SET (9)	6.00	15.00
COMMON CARD (1-9)	.75	2.00
STATED ODDS 1:4		

2016 Star Wars Rogue One Mission Briefing Dual Autographs

STATED PRINT RUN 3 SER.#'d SETS

UNPRICED DUE TO SCARCITY

1 C.Fisher

C.Blakiston

2 M.Hamill

D.Lawson

2016 Star Wars Rogue One Mission Briefing Heroes of the Rebel Alliance

GENERAL MADINE
HEROES OF THE REBEL ALLIANCE

COMPLETE SET (9)	10.00	25.00
COMMON CARD (1-9)	1.50	3.00
STATED ODDS 1:8		
1 Luke Skywalker	2.00	5.00
2 Princess Leia	2.00	5.00
3 Han Solo	2.00	5.00
4 Chewbacca	1.50	4.00
6 Obi-Wan Kenobi	1.50	4.00
7 R2-D2	1.50	4.00

2016 Star Wars Rogue One Mission Briefing Mission Briefing Monday

COMPLETE SET (36)	150.00	300.00
COMMON CARD	6.00	15.00
NOV.7, 2016 (MBME1-MBME6)/206*		
NOV.14, 2016 (MBM1-MBM5)/226*		
NOV.21, 2016 (MBM6-MBM10)/218*		
NOV.28, 2016 (MBM11-MBM15)/212*		
DEC.5, 2016 (MBM16-MBM20)/224*		
DEC.12, 2016 (MBM21-MBM25)/234*		
DEC.19, 2016 (MBM26-MBM30)/252*		

2016 Star Wars Rogue One Mission Briefing Montages

COMPLETE SET (9)	15.00	40.00
COMMON CARD (1-9)	3.00	8.00
STATED ODDS 1:24		
1 Storming the Beach	3.00	8.00
2 Imperial Assault	3.00	8.00
3 Jyn Erso	5.00	12.00
4 Within Rebel Base	3.00	8.00
5 Patrol of the Empire	3.00	8.00
6 Fearsome Death Trooper	3.00	8.00
7 Director Krennic	3.00	8.00
8 In Flames	3.00	8.00
9 Rebel Ensemble	3.00	8.00

2016 Star Wars Rogue One Mission Briefing NYCC Exclusives

COMPLETE SET (10)	12.00	30.00
COMMON CARD (E1-E10)	2.00	5.00
2016 NYCC EXCLUSIVE		

2016 Star Wars Rogue One Mission Briefing Patches

COMPLETE SET (12)	50.00	100.00
COMMON CARD (M1-M12)	3.00	8.00
*GRAY/100: .75X TO 2X BASIC CARDS		
*GOLD/50: 1.5X TO 4X BASIC CARDS		
*RED/10: 3X TO 8X BASIC CARDS		
STATED ODDS 1:26		
1 Jyn Erso	6.00	15.00
3 L-1 Droid	5.00	12.00
4 Admiral Raddus	4.00	10.00
6 TIE Fighter Pilot	4.00	10.00
7 Shoretrooper	4.00	10.00
10 Captain Cassian Andor	5.00	12.00
11 Bistan	4.00	10.00

2016 Star Wars Rogue One Mission Briefing Quad Autograph

STATED PRINT RUN 2 SER.#'d SETS

UNPRICED DUE TO SCARCITY

1 Hamill

Lawson

Klaff

Hagon

2016 Star Wars Rogue One Mission Briefing Stickers

DEATH TROOPER

COMPLETE SET (18)	10.00	25.00
COMMON CARD (1-18)	1.00	2.50
STATED ODDS 1:12		
1 Jyn Erso	1.50	4.00
13 Darth Vader	2.00	5.00

2016 Star Wars Rogue One Mission Briefing Triple Autographs

STATED PRINT RUN 3 SER.#'d SETS

UNPRICED DUE TO SCARCITY

1 Fisher

Blakiston

Crowley

2 Hamill

Lawson

Hagon

2016 Star Wars Rogue One Mission Briefing Villains of the Galactic Empire

GENERAL VEERS

VILLAINS OF THE GALACTIC EMPIRE

COMPLETE SET (8)	8.00	20.00
COMMON CARD (1-8)	1.25	3.00
STATED ODDS 1:8		
1 Darth Vader	1.25	5.00

1999 Star Wars Sci-Fi Expo Celebrity Promos

P1 Garrick Hagon	8.00	20.00
(Biggs Darklighter)		
P2 Peter Mayhew	8.00	20.00
(Chewbacca)		

2015 Star Wars SDCC Oversized Exclusives

COMPLETE SET (100)	120.00	250.00
COMMON CARD (1-100)	2.00	5.00

1997 Star Wars SE Trilogy 3-D Doritos Discs

COMPLETE SET (20)	5.00	12.00
COMMON CARD	.40	1.00

1997 Star Wars SE Trilogy 3-D Doritos-Cheetos

COMPLETE SET (6)	3.00	8.00
COMMON CARD (1-6)	.75	2.00

1996 Kenner Star Wars Shadows of the Empire

COMPLETE SET (100)	15.00	40.00
UNOPENED BOX (36 PACKS)	75.00	125.00
UNOPENED PACK (9 CARDS)	2.50	4.00
COMMON CARD (1-72, 83-100)	.15	.40
COMMON ETCHED (73-78)	2.00	5.00
COMMON EMBOSSED (79-82)	3.00	8.00
73-78 STATED ODDS 1:9		
79-82 STATED ODDS 1:18		

1996 Star Wars Shadows of the Empire Promos

COMMON CARD	1.00	2.50
SOTE1 Xizor	2.00	5.00
SOTE2 Darth Vader	2.00	5.00
SOTE3 Luke Skywalker	2.00	5.00
SOTE4 Dash Rendar & Leebo	2.00	5.00
SOTE5 Boba Fett	8.00	15.00
(Convention Exclusive)		
SOTE6 Guri	2.00	5.00
SOTE7 C-3PO & R2-D2	2.00	5.00
NNO SOTE3-SOTE1 (Luke Skywalker/Darth Vader)		

2021 Star Wars Signature Series Autographs

UNOPENED BOX (1 CARD)	100.00	150.00
AA Annabelle Davis	10.00	25.00
AS Stephen Stanton		
AA2 Annabelle Davis	10.00	25.00
AAF Anthony Forrest	6.00	15.00
AAG Anna Graves	6.00	15.00
AAH Alden Ehrenreich		
AAS Andy Serkis		
ABB Ben Burtt		
ABL Billie Lourd		
ABM Ben Mendelsohn		
ABW Billy Dee Williams		
ACC Cavin Cornwall	6.00	15.00
ACF Carrie Fisher		
ACH Clint Howard		

ACM Cameron Monaghan	15.00	40.00
ACW Carl Weathers		
ADA Derek Arnold	6.00	15.00
ADB Dee Bradley Baker	15.00	40.00
ADC Dave Chapman	8.00	20.00
ADF Donald Faison		
ADG Domhnall Gleeson		
ADL Daniel Logan	8.00	20.00
ADM Dominic Monaghan		
ADR Daisy Ridley		
ADT Dee Tails		
ADW Debra Wilson	10.00	25.00
ADY Donnie Yen		
AES Emily Swallow		
AEW Ewan McGregor		
AFJ Felicity Jones		
AFP Freddie Prinze Jr.		
AFW Forest Whitaker		
AGC Gwendoline Christie		
AGE Giancarlo Esposito	50.00	100.00
AGG Greg Grunberg	12.00	30.00
AGO Genevieve O'Reilly		
AGP Greg Proops	6.00	15.00
AHC Hayden Christensen		
AHD Harley Durst	6.00	15.00
AHF Harrison Ford		
AHS Horatio Sanz	15.00	40.00
AIM Ian McDiarmid		
AIR Ian Ruskin	6.00	15.00
AIW Ian Whyte	10.00	25.00
AJB John Boyega	30.00	75.00
AJK Jaime King	10.00	25.00
AJR Jerome Blake	8.00	20.00
AJS Joonas Suotamo	60.00	120.00
AJT James Arnold Taylor	15.00	40.00
AKB Kenny Baker		
AKT Kelly Marie Tran		
ALT Lee Towersey	15.00	40.00
AMD Matt Doran	6.00	15.00
AMM Mads Mikkelsen		
ANF Nika Futterman	10.00	25.00
ANK Nick Kellington	6.00	15.00
ANN Nick Nolte		
APA Philip Anthony-Rodriguez	10.00	25.00
APB Paul Bettany		
APM Peter Mayhew		
APP Pedro Pascal		
ARA Riz Ahmed		
ARD Robin Atkin Downes	6.00	15.00
ARP Ray Park		
AS2 Stephen Stanton		
AS3 Stephen Stanton		
ASJ Samuel L. Jackson		
ASW Sam Witwer	15.00	40.00
ATD Tim Dry	6.00	15.00
ATF Tovah Feldshuh	6.00	15.00
ATG Taylor Gray		
ATK Tom Kenny	8.00	20.00
ATM Temuera Morrison	50.00	100.00
ATR Tim Rose		
ATW Taika Waititi		
AWA Denis Lawson	12.00	30.00
AWD Warwick Davis	30.00	75.00
AWH Werner Herzog		
AAB2 Ahmed Best		
AAB3 Ahmed Best		
AAD2 Adam Driver		
AAD3 Adam Driver		
AAE2 Ashley Eckstein		
AAE3 Ashley Eckstein		
AAF2 Anthony Forrest	6.00	15.00
AAG2 Anna Graves	6.00	15.00
AAH2 Alden Ehrenreich		
AAS2 Andy Serkis		
AASG Arti Shah	5.00	12.00
ABB2 Ben Burtt		
ABBE Blair Bess	8.00	20.00
ABL2 Billie Lourd		
ABL3 Billie Lourd		
ABMR Bobby Moynihan	6.00	15.00
ABW2 Billy Dee Williams		
ABW3 Billy Dee Williams		
ACC2 Cavin Cornwall	6.00	15.00
ACDW Corey Dee Williams	12.00	30.00
ACF2 Carrie Fisher		
ADA2 Derek Arnold		
ADA3 Derek Arnold		
ADB2 Dee Bradley Baker	5.00	12.00
ADB3 Dee Bradley Baker	6.00	15.00
ADC2 Dave Chapman	12.00	30.00
ADG2 Domhnall Gleeson		
ADG3 Domhnall Gleeson		
ADL2 Daniel Logan	8.00	20.00
ADR2 Daisy Ridley		
ADR3 Daisy Ridley		
ADT2 Dee Tails		
ADT3 Dee Tails		
AEW2 Ewan McGregor		
AEW3 Ewan McGregor		
AFJ2 Felicity Jones		
AFJ3 Felicity Jones		
AFP2 Freddie Prinze Jr.		
AGC2 Gwendoline Christie		
AGCM Gina Carano		
AGG2 Greg Grunberg	12.00	30.00
AHC2 Hayden Christensen		
AHC3 Hayden Christensen		
AHF2 Harrison Ford		
AHF3 Harrison Ford		
AIM2 Ian McDiarmid		
AIM3 Ian McDiarmid		
AIW2 Ian Whyte	8.00	20.00
AJB2 John Boyega	30.00	75.00
AJB3 John Boyega	30.00	75.00
AJR2 Jerome Blake		
AJS2 Joonas Suotamo	60.00	120.00
AJT2 James Arnold Taylor	15.00	40.00
AJT3 James Arnold Taylor	12.00	30.00
AJTS John Tui	8.00	20.00
AKB2 Kenny Baker		
AKB3 Kenny Baker		
AKT2 Kelly Marie Tran		
ANF2 Nika Futterman	10.00	25.00
ANF3 Nika Futterman	10.00	25.00
ANK2 Nick Kellington	8.00	20.00
APM2 Peter Mayhew		
APM3 Peter Mayhew		
ARD2 Robin Atkin Downes	8.00	20.00
ARP2 Ray Park		
ARP3 Ray Park		
ARPC Ron Perlman		
ASJ2 Samuel L. Jackson		
ASJ3 Samuel L. Jackson		
ASW2 Sam Witwer	25.00	60.00
ASW3 Sam Witwer		
ATBS Thomas Brodie-Sangster	5.00	12.00
ATG2 Taylor Gray		
ATK2 Tom Kenny	10.00	25.00
ATK3 Tom Kenny	10.00	25.00
ATM2 Temuera Morrison	75.00	150.00
ATR2 Tim Rose		
ATR3 Tim Rose		
AWA2 Denis Lawson	12.00	30.00
AWA3 Denis Lawson	12.00	30.00
AWD2 Warwick Davis		
AWD3 Warwick Davis		

2021 Star Wars Signature Series Dual Autographs

STATED PRINT RUN 5 SER.#'d SETS

UNPRICED DUE TO SCARCITY

DABC G.Christie/J.Boyega

DACM I.McDiarmid/H.Christensen

DAEB A.Ehrenreich/P.Bettany

DAJM B.Mendelsohn/F.Jones

DALE A.Eckstein/M.Lanter

DAPE G.Esposito/P.Pascal

DARD D.Ridley/A.Driver

DAWM P.Mayhew/B.Williams

2021 Star Wars Signature Series Triple Autographs

STATED PRINT RUN 5 SER.#'d SETS

UNPRICED DUE TO SCARCITY

TADCG Driver/Christie/Gleeson

TAEFS Futterman/Eckstein/Salenger

TAESK Ehrenreich/Suotamo/Kellyman
TAJWA Jones/Whitaker/Ahmed
TAPGM Prinze Jr./Gray/Marshall
TAPWN Pascal/Waititi/Nolte
TARDB Ridley/Driver/Boyega
TARTL Ridley/Tran/Lourd

2019 Star Wars Skywalker Saga

COMPLETE SET (100)	8.00	20.00
UNOPENED BOX (24 PACKS)	100.00	150.00
UNOPENED PACK (8 CARDS)	4.00	6.00
COMMON CARD (1-100)	.20	.50

*ORANGE: .6X TO 1.5X BASIC CARDS
*BLUE: .75X TO 2X BASIC CARDS
*GREEN/99: 2.5X TO 6X BASIC CARDS
*PURPLE/25: 6X TO 15X BASIC CARDS

2019 Star Wars Skywalker Saga Allies

COMPLETE SET (10)	6.00	15.00
COMMON CARD (A1-A10)	.75	2.00

*GREEN/99: 1X TO 2.5X BASIC CARDS
*PURPLE/25: 3X TO 8X BASIC CARDS
STATED ODDS 1:12 HOBBY & BLASTER

2019 Star Wars Skywalker Saga Autographs

ERIN KELLYMAN as ENFYS NEST

STATED ODDS 1:39 HOBBY; 1:826 BLASTER

AAB Ahmed Best		
AAD Anthony Daniels		
AAS Andy Serkis		
AAT Alan Tudyk		
ABH Brian Herring	6.00	15.00
ABL Billie Lourd		
ABM Ben Mendelsohn		
ACF Carrie Fisher		
ADB David Barclay	6.00	15.00
ADG Domhnall Gleeson		
ADL Daniel Logan	5.00	12.00
ADR Daisy Ridley		
ADY Donnie Yen		
AEK Erin Kellyman	30.00	75.00
AEM Ewan McGregor		
AFJ Felicity Jones		
AFW Forest Whitaker		
AGH Garrick Hagon	6.00	15.00
AGO Genevieve O'Reilly		
AHC Hayden Christensen		
AHF Harrison Ford		
AIM Ian McDiarmid		
AJB Jerome Blake	5.00	12.00
AKB Kenny Baker		
AKK Katy Kartwheel	12.00	30.00
AML Matt Lanter		
AMM Mads Mikkelsen		
ANF Nika Futterman	5.00	12.00
APB Paul Bettany		
APL Phil LaMarr	6.00	15.00
APM Peter Mayhew		
ARA Riz Ahmed		
ARP Ray Park		
ASC Silas Carson	5.00	12.00
ATM Temuera Morrison		
AWD Warwick Davis		
AADK Adam Driver		
AAEH Alden Ehrenreich		
AASW Andy Secombe	5.00	12.00
ABDW Billy Dee Williams		
AHCV Hayden Christensen		
AIMS Ian McDiarmid		
AJAT James Arnold Taylor		
AJBF John Boyega		
AJSC Joonas Suotamo		
ASLJ Samuel L. Jackson		
ATKY Tom Kane	6.00	15.00

2019 Star Wars Skywalker Saga Commemorative Blueprint Relics

COMMON MEM	5.00	12.00

*ORANGE/99: SAME VALUE AS BASIC
*BLUE/50: .5X TO 1.2X BASIC MEM
*GREEN/25: .75X TO 2X BASIC MEM
STATED ODDS 1:64 HOBBY; 1:218 BLASTER

BPIS Imperial Speeder Bike	6.00	15.00
BPMF Millennium Falcon	8.00	20.00
BPSI Slave I	6.00	15.00
BPST AT-ST	6.00	15.00
BPTI Tie Interceptor	6.00	15.00
BPXW X-wing Fighter	6.00	15.00

2019 Star Wars Skywalker Saga Commemorative Nameplate Patches

COMMON ANAKIN	3.00	8.00
COMMON KYLO	4.00	10.00
COMMON LEIA	4.00	10.00
COMMON LUKE	5.00	12.00

*ORANGE/99: SAME VALUE AS BASIC
*BLUE/50: .5X TO 1.2X BASIC MEM
*GREEN/25: .75X TO 2X BASIC MEM

STATED ODDS 1:1 BLASTER

NPA General Leia Organa/A	4.00	10.00
NPE Princess Leia Organa/E	4.00	10.00
NPI General Leia Organa/I	4.00	10.00
NPL Princess Leia Organa/L	4.00	10.00
NPA2 Anakin Skywalker/A	3.00	8.00
NPAA Anakin Skywalker/A	3.00	8.00
NPAI Anakin Skywalker/I	3.00	8.00
NPAK Anakin Skywalker/K	3.00	8.00
NPAN Anakin Skywalker/N	3.00	8.00
NPKK Kylo Ren/K	4.00	10.00
NPKL Kylo Ren/L	4.00	10.00
NPKO Kylo Ren/O	4.00	10.00
NPKY Kylo Ren/Y	4.00	10.00
NPLE Luke Skywalker/E	5.00	12.00
NPLK Luke Skywalker/K	5.00	12.00
NPLL Luke Skywalker/L	5.00	12.00
NPLU Luke Skywalker/U	5.00	12.00
NPN2 Anakin Skywalker/N	3.00	8.00

2019 Star Wars Skywalker Saga Dual Autographs

STATED ODDS 1:7,572 HOBBY; 1:68,310 BLASTER

UNPRICED DUE TO SCARCITY

DAFD C.Fisher/A.Driver
DAJM S.L.Jackson/I.McDiarmid
DALD P.LeMarr/J.Dolan
DALE M.Lanter/A.Eckstein
DAPC K.Baker/R.Goffe
DAPM F.Prinze Jr./V.Marshall
DATG J.Taylor/A.Graves
DAWM B.Williams/P.Mayhew

2019 Star Wars Skywalker Saga Enemies

TUSKEN RAIDER

COMPLETE SET (10)	6.00	15.00
COMMON CARD (E1-E10)	.75	2.00

*GREEN/99: 1X TO 2.5X BASIC CARDS
*PURPLE/25: 3X TO 8X BASIC CARDS
STATED ODDS 1:12 HOBBY; 1:12 BLASTER

2019 Star Wars Skywalker Saga Iconic Looks

COMPLETE SET (10)	6.00	15.00
COMMON CARD (IL1-IL10)	.75	2.00
*GREEN/99: 1X TO 2.5X BASIC CARDS		
*PURPLE/25: 3X TO 8X BASIC CARDS		
STATED ODDS 1:4 HOBBY & BLASTER		

2019 Star Wars Skywalker Saga Path of the Jedi

COMPLETE SET (10)	6.00	15.00
COMMON CARD (PJ1-PJ10)	.75	2.00
*GREEN/99: 1X TO 2.5X BASIC CARDS		
*PURPLE/25: 3X TO 8X BASIC CARDS		
STATED ODDS 1:2 HOBBY & BLASTER		

2019 Star Wars Skywalker Saga Skywalker Legacy

COMPLETE SET (11)	6.00	15.00
COMMON CARD (FT1-FT11)	1.00	2.50
*GREEN/99: 1.5X TO 4X BASIC CARDS		
*PURPLE/25: 2.5X TO 6X BASIC CARDS		
STATED ODDS 1:12 HOBBY & BLASTER		

2019 Star Wars Skywalker Saga Triple Autographs

STATED ODDS 1:8,708 HOBBY; 1:168,310 BLASTER

UNPRICED DUE TO SCARCITY

- TABCR Blakiston/Crowley/Rose
- TABCT Taylor/Barclay/Carter
- TAFFD Driver/Fisher/Ford
- TAMBD Daniels/Baker/Mayhew
- TAWCB Carson/Wood/Blake

1978 Star Wars Spaceship Hang Gliders

COMPLETE SET (4)	75.00	150.00
COMMON CARD	20.00	50.00

2022 Star Wars Star File NYCC Set

1 Grogu
2 Boba Fett
3 Fennec Shand
4 The Mandalorian
5 Ahsoka Tano
6 Obi-Wan Kenobi
7 Princess Leia Organa
8 Reva
9 Darth Vader
10 The Grand Inquisitor

2017 Star Wars Stellar Signatures

COMMON AUTOS	25.00	60.00
*BLUE/25: .5X TO 1.2X BASIC AUTOS	30.00	75.00
STATED PRINT RUN 40 SER.#'d SETS		
100 TOTAL BOXES PRODUCED		
NNO Adam Driver	400.00	650.00
NNO Alan Tudyk	100.00	175.00
NNO Andy Serkis	75.00	150.00
NNO Ashley Eckstein	60.00	120.00

NNO Ben Mendelsohn EXCH		
NNO Billy Dee Williams	75.00	150.00
NNO Brian Herring	30.00	75.00
NNO Carrie Fisher	300.00	500.00
NNO Daisy Ridley	800.00	1200.00
NNO Donnie Yen	75.00	150.00
NNO Felicity Jones	300.00	500.00
NNO Forest Whitaker	75.00	150.00
NNO Freddie Prinze Jr.	50.00	100.00
NNO Genevieve O'Reilly	50.00	100.00
NNO Gwendoline Christie	250.00	400.00
NNO Harrison Ford	2500.00	4000.00
NNO Hayden Christensen	250.00	400.00
NNO Ian McDiarmid	250.00	400.00
NNO Jeremy Bulloch	30.00	75.00
NNO John Boyega	120.00	250.00
NNO Joonas Suotamo	30.00	75.00
NNO Kenny Baker	75.00	150.00
NNO Lars Mikkelsen	75.00	150.00
NNO Mark Hamill EXCH		
NNO Matthew Wood	30.00	75.00
NNO Peter Mayhew	75.00	150.00
NNO Ray Park	60.00	120.00
NNO Riz Ahmed	50.00	100.00
NNO Sarah Michelle Gellar	120.00	250.00
NNO Stephen Stanton EXCH		
NNO Temuera Morrison	30.00	75.00
NNO Tim Curry	100.00	175.00
NNO Tom Baker	100.00	200.00
NNO Warwick Davis	50.00	100.00

2018 Star Wars Stellar Signatures

COMMON AUTO	20.00	50.00
*BLUE/25: SAME VALUE AS BASIC AUTOS		
AAD Anthony Daniels	125.00	250.00
AAE Ashley Eckstein	30.00	75.00
AAS Andy Serkis	50.00	100.00
AAT Alan Tudyk	50.00	100.00
ABH Brian Herring	25.00	60.00
ACB Caroline Blakiston	25.00	60.00
ADG Domhnall Gleeson	125.00	250.00

ADR Daisy Ridley	400.00	600.00
AEB Erik Bauersfeld	50.00	100.00
AEK Erin Kellyman	125.00	250.00
AFW Forest Whitaker	60.00	120.00
AGG Greg Grunberg	25.00	60.00
AHC Hayden Christensen	125.00	250.00
AHF Harrison Ford	800.00	1400.00
AIM Ian McDiarmid	100.00	200.00
AJB Jeremy Bulloch	30.00	75.00
AJI Jason Isaacs	30.00	75.00
AJS Joonas Suotamo	50.00	100.00
AKB Kenny Baker	100.00	200.00
ALD Laura Dern	60.00	120.00
AMM Mads Mikkelsen	125.00	250.00
APR Paul Reubens	75.00	150.00
ARA Riz Ahmed	30.00	75.00
ARP Ray Park	50.00	100.00
ATC Tim Curry	50.00	100.00
AADR Adam Driver	200.00	350.00
ABDW Billy Dee Williams	75.00	150.00
ASLJ Samuel L. Jackson	600.00	800.00

2018 Star Wars Stellar Signatures Autographed Relics

COMMON AUTO	60.00	120.00
ARD Paul Bettany	150.00	300.00
ARJ Felicity Jones	200.00	350.00

2018 Star Wars Stellar Signatures Dual Autographs

- DABB J.Bulloch/D.Barclay
- DABM J.Bulloch/T.Morrison
- DABO C.Blakiston/G.O'Reilly
- DACW H.Christensen/M.Wood
- DAFB C.Fisher/K.Baker
- DAMM L.Mikkelsen/M.McGlynn
- DAMP I.McDiarmid/R.Park
- DAOM G.O'Reilly/I.McElhinney
- DARD D.Ridley/A.Driver
- DASV J.Suotamo/J.Vee
- DASW S.Stanton/S.Witwer
- DATL J.Taylor/M.Lanter
- DAWA F.Whitaker/R.Ahmed
- DAWQ B.Williams/M.Quinn

2019 Star Wars Stellar Signatures

HAN SOLO

COMPLETE SET (100)	750.00	1500.00
COMMON CARD (1-100)	10.00	25.00
STATED ODDS 1:SET PER BOXED SET		

2019 Star Wars Stellar Signatures Autographs

COMMON AUTO	15.00	40.00
AADR Adam Driver	125.00	250.00
AAB Ahmed Best	50.00	100.00
AAT Alan Tudyk	30.00	75.00
AAE Alden Ehrenreich	200.00	400.00
AAS Andy Serkis	30.00	75.00
ABL Billie Lourd	60.00	120.00
ABDW Billy Dee Williams	60.00	120.00
ABMY Bobby Moynihan	25.00	60.00
ADR Daisy Ridley	300.00	500.00
ADB David Barclay		
ADT David Tennant EXCH		
ADGL Domhnall Gleeson	100.00	200.00
ADFA Donald Faison	25.00	60.00
ADY Donnie Yen	50.00	100.00
AEK Erin Kellyman	50.00	100.00
AEM Ewan McGregor	500.00	1000.00
AFW Forest Whitaker	30.00	75.00
AFPJ Freddie Prinze Jr.	25.00	60.00
AHF Harrison Ford	600.00	1200.00
AHC Hayden Christensen	125.00	250.00
AHCO Hermione Corfield	25.00	60.00
AIM Ian McDiarmid	100.00	200.00
AJB Jeremy Bulloch	30.00	75.00
AKMT Kelly Marie Tran	75.00	150.00
AKB Kenny Baker	60.00	120.00
ALM Lars Mikkelsen	50.00	100.00
ALD Laura Dern	30.00	75.00
AMM Mads Mikkelsen	75.00	150.00
APB Paul Bettany	75.00	150.00
APR Paul Reubens	50.00	100.00
ARP Ray Park	25.00	60.00
ARA Riz Ahmed	20.00	50.00
ATC Tim Curry	20.00	50.00
AWD Warwick Davis	20.00	50.00

2019 Star Wars Stellar Signatures Dual Autographs

STATED ODDS 4:BOXED SET		
STATED PRINT RUN 25 SER.#'d SETS		
DALC A.Lawrence/H.Corfield		
DAES A.Eckstein/T.Sircar	75.00	200.00
DABW B.Williams/J.Bulloch		
DAMW B.Williams/P.Mayhew		
DARD D.Ridley/A.Driver		
DAKD E.Kellyman/W.Davis	60.00	120.00
DAMC E.McGregor/H.Christensen		
DAFD H.Ford/A.Driver		
DAMC I.McDiarmid/H.Christensen		
DATL J.Taylor/M.Lanter	25.00	60.00
DAIG J.Isaacs/T.Gray	25.00	60.00
DAMD L.Mikkelsen/W.Davis	50.00	100.00
DAFT N.Futterman/J.Taylor	25.00	60.00
DAPB R.Park/P.Bettany		
DAPW R.Park/S.Witwer	50.00	100.00
DAWB S.Witwer/P.Bettany		

2020 Star Wars Stellar Signatures

THE CLIENT

COMPLETE SET (100)	500.00	750.00
COMMON CARD (1-100)	6.00	15.00
STATED ODDS 1 SET PER BOX		

2020 Star Wars Stellar Signatures Autographs

UNOPENED BOX (141 CARDS)		
COMMON AUTO	25.00	60.00
100 TOTAL BOXES WERE PRODUCED		
AAB Ahmed Best	25.00	60.00
AAD Adam Driver	200.00	400.00
ABB Ben Burtt	60.00	120.00
ABL Billie Lourd	60.00	120.00
ACM Cameron Monaghan	25.00	60.00
ACW Carl Weathers	200.00	400.00
ADL Denis Lawson	50.00	100.00
ADM Dominic Monaghan	25.00	60.00
ADR Daisy Ridley	500.00	1000.00
ADW Debra Wilson	25.00	60.00
ADY Donnie Yen	75.00	150.00
AEM Ewan McGregor	500.00	1000.00

AES Emily Swallow	125.00	250.00
AGC Gina Carano	250.00	500.00
AGE Giancarlo Esposito	75.00	150.00
AGG Greg Grunberg	25.00	60.00
AHC Hayden Christensen	100.00	200.00
AHF Harrison Ford	1000.00	2000.00
AIM Ian McDiarmid	100.00	200.00
AJG Janina Gavankar	500.00	100.00
AKB Kenny Baker	75.00	150.00
ALD Laura Dern EXCH	30.00	75.00
ANA Naomi Ackie	50.00	100.00
ANN Nick Nolte	200.00	350.00
AOA Omid Abtahi	50.00	100.00
APP Pedro Pascal	750.00	1500.00
ASW Sam Witwer	50.00	100.00
ATM Temuera Morrison EXCH	25.00	60.00
ATW Taika Waititi	200.00	400.00
AWH Werner Herzog	100.00	200.00
AAE1 Alden Ehrenreich	150.00	300.00
AAE2 Ashley Eckstein	100.00	200.00
AASL Andy Serkis	50.00	100.00
ABDW Billy Dee Williams	75.00	150.00
AJBF Jeremy Bulloch	100.00	200.00
AJSC Joonas Suotamo	60.00	120.00

2020 Star Wars Stellar Signatures Dual Autographs

DABP B.Burtt/M.Pennington	
DAFW H.Ford/B.Williams	
DAGM G.Grunberg/D.Monaghan	
DAGT A.Graves/C.Taber	
DAHA W.Herzog/O.Abtahi	
DALE M.Lanter/A.Eckstein	
DAMC E.McGregor/H.Christensen	
DAMC I.McDiarmid/H.Christensen	
DAMM L.Mikkelsen/M.McGlynn	
DAMW C.Monaghan/D.Wilson	
DANC N.Nolte/G.Carano	
DARD D.Ridley/A.Driver	

2020 Star Wars Stellar Signatures Triple Autographs

TAFET Bulloch/Morrison/Logan	
TALMG Lourd/Monaghan/Grunberg	
TAOAA Taylor/Lanter/Eckstein	

2021 Star Wars Stellar Signatures

COMPLETE SET (100)	600.00	1200.00
COMMON CARD (1-100)	5.00	12.00
STATED PRINT RUN 100 SER.#'d SETS		

3	Omega	8.00	20.00
11	Qi'ra	30.00	75.00
14	Captian Cassian Andor	6.00	15.00
17	Crosshair	10.00	25.00
27	Cad Bane	15.00	40.00
28	General Leia Organa	6.00	15.00
29	Jyn Erso	15.00	40.00
31	Obi-Wan Kenobi	25.00	60.00
32	Captain Rex	20.00	50.00
35	C-3PO	6.00	15.00
36	Jango Fett	12.00	30.00
40	R2-D2	8.00	20.00
44	Greedo	6.00	15.00
45	Darth Vader	8.00	20.00
47	Ahsoka Tano	30.00	75.00
48	Hera Syndulla	10.00	25.00
53	Kanan Jarras	12.00	30.00
58	The Grand Inquisitor	8.00	20.00
59	Chewbacca	8.00	20.00
63	Zeb Orrelios	8.00	20.00
64	Darth Maul	8.00	20.00
67	Ezra Bridger	15.00	40.00
68	The Mandalorian	25.00	60.00
69	Darth Sidious	10.00	25.00
70	The Armorer	12.00	30.00
71	Wicket W. Warrick	12.00	30.00
72	Grand Admiral Thrawn	15.00	40.00
79	Jar Jar Binks	8.00	20.00
82	Rey	12.00	30.00
83	Moff Gideon	8.00	20.00
85	Boba Fett's Ship	8.00	20.00
88	Bo-Katan Kryze	10.00	25.00
89	Queen Amidala	12.00	30.00
91	Grogu	30.00	75.00
92	Ahsoka Tano	12.00	30.00
95	The Razor Crest	15.00	40.00
97	Boba Fett	10.00	25.00
98	Fennec Shand	12.00	30.00
99	Boba Fett	20.00	50.00

2021 Star Wars Stellar Signatures Autographs

COMMON AUTO	15.00	40.00
STATED PRINT RUN 40 SER.#'d SETS		
AAB Ahmed Best	30.00	75.00
AAD Adam Driver	300.00	600.00
AAE Ashley Eckstein	100.00	200.00
AAS Andy Serkis	60.00	120.00
ABL Billie Lourd	75.00	150.00
ACH Clint Howard	50.00	100.00
ACW Carl Weathers	125.00	250.00
ADR Daisy Ridley	400.00	800.00
AEC Emilia Clarke	1500.00	3000.00
AEK Erin Kellyman	30.00	75.00
AES Emily Swallow	75.00	150.00
AFJ Felicity Jones	450.00	900.00
AGE Giancarlo Esposito	60.00	120.00
AHC Hayden Christensen	300.00	600.00
AHF Harrison Ford EXCH	1500.00	3000.00
AHQ Hugh Quarshie	25.00	60.00
AKB Kenny Baker	100.00	200.00
ALM Lars Mikkelsen	50.00	100.00
AML Matt Lanter	30.00	75.00
AMP Michael Pennington	20.00	50.00
AMV Mercedes Varnado (Sasha Banks)	175.00	350.00
AMW Matthew Wood	50.00	100.00
ANA Naomi Ackie	20.00	50.00
ANP Natalie Portman	4000.00	6500.00
ARD Rosario Dawson	1000.00	2000.00
ASK Simon Kassianides	20.00	50.00
ATG Taylor Gray	25.00	60.00
ATW Taika Waititi	200.00	400.00
AWD Warwick Davis EXCH	30.00	75.00
AASP Amy Sedaris	75.00	150.00
ABDW Billy Dee Williams	100.00	200.00
ADLI Diana Lee Inosanto	25.00	60.00
AJAT James Arnold Taylor	50.00	100.00
AKMT Kelly Marie Tran	30.00	75.00

2021 Star Wars Stellar Signatures Dual Autographs

STATED PRINT RUN 25 SER.#'d SETS		
DABG Taylor Gray/Dee Bradley Baker	100.00	200.00
DADD Harrison Davis/Warwick Davis EXCH		
DAEB Dee Bradley Baker/Ashley Eckstein	150.00	300.00
DAFD Adam Driver/Harrison Ford EXCH		
DALE Matt Lanter/Ashley Eckstein		
DARD Daisy Ridley/Adam Driver	600.00	1200.00

DARW Billy Dee Williams/Daisy Ridley	500.00	1000.00
DAVK Simon Kassianides/Mercedes Varnado (Sasha Banks) EXCH	150.00	300.00

2021 Star Wars Stellar Signatures Quad Autographs

STATED PRINT RUN 40 SER.#'d SETS		
QDCW Dee Bradley Baker/Matt Lanter		
James Arnold Taylor/Ashley Eckstein	300.00	500.00

2022 Star Wars Signature Series

UNOPENED BOX (1 AUTO)	90.00	125.00
AAB Ahmed Best	30.00	75.00
AAE Ashley Eckstein	125.00	250.00
AAG Anna Graves	10.00	25.00
AAR Alan Ruscoe	10.00	25.00
AAW Andrew Woodall	8.00	20.00
ABS Bruce Spence	10.00	25.00
ACA Cas Anvar	10.00	25.00
ACB Chris Bartlett	15.00	40.00
ACE Chris Edgerly	10.00	25.00
ACH Clint Howard	20.00	50.00
ACO Candice Orwell	12.00	30.00
ACR Clive Revill	20.00	50.00
ADB Dee Bradley Baker	25.00	60.00
ADC Dave Chapman	15.00	40.00
ADI Diana Lee Inosanto	12.00	30.00
ADT David Tennant	30.00	75.00
AES Emily Swallow	30.00	75.00
AGE Giancarlo Esposito	60.00	125.00
AGG Greg Grunberg	10.00	25.00
AGH Garrick Hagon	12.00	30.00
AHD Harley Durst	8.00	20.00
AHQ Hugh Quarshie	10.00	25.00
AIR Ian Ruskin	8.00	20.00
AJB John Boyega	25.00	60.00
AJG Janina Gavankar	12.00	30.00
AJI Jason Isaacs	50.00	125.00
AJK Jack Klaff	8.00	20.00
AKL Ken Leung	10.00	25.00
AKM Cathy Munroe	15.00	40.00
AKO Katy O'Brian	15.00	40.00
ALC Lily Cole	8.00	20.00
ALM Lewis MacLeod	20.00	50.00

ALS	Leilani Shiu	25.00	60.00
ALT	Lee Towersey	15.00	40.00
ALW	Leeanna Walsman	8.00	20.00
AMA	Mark Austin	50.00	100.00
AMB	Mark Boone Jr.	15.00	40.00
AMD	Mark Dodson	15.00	40.00
AMW	Matthew Wood	30.00	75.00
ANA	Naomi Ackie	15.00	40.00
ANF	Nika Futterman	20.00	50.00
AOA	Omid Abtahi	10.00	25.00
AOD	Oliver Ford Davies	10.00	25.00
AOW	Oliver Walpole	8.00	20.00
APA	Philip Alexander	8.00	20.00
APK	Paul Kasey	8.00	20.00
APL	Paul Sun-Hyung Lee	15.00	40.00
APR	Paul Reubens	60.00	120.00
ARO	Rena Owen	10.00	25.00
ASC	Scott Capurro	15.00	40.00
ASK	Simon Kassianides	15.00	40.00
ASL	Scott Lawrence	8.00	20.00
ASS	Stephanie Silva	12.00	30.00
ATD	Tim Dry	8.00	20.00
ATG	Taylor Gray	30.00	75.00
AVK	Valene Kane	10.00	25.00
AAD1	Annabelle Davis	10.00	25.00
AAE2	Ashley Eckstein	125.00	250.00
AAG1	Anna Graves	10.00	25.00
AAH1	Amanda Hale	12.00	30.00
ADB2	Dee Bradley Baker	25.00	60.00
ADT1	Dee Tails	10.00	25.00
AJB2	Jeremy Bulloch	50.00	100.00
AKS1	Kath Soucie	15.00	40.00
ALM1	Lars Mikkelsen	60.00	120.00
AMB1	Michonne Bourriague	10.00	25.00
ANK1	Nick Kellington	8.00	20.00
ANK2	Nick Kellington	8.00	20.00
APB1	Paul Brooke	15.00	40.00
APB2	Paul Blake	12.00	30.00
ARB1	Richard Brake	12.00	30.00

2022 Star Wars Signature Series Autograph Variants

VALIN HESS

AVAD	Adam Driver
AVAE	Alden Ehrenreich
AVAS	Andy Serkis
AVAT	Alan Tudyk
AVBW	Billy Dee Williams
AVCB	Chris Bartlett
AVCR	Clive Revill
AVCW	Carl Weathers
AVDB	Dee Bradley Baker
AVDC	Dave Chapman
AVDG	Domhnall Gleeson
AVDY	Donnie Yen
AVEC	Emilia Clarke
AVEM	Ewan McGregor
AVFJ	Felicity Jones
AVFW	Forest Whitaker
AVGC	Gwendoline Christie
AVGE	Giancarlo Esposito
AVGG	Greg Grunberg
AVHC	Hayden Christensen
AVHF	Harrison Ford
AVIM	Ian McDiarmid
AVJB	John Boyega
AVJG	Janina Gavankar
AVKB	Kenny Baker
AVKC	Keisha Castle-Hughes
AVLD	Laura Dern
AVMB	Mark Boone Jr.
AVMC	Michael Carter
AVMK	Mercedes Varnado
AVML	Matt Lanter
AVMW	Matthew Wood
AVNF	Nika Futterman
AVNK	Nick Kellington
AVNN	Nick Nolte
AVOA	Omid Abtahi
AVPA	Philip Alexander
AVPB	Paul Bettany
AVRA	Robin Atkin Downes
AVRB	Richard Brake
AVRP	Ray Park
AVSB	Steve Blum
AVSG	Sarah Michelle Gellar
AVSK	Simon Kassianides
AVTG	Taylor Gray
AVTM	Temuera Morrison
AVTW	Taika Waititi
AVWD	Warwick Davis
AVWH	Werner Herzog
AVAD1	Annabelle Davis
AVAE1	Ashley Eckstein
AVAE2	Ashley Eckstein
AVDB1	Dmitrious Bistrevsky
AVFPJ	Freddie Prinze Jr.
AVJB1	Jeremy Bulloch
AVPB1	Paul Blake

2022 Star Wars Signature Series Dual Autographs

STATED ODDS 1:2,816

UNPRICED DUE TO SCARCITY

DAFJD F.Jones/D.Yen

DAJTA J.A.Taylor/A.Graves

DAMWT R.Park/M.Wood

2022 Star Wars Signature Series Quad Autographs

QACW Eckstein/Taylor/Lanter/Baker

QAFA Ford/Fisher/Ridley/Driver

QASA McDiarmid/Park/Christensen/Driver

2022 Star Wars Signature Series Triple Autographs

UNPRICED DUE TO SCARCITY

TALJ Ridley/Boyega/Dern

TARO Jones/Tudyk/Ahmed

TAFAW Driver/Gleeson/Serkis

2022 Star Wars Topps Industry Conference Exclusive Autographs

STATED PRINT RUN 15 SER.#'d SETS

UNPRICED DUE TO SCARCITY

AAD Adam Driver

ADR Daisy Ridley

AHC Hayden Christensen

ABDW Billy Dee Williams

AJBO John Boyega

1997 Star Wars Trilogy The Complete Story

COMPLETE SET (72)		6.00	15.00
COMMON CARD (1-72)		.25	.60
0 Promo		1.00	2.00

1997 Star Wars Trilogy The Complete Story Laser

COMPLETE SET (6)		6.00	15.00
COMMON CARD (LC1-LC6)		1.25	3.00
STATED ODDS 1:9			

1997 Star Wars Trilogy Merlin

COMPLETE SET (125)	10.00	25.00
UNOPENED BOX (48 PACKS)	25.00	40.00
UNOPENED PACK (5 CARDS)	1.00	1.25
COMMON CARD (1-125)	.15	.40

1997 Star Wars Trilogy Merlin Case-Toppers

COMPLETE SET (3)	20.00	50.00
COMMON CARD (P1-P3)	8.00	20.00
STATED ODDS 1:CASE		

1997 Star Wars Trilogy Special Edition

COMPLETE SET (72)	6.00	15.00
UNOPENED BOX (36 PACKS)	100.00	200.00
UNOPENED PACK (9 CARDS)	3.00	6.00
COMMON CARD (1-72)	.15	.40
13D ISSUED AS BOX TOPPER		
13D X-Wings Departing	6.00	15.00

1997 Star Wars Trilogy Special Edition Holograms

COMPLETE SET (2)	10.00	25.00
COMMON CARD (1-2)	6.00	15.00
STATED ODDS 1:18		

1997 Star Wars Trilogy Special Edition Laser

COMPLETE SET (6)	6.00	15.00
COMMON CARD (LC1-LC6)	1.25	3.00
STATED ODDS 1:9		

1997 Star Wars Trilogy Special Edition Promos

COMPLETE SET (8)	10.00	25.00
COMMON CARD (P1-P8)	1.25	3.00
P1 Three Stormtroopers	4.00	10.00
P4 Sandcrawler	3.00	8.00
P5 Jawa and Landspeeder	3.00	8.00
P6 Millennium Falcon	3.00	8.00

1997 Star Wars Trilogy Special Edition Kenner Promos

COMPLETE SET (4)	10.00	25.00
COMMON CARD (H1-H4)	4.00	10.00

1997 Star Wars Trilogy Special Edition Micro Machine Promos

COMPLETE SET (5)	12.00	30.00
COMMON CARD (G1-G5)	4.00	10.00

1997 Kenner Star Wars Vehicles

COMPLETE SET (72)	5.00	12.00
UNOPENED BOX (36 PACKS)	40.00	60.00
UNOPENED PACK (5 CARDS)	1.50	2.50
COMMON CARD (1-72)	.15	.40

1997 Star Wars Vehicles 3-D

COMPLETE SET (3)	25.00	60.00
COMMON CARD	8.00	20.00
STATED ODDS 1:36		

3 Princess Leia	15.00	40.00
Luke Skywalker		

1997 Star Wars Vehicles Cut-Away

COMPLETE SET (4)	7.50	20.00
COMMON CARD (C1-C4)	2.50	6.00
STATED ODDS 1:18		

1997 Star Wars Vehicles Promos

P1A Darth Vader & Stormtroopers on Speeder Bikes chromium)/3200*	12.00	30.00
P1B Darth Vader & Stormtroopers on Speeder Bikes (refractor)/320*	30.00	75.00
P2A Stormtroopers on Speeder Bikes (chromium)/1600*	20.00	50.00
P2B Stormtroopers on Speeder Bikes (refractor)/160*	50.00	100.00
NNO 2-Card Sheet		

2021 Star Wars Visions Episode 1 The Duel

COMPLETE SET (5)	8.00	20.00
COMMON CARD (1-5)	2.50	6.00
STATED PRINT RUN 665 ANNCD SETS		

2021 Star Wars Visions Episode 2 Tatooine Rhapsody

COMPLETE SET (5)	8.00	20.00
COMMON CARD (1-5)	2.50	6.00
STATED PRINT RUN 501 ANNCD SETS		

2021 Star Wars Visions Episode 3 The Twins

COMPLETE SET (5)	8.00	20.00
COMMON CARD (1-5)	2.50	6.00
STATED PRINT RUN 461 ANNCD SETS		

2021 Star Wars Visions Episode 4 The Elder

COMPLETE SET (5)	8.00	20.00
COMMON CARD (1-5)	2.50	6.00
STATED PRINT RUN 539 ANNCD SETS		

2021 Star Wars Visions Episode 5 The Village Bride

COMPLETE SET (5)	8.00	20.00
COMMON CARD (1-5)	2.50	6.00
STATED PRINT RUN 463 ANNCD SETS		

2021 Star Wars Visions Episode 6 Akakiri

COMPLETE SET (5)	8.00	20.00
COMMON CARD (1-5)	2.50	6.00
STATED PRINT RUN 484 ANNCD SETS		

2021 Star Wars Visions Episode 7 T0-B1

COMPLETE SET (5)	8.00	20.00
COMMON CARD (1-5)	2.50	6.00
STATED PRINT RUN 517 ANNCD SETS		

2021 Star Wars Visions Episode 8 The Ninth Jedi

COMPLETE SET (5)	8.00	20.00
COMMON CARD (1-5)	2.50	6.00
STATED PRINT RUN 474 ANNCD SETS		

2021 Star Wars Visions Episode 9 Lop and Ocho

COMPLETE SET (5)	8.00	20.00
COMMON CARD (1-5)	2.50	6.00
STATED PRINT RUN 466 ANNCD SETS		

2017 Star Wars Widevision Bonus Abrams

1 Display Box, 1995
2 Foil Wrapper, 1995
3 Card No.1, 1995
Art By John Berkey
4 Topps Finest Card No. C-1, 1995

2022 Star Wars Wrapper Art Collection Set

1 Rey/632*
2 Kylo Ren/536*
3 BB-8/572*
4 Finn/473*
5 Darth Maul/614*
6 Qui-Gon Jinn/536*
7 Anakin Skywalker/500*
8 Queen Amidala/556*
9 Obi-Wan Kenobi/
10 Princess Leia Organa/
11 Reva/
12 Grand Inquisitor/
13 Ahsoka Tano/
14 Moff Gideon/
15 Krrsantan/
16 Cad Bane/

2015 Star Wars Wrapper Metal Card Set

1 Star Wars Series 1 C-3PO
2 Star Wars Series 2 Darth Vader
3 Star Wars Series 3 R2-D2
4 Star Wars Series 4 Luke and Obi-Wan
5 Star Wars Series 5 X-Wing Fighter
6 Empire Strikes Back Series 1 Darth Vader Red
7 Empire Strikes Back Series 2 Darth Vader Blue
8 Empire Strikes Back Series 3 Darth Vader Yellow
9 Return of the Jedi Series 1 Darth Vader
10 Return of the Jedi Series 1 Jabba the Hutt
11 Return of the Jedi Series 1 Luke Skywalker
12 Return of the Jedi Series 1 Wicket
13 Return of the Jedi Series 2 C-3PO
14 Return of the Jedi Series 2 Lando Calrissian
15 Return of the Jedi Series 2 Princess Leia

1999 Star Wars X-Wing Rogue Squadron

COMMON CARD	2.50	6.00

2020 Women of Star Wars

COMPLETE SET (100)	8.00	20.00
UNOPENED BOX (7 PACKS)	125.00	200.00
UNOPENED PACK (8 CARDS)	20.00	30.00
COMMON CARD (1-100)	.20	.50
*ORANGE: .5X TO 1.2X BASIC CARDS		
*BLUE: .6X TO 1.5X BASIC CARDS		
*GREEN/99: 4X TO 10X BASIC CARDS		
*PURPLE/25: 8X TO 20X BASIC CARDS		

2020 Women of Star Wars Autographs

LEEANNA WALSMAN
AS ZAM WESELL

COMMON AUTO	4.00	10.00

*ORANGE/99: .5X TO 1.2X BASIC AUTOS
*BLUE/50: .6X TO 1.5X BASIC AUTOS
*PURPLE/25: .75X TO 2X BASIC AUTOS
STATED ODDS 1:14

AAA	Amy Allen	10.00	25.00
AAF	Anna Francolini	5.00	12.00
AAG	Anna Graves	5.00	12.00
AAP	Angelique Perrin	6.00	15.00
ACC	Crystal Clarke	5.00	12.00
ACL	Charlotte Louise	5.00	12.00
ACT	Catherine Taber	5.00	12.00
AJD	Julie Dolan	5.00	12.00
AJK	Jaime King	8.00	20.00
ALC	Lily Cole	5.00	12.00
ALW	Leeanna Walsman	8.00	20.00
AML	Misty Lee	6.00	15.00
AMV	Myrna Velasco	6.00	15.00
ANC	Nazneen Contractor	5.00	12.00
AOS	Orli Shoshan	8.00	20.00
ATS	Tiya Sircar	10.00	25.00

2020 Women of Star Wars Autographs Blue

STATED PRINT RUN 50 SER.#'d SETS

AAH	Amanda Hale	8.00	20.00
AJH	Jessica Henwick	12.00	30.00
AMB	Michonne Bourriague	12.00	30.00
ANF	Nika Futterman	15.00	40.00
ASM	Suzie McGrath	6.00	15.00
AVR	Vinette Robinson	10.00	25.00

2020 Women of Star Wars Autographs Orange

STATED PRINT RUN 99 SER.#'d SETS

AAB	Anna Brewster	6.00	15.00
ADW	Debra Wilson	10.00	25.00
AEK	Erin Kellyman	15.00	40.00
AHC	Hermione Corfield	12.00	30.00
AJG	Janina Gavankar	15.00	40.00
AVM	Vanessa Marshall	10.00	25.00

2020 Women of Star Wars Autographs Purple

STATED PRINT RUN 25 SER.#'d SETS

AAE	Ashley Eckstein	50.00	100.00
ACB	Caroline Blakiston	20.00	50.00
ANA	Naomi Ackie	60.00	120.00
AGCM	Gina Carano	200.00	400.00
AKCH	Keisha Castle-Hughes	25.00	60.00

2020 Women of Star Wars Dual Autographs

MYRNA VELASCO AS TORRA DOZA

SUZIE McGRATH AS TAM RYVORA

UNPRICED DUE TO SCARCITY

DAAS A.Allen/O.Shoshan
DADL L.Dern/A.Lawrence
DADS O.d'Abo/M.Salenger
DAEF A.Eckstein/N.Futterman
DAHC J.Henwick/H.Corfield
DAJK F.Jones/V.Kane
DALA B.Lourd/N.Ackie
DAMS V.Marshall/T.Sircar
DART D.Ridley/K.Tran
DASL S.Smart/C.Louise
DATN K.Tran/V.Ngo
DAVM M.Velasco/S.McGrath

2020 Women of Star Wars Iconic Moments

COMPLETE SET (22)	12.00	30.00
COMMON CARD (IM1-IM22)	1.25	3.00

*GREEN/99: .6X TO 1.5X BASIC CARDS
*PURPLE/25: 1.2X TO 3X BASIC CARDS
RANDOMLY INSERTED INTO PACKS

2020 Women of Star Wars Journey of Leia Organa

THE JOURNEY OF
LEIA ORGANA

COMPLETE SET (8)	10.00	25.00
COMMON CARD (JL1-JL8)	1.50	4.00

STATED ODDS 1:7

2020 Women of Star Wars Powerful Pairs

PADMÉ AMIDALA   DORMÉ

COMPLETE SET (28)	15.00	40.00
COMMON CARD (PP1-PP28)	.75	2.00

*GREEN/99: .6X TO 1.5X BASIC CARDS
*PURPLE/25: 1.2X TO 3X BASIC CARDS
STATED ODDS 1:3

2020 Women of Star Wars Triple Autographs

UNPRICED DUE TO SCARCITY

NNO Allen/d'Abo/Futterman
NNO Fisher/Jones/Ridley
NNO Ridley/Tran/Lourd
NNO Dern/Lawrence/Lourd
NNO Velasco/McGrath/McGlynn
NNO Gellar/Eckstein/Sircar

2020 Women of Star Wars Weapon of Choice

STAFF
ENFYS NEST

COMPLETE SET (24)	12.00	30.00
COMMON CARD (WC1-WC24)	1.00	2.50

*GREEN/99: .6X TO 1.5X BASIC CARDS
*PURPLE/25: 1.5X TO 4X BASIC CARDS

TCG

1995 Star Wars Premiere

RELEASED IN DECEMBER 1995

#			
1	5D6-RA-7 (Fivedesix) R1	2.00	4.00
2	Admiral Motti R2	1.25	2.50
3	Chief Bast U1	.50	1.00
4	Colonel Wullf Yularen U1	.50	1.00
5	Commander Praji U2	.50	1.00
6	Darth Vader R1	.50	1.00
7	Dathcha U1	5.00	10.00
8	Death Star Trooper C2	15.00	30.00
9	Djas Puhr R2	.50	1.00
10	Dr. Evazan R2	.20	.40
11	DS-61-2 U1	1.25	2.50
12	DS-61-3 R1	1.25	2.50
13	EG-6 (Eegee-Six) U2	.50	1.00
14	Feltipern Trevagg U1	.50	1.00
15	Garindan R2	1.25	2.50
16	General Tagge R2	1.25	2.50
17	Grand Moff Tarkin R1	5.00	10.00
18	Imperial Pilot C2	.20	.40
19	Imperial Trooper Guard C2	.20	.40
20	Jawa DARK C2	.20	.40
21	Kitik Keed'kak R1	2.00	4.00
22	Labria R2	.20	.40
23	Lieutenant Tanbris U2	1.25	2.50
24	LIN-V8M (Elleyein-Veeateemm) C1	.50	1.00
25	Miiiyoom Onith U2	.50	1.00
26	MSE-6 ëMouseí Droid U1	.50	1.00
27	Myo R2	1.25	2.50
28	Ponda Baba U1	.50	1.00
29	Prophetess U1	.50	1.00
30	R1-G4 (Arone-Geefour) C2	.20	.40
31	R4-M9 (Arfour-Emmnine) C2	.20	.40
32	Stormtrooper C3	.20	.40
33	Tonnika Sisters R1	2.00	4.00
34	Tusken Raider C2	.20	.40
35	WED-9-M1 ëBanthaí Droid R2	1.25	2.50
36	Wuher U2	.50	1.00
37	Blaster Scope U1	.50	1.00
38	Caller DARK U2	.50	1.00
39	Comlink C1	.20	.40
40	Droid Detector C2	.20	.40
41	Fusion Generator Supply Tanks DARK C2	.20	.40
42	Observation Holocam U2	.50	1.00
43	Restraining Bolt DARK C2	.20	.40
44	Stormtrooper Backpack C2	.20	.40
45	Stormtrooper Utility Belt C2	.20	.40
46	A Disturbance In The Force U1	.50	1.00
47	Baniss Keeg C2	.20	.40
48	Blast Door Controls U2	.50	1.00
49	Blaster Rack U1	.50	1.00
50	Dark Hours U2	.50	1.00
51	Death Star Sentry U1	.50	1.00
52	Disarmed DARK R1	2.00	4.00
53	Expand The Empire R1	2.00	4.00
54	Fear Will Keep Them In Line R2	1.25	2.50
55	I Find Your Lack Of Faith Disturbing R1	2.00	4.00
56	Iíve Lost Artoo! U1	.50	1.00
57	Jawa Pack U1	.50	1.00
58	Juri Juice R2	1.25	2.50
59	Ket Maliss C2	.20	.40
60	Lateral Damage R2	1.25	2.50
61	Luke? Luuuuke! U1	.50	1.00
62	Macroscan C2	.20	.40
63	Molator R1	2.00	4.00
64	Organaís Ceremonial Necklace R1	2.00	4.00
65	Presence Of The Force R1	2.00	4.00
66	Reactor Terminal U2	.50	1.00
67	Send A Detachment Down R1	2.00	4.00
68	Sunsdown U1	.50	1.00
69	Tactical Re-Call R2	1.25	2.50
70	Wrong Turn U1	.50	1.00
71	Your Eyes Can Deceive You U1	2.00	4.00
72	Alter DARK U1	.50	1.00
73	Boring Conversation Anyway R1	2.00	4.00
74	Charming To The Last R2	1.25	2.50
75	Collateral Damage C2	.20	.40
76	Counter Assault C1	.20	.40
77	Dark Collaboration R1	2.00	4.00
78	Dark Jedi Presence R1	6.00	12.00
79	Dark Maneuvers C2	.20	.40
80	Dead Jawa C2	.20	.40
81	Elis Helrot U2	.50	1.00
82	Emergency Deployment U1	.50	1.00
83	Evacuate? U2	.50	1.00
84	Full Scale Alert U2	.50	1.00
85	Gravel Storm U2	.50	1.00
86	I Have You Now R2	1.25	2.50
87	Iíve Got A Problem Here C2	.20	.40
88	Imperial Reinforcements C1	.20	.40
89	Imperial Code Cylinder C2	.20	.40
90	Itís Worse C2	.20	.40
91	Imperial Barrier DARK C2	.20	.40
92	Kintan Strider C1	.20	.40
93	Limited Resources U2	.50	1.00
94	Local Trouble R1	2.00	4.00
95	Lone Pilot R2	1.25	2.50
96	Lone Warrior R2	1.25	2.50
97	Look Sir, Droids R1	2.00	4.00
98	Moment Of Triumph R2	1.25	2.50
99	Nevar Yalnal R2	1.25	2.50
100	Ommni Box C2	.20	.40
101	Overload C2	.20	.40
102	Physical Choke R1	2.00	4.00
103	Precise Attack C2	.20	.40
104	Scanning Crew C2	.20	.40
105	Sense DARK U1	.50	1.00
106	Set For Stun C2	.20	.40
107	Takeel C2	.20	.40
108	Tallon Roll C2	.20	.40
109	The Circle Is Now Complete R1	2.00	4.00
110	The Empireís Back U1	.50	1.00
111	Trinto Duaba U1	.50	1.00
112	Trooper Charge U2	.50	1.00
113	Tusken Scavengers C2	.20	.40
114	Utinni! DARK R1	2.00	4.00
115	Vaderís Eye R1	2.00	4.00
116	Weíre All Gonna Be A Lot Thinner! R1	2.00	4.00
117	You Overestimate Their Chances C1	.50	1.00
118	Your Powers Are Weak, Old Man R1	.20	.40
119	Alderaan DARK R1	2.00	4.00
120	Dantooine DARK U1	.50	1.00
121	Death Star: Central Core U2	.50	1.00
122	Death Star: Detention Block Corridor C1	.20	.40
123	Death Star: Docking Bay 327 DARK C2	.20	.40
124	Death Star: Level 4 Military Corridor U1	.50	1.00
125	Death Star: War Room U2	.50	1.00
126	Kessel U2	1.25	2.50
127	Tatooine DARK C2	.20	.40
128	Tatooine: Cantina DARK R2	1.25	2.50
129	Tatooine: Docking Bay 94 DARK C2	.20	.40
130	Tatooine: Jawa Camp DARK C1	.20	.40
131	Tatooine: Jundland Wastes C1	.20	.40
132	Tatooine: Larsí Moisture Farm DARK C1	.20	.40
133	Tatooine: Mos Eisley DARK C1	.20	.40
134	Yavin 4 DARK C2	.20	.40
135	Yavin 4: Docking Bay DARK C2	.20	.40
136	Yavin 4: Jungle DARK U2	.50	1.00
137	Black 2 R1	4.00	8.00
138	Black 3 U1	.50	1.00
139	Devastator R1	4.00	8.00
140	Imperial-Class Star Destroyer U1	1.25	2.50
141	TIE Advanced x1 U2	.50	1.00
142	TIE Fighter C2	.20	.40
143	TIE Scout C2	.20	.40
144	Vaderís Custom TIE R1	6.00	12.00
145	Bantha U2	.50	1.00
146	Lift Tube DARK C2	.20	.40
147	Sandcrawler DARK R2	1.25	2.50
148	Ubrikkian 9000 Z001 C2	.20	.40
149	Assault Rifle R2	1.25	2.50

150 Blaster Rifle DARK C1	.20	.40
151 Boosted TIE Cannon U1	.50	1.00
152 Dark Jedi Lightsaber U1	.60	1.25
153 Gaderffii Stick C2	.20	.40
154 Han Seeker R2	1.25	2.50
155 Imperial Blaster DARK C2	.20	.40
156 Ion Cannon U1	.50	1.00
157 Laser Projector U2	.50	1.00
158 Light Repeating Blaster Rifle R1	2.00	4.00
159 Luke Seeker R2	1.25	2.50
160 Timer Mine DARK C2	.20	.40
161 Turbolaser Battery R2	1.25	2.50
162 Vader's Lightsaber R1	5.00	10.00
163 2X-3KPR (Tooex) U1	.50	1.00
164 Beru Lars U2	.50	1.00
165 Biggs Darklighter R2	1.25	2.50
166 BoShek U1	.50	1.00
167 C-3PO (See-Threepio) R1	5.00	10.00
168 CZ-3 (Seezee-Three) C1	.20	.40
169 Dice Ibegon R2	1.25	2.50
170 Dutch R1	4.00	8.00
171 Figrin D'an U2	.50	1.00
172 General Dodonna U1	.50	1.00
173 Han Solo R1	7.50	15.00
174 Jawa LIGHT C2	.20	.40
175 Jek Porkins U1	.50	1.00
176 Kabe U1	.50	1.00
177 KaliFalnI Cindros R1	2.00	4.00
178 Leesub Sirln R2	.20	.40
179 Leia Organa R1	1.25	2.50
180 LIN-V8K (Elleyein-Veeatekay) C1	6.00	12.00
181 Luke Skywalker R1	10.00	20.00
182 Momaw Nadon U2	.50	1.00
183 Obi-Wan Kenobi R1	6.00	12.00
184 Owen Lars U1	.50	1.00
185 Pops U1	.50	1.00
186 R2-X2 (Artoo-Extoo) C2	.20	.40
187 R4-E1 (Arfour-Eeone) C2	.20	.40
188 Rebel Guard C2	.20	.40
189 Rebel Pilot C2	.20	.40
190 Rebel Trooper C3	.20	.40
191 Red Leader R1	4.00	8.00
192 Shistavanen Wolfman C2	.20	.40
193 Talz C2	.20	.40
194 WED-9-M1 'Bantha' Droid R2	1.25	2.50
195 Wioslea U1	.50	1.00
196 Caller LIGHT U2	.50	1.00
197 Electrobinoculars C2	.20	.40
198 Fusion Generator Supply Tanks LIGHT C2	.20	.40
199 Hydroponics Station C2	.50	1.00
200 Restraining Bolt LIGHT C2	.20	.40
201 Targeting Computer U1	.50	1.00
202 Tatooine Utility Belt C2	.20	.40
203 Vaporator C2	.20	.40
204 A Tremor In The Force U1	.50	1.00
205 Affect Mind R1	2.00	4.00
206 Beggar R1	2.00	4.00
207 Crash Site Memorial U1	.50	1.00
208 Death Star Plans R1	2.00	4.00
209 Demotion R2	1.25	2.50
210 Disarmed Light R1	2.00	4.00
211 Ellorrs Madak C2	.20	.40
212 Eyes In The Dark U1	.50	1.00
213 Jawa Siesta U1	.50	1.00
214 Kessel LIGHT U2	2.00	4.00
215 K'lor'slug R1	.50	1.00
216 Lightsaber Proficiency R1	2.00	4.00
217 Mantellian Savrip R2	1.25	2.50
218 Nightfall U1	.50	1.00
219 Obi-Wan's Cape R1	2.00	4.00
220 Our Most Desperate Hour R1	2.00	4.00
221 Plastoid Armor U2	.50	1.00
222 Rebel Planners R2	1.25	2.50

223 Restricted Deployment U1	.50	1.00
224 Revolution R1	2.00	4.00
225 Rycar Ryjerd U1	.50	1.00
226 Sailtorr Kal Fas C2	.20	.40
227 Special Modifications U1	.50	1.00
228 Traffic Control U2	.50	1.00
229 Tusken Breath Mask U1	.50	1.00
230 Yavin Sentry U2	.50	1.00
231 Yerka Mig U1	.20	.40
232 A Few Maneuvers C2	.20	.40
233 Alter LIGHT U1	.50	1.00
234 Beru Stew U2	.50	1.00
235 Cantina Brawl R1	2.00	4.00
236 Collision! C2	.20	.40
237 Combined Attack C2	.20	.40
238 Don't Get Cocky R1	2.00	4.00
239 Don't Underestimate Our Chances C1	.20	.40
240 Droid Shutdown C2	.20	.40
241 Escape Pod U2	.50	1.00
242 Friendly Fire C2	.20	.40
243 Full Throttle R2	1.25	2.50
244 Gift Of The Mentor R1	2.00	4.00
245 Han's Back U2	.50	1.00
246 Han's Dice C2	.20	.40
247 Hear Me Baby, Hold Together C2	.20	.40
248 Help Me Obi-Wan Kenobi R1	2.00	4.00
249 How Did We Get Into This Mess? U2	.50	1.00
250 Hyper Escape C2	.20	.40
251 I've Got A Bad Feeling About This C2	.20	.40
252 It Could Be Worse C2	1.25	2.50
253 Into The Garbage Chute, Flyboy R2	.20	.40
254 Jedi Presence R1	2.00	4.00
255 Krayt Dragon Howl R1	2.00	4.00
256 Leia's Back U2	.50	1.00
257 Luke's Back U2	.50	1.00
258 Move Along... R1	2.00	4.00
259 Nabrun Leids U2	.50	1.00
260 Narrow Escape C2	.20	.40
261 Noble Sacrifice R2	1.25	2.50
262 Old Ben C2	.20	.40
263 On The Edge R2	1.25	2.50
264 Out Of Nowhere U2	.50	1.00
265 Panic U1	.50	1.00
266 Radar Scanner C2	.20	.40
267 Rebel Barrier C2	.20	.40
268 Rebel Reinforcements C1	.20	.40
269 Return Of A Jedi U2	.50	1.00
270 Scomp Link Access C2	.20	.40
271 Sense LIGHT U1	.50	1.00
272 Skywalkers R1	2.00	4.00
273 Solo Han R2	1.25	2.50
274 Spaceport Speeders U2	.50	1.00
275 Surprise Assault C1	.20	.40
276 Thank The Maker R2	1.25	2.50
277 The Bith Shuffle C2	.20	.40
278 The Force Is Strong With This One R2	1.25	2.50
279 This Is All Your Fault U1	.50	1.00
280 Utinni! LIGHT R1	2.00	4.00
281 Warrior's Courage R2	1.25	2.50
282 We're Doomed C2	.20	.40
283 Alderaan LIGHT U2	1.25	2.50
284 Dantooine LIGHT U1	.50	1.00
285 Death Star: Detention Block Control Room U2	.50	1.00
286 Death Star: Docking Bay 327 LIGHT C2	.20	.40
287 Death Star: Trash Compactor U1	.50	1.00
288 Kessel LIGHT U2	.50	1.00
289 Tatooine LIGHT C2	.20	.40
290 Tatooine: Cantina LIGHT R2	1.25	2.50
291 Tatooine: Docking Bay 94 LIGHT C2	.20	.40
292 Tatooine: Dune Sea C1	.20	.40
293 Tatooine: Jawa Camp LIGHT C1	.20	.40
294 Tatooine: Lars' Moisture Farm LIGHT U2	.50	1.00
295 Tatooine: Mos Eisley LIGHT C1	.50	1.00

296 Tatooine: Obi-Wan's Hut R1	2.00	4.00
297 Yavin 4: LIGHT C2	.20	.40
298 Yavin 4: Docking Bay LIGHT C1	.20	.40
299 Yavin 4: Jungle LIGHT C2	2.00	4.00
300 Yavin 4: Massassi Throne Room R1	.50	1.00
301 Yavin 4: Massassi War Room U2	.50	1.00
302 Corellian Corvette U2	.60	1.25
303 Gold 1 R2	1.25	2.50
304 Gold 5 R2	1.25	2.50
305 Millenium Falcon R1	5.00	10.00
306 Red 1 U1	.50	1.00
307 Red 3 R2	1.25	2.50
308 X-wing C2	.20	.40
309 Y-wing C2	.20	.40
310 Lift Tube LIGHT C2	.20	.40
311 Luke's X-34 Landspeeder U2	.50	1.00
312 Sandcrawler LIGHT R2	1.25	2.50
313 SoroSuub V-35 Landspeeder C2	.20	.40
314 Blaster C2	.20	.40
315 Blaster Rifle LIGHT C2	.20	.40
316 Han's Heavy Blaster Pistol R2	1.25	2.50
317 Jedi Lightsaber U1	.50	1.00
318 Leia's Sporting Blaster U1	.50	1.00
319 Obi-Wan's Lightsaber R1	4.00	8.00
320 Proton Torpedoes C2	.20	.40
321 Quad Laser Cannon U1	.50	1.00
322 Tagge Seeker R2	1.25	2.50
323 Tarkin Seeker R2	1.25	2.50
324 Timer Mine LIGHT C2	.20	.40

1996 Star Wars Hoth

RELEASED IN NOVEMBER 1996

1 AT-AT Driver C2	.20	.40
2 Admiral Ozzel R1	2.00	4.00
3 Captain Lennox U1	.60	1.25
4 Captain Piett R2	2.00	4.00
5 FX-10 (Effex-ten) C2	.20	.40
6 General Veers R1	5.00	10.00
7 Imperial Gunner C2	.20	.40
8 Lieutenant Cabbel U2	.60	1.25
9 Probe Droid C2	.20	.40
10 Snowtrooper C3	.20	.40
11 Snowtrooper Officer C1	.20	.40
12 Wampa R2	2.00	4.00
13 Deflector Shield Generators U2	.60	1.25
14 Evacuation Control U1	.60	1.25
15 Portable Fusion Generator C2	.20	.40
16 Probe Antennae U2	.60	1.25
17 Breached Defenses U2	.60	1.25
18 Death Mark R1	2.00	4.00
19 Death Squadron U1	.60	1.25
20 Frostbite LIGHT C2	.20	.40
21 Frozen Dinner R1	2.00	4.00

TRADING CARD GAMES AND MINIATURES

22 High Anxiety R1	2.00	4.00
23 Ice Storm LIGHT U1	.60	1.25
24 Image Of The Dark Lord R2	2.00	4.00
25 Imperial Domination U1	.60	1.25
26 Meteor Impact? R1	2.00	4.00
27 Mournful Roar R1	2.00	4.00
28 Responsibility Of Command R1	2.00	4.00
29 Silence Is Golden U2	.60	1.25
30 The Shield Doors Must Be Closed U1	.60	1.25
31 This Is Just Wrong R1	2.00	4.00
32 Too Cold For Speeders U1	.60	1.25
33 Weapon Malfunction R1	2.00	4.00
34 Target The Main Generator R2	2.00	4.00
35 A Dark Time For The Rebellion C1	.20	.40
36 Cold Feet C2	.20	.40
37 Collapsing Corridor R2	2.00	4.00
38 ComScan Detection C2	.20	.40
39 Crash Landing U1	.60	1.25
40 Debris Zone R2	2.00	4.00
41 Direct Hit U1	.60	1.25
42 Exhaustion U2	.60	1.25
43 Exposure U1	.60	1.25
44 Furry Fury R2	2.00	4.00
45 He Hasnít Come Back Yet C2	.20	.40
46 Iíd Just As Soon Kiss A Wookiee C2	.20	.40
47 Imperial Supply C1	.20	.40
48 Lightsaber Deficiency U1	.60	1.25
49 Oh, Switch Off C2	.20	.40
50 Our First Catch Of The Day C2	.20	.40
51 Probe Telemetry C2	.20	.40
52 Scruffy-Looking Nerf Herder R2	2.00	4.00
53 Self-Destruct Mechanism U1	.60	1.25
54 Stop Motion C2	.20	.40
55 Tactical Support R2	2.00	4.00
56 Thatís It, The Rebels Are There! U2	.60	1.25
57 Trample R1	2.00	4.00
58 Turn It Off! Turn It Off! C1	.20	.40
59 Walker Barrage U1	.60	1.25
60 Wall Of Fire U1	.60	1.25
61 Yaggle Gakkle R2	2.00	4.00
62 Hoth DARK U2	.60	1.25
63 Hoth: Defensive Perimeter LIGHT C2	.20	.40
64 Hoth: Echo Command Center	.60	1.25
65 Hoth: Echo Corridor DARK U2	.60	1.25
66 Hoth: Echo Docking Bay LIGHT C2	.20	.40
67 Hoth: Ice Plains C2	.20	.40
68 Hoth: North Ridge LIGHT C2	.20	.40
69 Hoth: Wampa Cave R2	2.00	4.00
70 Ord Mantell LIGHT U2	.60	1.25
71 Stalker R1	6.00	12.00
72 Tyrant R1	5.00	10.00
73 Blizzard 1 R1	4.00	8.00
74 Blizzard 2 R2	2.00	4.00
75 Blizzard Scout 1 R1	4.00	8.00
76 Blizzard Walker U2	.60	1.25
77 AT-AT Cannon U1	.60	1.25
78 Echo Base Operations R2	2.00	4.00
79 Infantry Mine LIGHT C2	.20	.40
80 Probe Droid Laser U2	.60	1.25
81 Vehicle Mine LIGHT C2	.20	.40
82 2-1B (Too-Onebee) R1	2.00	4.00
83 Cal Alder U2	.60	1.25
84 Commander Luke Skywalker R1	10.00	20.00
85 Dack Ralter R2	2.00	4.00
86 Derek ëHobbieí Klivian U1	.60	1.25
87 Electro-Rangefinder U1	.60	1.25
88 Echo Base Trooper Officer C1	.20	.40
89 Echo Trooper Backpack C2	.20	.40
90 FX-7 (Effex-Seven) C2	.20	.40
91 General Carlist Rieekan R2	2.00	4.00
92 Jeroen Webb U1	.60	1.25
93 K-3PO (Kay-Threepio) R1	2.00	4.00
94 Major Bren Derlin R2	2.00	4.00

95 R2 Sensor Array C2	.20	.40
96 R5-M2 (Arfive-Emmtoo) C2	.20	.40
97 Rebel Scout C1	.20	.40
98 Rogue Gunner C2	.20	.40
99 Romas Lock Navander U2	.60	1.25
100 Shawn Valdez U1	.60	1.25
101 Tamizander Rey U2	.60	1.25
102 Tauntaun Handler C2	.20	.40
103 Tigran Jamiro U1	.60	1.25
104 Toryn Farr U1	.60	1.25
105 WED-1016 ëTechieí Droid C1	.20	.40
106 Wes Janson R2	2.00	4.00
107 Wyron Serper U2	.60	1.25
108 Zev Senesca R2	2.00	4.00
109 Artillery Remote R2	2.00	4.00
110 EG-4 (Eegee-Four) C1	.20	.40
111 Hoth LIGHT U2	.60	1.25
112 R-3PO (Ar-Threepio) DARK R2	2.00	4.00
112 R-3PO (Ar-Threepio) LIGHT R2	2.00	4.00
113 Bacta Tank R2	3.00	6.00
114 Disarming Creature R1	2.00	4.00
115 Echo Base Trooper C3	.20	.40
116 E-web Blaster C1	.20	.40
117 Frostbite DARK C2	.20	.40
118 Ice Storm DARK U1	.60	1.25
119 Tauntaun Bones U1	.60	1.25
120 The First Transport Is Away! R1	2.00	4.00
121 Attack Pattern Delta U1	.60	1.25
122 Dark Dissension R1	2.00	4.00
123 Fall Back! C2	.20	.40
124 I Thought They Smelled Bad	2.00	4.00
125 It Can Wait C2	.20	.40
126 Lucky Shot U1	.60	1.25
127 Nice Of You Guys To Drop By C2	.20	.40
128 One More Pass U1	.60	1.25
129 Perimeter Scan C2	.20	.40
130 Rug Hug R1	2.00	4.00
131 Under Attack U1	.60	1.25
132 Walker Sighting U2	.60	1.25
133 Whoís Scruffy-Looking? R1	2.00	4.00
134 You Have Failed Me	2.00	4.00
135 You Will Go To The Dagobah System R1	2.00	4.00
136 Hoth Survival Gear C2	.20	.40
137 Hoth: Defensive Perimeter DARK C2	.20	.40
138 Hoth: Echo Command Center	.60	1.25
139 Hoth: Echo Corridor LIGHT C2	.20	.40
140 Hoth: Echo Docking Bay DARK C2	.20	.40
141 Hoth: Echo Med Lab C2	.20	.40
142 Hoth: Main Power Generators U2	.60	1.25
143 Hoth: North Ridge DARK C2	.20	.40
144 Hoth: Snow Trench C2	.20	.40
145 Ord Mantell DARK C2	.20	.40
146 Medium Transport U2	.60	1.25
147 Rogue 1 R1	4.00	8.00
148 Rogue 2 R2	2.00	4.00
149 Rogue 3 R1	4.00	8.00
150 Snowspeeder U2	.60	1.25
151 Tauntaun C2	.20	.40
152 Anakinís Lightsaber R1	10.00	20.00
153 Atgar Laser Cannon U2	.60	1.25
154 Concussion Grenade R1	2.00	4.00
155 Dual Laser Cannon U1	.60	1.25
156 Golan Laser Battery U1	.60	1.25
157 Infantry Mine DARK C2	.20	.40
158 Medium Repeating Blaster Cannon C1	.20	.40
159 Planet Defender Ion Cannon R2	2.00	4.00
160 Power Harpoon U1	.60	1.25
161 Surface Defense Cannon R2	2.00	4.00
162 Vehicle Mine DARK C2	.20	.40

1996 Star Wars Jedi Pack

RELEASED IN 1996

1 Hyperoute Navigation Chart PM	.60	1.25
2 Dark Forces PM	.60	1.25
3 Eriadu PM	.60	1.25
4 For Luck PM	.60	1.25
5 Gravity Shadow PM	.60	1.25
6 Han PM	.60	1.25
7 Leia PM	.60	1.25
8 Lukeís T-16 Skyhopper PM	.60	1.25
9 Motti PM	.60	1.25
10 Tarkin PM	.60	1.25
11 Tedn Dahai PM	.60	1.25

1996 Star Wars A New Hope

RELEASED IN JULY 1996

1 Advosze C2	.20	.40
2 Captain Khurgee U1	.60	1.25
3 DS-61-4 R2	2.00	4.00
4 Dannik Jerriko R1	2.00	4.00
5 Danz Borin U2	.60	1.25
6 Death Star R2	6.00	12.00
7 Defel C2	.20	.40
8 Greedo R1	5.00	10.00
9 Hem Dazon R1	2.00	4.00
10 IT-O (Eyetee-Oh) R1	2.00	4.00
11 Imperial Commander C2	.20	.40
12 Imperial Squad Leader C3	.20	.40
13 Lirin Carín U2	.60	1.25
14 Lt. Pol Treidum C1	.20	.40
15 Lt. Shann Childsen U1	.60	1.25
16 Mosep U2	.60	1.25
17 Officer Evax C1	.20	.40
18 R2-Q2 (Artoo-Kyootoo) C2	.20	.40
19 R3-T6 (Arthree-Teesix) R1	2.00	4.00
20 R5-A2 (Arfive-Aytoo) C2	.20	.40
21 Reegesk U2	.60	1.25
22 Reserve Pilot U1	.60	1.25
23 Rodian C2	.20	.40
24 Tech Moír U2	.60	1.25
25 Trooper Davin Felth R2	2.00	4.00
26 U-3PO (Yoo-Threepio) R1	2.00	4.00
27 URoRRuRiRiR U2	.60	1.25
28 WED15-I7 ëSeptoidí Droid U2	.60	1.25
29 Dianoga R2	2.00	4.00
30 Death Star Tractor Beam R2	2.00	4.00
31 Hypo R1	2.00	4.00
32 Laser Gate U2	.60	1.25
33 Maneuver Check R2	2.00	4.00
34 Tractor Beam U1	.60	1.25
35 Astromech Shortage U2	.60	1.25
36 Besieged R2	2.00	4.00
37 Come With Me C2	.20	.40

#	Card		
38	Dark Waters R2	2.00	4.00
39	Hyperwave Scan U1	.60	1.25
40	Imperial Justice C2	.20	.40
41	Krayt Dragon Bones U1	.60	1.25
42	Merc Sunlet C2	.20	.40
43	Program Trap U1	.60	1.25
44	Spice Mines Of Kessel R1	2.00	4.00
45	Swilla Corey C2	.20	.40
46	Tentacle C2	.20	.40
47	Thereíll Be Hell To Pay U2	.60	1.25
48	Undercover LIGHT U2	.60	1.25
49	Commence Primary Ignition R2	2.00	4.00
50	Evader U1	.60	1.25
51	Ghhhk C2	.20	.40
52	Iím On The Leader R1	2.00	4.00
53	Informant U1	.60	1.25
54	Monnok C2	.20	.40
55	Ngíok C2	.20	.40
56	Oo-ta Goo-ta, Solo? C2	.20	.40
57	Retract the Bridge R1	2.00	4.00
58	Sniper U1	.60	1.25
59	Stunning Leader C2	.20	.40
60	This Is Some Rescue! U1	.60	1.25
61	We Have A Prisoner C2	.20	.40
62	Death Star Gunner C1	.20	.40
63	Death Star: Conference Room U1	.60	1.25
64	Imperial Holotable R1	2.00	4.00
65	Kashyyyk LIGHTC1	.20	.40
66	Kiffex R1	2.00	4.00
67	Ralltiir LIGHT C1	.20	.40
68	Sandcrawler: Droid Junkheap R1	2.00	4.00
69	Tatooine: Bluffs R1	2.00	4.00
70	Black 4 U2	.60	1.25
71	Conquest R1	6.00	12.00
72	TIE Assault Squadron U1	.60	1.25
73	TIE Vanguard C2	.20	.40
74	Victory-Class Star Destroyer U1	.60	1.25
75	Bespin Motors Void Spider THX 1138 C2	.20	.40
76	Mobquet A-1 Deluxe Floater C2	.20	.40
77	Enhanced TIE Laser Cannon C2	.20	.40
78	Jawa Blaster C2	.20	.40
79	Leia Seeker R2	2.00	4.00
80	Superlaser R2	3.00	6.00
81	URoRRuRiRiRís Hunting Rifle U1	.60	1.25
82	Arcona C2	.20	.40
83	Brainiac R1	4.00	8.00
84	Chewbacca R2	10.00	20.00
85	Commander Evram Lajaie C1	.20	.40
86	Commander Vanden Willard U2	.60	1.25
87	Corellian C2	.20	.40
88	Doikk Naíts U2	.60	1.25
89	Garouf Lafoe U2	.60	1.25
90	Het Nkik U2	.60	1.25
91	Hunchback R1	2.00	4.00
92	Ickabel Gíont U2	.60	1.25
93	Magnetic Suction Tube DARK R2	2.00	4.00
94	Nalan Cheel U2	.60	1.25
95	R2-D2 (Artoo-Detoo) R2	10.00	20.00
96	R5-D4 (Arfive-Defour) C2	.20	.40
97	RA-7 (Aray-Seven) C2	.20	.40
98	Rebel Commander C2	.20	.40
99	Rebel Squad Leader C3	.20	.40
100	Rebel Tech C1	.20	.40
101	Saurin C2	.20	.40
102	Tiree U2	.60	1.25
103	Tzizvvt R2	2.00	4.00
104	Wedge Antilles R1	10.00	20.00
105	Zutton C1	.20	.40
106	Fire Extinguisher U2	.60	1.25
107	Magnetic Suction Tube LIGHT R2	2.00	4.00
108	Rectenna C2	.20	.40
109	Remote C2	.20	.40
110	Sensor Panel U1	.60	1.25
111	Cell 2187 R1	2.00	4.00
112	Commence Recharging R2	2.00	4.00
113	Eject! Eject! C2	.20	.40
114	Grappling Hook C2	.20	.40
115	Logistical Delay U2	.60	1.25
116	Lukeís Cape R1	2.00	4.00
117	M-HYD ëBinaryí Droid U1	.60	1.25
118	Scanner Techs U1	.60	1.25
119	Solomahal C2	.20	.40
120	Theyíre On Dantooine R1	2.00	4.00
121	Undercover DARK U2	.60	1.25
122	Whatíre You Tryiní To Push On Us? U2	.60	1.25
123	Attack Run R2	2.00	4.00
124	Advance Preparation U1	.60	1.25
125	Alternatives To Fighting U1	.60	1.25
126	Blast The Door, Kid! C2	.20	.40
127	Blue Milk C2	.20	.40
128	Corellian Slip C2	.20	.40
129	Double Agent R2	2.00	4.00
130	Grimtaash C2	.20	.40
131	Houjix C2	.20	.40
132	I Have A Very Bad Feeling About This C2	.20	.40
133	Iím Here To Rescue You U1	.60	1.25
134	Let The Wookiee Win R1	7.50	15.00
135	Out Of Commission U2	.60	1.25
136	Quite A Mercenary C2	.20	.40
137	Sabotage U1	.60	1.25
138	Sorry About The Mess U1	.60	1.25
139	Wookiee Roar R1	2.00	4.00
140	Y-wing Assault Squadron U1	.60	1.25
141	Clakídor VII R2	2.00	4.00
142	Corellia R1	2.00	4.00
143	Death Star: Trench R2	2.00	4.00
144	Dejarik Hologameboard R1	2.00	4.00
145	Kashyyyk DARK C1	.20	.40
146	Ralltiir DARK C1	.20	.40
147	Sandcrawler: Loading Bay R1	2.00	4.00
148	Yavin 4: Massassi Ruins U1	.60	1.25
149	Youíre All Clear Kid! R1	2.00	4.00
150	Gold 2 U1	.60	1.25
151	Red 2 R1	2.00	4.00
152	Red 5 R1	5.00	10.00
153	Red 6 U1	.60	1.25
154	Tantive IV R1	6.00	12.00
155	Yavin 4: Briefing Room U1	.60	1.25
156	Incom T-16 Skyhopper C2	.20	.40
157	Rogue Bantha U1	.60	1.25
158	Bowcaster R2	2.00	4.00
159	Jawa Ion Gun C2	.20	.40
160	Lukeís Hunting Rifle U1	.60	1.25
161	Motti Seeker R2	2.00	4.00
162	SW-4 Ion Cannon R2	2.00	4.00

1997 Star Wars Cloud City

RELEASED IN NOVEMBER 1997			
1	Ability, Ability, Ability C	.20	.40
2	Abyss U	.60	1.25
3	Access Denied C	.20	.40
4	Advantage R	2.00	4.00
5	Aiiii! Aaa! Aggggggggggg! R	2.00	4.00
6	All My Urchins R	2.00	4.00
7	All Too Easy R	2.00	4.00
8	Ambush R	2.00	4.00
9	Armed And Dangerous U	.60	1.25
10	Artoo, Come Back At Once! R	2.00	4.00
11	As Good As Gone C	.20	.40
12	Atmospheric Assault R	2.00	4.00
13	Beldonís Eye R	2.00	4.00
14	Bespin DARK U	.60	1.25
15	Bespin LIGHT U	.60	1.25
16	Bespin: Cloud City DARK U	.60	1.25
17	Bespin: Cloud City LIGHT U	.60	1.25
18	Binders C	.20	.40
19	Bionic Hand R	2.00	4.00
20	Blasted Droid C	.20	.40
21	Blaster Proficiency C	.20	.40
22	Boba Fett R	12.00	25.00
23	Boba Fettís Blaster Rifle R	5.00	10.00
24	Bounty C	.20	.40
25	Brief Loss Of Control R	2.00	4.00
26	Bright Hope R	2.00	4.00
27	Captain Bewil R	2.00	4.00
28	Captain Han Solo R	12.00	25.00
29	Captive Fury U	.60	1.25
30	Captive Pursuit C	.20	.40
31	Carbon-Freezing U	.60	1.25
32	Carbonite Chamber Console U	.60	1.25
33	Chasm U	.60	1.25
34	Chief Retwin R	2.00	4.00
35	Civil Disorder C	.20	.40
36	Clash Of Sabers U	.60	1.25
37	Cloud Car DARK C	.20	.40
38	Cloud Car LIGHT C	.20	.40
39	Cloud City Blaster DARK C	.20	.40
40	Cloud City Blaster LIGHT C	.20	.40
41	Cloud City Engineer C	.20	.40
42	Cloud City Sabacc DARK U	.60	1.25
43	Cloud City Sabacc LIGHT U	.60	1.25
44	Cloud City Technician C	.20	.40
45	Cloud City Trooper DARK C	.20	.40
46	Cloud City Trooper LIGHT C	.20	.40
47	Cloud City: Carbonite Chamber DARK U	.60	1.25
48	Cloud City: Carbonite Chamber LIGHT U	.60	1.25
49	Cloud City: Chasm Walkway DARK C	.20	.40
50	Cloud City: Chasm Walkway LIGHT C	.20	.40
51	Cloud City: Dining Room R	2.00	4.00
52	Cloud City: East Platform	.20	.40
53	Cloud City: Guest Quarters R	2.00	4.00
54	Cloud City: Incinerator DARK C	.20	.40
55	Cloud City: Incinerator LIGHT C	.20	.40
56	Cloud City: Lower Corridor DARK U	.60	1.25
57	Cloud City: Lower Corridor LIGHT U	.60	1.25
58	Cloud City: Platform 327	.20	.40
59	Cloud City: Security Tower C	.20	.40
60	Cloud City: Upper Plaza	.20	.40
61	Cloud City: Upper Plaza	.60	1.25
62	Clouds DARK C	.20	.40
63	Clouds LIGHT C	.20	.40
64	Commander Desanne U	.60	1.25
65	Computer Interface C	.20	.40
66	Courage Of A Skywalker R	2.00	4.00
67	Crack Shot U	.60	1.25
68	Cyborg Construct U	.60	1.25
69	Dark Approach R	2.00	4.00
70	Dark Deal R	2.00	4.00
71	Dark Strike C	.20	.40
72	Dash C	.20	.40

73	Despair R	2.00	4.00
74	Desperate Reach U	.60	1.25
75	Dismantle On Sight R	2.00	4.00
76	Dodge C	.20	.40
77	Double Back U	.60	1.25
78	Double-Crossing, No-Good Swindler C	.20	.40
79	E Chu Ta C	.20	.40
80	E-3PO R	2.00	4.00
81	End This Destructive Conflict R	2.00	4.00
82	Epic Duel R	3.00	6.00
83	Fall Of The Empire U	.60	1.25
84	Fall Of The Legend U	.60	1.25
85	Flight Escort R	2.00	4.00
86	Focused Attack R	2.00	4.00
87	Force Field R	2.00	4.00
88	Forced Landing R	2.00	4.00
89	Frozen Assets R	2.00	4.00
90	Gambleris Luck R	2.00	4.00
91	Glancing Blow R	2.00	4.00
92	Haven R	2.00	4.00
93	Heis All Yours, Bounty Hunter R	2.00	4.00
94	Heart Of The Chasm U	.60	1.25
95	Hero Of A Thousand Devices U	.60	1.25
96	Higher Ground R	2.00	4.00
97	Hindsight R	2.00	4.00
98	Hopping Mad R	2.00	4.00
99	Human Shield C	.20	.40
100	I Am Your Father R	2.00	4.00
101	I Donit Need Their Scum, Either R	2.00	4.00
102	I Had No Choice R	2.00	4.00
103	Imperial Decree U	.60	1.25
104	Imperial Trooper Guard Dainsom U	.60	1.25
105	Impressive, Most Impressive R	2.00	4.00
106	Innocent Scoundrel U	.60	1.25
107	Interrogation Array R	2.00	4.00
108	Into The Ventilation Shaft, Lefty R	2.00	4.00
109	Itis A Trap! U	.60	1.25
110	Kebyc U	.60	1.25
111	Keep Your Eyes Open C	.20	.40
112	Lando Calrissian DARK R	7.50	15.00
113	Lando Calrissian LIGHT R	7.50	15.00
114	Landois Wrist Comlink U	.60	1.25
115	Leia Of Alderaan R	3.00	6.00
116	Levitation Attack U	.60	1.25
117	Lieutenant Cecius U	.60	1.25
118	Lieutenant Sheckil R	2.00	4.00
119	Lift Tube Escape C	.20	.40
120	Lobot R	4.00	8.00
121	Lukeis Blaster Pistol R	2.00	4.00
122	Mandalorian Armor R	3.00	6.00
123	Mostly Armless R	2.00	4.00
124	NOOOOOOOOOOOO! R	2.00	4.00
125	Obsidian 7 R	3.00	6.00
126	Obsidian 8 R	3.00	6.00
127	Off The Edge R	2.00	4.00
128	Old Pirates R	2.00	4.00
129	Out Of Somewhere U	.60	1.25
130	Path Of Least Resistance C	.20	.40
131	Point Man R	2.00	4.00
132	Prepare The Chamber U	.60	1.25
133	Princess Leia R	6.00	12.00
134	Projective Telepathy U	.60	1.25
135	Protector R	2.00	4.00
136	Punch It! R	2.00	4.00
137	Put That Down C	.20	.40
138	Redemption R	4.00	8.00
139	Release Your Anger R	2.00	4.00
140	Rendezvous Point On Tatooine R	2.00	4.00
141	Rescue In The Clouds C	.20	.40
142	Restricted Access C	.20	.40
143	Rite Of Passage C	.20	.40
144	Shattered Hope U	.60	1.25
145	Shocking Information C	.20	.40
146	Shocking Revelation C	.20	.40
147	Slave I R	6.00	12.00
148	Slip Sliding Away R	2.00	4.00
149	Smoke Screen R	2.00	4.00
150	Somersault C	.20	.40
151	Sonic Bombardment U	.60	1.25
152	Special Delivery C	.20	.40
153	Surprise R	2.00	4.00
154	Surreptitious Glance R	2.00	4.00
155	Swing-And-A-Miss U	.60	1.25
156	The Emperoris Prize R	2.00	4.00
157	This Is Even Better R	2.00	4.00
158	This Is Still Wrong R	2.00	4.00
159	Tibanna Gas Miner DARK C	.20	.40
160	Tibanna Gas Miner LIGHT C	.20	.40
161	TIE Sentry Ships C	.20	.40
162	Treva Horme U	.60	1.25
163	Trooper Assault C	.20	.40
164	Trooper Jerrol Blendin U	.60	1.25
165	Trooper Utris Mitoc U	.60	1.25
166	Ugloste R	2.00	4.00
167	Ugnaught C	.20	.40
168	Uncontrollable Fury R	2.00	4.00
169	Vaderis Bounty R	2.00	4.00
170	Vaderis Cape R	2.00	4.00
171	Weill Find Han R	2.00	4.00
172	Weire The Bait R	2.00	4.00
173	Weapon Levitation U	.60	1.25
174	Weapon Of An Ungrateful Son U	.60	1.25
175	Weather Vane DARK U	.60	1.25
176	Weather Vane LIGHT U	.60	1.25
177	Why Didnit You Tell Me? R	2.00	4.00
178	Wiorkettle U	.60	1.25
179	Wookiee Strangle R	2.00	4.00
180	You Are Beaten U	.60	1.25

1997 Star Wars Dagobah

RELEASED ON APRIL 23, 1997

1	3,720 To 1 C	.20	.40
2	4-LOM R	4.00	8.00
3	4-LOMis Concussion Rifle R	3.00	6.00
4	A Dangerous Time C	.20	.40
5	A Jediis Strength U	.60	1.25
6	Anger, Fear, Aggression C	.20	.40
7	Anoat DARK U	.60	1.25
8	Anoat LIGHT U	.60	1.25
9	Apology Accepted C	.20	.40
10	Asteroid Field DARK C	.20	.40
11	Asteroid Field LIGHT C	.20	.40
12	Asteroid Sanctuary C	.20	.40
13	Asteroids Do Not Concern Me R	2.00	4.00
14	Astroid Sanctuary C	.20	.40
15	Astromech Translator C	.20	.40
16	At Peace R	2.00	4.00
17	Avenger R	6.00	12.00
18	Away Put Your Weapon U	.60	1.25
19	Awwww, Cannot Get Your Ship Out C	.20	.40
20	Bad Feeling Have I R	2.00	4.00
21	Big One DARK U	.60	1.25
22	Big One LIGHT U	.60	1.25
23	Big One: Asteroid Cave	.60	1.25
24	Big One: Asteroid Cave	.60	1.25
25	Blasted Varmints C	.20	.40
26	Bog-wing DARK C	.20	.40
27	Bog-wing LIGHT C	.20	.40
28	Bombing Run R	2.00	4.00
29	Bossk R	5.00	10.00
30	Bosskis Mortar Gun R	3.00	6.00
31	Broken Concentration R	2.00	4.00
32	Captain Needa R	3.00	6.00
33	Close Call C	.20	.40
34	Closer?! U	.60	1.25
35	Comm Chief C	.20	.40
36	Commander Brandei U	.60	1.25
37	Commander Gherant U	.60	1.25
38	Commander Nemet U	.60	1.25
39	Control DARK U	.60	1.25
40	Control LIGHT U	.60	1.25
41	Corporal Derdram U	.60	1.25
42	Corporal Vandolay U	.60	1.25
43	Corrosive Damage R	2.00	4.00
44	Dagobah U	.60	1.25
45	Dagobah: Bog Clearing R	2.00	4.00
46	Dagobah: Cave R	2.00	4.00
47	Dagobah: Jungle U	.60	1.25
48	Dagobah: Swamp U	.60	1.25
49	Dagobah: Training Area C	.20	.40
50	Dagobah: Yodais Hut R	3.00	6.00
51	Defensive Fire C	.20	.40
52	Dengar R	2.00	4.00
53	Dengaris Blaster Carbine R	2.00	4.00
54	Descent Into The Dark R	2.00	4.00
55	Do, Or Do Not C	.20	.40
56	Domain Of Evil U	.60	1.25
57	Dragonsnake R	2.00	4.00
58	Droid Sensorscope C	.20	.40
59	Effective Repairs R	2.00	4.00
60	Egregious Pilot Error R	2.00	4.00
61	Encampment C	.20	.40
62	Executor R	12.00	25.00
63	Executor: Comm Station U	.60	1.25
64	Executor: Control Station U	.60	1.25
65	Executor: Holotheatre R	2.00	4.00
66	Executor: Main Corridor C	.20	.40
67	Executor: Meditation Chamber R	2.00	4.00
68	Failure At The Cave R	2.00	4.00
69	Fear C	.20	.40
70	Field Promotion R	2.00	4.00
71	Flagship R	2.00	4.00
72	Flash Of Insight U	.60	1.25
73	Found Someone You Have U	.60	1.25
74	Frustration R	2.00	4.00
75	Great Warrior C	.20	.40
76	Grounded Starfighter U	.60	1.25
77	Hanis Toolkit R	2.00	4.00
78	He Is Not Ready C	.20	.40
79	Hiding In The Garbage R	2.00	4.00
80	HoloNet Transmission U	.60	1.25
81	Hounds Tooth R	4.00	8.00
82	I Have A Bad Feeling About This R	2.00	4.00
83	I Want That Ship R	2.00	4.00
84	IG-2000 R	3.00	6.00
85	IG-88 R	6.00	12.00
86	IG-88is Neural Inhibitor R	3.00	6.00
87	IG-88is Pulse Cannon R	3.00	6.00
88	Imbalance U	.60	1.25

89 Imperial Helmsman C	.20	.40
90 Ineffective Maneuver U	.60	1.25
91 It Is The Future You See R	2.00	4.00
92 Jedi Levitation R	2.00	4.00
93 Knowledge And Defense C	.20	.40
94 Landing Claw R	2.00	4.00
95 Lando System? R	2.00	4.00
96 Levitation U	.60	1.25
97 Lieutenant Commander Ardan U	.60	1.25
98 Lieutenant Suba R	2.00	4.00
99 Lieutenant Venka U	.60	1.25
100 Light Maneuvers R	2.00	4.00
101 Location, Location, Location R	2.00	4.00
102 Lost In Space R	2.00	4.00
103 Lost Relay C	.20	.40
104 Lukeís Backpack R	2.00	4.00
105 Mist Hunter R	3.00	6.00
106 Moving To Attack Position C	.20	.40
107 Much Anger In Him R	2.00	4.00
108 Mynock DARK C	.20	.40
109 Mynock LIGHT C	.20	.40
110 Never Tell Me The Odds C	.20	.40
111 No Disintegrations! R	2.00	4.00
112 Nudj C	.20	.40
113 Obi-Wanís Apparition R	2.00	4.00
114 Order To Engage R	2.00	4.00
115 Polarized Negative Power Coupling R	2.00	4.00
116 Portable Fusion Generator C	.20	.40
117 Precision Targeting U	.60	1.25
118 Proton Bombs U	.60	1.25
119 Punishing One R	3.00	6.00
120 Quick Draw C	.20	.40
121 Raithal DARK R	2.00	4.00
122 Raithal LIGHT U	.60	1.25
123 Rebel Flight Suit C	.20	.40
124 Recoil In Fear C	.20	.40
125 Reflection R	2.00	4.00
126 Report To Lord Vader R	2.00	4.00
127 Res Luk Raíauf R	2.00	4.00
128 Retractable Arm C	.20	.40
129 Rogue Asteroid DARK C	.20	.40
130 Rogue Asteroid LIGHT C	.20	.40
131 Rycarís Run R	2.00	4.00
132 Scramble U	.60	1.25
133 Shoo! Shoo! U	.60	1.25
134 Shot In The Dark U	.60	1.25
135 Shut Him Up Or Shut Him Down U	.60	1.25
136 Size Matters Not R	2.00	4.00
137 Sleen C	.20	.40
138 Smugglerís Blues R	2.00	4.00
139 Something Hit Us! U	.60	1.25
140 Son of Skywalker R	12.00	25.00
141 Space Slug DARK R	2.00	4.00
142 Space Slug LIGHT U	.60	1.25
143 Star Destroyer: Launch Bay C	.20	.40
144 Starship Levitation U	.60	1.25
145 Stone Pile R	2.00	4.00
146 Sudden Impact U	.60	1.25
147 Take Evasive Action C	.20	.40
148 The Dark Path R	2.00	4.00
149 The Professor R	2.00	4.00
150 There Is No Try C	.20	.40
151 Theyíd Be Crazy To Follow Us C	.20	.40
152 This Is More Like It R	2.00	4.00
153 This Is No Cave R	2.00	4.00
154 Those Rebels Wonít Escape Us C	.20	.40
155 Through The Force Things	2.00	4.00
156 TIE Avenger C	.20	.40
157 TIE Bomber U	.60	1.25
158 Tight Squeeze R	2.00	4.00
159 Transmission Terminated U	.60	1.25
160 Tunnel Vision U	.60	1.25
161 Uncertain Is The Future C	.20	.40
162 Unexpected Interruption R	2.00	4.00

163 Vine Snake DARK C	.20	.40
164 Vine Snake LIGHT C	.20	.40
165 Visage Of The Emperor R	2.00	4.00
166 Visored Vision C	.20	.40
167 Voyeur C	.20	.40
168 Warrant Officer MiKae U	.60	1.25
169 Wars Not Make One Great U	.60	1.25
170 We Can Still Outmaneuver Them R	2.00	4.00
171 We Donít Need Their Scum R	2.00	4.00
172 WHAAAAAAAAOOOOW! R	2.00	4.00
173 What Is Thy Bidding, My Master? R	2.00	4.00
174 Yoda R	12.00	25.00
175 Yoda Stew U	.60	1.25
176 Yoda, You Seek Yoda R	2.00	4.00
177 Yodaís Gimer Stick R	2.00	4.00
178 Yodaís Hope U	.60	1.25
179 You Do Have Your Moments U	.60	1.25
180 Zuckuss R	3.00	6.00
181 Zuckussí Snare Rifle R	2.00	4.00

1997 Star Wars First Anthology

RELEASED IN 1997

1 Boba Fett PV	1.25	2.50
2 Commander Wedge Antilles PV	1.25	2.50
3 Death Star Assault Squadron PV	1.25	2.50
4 Hit And Run PV	1.25	2.50
5 Jabbaís Influence PV	1.25	2.50
6 X-wing Assault Squadron PV	1.25	2.50

1997 Star Wars Rebel Leaders

RELEASED IN 1997

1 Gold Leader In Gold 1 PM	1.50	3.00
2 Red Leader In Red 1 PM	1.50	3.00

1998 Star Wars Enhanced Premiere

RELEASED IN 1998

1 Boba Fett With Blaster Rifle PM	1.25	2.50
2 Darth Vader With Lightsaber PM	1.25	2.50
3 Han With Heavy Blaster Pistol PM	1.25	2.50
4 Leia With Blaster Rifle PM	1.25	2.50
5 Luke With Lightsaber PM	1.25	2.50
6 Obi-Wan With Lightsaber PM	1.25	2.50

1998 Star Wars Jabba's Palace

RELEASED IN MAY 1998

1 8D8 R	2.00	4.00
2 A Gift U	.60	1.25
3 Abyssin C	.20	.40
4 Abyssin Ornament U	.60	1.25
5 All Wrapped Up U	.60	1.25
6 Amanaman R	2.00	4.00
7 Amanin C	.20	.40
8 Antipersonnel Laser Cannon U	.60	1.25
9 Aqualish C	.20	.40
10 Arc Welder U	.60	1.25
11 Ardon Vapor Crell R	2.00	4.00
12 Artoo R	5.00	10.00
13 Artoo, I Have A Bad	.60	1.25
14 Attark R	2.00	4.00
15 Aved Luun R	2.00	4.00
16 Bíomarr Monk C	.20	.40
17 .Bane Malar R	2.00	4.00
18 Bantha Fodder C	.20	.40
19 Barada R	2.00	4.00
20 Baragwin C	.20	.40
21 Bargaining Table U	.60	1.25
22 Beedo R	2.00	4.00
23 BG-J38 R	2.00	4.00
24 Bib Fortuna R	2.00	4.00
25 Blaster Deflection R	2.00	4.00
26 Bo Shuda U	.60	1.25
27 Bubo U	.60	1.25
28 Cane Adiss U	.60	1.25
29 Chadra-Fan C	.20	.40
30 Chevin C	.20	.40
31 Choke C	.20	.40
32 Corellian Retort U	.60	1.25
33 CZ-4 C	.20	.40
34 Den Of Thieves U	.60	1.25
35 Dengarís Modified Riot Gun R	2.00	4.00
36 Devaronian C	.20	.40
37 Donít Forget The Droids C	.20	.40
38 Double Laser Cannon R	2.00	4.00
39 Droopy McCool R	2.00	4.00
40 Dune Sea Sabacc DARK U	.60	1.25
41 Dune Sea Sabacc LIGHT U	.60	1.25

42 Elom C		.20	.40
43 Ephant Mon R		2.00	4.00
44 EV-9D9 R		2.00	4.00
45 Fallen Portal U		.60	1.25
46 Florn Lamproid C		.20	.40
47 Fozec R		2.00	4.00
48 Gailid R		2.00	4.00
49 Gamorrean Ax C		.20	.40
50 Gamorrean Guard C		.20	.40
51 Garon Nas Tal R		2.00	4.00
52 Geezum R		2.00	4.00
53 Ghoel R		2.00	4.00
54 Giran R		2.00	4.00
55 Gran C		.20	.40
56 Hinemthe C		.20	.40
57 Herat R		2.00	4.00
58 Hermi Odle R		2.00	4.00
59 Hidden Compartment U		.60	1.25
60 Hidden Weapons U		.60	1.25
61 Holoprojector U		.60	1.25
62 Hutt Bounty R		2.00	4.00
63 Hutt Smooch U		.60	1.25
64 I Must Be Allowed To Speak R		2.00	4.00
65 Information Exchange U		.60	1.25
66 Ishi Tib C		.20	.40
67 Ithorian C		.20	.40
68 Ji'Quille R		2.00	4.00
69 Jabba the Hutt R		6.00	12.00
70 Jabba's Palace Sabacc DARK U		.60	1.25
71 Jabba's Palace Sabacc LIGHT U		.60	1.25
72 Jabba's Palace:		.60	1.25
73 Jabba's Palace:		.60	1.25
74 Jabba's Palace: Droid Workshop U		.60	1.25
75 Jabba's Palace: Dungeon U		.60	1.25
76 Jabba's Palace:		.60	1.25
77 Jabba's Palace:		.60	1.25
78 Jabba's Palace: Rancor Pit U		.60	1.25
79 Jabba's Sail Barge R		4.00	8.00
80 Jabba's Sail Barge: Passenger Deck R		2.00	4.00
81 Jedi Mind Trick R		2.00	4.00
82 Jess R		2.00	4.00
83 Jet Pack U		.60	1.25
84 Kalit R		2.00	4.00
85 Ke Chu Ke Kakuta? C		.20	.40
86 Kiffex R		2.00	4.00
87 Kirdo III R		2.00	4.00
88 Kithaba R		2.00	4.00
89 Kitonak C		.20	.40
90 Klaatu R		2.00	4.00
91 Klatooinian Revolutionary C		.20	.40
92 Laudica R		2.00	4.00
93 Leslomy Tacema R		2.00	4.00
94 Life Debt R		2.00	4.00
95 Loje Nella R		2.00	4.00
96 Malakili R		2.00	4.00
97 Mandalorian Mishap U		.60	1.25
98 Max Rebo R		2.00	4.00
99 Mos Eisley Blaster DARK C		.20	.40
100 Mos Eisley Blaster LIGHT C		.20	.40
101 Murttoc Yine R		2.00	4.00
102 Nal Hutta R		2.00	4.00
103 Nar Shaddaa Wind Chimes U		.60	1.25
104 Nikto C		.20	.40
105 Nizuc Bek R		2.00	4.00
106 None Shall Pass C		.20	.40
107 Nysad R		2.00	4.00
108 Oola R		2.00	4.00
109 Ortolan C		.20	.40
110 Ortugg R		2.00	4.00
111 Palejo Reshad R		2.00	4.00
112 Pote Snitkin R		2.00	4.00
113 Princess Leia Organa R		5.00	10.00
114 Projection Of A Skywalker U		.60	1.25

115 Pucumir Thryss R		2.00	4.00
116 Quarren C		.20	.40
117 Quick Reflexes C		.20	.40
118 Rikik Dinec, Hero Of The Dune Sea R		2.00	4.00
119 Rancor R		4.00	8.00
120 Rayc Ryjerd R		2.00	4.00
121 Ree-Yees R		2.00	4.00
122 Rennek R		2.00	4.00
123 Resistance U		.60	1.25
124 Revealed U		.60	1.25
125 Saelt-Marae R		2.00	4.00
126 Salacious Crumb R		2.00	4.00
127 Sandwhirl DARK U		.60	1.25
128 Sandwhirl LIGHT U		.60	1.25
129 Scum And Villainy R		2.00	4.00
130 Sergeant Doallyn R		2.00	4.00
131 Shasa Tiel R		2.00	4.00
132 Sic-Six C		.20	.40
133 Skiff DARK C		.20	.40
134 Skiff LIGHT C		.20	.40
135 Skrilling C		.20	.40
136 Skull U		.60	1.25
137 Snivvian C		.20	.40
138 Someone Who Loves You U		.60	1.25
139 Strangle R		2.00	4.00
140 Tamtel Skreej R		4.00	8.00
141 Tanus Spijek R		2.00	4.00
142 Tatooine: Desert DARK C		.20	.40
143 Tatooine: Desert LIGHT C		.20	.40
144 Tatooine: Great Pit Of Carkoon U		.60	1.25
145 Tatooine: Hutt Canyon U		.60	1.25
146 Tatooine: Jabba's Palace U		.60	1.25
147 Taym Dren-garen R		2.00	4.00
148 Tessek R		2.00	4.00
149 The Signal C		.20	.40
150 Thermal Detonator R		3.00	6.00
151 Thul Fain R		2.00	4.00
152 Tibrin R		2.00	4.00
153 Torture C		.20	.40
154 Trandoshan C		.20	.40
155 Trap Door U		.60	1.25
156 Twi'lek Advisor C		.20	.40
157 Ultimatum U		.60	1.25
158 Unfriendly Fire R		2.00	4.00
159 Vedain R		2.00	4.00
160 Velken Tezeri R		2.00	4.00
161 Vibro-Ax DARK C		.20	.40
162 Vibro-Ax LIGHT C		.20	.40
163 Vizam R		2.00	4.00
164 Vul Tazaene R		2.00	4.00
165 Weapon Levitation U		.60	1.25
166 Weequay Guard C		.20	.40
167 Weequay Hunter C		.20	.40
168 Weequay Marksman U		.60	1.25
169 Weequay Skiff Master C		.20	.40
170 Well Guarded U		.60	1.25
171 Whiphid C		.20	.40
172 Wittin R		2.00	4.00
173 Wooof R		2.00	4.00
174 Worrt U		.60	1.25
175 Wounded Wookiee U		.60	1.25
176 Yarkora C		.20	.40
177 Yarna d'al' Gargan U		.60	1.25
178 You Will Take Me To Jabba Now C		.20	.40
179 Yoxgit R		2.00	4.00
180 Yuzzum C		.20	.40

1998 Star Wars Official Tournament Sealed Deck

RELEASED IN 1998

1 Arleil Schous PM		.60	1.25
2 Black Squadron TIE PM		.60	1.25

3 Chall Bekan PM		.60	1.25
4 Corulag DARK PM		.60	1.25
5 Corulag LIGHT PM		.60	1.25
6 Dreadnaught-Class Heavy Cruiser PM		.60	1.25
7 Faithful Service PM		.60	1.25
8 Forced Servitude PM		.60	1.25
9 Gold Squadron Y-wing PM		.60	1.25
10 It's a Hit! PM		.60	1.25
11 Obsidian Squadron TIE PM		.60	1.25
12 Rebel Trooper Recruit PM		.60	1.25
13 Red Squadron X-wing PM		.60	1.25
14 Stormtrooper Cadet PM		.60	1.25
15 Tarkin's Orders PM		.60	1.25
16 Tatooine: Jundland Wastes PM		.60	1.25
17 Tatooine: Tusken Canyon PM		.60	1.25
18 Z-95 Headhunter PM		.60	1.25

1998 Star Wars Second Anthology

RELEASED IN 1998

1 Flagship Operations PV		1.50	3.00
2 Mon Calamari Star Cruiser PV		1.50	3.00
3 Mon Mothma PV		1.50	3.00
4 Rapid Deployment PV		1.50	3.00
5 Sarlacc PV		1.50	3.00
6 Thunderflare PV		1.50	3.00

1998 Star Wars Special Edition

RELEASED IN NOVEMBER 1998

1 ISB Operations / Empire's Sinister Agents R		1.50	3.00
2 2X-7KPR (Tooex) C		.20	.40
3 A Bright Center To The Universe U		.60	1.25
4 A Day Long Remembered U		.60	1.25
5 A Real Hero R		1.50	3.00

#	Card	Price 1	Price 2
6	Air-2 Racing Swoop C	.20	.40
7	Ak-rev U	.60	1.25
8	Alderaan Operative C	.20	.40
9	Alert My Star Destroyer! C	.20	.40
10	All Power To Weapons C	.20	.40
11	All Wings Report In R	1.50	3.00
12	Anoat Operative DARK C	.20	.40
13	Anoat Operative LIGHT C	.20	.40
14	Antilles Maneuver C	.20	.40
15	ASP-707 (Ayesspee) F	1.00	2.00
16	Balanced Attack U	.60	1.25
17	Bantha Herd R	1.25	2.50
18	Barquin Dían U	.60	1.25
19	Ben Kenobi R	3.00	6.00
20	Blast Points C	.20	.40
21	Blown Clear U	.60	1.25
22	Boba Fett R	2.50	5.00
23	Boelo R	1.50	3.00
24	Bossk In Houndís Tooth R	1.50	3.00
25	Bothan Spy C	.20	.40
26	Bothawui F	1.00	2.00
27	Bothawui Operative C	.20	.40
28	Brangus Glee R	1.25	2.50
29	Bren Quersey U	.60	1.25
30	Bron Burs R	1.25	2.50
31	B-wing Attack Fighter F	1.00	2.00
32	Camie R	1.50	3.00
33	Carbon Chamber Testing	1.50	3.00
34	Chyler U	.60	1.25
35	Clakidor VII Operative U	.60	1.25
36	Cloud City Celebration R	1.50	3.00
37	Cloud City Occupation R	2.00	4.00
38	Cloud City: Casino DARK U	.60	1.25
39	Cloud City: Casino LIGHT U	.60	1.25
40	Cloud City: Core Tunnel U	.60	1.25
41	Cloud City: Downtown Plaza DARK R	1.50	3.00
42	Cloud City: Downtown Plaza LIGHT R	1.50	3.00
43	Cloud City: Interrogation Room C	.20	.40
44	Cloud City: North Corridor C	.20	.40
45	Cloud City: Port Town District U	.60	1.25
46	Cloud City: Upper Walkway C	.20	.40
47	Cloud City: West Gallery DARK C	.20	.40
48	Cloud City: West Gallery LIGHT C	.20	.40
49	Colonel Feyn Gospic R	1.50	3.00
50	Combat Cloud Car F	1.00	2.00
51	Come Here You Big Coward! C	.20	.40
52	Commander Wedge Antilles R	1.50	3.00
53	Coordinated Attack C	.20	.40
54	Corellia Operative U	.60	1.25
55	Corellian Engineering Corporation R	1.50	3.00
56	Corporal Grenwick R	1.25	2.50
57	Corporal Prescott U	.60	1.25
58	Corulag Operative C	.20	.40
59	Coruscant Celebration R	1.25	2.50
60	Coruscant DARK R	4.00	8.00
61	Coruscant LIGHT R	1.50	3.00
62	Coruscant: Docking Bay C	.20	.40
63	Coruscant: Imperial City U	.60	1.25
64	Coruscant: Imperial Square R	2.00	4.00
65	Counter Surprise Assault R	1.50	3.00
66	Dagobah U	.60	1.25
67	Dantooine Base Operations	1.25	2.50
68	Dantooine Operative C	.20	.40
69	Darklighter Spin C	.20	.40
70	Darth Vader, Dark Lord Of The Sith R	10.00	20.00
71	Death Squadron Star Destroyer R	1.50	3.00
72	Death Star Assault Squadron R	1.50	3.00
73	Death Star R	2.00	4.00
74	Death Star: Detention Block Control Room C	.20	.40
75	Death Star: Detention Block Corridor C	.20	.40
76	Debnoli R	1.50	3.00
77	Desert DARK F	1.00	2.00
78	Desert LIGHT F	1.00	2.00
79	Desilijic Tattoo U	.60	1.25
80	Desperate Tactics C	.20	.40
81	Destroyed Homestead R	1.50	3.00
82	Dewback C	.20	.40
83	Direct Assault C	.20	.40
84	Disruptor Pistol DARK F	1.00	2.00
85	Disruptor Pistol LIGHT F	1.00	2.00
86	Docking And Repair Facilities R	1.50	3.00
87	Dodo Bodonawieedo U	.60	1.25
88	Donít Tread On Me R	1.50	3.00
89	Down With The Emperor! U	.60	1.25
90	Dr. Evazanis Sawed-off Blaster U	.60	1.25
91	Draw Their Fire U	.60	1.25
92	Dreaded Imperial Starfleet R	2.00	4.00
93	Droid Merchant C	.20	.40
94	Dune Walker R	2.00	4.00
95	Echo Base Trooper Rifle C	.20	.40
96	Elyhek Rue U	.60	1.25
97	Entrenchment R	1.25	2.50
98	Eriadu Operative C	.20	.40
99	Executor: Docking Bay U	.60	1.25
100	Farm F	1.00	2.00
101	Feltipern Trevaggís Stun Rifle U	.60	1.25
102	Firepower C	.20	.40
103	Firin Morett U	.60	1.25
104	First Aid F	1.00	2.00
105	First Strike U	.60	1.25
106	Flare-S Racing Swoop C	.20	.40
107	Flawless Marksmanship C	.20	.40
108	Floating Refinery C	.20	.40
109	Fondor U	.60	1.25
110	Forest DARK F	1.00	2.00
111	Forest LIGHT F	1.00	2.00
112	Gela Yeens U	.60	1.25
113	General McQuarrie R	1.25	2.50
114	Gold 3 U	.60	1.25
115	Gold 4 U	.60	1.25
116	Gold 6 U	.60	1.25
117	Goo Nee Tay R	1.50	3.00
118	Greeata U	.60	1.25
119	Grondorn Muse R	1.25	2.50
120	Harc Seff U	.60	1.25
121	Harvest R	2.00	4.00
122	Heavy Fire Zone C	.20	.40
123	Heroes Of Yavin R	1.25	2.50
124	Heroic Sacrifice U	.60	1.25
125	Hidden Base	2.50	5.00
126	Hit And Run R	1.25	2.50
127	Hol Okand U	.60	1.25
128	Homing Beacon R	1.50	3.00
129	Hoth Sentry U	.60	1.25
130	Hunt Down And Destroy The Jedi	2.50	5.00
131	Hunting Party R	1.50	3.00
132	I Canít Shake Him! C	.20	.40
133	Iasa, The Traitor Of Jawa Canyon R	1.25	2.50
134	IM4-099 F	1.00	2.00
135	Imperial Atrocity R	5.00	10.00
136	Imperial Occupation / Imperial Control R	1.50	3.00
137	Imperial Propaganda R	5.00	10.00
138	In Range C	.20	.40
139	Incom Corporation R	1.25	2.50
140	InCom Engineer C	.20	.40
141	Intruder Missile DARK F	1.00	2.00
142	Intruder Missile LIGHT F	1.00	2.00
143	Itís Not My Fault! F	1.00	2.00
144	Jabba R	1.50	3.00
145	Jabbaís Influence R	1.25	2.50
146	Jabbaís Space Cruiser R	2.00	4.00
147	Jabbaís Through With You U	.60	1.25
148	Jabbaís Twerps U	.60	1.25
149	Joh Yowza R	1.25	2.50
150	Jungle DARK F	1.00	2.00
151	Jungle LIGHT F	1.00	2.00
152	Kalitis Sandcrawler R	1.50	3.00
153	Kashyyyk Operative DARK U	.60	1.25
154	Kashyyyk Operative LIGHT U	.60	1.25
155	Kessel Operative U	.60	1.25
156	Ketwol R	1.25	2.50
157	Kiffex Operative DARK U	.60	1.25
158	Kiffex Operative LIGHT U	.60	1.25
159	Kirdo III Operative C	.20	.40
160	Koensayr Manufacturing R	1.50	3.00
161	Krayt Dragon R	1.50	3.00
162	Kuat Drive Yards R	2.00	4.00
163	Kuat U	.60	1.25
164	Landois Blaster Rifle R	1.50	3.00
165	Legendary Starfighter C	.20	.40
166	Leiaís Blaster Rifle R	1.50	3.00
167	Lieutenant Lepira U	.60	1.25
168	Lieutenant Naytaan U	.60	1.25
169	Lieutenant Tarn Mison R	1.50	3.00
170	Lobel C	.20	.40
171	Lobot R	1.50	3.00
172	Local Defense U	.60	1.25
173	Local Uprising / Liberation R	1.50	3.00
174	Lyn Me U	.60	1.25
175	Major Palo Torshan R	1.50	3.00
176	Makurth F	1.00	2.00
177	Maneuvering Flaps C	.20	.40
178	Masterful Move C	.20	.40
179	Mechanical Failure R	1.25	2.50
180	Meditation R	2.00	4.00
181	Medium Bulk Freighter U	.60	1.25
182	Melas R	1.50	3.00
183	Mind What You Have Learned	2.00	4.00
184	Moisture Farmer C	.20	.40
185	Nal Hutta Operative C	.20	.40
186	Neb Dulo U	.60	1.25
187	Nebit R	1.50	3.00
188	Niado Duegad U	.60	1.25
189	Nick Of Time U	.60	1.25
190	No Bargain U	.60	1.25
191	Old Times R	1.25	2.50
192	On Target C	.20	.40
193	One-Arm R	1.50	3.00
194	Oppressive Enforcement U	.60	1.25
195	Ord Mantell Operative C	.20	.40
196	Organized Attack C	.20	.40
197	OS-72-1 In Obsidian 1 R	1.50	3.00
198	OS-72-10 R	1.50	3.00
199	OS-72-2 In Obsidian 2 R	1.50	3.00
200	Outer Rim Scout R	2.50	5.00
201	Overwhelmed C	.20	.40
202	Patrol Craft DARK C	.20	.40
203	Patrol Craft LIGHT C	.20	.40
204	Planetary Subjugation U	.60	1.25
205	Ponda Babaís Hold-out Blaster U	.60	1.25
206	Portable Scanner C	.20	.40
207	Power Pivot C	.20	.40
208	Precise Hit C	.20	.40
209	Pride Of The Empire C	.20	.40
210	Princess Organa R	2.00	4.00
211	Put All Sections On Alert C	.20	.40
212	R2-A5 (Artoo-Ayfive) U	.60	1.25
213	R3-A2 (Arthree-Aytoo) U	.60	1.25
214	R3-T2 (Arthree-Teetoo) R	1.50	3.00
215	Raithal Operative C	.20	.40
216	Ralltiir Freighter Captain F	1.00	2.00
217	Ralltiir Operations	2.50	5.00
218	Ralltiir Operative C	.20	.40
219	Rapid Fire C	.20	.40
220	Rappertunie U	.60	1.25
221	Rebel Ambush C	.20	.40
222	Rebel Base Occupation R	1.25	2.50
223	Rebel Fleet R	1.50	3.00
224	Red 10 U	.60	1.25

225 Red 7 U	.60	1.25
226 Red 8 U	.60	1.25
227 Red 9 U	.60	1.25
228 Relentless Pursuit C	.20	.40
229 Rendezvous Point R	1.50	3.00
230 Rendili F	1.00	2.00
231 Rendili StarDrive R	1.25	2.50
232 Rescue The Princess	1.50	3.00
233 Return To Base R	1.50	3.00
234 Roche U	.60	1.25
235 Rock Wart F	1.00	2.00
236 Rogue 4 R	2.50	5.00
237 Ronto DARK C	.20	.40
238 Ronto LIGHT C	.20	.40
239 RRiuruurrr R	1.50	3.00
240 Ryle Torsyn U	.60	1.25
241 Rystall R	2.50	5.00
242 Sacrifice F	1.00	2.00
243 Sandspeeder F	1.00	2.00
244 Sandtrooper F	1.00	2.00
245 Sarlacc R	1.50	3.00
246 Scrambled Transmission U	.60	1.25
247 Scurrier F	1.00	2.00
248 Secret Plans U	.60	1.25
249 Sentinel-Class Landing Craft F	1.00	2.00
250 Sergeant Edian U	.60	1.25
251 Sergeant Hollis R	1.50	3.00
252 Sergeant Major Bursk U	.60	1.25
253 Sergeant Major Enfield R	1.25	2.50
254 Sergeant Merril U	.60	1.25
255 Sergeant Narthax R	1.50	3.00
256 Sergeant Torent R	1.50	3.00
257 S-Foils C	.20	.40
258 SFS L-s9.3 Laser Cannons C	.20	.40
259 Short-Range Fighters R	1.50	3.00
260 Sienar Fleet Systems R	1.50	3.00
261 Slayn and Korpil Facilities R	1.25	2.50
262 Slight Weapons Malfunction C	.20	.40
263 Soth Petikkin R	1.25	2.50
264 Spaceport City DARK F	1.00	2.00
265 Spaceport City LIGHT F	1.00	2.00
266 Spaceport Docking Bay DARK F	1.00	2.00
267 Spaceport Docking Bay LIGHT F	1.00	2.00
268 Spaceport Prefectis Office F	1.00	2.00
269 Spaceport Street DARK F	1.00	2.00
270 Spaceport Street LIGHT F	1.00	2.00
271 Spiral R	2.00	4.00
272 Star Destroyer! R	1.50	3.00
273 Stay Sharp! U	.60	1.25
274 Steady Aim C	.20	.40
275 Strategic Reserves R	1.50	3.00
276 Suppressive Fire C	.20	.40
277 Surface Defense R	1.50	3.00
278 Swamp DARK F	1.00	2.00
279 Swamp LIGHT F	1.00	2.00
280 Swoop Mercenary F	1.00	2.00
281 Sy Snootles R	1.50	3.00
282 T-47 Battle Formation R	1.50	3.00
283 Tarkinís Bounty U	.60	1.25
284 Tatooine Celebration R	2.00	4.00
285 Tatooine Occupation R	2.50	5.00
286 Tatooine: Anchorhead F	1.00	2.00
287 Tatooine: Beggarís Canyon R	1.25	2.50
288 Tatooine: Jabbaís Palace C	.20	.40
289 Tatooine: Jawa Canyon DARK U	.60	1.25
290 Tatooine: Jawa Canyon LIGHT U	.60	1.25
291 Tatooine: Krayt Dragon Pass F	1.00	2.00
292 Tatooine: Tosche Station C	.20	.40
293 Tauntaun Skull C	.20	.40
294 Tawss Khaa R	1.25	2.50
295 The Planet That Itís Farthest From U	.60	1.25
296 Thedit R	1.50	3.00
297 Theron Nett U	.60	1.25

298 Theyíre Coming In Too Fast! C	.20	.40
299 Theyíre Tracking Us C	.20	.40
300 Theyíve Shut Down The Main Reactor C	.20	.40
301 Tibrin Operative C	.20	.40
302 TIE Defender Mark I F	1.00	2.00
303 TK-422 R	1.50	3.00
304 Trooper Sabacc DARK F	1.00	2.00
305 Trooper Sabacc LIGHT F	1.00	2.00
306 Uh-oh! U	.60	1.25
307 Umpass-stay R	1.25	2.50
308 UriRuir R	1.50	3.00
309 URoRRuRiRiRís Bantha R	1.50	3.00
310 Uutkik R	1.50	3.00
311 Vaderís Personal Shuttle R	1.50	3.00
312 Vengeance R	1.50	3.00
313 Wakeelmui U	.60	1.25
314 Watch Your Back! C	.20	.40
315 Weapons Display C	.20	.40
316 Wise Advice U	.60	1.25
317 Wittinís Sandcrawler R	1.50	3.00
318 Womp Rat C	.20	.40
319 Wookiee F	1.00	2.00
320 Wrist Comlink C	.20	.40
321 X-wing Assault Squadron R	1.50	3.00
322 X-wing Laser Cannon C	.20	.40
323 Yavin 4 Trooper F	1.00	2.00
324 Yavin 4: Massassi Headquarters R	1.50	3.00

1999 Star Wars Endor

RELEASED IN JUNE 1999

1 AT-ST Pilot C	.20	.40
2 Biker Scout Trooper C	.20	.40
3 Colonel Dyer R	2.00	4.00
4 Commander Igar R	2.00	4.00
5 Corporal Avarik U	.60	1.25
6 Corporal Drazin U	.60	1.25
7 Corporal Drelosyn R	2.00	4.00
8 Corporal Misik R	1.50	3.00
9 Corporal Oberk R	2.00	4.00
10 Elite Squadron Stormtrooper C	.20	.40
11 Lieutenant Arnet U	.60	1.25
12 Lieutenant Grond U	.60	1.25
13 Lieutenant Renz R	1.25	2.50
14 Lieutenant Watts R	2.00	4.00
15 Major Hewex R	1.25	2.50
16 Major Marquand R	2.50	5.00
17 Navy Trooper C	.20	.40
18 Navy Trooper Fenson R	1.50	3.00
19 Navy Trooper Shield Technician C	.20	.40
20 Navy Trooper Vesden U	.60	1.25
21 Sergeant Barich R	3.00	6.00
22 Sergeant Elsek U	.60	1.25
23 Sergeant Irol R	2.50	5.00

24 Sergeant Tarl U	.60	1.25
25 Sergeant Wallen R	2.50	5.00
26 An Entire Legion Of My Best Troops U	.60	1.25
27 Aratech Corporation R	1.50	3.00
28 Battle Order U	.30	.80
29 Biker Scout Gear U	.60	1.25
30 Closed Door R	1.25	2.50
31 Crossfire R	5.00	10.00
32 Early Warning Network R	1.25	2.50
33 Empireís New Order R	1.25	2.50
34 Establish Secret Base R	2.50	5.00
35 Imperial Academy Training C	.20	.40
36 Imperial Arrest Order U	.60	1.25
37 Ominous Rumors R	1.25	2.50
38 Perimeter Patrol R	1.50	3.00
39 Pinned Down U	.60	1.25
40 Relentless Tracking R	1.25	2.50
41 Search And Destroy U	.60	1.25
42 Security Precautions R	4.00	8.00
43 Well-earned Command R	1.25	2.50
44 Accelerate C	.20	.40
45 Always Thinking With Your Stomach R	4.00	8.00
46 Combat Readiness C	.20	.40
47 Compact Firepower C	.20	.40
48 Counterattack R	1.25	2.50
49 Dead Ewok C	.20	.40
50 Donit Move! C	.20	.40
51 Eee Chu Wawa! C	.20	.40
52 Endor Scout Trooper C	.20	.40
53 Freeze! U	.60	1.25
54 Go For Help! C	.20	.40
55 High-speed Tactics U	.60	1.25
56 Hot Pursuit C	.20	.40
57 Imperial Tyranny C	.20	.40
58 Itís An Older Code R	1.25	2.50
59 Main Course U	.60	1.25
60 Outflank C	.20	.40
61 Pitiful Little Band C	.20	.40
62 Scout Recon C	.20	.40
63 Sneak Attack C	.20	.40
64 Wounded Warrior R	2.50	5.00
65 You Rebel Scum R	1.50	3.00
66 Carida U	.60	1.25
67 Endor Occupation R	1.25	2.50
68 Endor: Ancient Forest U	.60	1.25
69 Endor: Back Door LIGHT U	.60	1.25
70 Endor: Bunker LIGHT U	.60	1.25
71 Endor: Dark Forest R	4.00	8.00
72 Endor: Dense Forest LIGHT C	.20	.40
73 Endor: Ewok Village LIGHT U	.60	1.25
74 Endor: Forest Clearing U	.60	1.25
75 Endor: Great Forest LIGHT C	.20	.40
76 Endor: Landing Platform	.20	.40
77 Endor DARK U	.60	1.25
78 Lambda-class Shuttle C	.20	.40
79 Speeder Bike LIGHT C	.20	.40
80 Tempest 1 R	1.25	2.50
81 Tempest Scout 1 R	1.50	3.00
82 Tempest Scout 2 R	3.00	6.00
83 Tempest Scout 3 R	1.25	2.50
84 Tempest Scout 4 R	4.00	8.00
85 Tempest Scout 5 R	3.00	6.00
86 Tempest Scout 6 R	4.00	8.00
87 Tempest Scout U	.60	1.25
88 AT-ST Dual Cannon R	10.00	20.00
89 Scout Blaster C	.20	.40
90 Speeder Bike Cannon U	.60	1.25
91 Captain Yutani U	.60	1.25
92 Chewbacca of Kashyyyk R	1.25	2.50
93 Chief Chirpa R	1.50	3.00
94 Corporal Beezer U	.60	1.25
95 Corporal Delevar U	.60	1.25
96 Corporal Janse U	.60	1.25
97 Corporal Kensaric R	2.00	4.00

#	Card		
98	Daughter of Skywalker R	12.00	25.00
99	Dressellian Commando C	.20	.40
100	Endor LIGHT U	.60	1.25
101	Ewok Sentry C	.20	.40
102	Ewok Spearman C	.20	.40
103	Ewok Tribesman C	.20	.40
104	General Crix Madine R	1.50	3.00
105	General Solo R	1.25	2.50
106	Graak R	1.25	2.50
107	Kazak R	1.50	3.00
108	Lieutenant Greeve R	1.25	2.50
109	Lieutenant Page R	2.50	5.00
110	Logray R	1.25	2.50
111	Lumat U	.60	1.25
112	Mon Mothma R	2.00	4.00
113	Orrimaarko R	1.25	2.50
114	Paploo U	.60	1.25
115	Rabin U	.60	1.25
116	Romba R	1.25	2.50
117	Sergeant Brooks Carlson R	1.25	2.50
118	Sergeant Bruckman R	1.25	2.50
119	Sergeant Junkin U	.60	1.25
120	Teebo R	1.25	2.50
121	Threepio R	2.00	4.00
122	Wicket R	1.25	2.50
123	Wuta U	.60	1.25
124	Aim High R	1.50	3.00
125	Battle Plan U	.60	1.25
126	Commando Training C	.20	.40
127	Count Me In R	1.25	2.50
128	I Hope She's All Right U	.60	1.25
129	I Wonder Who They Found U	.60	1.25
130	Insurrection U	.60	1.25
131	That's One R	1.25	2.50
132	Wokling R	10.00	20.00
133	Deactivate The Shield Generator R	2.00	4.00
134	Careful Planning C	.20	.40
135	Covert Landing U	.60	1.25
136	Endor Operations / Imperial Outpost R	4.00	8.00
137	Ewok And Roll C	.20	.40
138	Ewok Log Jam C	.20	.40
139	Ewok Rescue C	.20	.40
140	Firefight C	.20	.40
141	Fly Casual R	1.25	2.50
142	Free Ride U	.60	1.25
143	Get Alongside That One U	.60	1.25
144	Here We Go Again R	1.25	2.50
145	I Have A Really Bad	.20	.40
146	I Know R	2.00	4.00
147	Lost In The Wilderness R	1.25	2.50
148	Rapid Deployment R	1.25	2.50
149	Sound The Attack C	.20	.40
150	Surprise Counter Assault R	1.25	2.50
151	Take The Initiative C	.20	.40
152	This Is Absolutely Right R	1.25	2.50
153	Throw Me Another Charge U	.60	1.25
154	Were You Looking For Me? R	6.00	12.00
155	Wookiee Guide C	.20	.40
156	Yub Yub! C	.20	.40
157	Chandrila U	.60	1.25
158	Endor Celebration R	1.25	2.50
159	Endor: Back Door DARK U	.60	1.25
160	Endor: Bunker DARK U	.60	1.25
161	Endor: Chief Chirpa's Hut R	5.00	10.00
162	Endor: Dense Forest DARK C	.20	.40
163	Endor: Ewok Village DARK U	.60	1.25
164	Endor: Great Forest DARK C	.20	.40
165	Endor: Hidden Forest Trail U	.60	1.25
166	Endor: Landing Platform	.20	.40
167	Endor: Rebel Landing Site (Forest) R	4.00	8.00
168	Rebel Strike Team	2.00	4.00
169	Tydirium R	2.00	4.00
170	YT-1300 Transport C	.20	.40
171	Chewie's AT-ST R	5.00	10.00

172	Ewok Glider C	.20	.40
173	Speeder Bike DARK C	.20	.40
174	A280 Sharpshooter Rifle R	4.00	8.00
175	BlasTech E-11B Blaster Rifle C	.20	.40
176	Chewbacca's Bowcaster R	4.00	8.00
177	Ewok Bow C	.20	.40
178	Ewok Catapult U	.60	1.25
179	Ewok Spear C	.20	.40
180	Explosive Charge U	.60	1.25

1999 Star Wars Enhanced Cloud City

RELEASED IN 1999

1	4-LOM With Concussion Rifle PM	2.50	5.00
2	Any Methods Necessary PM	3.00	6.00
3	Boba Fett in Slave I PM	1.50	3.00
4	Chewie With Blaster Rifle PM	1.50	3.00
5	Crush The Rebellion PM	2.00	4.00
6	Dengar In Punishing One PM	1.50	3.00
7	IG-88 With Riot Gun PM	5.00	10.00
8	Lando In Millennium Falcon PM	1.50	3.00
9	Lando With Blaster Pistol PM	1.50	3.00
10	Quiet Mining Colony	1.50	3.00
11	This Deal Is Getting Worse All The Time	1.50	3.00
12	Z-95 Bespin Defense Fighter PM	1.50	3.00

1999 Star Wars Enhanced Jabba's Palace

RELEASE IN 1999

1	Bossk With Mortar Gun PM	1.50	3.00
2	Boushh PM	2.00	4.00
3	Court Of The Vile Gangster PM	1.50	3.00
4	Dengar With Blaster Carbine PM	1.50	3.00
5	IG-88 In IG-2000 PM	1.50	3.00
6	Jodo Kast PM	2.50	5.00
7	Mara Jade, The Emperor's Hand PM	12.00	25.00
8	Mara Jade's Lightsaber PM	2.50	5.00
9	Master Luke PM	4.00	8.00
10	See-Threepio PM	1.50	3.00
11	You Can Either Profit By This...	1.50	3.00
12	Zuckuss In Mist Hunter PM	2.00	4.00

2000 Star Wars Death Star II

RELEASED IN JULY 2000

1	Accuser R	1.50	3.00
2	Admiral Ackbar XR	1.50	3.00
3	Admiral Chiraneau R	2.00	4.00
4	Admiral Piett XR	1.25	2.50
5	Anakin Skywalker R	1.25	2.50
6	Aquaris C	.15	.30
7	A-wing C	.15	.30
8	A-wing Cannon C	.15	.30
9	Baron Soontir Fel R	2.00	4.00
10	Battle Deployment R	1.50	3.00

#	Card		
11	Black 11 R	1.25	2.50
12	Blue Squadron 5 U	.50	1.00
13	Blue Squadron B-wing R	2.00	4.00
14	Bring Him Before Me	1.25	2.50
	Take Your Father's Place R		
15	B-wing Attack Squadron R	1.25	2.50
16	B-wing Bomber C	.15	.30
17	Capital Support R	1.25	2.50
18	Captain Godherdt U	.50	1.00
19	Captain Jonus U	.50	1.00
20	Captain Sarkli R	1.25	2.50
21	Captain Verrack U	.50	1.00
22	Captain Yorr U	.50	1.00
23	Chimaera R	3.00	6.00
24	Close Air Support C	.15	.30
25	Colonel Cracken R	1.25	2.50
26	Colonel Davod Jon U	.50	1.00
27	Colonel Jendon R	1.25	2.50
28	Colonel Salm U	.50	1.00
29	Combat Response C	.15	.30
30	Combined Fleet Action R	1.25	2.50
31	Commander Merrejk R	1.50	3.00
32	Concentrate All Fire R	1.25	2.50
33	Concussion Missiles DARK C	.15	.30
34	Concussion Missiles LIGHT C	.15	.30
35	Corporal Marmor U	.50	1.00
36	Corporal Midge U	.50	1.00
37	Critical Error Revealed C	.15	.30
38	Darth Vader's Lightsaber R	1.25	2.50
39	Death Star II R	1.50	3.00
40	Death Star II: Capacitors C	.15	.30
41	Death Star II: Coolant Shaft C	.15	.30
42	Death Star II: Docking Bay C	.15	.30
43	Death Star II: Reactor Core C	.15	.30
44	Death Star II: Throne Room R	1.25	2.50
45	Defiance R	1.50	3.00
46	Desperate Counter C	.15	.30
47	Dominator R	1.25	2.50
48	DS-181-3 U	.50	1.00
49	DS-181-4 U	.50	1.00
50	Emperor Palpatine UR	30.00	60.00
51	Emperor's Personal Shuttle R	1.25	2.50
52	Emperor's Power U	.50	1.00
53	Endor Shield U	.50	1.00
54	Enhanced Proton Torpedoes C	.15	.30
55	Fighter Cover R	2.50	5.00
56	Fighters Coming In R	1.25	2.50
57	First Officer Thaneespi R	1.25	2.50
58	Flagship Executor R	1.50	3.00
59	Flagship Operations R	1.25	2.50
60	Force Lightning R	2.50	5.00
61	Force Pike C	.15	.30
62	Gall C	.15	.30
63	General Calrissian R	1.25	2.50
64	General Walex Blissex U	.50	1.00
65	Gold Squadron 1 R	1.25	2.50
66	Gray Squadron 1 U	.50	1.00
67	Gray Squadron 2 U	.50	1.00
68	Gray Squadron Y-wing Pilot C	.15	.30
69	Green Leader R	1.25	2.50
70	Green Squadron 1 R	1.25	2.50
71	Green Squadron 3 R	1.25	2.50
72	Green Squadron A-wing R	1.50	3.00
73	Green Squadron Pilot C	.15	.30
74	Head Back To The Surface C	.15	.30
75	Heading For The Medical Frigate C	.15	.30
76	Heavy Turbolaser Battery DARK C	.15	.30
77	Heavy Turbolaser Battery LIGHT C	.15	.30
78	Home One R	5.00	10.00
79	Home One: Docking Bay C	.15	.30
80	Home One: War Room R	1.50	3.00
81	Honor Of The Jedi U	.50	1.00
82	I Feel The Conflict U	.50	1.00
83	I'll Take The Leader R	3.00	6.00

84 Iím With You Too R	2.00	4.00
85 Imperial Command R	5.00	10.00
86 Inconsequential Losses C	.15	.30
87 Independence R	1.50	3.00
88 Insertion Planning C	.15	.30
89 Insignificant Rebellion U	.50	1.00
90 Intensify The Forward Batteries R	1.25	2.50
91 Janus Greejatus R	1.25	2.50
92 Judicator R	2.00	4.00
93 Karie Neth U	.50	1.00
94 Keir Santage U	.50	1.00
95 Kin Kian U	.50	1.00
96 Launching The Assault R	1.25	2.50
97 Leave Them To Me C	.15	.30
98 Letís Keep A Little Optimism Here C	.15	.30
99 Liberty R	1.50	3.00
100 Lieutenant Blount R	1.25	2.50
101 Lieutenant Endicott U	.50	1.00
102 Lieutenant Hebsly U	.50	1.00
103 Lieutenant síToo Vees U	.50	1.00
104 Lieutenant Telsij U	.50	1.00
105 Lord Vader R	10.00	20.00
106 Luke Skywalker, Jedi Knight UR	30.00	60.00
107 Lukeís Lightsaber R	2.00	4.00
108 Luminous U	.50	1.00
109 Major Haashín U	.50	1.00
110 Major Mianda U	.50	1.00
111 Major Olander Brit U	.50	1.00
112 Major Panno U	.50	1.00
113 Major Rhymer U	.50	1.00
114 Major Turr Phennir U	.50	1.00
115 Masanya R	2.00	4.00
116 Menace Fades C	.15	.30
117 Mobilization Points C	.15	.30
118 Moff Jerjerrod R	1.25	2.50
119 Mon Calamari DARK C	.15	.30
120 Mon Calamari LIGHT C	.15	.30
121 Mon Calamari Star Cruiser R	1.50	3.00
122 Myn Kyneugh R	1.25	2.50
123 Nebulon-B Frigate U	.50	1.00
124 Nien Nunb R	1.50	3.00
125 Obsidian 10 U	.50	1.00
126 Onyx 1 R	1.50	3.00
127 Onyx 2 U	.50	1.00
128 Operational As Planned C	.15	.30
129 Orbital Mine C	.15	.30
130 Our Only Hope U	.50	1.00
131 Overseeing It Personally R	1.25	2.50
132 Prepared Defenses C	.15	.30
133 Rebel Leadership R	4.00	8.00
134 Red Squadron 1 R	1.25	2.50
135 Red Squadron 4 U	.50	1.00
136 Red Squadron 7 U	.50	1.00
137 Rise, My Friend R	1.25	2.50
138 Royal Escort C	.15	.30
139 Royal Guard C	.15	.30
140 Saber 1 R	7.50	15.00
141 Saber 2 U	.50	1.00
142 Saber 3 U	.50	1.00
143 Saber 4 U	.50	1.00
144 Scimitar 1 U	.50	1.00
145 Scimitar 2 U	.50	1.00
146 Scimitar Squadron TIE C	.15	.30
147 Scythe 1 U	.50	1.00
148 Scythe 3 U	.50	1.00
149 Scythe Squadron TIE C	.15	.30
150 SFS L-s7.2 TIE Cannon C	.15	.30
151 Sim Aloo R	1.25	2.50
152 Something Special Planned For Them C	.15	.30
153 Squadron Assignments C	.15	.30
154 Staging Areas C	.15	.30
155 Strike Planning R	1.25	2.50
156 Strikeforce C	.15	.30
157 Sullust DARK C	.15	.30

158 Sullust LIGHT C	.15	.30
159 Superficial Damage C	.15	.30
160 Superlaser Mark II U	.50	1.00
161 Taking Them With Us R	1.50	3.00
162 Tala 1 R	1.25	2.50
163 Tala 2 R	1.25	2.50
164 Ten Numb R	1.25	2.50
165 That Thingís Operational R	1.25	2.50
166 The Emperorís Shield R	1.25	2.50
167 The Emperorís Sword R	1.25	2.50
168 The Time For Our Attack Has Come C	.15	.30
169 The Way Of Things U	.50	1.00
170 There Is Good In Him I Can Save Him R	1.25	2.50
171 Thunderflare R	1.25	2.50
172 TIE Interceptor C	.15	.30
173 Twilight Is Upon Me R	1.25	2.50
174 Tycho Celchu R	1.50	3.00
175 Visage R	1.25	2.50
176 Weíre In Attack Position Now R	3.00	6.00
177 Wedge Antilles, Red Squadron Leader R	2.00	4.00
178 You Cannot Hide Forever U	.50	1.00
179 You Must Confront Vader R	2.00	4.00
180 Young Fool R	1.25	2.50
181 Your Destiny C	.15	.30
182 Your Insight Serves You Well U	.50	1.00

2000 Star Wars Jabba's Palace Sealed Deck

RELEASE DATE FALL, 2000

1 Agents In The Court No Love For The Empire PM	.50	1.00
2 Hutt Influence PM	.50	1.00
3 Jabbaís Palace: Antechamber PM	.50	1.00
4 Jabbaís Palace: Lower Passages PM	.50	1.00
5 Lando With Vibro-Ax PM	.50	1.00
6 Let Them Make The First Move / My Kind Of Scum Fearless And Inventive PM	.50	1.00
7 Mercenary Pilot PM	.50	1.00
8 Mighty Jabba PM	.50	1.00
9 No Escape PM	.50	1.00
10 Ounee Ta PM	.50	1.00
11 Palace Raider PM	.50	1.00
12 Power Of The Hutt PM	.50	1.00
13 Racing Skiff DARK PM	.50	1.00
14 Racing Skiff LIGHT PM	.50	1.00
15 Seeking An Audience PM	.50	1.00
16 Stun Blaster DARK PM	.50	1.00
17 Stun Blaster LIGHT PM	.50	1.00
18 Tatooine: Desert Heart PM	.50	1.00
19 Tatooine: Hutt Trade Route (Desert) PM	.50	1.00
20 Underworld Contacts PM	.50	1.00

2000 Star Wars Reflections II

RELEASED IN DECEMBER 2000		
1 There Is No Try and Oppressive Enforcement PM	.75	1.50
2 Abyssin Ornament and Wounded Wookiee PM	.50	1.00
3 Agents Of Black Sun Vengence Of The Dark Prince PM	.50	1.00
4 Alter and Collateral Damage PM	.75	1.50
5 Alter and Friendly Fire PM	.75	1.50
6 Arica PM	2.50	5.00
7 Artoo and Threepio PM	.75	1.50
8 Black Sun Fleet PM	.50	1.00
9 Captain Gilad Pellaeon PM	.75	1.50
10 Chewbacca, Protector PM	.75	1.50
11 Control and Set For Stun PM	.75	1.50
12 Control and Tunnel Vision PM	1.25	2.50
13 Corran Horn PM	2.00	4.00
14 Dark Maneuvers and Tallon Roll PM	1.25	2.50
15 Dash Rendar PM	1.50	3.00
16 Defensive Fire and Hutt Smooch PM	.50	1.00
17 Do, Or Do Not and Wise Advice PM	.50	1.00
18 Dr Evazan and Ponda Baba PM	.50	1.00
19 Evader and Monnok PM	.75	1.50
20 Ghhhk and Those Rebels Wonít Escape Us PM	.50	1.00
21 Grand Admiral Thrawn PM	3.00	6.00
22 Guri PM	1.50	3.00
23 Houjix and Out Of Nowhere PM	.75	1.50
24 Jabbaís Prize PM	.50	1.00
25 Kir Kanos PM	.50	1.00
26 LE-BO2D9 [Leebo] PM	.50	1.00
27 Luke Skywalker, Rebel Scout PM	1.25	2.50
28 Mercenary Armor PM	.50	1.00
29 Mirax Terrik PM	.75	1.50
30 Nar Shaddaa Wind Chimes and Out Of Somewhere PM	.50	1.00
31 No Questions Asked PM	.50	1.00
32 Obi-Wanís Journal PM	.50	1.00
33 Ommni Box and Itís Worse PM	.50	1.00
34 Out of Commission and Transmission Terminated PM	1.25	2.50
35 Outrider PM	.75	1.50
36 Owen Lars and Beru Lars PM	.50	1.00
37 Path Of Least Resistance and Revealed PM	.50	1.00
38 Prince Xizor PM	2.00	4.00
39 Pulsar Skate PM	.50	1.00
40 Sense and Recoil In Fear PM	.75	1.50
41 Sense and Uncertain Is The Future PM	.75	1.50
42 Shocking Information and Grimtaash PM	.50	1.00
43 Sniper and Dark Strike PM	.50	1.00
44 Snoova PM	1.25	2.50
45 Sorry About The Mess and Blaster Proficiency PM	.75	1.50
46 Stinger PM	.50	1.00
47 Sunsdown and Too Cold For Speeders PM	.50	1.00
48 Talon Karrde PM	.75	1.50
49 The Bith Shuffle and Desperate Reach PM	.50	1.00
50 The Emperor PM	2.00	4.00
51 Vigo PM	2.00	4.00
52 Virago PM	.50	1.00
53 Watch Your Step This Place Can Be A Little Rough PM	.50	1.00
54 Yoda Stew and You Do Have Your Moments PM	.50	1.00

2000 Star Wars Third Anthology

RELEASED IN 2000

1 A New Secret Base PM	1.25	2.50
2 Artoo-Detoo In Red 5 PM	1.25	2.50
3 Echo Base Garrison PM	1.25	2.50
4 Massassi Base Operations	1.25	2.50
One In A Million PM		
5 Prisoner 2187 PM	1.25	2.50
6 Set Your Course For Alderaan	1.25	2.50
The Ultimate Power In The Universe PM		

2001 Star Wars Coruscant

RELEASED IN AUGUST 2001

1 A Tragedy Has Occurred U	.50	1.00
2 A Vergence In The Force U	.50	1.00
3 Accepting Trade Federation Control U	.50	1.00
4 Aks Moe R	1.50	3.00
5 All Wings Report In and Darklighter Spin R	7.50	15.00
6 Allegations Of Corruption U	.50	1.00
7 Alter DARK U	.50	1.00
8 Alter LIGHT U	.50	1.00
9 Another Pathetic Lifeform U	.50	1.00
10 Are You Brain Dead?! R	2.00	4.00
11 Ascertaining The Truth U	.50	1.00
12 Baseless Accusations C	.15	.30
13 Baskol Yeesrim U	.50	1.00
14 Battle Droid Blaster Rifle C	.15	.30
15 Battle Order and First Strike R	1.25	2.50
16 Battle Plan and Draw Their Fire R	2.00	4.00

17 Begin Landing Your Troops U	.50	1.00
18 Blockade Flagship: Bridge R	4.00	8.00
19 Captain Madakor R	1.25	2.50
20 Captain Panaka R	1.25	2.50
21 Chokk U	.50	1.00
22 Control DARK U	.50	1.00
23 Control LIGHT U	.50	1.00
24 Coruscant DARK C	.15	.30
25 Coruscant LIGHT C	.15	.30
26 Coruscant Guard DARK C	.15	.30
27 Coruscant Guard LIGHT C	.15	.30
28 Coruscant: Docking Bay DARK C	.15	.30
29 Coruscant: Docking Bay LIGHT C	.15	.30
30 Coruscant: Galactic Senate DARK C	.15	.30
31 Coruscant: Galactic Senate LIGHT C	.15	.30
32 Coruscant: Jedi Council Chamber R	4.00	8.00
33 Credits Will Do Fine C	.15	.30
34 Darth Maul, Young Apprentice R	15.00	30.00
35 Daultay Dofine R	1.50	3.00
36 Depa Billaba R	1.50	3.00
37 Destroyer Droid R	12.00	25.00
38 Dioxis R	1.25	2.50
39 Do They Have A Code Clearance? R	1.25	2.50
40 Droid Starfighter C	.15	.30
41 Drop! U	.50	1.00
42 Edcel Bar Gane C	.15	.30
43 Enter The Bureaucrat U	.50	1.00
44 Establish Control U	.50	1.00
45 Free Ride and Endor Celebration R	2.00	4.00
46 Freon Drevan U	.50	1.00
47 Gardulla The Hutt U	.50	1.00
48 Graxol Kelvyyn U	.50	1.00
49 Grotto Werribee R	1.50	3.00
50 Gungan Warrior C	.15	.30
51 Horox Ryyder C	.15	.30
52 I Will Not Defer U	.50	1.00
53 Iive Decided To Go Back C	.15	.30
54 Imperial Arrest Order and Secret Plans R	4.00	8.00
55 Imperial Artillery R	4.00	8.00
56 Inconsequential Barriers C	.15	.30
57 Insurrection and Aim High R	3.00	6.00
58 Jawa DARK C	.15	.30
59 Jawa LIGHT C	.15	.30
60 Keder The Black R	1.25	2.50
61 Ki-Adi-Mundi U	.50	1.00
62 Kill Them Immediately C	.15	.30
63 Lana Dobreed U	.50	1.00
64 Laser Cannon Battery U	.50	1.00
65 Liana Merian U	.50	1.00
66 Lieutenant Williams U	.50	1.00
67 Little Real Power C	.15	.30
68 Lott Dod R	1.50	3.00
69 Mace Windu R	10.00	20.00
70 Malastare DARK U	.50	1.00
71 Malastare LIGHT U	.50	1.00
72 Mas Amedda U	.50	1.00
73 Master Qui-Gon R	4.00	8.00
74 Masterful Move and Endor Occupation R	2.50	5.00
75 Maul Strikes R	2.50	5.00
76 Mauls Sith Infiltrator R	4.00	8.00
77 Might Of The Republic R	3.00	6.00
78 Mind Tricks Donit Work On Me U	.50	1.00
79 Mindful Of The Future C	.15	.30
80 Motion Supported U	.50	1.00
81 Murr Danod R	1.25	2.50
82 My Lord, Is That Legal?	.50	1.00
I Will Make It Legal U		
83 My Loyal Bodyguard U	.50	1.00
84 Naboo Blaster C	.15	.30
85 Naboo Blaster Rifle DARK C	.15	.30

86 Naboo Blaster Rifle LIGHT C	.15	.30
87 Naboo Defense Fighter C	.15	.30
88 Naboo Fighter Pilot C	.15	.30
89 Naboo Security Officer Blaster C	.15	.30
90 Naboo DARK U	.50	1.00
91 Naboo LIGHT U	.50	1.00
92 Naboo: Battle Plains DARK C	.15	.30
93 Naboo: Battle Plains LIGHT C	.15	.30
94 Naboo: Swamp DARK C	.15	.30
95 Naboo: Swamp LIGHT C	.15	.30
96 Naboo: Theed Palace	.15	.30
Courtyard DARK C		
97 Naboo: Theed Palace	.15	.30
Courtyard LIGHT C		
98 Naboo: Theed Palace	.15	.30
Docking Bay DARK C		
99 Naboo: Theed Palace	.15	.30
Docking Bay LIGHT C		
100 Naboo: Theed Palace	.15	.30
Throne Room DARK C		
101 Naboo: Theed Palace	.15	.30
Throne Room LIGHT C		
102 Neimoidian Advisor U	.50	1.00
103 Neimoidian Pilot C	.15	.30
104 New Leadership Is Needed C	.15	.30
105 No Civility, Only Politics C	.15	.30
106 No Money, No Parts, No Deal!	.50	1.00
Youire A Slave? U		
107 Nute Gunray R	1.25	2.50
108 Odin Nesloor U	.50	1.00
109 On The Payroll Of The Trade Federation C	.15	.30
110 Orn Free Taa C	.15	.30
111 Our Blockade Is Perfectly Legal U	.50	1.00
112 P-59 R	4.00	8.00
113 P-60 R	2.00	4.00
114 Panakaís Blaster R	1.50	3.00
115 Passel Argente C	.15	.30
116 Phylo Gandish R	2.00	4.00
117 Plea To The Court U	.50	1.00
118 Plead My Case To The Senate	.50	1.00
Sanity And Compassion U		
119 Plo Koon R	4.00	8.00
120 Queen Amidala, Ruler Of Naboo R	5.00	10.00
121 Queenis Royal Starship R	1.50	3.00
122 Radiant VII R	2.00	4.00
123 Rebel Artillery R	4.00	8.00
124 Republic Cruiser C	.15	.30
125 Reveal Ourselves To The Jedi C	.15	.30
126 Ric Olie R	1.25	2.50
127 Rune Haako R	1.25	2.50
128 Sabe R	1.50	3.00
129 Sache U	.50	1.00
130 Secure Route U	.50	1.00
131 Security Battle Droid C	.15	.30
132 Security Control U	.50	1.00
133 Sei Taria U	.50	1.00
134 Senator Palpatine	4.00	8.00
(head and shoulders) R		
135 Senator Palpatine (head shot) R	15.00	30.00
136 Sense DARK U	.50	1.00
137 Sense LIGHT U	.50	1.00
138 Short Range Fighters and	3.00	6.00
Watch Your Back! R		
139 Speak With The Jedi Council R	4.00	8.00
140 Squabbling Delegates R	1.50	3.00
141 Stay Here, Where Itís Safe C	.15	.30
142 Supreme Chancellor Valorum R	1.25	2.50
143 Tatooine DARK U	.50	1.00
144 Tatooine LIGHT U	.50	1.00
145 Tatooine: Marketplace DARK C	.15	.30
146 Tatooine: Marketplace LIGHT C	.15	.30

147	Tatooine: Mos Espa Docking Bay DARK C	.15	.30
148	Tatooine: Mos Espa Docking Bay LIGHT C	.15	.30
149	Tatooine: Wattoís Junkyard DARK C	.15	.30
150	Tatooine: Wattoís Junkyard LIGHT C	.15	.30
151	TC-14 R	1.25	2.50
152	Televan Koreyy R	1.25	2.50
153	Tendau Bendon U	.50	1.00
154	Tey How U	.50	1.00
155	The Gravest Of Circumstances U	.50	1.00
156	The Hyperdrive Generatorís Gone Weíll Need A New One U	.50	1.00
157	The Phantom Menace R	5.00	10.00
158	The Point Is Conceded C	.15	.30
159	They Will Be No Match For You R	1.25	2.50
160	Theyíre Still Coming Through! U	.50	1.00
161	This Is Outrageous! U	.50	1.00
162	Thrown Back C	.15	.30
163	Tikkes C	.15	.30
164	Toonbuck Toora U	.50	1.00
165	Trade Federation Battleship U	.50	1.00
166	Trade Federation Droid Control Ship R	1.50	3.00
167	Tusken Raider C	.15	.30
168	Vote Now! DARK R	1.25	2.50
169	Vote Now! LIGHT R	1.50	3.00
170	We Must Accelerate Our Plans R	10.00	20.00
171	We Wish To Board At Once R	2.50	5.00
172	Weíre Leaving C	.15	.30
173	Wipe Them Out, All Of Them U	.50	1.00
174	Yade Mírak U	.50	1.00
175	YanÈ U	.50	1.00
176	Yarua U	.50	1.00
177	Yeb Yeb Ademithorn C	.15	.30
178	Yoda, Senior Council Member R	3.00	6.00
179	You Cannot Hide Forever and Mobilization Points R	3.00	6.00
180	You've Got A Lot Of Guts Coming Here R	1.50	3.00
181	Your Insight Serves You Well and Staging Areas R	1.25	2.50
182	Coruscant Dark Side List 1	.15	.30
183	Coruscant Dark Side List 2	.15	.30
184	Coruscant Light Side List 1	.15	.30
185	Coruscant Light Side List 2	.15	.30
186	Coruscant Rule Card 1	.15	.30
187	Coruscant Rule Card 2	.15	.30
188	Coruscant Rule Card 3	.15	.30

2001 Star Wars Reflections III

RELEASED IN 2001

1	A Close Race PM	1.25	2.50
2	A Remote Planet PM	1.25	2.50
3	A Tragedy Has Occured PM	1.50	3.00
4	A Useless Gesture PM	1.25	2.50
5	Aim High PM	1.50	3.00
6	Allegations of Coruption PM	1.25	2.50
7	An Unusual Amount Of Fear PM	1.25	2.50
8	Another Pathetic Lifeform PM	1.25	2.50
9	Armarment Dismantled PM	1.25	2.50
10	Battle Order PM	1.25	2.50
11	Battle Plan PM	1.50	3.00
12	Bib Fortuna PM	1.25	2.50
13	Blizzard 4 PM	2.50	5.00
14	Blockade Flagship: Hallway PM	1.25	2.50
15	Blow Parried PM	1.25	2.50
16	Boba Fett, Bounty Hunter PM	6.00	12.00
17	Chewie, Enraged PM	2.00	4.00
18	Clinging To The Edge PM	1.25	2.50
19	Colo Claw Fish DARK PM	1.25	2.50
20	Colo Claw Fish LIGHT PM	1.25	2.50
21	Come Here You Big Coward PM	1.50	3.00
22	Conduct Your Search PM	1.50	3.00
23	Crossfire PM	1.25	2.50
24	Dark Rage PM	1.25	2.50
25	Darth Maulís Demise PM	1.25	2.50
26	Deep Hatred PM	1.25	2.50
27	Desperate Times PM	1.25	2.50
28	Diversionary Tactics PM	1.25	2.50
29	Do They Have A Code Clearance? PM	1.50	3.00
30	Do, Or Do Not PM	1.25	2.50
31	Donít Do That Again PM	1.25	2.50
32	Echo Base Sensors PM	1.50	3.00
33	Energy Walls DARK PM	1.25	2.50
34	Energy Walls LIGHT PM	1.25	2.50
35	Ewok Celebration PM	1.25	2.50
36	Fall Of A Jedi PM	1.25	2.50
37	Fanfare PM	1.25	2.50
38	Fear Is My Ally PM	1.25	2.50
39	Force Push PM	1.50	3.00
40	Han, Chewie, and The Falcon PM	6.00	12.00
41	He Can Go About His Business PM	1.25	2.50
42	Horace Vancil PM	1.25	2.50
43	Inner Strength PM	1.25	2.50
44	Jabba Desilijic Tiure PM	1.25	2.50
45	Jar Jarís Electropole PM	1.25	2.50
46	Jedi Leap PM	1.25	2.50
47	Lando Calrissian, Scoundrel PM	2.50	5.00
48	Landoís Not A System, Heís A Man PM	1.25	2.50
49	Leave them to Me PM	1.25	2.50
50	Leia, Rebel Princess PM	3.00	6.00
51	Letís Keep A Little Optimism Here PM	1.25	2.50
52	Lord Maul PM	7.50	15.00
53	Maulís Double-Bladed Lightsaber PM	2.50	5.00
54	Naboo: Theed Palace Generator Core DARK PM	1.25	2.50
55	Naboo: Theed Palace Generator Core LIGHT PM	1.25	2.50
56	Naboo: Theed Palace Generator DARK PM	1.25	2.50
57	Naboo: Theed Palace Generator LIGHT PM	1.25	2.50
58	No Escape PM	1.25	2.50
59	No Match For A Sith PM	1.25	2.50
60	Obi-Wan Kenobi, Jedi Knight PM	2.00	4.00
61	Obi-Wanís Lightsaber PM	1.25	2.50
62	Only Jedi Carry That Weapon PM	1.25	2.50
63	Opee Sea Killer DARK PM	1.25	2.50
64	Opee Sea Killer LIGHT PM	1.25	2.50
65	Oppressive Enforcement PM	1.25	2.50
66	Ounee Ta PM	1.25	2.50
67	Planetary Defenses PM	1.25	2.50
68	Prepare For A Surface Attack PM	1.25	2.50
69	Qui-Gon Jinn, Jedi Master PM	3.00	6.00
70	Qui-Gonís End PM	1.50	3.00
71	Reistance PM	1.25	2.50
72	Sando Aqua Monster DARK PM	1.25	2.50
73	Sando Aqua Monster LIGHT PM	1.25	2.50
74	Secret Plans PM	1.25	2.50
75	Sio Bibble PM	1.25	2.50
76	Stormtrooper Garrison PM	5.00	10.00
77	Strike Blockaded PM	1.25	2.50
78	The Ebb Of Battle PM	1.25	2.50
79	The Hutts Are Gangsters PM	1.25	2.50
80	There Is No Try PM	1.50	3.00
81	They Must Never Again Leave This City PM	1.25	2.50
82	Thok and Thug PM	1.25	2.50
83	Through The Corridor PM	1.25	2.50
84	Ultimatum PM	1.25	2.50
85	Unsalvageable PM	1.25	2.50
86	Weíll Let Fate-a Decide, Huh? PM	1.25	2.50
87	Weapon Of A Fallen Mentor PM	1.25	2.50
88	Weapon Of A Sith PM	1.25	2.50
89	Where Are Those Droidekas?! PM	1.25	2.50
90	Wipe Them Out, All Of Them PM	1.25	2.50
91	Wise Advice PM	1.25	2.50
92	Yoda, Master Of The Force PM	5.00	10.00
93	You Cannot Hide Forever PM	1.25	2.50
94	Youíve Never Won A Race? PM	1.25	2.50
95	Your Insight Serves You Well PM	1.25	2.50
96	Your Ship? PM	1.50	3.00

2001 Star Wars Tatooine

RELEASED IN MAY 2001

1	A Jediís Concentration C	.15	.30
2	A Jediís Focus C	.15	.30
3	A Jediís Patience C	.15	.30
4	A Jediís Resilience U	.50	1.00
5	A Million Voices Crying Out R	1.00	2.00
6	A Step Backward U	.50	1.00
7	Anakinís Podracer R	1.00	2.00
8	Aurra Sing R	2.00	4.00
9	Ben Quadinarosí Podracer C	.15	.30
10	Boonta Eve Podrace DARK R	1.25	2.50
11	Boonta Eve Podrace LIGHT R	1.00	2.00
12	Brisky Morning Munchen R	1.00	2.00
13	Caldera Righim C	.15	.30
14	Changing The Odds C	.15	.30
15	Daroe R	1.00	2.00
16	Darth Maul R	2.00	4.00
17	Deneb Both U	.50	1.00
18	Donít Do That Again C	.15	.30
19	Dud Boltís Podracer C	.15	.30
20	Either Way, You Win U	.50	1.00
21	End Of A Reign R	1.00	2.00

#	Card			
22	Entering The Arena U	.50	1.00
23	Eopie C	.15	.30
24	Eventually Youíll Lose U	.50	1.00
25	Fanfare C	.15	.30
26	Gamall Wironicc U	.50	1.00
27	Ghana Gleemort U	.50	1.00
28	Gragra U	.50	1.00
29	Great Shot, Kid! R	1.00	2.00
30	Grugnak U	.50	1.00
31	His Name Is Anakin C	.15	.30
32	Hit Racer U	.50	1.00
33	I Canít Believe Heís Gone C	.15	.30
34	I Did It! R	1.00	2.00
35	I Will Find Them Quickly, Master R	1.00	2.00
36	Iím Sorry R	1.00	2.00
37	If The Trace Was Correct U	.50	1.00
38	Jar Jar Binks R	1.00	2.00
39	Jedi Escape C	.15	.30
40	Join Me! U	.50	1.00
41	Keeping The Empire Out Forever R	1.00	2.00
42	Lathe U	.50	1.00
43	Lightsaber Parry C	.15	.30
44	Loci Rosen U	.50	1.00
45	Losing Track C	.15	.30
46	Maulís Electrobinoculars C	.15	.30
47	Maulís Lightsaber R	1.00	2.00
48	Neck And Neck U	.50	1.00
49	Ni Chuba Na?? C	.15	.30
50	Obi-wan Kenobi, Padawan Learner R	1.25	2.50
51	Padme Naberrie R	2.50	5.00
52	Pit Crews U	.50	1.00
53	Pit Droid C	.15	.30
54	Podrace Prep U	.50	1.00
55	Podracer Collision U	.50	1.00
56	Quietly Observing U	.50	1.00
57	Qui-Gon Jinn R	2.00	4.00
58	Qui-Gon Jinnís Lightsaber R	1.25	2.50
59	Rachalt Hyst U	.50	1.00
60	Sebulba R	1.00	2.00
61	Sebulbaís Podracer R	1.00	2.00
62	Shmi Skywalker R	1.00	2.00
63	Sith Fury C	.15	.30
64	Sith Probe Droid R	1.25	2.50
65	Start Your Engines! U	.50	1.00
66	Tatooine: City Outskirts U	.50	1.00
67	Tatooine: Desert Landing Site R	1.00	2.00
68	Tatooine: Mos Espa DARK C	.15	.30
69	Tatooine: Mos Espa LIGHT C	.15	.30
70	Tatooine: Podrace Arena DARK C	.15	.30
71	Tatooine: Podrace Arena LIGHT C	.15	.30
72	Tatooine: Podracer Bay C	.15	.30
73	Tatooine: Slave Quarters U	.50	1.00
74	Teemto Pagaliesí Podracer C	.15	.30
75	The Camp C	.15	.30
76	The Shield Is Down! R	1.00	2.00
77	There Is No Conflict C	.15	.30
78	Threepio With His Parts Showing R	1.50	3.00
79	Too Close For Comfort U	.50	1.00
80	Vaderís Anger C	.15	.30
81	Watto R	1.50	3.00
82	Wattoís Box C	.15	.30
83	Wattoís Chance Cube U	.50	1.00
84	We Shall Double Our Efforts! R	1.00	2.00
85	What Was It U	.50	1.00
86	Yotts Orren U	.50	1.00
87	You May Start Your Landing R	1.00	2.00
88	You Swindled Me! U	.50	1.00
89	You Want This, Donít You? C	.15	.30
90	Youíll Find ím Full Of Surprises U	.50	1.00
91	Tatooine Dark Side List	.15	.30
92	Tatooine Light Side List	.15	.30
93	Tatooine Rule Card 1	.15	.30
94	Tatooine Rule Card 2	.15	.30
95	Tatooine Rule Card 3	.15	.30

2001 Star Wars Theed Palace

RELEASED IN DECEMBER 2001

#	Card		
1	3B3-10 U	.30	.75
2	3B3-1204 U	.30	.75
3	3B3-21 U	.30	.75
4	3B3-888 U	.30	.75
5	AAT Assault Leader R	1.25	2.50
6	AAT Laser Cannon U	.30	.75
7	Activate The Droids C	.15	.30
8	After Her! R	1.00	2.00
9	Amidalaís Blaster R	1.00	2.00
10	Armored Attack Tank U	.30	.75
11	Artoo, Brave Little Droid R	2.00	4.00
12	Ascension Guns U	.30	.75
13	At Last We Are Getting Results C	.15	.30
14	Battle Droid Officer C	.15	.30
15	Battle Droid Pilot C	.15	.30
16	Big Boomers! C	.15	.30
17	Blockade Flaghip R	2.00	4.00
18	Blockade Flagship: Docking Bay DARK U	.30	.75
19	Blockade Flagship: Docking Bay LIGHT U	.30	.75
20	Bok Askol U	.30	.75
21	Booma C	.15	.30
22	Boss Nass R	1.50	3.00
23	Bravo 1 R	1.00	2.00
24	Bravo 2 U	.30	.75
25	Bravo 3 U	.30	.75
26	Bravo 4 U	.30	.75
27	Bravo 5 U	.30	.75
28	Bravo Fighter R	1.00	2.00
29	Captain Tarpals R	1.00	2.00
30	Captain Tarpalsí Electropole C	.15	.30
31	Captian Daultay Dofine R	1.00	2.00
32	Cease Fire! C	.15	.30
33	Corporal Rushing U	.30	.75
34	Dams Denna U	.30	.75
35	Darth Maul With Lightsaber R	12.00	25.00
36	Darth Sidious R	25.00	50.00
37	DFS Squadron Starfighter C	.15	.30
38	DFS-1015 U	.30	.75
39	DFS-1308 R	1.00	2.00
40	DFS-327 C	.15	.30
41	Droid Racks R	1.50	3.00
42	Droid Starfighter Laser Cannons C	.15	.30
43	Drop Your Weapons C	.15	.30
44	Electropole C	.15	.30
45	Energy Shell Launchers C	.15	.30
46	Fambaa C	.15	.30
47	Fighters Straight Ahead U	.30	.75
48	General Jar Jar R	1.50	3.00
49	Get To Your Ships! C	.15	.30

#	Card		
50	Gian Speeder C	.15	.30
51	Gimme A Lift! R	1.00	2.00
52	Gungan Energy Shield C	.15	.30
53	Gungan General C	.15	.30
54	Gungan Guard C	.15	.30
55	Halt! C	.15	.30
56	Iíll Try Spinning R	1.00	2.00
57	Infantry Battle Droid C	.15	.30
58	Invasion / In Complete Control U	.30	.75
59	Itís On Automatic Pilot C	.15	.30
60	Jerus Jannick U	.30	.75
61	Kaadu C	.15	.30
62	Letís Go Left R	1.00	2.00
63	Lieutenant Arven Wendik U	.30	.75
64	Lieutenant Chamberlyn U	.30	.75
65	Lieutenant Rya Kirsch U	.30	.75
66	Mace Windu, Jedi Master R	7.50	15.00
67	Master, Destroyers! R	1.25	2.50
68	Multi Troop Transport U	.30	.75
69	Naboo Celebration R	1.00	2.00
70	Naboo Occupation R	1.25	2.50
71	Naboo: Boss Nassís Chambers U	.30	.75
72	Naboo: Otoh Gunga Entrance U	.30	.75
73	Naboo: Theed Palace Hall U	.30	.75
74	Naboo: Theed Palace Hallway U	.30	.75
75	No Giben Up, General Jar Jar! R	1.00	2.00
76	Nothing Can Get Through Are Shield R	1.25	2.50
77	Nute Gunray, Neimoidian Viceroy R	2.50	5.00
78	Officer Dolphe U	.30	.75
79	Officer Ellberger U	.30	.75
80	Officer Perosei U	.30	.75
81	OOM-9 U	.30	.75
82	Open Fire! C	.15	.30
83	OWO-1 With Backup R	1.50	3.00
84	Panaka, Protector Of The Queen R	3.00	6.00
85	Proton Torpedoes C	.15	.30
86	Queen Amidala R	10.00	20.00
87	Qui-Gon Jinn With Lightsaber R	7.50	15.00
88	Rayno Vaca C	.30	.75
89	Rep Been U	.30	.75
90	Ric Olie, Bravo Leader R	1.00	2.00
91	Rolling, Rolling, Rolling R	1.25	2.50
92	Royal Naboo Security Officer C	.15	.30
93	Rune Haako, Legal Counsel R	1.50	3.00
94	Senate Hovercam DARK R	1.25	2.50
95	Senate Hovercam LIGHT R	1.25	2.50
96	Sil Unch U	.30	.75
97	Single Trooper Aerial Platform C	.15	.30
98	SSA-1015 U	.30	.75
99	SSA-306 U	.30	.75
100	SSA-719 R	1.50	3.00
101	STAP Blaster Cannons C	.15	.30
102	Steady, Steady C	.15	.30
103	Take Them Away C	.15	.30
104	Take This! C	.15	.30
105	Tank Commander C	.15	.30
106	The Deflector Shield Is Too Strong R	1.00	2.00
107	There They Are! U	.30	.75
108	They Win This Round R	1.00	2.00
109	This Is Not Good C	.15	.30
110	Trade Federation Landing Craft C	.15	.30
111	TT-6 R	1.25	2.50
112	TT-9 R	1.00	2.00
113	We Didnít Hit It C	.15	.30
114	We Donít Have Time For This R	1.25	2.50
115	We Have A Plan / They Will Be Lost And Confused C	.15	.30
116	Weíre Hit Artoo C	.15	.30
117	Wesa Gotta Grand Army C	.15	.30
118	Wesa Ready To Do Our-sa Part C	.15	.30
119	Whoooo! C	.15	.30
120	Theed Palace Dark Side List	.15	.30
121	Theed Palace Light Side List	.15	.30

2002 Star Wars Attack of the Clones

Darth Tyranus
CHARACTER · DARK JEDI MASTER

Pay 1 Force → Tyranus gets +2 power for this attack.
Pay 3 Force → Evade 3 (Prevent up to 3 damage to Tyranus.)
Pay 2 Force → Deflect 1 (Prevent 1 damage to Tyranus, and Tyranus may do that much damage to a unit of your choice in the Character arena.)

"The battle is far from over."

2002 LUCASFILM LTD. & ™ TM GAME DESIGN. WIZARDS.   14/180 *

RELEASED IN APRIL 2002

1 Anakin Skywalker (A) R	.75	1.50
2 Anakin Skywalker (B) R	.75	1.50
3 Assassin Droid ASN-121 (A) R	.75	1.50
4 Bail Organa (A) R	.75	1.50
5 Battle Fatigue R	.75	1.50
6 Boba Fett (A) R	.75	1.50
7 Captain Typho (A) R	.75	1.50
8 Clear the Skies R	.75	1.50
9 Clone Officer R	.75	1.50
10 Dark Rendezvous R	.75	1.50
11 Dark Side's Command R	.75	1.50
12 Dark Side's Compulsion R	.75	1.50
13 Darth Sidious (A) R	.75	1.50
14 Darth Tyranus (A) R	.75	1.50
15 Destruction of Hope R	.75	1.50
16 Dexter Jettster (A) R	.75	1.50
17 Geonosian Sentry R	.75	1.50
18 Hero's Duty R	.75	1.50
19 Hero's Flaw R	.75	1.50
20 Interference in the Senate R	.75	1.50
21 Jango Fett (A) R	.75	1.50
22 Jango Fett (B) R	.75	1.50
23 Jar Jar Binks (A) R	.75	1.50
24 Jedi Call for Help R	.75	1.50
25 Jedi Council Summons R	.75	1.50
26 Jedi Knight's Deflection R	.75	1.50
27 Lama Su (A) R	.75	1.50
28 Luxury Airspeeder U	.25	.50
29 A Moment's Rest R	.75	1.50
30 Naboo Defense Station R	.75	1.50
31 Obi-Wan Kenobi (A) R	.75	1.50
32 Obi-Wan's Starfighter (A) R	.75	1.50
33 Order Here R	.75	1.50
34 Padmè Amidala (A) R	.75	1.50
35 Padmè Amidala (B) R	.75	1.50
36 Padmè's Yacht (A) R	.75	1.50
37 Plo Koon (A) R	.75	1.50
38 Plot the Secession R	.75	1.50
39 Power Dive R	.75	1.50
40 Queen Jamillia (A) R	.75	1.50
41 R2-D2 (A) R	.75	1.50
42 San Hill (A) U	.25	.50
43 Second Effort R	.75	1.50
44 Seek the Council's Wisdom R	.75	1.50
45 Shu Mai (A) U	.25	.50
46 Slave I (A) R	.75	1.50
47 Spirit of the Fallen R	.75	1.50
48 Target the Senator R	.75	1.50
49 Taun We (A) R	.75	1.50
50 Trade Federation Battleship Core R	.75	1.50
51 Tyranus's Edict R	.75	1.50
52 Tyranus's Geonosian Speeder (A) R	.75	1.50
53 Tyranus's Solar Sailer (A) R	.75	1.50
54 Tyranus's Wrath R	.75	1.50
55 War Will Follow R	.75	1.50
56 Ward of the Jedi R	.75	1.50
57 Windu's Solution R	.75	1.50
58 Yoda (A) R	.75	1.50
59 Yoda's Intervention R	.75	1.50
60 Zam Wesell (A) R	.75	1.50
61 Acklay U	.25	.50
62 Anakin Skywalker (C) U	.25	.50
63 Anakin's Inspiration U	.25	.50
64 AT-TE Walker 23X U	.25	.50
65 AT-TE Walker 71E R	.75	1.50
66 Attract Enemy Fire U	.25	.50
67 C-3PO (A) U	.25	.50
68 Capture Obi-Wan U	.25	.50
69 Chancellor Palpatine (A) R	.75	1.50
70 Chase the Villain U	.25	.50
71 Cheat the Game U	.25	.50
72 Cliegg Lars (A) U	.25	.50
73 Clone Warrior 4/163 U	.25	.50
74 Clone Warrior 5/373 U	.25	.50
75 Commerce Guild Droid Platoon U	.25	.50
76 Cordè (A) U	.25	.50
77 Coruscant Freighter AA-9 (A) U	.25	.50
78 Dark Speed U	.25	.50
79 Darth Tyranus (B) U	.25	.50
80 Departure Time U	.25	.50
81 Destroyer Droid, P Series U	.25	.50
82 Down in Flames U	.25	.50
83 Droid Control Ship U	.25	.50
84 Elan Sleazebaggano (A) R	.75	1.50
85 Geonosian Guard U	.25	.50
86 Geonosian Warrior U	.25	.50
87 Go to the Temple U	.25	.50
88 Infantry Battle Droid, B1 Series U	.25	.50
89 Jango Fett (C) U	.25	.50
90 Jawa Sandcrawler U	.25	.50
91 Jedi Patrol U	.25	.50
92 Kaminoan Guard U	.25	.50
93 Kit Fisto (A) U	.25	.50
94 Master and Apprentice U	.25	.50
95 Naboo Security Guard U	.25	.50
96 Naboo Spaceport U	.25	.50
97 Nexu U	.25	.50
98 Nute Gunray (A) U	.25	.50
99 Obi-Wan Kenobi (B) U	.25	.50
100 Padmè Amidala (C) U	.25	.50
101 Poggle the Lesser (A) U	.25	.50
102 Reek U	.25	.50
103 Republic Assault Ship U	.25	.50
104 Republic Cruiser C	.12	.25
105 Shaak Ti (A) U	.25	.50
106 Ship Arrival U	.25	.50
107 Splinter the Republic U	.25	.50
108 Strength of Hate U	.25	.50
109 Subtle Assassination U	.25	.50
110 Super Battle Droid 8EX U	.25	.50
111 Trade Federation Battleship U	.25	.50
112 Trade Federation C-9979 U	.25	.50
113 Tyranus's Gift U	.25	.50
114 Underworld Connections U	.25	.50
115 Wat Tambor (A) U	.25	.50
116 Watto (A) U	.25	.50
117 Weapon Response U	.25	.50
118 Wedding of Destiny U	.25	.50
119 Yoda (B) U	.25	.50
120 Zam's Airspeeder (A) U	.25	.50
121 Anakin Skywalker (D) C	.12	.25
122 Battle Droid Squad C	.12	.25
123 Bravo N-1 Starfighter C	.12	.25
124 Chancellor's Guard Squad C	.12	.25
125 Clone Platoon C	.12	.25
126 Clone Squad C	.12	.25
127 Commerce Guild Droid 81 C	.12	.25
128 Commerce Guild Starship C	.12	.25
129 Corellian Star Shuttle C	.12	.25
130 Darth Tyranus (C) C	.12	.25
131 Destroyer Droid Squad C	.12	.25
132 Droid Starfighter DFS-4CT C	.12	.25
133 Droid Starfighter Squadron C	.12	.25
134 Droid Starfighter Wing C	.12	.25
135 Elite Jedi Squad C	.12	.25
136 Flying Geonosian Squad C	.12	.25
137 Geonosian Defense Platform C	.12	.25
138 Geonosian Fighter C	.12	.25
139 Geonosian Squad C	.12	.25
140 Gozanti Cruiser C	.12	.25
141 Hatch a Clone C	.12	.25
142 Hero's Dodge C	.12	.25
143 High-Force Dodge C	.12	.25
144 Hyperdrive Ring C	.12	.25
145 InterGalactic Banking Clan Starship C	.12	.25
146 Jango Fett (D) C	.12	.25
147 Jedi Starfighter 3R3 C	.12	.25
148 Knockdown C	.12	.25
149 Lost in the Asteroids C	.12	.25
150 Lull in the Fighting C	.12	.25
151 Mending C	.12	.25
152 N-1 Starfighter C	.12	.25
153 Naboo Cruiser C	.12	.25
154 Naboo Royal Starship C	.12	.25
155 Naboo Senatorial Escort C	.12	.25
156 Naboo Starfighter Squadron C	.12	.25
157 Obi-Wan Kenobi (C) C	.12	.25
158 Padawan's Deflection C	.12	.25
159 Padmè Amidala (D) C	.12	.25
160 Patrol Speeder C	.12	.25
161 Peace on Naboo C	.12	.25
162 Pilot's Dodge C	.12	.25
163 Recon Speeder U	.12	.25
164 Republic Attack Gunship UH-478 C	.12	.25
165 Repulsorlift Malfunction C	.12	.25
166 Return to Spaceport C	.12	.25
167 Rickshaw C	.12	.25
168 Slumming on Coruscant C	.12	.25
169 Sonic Shockwave C	.12	.25
170 Speeder Bike Squadron C	.12	.25
171 Starship Refit C	.12	.25
172 Surge of Power C	.12	.25
173 Swoop Bike C	.12	.25
174 Take the Initiative C	.12	.25
175 Target Locked C	.12	.25
176 Taylander Shuttle C	.12	.25
177 Techno Union Starship C	.12	.25
178 Trade Federation War Freighter C	.12	.25
179 Walking Droid Fighter C	.12	.25
180 Zam Wesell (B) C	.12	.25

2002 Star Wars A New Hope

RELEASED IN OCTOBER 2002

1 Admiral Motti (A) R	.75	1.50
2 Beru Lars (A) R	.75	1.50
3 Blaster Barrage R	.75	1.50
4 Capture the Falcon R	.75	1.50
5 Contingency Plan R	.75	1.50
6 Dannik Jerriko (A) R	.75	1.50
7 Darth Vader (A) R	1.50	3.00
8 Desperate Confrontation R	1.00	2.00
9 Destroy Alderaan R	.75	1.50
10 Dianoga (A) R	.75	1.50
11 Disturbance in the Force R	.75	1.50
12 It's Not Over Yet R	.75	1.50
13 EG-6 Power Droid R	.75	1.50

14 Elite Stormtrooper Squad R	.75	1.50
15 Figrin D'an (A) R	1.00	2.00
16 Greedo (A) R	.75	1.50
17 Hold 'Em Off R	.75	1.50
18 Imperial Blockade R	.75	1.50
19 Imperial Navy Helmsman R	.75	1.50
20 Imperial Sentry Droid R	.75	1.50
21 IT-0 Interrogator Droid R	1.00	2.00
22 Jawa Leader R	.75	1.50
23 Krayt Dragon R	.75	1.50
24 Leia's Kiss R	.75	1.50
25 Luke Skywalker (B) R	.75	1.50
26 Luke Skywalker (A) R	.75	1.50
27 Luke's Speeder (A) R	.75	1.50
28 Luke's X-Wing (A) R	.75	1.50
29 Momaw Nadon (A) R	1.25	2.50
30 Most Desperate Hour R	.75	1.50
31 No Escape R	.75	1.50
32 Obi-Wan Kenobi (E) R	.75	1.50
33 Obi-Wan's Prowess R	.75	1.50
34 Obi-Wan's Task R	.75	1.50
35 Our Only Hope R	.75	1.50
36 Owen Lars (A) R	.75	1.50
37 Plan of Attack R	.75	1.50
38 Princess Leia (A) R	.75	1.50
39 Protection of the Master R	.75	1.50
40 R5-D4 (A) R	.75	1.50
41 Rebel Crew Chief R	.75	1.50
42 Rebel Lieutenant R	.75	1.50
43 Regroup on Yavin R	.75	1.50
44 Sandtrooper R	.75	1.50
45 Starfighter's End R	.75	1.50
46 Stormtrooper TK-421 R	.75	1.50
47 Strategy Session R	.75	1.50
48 Strike Me Down R	.75	1.50
49 Surprise Attack R	.75	1.50
50 Tantive IV (A) R	.75	1.50
51 Tarkin's Stench R	.75	1.50
52 TIE Fighter Elite Pilot U	.25	.50
53 Tiree (A) R	.75	1.50
54 Tractor Beam R	.75	1.50
55 URoRRuR'R'R (A) R	.75	1.50
56 Imperial Manipulation R	.75	1.50
57 Vader's Leadership R	.75	1.50
58 Vader's TIE Fighter (A) R	.75	1.50
59 Wedge Antilles (A) R	.75	1.50
60 Yavin 4 Hangar Base R	.75	1.50
61 Astromech Assistance U	.25	.50
62 Benefits of Training U	.25	.50
63 Biggs Darklighter (A) U	.25	.50
64 C-3PO (C) U	.25	.50
65 Commander Praji (A) U	.25	.50
66 Tatooine Sandcrawler U	.25	.50
67 Darth Vader (B) U	.25	.50
68 Death Star Hangar Bay U	.25	.50
69 Death Star Plans U	.25	.50
70 Death Star Scanning Technician U	.25	.50
71 Death Star Superlaser Gunner U	.25	.50
72 Death Star Turbolaser Gunner U	.25	.50
73 Demonstration of Power U	.25	.50
74 Devastator (A) U	.25	.50
75 Dissolve the Senate U	.25	.50
76 Error in Judgment U	.25	.50
77 Fate of the Dragon U	.25	.50
78 General Dodonna (A) U	.25	.50
79 General Tagge (A) U	.25	.50
80 Han's Courage U	.25	.50
81 Imperial Control Station U	.25	.50
82 Imperial Navy Lieutenant U	.25	.50
83 Insignificant Power U	.25	.50

84 Into the Garbage Chute C	.12	.25
85 Jawa U	.25	.50
86 Jawa Collection Team U	.25	.50
87 Jedi Extinction U	.25	.50
88 Jon Dutch Vander (A) U	.25	.50
89 Learning the Force U	.25	.50
90 Lieutenant Tanbris (A) U	.25	.50
91 LIN Demolitionmech U	.25	.50
92 Luke Skywalker (C) U	.25	.50
93 Luke's Warning U	.25	.50
94 Mounted Stormtrooper U	.25	.50
95 Mouse Droid U	.25	.50
96 Obi-Wan Kenobi (F) U	.25	.50
97 Oil Bath U	.25	.50
98 Princess Leia (B) U	.25	.50
99 R2-D2 (C) U	.25	.50
100 Rebel Blockade Runner U	.25	.50
101 Rebel Control Officer U	.25	.50
102 Rebel Control Post U	.25	.50
103 Rebel Marine U	.25	.50
104 Rebel Surrender U	.25	.50
105 Rebel Trooper U	.25	.50
106 Remote Seeker Droid U	.25	.50
107 Press the Advantage U	.25	.50
108 Stabilize Deflectors U	.25	.50
109 Star Destroyer Commander U	.25	.50
110 Stormtrooper Charge U	.25	.50
111 Stormtrooper DV-692 U	.25	.50
112 Stormtrooper Squad Leader U	.25	.50
113 Stormtrooper TK-119 U	.25	.50
114 Support in the Senate U	.25	.50
115 Disrupt the Power System U	.25	.50
116 Tatooine Speeder U	.25	.50
117 Tusken Sharpshooter U	.25	.50
118 Vader's Interference U	.25	.50
119 Vader's TIE Fighter (B) U	.75	1.50
120 Wuher (A) U	.25	.50
121 Air Cover C	.12	.25
122 Precise Blast C	.12	.25
123 Stay Sharp C	.12	.25
124 Carrack Cruiser C	.12	.25
125 Darth Vader (C) C	.12	.25
126 Death Star Cannon Tower C	.12	.25
127 Death Star Guard Squad C	.12	.25
128 Domesticated Bantha C	.12	.25
129 Flare-S Swoop C	.12	.25
130 Ground Support C	.12	.25
131 Imperial Detention Block C	.12	.25
132 Imperial Star Destroyer C	.12	.25
133 Incom T-16 Skyhopper C	.12	.25
134 Into Hiding C	.12	.25
135 Jawa Squad C	.12	.25
136 Jawa Supply Trip C	.12	.25
137 Jump to Lightspeed C	.12	.25
138 Luke Skywalker (D) C	.12	.25
139 Luke's Repairs C	.12	.25
140 Moisture Farm C	.12	.25
141 Planetary Defense Turret C	.12	.25
142 Nowhere to Run C	.12	.25
143 Obi-Wan Kenobi (G) C	.12	.25
144 Jedi Intervention C	.12	.25
145 Obi-Wan's Plan C	.12	.25
146 Penetrate the Shields C	.12	.25
147 Preemptive Shot C	.12	.25
148 Princess Leia (C) C	.12	.25
149 Rebel Fighter Wing C	.12	.25
150 Rebel Honor Company C	.12	.25
151 Rebel Marine Squad C	.12	.25
152 Rebel Pilot C	.12	.25
153 Rebel Squad C	.12	.25

154 Rescue C	.12	.25
155 Slipping Through C	.12	.25
156 SoruSuub V-35 Courier C	.12	.25
157 Synchronized Assault C	.12	.25
158 Stormtrooper Assault Team C	.12	.25
159 Stormtrooper DV-523 C	.12	.25
160 Stormtrooper Patrol C	.12	.25
161 Stormtrooper Squad C	.12	.25
162 TIE Fighter DS-3-12 C	.12	.25
163 TIE Fighter DS-73-3 C	.12	.25
164 TIE Fighter DS-55-6 C	.12	.25
165 TIE Fighter DS-61-9 C	.12	.25
166 TIE Fighter Pilot C	.12	.25
167 TIE Fighter Squad C	.12	.25
168 Tusken Squad C	.12	.25
169 Vader's Grip U	.12	.25
170 Victory-Class Star Destroyer C	.12	.25
171 Well-Aimed Shot C	.12	.25
172 X-wing Red One C	.12	.25
173 X-wing Red Three C	.12	.25
174 X-wing Red Two C	.12	.25
175 X-wing Attack Formation C	.12	.25
176 Y-wing Gold One C	.12	.25
177 Y-wing Gold Squadron C	.12	.25
178 YT-1300 Transport C	.12	.25
179 YV-664 Light Freighter C	.12	.25
180 Z-95 Headhunter C	.12	.25

2002 Star Wars Sith Rising

RELEASED IN JULY 2002

1 Aayla Secura (A) R	.75	1.50
2 Anakin Skywalker (E) R	.75	1.50
3 Aurra Sing (A) R	.75	1.50
4 Chancellor Palpatine (B) R	.75	1.50
5 Clone Captain R	.75	1.50
6 Clone Facility R	.75	1.50
7 Darth Maul (A) R	.75	1.50
8 Darth Maul (C) R	.75	1.50
9 Darth Sidious (B) R	.75	1.50
10 Darth Tyranus (D) R	.75	1.50
11 Geonosian Picadors R	.75	1.50
12 Impossible Victory R	.75	1.50
13 Jango Fett (E) R	.75	1.50
14 Jedi Bravery R	.75	1.50
15 Jedi Starfighter Wing R	.75	1.50
16 Jocasta Nu (A) R	.75	1.50
17 Mace Windu (A) R	.75	1.50
18 Mace Windu (C) R	.75	1.50
19 Massiff R	.75	1.50
20 Nute Gunray (B) R	.75	1.50

21	Republic Drop Ship R	.75	1.50
22	Sio Bibble (A) R	.75	1.50
23	Sith Infiltrator (A) R	.75	1.50
24	Slave I (B) R	.75	1.50
25	Super Battle Droid 5TE R	.75	1.50
26	Trade Federation Control Core R	.75	1.50
27	Tusken Camp R	.75	1.50
28	Twilight of the Republic R	.75	1.50
29	Unfriendly Fire R	.75	1.50
30	Yoda (C) R	.75	1.50
31	Aiwha Rider U	.25	.50
32	C-3PO (B) U	.25	.50
33	Careful Targeting U	.25	.50
34	Clever Escape U	.25	.50
35	Clone Trooper 6/298 U	.25	.50
36	Darth Maul (B) U	.25	.50
37	Darth Tyranus (E) U	.25	.50
38	Destroyer Droid, W Series U	.25	.50
39	Female Tusken Raider U	.25	.50
40	Fog of War U	.25	.50
41	Geonosian Scout U	.25	.50
42	Hailfire Droid U	.25	.50
43	Homing Spider Droid U	.25	.50
44	Infantry Battle Droid U	.25	.50
45	Jedi Heroes U	.25	.50
46	Jedi Starfighter Scout U	.25	.50
47	Mace Windu (B) U	.25	.50
48	Moment of Truth U	.25	.50
49	Obi_Wan Kenobi (D) U	.25	.50
50	Out of His Misery U	.25	.50
51	PadmÈ Amidala (E) U	.25	.50
52	Passel Argente (A) U	.25	.50
53	Price of Failure U	.25	.50
54	R2-D2 (B) U	.25	.50
55	Recognition of Valor U	.25	.50
56	Sun Fac (A) U	.25	.50
57	Techno Union Warship U	.25	.50
58	Trade Federation Offensive U	.25	.50
59	Tusken Raider U	.25	.50
60	Visit the Lake Retreat U	.25	.50
61	Acclamator-Class Assault Ship C	.12	.25
62	Aggressive Negotiations C	.12	.25
63	Anakin Skywalker (F) C	.12	.25
64	AT-TE Troop Transport C	.12	.25
65	Battle Droid Assault Squad C	.12	.25
66	Brutal Assault C	.12	.25
67	Clone Trooper Legion C	.12	.25
68	Commerce Guild Cruiser C	.12	.25
69	Commerce Guild Spider Droid C	.12	.25
70	Concentrated Fire C	.12	.25
71	Corsucant Speeder C	.12	.25
72	Darth Maul (D) C	.12	.25
73	Diplomatic Cruiser C	.12	.25
74	Droid Starfighter DFS-1VR C	.12	.25
75	Geonosian Artillery Battery C	.12	.25
76	Geonosian Defense Fighter C	.12	.25
77	Maul's Strategy C	.12	.25
78	Mobile Assault Cannon C	.12	.25
79	Naboo Starfighter Wing C	.12	.25
80	Nubian Yacht C	.12	.25
81	Padawan and Senator C	.12	.25
82	Reassemble C-3PO C	.12	.25
83	Republic LAAT/i Gunship C	.12	.25
84	Retreat Underground R	.12	.25
85	Run the Gauntlet C	.12	.25
86	Senatorial Cruiser C	.12	.25
87	Shoot Her or Something C	.12	.25
88	Super Battle Droid Squad C	.12	.25
89	Suppressing Fire C	.12	.25
90	Trade Federation Warship C	.12	.25

2003 Star Wars Battle of Yavin

RELEASED IN MARCH 2003

1	Artoo's Repairs R	2.50	5.00
2	Blow This Thing R	2.00	4.00
3	Celebrate the Victory R	1.00	2.00
4	Chariot Light Assault Vehicle R	1.00	2.00
5	Chewbacca (B) R	5.00	10.00
6	Chewbacca (A) R	5.00	10.00
7	Chief Bast (A) R	2.50	5.00
8	Colonel Wullf Yularen (A) R	2.50	5.00
9	Darth Vader (D) R	5.00	10.00
10	Death Star (A) R	4.00	8.00
11	Death Star (C) R	4.00	8.00
12	Garven Dreis (A) R	1.50	3.00
13	Grand Moff Tarkin (A) R	4.00	8.00
14	Han Solo (B) R	6.00	12.00
15	Han Solo (A) R	5.00	10.00
16	Hero's Potential R	.25	.50
17	Jek Porkins (A) R	.75	1.50
18	Lieutenant Shann Childsen (A) R	1.50	3.00
19	Luke Skywalker (E) R	5.00	10.00
20	Luke's Skyhopper (A) R	.25	.50
21	Luke's X-wing (B) R	2.50	5.00
22	Millennium Falcon (A) R	2.50	5.00
23	Millennium Falcon (B) R	2.50	5.00
24	Millennium Falcon (C) R	2.50	5.00
25	Obi-Wan Kenobi (H) R	5.00	10.00
26	Obi-Wan's Guidance R	1.00	2.00
27	Princess Leia (D) R	1.50	3.00
28	R2-X2 (A) R	1.50	3.00
29	R2-Q5 (A) R	1.50	3.00
30	Rebel Ground Crew Chief R	1.00	2.00
31	Second Wave R	1.50	3.00
32	Stormtrooper Commander R	5.00	10.00
33	Vader's Fury R	2.50	5.00
34	X-wing Squadron R	2.50	5.00
35	Your Powers Are Weak R	1.50	3.00
36	Alien Rage U	.50	1.00
37	C-3PO (D) U	.50	1.00
38	Chewbacca (C) U	.50	1.00
39	Commander Willard (A) U	.50	1.00
40	Countermeasures U	.50	1.00
41	Darth Vader (E) U	.50	1.00
42	Death Star (B) U	.50	1.00
43	Death Star Trooper U	.50	1.00
44	Deflectors Activated U	.50	1.00
45	Grand Moff Tarkin (B) U	.50	1.00
46	Grand Moff Tarkin (C) U	.50	1.00
47	Han Solo (C) U	.50	1.00
48	Heavy Fire Zone U	.50	1.00
49	Imperial Dewback U	.50	1.00
50	Interrogation Droid U	.50	1.00
51	Jawa Crawler U	.50	1.00
52	Jawa Scavenger U	.50	1.00
53	Labria (A) U	.50	1.00
54	Let the Wookiee Win U	.50	1.00
55	Luke Skywalker (F) U	.50	1.00
56	Luke's Speeder (B) U	.50	1.00
57	Mobile Command Base U	.50	1.00
58	Obi-Wan's Handiwork U	.50	1.00
59	Princess Leia (E) U	.50	1.00
60	R2-D2 (D) U	.50	1.00
61	Rebel Armored Freerunner U	.50	1.00
62	Refit on Yavin U	.50	1.00
63	Sabers Locked U	.50	1.00
64	Stormtrooper KE-829 U	.50	1.00
65	Tatooine Hangar U	.50	1.00
66	Tusken Raider Squad U	.50	1.00
67	Tusken War Party U	.50	1.00
68	Untamed Ronto U	.50	1.00
69	WED Treadwell U	.50	1.00
70	Womp Rat U	.50	1.00
71	Accelerate C	.25	.50
72	Blast It! C	.25	.50
73	Chewbacca (D) C	.25	.50
74	Corellian Corvette C	.25	.50
75	Creature Attack C	.25	.50
76	Luke Skywalker (G) C	.25	.50
77	Darth Vader (F) C	.25	.50
78	Death Star Turbolaser Tower C	.25	.50
79	Dewback Patrol C	.25	.50
80	Escape Pod C	.25	.50
81	Greedo's Marksmanship C	.25	.50
82	Han Solo (D) C	.25	.50
83	Han's Evasion C	.25	.50
84	Imperial Landing Craft C	.25	.50
85	Jawa Salvage Team C	.25	.50
86	Juggernaut U	.25	.50
87	Star Destroyer C	.25	.50
88	Malfunction C	.25	.50
89	Outrun C	.25	.50
90	Pilot's Speed C	.25	.50
91	Rebel Defense Team C	.25	.50
92	Sandtrooper Squad C	.25	.50
93	Stormtrooper Assault C	.25	.50
94	Stormtrooper TK-875 C	.25	.50
95	Stormtrooper Platoon C	.25	.50
96	Stormtrooper Regiment C	.25	.50
97	TIE Defense Squadron C	.25	.50
98	TIE Fighter DS-73-5 C	.25	.50
99	TIE Fighter DS-29-4 C	.25	.50
100	TIE Fighter DS-55-2 C	.25	.50
101	Trust Your Feelings C	.25	.50
102	Visit to Mos Eisley C	.25	.50
103	X-wing Red Squadron C	.25	.50
104	X-wing Red Ten C	.25	.50
105	Y-wing Gold Two C	.25	.50

2003 Star Wars The Empire Strikes Back

RELEASED IN NOVEMBER 2003

1	2-1B Medical Droid (A) R	1.50	3.00
2	Admiral Firmus Piett (B) R	1.50	3.00
3	AT-AT Assault Group R	1.50	3.00
4	Avenger (A) R	5.00	10.00
5	Blizzard Force Snowtrooper R	1.50	3.00
6	Blizzard One (A) R	1.50	3.00
7	C-3PO (E) R	1.50	3.00
8	Captain Lorth Needa (A) R	1.50	3.00
9	Carbon Freezing Chamber R	6.00	12.00
10	Chewbacca (E) U	1.50	3.00
11	Chewbacca (G) R	1.50	3.00
12	Dack Ralter (A) R	1.50	3.00
13	Dangerous Gamble R	1.50	3.00
14	Dark Cave R	1.50	3.00
15	Darth Vader (H) R	2.50	5.00
16	Darth Vader (I) R	4.00	8.00
17	Decoy Tactics R	1.50	3.00
18	Desperate Times R	1.50	3.00
19	Echo Base R	4.00	8.00
20	Emperor's Bidding R	1.50	3.00
21	Emperor's Prize R	1.50	3.00
22	Executor (A) R	1.50	3.00
23	Failed for the Last Time R	1.50	3.00
24	Future Sight R	1.50	3.00
25	FX-7 Medical Droid (A) R	1.50	3.00
26	General Carlist Rieekan (A) R	1.50	3.00
27	General Maximilian Veers (B) R	1.50	3.00
28	Go for the Legs R	1.50	3.00
29	Han Solo (G) R	2.50	5.00
30	Jedi Test R	1.50	3.00
31	Jedi's Failure R	1.50	3.00
32	K-3PO (A) R	1.50	3.00
33	Kiss From Your Sister R	1.50	3.00
34	Lando Calrissian (A) R	3.00	6.00
35	Lando Calrissian (D) R	3.00	6.00
36	Lieutenant Wes Janson (A) R	2.50	5.00
37	Lobot (A) R	1.50	3.00
38	Luke Skywalker (J) R	7.50	15.00
39	Luke Skywalker (K) R	6.00	12.00
40	Luke's Snowspeeder (A) R	5.00	10.00
41	Luke's Wrath R	1.50	3.00
42	Luke's X-wing (c) R	2.50	5.00
43	Major Bren Derlin (A) R	1.50	3.00
44	Mara Jade (A) R	1.50	3.00
45	Millennium Falcon (E) R	2.50	5.00
46	Millennium Falcon (F) R	2.50	5.00
47	Millennium Falcon (G) R	2.50	5.00
48	Obi-Wan's Spirit (A) R	1.50	3.00
49	Occupation R	1.50	3.00
50	Parting of Heroes R	1.50	3.00
51	Planetary Ion Cannon R	1.50	3.00
52	Princess Leia (G) R	2.50	5.00
53	Quest for Truth R	1.50	3.00
54	R2-D2 (G) R	1.50	3.00
55	R2-D2's Heroism R	1.50	3.00
56	Rally the Defenders R	1.50	3.00
57	Sacrifice R	1.50	3.00
58	Search for the Rebels R	1.50	3.00
59	Stormtrooper Swarm R	1.50	3.00
60	Streets of Cloud City R	1.50	3.00
61	Toryn Farr (A) R	1.50	3.00
62	Vader's Imperial Shuttle (A) R	2.50	5.00
63	Wampa Cave R	1.50	3.00
64	Wedge Antilles (B) R	5.00	10.00
65	Wedge's Snowspeeder (A) R	5.00	10.00
66	Yoda (F) R	1.50	3.00
67	Yoda (G) R	1.50	3.00
68	Yoda (H) R	1.50	3.00
69	Yoda's Training R	1.50	3.00
70	Zev Senesca (A) R	1.50	3.00
71	3,720 to 1 U	.50	1.00
72	Admiral Firmus Piett (A) U	.50	1.00
73	Admiral Kendal Ozzel (A) U	.50	1.00
74	Outmaneuver Them U	.50	1.00
75	All Terrain Troop Transport U	.50	1.00
76	Anti-Infantry Laser Battery U	.50	1.00
77	Asteroid Field U	.50	1.00
78	AT-AT Driver U	.50	1.00
79	Blizzard Force AT-ST U	.50	1.00
80	Battle the Wampa U	.50	1.00
81	Cloud City Penthouse U	.50	1.00
82	Cloud City Prison U	.50	1.00
83	Bespin Twin-Pod Cloud Car U	.50	1.00
84	Blockade U	.50	1.00
85	Bright Hope (A) U	.50	1.00
86	C-3PO (F) U	.50	1.00
87	Change in Destiny U	.50	1.00
88	Chewbacca (F) R	.50	1.00
89	Darth Vader (G) R	.50	1.00
90	Darth Vader (K) U	.50	1.00
91	Death Mark U	.50	1.00
92	Derek Hobbie Klivian (A) U	.50	1.00
93	Don't Get All Mushy U	.50	1.00
94	Dragonsnake U	.50	1.00
95	Emergency Repairs U	.50	1.00
96	Carbon Freeze U	.50	1.00
97	Executor Bridge U	.50	1.00
98	Executor Hangar U	.50	1.00
99	Quicker Easier More Seductive U	.50	1.00
100	General Maximilian Veers (A) U	.50	1.00
101	Han Enchained U	.50	1.00
102	Han Solo (F) U	.50	1.00
103	Hoth Icefields U	.50	1.00
104	Imperial Fleet U	.50	1.00
105	Imperial Misdirection U	.50	1.00
106	Jungles of Dagobah U	.50	1.00
107	Lambda-Class Shuttle U	.50	1.00
108	Lando Calrissian (C) U	.50	1.00
109	Leia's Warning U	.50	1.00
110	Luke Skywalker (I) U	.50	1.00
111	Medical Center U	.50	1.00
112	Millennium Falcon (D) U	.50	1.00
113	Mynock U	.50	1.00
114	Painful Reckoning U	.50	1.00
115	Princess Leia (H) U	.50	1.00
116	Probe Droid U	.50	1.00
117	Probot U	.50	1.00
118	R2-D2 (F) U	.50	1.00
119	Rebel Fleet U	.50	1.00
120	Rebel Hoth Army U	.50	1.00
121	Rebel Trenches U	.50	1.00
122	Rebel Troop Cart U	.50	1.00
123	Redemption (A) U	.50	1.00
124	See You In Hell U	.50	1.00
125	Self Destruct U	.50	1.00
126	Shield Generator U	.50	1.00
127	Snowspeeder Rogue Ten U	.50	1.00
128	Snowspeeder Squad U	.50	1.00
129	Snowtrooper Elite Squad U	.50	1.00
130	Stormtrooper Sentry U	.50	1.00
131	Surprise Reinforcements U	.50	1.00
132	TIE Bomber Pilot U	.50	1.00
133	TIE Bomber Squad U	.50	1.00
134	TIE Pursuit Pilot U	.50	1.00
135	Torture Room U	.50	1.00
136	Vader's Call U	.50	1.00
137	Vicious Attack U	.50	1.00
138	Wampa U	.50	1.00
139	Yoda's Hut U	.50	1.00
140	725 to 1 C	.25	.50
141	All Terrain Armored Transport C	.25	.50
142	All Terrain Scout Transport C	.25	.50
143	Alter the Deal C	.25	.50
144	Antivehicle Laser Cannon C	.25	.50
145	Armor Plating C	.25	.50
146	Space Slug C	.25	.50
147	Blizzard Force AT-AT C	.25	.50
148	Precise Attack C	.25	.50
149	Belly of the Beast C	.25	.50
150	Cloud City Battleground C	.25	.50
151	Cloud City Dining Hall C	.25	.50
152	Cloud City Landing Platform C	.25	.50
153	Bespin System C	.25	.50
154	Blizzard C	.25	.50
155	Bogwing C	.25	.50
156	Close the Shield Doors C	.25	.50
157	Darth Vader (J) C	.25	.50
158	Vader's Vengeance C	.25	.50
159	Dagobah System C	.25	.50
160	Explore the Swamps C	.25	.50
161	Float Away C	.25	.50
162	Force Throw C	.25	.50
163	Gallofree Medium Transport C	.25	.50
164	Ground Assault C	.25	.50
165	Han Solo (E) C	.25	.50
166	Han's Attack C	.25	.50
167	Han's Promise C	.25	.50
168	Hanging Around C	.25	.50
169	Hope of Another C	.25	.50
170	Hoth Battle Plains C	.25	.50
171	Hoth System C	.25	.50
172	Imperial II-Class Star Destroyer C	.25	.50
173	Jedi Master's Meditation C	.25	.50
174	Jedi Trap C	.25	.50
175	Kuat Lancer-Class Frigate C	.25	.50
176	Kuat Nebulon-B Frigate C	.25	.50
177	Lando Calrissian (B) C	.25	.50
178	Lando's Repairs C	.25	.50
179	Leap into the Chasm C	.25	.50
180	Luke Skywalker (H) C	.25	.50
181	Meditation Chamber C	.25	.50
182	Navy Trooper C	.25	.50
183	Princess Leia (F) C	.25	.50
184	Probe the Galaxy C	.25	.50
185	Rebel Command Center C	.25	.50
186	Rebel Escape Squad C	.25	.50
187	Rebel Hangar C	.25	.50
188	Rebel Trench Defenders C	.25	.50
189	Rebel Assault Frigate C	.25	.50
190	Dreadnaught Heavy Cruiser C	.25	.50
191	Snowspeeder Rogue Two C	.25	.50
192	Snowstorm C	.25	.50
193	Snowtrooper Heavy Weapons Team C	.25	.50
194	Snowtrooper Squad C	.25	.50

195 Snowtrooper Guard C		.25	.50
196 Imperial II Star Destroyer C		.25	.50
197 Strange Lodgings C		.25	.50
198 Swamps of Dagobah C		.25	.50
199 Tauntaun C		.25	.50
200 Tauntaun Mount C		.25	.50
201 TIE Bomber EX-1-2 C		.25	.50
202 TIE Bomber EX-1-8 C		.25	.50
203 TIE Fighter EX-4-9 C		.25	.50
204 TIE Fighter OS-72-8 C		.25	.50
205 TIE Pursuit Squad C		.25	.50
206 Trust Her Instincts C		.25	.50
207 Visions of the Future C		.25	.50
208 Well-Earned Meal C		.25	.50
209 X-wing Rogue Seven C		.25	.50
210 Y-wing Gold Six C		.25	.50

2003 Star Wars Jedi Guardians

RELEASED IN JULY 2003

1 Adi Gallia (A) R		1.50	3.00
2 Anakin Skywalker (H) R		1.50	3.00
3 Aurra Sing (B) R		1.50	3.00
4 Boba Fett (B) R		1.50	3.00
5 Coup de Grace U		1.50	3.00
6 Dark Dreams R		1.50	3.00
7 Darth Maul (E) R		4.00	8.00
8 Darth Sidious (C) R		1.50	3.00
9 Darth Tyranus (F) R		2.50	5.00
10 Eeth Koth (A) R		1.50	3.00
11 Even Piell (A) R		1.50	3.00
12 Furious Charge C		1.50	3.00
13 Gather the Council R		1.50	3.00
14 Guidance of the Chancellor C		1.50	3.00
15 Homing Missile R		1.50	3.00
16 Jango Fett (G) R		1.50	3.00
17 Jedi Council Quorum R		1.50	3.00
18 Jedi Youngling R		1.50	3.00
19 Ki-Adi-Mundi (A) R		1.50	3.00
20 Kouhun R		1.50	3.00
21 Mace Windu (D) R		3.00	6.00
22 Trade Federation Battle Freighter C		1.50	3.00
23 Obi-Wan Kenobi (I) R		1.50	3.00
24 Obi-Wan's Starfighter (B) R		2.50	5.00
25 Oppo Rancisis (A) R		1.50	3.00
26 Padme Amidala (F) R		2.50	5.00
27 Plo Koon (B) R		1.50	3.00
28 R2-D2 (E) R		1.50	3.00
29 Remember the Prophecy R		1.50	3.00
30 Saesee Tiin (A) R		2.50	5.00
31 Senator Tikkes (A) R		1.50	3.00
32 Shaak Ti (B) R		2.50	5.00
33 Shmi Skywalker (A) R		2.50	5.00

34 Slave I (C) R		1.50	3.00
35 Trade Federation Blockade Ship C		1.50	3.00
36 Rapid Recovery R		1.50	3.00
37 Tipoca Training Ground R		1.50	3.00
38 Trade Federation Core Ship C		1.50	3.00
39 Tyranus's Geonosis Speeder (B) C		1.50	3.00
40 Unified Attack U		1.50	3.00
41 Yoda (D) R		6.00	12.00
42 Zam Wesell (D) R		1.50	3.00
43 Zam's Airspeeder (B) R		1.50	3.00
44 Battle Droid Division U		.50	1.00
45 Battle Protocol Droid (A) U		.50	1.00
46 Call for Reinforcements U		.50	1.00
47 Tyranus's Power C		.50	1.00
48 Clone Cadet U		.50	1.00
49 Coleman Trebor (A) U		.50	1.00
50 Corporate Alliance Tank Droid U		.50	1.00
51 Coruscant Air Bus U		.50	1.00
52 Depa Billaba (A) U		.50	1.00
53 Executioner Cart U		.50	1.00
54 FA-4 (A) U		.50	1.00
55 Jango Fett (F) U		.50	1.00
56 Jedi Arrogance U		.50	1.00
57 Jedi Training Exercise U		.50	1.00
58 Jedi Knight's Survival U		.50	1.00
59 Jedi Superiority U		.50	1.00
60 Lightsaber Gift U		.50	1.00
61 Lightsaber Loss U		.50	1.00
62 Neimoidian Shuttle (A) U		.50	1.00
63 Obi-Wan Kenobi (J) U		.50	1.00
64 Orray U		.50	1.00
65 Padme's Yacht (B) U		.50	1.00
66 Underworld Investigations C		.50	1.00
67 Protocol Battle Droid (A) U		.50	1.00
68 Qui-Gon Jinn (B) U		.50	1.00
69 Republic Communications Tower U		.50	1.00
70 RIC-920 U		.50	1.00
71 Sun-Fac (B) U		.50	1.00
72 Tactical leadership U		.50	1.00
73 Tame the Beast U		.50	1.00
74 Train For War U		.50	1.00
75 Tyranus's Return U		.50	1.00
76 Tyranus's Solar Sailer (B) U		.50	1.00
77 Yoda (E) U		.50	1.00
78 Zam Wesell (C) U		.50	1.00
79 Anakin Skywalker (I) C		.25	.50
80 Mobile Artillery Division C		.25	.50
81 Captured Reek C		.25	.50
82 Clone Fire Team C		.25	.50
83 Close Pursuit C		.25	.50
84 Darth Tyranus (G) C		.25	.50
85 Destroyer Droid Team U		.25	.50
86 Diplomatic Barge C		.25	.50
87 Droid Deactivation C		.25	.50
88 Droid Starfighter Assault Wing C		.25	.50
89 Trade Federation Droid Bomber C		.25	.50
90 Forward Command Center C		.25	.50
91 Geonosian Fighter Escort C		.25	.50
92 Gondola Speeder C		.25	.50
93 Gunship Offensive C		.25	.50
94 Jedi Starfighter Squadron C		.25	.50
95 Obi-Wan's Maneuver C		.25	.50
96 Plan for the Future C		.25	.50
97 Republic Assault Transport C		.25	.50
98 Republic Attack Gunship C		.25	.50
99 Republic Light Assault Cruiser C		.25	.50
100 Republic Hyperdrive Ring C		.25	.50
101 Sabaoth Starfighter C		.25	.50
102 Scurrier C		.25	.50
103 Separatist Battle Droid C		.25	.50
104 Shaak C		.25	.50
105 Synchronized Systems C		.25	.50

2004 Star Wars The Phantom Menace

RELEASED IN JULY 2004

1 Ann and Tann Gella (A) R		2.50	5.00
2 Aurra Sing (C) R		1.50	3.00
3 Bongo Sub R		1.50	3.00
4 Boss Nass (A) R		1.50	3.00
5 C-9979 R		1.50	3.00
6 Corridors of Power R		1.50	3.00
7 Dark Woman (A) R		2.50	5.00
8 Darth Maul (F) R		2.50	5.00
9 Duel of the Fates R		1.50	3.00
10 Fambaa Shield Beast R		1.50	3.00
11 Fight on All Fronts R		1.50	3.00
12 Gardulla the Hutt (A) R		1.50	3.00
13 Gas Attack R		1.50	3.00
14 Gungan Grand Army R		2.00	4.00
15 Guardian Mantis (A) R		1.50	3.00
16 In Disguise R		1.50	3.00
17 Jar Jar Binks (B) R		1.50	3.00
18 Jedi Temple R		1.50	3.00
19 Ki-Adi-Mundi (B) R		2.50	5.00
20 Marauder-Class Corvette R		1.50	3.00
21 Negotiate the Peace R		1.50	3.00
22 Nute Gunray (C) R		1.50	3.00
23 Orn Free Taa (A) R		1.50	3.00
24 Otoh Gunga R		1.50	3.00
25 Podracing Course R		1.50	3.00
26 Quinlan Vos (A) R		1.50	3.00
27 Sando Aqua Monster R		1.50	3.00
28 Sith Infiltrator (B) R		1.50	3.00
29 Walking Droid Starfighter R		1.50	3.00
30 Watto's Shop R		1.50	3.00
31 A'Sharad Hett (A) U		1.50	3.00
32 Anakin Skywalker (J) U		4.00	8.00
33 Anakin's Podracer (A) U		2.50	5.00
34 Bravo Starfighter U		.50	1.00
35 Captain Panaka (A) U		.50	1.00
36 Captain Tarpals (A) U		.50	1.00
37 Citadel Cruiser U		.50	1.00
38 Colo Claw Fish U		.50	1.00
39 Discuss It in Committee U		.50	1.00
40 Durge (A) U		.50	1.00
41 Falumpaset U		.50	1.00
42 Gungan Battle Wagon U		.50	1.00
43 Gungan Catapult U		.50	1.00
44 Inferno (A) U		.50	1.00
45 Kaadu Scout U		.50	1.00
46 Let the Cube Decide U		.50	1.00
47 Modified YV-330 (A) U		.50	1.00
48 Naboo System U		.50	1.00
49 Qui-Gon Jinn (D) U		.50	1.00
50 Ric Olié (A) U		.50	1.00

51	Royal Cruiser U	.50	1.00
52	Rune Haako (A) U	.50	1.00
53	Sebulba (A) U	.50	1.00
54	Sebulba's Podracer (A) U	.50	1.00
55	Streets of Theed U	.50	1.00
56	Trade Federation Hangar U	.50	1.00
57	Trade Federation MTT U	.50	1.00
58	Vilmarh Grahrk (A) U	.50	1.00
59	Watto (B) U	.50	1.00
60	Yaddle (A) U	.50	1.00
61	A Bigger Fish C	.25	.50
62	Aayla Secura (B) C	.25	.50
63	Blockade {TPM} C	.25	.50
64	Blockade Battleship C	.25	.50
65	CloakShape Fighter C	.25	.50
66	Darth Sidious (D) C	.25	.50
67	Delta Six Jedi Starfighter C	.25	.50
68	Eopie C	.25	.50
69	Finis Valorum (B) C	.25	.50
70	Flash Speeder C	.25	.50
71	Gian Speeder C	.25	.50
72	Gungan Kaadu Squad C	.25	.50
73	Jedi Transport C	.25	.50
74	Melt Your Way In C	.25	.50
75	Mos Espa C	.25	.50
76	Naboo Pilot C	.25	.50
77	Obi-Wan Kenobi (K) C	.25	.50
78	Opee Sea Killer C	.25	.50
79	Podrace C	.25	.50
80	Qui-Gon Jinn (C) C	.25	.50
81	Sith Probe Droid C	.25	.50
82	Sneak Attack C	.25	.50
83	Swamps of Naboo C	.25	.50
84	TC-14 (A) C	.25	.50
85	Theed Power Generator C	.25	.50
86	Theed Royal Palace C	.25	.50
87	Trade Federation AAT C	.25	.50
88	Trade Federation STAP C	.25	.50
89	Unconventional Maneuvers C	.25	.50
90	Yinchorri Fighter C	.25	.50

2004 Star Wars Return of the Jedi

RELEASED IN OCTOBER 2004

1	Admiral Ackbar (A) R	1.50	3.00
2	Anakin Skywalker (K) R	1.50	3.00
3	Anakin's Spirit (A) R	1.50	3.00
4	Bargain with Jabba R	1.50	3.00
5	Bib Fortuna (A) R	1.50	3.00
6	Chewbacca (J) R	1.50	3.00
7	Darth Vader (P) R	1.50	3.00
8	Death Star II (B) R	1.50	3.00
9	Emperor Palpatine (E) R	1.50	3.00

10	Endor Imperial Fleet R	1.50	3.00
11	Endor Rebel Fleet R	1.50	3.00
12	Endor Shield Generator R	1.50	3.00
13	Ephant Mon (A) R	1.50	3.00
14	Endor Regiment R	1.50	3.00
15	Free Tatooine R	1.50	3.00
16	Han Solo (K) R	1.50	3.00
17	Home One (A) R	1.50	3.00
18	Honor the Fallen R	1.50	3.00
19	Jabba the Hutt (A) R	1.50	3.00
20	Jabba's Dancers R	1.50	3.00
21	Jabba's Palace R	1.50	3.00
22	Jabba's Spies R	1.50	3.00
23	Lando Calrissian (H) R	1.50	3.00
24	Luke Skywalker (N) R	1.50	3.00
25	Malakili (A) R	1.50	3.00
26	Max Rebo Band (A) R	1.50	3.00
27	Mixed Battlegroup R	1.50	3.00
28	Mon Mothma (A) R	1.50	3.00
29	Nien Nunb (A) R	1.50	3.00
30	Occupied Tatooine R	1.50	3.00
31	Progress Report R	1.50	3.00
32	Rancor R	1.50	3.00
33	Reactor Core R	1.50	3.00
34	Salacious B. Crumb (A) R	1.50	3.00
35	Sarlacc (A) R	1.50	3.00
36	Scythe Squadron (A) R	1.50	3.00
37	Throne Room R	1.50	3.00
38	Trap Door! R	1.50	3.00
39	Vader's Guile R	1.50	3.00
40	Yoda's Spirit (A) R	1.50	3.00
41	Baited Trap U	.50	1.00
42	Boba Fett (H) U	.50	1.00
43	C-3PO (H) U	.50	1.00
44	Captain Lennox (A) U	.50	1.00
45	Chief Chirpa (A) U	.50	1.00
46	Darth Vader (N) U	.50	1.00
47	Desperate Bluff U	.50	1.00
48	Emperor Palpatine (D) U	.50	1.00
49	Ewok Village U	.50	1.00
50	Free Bespin U	.50	1.00
51	Free Endor U	.50	1.00
52	Han Solo (J) U	.50	1.00
53	Ionization Weapons U	.50	1.00
55	Jabba the Hutt (C) U	.50	1.00
56	Jabba's Sail Barge (A) U	.50	1.00
57	Lando Calrissian (I) U	.50	1.00
58	Luke Skywalker (O) U	.50	1.00
59	Millennium Falcon (J) U	.50	1.00
60	Occupied Bespin U	.50	1.00
61	Occupied Endor U	.50	1.00
62	Princess Leia (J) U	.50	1.00
63	R2-D2 (I) U	.50	1.00
64	Rancor Pit U	.50	1.00
65	Red Squadron X-wing U	.50	1.00
66	Skiff U	.50	1.00
67	Vader's Summons U	.50	1.00
68	Wicket W. Warrick (A) U	.50	1.00
69	Wookiee Hug U	.50	1.00
70	Worrt U	.50	1.00
71	A-wing C	.25	.50
72	B-wing C	.25	.50
73	Cantina Bar Mob C	.25	.50
74	Chewbacca (K) C	.25	.50
75	Close Quarters C	.25	.50
76	Elite Royal Guard C	.25	.50
77	Darth Vader (O) C	.25	.50
78	Death Star Battalion C	.25	.50
79	Death Star II (A) C	.25	.50
80	Decoy C	.25	.50
81	Dune Sea C	.25	.50

82	Elite Squad C	.25	.50
83	Emperor Palpatine (C) C	.25	.50
84	Ewok Artillery C	.25	.50
85	Ewok Glider C	.25	.50
86	Fly Casual C	.25	.50
87	Force Lightning C	.25	.50
88	Forest AT-AT C	.25	.50
89	Forest AT-ST C	.25	.50
90	Endor Attack Squad C	.25	.50
91	Forests of Endor C	.25	.50
92	Free Coruscant C	.25	.50
93	Gray Squadron Y-wing C	.25	.50
94	High-Speed Dodge C	.25	.50
95	Imperial Speeder Bike C	.25	.50
96	Imperial-Class Star Destroyer C	.25	.50
97	Jabba's Guards C	.25	.50
98	Lightsaber Throw C	.25	.50
99	Log Trap C	.25	.50
100	Luke Skywalker (M) C	.25	.50
101	Mon Calamari Cruiser C	.25	.50
102	Occupied Coruscant C	.25	.50
103	Oola (A) C	.25	.50
104	Princess Leia (K) C	.25	.50
105	Rebel Scouts C	.25	.50
106	Royal Guards C	.25	.50
107	Scout Trooper C	.25	.50
108	Surprising Strength C	.25	.50
109	TIE Interceptor C	.25	.50
110	Savage Attack C	.25	.50

2004 Star Wars Rogues and Scoundrels

RELEASED IN APRIL 2004

1	Admiral Firmus Piett (C) R	1.50	3.00
2	Boba Fett (G) R	1.50	3.00
3	Bossk (A) R	1.50	3.00
4	Call For Hunters R	1.50	3.00
5	Chewbacca (I) R	1.50	3.00
6	Commander Nemet (A) R	1.50	3.00
7	Dantooine System R	1.50	3.00
8	Dark Sacrifice R	1.50	3.00
9	Dengar (A) R	1.50	3.00
10	Doctor Evazan (A) R	1.50	3.00
11	Guri (A) R	1.50	3.00
12	Han Solo (I) R	1.50	3.00
13	Het Nkik (A) R	1.50	3.00
14	Hounds Tooth (A) R	1.50	3.00
15	IG-2000 (A) R	1.50	3.00
16	IG-88 (A) R	1.50	3.00
17	Dune Sea Krayt Dragon R	1.50	3.00
18	Lando Calrissian (F) R	1.50	3.00
19	Lando Calrissian (G) R	1.50	3.00
20	Lando's Influence R	1.50	3.00

21 Lobot (B) R	1.50	3.00
22 Mara Jade (B) R	1.50	3.00
23 Millennium Falcon (I) R	1.50	3.00
24 Mist Hunter (A) R	1.50	3.00
25 Modal Nodes (A) R	1.50	3.00
26 Prince Xizor (A) R	1.50	3.00
27 Princess Leia (I) R	1.50	3.00
28 Slave 1 (F) R	1.50	3.00
29 Stinger (A) R	1.50	3.00
30 Take A Prisoner R	1.50	3.00
31 Trash Compactor R	1.50	3.00
32 Virago (A) R	1.50	3.00
33 Yoda (I) R	1.50	3.00
34 Yoda's Lesson R	1.50	3.00
35 Zuckuss (A) R	1.50	3.00
36 4 Lom (A) U	.50	1.00
37 AT-AT U	.50	1.00
38 Bespin Cloud Car Squad U	.50	1.00
39 Big Asteroid U	.50	1.00
40 Boba Fett (F) U	.50	1.00
41 C 3P0 (G) U	.50	1.00
42 Chewbacca (H) U	.50	1.00
43 Cloud City Wing Guard U	.50	1.00
44 Darth Vader (M) U	.50	1.00
45 Death Star Control Room U	.50	1.00
46 Garindan (A) U	.50	1.00
47 Greedo (B) U	.50	1.00
48 Han Solo (H) U	.50	1.00
49 Han's Sacrifice U	.50	1.00
50 Holoprojection Chamber U	.50	1.00
51 Human Shield U	.50	1.00
52 Kessel System U	.50	1.00
53 Lando Calrissian (E) U	.50	1.00
54 Lando's Trickery U	.50	1.00
55 Luke Skywalker (L) U	.50	1.00
56 Luke's X-wing (D) U	.50	1.00
57 Millennium Falcon (H) U	.50	1.00
58 Ponda Baba (A) U	.50	1.00
59 Punishing One (A) U	.50	1.00
60 R2-D2 (H) U	.50	1.00
61 Redoubled Effort U	.50	1.00
62 E-3P0 (A) U	.50	1.00
63 Slave 1 (E) U	.50	1.00
64 Slave 1 (D) U	.50	1.00
65 Space Slug {RaS} U	.50	1.00
66 Outrider (A) U	.50	1.00
67 Ugnaught U	.50	1.00
68 Vendetta U	.50	1.00
69 Enraged Wampa U	.50	1.00
70 Lars Homestead U	.50	1.00
71 2-1B's Touch C	.25	.50
72 Bantha Herd C	.25	.50
73 Base Guards C	.25	.50
74 Bespin Patrol Cloud Car C	.25	.50
75 Boba Fett (C) C	.25	.50
76 Boba Fett (D) C	.25	.50
77 Boba Fett (E) C	.25	.50
78 Darth Vader (L) C	.25	.50
79 Dash Rendar (A) C	.25	.50
80 Disrupting Strike C	.25	.50
81 Falcon's Needs C	.25	.50
82 Jabba's Death Mark C	.25	.50
83 Kabe (A) C	.25	.50
84 Kyle Katarn (A) C	.25	.50
85 Lando System? C	.25	.50
86 Leebo (A) C	.25	.50
87 Luke's Garage C	.25	.50
88 Luke's Vow C	.25	.50
89 Medium Asteroid C	.25	.50
90 Mos Eisley C	.25	.50
91 Mos Eisley Cantina C	.25	.50
92 Muftak C	.25	.50
93 No Good To Me Dead C	.25	.50
94 Ord Mantell System C	.25	.50
95 Sleen C	.25	.50
96 Small Asteroid C	.25	.50
97 Zutton (A) C	.25	.50
98 Star Destroyer {RaS} C	.25	.50
99 Stormtrooper Detachment C	.25	.50
100 Streets Of Tatooine C	.25	.50
101 Tatooine Desert C	.25	.50
102 Tie Fighter C	.25	.50
103 Tusken Warrior C	.25	.50
104 Unmodified Snowspeeder C	.25	.50
105 X Wing Escort C	.25	.50

2005 Star Wars Revenge of the Sith

RELEASED IN MAY 2005

1 Anakin Skywalker (M) R	1.50	3.00
2 Bail Organa (B) R	1.50	3.00
3 Chewbacca (M) R	1.50	3.00
4 Commerce Guild Droid 81-X R	1.50	3.00
5 Commerce Guild Starship (ROTS) R	1.50	3.00
6 Coruscant Shuttle R	1.50	3.00
7 Darth Sidious (G) R	1.50	3.00
8 Darth Tyranus (I) R	1.50	3.00
9 Darth Vader (R) R	1.50	3.00
10 Darth Vader (S) R	1.50	3.00
11 Dismiss R	1.50	3.00
12 Droid Security Escort R	1.50	3.00
13 Engine Upgrade R	1.50	3.00
14 Foil R	1.50	3.00
15 Palpatine's Sanctum R	1.50	3.00
16 Grand Moff Tarkin (D) R	1.50	3.00
17 It Just Might Work R	1.50	3.00
18 Jar Jar Binks (C) R	1.50	3.00
19 Lightsaber Quick Draw R	1.50	3.00
20 Mace Windu (F) R	1.50	3.00
21 Mas Amedda (A) R	1.50	3.00
22 Mustafar Battle Grounds R	1.50	3.00
23 Mustafar System R	1.50	3.00
24 Nos Monster R	1.50	3.00
25 Obi-Wan Kenobi (N) R	1.50	3.00
26 PadmÈ Amidala (G) R	1.50	3.00
27 R4-P17 (A) R	1.50	3.00
28 Rage of Victory R	1.50	3.00
29 Recusant-Class Light Destroyer R	1.50	3.00
30 Republic Fighter Wing R	1.50	3.00
31 Sacrifice the Expendable R	1.50	3.00
32 Separatist Fleet R	1.50	3.00
33 Spinning Slash R	1.50	3.00
34 Strike with Impunity R	1.50	3.00
35 Stubborn Personality R	1.50	3.00
36 Super Battle Droid 7EX R	1.50	3.00
37 Theta-Class Shuttle R	1.50	3.00
38 Unexpected Attack R	1.50	3.00
39 Venator-Class Destroyer R	1.50	3.00
40 Yoda (K) R	1.50	3.00
41 Acclamator II-Class Assault Ship U	.50	1.00
42 AT-AP U	.50	1.00
43 C-3PO (I) U	.50	1.00
44 Chancellor's Office U	.50	1.00
45 Combined Squadron Tactics U	.50	1.00
46 Confusion U	.50	1.00
47 Darth Sidious (F) U	.50	1.00
48 Darth Vader (Q) U	.50	1.00
49 Destroyer Droid, Q Series U	.50	1.00
50 Droid Missiles U	.50	1.00
51 Elite Guardian U	.50	1.00
52 Hardcell-Class Transport U	.50	1.00
53 Jedi Concentration U	.50	1.00
54 Jedi Master's Deflection U	.50	1.00
55 Kashyyyk System U	.50	1.00
56 Naboo Star Skiff U	.50	1.00
57 Nute Gunray (D) U	.50	1.00
58 Obi-Wan Kenobi (L) U	.50	1.00
59 PadmÈ Amidala (H) U	.50	1.00
60 Patrol Mode Vulture Droid U	.50	1.00
61 GH-7 Medical Droid U	.50	1.00
62 R2-D2 (J) U	.50	1.00
63 Thread The Needle U	.50	1.00
64 Thwart U	.50	1.00
65 Treachery U	.50	1.00
66 Techno Union Interceptor U	.50	1.00
67 Utapau System U	.50	1.00
68 Vehicle Shields Package U	.50	1.00
69 Vehicle Weapons Package U	.50	1.00
70 Yoda (J) U	.50	1.00
71 Anakin Skywalker (L) C	.25	.50
72 Anakin's Starfighter (A) C	.25	.50
73 ARC-170 Starfighter C	.25	.50
74 AT-RT C	.25	.50
75 BARC Speeder C	.25	.50
76 Blaster Pistol C	.25	.50
77 Blaster Rifle C	.25	.50
78 Buzz Droid C	.25	.50
79 Chewbacca (L) C	.25	.50
80 Coruscant Emergency Ship C	.25	.50
81 Darth Sidious (E) C	.25	.50
82 Darth Tyranus (H) C	.25	.50
83 DC0052 Intergalactic Airspeeder C	.25	.50
84 Diving Attack C	.25	.50
85 Droid Battlestaff C	.25	.50
86 Droid Tri-Fighter C	.25	.50
87 Force Dodge C	.25	.50
88 HAVw A6 Juggernaut C	.25	.50
89 Homing Missiles Salvo C	.25	.50
90 IBC Hailfire Droid C	.25	.50
91 Instill Doubt C	.25	.50
92 InterGalactic Banking Clan Cruiser C	.25	.50
93 Jedi Lightsaber C	.25	.50
94 Jedi Piloting C	.25	.50
95 Meditate C	.25	.50
96 Obi-Wan Kenobi (M) C	.25	.50
97 Plo Koon's Starfighter (A) C	.25	.50
98 Power Attack C	.25	.50
99 Republic Assault Gunboat C	.25	.50
100 Security Droid C	.25	.50
101 Sith Lightsaber C	.25	.50
102 STAP Squad C	.25	.50
103 Surge of Strength C	.25	.50
104 Tank Droid C	.25	.50
105 TF Battle Droid Army C	.25	.50
106 Trade Federation Cruiser C	.25	.50
107 Unity of the Jedi C	.25	.50
108 Utapau Sinkhole C	.25	.50
109 Vulture Droid Starfighter C	.25	.50
110 V-wing Clone Starfighter C	.25	.50

2015 Star Wars Between the Shadows

12710633 A Hero's Trial	1.00	2.00
12720634 Luke Skywalker	1.00	2.00
12730635 Speeder Bike	1.00	2.00
12740636 Luke's Lightsaber	1.00	2.00
12750637 I Am a Jedi	1.00	2.00
12760065 Heat of Battle	1.00	2.00
12810638 The Master's Domain	1.00	2.00
12820639 Yoda	1.00	2.00
12830640 Bogwing	1.00	2.00
12840641 Yoda's Hut	1.00	2.00
12850089 Lightsaber Deflection	1.00	2.00
12860642 The Jedi's Resolve	1.00	2.00
12910643 Following Fate	1.00	2.00
12920644 Obi-Wan Kenobi	1.00	2.00
12930106 R2-D2	1.00	2.00
12940645 Obi-Wan's Lightsaber	1.00	2.00
12950646 Noble Sacrifice	1.00	2.00
12960133 Target of Opportunity	1.00	2.00
13010647 Journey Through the Swamp	1.00	2.00
13020648 Jubba Bird	1.00	2.00
13030648 Jubba Bird	1.00	2.00
13040649 Knobby White Spider	1.00	2.00
13050650 Life Creates It	1.00	2.00
13060651 Size Matters Not	1.00	2.00
13110652 Sacrifice at Endor	1.00	2.00
13120653 Ewok Hunter	1.00	2.00
13130653 Ewok Hunter	1.00	2.00
13140654 Funeral Pyre	1.00	2.00
13150655 Unexpected Assistance	1.00	2.00
13160656 Retreat to the Forest	1.00	2.00
13210657 Commando Raid	1.00	2.00
13220658 Lieutenant Judder Page	1.00	2.00
13230659 Page's Commandos	1.00	2.00
13240659 Page's Commandos	1.00	2.00
13250065 Heat of Battle	1.00	2.00
13260133 Target of Opportunity	1.00	2.00
13310660 Calling In Favors	1.00	2.00
13320661 Talon Karrde	1.00	2.00
13330662 Skipray Blastboat	1.00	2.00
13340662 Skipray Blastboat	1.00	2.00
13350663 Dirty Secrets	1.00	2.00
13360664 Clever Ruse	1.00	2.00
13410665 No Disintegrations	1.00	2.00
13420666 Boba Fett	1.00	2.00
13430667 Freelance Hunter	1.00	2.00
13440668 Flamethrower	1.00	2.00
13450378 Prized Possession	1.00	2.00
13460669 Entangled	1.00	2.00
13510670 Masterful Manipulation	1.00	2.00
13520671 Prince Xizor	1.00	2.00
13530672 Black Sun Headhunter	1.00	2.00
13540673 Debt Collector	1.00	2.00
13550674 Shadows of the Empire	1.00	2.00
13560675 The Prince's Scheme	1.00	2.00
13610676 All Out Brawl	1.00	2.00
13620677 Zekka Thyne	1.00	2.00
13630673 Debt Collector	1.00	2.00
13640678 Armed to the Teeth	1.00	2.00
13650669 Entangled	1.00	2.00
13660169 Heat of Battle	1.00	2.00
13710679 The Best That Credits Can Buy	1.00	2.00
13720680 Virago	1.00	2.00
13730672 Black Sun Headhunter	1.00	2.00
13740681 Rise of the Black Sun	1.00	2.00
13750682 Warning Shot	1.00	2.00
13760170 Target of Opportunity	1.00	2.00
13810683 The Hunters	1.00	2.00
13820684 Boushh	1.00	2.00
13830685 Snoova	1.00	2.00
13840686 A Better Offer	1.00	2.00
13850542 Pay Out	1.00	2.00
13860687 Show of Force	1.00	2.00
13910688 The Investigation	1.00	2.00
13920689 Ysanne Isard	1.00	2.00
13930690 Imperial Intelligence Officer	1.00	2.00
13940690 Imperial Intelligence Officer	1.00	2.00
13950691 Confiscation	1.00	2.00
13960692 Official Inquiry	1.00	2.00
14010693 Family Connections	1.00	2.00
14020694 General Tagge	1.00	2.00
14030695 Security Task Force	1.00	2.00
14040695 Security Task Force	1.00	2.00
14050696 Imperial Discipline	1.00	2.00
14060697 Precision Fire	1.00	2.00

2015 Star Wars Chain of Command

1611 A Hero's Beginning	1.00	2.00
1612 Luke's X-34 Landspeeder	1.00	2.00
1613 Owen Lars	1.00	2.00
1614 Moisture Vaporator	1.00	2.00
1615 Unfinished Business	1.00	2.00
1616 Supporting Fire	1.00	2.00
1621 Breaking the Blockade	1.00	2.00
1622 Smuggling Freighter	1.00	2.00
1623 Smuggling Freighter	1.00	2.00
1624 Duros Smuggler	1.00	2.00
1625 Duros Smuggler	1.00	2.00
1626 Surprising Maneuver	1.00	2.00
1631 The Imperial Bureaucracy	1.00	2.00
1632 Sate Pestage	1.00	2.00
1633 Advisor to the Emperor	1.00	2.00
1634 Quarren Bureaucrat	1.00	2.00
1635 Endless Bureaucracy	1.00	2.00
1636 Supporting Fire	1.00	2.00
1641 The Last Grand Admiral	1.00	2.00
1642 Grand Admiral Thrawn	1.00	2.00
1643 Noghri Bodyguard	1.00	2.00
1644 Noghri Bodyguard	1.00	2.00
1645 Chain of Command	2.50	5.00
1646 Supporting Fire	1.00	2.00
1651 Nar Shaddaa Drift	1.00	2.00
1652 Race Circuit Champion	1.00	2.00
1653 Racing Swoop	1.00	2.00
1654 Racing Swoop	1.00	2.00
1655 Black Market Exchange	1.00	2.00
1656 Cut Off	1.00	2.00

2015 Star Wars Draw Their Fire

14610722 The Survivors	1.00	2.00
14620723 Qu Rahn	1.00	2.00
14630724 Sulon Sympathizer	1.00	2.00
14640725 Shien Training	1.00	2.00
14650061 Force Rejuvenation	1.00	2.00
14660256 Protection	1.00	2.00
14710726 Called to Arms	1.00	2.00
14720727 Gray Squadron Gunner	1.00	2.00
14730728 Gray Squadron Y-Wing	1.00	2.00
14740729 Advanced Proton Torpedoes	1.00	2.00
14750730 Desperation	1.00	2.00
14760133 Target of Opportunity	1.00	2.00
14810731 The Daring Escape	1.00	2.00
14820732 LE-B02D9	1.00	2.00
14830733 Outrider	1.00	2.00
14840734 Spacer Cantina	1.00	2.00
14850735 Punch It	1.00	2.00
14860702 Stay on Target	1.00	2.00
14910736 The Emperor's Sword	1.00	2.00
14920737 Maarek Stele	1.00	2.00
14930738 Delta One	1.00	2.00
14940739 Advanced Concussion Missiles	1.00	2.00
14950740 Hand of the Emperor	1.00	2.00
14960169 Heat of Battle	1.00	2.00
15010741 Guarding the Wing	1.00	2.00
15020742 DS-61-3	1.00	2.00
15030743 Black Squadron Fighter	1.00	2.00
15040743 Black Squadron Fighter	1.00	2.00
15050744 Elite Pilot Training	1.00	2.00
15060170 Target of Opportunity	1.00	2.00

2015 Star Wars Imperial Entanglement

17110838	House Edge	1.00	2.00		18230892	TIE Phantom	1.00	2.00
17120839	Lando Calrissian	1.00	2.00		18240893	Enhanced Laser Cannon	1.00	2.00
17130840	Herglic Sabacc Addict	1.00	2.00		18250894	Fighters Coming In!	1.00	2.00
17140022	Cloud City Casino	1.00	2.00		18260169	Heat of Battle	1.00	2.00
17150841	Sabacc Shift	1.00	2.00		18310895	Brothers of the Sith	1.00	2.00
17160842	The Gamblerís Trick	1.00	2.00		18320896	Gorc	1.00	2.00
17210843	Debt of Honor	1.00	2.00		18330897	Pic	1.00	2.00
17220844	Chewbacca	1.00	2.00		18340898	Telepathic Connection	1.00	2.00
17230845	Wookiee Defender	1.00	2.00		18350062	Force Stasis	1.00	2.00
17240846	Kashyyyk Resistance Hideout	1.00	2.00		18360899	Force Invisibility	1.00	2.00
17250847	Wookiee Rage	1.00	2.00		18410900	The Huttís Menagerie	1.00	2.00
17260256	Protection	1.00	2.00		18420901	Malakili	1.00	2.00
17310848	Fortune and Fate	1.00	2.00		18430902	Jabbaís Rancor	1.00	2.00
17320849	Lady Luck	1.00	2.00		18440903	Bubo	1.00	2.00
17330850	Cloud City Technician	1.00	2.00		18450904	Underground Entertainment	1.00	2.00
17340850	Cloud City Technician	1.00	2.00		18460905	Jabbaís Summons	1.00	2.00
17350851	Central Computer	1.00	2.00					
17360133	Target of Opportunity	1.00	2.00			**2015 Star Wars Jump to Lightspeed**		
17410852	Honor Among Thieves	1.00	2.00					
17420853	Mirax Terrik	1.00	2.00					
17430854	Fringer Captain	1.00	2.00					
17440854	Fringer Captain	1.00	2.00					
17450855	Special Discount	1.00	2.00					
17460856	One Last Trick	1.00	2.00					
17510857	Renegade Reinforcements	1.00	2.00					
17520858	Corporal Dansra Beezer	1.00	2.00					
17530210	Renegade Squadron Operative	1.00	2.00					
17540859	Hidden Backup	1.00	2.00					
17550860	Directed Fire	1.00	2.00					
17560861	Last Minute Reinforcements	1.00	2.00					
17610862	Mysteries of the Rim	1.00	2.00					
17620863	Outer Rim Mystic	1.00	2.00					
17630863	Outer Rim Mystic	1.00	2.00					
17640864	Niman Training	1.00	2.00					
17650864	Niman Training	1.00	2.00					
17660865	Force Illusion	1.00	2.00					
17710866	Planning the Rescue	1.00	2.00		1661	The Forgotten Masters	1.00	2.00
17720867	General Airen Cracken	1.00	2.00		1662	Tira Saa	1.00	2.00
17730868	Alliance Infiltrator	1.00	2.00		1663	Lost Master	1.00	2.00
17740869	Superior Intelligence	1.00	2.00		1664	Lost Master	1.00	2.00
17750870	Undercover	1.00	2.00		1665	A Gift from the Past	1.00	2.00
17760117	Rescue Mission	1.00	2.00		1666	Echoes of the Force	1.00	2.00
17810871	The Tarkin Doctrine	1.00	2.00		1671	Heroes of the Rebellion	1.00	2.00
17820872	Grand Moff Tarkin	1.00	2.00		1672	Tycho Celchu	1.00	2.00
17830873	Stormtrooper Assault Team	1.00	2.00		1673	Wes Janson	1.00	2.00
17840874	Rule by Fear	1.00	2.00		1674	Rogue Six	1.00	2.00
17850875	Moment of Triumph	1.00	2.00		1675	Rogue Nine	1.00	2.00
17860171	Twist of Fate	1.00	2.00		1676	Ready for Takeoff	1.00	2.00
17910876	Might of the Empire	1.00	2.00		1681	That Bucket oí Bolts	1.00	2.00
17920877	Chimaera	1.00	2.00		1682	Han Solo	1.00	2.00
17930878	DP20 Corellian Gunship	1.00	2.00		1683	Millennium Falcon	1.00	2.00
17940879	Fleet Staging Area	1.00	2.00		1684	Well Paid	1.00	2.00
17950392	Tractor Beam	1.00	2.00		1685	Well Paid	1.00	2.00
17960880	The Empire Strikes Back	1.00	2.00		1686	Heat of Battle	1.00	2.00
18010881	Enforced Loyalty	1.00	2.00		1691	The Reawakening	1.00	2.00
18020882	Colonel Yularen	1.00	2.00		1692	Arden Lyn	1.00	2.00
18030883	Lieutenant Mithel	1.00	2.00		1693	Dark Side Apprentice	1.00	2.00
18040884	MSE-6 íMouseí Droid	1.00	2.00		1694	Return to Darkness	1.00	2.00
18050024	Control Room	1.00	2.00		1695	Give in to Your Anger	1.00	2.00
18060885	The Imperial Fist	1.00	2.00		1696	Give in to Your Anger	1.00	2.00
18110886	Imperial Entanglements	1.00	2.00		1701	Behind the Black Sun	1.00	2.00
18120887	Imperial Raider	1.00	2.00		1702	Guri	1.00	2.00
18130888	VT-49 Decimator	1.00	2.00		1703	Freelance Assassin	1.00	2.00
18140888	VT-49 Decimator	1.00	2.00		1704	Hidden Vibroknife	1.00	2.00
18150889	Customs Blockade	1.00	2.00		1705	Threat Removal	1.00	2.00
18160890	Ion Cannon	1.00	2.00		1706	Heat of Battle	1.00	2.00
18210891	Phantoms of Imdaar	1.00	2.00					
18220892	TIE Phantom	1.00	2.00					

2015 Star Wars Ready for Takeoff

14110698	Rogue Squadron Assault	1.00	2.00
14120699	Derek íHobbieí Klivian	1.00	2.00
14130700	Rogue Squadron X-Wing	1.00	2.00
14140700	Rogue Squadron X-Wing	1.00	2.00
14150701	Pilot Ready Room	1.00	2.00
14160702	Stay on Target	1.00	2.00
14210703	Memories of Taanab	1.00	2.00
14220704	Lando Calrissian	1.00	2.00
14230705	System Patrol Craft	1.00	2.00
14240705	System Patrol Craft	1.00	2.00
14250706	Conner Net	1.00	2.00
14260707	A Little Maneuver	1.00	2.00
14310708	Black Squadron Formation	1.00	2.00
14320709	íMaulerí Mithel	1.00	2.00
14330710	Black Two	1.00	2.00
14340146	TIE Advanced	1.00	2.00
14350711	Death Star Ready Room	1.00	2.00
14360712	Stay on Target	1.00	2.00
14410713	The Empireís Elite	1.00	2.00
14420714	Baron Fel	1.00	2.00
14430715	181st TIE Interceptor	1.00	2.00
14440715	181st TIE Interceptor	1.00	2.00
14450716	Flight Academy	1.00	2.00
14460712	Stay on Target	1.00	2.00
14510717	The Grand Heist	1.00	2.00
14520718	Niles Ferrier	1.00	2.00
14530719	Novice Starship Thief	1.00	2.00
14540719	Novice Starship Thief	1.00	2.00
14550720	Pirate Hideout	1.00	2.00
14560721	Salvage Operation	1.00	2.00

2016 Star Wars Destiny Awakening

RELEASED IN DECEMBER 2016

1	Captain Phasma L	7.50	15.00
2	First Order Stormtrooper R	2.50	5.00
3	General Grievous R	2.50	5.00
4	General Veers R	2.50	5.00
5	AT ST L	6.00	12.00
6	First Order TIE Fighter R	2.50	5.00
7	Commanding Presence L	7.50	15.00
8	F 11D Rifle S	2.00	4.00

#	Card	Low	High
9	Count Dooku R	2.50	5.00
10	Darth Vader L	15.00	30.00
11	Kylo Ren S	1.25	2.50
12	Nightsister R	2.50	5.00
13	Force Choke L	10.00	20.00
14	Immobilize R	2.50	5.00
15	Kylo Rens Lightsaber L	10.00	20.00
16	Sith Holocron R	7.50	13.00
17	Infantry Grenades R	2.50	5.00
18	Speeder Bike Scout R	2.50	5.00
19	Bala Tik R	2.50	5.00
20	Jabba the Hutt L	12.00	25.00
21	Jango Fett R	2.50	5.00
22	Tusken Raider R	2.50	5.00
23	Crime Lord L	7.50	15.00
24	Flame Thrower R	2.50	5.00
25	Gaffi Stick R	2.50	5.00
26	On the Hunt R	2.50	5.00
27	Admiral Ackbar R	2.50	5.00
28	Leia Organa R	2.50	5.00
29	Poe Dameron L	12.00	25.00
30	Rebel Trooper R	2.50	5.00
31	Launch Bay L	5.00	10.00
32	Black One L	4.00	8.00
33	Scout R	2.50	5.00
34	Survival Gear R	2.50	5.00
35	Luke Skywalker L	12.00	25.00
36	Padawan R	2.50	5.00
37	Qui Gon Jinn R	2.50	5.00
38	Rey S	2.00	4.00
39	Force Protection R	2.50	5.00
40	Jedi Robes R	2.50	5.00
41	Luke Skywalkers Lightsaber L	7.50	15.00
42	One With the Force L	12.00	25.00
43	BB 8 R	2.50	5.00
44	Reys Staff R	2.50	5.00
45	Finn S	2.00	4.00
46	Han Solo L	10.00	20.00
47	Hired Gun R	2.50	5.00
48	Padme Amidala R	2.50	5.00
49	Millennium Falcon L	7.50	15.00
50	Diplomatic Immunity R	2.50	5.00
51	DL 44 Heavy Blaster Pistol R	2.50	5.00
52	Infiltrate R	2.50	5.00
53	Outpost R	2.50	5.00
54	DH 17 Blaster Pistol R	2.50	5.00
55	IQA 11 Blaster Rifle R	2.50	5.00
56	Promotion R	2.50	5.00
57	Force Throw S	5.00	10.00
58	Force Training R	2.50	5.00
59	Lightsaber S	2.00	4.00
60	Mind Probe S	4.00	8.00
61	Comlink R	2.50	5.00
62	Datapad R	2.50	5.00
63	Holdout Blaster R	10.00	20.00
64	Black Market R	2.50	5.00
65	Cunning R	2.50	5.00
66	Jetpack R	2.50	5.00
67	Thermal Detonator L	12.00	25.00
68	Cannon Fodder C	.10	.20
69	Closing the Net C	.10	.20
70	Endless Ranks U	1.00	2.00
71	Occupation C	.10	.20
72	Probe C	.10	.20
73	Sweep the Area C	.10	.20
74	Tactical Mastery U	2.00	4.00
75	The Best Defense U	.20	.40
76	Drudge Work C	.10	.20
77	Local Garrison U	.20	.40
78	Personal Escort C	.10	.20
79	Abandon All Hope U	.20	.40
80	Boundless Ambition C	.10	.20
81	Enrage C	.10	.20

#	Card	Low	High
82	Feel Your Anger C	.10	.20
83	Force Strike U	.60	1.25
84	Intimidate C	.10	.20
85	Isolation C	.10	.20
86	No Mercy U	2.00	4.00
87	Pulling the Strings C	.10	.20
88	Emperors Favor U	.20	.40
89	Power of the Dark Side S	.30	.60
90	Hidden in Shadow U	.20	.40
91	Nowhere to Run U	.20	.40
92	Ace in the Hole U	.60	1.25
93	Armed to the Teeth C	.10	.20
94	Confiscation U	.20	.40
95	Fight Dirty U	.20	.40
96	Go for the Kill C	.10	.20
97	He Doesnt Like You C	.10	.20
98	Lying in Wait C	.10	.20
99	Backup Muscle C	.10	.20
100	My Kind of Scum C	.10	.20
101	Underworld Connections U	.75	1.50
102	Prized Possession U	.20	.40
103	Commando Raid U	.20	.40
104	Defensive Position C	.10	.20
105	Field Medic C	.10	.20
106	Hit and Run C	.10	.20
107	Its a Trap U	.60	1.25
108	Natural Talent C	.10	.20
109	Rearm U	.20	.40
110	Retreat U	.20	.40
111	Strategic Planning C	.10	.20
112	Surgical Strike C	.10	.20
113	Resistance HQ U	.20	.40
114	Anticipate U	.20	.40
115	Defensive Stance C	.10	.20
116	Force Misdirection C	.10	.20
117	Heroism C	.10	.20
118	Noble Sacrifice C	.10	.20
119	Patience C	.10	.20
120	Return of the Jedi U	.20	.40
121	Riposte C	.10	.20
122	Willpower U	.30	.60
123	Jedi Council U	.20	.40
124	Awakening S	.50	1.00
125	The Force is Strong C	.10	.20
126	Daring Escape U	.20	.40
127	Dont Get Cocky C	.10	.20
128	Draw Attention C	.10	.20
129	Hyperspace Jump U	.20	.40
130	Let the Wookiee Win U	.20	.40
131	Negotiate C	.10	.20
132	Scavenge C	.10	.20
133	Shoot First U	.20	.40
134	Smuggling C	.10	.20
135	Play the Odds U	.20	.40
136	Street Informants C	.10	.20
137	Second Chance U	1.25	2.50
138	Award Ceremony C	.10	.20
139	Dug In U	2.00	4.00
140	Firepower C	.10	.20
141	Leadership U	.30	.60
142	Logistics C	.10	.20
143	Squad Tactics C	.10	.20
144	Supporting Fire U	.20	.40
145	Deflect C	.10	.20
146	Disturbance in the Force C	.10	.20
147	Mind Trick U	.30	.60
148	The Power of the Force C	.10	.20
149	Use the Force S	.60	1.25
150	It Binds All Things U	1.00	2.00
151	Aim S	.30	.75
152	All In U	1.00	2.00
153	Block C	.10	.20
154	Close Quarters Assault S	.75	1.50

#	Card	Low	High
155	Dodge C	.10	.20
156	Flank U	.20	.40
157	Take Cover C	.10	.20
158	Disarm C	.10	.20
159	Electroshock U	3.00	6.00
160	Reversal U	.75	1.50
161	Scramble C	.10	.20
162	Unpredictable C	.10	.20
163	Infamous U	1.25	2.50
164	Hunker Down C	.10	.20
165	Command Center U	.20	.40
166	Echo Base U	.20	.40
167	Emperors Throne Room U	.20	.40
168	Frozen Wastes S	.50	1.00
169	Imperial Armory C	.10	.20
170	Jedi Temple C	.10	.20
171	Rebel War Room C	.10	.20
172	Mos Eisley Spaceport C	.10	.20
173	Separatist Base C	.10	.20
174	Starship Graveyard S	1.25	2.50

2017 Star Wars Destiny Spirit of Rebellion

RELEASED ON MAY 4, 2017

#	Card	Low	High
1	Death Trooper R	3.00	6.00
2	FN 2199 R	2.00	4.00
3	Director Krennic L	6.00	12.00
4	TIE Pilot R	2.00	4.00
5	E Web Emplacement R	5.00	10.00
6	Imperial Discipline R	2.00	4.00
7	DT 29 Heavy Blaster Pistol R	2.00	4.00
8	Z6 Riot Control Baton L	12.00	25.00
9	Asajj Ventress R	2.00	4.00
10	Darth Vader R	2.00	4.00
11	Palpatine L	12.00	25.00
12	Royal Guard R	2.00	4.00
13	Commando Shuttle R	2.00	4.00
14	Force Lightning L	10.00	20.00
15	Lightsaber Pike R	5.00	10.00
16	Lure of Power R	2.00	4.00
17	Interrogation Droid R	2.00	4.00
18	Aurra Sing R	2.00	4.00
19	Guavian Enforcer R	2.00	4.00
20	IG 88 L	6.00	12.00
21	Unkar Plutt R	2.00	4.00
22	Slave I L	6.00	12.00
23	Blackmail L	6.00	12.00
24	Personal Shield R	2.00	4.00
25	Vibroknucklers R	2.00	4.00
26	Baze Malbus L	6.00	12.00
27	Mon Mothma R	2.00	4.00
28	Rebel Commando R	2.00	4.00
29	Temmin "Snap" Wexley R	2.00	4.00
30	C 3PO R	2.00	4.00
31	U Wing L	6.00	12.00

#	Card	Lo	Hi
32	A180 Blaster R	2.00	4.00
33	Overkill R	2.00	4.00
34	Jedi Acolyte R	2.00	4.00
35	Chirrut Œmwe R	2.00	4.00
36	Luminara Unduli R	2.00	4.00
37	Obi Wan Kenobi L	6.00	12.00
38	Delta 7 Interceptor R	2.00	4.00
39	Handcrafted Light Bow L	6.00	12.00
40	Force Heal R	2.00	4.00
41	Journals of Ben Kenobi R	2.00	4.00
42	R2 D2 R	2.00	4.00
43	Chewbacca L	6.00	12.00
44	Jyn Erso R	2.00	4.00
45	Maz Kanata R	2.00	4.00
46	Outer Rim Smuggler R	2.00	4.00
47	Smuggling Freighter R	2.00	4.00
48	Bowcaster L	6.00	12.00
49	Lone Operative R	2.00	4.00
50	Mazs Goggles L	6.00	12.00
51	Supply Line R	2.00	4.00
52	Astromech R	2.00	4.00
53	Rocket Launcher L	20.00	35.00
54	Force Push R	2.00	4.00
55	Force Speed L	50.00	100.00
56	Makashi Training R	2.00	4.00
57	Vibroknife R	10.00	20.00
58	Quadjumper L	6.00	12.00
59	Ascension Gun R	5.00	10.00
60	Con Artist R	2.00	4.00
61	Battle Formation C	.10	.20
62	Imperial War Machine U	.20	.40
63	Lockdown C	.10	.20
64	Sustained Fire U	.20	.40
65	Traitor U	.20	.40
66	Trench Warfare C	.10	.20
67	Undying Loyalty C	.10	.20
68	We Have Them Now U	.30	.60
69	Attrition C	.10	.20
70	Imperial Inspection U	.30	.60
71	Anger U	.60	1.25
72	Lightsaber Throw U	.50	1.00
73	Manipulate C	.10	.20
74	No Disintegrations C	.10	.20
75	Now You Will Die C	.10	.20
76	Rise Again U	.75	1.50
77	The Price of Failure C	.10	.20
78	Dark Presence U	.75	1.50
79	Now I Am The Master C	.10	.20
80	Doubt C	.10	.20
81	Arms Deal C	.10	.20
82	Bait and Switch C	.10	.20
83	Friends in High Places U	.20	.40
84	Loose Ends U	.20	.40
85	One Quarter Portion C	.10	.20
86	Relentless Pursuit C	.10	.20
87	Scrap Buy U	.20	.40
88	Salvage Stand C	.10	.20
89	Armor Plating U	.50	1.00
90	Emergency Evacuation U	.20	.40
91	Friendly Fire U	.20	.40
92	Guerrilla Warfare C	.10	.20
93	Our Only Hope U	.20	.40
94	Rebel Assault C	.10	.20
95	Sensor Placement U	.20	.40
96	Spirit of Rebellion C	.10	.20
97	Planetary Uprising U	.50	1.00
98	Spy Net C	.10	.20
99	Tactical Aptitude C	.10	.20
100	Caution U	.60	1.25
101	Destiny C	.10	.20
102	Determination C	.10	.20
103	Guard U	.20	.40
104	Krayt Dragon Howl C	.10	.20
105	My Ally Is The Force U	.50	1.00
106	Synchronicity C	.10	.20
107	Your Eyes Can Decive You U	.20	.40
108	Protective Mentor C	.10	.20
109	Confidence U	.20	.40
110	Garbagell Do C	.10	.20
111	Hold On C	.10	.20
112	Rebel U	.20	.40
113	Long Con C	.10	.20
114	Loth Cat and Mouse C	.10	.20
115	Never Tell Me the Odds U	.20	.40
116	Planned Explosion U	.20	.40
117	Double Dealing C	.10	.20
118	Life Debt U	.20	.40
119	Bombing Run U	.20	.40
120	Collateral Damage C	.10	.20
121	Salvo U	.30	.60
122	Suppression C	.10	.20
123	Aftermath C	.10	.20
124	Air Superiority C	.10	.20
125	Training U	2.00	4.00
126	Wingman C	.10	.20
127	Decisive Blow C	.10	.20
128	High Ground C	.10	.20
129	Momentum Shift U	.20	.40
130	Overconfidence C	.10	.20
131	Premonitions U	.20	.40
132	Rejuvenate C	.10	.20
133	Trust Your Instincts U	1.00	2.00
134	Meditate C	.10	.20
135	Force Illusion U	2.00	4.00
136	Evade C	.10	.20
137	New Orders U	.50	1.00
138	Parry C	.10	.20
139	Swiftness C	.10	.20
140	Resolve U	.20	.40
141	Ammo Belt C	.10	.20
142	Bolt Hole C	.10	.20
143	Cheat U	.60	1.25
144	Diversion C	.10	.20
145	Fair Trade U	.20	.40
146	Friends in Low Places C	.10	.20
147	Sabotage U	.20	.40
148	Improvisation C	.10	.20
149	Outmaneuver C	.10	.20
150	Fast Hands U	4.00	7.00
151	Carbon Freezing Chamber U	.20	.40
152	Cargo Hold C	.10	.20
153	Docking Bay C	.10	.20
154	Ewok Village C	.10	.20
155	Mazs Castle U	.20	.40
156	Moisture Farm U	.20	.40
157	Otoh Gunga C	.10	.20
158	Secluded Beach C	.10	.20
159	Secret Facility U	.20	.40
160	War Torn Streets C	.10	.20

2018 Star Wars Destiny Empire at War

RELEASED ON DECEMBER 10, 2018

#	Card	Lo	Hi
1	†Ciena Reet† Adept Pilot R	2.50	5.00
2	General Hux†- Aspiring Commander R	2.50	5.00
3	MagnaGuard R	2.50	5.00
4	Thrawn -†Master Strategist L	10.00	20.00
5	AT-DP R	2.50	5.00
6	Probe Droid R	2.50	5.00
7	T-7 Ion Disruptor Rifle L	7.50	15.00
8	Quinlan Vos†- Dark Disciple R	2.50	5.00
9	Servant of the Dark Side R	2.50	5.00
10	Seventh Sister†- Agile Inquisitor L	7.50	15.00
11	Grand Inquisitor†- Sith Loyalist L	7.50	15.00
12	Darth Vader's TIE Advanced R	2.50	5.00
13	ID9 Seeker Droid R	2.50	5.00
14	Temptation R	2.50	5.00
15	Grand Inquisitor's Lightsaber L	7.50	15.00
16	Bazine Netal†- Master Manipulator R	2.50	5.00
17	†Bosskt† Wookiee Slayer R	2.50	5.00
18	Cad Bane†- Vicious Mercenary L	10.00	20.00
19	Gamorrean Guard R	2.50	5.00
20	Hound's Tooth L	7.50	15.00
21	Cable Launcher R	2.50	5.00
22	LL-30 Blaster Pistol R	2.50	5.00
23	Relby-V10 Mortar Gun R	2.50	5.00
24	General Rieekan†- Defensive Mastermind R	2.50	5.00
25	Hera Syndulla - Phoenix Leader R	2.50	5.00
26	K-2SO†Reprogrammed Droid L	7.50	15.00
27	Rookie Pilot R	2.50	5.00
28	Ghost L	7.50	15.00
29	Y-Wing R	2.50	5.00
30	A280 Blaster Rifle R	2.50	5.00
31	Ahsoka Tano†- Force Operative L	12.00	25.00
32	Jedi Instructor R	2.50	5.00
33	Kanan Jarrus†- Rebel Jedi R	2.50	5.00
34	Mace Windu†- Jedi Champion L	7.50	15.00
35	Training Remote R	2.50	5.00
36	Master of the Council L	7.50	15.00
37	Coordination R	2.50	5.00
38	Ezra Bridger†- Force-sensitive Thief R	2.50	5.00
39	Lando Calrissian†- Galactic Entrepreneur R	2.50	5.00
40	Sabine Wren†- Explosives Expert L	7.50	15.00
41	Wookiee Warrior R	2.50	5.00
42	Chopper L	7.50	15.00
43	Energy Slingshot R	2.50	5.00
44	Tough Haggler R	2.50	5.00
45	T-47 Airspeeder R	2.50	5.00
46	LR1K Sonic Cannon L	7.50	15.00
47	Electrostaff R	2.50	5.00
48	Natural Pilot R	2.50	5.00
49	Ancient Lightsaber L	25.00	45.00
50	Psychometry R	2.50	5.00
51	Shoto Lightsaber R	2.50	5.00
52	Weapons Cache R	2.50	5.00
53	BD-1 Cutter Vibro AX R	2.50	5.00
54	Extortion R	2.50	5.00
55	X-8 Night Sniper L	7.50	15.00
56	Z-95 Headhunter R	2.50	5.00
57	Chance Cube R	2.50	5.00
58	EMP Grenades R	2.50	5.00
59	Lead by Example R	2.50	5.00
60	Scatterblaster R	2.50	5.00
61	Commander U	.30	.60
62	Crossfire C	.10	.20
63	Drop Your Weapon! U	.30	.60
64	Imperial Backing U	.30	.60
65	Prepare for War C	.10	.20
66	Red Alert C	.10	.20
67	Ruthless Tactics C	.10	.20
68	Take Prisoner U	.30	.60
69	Imperial HQ C	.10	.20
70	As You Command C	.10	.20
71	Cornered Prey C	.10	.20
72	Indomitable C	.10	.20
73	It Will All Be Mine U	.30	.60
74	Kill Them All C	.10	.20
75	Unyielding U	.30	.60
76	Insidious C	.10	.20
77	Hate U	.30	.60
78	Anarchy U	.30	.60
79	Bounty Postings C	.10	.20
80	Buy Out U	.30	.60
81	Coercion U	.30	.60
82	Only Business Matters C	.10	.20
83	Pilfered Goods U	.30	.60
84	Twin Shadows U	.30	.60

#	Card		
85	Hutt Ties C	.10	.20
86	Deadly U	.30	.60
87	No Survivors C	.10	.20
88	Detention Center U	.30	.60
89	All Quiet On The Front U	.30	.60
90	Entrenched U	.30	.60
91	Fortuitous Strike C	.10	.20
92	Rearguard C	.10	.20
93	Reckless Reentry U	.30	.60
94	Strike Briefing C	.10	.20
95	Swift Strike C	.10	.20
96	Rally Aid U	.30	.60
97	Shield Generator C	.10	.20
98	At Peace C	.10	.20
99	Bestow C	.10	.20
100	Bring Balance U	.30	.60
101	Reaping The Crystal U	.30	.60
102	Secret Mission C	.10	.20
103	Trust The Force C	.10	.20
104	Funeral Pyre C	.10	.20
105	Yoda's Quarters U	.30	.60
106	Fearless U	.30	.60
107	Against The Odds C	.10	.20
108	Appraise C	.10	.20
109	Bad Feeling C	.10	.20
110	Double Cross U	.30	.60
111	Impersonate U	.30	.60
112	Local Patrol C	.10	.20
113	Quick Escape U	.30	.60
114	Tenacity C	.10	.20
115	Running Interference U	.30	.60
116	Thermal Paint C	.10	.20
117	Defiance C	.10	.20
118	Covering Fire C	.10	.20
119	Deploy Squadron C	.10	.20
120	Fall Back U	.30	.60
121	Feint U	.30	.60
122	Flanking Maneuver U	.30	.60
123	Heat Of Battle C	.10	.20
124	Pinned Down C	.10	.20
125	The Day is Ours C	.10	.20
126	Drop Zone U	.30	.60
127	Tech Team C	.10	.20
128	Battle of Wills U	.30	.60
129	Force Vision C	.10	.20
130	Lightsaber Pull C	.10	.20
131	Lightsaber Training C	.10	.20
132	No Surrender C	.10	.20
133	Something familiar U	.30	.60
134	Voices Cry Out C	.10	.20
135	Keen Instincts U	.30	.60
136	Battle Rage C	.10	.20
137	Disable C	.10	.20
138	Persuade C	.10	.20
139	Pickpocket C	.10	.20
140	Threaten U	.30	.60
141	Trickery U	.30	.60
142	Truce C	.10	.20
143	Stolen Cache C	.10	.20
144	Hidden Agenda U	.30	.60
145	Mandalorian Armor C	.10	.20
146	Dangerous Mission C	.10	.20
147	Endurance U	.30	.60
148	Partnership C	.10	.20
149	Recycle C	.10	.20
150	Rend C	.10	.20
151	Roll On C	.10	.20
152	Plastoid Armor C	.10	.20
153	B'Omarr Monastery†- Teth C	.10	.20
154	Fort Anaxes†- Anaxes U	.30	.60
155	Garel Spaceport†- Garel U	.30	.60
156	Imperial Academy†- Lothal U	.30	.60
157	Main Plaza†- Vashka C	.10	.20

#	Card		
158	Medical Center†- Kaliida Shoals U	.30	.60
159	Port District†- Bespin U	.30	.60
160	Weapons Factory Alpha†- Cymoon 1 U	.30	.60

2018 Star Wars Destiny Rivals Starter Deck

RELEASED ON FEBRUARY 15, 2018

1 Anakin Skywalker - Conflicted Apprentice
2 Lobot - Cyborg Aide
3 Ketsu Onyo - Black Sun Operative
4 Jawa Scavenger
5 Hidden Motive
6 Crafted Lightsaber
7 Targeting Computer
8 Fang Fighter
9 Tinker
10 Verpine Sniper Rifle
11 Emulate
12 Fight Back
13 Resourceful
14 Surprise Attack
15 Supply Pack
16 T-21 Repeating Blaster
17 Vibrosword
18 Bespin Wing Guard
19 Dry Fields - Atollon
20 Sith Temple - Malachor

2018 Star Wars Destiny Legacies

RELEASED ON FEBRUARY 1, 2018

#	Card		
1	Dark Advisor R	.50	1.00
2	Maul - Vengeful One L	7.50	15.00
3	Mother Talzin - Nightsister Matriarch R	.50	1.00
4	Palpatine - Darth Sidious R	.50	1.00
5	Kylo Ren's Starfighter L	2.00	4.00
6	Crystal Ball R	.50	1.00
7	Force Rend R	.50	1.00
8	Maul's Lightsaber L	10.00	20.00
9	Battle Droid R	.50	1.00
10	Kallus - Agent of the Empire R	.50	1.00
11	Nute Gunray - Separatist Viceroy R	.50	1.00
12	Tarkin - Grand Moff L	2.50	5.00
13	Veteran Stormtrooper ST		
14	Separatist Landing Craft R	.50	1.00
15	Fragmentation Grenade R	.50	1.00
16	Grand Moff L	3.00	6.00
17	Kallus' Bo-Rifle L	1.00	2.00
18	Bib Fortuna - Majordomo R	.50	1.00
19	Boba Fett - Deadly Mercenary ST		
20	Doctor Aphra - Artifact Hunter L	7.50	15.00
21	Greedo - Unlucky Mercenary L	1.50	3.00
22	Rebel Traitor R	.50	1.00
23	Ark Angel R	.50	1.00
24	BT-1 R	.50	1.00
25	Slave I ST		

#	Card		
26	Hunter Instinct ST		
27	Wrist Rockets ST		
28	BB-9E R	.50	1.00
29	Aayla Secura - Jedi General R	.50	1.00
30	Jedi Temple Guard R	.50	1.00
31	Luke Skywalker - Unlikely Hero ST		
32	Obi-Wan Kenobi - Jedi Master R	.50	1.00
33	Yoda - Wizened Master L	12.00	25.00
34	ETA-2 Interceptor R	.50	1.00
35	R2-D2 ST		
36	Force Meditation R	.50	1.00
37	Obi-Wan Kenobi's Lightsaber L	6.00	12.00
38	Clone Trooper R	.50	1.00
39	Finn - Soldier of Necessity L	1.50	3.00
40	Rose - Skilled Mechanic R	.50	1.00
41	Wedge Antilles - Squad Leader R	.50	1.00
42	Mortar Team R	.50	1.00
43	Resistance Bomber R	.50	1.00
44	Camouflaged Rifle R	.50	1.00
45	Rebellion Leader L	1.00	2.00
46	Han Solo - Savvy Smuggler ST		
47	Jar Jar Binks - Clumsy Outcast R	.50	1.00
48	Jedha Partisan R	.50	1.00
49	Saw Gerrera - Extremist Leader L	3.00	6.00
50	Zeb Orrelios - The Last Lasat L	7.50	15.00
51	Runaway Boomas R	.50	1.00
52	Millennium Falcon ST		
53	Roguish Charm R	.50	1.00
54	Zeb Orrelios' Bo-Rifle L	1.50	3.00
55	Republic Cruiser R	.50	1.00
56	Force Focus ST		
57	Force Wave L	7.50	15.00
58	Heirloom Lightsaber ST		
59	Hush-98 Comlink R	.50	1.00
60	Ground Battalion R	.50	1.00
61	Lookout Post R	.50	1.00
62	Auto Cannon R	.50	1.00
63	E-11 Blaster R	.50	1.00
64	74-Z Speeder Bike ST		
65	Hondo Ohnaka - Respected Businessman R	.50	1.00
66	Pirate Speeder Tank L		
67	Bartering R	.50	1.00
68	Gang Up R	.50	1.00
69	Vibrocutlass R	.50	1.00
70	Modified HWK-290 R	.50	1.00
71	Canto Bight Pistol R	.50	1.00
72	Hidden Blaster ST		
73	Hunting Rifle ST		
74	Stun Baton R	.50	1.00
75	Consumed By The Dark Side C	.15	.30
76	Dark Scheme C	.15	.30
77	Double Strike U	.20	.40
78	Frighten C	.15	.30
79	I Am Your Father U	.20	.40
80	Snare U	.20	.40
81	Spell of Removal C	.15	.30
82	Witch Magick C	.15	.30
83	Nightsister Coven U	.20	.40
84	Battle Fatigue C	.15	.30
85	Crush the Rebellion U	.20	.40
86	Imperial Might C	.15	.30
87	Scorched Earth U	.20	.40
88	Shrapnel Blast C	.15	.30
89	Target Practice C	.15	.30
90	Three Steps Ahead U	.20	.40
91	Command Bridge U	.20	.40
92	Delve U	.20	.40
93	Free-For-All U	.20	.40
94	In Pursuit U	.20	.40
95	No Good To Me Dead C	.15	.30
96	Rumors C	.15	.30
97	Subdue C	.15	.30
98	Take Flight C	.15	.30

99 Outnumber C	.15	.30	
100 Adapt C	.15	.30	
101 Ataru Strike U	.20	.40	
102 Heightened Awareness ST			
103 Investigate C	.15	.30	
104 Strength Through Weakness U	.20	.40	
105 Unbreakable C	.15	.30	
106 Defensive Teaching U	.20	.40	
107 Yoda's Hut U	.20	.40	
108 Attack Run C	.15	.30	
109 Equip C	.15	.30	
110 Final Moment U	.20	.40	
111 Light 'Em Up C	.15	.30	
112 Mend U	.20	.40	
113 Refit C	.15	.30	
114 Special Modification U	.20	.40	
115 Suppression Field U	.20	.40	
116 Bravado C	.15	.30	
117 Easy Pickings U	.20	.40	
118 Explosive Tactics U	.20	.40	
119 Impulsive C	.15	.30	
120 Scruffy Looking Nerf-Herder C	.15	.30	
121 Smuggler's Run C	.15	.30	
122 Maz's Vault U	.20	.40	
123 Diplomatic Protection U	.20	.40	
124 Into The Garbage Chute U	.20	.40	
125 Alter C	.15	.30	
126 Ancient Wisdom C	.15	.30	
127 Feel The Force C	.15	.30	
128 Invigorate ST			
129 Legacies U	.20	.40	
130 Mislead C	.15	.30	
131 Respite C	.15	.30	
132 Stronger You Have Become U	.20	.40	
133 The Force Is With Me C	.15	.30	
134 Perseverance C	.15	.30	
135 Resilient U	.20	.40	
136 Crackdown C	.15	.30	
137 Crash Landing ST			
138 Law and Order C	.15	.30	
139 Locked and Loaded C	.15	.30	
140 Reinforce U	.20	.40	
141 Strength in Numbers C	.15	.30	
142 Sudden Impact U	.20	.40	
143 Superior Position C	.15	.30	
144 Target Intel C	.15	.30	
145 Bubble Shield U	.20	.40	
146 Cover Team C	.15	.30	
147 Bamboozle C	.15	.30	
148 Cantina Brawl U	.20	.40	
149 Counter Strike C	.15	.30	
150 Dangerous Maneuver C	.15	.30	
151 Entangle ST			
152 Face-Off C	.15	.30	
153 Hasty Exit C	.15	.30	
154 Lure U	.20	.40	
155 Quick Draw C	.15	.30	
156 Vandalize U	.20	.40	
157 Well-Connected C	.15	.30	
158 Defend C	.15	.30	
159 Dive C	.15	.30	
160 Ice Storm C	.15	.30	
161 No Cheating U	.20	.40	
162 Shelter C	.15	.30	
163 Backup Specialist C	.15	.30	
164 Remote Stockpile C	.15	.30	
165 Scrap Heap U	.20	.40	
166 Bodyguard U	.20	.40	
167 Quickdraw Holster C	.15	.30	
168 Espionage U	.20	.40	
169 Fortify U	.20	.40	
170 Preemptive Strike U	.20	.40	
171 Profitable Connection U	.20	.40	

172 Stolen Intel C	.15	.30
173 Taking Ground C	.15	.30
174 Arid Wasteland - Geonosis ST		
175 Citadel Landing Zone - Scarif ST		
176 Imperial Palace - Coruscant U	.20	.40
177 Launch Deck - Home One U	.20	.40
178 Outer Rim Outpost - Nal Hutta ST		
179 Petranaki Arena - Geonosis C	.15	.30
180 Power Generator Trench - Death Star I U	.20	.40

2018 Star Wars Destiny Way of the Force

RELEASED ON JULY 5, 2018

1 Count Dooku - Darth Tyranus R
2 Fifth Brother - Intimidating Enforcer R
3 Force Sensitive Outcast R
4 Snoke - Supreme Leader L
5 Crush Hope U
6 Dark Ritual U
7 Lack of Faith U
8 No Escape C
9 Power From Pain U
10 Triple Threat C
11 Undermine C
12 Dark Empowerment C
13 Count Dooku's Solar Sailer R
14 Bardottan Sphere R
15 Fifth Brother's Lightsaber L
16 Force Fear R
17 Torment C
18 Arihnda Pryce - Unscrupulous Governor R
19 Executioner R
20 Firmus Piett - Ambitious Admiral R
21 General Grievous - Fearsome Cyborg L
22 Art of War U
23 Furious Assault U
24 Machine Replacement C
25 Opening Volley C
26 Overrun U
27 Testing Procedure C
28 Well-armed C
29 Blockade U
30 Climate Disruption Array U
31 General Grievous' Wheel Bike L
32 Imperial Troop Transport R
33 Planetary Bombardment L
34 Executioner's Axe R
35 DJ - Treacherous Rogue L
36 Jabba The Hutt - Renowned Gangster R
37 Mandalorian Super Commando R
38 Sebulba - Cutthroat Podracer R
39 By Any Means C
40 Cocky C
41 Extreme Hubris U
42 Nefarious Deed C

43 Paid Off U		
44 Partners in Crime C		
45 Quarrel C		
46 Rancorous U		
47 Sebulba Always Wins U		
48 Sticky Situation C		
49 0-0-0 R		
50 Sebulba's Podracer R		
51 Formidable L		
52 Underhanded Tactics R		
53 Way of the Dark C		
54 Ezra Bridger - Aspiring Jedi R		
55 Jedi Sentinel R		
56 Luke Skywalker - Reluctant Instructor L		
57 Plo Koon - Jedi Protector R		
58 Fond Memories C		
59 Loth-Wolf Bond C		
60 Luke's Training U		
61 Pacify U		
62 Propel C		
63 Renewed Purpose C		
64 Steadfast C		
65 Plo Koon's Starfighter R		
66 A99 Aquata Breather U		
67 Ezra Bridger's Lightsaber L		
68 Guardian of the Whills U		
69 Luke Skywalker's Lightning Rod R		
70 There Is No Try R		
71 Boss Nass - Bombastic Ruler R		
72 Gungan Warrior R		
73 Leia Organa - Heart of the Resistance L		
74 Rex - Clone Captain L		
75 Blaze of Glory C		
76 Desperate Hour C		
77 First Aid C		
78 Gungan Offensive U		
79 Motivate U		
80 Reposition C		
81 Long-Term Plan U		
82 Gungan Catapult R		
83 Resistance Crait Speeder R		
84 Suppressive Fire U		
85 Electropole R		
86 Inspiring Presence U		
87 Rex's Blaster Pistol L		
88 Anakin Skywalker - Podracing Prodigy R		
89 Bo-Katan Kryze - Deathwatch Lieutenant R		
90 Cassian Andor - Rebellion Operative L		
91 Trusted Informant R		
92 Clandestine Operation U		
93 Closing the Deal C		
94 Defensive Racing U		
95 Dumb Luck U		
96 Mechanical Insight C		
97 Narrow Escape C		
98 Rigged Detonation C		
99 Righteous Cause C		
100 Scoping the Target U		
101 Shootout C		
102 Anakin Skywalker's Podracer R		
103 N-1 Starfighter R		
104 CR-2 Heavy Blaster R		
105 Stealthy L		
106 Way of the Light C		
107 Dex's Diner U		
108 Become One C		
109 Beguile C		
110 Control U		
111 Division in the Force C		
112 Flames of the Past U		
113 Peace and Quiet C		
114 Turn the Tide C		
115 Built to Last U		

#	Name		
116	Honed Skills C		
117	Dagger of Mortis L		
118	Force Jump R		
119	Way of the Force U		
120	Change of Fate C		
121	Glancing Shot C		
122	Grand Entrance C		
123	Hostile Takeover U		
124	Overload C		
125	Reconstruct C		
126	Take the Fight to Them C		
127	Home Turf Advantage U		
128	Ammo Reserves C		
129	ARC-170 Starfighter R		
130	Hailfire Droid Tank L		
131	Weapon Master C		
132	Friend or Foe C		
133	In The Crosshairs C		
134	Podracer Betting U		
135	Reprogram U		
136	Risky Move U		
137	Start Your Engines! U		
138	Calling in Favors U		
139	Prized Goods C		
140	Streetwise C		
141	XS Stock Light Freighter R		
142	Darksaber L		
143	Mandalorian Vambraces R		
144	Respected Businessman C		
145	V-1 Thermal Detonator R		
146	Extract C		
147	Free Fall C		
148	Made to Suffer U		
149	Nature's Charm C		
150	Quell C		
151	Under Attack C		
152	Lotho Minor Junkers R		
153	Podracer R		
154	Macrobinoculars R		
155	Boonta Eve Classic U		
156	Arena of Death - Nar Shaddaa U		
157	Bendu's Lair - Atollon R		
158	Comm Tower - Scarif C		
159	Mos Espa Arena - Tatooine U		
160	Rift Valley - Dathomir U		

2018 Star Wars Destiny Across the Galaxy

RELEASED ON NOVEMBER 9, 2018

#	Name		
1	Darth Vader - Terror To Behold L	25.00	50.00
2	Luce - Callous Nightsister R	.50	1.00
3	Nightbrother R	.50	1.00
4	Savage Opress - Reckless Warrior R	.50	1.00
5	Burst Of Lightning C	.15	.30
6	Endow U	.20	.40
7	Fear and Dead Men U	.20	.40
8	I Am The Senate U	.20	.40
9	Let The Hate Flow U	.15	.30
10	Darth Vader's Meditation Chamber U	.20	.40
11	Galactic Deception C	.15	.30
12	Stifle U	.20	.40
13	Vader's Fist L		
14	Bloodlust C	.15	.30
15	Chain Sickle R	.50	1.00
16	Darth Vader's Lightsaber L	15.00	30.00
17	Energy Bow R	.50	1.00
18	Iden Versio - Inferno Squad Commander L		
19	Mauler Mithel - Vader's Wingman R	.50	1.00
20	Super Battle Droid R	.50	1.00
21	Wulff Yularen - ISB Colonel R	.50	1.00
22	Browbeat C	.15	.30
23	Commence Primary Ignition U	.20	.40
24	Drop 'Em U	.20	.40
25	Hatching A Plan C	.15	.30
26	Imposing Presence C	.15	.30
27	In Tandem C	.15	.30
28	Questioned Loyalty U	.20	.40
29	Reach The Stars C	.15	.30
30	Black Two R	.50	1.00
31	TIE Fighter R	.50	1.00
32	Umbaran Hover Tank L		
33	Vigilance C	.15	.30
34	Inferno Squad ID10 Seeker Droid R	.50	1.00
35	Dryden Voss - Ruthless Crime Lord L	6.00	12.00
36	Tobias Beckett - Thief For Hire L		
37	Val - Headstrong Renegade R	.50	1.00
38	Act Of Cruelty C	.15	.30
39	Cunning Ruse C	.15	.30
40	Exploit C	.15	.30
41	First Claim C	.15	.30
42	Heated Confrontation C	.15	.30
43	In a Bind U	.20	.40
44	Shakedown C	.15	.30
45	Sidestep U	.20	.40
46	Wanton Destruction U	.20	.40
47	Dèj‡ Vu U	.20	.40
48	Firespray-31 R	.50	1.00
49	Relentless C	.15	.30
50	Donderbus Blaster Pistol R	.50	1.00
51	Grappling Boa R	.50	1.00
52	Tobias Beckett's Rifle R	.50	1.00
53	Vow Of Vengeance U	.20	.40
54	Retribution U	.20	.40
55	Barriss Offee - Studious Padawan R	.50	1.00
56	Force Mystic R	.50	1.00
57	Kit Fisto - Shii-cho Master R	.50	1.00
58	Qui-Gon Jinn - Defiant Jedi Master L		
59	Bewilder C	.15	.30
60	Finishing Strike U	.20	.40
61	Gathering Intelligence C	.15	.30
62	Hold Off C	.15	.30
63	Insight C	.15	.30
64	Into Exile U	.20	.40
65	Repulse C	.15	.30
66	Safeguard C	.15	.30
67	Immutability C	.15	.30
68	Counterstroke R	.50	1.00
69	Lightsaber Training Staff R	.50	1.00
70	Pillio Star Compass R	.50	1.00
71	Qui-Gon Jinn's Lightsaber L		
72	Biggs Darklighter - Rebellion Ace R	.50	1.00
73	Clone Commander Cody - Loyal Strategist R	.50	1.00
74	Jyn Erso - Daring Infiltrator L		
75	Rebel Engineer R	.50	1.00
76	Aerial Advantage C	.15	.30
77	Attack of The Clones U	.20	.40
78	Dogfight U	.20	.40
79	Evacuate U	.20	.40
80	Inflame C	.15	.30
81	Outgun C	.15	.30
82	Turn The Tables U	.20	.40
83	Armed Escort C	.15	.30
84	BB-8 L	2.50	5.00
85	Black One R	.50	1.00
86	X-Wing R	.50	1.00
87	Jyn Erso's Blaster L		
88	R2 Astromech C	.15	.30
89	Lando Calrissian - Smooth and Sophisticated L		
90	Leia Organa - Boushh R	.50	1.00
91	L3-37 - Droid Revolutionary R	.50	1.00
92	A Good Investment C	.15	.30
93	Aid From Above U	.20	.40
94	Daring Gambit U	.20	.40
95	Drop In C	.15	.30
96	Hijack U	.20	.40
97	Karabast! C	.15	.30
98	Leverage C	.15	.30
99	Reluctance U	.20	.40
100	Slice And Dice U	.20	.40
101	Through The Pass C	.15	.30
102	Escape Craft R	.50	1.00
103	Millennium Falcon L		
104	On The Mark C	.15	.30
105	Decoy U	.20	.40
106	Energy Pike R	.50	1.00
107	Token Of Affection R	.50	1.00
108	At Odds C	.15	.30
109	Common Cause U	.20	.40
110	Conflicted C	.15	.30
111	Deadly Advance C	.15	.30
112	No Questions Asked U	.20	.40
113	Relinquish C	.15	.30
114	You Were My Friend C	.15	.30
115	Bitter Rivalry U	.20	.40
116	Foresight C	.15	.30
117	Nexus Of Power R	.50	1.00
118	Force Lift R	.50	1.00
119	Shatterpoint R	.50	1.00
120	Treasured Lightsaber R	.50	1.00
121	Attack Formation C	.15	.30
122	Barrel Roll C	.15	.30
123	Deployment C	.15	.30
124	Fleet Command C	.15	.30
125	Intense Fire C	.15	.30
126	Revised Order C	.15	.30
127	Snuff Out U	.20	.40
128	Transfer U	.20	.40
129	Armored Reinforcement U	.20	.40
130	Senate Chamber R	.50	1.00
131	Dorsal Turret R	.50	1.00
132	Handheld L-S1 Cannon L		
133	Triple Laser Turret R	.50	1.00
134	Han Solo - Independent Hotshot L	5.00	10.00
135	Qi'Ra - Street Savvy R	.50	1.00
136	Across The Galaxy C	.15	.30
137	Cash Out C	.15	.30
138	Dismantle U	.20	.40
139	Fight Fire With Fire C	.15	.30
140	Indifferent C	.15	.30
141	Quick Thinking C	.15	.30
142	Shock Tactic U	.20	.40
143	Double Down U	.20	.40
144	Improvised Defense C	.15	.30
145	Shadow Caster L		
146	Arc Caster R	.50	1.00
147	Black Sun Blaster Pistol R	.50	1.00
148	Flame Projector R	.50	1.00
149	Shriek C	.15	.30
150	T-16 Skyhopper C	.15	.30
151	X-34 Landspeeder C	.15	.30
152	Laser Cannon C	.15	.30

153 Systems Gauge U	.20	.40
154 Targeting Astromech U	.20	.40
155 No Allegiance U	.20	.40
156 Solidarity U	.20	.40
157 Landing Dock - Scipio U	.20	.40
158 Occupied City - Lothal U	.20	.40
159 Theed Royal Palace - Naboo U	.20	.40
160 Training Room - Kamino U	.20	.40

2019 Star Wars Destiny Convergence

RELEASED ON MARCH 28, 2019

1 Asajj Ventress - Swift And Cunning R
2 Palpatine - Unlimited Power L
3 Sentinel Messenger R
4 Sly Moore - Aide to the Emperor R
5 Mind Extraction U
6 A Tale of Tragedy C
7 Breaking Bonds C
8 Fit of Rage C
9 Forsaken U
10 Isolation C
11 No Mercy U
12 Forbidden Lore U
13 Imperialis R
14 Force Storm L
15 Malice R
16 Palpatine's Lightsaber L
17 Sith Teachings R
18 Captain Phasma - Stormtrooper Commander L
19 Commando Droid ST
20 First Order Stormtrooper R
21 General Grievous - Droid Armies Commander ST
22 Wat Tambor - Techno Union Foreman R
23 A Sinister Peace C
24 Make Demands C
25 Probe C
26 Pulverize C
27 Roger, Roger ST
28 The Best Defense... C
29 Defoliator Tank ST
30 Imperial Officer R
31 Megablaster Troopers L
32 Stap Droid ST
33 E-5 Blaster Carbine ST
34 Modular Frame ST
35 Dengar - Ruthless Tracker R
36 Jabba The Hutt - Influential Kingpin L
37 Quarren Tracker R
38 Watto - Stubborn Gambler R
39 Death Mark C
40 Enticing Reward U
41 Barter With Blood U
42 Conveyex Robbery U
43 Exterminate U

44 Fight Dirty U
45 Hard Bargain U
46 Hunt Them Down C
47 Bounty Board U
48 Punishing One R
49 Crime Lord L
50 Dengar's Fire Blade R
51 Skilled Tracker R
52 Separatist Conspiracy U
53 Assassin Droid ST
54 Ahsoka Tano - Brash Prodigy R
55 Lor San Tekka - True Believer R
56 Mace Windu - Inspiring Master R
57 Obi-Wan Kenobi - Ardent Avenger ST
58 Vigilant Jedi R
59 A Friend Lost C
60 Channel The Force C
61 Defensive Stance C
62 Disciplined Mind C
63 Strong Intuition C
64 Upper Hand ST
65 Obi-Wan Kenobi's Interceptor ST
66 Uneti Force Tree U
67 Yoda's Spirit L
68 Jedi Holocron R
69 Lore Hunter C
70 Mace Windu's Lightsaber L
71 Republic Jedi Armor ST
72 K-2SO - Incognito R
73 Kes Dameron - Courageous Sergeant R
74 Naboo Palace Guard R
75 PadmÈ Amidala - Resolute Senator L
76 Target Acquired U
77 Aggressive Negotiations U
78 Field Medic C
79 Honorable Sacrifice U
80 Power Surge U
81 Unfetter C
82 A-Wing R
83 Concerted Effort U
84 LAAT Gunship L
85 PadmÈ Amidala's Royal Starship R
86 Overkill R
87 Resistance Ring R
88 Chewbacca - The Beast L
89 Ezra Bridger - Resourceful Cutpurse R
90 Maz Kanata - Canny Negotiator R
91 Satine Kryze - Hope of Mandalore ST
92 Calculated Risk C
93 Convergence U
94 Draw Attention U
95 Flee the Scene U
96 Instigate C
97 Reap the Reward U
98 Sure Shot C
99 We're Home U
100 Laser Tripwire U
101 Rebel Cache R
102 Chewbacca's Blaster Rifle L
103 Custom Bandolier C
104 Moxie R
105 Secrets Laid Bare C
106 Attunement C
107 Circle of Shelter U
108 Deflecting Slash U
109 Fatal Blow C
110 Overqualified C
111 Twin Strike C
112 Use The Force C
113 Force Flow ST
114 Lightsaber Mastery U
115 Diatium Power Cell U
116 It Binds All Things U

117 Force Pull R
118 Lightsaber ST
119 Soresu Mastery L
120 Soresu Training R
121 Hampered U
122 Automated Defense C
123 Domination U
124 Energize C
125 Forced Compliance C
126 Fresh Supplies C
127 Measure for Measure C
128 No Answer C
129 Rout U
130 Seize the Day C
131 Squad Tactics C
132 Strike Back C
133 Advanced Training U
134 Conscript Squad R
135 Press the Advantage C
136 Tech Team C
137 V-Wing R
138 A300 Blaster R
139 Quicksilver Baton L
140 Riot Shield U
141 Enfys Nest - Fearsome Outlaw L
142 Enfys Nest's Marauder R
143 Wanted C
144 Electroshock U
145 For a Price C
146 Prey Upon C
147 Rendezvous C
148 Skullduggery C
149 Truce C
150 Unpredictable C
151 Profiteering U
152 Entourage L
153 Seeking The Truth C
154 Smuggling Ring C
155 Starviper R
156 Enfys Nest's Electroripper R
157 Mandalorian Jetpack ST
158 Ordnance Launcher R
159 Unscrupulous R
160 Shock Collar C
161 Wounded C
162 Bacta Therapy U
163 Block C
164 Dodge C
165 Electromagnetic Pulse C
166 Near Miss C
167 Unshackle C
168 Fickle Mercenaries R
169 Grievance Striker ST
170 Protective Suit U
171 Punch Dagger ST
172 Sonic Detonators R
173 Command Center - Lothal U
174 Deathwatch Hideout - Concordia ST
175 Fighting Pit - Mimban U
176 Lair of General Grievous - Vassek 3 ST
177 Mean Streets - Corellia U
178 Military Camp - Kaller U
179 Salt Flats - Crait U
180 Watto's Shop - Tatooine U

2019 Star Wars Destiny Allies of Necessity Starter Deck

RELEASED ON APRIL 25, 2019

1 Count Dooku - Corrupted Politician	2.50	5.00
2 Count Dooku's Lightsaber	4.00	8.00
3 Sniper Team	1.00	2.00
4 Astrogation	.50	1.00

5 Knighthood	1.50	3.00
6 Fenn Rau - Mandalorian Protector	.50	1.00
7 Test of Character	.50	1.00
8 Grand Design	.50	1.00
9 Outer Rim Outlaw	.50	1.00
10 Shadowed	.50	1.00
11 Perilous Escapade	.50	1.00
12 Hired Muscle	.50	1.00
13 Clawdite Shapeshifter	.50	1.00
14 Chance Encounter	.50	1.00
15 Flank	.50	1.00
16 Allies of Necessity	.50	1.00
17 LR-57 Combat Droid	.50	1.00
18 Electro Sword	.50	1.00
19 Chalmun's Cantina - Tatooine	.50	1.00
20 Wheeta Palace - Nal Hutta	.50	1.00

2019 Star Wars Destiny Spark of Hope

RELEASED ON JULY 5, 2019

1 Dark Mystic R
2 Kylo Ren - Bound By The Force R
3 Maul - Skilled Duelist L
4 Nightsister Zombie C
5 Old Daka - Nightsister Necromancer R
6 Chancellor's Edict C
7 Hex C
8 Possessed U
9 Uncontrollable Rage C
10 Act of Betrayal C
11 Dark Magick C
12 Sinister Ruse C
13 Tantrum C
14 Weave The Ichor C
15 Order 66 U
16 Scimitar R
17 Ancient Magicks R
18 Recovered Sith Lightsaber R
19 Talisman of Resurrection L
20 Conan Motti - Overconfident Officer R
21 Gideon Hask - Inferno Squad Commando R
22 Mudtrooper R
23 Thrawn - Grand Admiral L
24 Priority Target C
25 Counterintelligence C
26 Crushing Advantage C
27 Execute Order 66 U
28 Rally the Troops C
29 To Victory C
30 Warning Siren C
31 Cultural Records R
32 Hostile Territory U
33 Separatist Embargo U
34 Superlaser Siege Cannon L
35 Crimson Star U
36 Mastermind R
37 TL-50 Heavy Repeater R
38 4-LOM - Calculating Criminal R
39 IG-88 - Single-Minded R
40 Jango Fett - Armed To The Teeth L
41 Zuckuss - The Uncanny One R
42 Armed To The Teeth C
43 Desperate Measures C
44 Misinformation C
45 Tireless Pursuit C
46 Bounty Hunters' Guild U
47 IG-2000 R
48 Impound U
49 Mist Hunter R
50 Predatory Banker U
51 0-0-0 Protocol Matrix R
52 Armor Plating C
53 Gauntlet Rockets R

54 Pulse Cannon L
55 Acceptable Losses C
56 R2-D2 - Loyal Companion L
57 Rey - Bound By The Force R
58 Yoda - Mystical Mentor R
59 Youngling U
60 Refusal U
61 Destiny Fulfilled U
62 Exchange Of Information C
63 Heroic Stand U
64 Humble Service C
65 Jedi Mind Trick U
66 Moving Rocks U
67 Yoda's Protection C
68 Caretaker Village U
69 Professor Huyang R
70 Qui-Gon Jinn's Spirit L
71 Three Lessons U
72 Jedi Lightsaber R
73 Sacred Jedi Texts R
74 Yoda's Lightsaber L
75 Amilyn Holdo - Vice Admiral L
76 Bail Organa - Alderaanian Senator R
77 C-3PO - Perfect Gentleman L
78 Hoth Trooper U
79 Droids' Day Out U
80 Happy Beeps C
81 Lightspeed Assault U
82 Our Situation is Desperate C
83 Rebel Assault C
84 Spark of Hope C
85 Take Control U
86 B-Wing R
87 Firm Resolve U
88 GH-7 Droid R
89 Resistance Trench Fighters R
90 EL-16 Heavy Field Blaster R
91 Salvaged Arm U
92 Tico Pendant C
93 Chief Chirpa - Bright Tree Village Elder R
94 Chopper - Metal Menace R
95 Ewok Warrior C
96 Han Solo - Old Swindler L
97 Wicket - Crafty Scout R
98 Ensnare U
99 Net Trap C
100 Rolling Logs C
101 Ewok Ambush C
102 Glider Attack U
103 Jump To Lightspeed U
104 Reassemble U
105 Chief Chirpa's Hut R
106 Mr. Bones L
107 Ewok Bow R
108 Han Solo's Blaster L
109 Han Solo's Dice R
110 Support of the Tribe C
111 Fateful Companions U
112 Alter Fate C
113 Clever Distraction C
114 Dark Reflections C
115 Decisive Blow C
116 Draw Closer U
117 Polarity C
118 Pushing Slash C
119 Temporary Truce U
120 Force Connection U
121 Mysteries Of The Force U
122 Niman Mastery L
123 Niman Training R
124 Untamed Power R
125 Chain Lightning C
126 Focused Fire C

127 Hull Breach C
128 Off The Sensors C
129 Seizing Territory C
130 Shields Are Down C
131 Shortcut U
132 You Are In Command Now U
133 Aftermath C
134 AT-RT R
135 Coruscant Police R
136 Admiral L
137 Communication Module U
138 Dead Or Alive C
139 Bad Credit U
140 Disassemble C
141 Encircle U
142 I Performed Violence C
143 Kinship U
144 Outpace C
145 Practice Makes Perfect C
146 Reversal C
147 Simple Mistake U
148 Unify C
149 Any Means Necessary U
150 Canto Bight Security L
151 Mining Guild TIE Fighter R
152 Bounty Hunter Mask C
153 DX-2 Disruptor Blaster Pistol R
154 Inflict Pain U
155 Grappling Arm R
156 Rocket Booster R
157 Canto Casino - Canto Bight U
158 Jabba's Palace - Tatooine U
159 Nightsister Lair - Dathomir C
160 Snoke's Throne Room - Supremacy U

2020 Star Wars Destiny Covert Missions

RELEASED ON MARCH 6, 2020

1 Darth Bane - Ancient Master L		
2 Darth Vader - Victor Leader R	.50	1.00
4 Snoke's Praetorian Guard R	.50	1.00
5 Recurring Nightmare R	.50	1.00
6 Entropic Blast C	.15	.30
7 Legacy of the Sith U	.30	.75
8 Pincer Movement U	.30	.75
9 Quad Slam U	.30	.75
10 Trap the Blade C	.15	.30
11 Treason U	.30	.75
12 Rule of Two U	.30	.75
13 Bloodletting C	.15	.30
14 Darth Vader's Tie Advanced R	.50	1.00
15 Ancient Sith Armor U	.30	.75
16 Death Field L		
17 Pong Krell's Lightsaber R	.50	1.00

#	Card		
18	Sith Lord L		
19	Vibro-Arbir Blades R	.50	1.00
20	Commander Pyre - Harsh Negotiator R	.50	1.00
21	Director Krennic - Death Star Mastermind L		
22	Elrik Vonreg - Major Baron R	.50	1.00
23	Imperial Death Trooper R	.50	1.00
24	Imperial Pilot U	.30	.75
25	Cruel Methods C	.15	.30
26	Call to Action C	.15	.30
27	Face the Enemy U	.30	.75
28	I'll Handle This Myself C	.15	.30
29	Taking Charge C	.15	.30
30	Construct the Death Star U	.30	.75
31	Elrik Vonreg's TIE Interceptor R	.50	1.00
32	The "Duchess" L		
33	TIE Bomber R	.50	1.00
34	Viper Probe Droid U	.30	.75
35	Commander Pyre's Blaster R	.50	1.00
36	Director U	.30	.75
37	E-11D Blaster Rifle R	.50	1.00
38	Boba Fett - Infamous and Ruthless L		
39	Kragan Gorr - Pirate Captain R	.50	1.00
40	Pyke Sentinel U	.30	.75
41	Synara San - Opportunistic Infiltrator R	.50	1.00
42	Trandoshan Hunter R	.50	1.00
43	Forced Labor C	.15	.30
44	Pestering R	.50	1.00
45	Change of Fortune C	.15	.30
46	Opportune Strike C	.15	.30
47	Plunder U	.30	.75
48	Warning Shot C	.15	.30
49	Pirate Ship R	.50	1.00
50	Slave I L		
51	Boba Fett's Wrist Laser R	.50	1.00
52	Pyke Blaster R	.50	1.00
53	Anakin Skywalker - Dedicated Mentor L		
54	Jedi Knight R	.50	1.00
55	Kanan Jarrus - Jedi Exile R	.50	1.00
56	Luke Skywalker - Red Five R	.50	1.00
57	Forestall C	.15	.30
58	Fresh Start C	.15	.30
59	Luminous Beings Are We U	.30	.75
60	Nullify C	.15	.30
61	Skillful Deterrence U	.30	.75
62	Stand Firm C	.15	.30
63	Trust Your Feelings C	.15	.30
64	Valiant Deed C	.15	.30
65	Jedi Trails U	.30	.75
66	Luke Skywalker's X-Wing R	.50	1.00
67	Anakin Skywalker's Lightsaber L		
68	Kanan Jarrus' Lightsaber R	.50	1.00
69	Padawan Braid C	.15	.30
70	Hera Syndulla - Seasoned Captain L		
71	Kashyyyk Warrior R	.50	1.00
72	Kazuda Xiono - Naive Hotshot R	.50	1.00
73	Poe Dameron - Reckless Aviator L		
74	Tarfful - Chieftain of Kachirho R	.50	1.00
75	Feat of Strength C	.15	.30
76	Imposing Force C	.15	.30
77	Plan of Attack C	.15	.30
78	Run To Safety C	.15	.30
79	Swing In C	.15	.30
80	Trench Run U	.30	.75
81	Destroy the Death Star U	.30	.75
82	Fireball R	.50	1.00
83	Ghost L		
83	Rebel Hangar L		
84	Phantom R	.50	1.00
85	Wookiee Protection U	.30	.75
86	Fortitude C	.15	.30
87	[illegible]		
88	Master Smuggler R	.50	1.00
89	Sabine Wren - Artistic and Resourceful R	.50	1.00
90	Sinjir Rath Velus - Ex-Loyalty Officer L		
91	Torra Doza - Energetic Thrill-Seeker R	.50	1.00
92	Vengeful Wookiee U	.30	.75
93	As One C	.15	.30
94	Lead From the Front U	.30	.75
95	Loth-Cat and Mouse C	.15	.30
96	Pride and Joy U	.30	.75
97	Reciprocate C	.15	.30
98	Blue Ace R	.50	1.00
99	Bucket R	.50	1.00
100	Sabine Wren's TIE Fighter R	.50	1.00
101	Custom Paint Job U	.30	.75
102	Fling U	.30	.75
103	Wookiee Rage U	.30	.75
104	Spectre Cell U	.30	.75
105	Valorous Tribe U	.30	.75
106	Acute Awareness C	.15	.30
107	Bestow Wisdom U	.30	.75
108	Falling Avalanche U	.30	.75
109	Fluid Riposte C	.15	.30
110	Infuse the Force C	.15	.30
111	On Guard C	.15	.30
112	Side By Side C	.15	.30
113	Seeking Knowledge C	.15	.30
114	Shien Mastery L		
115	Shien Training R	.50	1.00
116	Systems Malfunction R	.50	1.00
117	Assail C	.15	.30
118	Command and Conquer C	.15	.30
119	Covert Mission C	.15	.30
120	Embark C	.15	.30
121	Flanked by Wingmen C	.15	.30
122	Joint Maneuver U	.30	.75
123	Sneak Attack U	.30	.75
124	Under Fire C	.15	.30
125	Tactical Delay C	.15	.30
126	Death Star Plans U	.30	.75
127	Experimental Booster R	.50	1.00
128	Licensed to Fly C	.15	.30
129	Nar Shaddaa Thief U	.30	.75
130	Controlled Chaos U	.30	.75
131	Dangerous Escape C	.15	.30
132	Deadlock C	.15	.30
133	Monopolize C	.15	.30
134	Reap C	.15	.30
135	Rogue Tendencies C	.15	.30
136	Survival Instinct C	.15	.30
137	Taken by Surprise C	.15	.30
138	Think on Your Feet C	.15	.30
139	Coaxium Heist U	.30	.75
140	Cloud Car R	.50	1.00
141	Double Agent U	.30	.75
142	Improvised Explosive C	.15	.30
143	Raiding Party R	.50	1.00
144	Repurposing U	.30	.75
145	Magna-Glove L		
146	Z-6 Jetpack L		
147	Jawa Junk Dealer C	.15	.30
148	Outdated Tech U	.30	.75
149	Eject U	.30	.75
150	Harmless Trick C	.15	.30
151	Salvaged Parts C	.15	.30
152	Standoff C	.15	.30
153	Utinni! C	.15	.30
154	Merchant Freighter C	.15	.30
155	Sandcrawler R	.50	1.00
156	Wretched Hive U	.30	.75
157	Abandoned Refinery - Savareen U	.30	.75
158	Colossus - Castilon U	.30	.75
159	Pyke Syndicate Mine - Kessel U	.30	.75
160	Valley of the Dark Lords - Moraband U	.15	.30

1999 Young Jedi Menace of Darth Maul

RELEASED ON MAY 12, 1999

#	Card		
1	Obi-Wan Kenobi, Young Jedi R	3.00	6.00
2	Qui-Gon Jinn, Jedi Master R	2.50	5.00
3	Jar Jar Binks, Gungan Chuba Thief R	1.50	3.00
4	Anakin Skywalker, Podracer Pilot R	1.25	2.50
5	Padme Naberrie, Handmaiden R	2.00	4.00
6	Captain Panaka, Protector of the Queen R	1.25	2.50
7	Mace Windu, Jedi Master R	1.50	3.00
8	Queen Amidala, Ruler of Naboo R	2.00	4.00
9	Queen Amidala, Royal Leader R	2.00	4.00
10	Yoda, Jedi Master R	2.00	4.00
11	R2-D2, Astromech Droid R	1.50	3.00
12	C-3PO, Anakin's Creation R	1.50	3.00
13	Boss Nass, Leader of the Gungans U	.50	1.00
14	Ric Olie, Ace Pilot U	.50	1.00
15	Captain Tarpals, Gungan Guard U	.50	1.00
16	Rabe, Handmaiden U	.50	1.00
17	Rep Been, Gungan U	.50	1.00
18	Mas Amedda, Vice Chancellor U	.50	1.00
19	Naboo Officer, Battle Planner U	.50	1.00
20	Naboo Security, Guard C	.15	.30
21	Bravo Pilot, Veteran Flyer C	.15	.30
22	Gungan Official, Bureaucrat C	.15	.30
23	Gungan Soldier, Scout C	.15	.30
24	Gungan Guard C	.15	.30
25	Gungan Warrior, Infantry C	.15	.30
26	Gungan Soldier, Veteran C	.15	.30
27	Ishi Tib, Warrior C	.15	.30
28	Ithorian, Merchant C	.15	.30
29	Jawa, Thief C	.15	.30
30	Jawa, Bargainer S	.15	.30
31	Royal Guard, Leader C	.15	.30
32	Royal Guard, Veteran C	.15	.30
33	Obi-Wan Kenobi, Jedi Padawan S	.15	.30
34	Obi-Wan Kenobi's Lightsaber R	1.50	3.00
35	Jedi Lightsaber	.50	1.00
36	Anakin Skywalker's Podracer R	1.25	2.50
37	Captain Panaka's Blaster C	.15	.30
38	Jar Jar Binks' Electropole U	.50	1.00
39	Electropole C	.15	.30
40	Eopie C	.15	.30
41	Kaadu C	.15	.30
42	Flash Speeder C	.15	.30
43	Jawa Ion Blaster C	.15	.30
44	Naboo Blaster C	.15	.30
45	Blaster C	.15	.30
46	Blaster Rifle C	.15	.30
47	Anakin Skywalker	.50	1.00
48	Are You An Angel? U	.50	1.00
49	Cha Skrunee Da Pat, Sleemo C	.15	.30
50	Counterparts U	.50	1.00
51	Da Beings Hereabouts Cawazy C	.15	.30

52	Enough Of This Pretense U	.50	1.00
53	Fear Attracts The Fearful U	.50	1.00
54	Gungan Curiosity C	.15	.30
55	He Was Meant To Help You U	.50	1.00
56	I Have A Bad Feeling About This U	.50	1.00
57	I've Been Trained In Defense U	.50	1.00
58	Security Volunteers C	.15	.30
59	Shmi's Pride U	.50	1.00
60	The Federation Has Gone Too Far C	.15	.30
61	The Negotiations Were Short C	.15	.30
62	The Queen's Plan C	.15	.30
63	We're Not In Trouble Yet U	.50	1.00
64	Yousa Guys Bombad! R	1.00	2.00
65	Tatooine Podrace Arena S	.15	.30
66	Coruscant Capital City S	.15	.30
67	Naboo Theed Palace S	.15	.30
68	Bravo 1, Naboo Starfighter U	.50	1.00
69	Naboo Starfighter C	.15	.30
70	Republic Cruiser, Transport C	.15	.30
71	Darth Maul, Sith Apprentice R	4.00	8.00
72	Darth Sidious, Sith Master R	2.50	5.00
73	Sebulba, Bad-Tempered Dug R	1.50	3.00
74	Watto, Slave Owner R	1.25	2.50
75	Aurra Sing, Bounty Hunter R	2.00	4.00
76	Jabba the Hutt, Vile Crime Lord R	1.50	3.00
77	Gardulla the Hutt, Crime Lord U	.50	1.00
78	Destroyer Droid Squad	1.00	2.00
79	Battle Droid Squad, Assault Unit R	1.25	2.50
80	Ben Quadinaros, Podracer Pilot U	.50	1.00
81	Gasgano, Podracer Pilot U	.50	1.00
82	Mawhonic, Podracer Pilot U	.50	1.00
83	Teemto Pagalies, Podracer Pilot U	.50	1.00
84	Bib Fortuna, Twi'lek Advisor U	.50	1.00
85	Ann and Tann Gella	.50	1.00
86	Gragra, Chuba Peddler C	.15	.30
87	Passel Argente, Senator C	.15	.30
88	Trade Federation Tank	1.25	2.50
89	Destroyer Droid, Wheel Droid C	.15	.30
90	Destroyer Droid, Defense Droid C	.15	.30
91	Sith Probe Droid, Spy Drone C	.15	.30
92	Pit Droid, Engineer C	.15	.30
93	Pit Droid, Heavy Lifter C	.15	.30
94	Pit Droid, Mechanic C	.15	.30
95	Tusken Raider, Nomad C	.15	.30
96	Tusken Raider, Marksman C	.15	.30
97	Battle Droid: Pilot, MTT Division C	.15	.30
98	Battle Droid: Security, MTT Division C	.15	.30
99	Battle Droid: Infantry, MTT Division C	.15	.30
100	Battle Droid: Officer, MTT Division C	.15	.30
101	Battle Droid: Pilot, AAT Division C	.15	.30
102	Battle Droid: Security, AAT Division C	.15	.30
103	Battle Droid: Infantry, AAT Division C	.15	.30
104	Battle Droid: Officer, AAT Division C	.15	.30
105	Neimoidian, Trade Federation Pilot S	.15	.30
106	Darth Maul, Sith Lord S	.60	1.25
107	Sith Lightsaber R	1.25	2.50
108	Aurra Sing's Blaster Rifle R	1.00	2.00
109	Sebulba's Podracer R	1.00	2.00
110	Ben Quadinaros' Podracer U	.50	1.00
111	Gasgano's Podracer U	.50	1.00
112	Mawhonic's Podracer U	.50	1.00
113	Teemto Pagalies' Podracer U	.50	1.00
114	Trade Federation Tank Laser Cannon U	.50	1.00
115	Multi Troop Transport U	.50	1.00
116	STAP U	.50	1.00
117	Tatooine Thunder Rifle C	.15	.30
118	Battle Droid Blaster Rifle C	.15	.30
119	Blaster C	.15	.30
120	Blaster Rifle C	.15	.30
121	At Last We Will Have Revenge R	1.00	2.00
122	Begin Landing Your Troops C	.15	.30
123	Boonta Eve Podrace U	.50	1.00
124	Grueling Contest U	.50	1.00
125	In Complete Control C	.15	.30
126	Kaa Bazza Kundee Hodrudda! U	.50	1.00
127	Opee Sea Killer C	.15	.30
128	Podrace Preparation U	.50	1.00
129	Sandstorm C	.15	.30
130	Sniper C	.15	.30
131	The Invasion Is On Schedule C	.15	.30
132	Vile Gangsters U	.50	1.00
133	Watto's Wager U	.50	1.00
134	You Have Been Well Trained R	1.00	2.00
135	Tatooine Desert Landing Site S	.15	.30
136	Coruscant Jedi Council Chamber S	.15	.30
137	Naboo Gungan Swamp S	.15	.30
138	Darth Maul's Starfighter	1.50	3.00
139	Droid Starfighter C	.15	.30
140	Battleship	.15	.30

1999 Young Jedi Menace of Darth Maul Foil

RELEASED ON MAY 12, 1999

F1	Obi-Wan Kenobi, Young Jedi R	4.00	8.00
F2	Jar-Jar Binks, Gungan Chuba Thief R	2.00	4.00
F3	Mace Windu, Jedi Master U	2.00	4.00
F4	Queen Amidala, Ruler of Naboo U	3.00	6.00
F5	C-3PO, Anakin's Creation U	2.00	4.00
F6	Obi-Wan Kenobi's Lightsaber C	1.50	3.00
F7	Anakin Skywalker's Podracer C	1.25	2.50
F8	Bravo 1, Naboo Starfighter C	.60	1.25
F9	Republic Cruiser, Transport C	.60	1.25
F10	Darth Maul, Sith Apprentice R	5.00	10.00
F11	Darth Sidious, Sith Master R	3.00	6.00
F12	Destroyer Droid Squad	1.00	2.00
F13	Battle Droid Squad, Assault Unit U	1.00	2.00
F14	Sebulba's Podracer U	1.00	2.00
F15	Ben Quadinaros' Podracer C	.60	1.25
F16	Gasgano's Podracer C	.60	1.25
F17	Mawhonic's Podracer C	.60	1.25
F18	Teemto Pagalies' Podracer C	.60	1.25

1999 Young Jedi The Jedi Council

Queen Amidala
Voice of Her People

"I was not elected to watch my people suffer and die..." – Queen Amidala

RELEASED ON OCTOBER 27, 1999

1	Obi-Wan Kenobi, Jedi Apprentice R	2.50	5.00
2	Qui-Gon Jinn, Jedi Protector R	2.00	4.00
3	Jar Jar Binks, Gungan Outcast R	1.25	2.50
4	Anakin Skywalker, Child of Prophecy R	1.25	2.50
5	Padme Naberrie, Queen's Handmaiden R	1.50	3.00
6	Captain Panaka, Amidala's Bodyguard R	1.00	2.00
7	Mace Windu	1.25	2.50
8	Queen Amidala, Representative of Naboo R	1.50	3.00
9	Queen Amidala, Voice of Her People R	1.50	3.00
10	Yoda, Jedi Council Member R	1.50	3.00
11	R2-D2, Loyal Droid R	1.25	2.50
12	Ki-Adi-Mundi, Cerean Jedi Knight R	1.25	2.50
13	Adi Gallia, Corellian Jedi Master R	.50	1.00
14	Depa Billaba, Jedi Master U	.50	1.00
15	Eeth Koth, Zabrak Jedi Master U	.50	1.00
16	Even Piell, Lannik Jedi Master U	.50	1.00
17	Oppo Rancisis, Jedi Master U	.50	1.00
18	Plo Koon, Jedi Master U	.50	1.00
19	Saesee Tiin, Iktotchi Jedi Master U	.50	1.00
20	Yaddle, Jedi Master U	.50	1.00
21	Yarael Poof, Quermian Jedi Master U	.50	1.00
22	Boss Nass, Gungan Leader U	.50	1.00
23	Ric Olié, Chief Pilot U	.50	1.00
24	Captain Tarpals, Gungan Battle Leader U	.50	1.00
25	Eirtae, Handmaiden U	.50	1.00
26	Valorum, Supreme Chancellor C	.15	.30
27	Sci Taria, Chancellor's Aide C	.15	.30
28	Naboo Officer, Liberator C	.15	.30
29	Bravo Pilot, Naboo Volunteer C	.15	.30
30	Naboo Security, Amidala's Guard C	.15	.30
31	Republic Captain, Officer C	.15	.30
32	Republic Pilot, Veteran C	.15	.30
33	Coruscant Guard	.15	.30
34	Coruscant Guard, Peacekeeper C	.15	.30
35	Coruscant Guard, Officer C	.15	.30
36	Coruscant Guard, Chancellor's Guard C	.15	.30
37	Wookiee Senator, Representative C	.15	.30
38	Galactic Senator, Delegate S	.15	.30
39	Obi-Wan Kenobi, Jedi Warrior S	.15	.30
40	Qui-Gon Jinn's Lightsaber R	1.00	2.00
41	Amidala's Blaster R	1.00	2.00
42	Adi Gallia's Lightsaber U	.50	1.00
43	Coruscant Guard Blaster Rifle U	.50	1.00
44	Ascension Gun C	.15	.30
45	Electropole C	.15	.30
46	Kaadu C	.15	.30
47	Flash Speeder C	.15	.30
48	Gian Speeder C	.15	.30
49	Naboo Blaster C	.15	.30
50	Blaster C	.15	.30
51	Blaster Rifle C	.15	.30
52	Balance To The Force U	.50	1.00
53	Brave Little Droid U	.50	1.00
54	Dos Mackineeks No Comen Here! C	.15	.30
55	Galactic Chancellor C	.15	.30
56	Hate Leads To Suffering U	.50	1.00
57	I Will Not Cooperate U	.50	1.00
58	Invasion! C	.15	.30
59	May The Force Be With You C	.15	.30
60	Senator Palpatine C	.15	.30
61	The Might Of The Republic C	.15	.30
62	We Don't Have Time For This C	.15	.30
63	We Wish To Board At Once C	.15	.30
64	Wisdom Of The Council R	1.00	2.00
65	Tatooine Mos Espa S	.15	.30
66	Coruscant Jedi Council Chamber S	.15	.30
67	Naboo Gungan Swamp S	.15	.30
68	Bravo 2, Naboo Starfighter U	.50	1.00
69	Naboo Starfighter C	.15	.30
70	Radiant VII, Republic Cruiser Transport C	.15	.30
71	Darth Maul, Master of Evil R	3.00	6.00
72	Darth Sidious, Lord of the Sith R	2.00	4.00
73	Sebulba, Podracer Pilot R	1.25	2.50
74	Watto, Junk Merchant R	1.00	2.00
75	Jabba the Hutt, Gangster R	1.25	2.50
76	Nute Gunray, Neimoidian Viceroy R	1.00	2.00
77	Rune Haako, Neimoidian Advisor R	1.00	2.00
78	Destroyer Droid Squad, Defense Division R	1.00	2.00
79	Battle Droid Squad, Escort Unit R	1.00	2.00
80	Trade Federation Tank, Assault Division R	1.00	2.00
81	Lott Dod, Neimoidian Senator R	1.00	2.00
82	Fode and Beed, Podrace Announcer R	1.00	2.00
83	Clegg Holdfast, Podracer Pilot U	.50	1.00
84	Dud Bolt, Podracer Pilot U	.50	1.00
85	Mars Guo, Podracer Pilot U	.50	1.00
86	Ody Mandrell, Podracer Pilot U	.50	1.00

87	Ratts Tyerell, Podracer Pilot U	.50	1.00
88	Aks Moe, Senator C	.15	.30
89	Horox Ryyder, Senator C	.15	.30
90	Edcel Bar Gane, Roona Senator C	.15	.30
91	Galactic Delegate, Representative C	.15	.30
92	Destroyer Droid, Assault Droid C	.15	.30
93	Destroyer Droid, Battleship Security C	.15	.30
94	Sith Probe Droid, Hunter Droid C	.15	.30
95	Rodian, Mercenary C	.15	.30
96	Battle Droid: Pilot, Assault Division C	.15	.30
97	Battle Droid: Security, Assault Division C	.15	.30
98	Battle Droid: Infantry, Assault Division C	.15	.30
99	Battle Droid: Officer, Assault Division C	.15	.30
100	Battle Droid: Pilot, Guard Division C	.15	.30
101	Battle Droid: Security, Guard Division C	.15	.30
102	Battle Droid: Infantry, Guard Division C	.15	.30
103	Battle Droid: Officer, Guard Division C	.15	.30
104	Neimoidian Aide	.15	.30
105	Darth Maul, Sith Warrior S	.15	.30
106	Darth Maul's Lightsaber R	1.00	2.00
107	Darth Maul's Sith Speeder R	1.00	2.00
108	Clegg Holdfast's Podracer U	.50	1.00
109	Dud Bolt's Podracer U	.50	1.00
110	Mars Guo's Podracer U	.50	1.00
111	Ody Mandrell's Podracer U	.50	1.00
112	Ratts Tyerell's Podracer U	.50	1.00
113	Trade Federation Tank Laser Cannon U	.50	1.00
114	Multi Troop Transport U	.50	1.00
115	STAP U	.50	1.00
116	Thermal Detonator U	.50	1.00
117	Battle Droid Blaster Rifle C	.15	.30
118	Blaster C	.15	.30
119	Blaster Rifle C	.15	.30
120	I Object! C	.15	.30
121	I Will Deal With Them Myself C	.15	.30
122	Let Them Make The First Move R	1.00	2.00
123	Move Against The Jedi First C	.15	.30
124	Open Fire! U	.50	1.00
125	Seal Off The Bridge U	.50	1.00
126	Start Your Engines! U	.50	1.00
127	Switch To Bio C	.15	.30
128	Take Them To Camp Four C	.15	.30
129	Very Unusual C	.15	.30
130	Vote Of No Confidence C	.15	.30
131	We Are Meeting No Resistance C	.15	.30
132	We Have Them On The Run U	.50	1.00
133	Yoka To Bantha Poodoo C	.15	.30
134	Your Little Insurrection Is At An End U	.50	1.00
135	Tatooine Podrace Arena S	.15	.30
136	Coruscant Galactic Senate S	.15	.30
137	Naboo Battle Plains S	.15	.30
138	Sith Infiltrator, Starfighter U	.50	1.00
139	Droid Starfighter C	.15	.30
140	Battleship, Trade Federation Transport C	.15	.30

1999 Young Jedi The Jedi Council Foil

RELEASED ON OCTOBER 27, 1999

F1	Obi-Wan Kenobi, Jedi Apprentice UR	3.00	6.00
F2	Qui-Gon Jinn, Jedi Protector SR	1.25	2.50
F3	PadmÈ Naberrie	1.25	2.50
F4	Captain Panaka	1.00	2.00
F5	Mace Windu	1.50	3.00
F6	Queen Amidala	2.00	4.00
F7	R2-D2, Loyal Droid VR	2.00	4.00
F8	Qui-Gon Jinn's Lightsaber VR	.60	1.25
F9	Amidala's Blaster VR	.60	1.25
F10	Darth Maul, Master of Evil UR	3.00	6.00
F11	Darth Sidious, Lord of the Sith UR	2.00	4.00
F12	Watto, Junk Merchant SR	1.00	2.00
F13	Jabba the Hutt, Gangster SR	1.00	2.00
F14	Nute Gunray, Neimoidian Viceroy SR	1.00	2.00
F15	Rune Haako, Neimoidian Advisor VR	.60	1.25

F16	Lott Dod, Neimoidian Senator VR	.60	1.25
F17	Darth Maul's Lightsaber VR	.60	1.25
F18	Darth Maul's Sith Speeder VR	.60	1.25

2000 Young Jedi Battle of Naboo

RELEASED ON APRIL 5, 2000

1	Obi-Wan Kenobi, Jedi Knight R	2.00	4.00
2	Qui-Gon Jinn, Jedi Ambassador R	1.50	3.00
3	Jar Jar Binks, Bombad Gungan General R	1.00	2.00
4	Anakin Skywalker, Padawan R	1.00	2.00
5	Padme Naberrie, Amidala's Handmaiden R	1.25	2.50
6	Captain Panaka, Veteran Leader R	.75	1.50
7	Mace Windu, Jedi Speaker R	1.00	2.00
8	Queen Amidala, Resolute Negotiator R	1.25	2.50
9	Queen Amidala, Keeper of the Peace R	1.25	2.50
10	Yoda, Jedi Elder R	1.25	2.50
11	R2-D2, The Queen's Hero R	1.00	2.00
12	Boss Nass, Gungan Chief U	.30	.75
13	Ric Olie, Bravo Leader U	.30	.75
14	Captain Tarpals, Gungan Officer U	.30	.75
15	Sio Bibble, Governor of Naboo U	.30	.75
16	Sabe, Handmaiden Decoy Queen U	.30	.75
17	Sache, Handmaiden U	.30	.75
18	Yane, Handmaiden U	.30	.75
19	Naboo Officer, Squad Leader U	.30	.75
20	Naboo Officer, Commander C	.12	.25
21	Naboo Bureaucrat, Official C	.12	.25
22	Naboo Security, Trooper C	.12	.25
23	Naboo Security, Defender C	.12	.25
24	Bravo Pilot, Ace Flyer C	.12	.25
25	Coruscant Guard, Chancellor's Escort C	.12	.25
26	Alderaan Diplomat, Senator C	.12	.25
27	Council Member, Naboo Governor C	.12	.25
28	Gungan Warrior, Veteran C	.12	.25
29	Gungan Guard, Lookout C	.12	.25
30	Gungan General, Army Leader C	.12	.25
31	Gungan Soldier, Infantry C	.12	.25
32	Rep Officer, Gungan Diplomat S	.12	.25
33	Obi-Wan Kenobi, Jedi Negotiator S	.12	.25
34	Mace Windu's Lightsaber R	.75	1.50
35	Eeth Koth's Lightsaber U	.30	.75
36	Captain Tarpals' Electropole U	.30	.75
37	Planetary Shuttle C	.12	.25
38	Fambaa C	.12	.25
39	Electropole C	.12	.25
40	Kaadu C	.12	.25
41	Flash Speeder C	.12	.25
42	Blaster C	.12	.25
43	Heavy Blaster C	.12	.25
44	Capture The Viceroy C	.12	.25
45	Celebration C	.12	.25
46	Guardians Of The Queen U	.30	.75
47	Gunga City C	.12	.25

48	Gungan Battle Cry U	.30	.75
49	How Wude! U	.30	.75
50	I Will Take Back What Is Ours C	.12	.25
51	Jedi Force Push U	.30	.75
52	Meeeesa Lika Dis! C	.12	.25
53	NOOOOOOOOOO! R	.75	1.50
54	Thanks, Artoo! U	.30	.75
55	The Chancellor's Ambassador U	.30	.75
56	The Will Of The Force R	.75	1.50
57	Young Skywalker U	.30	.75
58	Your Occupation Here Has Ended C	.12	.25
59	Bombad General U	.30	.75
60	Kiss Your Trade Franchise Goodbye U	.30	.75
61	There's Always A Bigger Fish C	.12	.25
62	Uh-Oh! C	.12	.25
63	We Wish To Form An Alliance C	.12	.25
64	Tatooine Desert Landing Site S	.12	.25
65	Coruscant Galactic Senate S	.12	.25
66	Naboo Battle Plains S	.12	.25
67	Amidala's Starship, Royal Transport R	.75	1.50
68	Bravo 3, Naboo Starfighter U	.30	.75
69	Naboo Starfighter U	.12	.25
70	Republic Cruiser, Transport C	.12	.25
71	Darth Maul, Dark Lord of the Sith R	2.50	5.00
72	Darth Sidious, Sith Manipulator R	1.50	3.00
73	Sebulba, Dangerous Podracer Pilot R	.75	1.50
74	Watto, Toydarian Gambler R	.75	1.50
75	Aurra Sing, Mercenary R	1.00	2.00
76	Jabba The Hutt, Crime Lord R	.75	1.50
77	Nute Gunray, Neimoidian Despot R	.75	1.50
78	Rune Haako, Neimoidian Deputy R	.75	1.50
79	Destroyer Droid Squad, Guard Division R	.75	1.50
80	Battle Droid Squad, Guard Unit R	.75	1.50
81	Trade Federation Tank, Guard Division R	.75	1.50
82	Trade Federation Tank, Patrol Division R	.75	1.50
83	P-59, Destroyer Droid Commander U	.30	.75
84	OOM-9, Battle Droid Commander U	.30	.75
85	Daultay Dofine, Neimoidian Attendant U	.30	.75
86	Diva Shaliqua, Singer U	.30	.75
87	Diva Funquita, Dancer U	.30	.75
88	Bith, Musician U	.30	.75
89	Quarren, Smuggler U	.30	.75
90	Toonbuck Toora, Senator U	.30	.75
91	Aqualish, Galactic Senator C	.12	.25
92	Twi'lek Diplomat, Senator C	.12	.25
93	Weequay, Enforcer C	.12	.25
94	Nikto, Slave C	.12	.25
95	Pacithhip, Prospector C	.12	.25
96	Destroyer Droid, Vanguard Droid C	.12	.25
97	Destroyer Droid, MTT Infantry C	.12	.25
98	Sith Probe Droid, Remote Tracker C	.12	.25
99	Battle Droid: Pilot, Patrol Division C	.12	.25
100	Battle Droid: Security, Patrol Division C	.12	.25
101	Battle Droid: Infantry, Patrol Division C	.12	.25
102	Battle Droid: Officer, Patrol Division C	.12	.25
103	Battle Droid: Pilot, Defense Division C	.12	.25
104	Battle Droid: Security, Defense Division C	.12	.25
105	Battle Droid: Infantry, Defense Division C	.12	.25
106	Battle Droid: Officer, Defense Division C	.12	.25
107	Neimoidian Advisor, Bureaucrat S	.12	.25
108	Darth Maul, Evil Sith Lord S	.12	.25
109	Darth Maul's Lightsaber R	1.00	2.00
110	Sith Lightsaber R	.75	1.50
111	Darth Maul's Electrobinoculars U	.30	.75
112	Trade Federation Tank Laser Cannon U	.30	.75
113	Multi Troop Transport U	.30	.75
114	STAP U	.30	.75
115	Battle Droid Blaster Rifle C	.12	.25
116	Blaster C	.12	.25
117	Blaster Rifle C	.12	.25
118	A Thousand Terrible Things C	.12	.25
119	Armored Assault C	.12	.25
120	Death From Above C	.12	.25

121 Don't Spect A Werm Welcome C	.12	.25
122 I Will Make It Legal C	.12	.25
123 Not For A Sith R	.75	1.50
124 Now There Are Two Of Them U	.30	.75
125 Sith Force Push U	.30	.75
126 The Phantom Menace U	.30	.75
127 They Win This Round C	.12	.25
128 We Are Sending All Troops C	.12	.25
129 After Her! C	.12	.25
130 Da Dug Chaaa! U	.30	.75
131 Sando Aqua Monster C	.12	.25
132 They Will Not Stay Hidden For Long C	.12	.25
133 This Is Too Close! U	.30	.75
134 Tatooine Mos Espa S	.12	.25
135 Coruscant Capital City S	.12	.25
136 Naboo Theed Palace S	.12	.25
137 Droid Control Ship	.30	.75
Trade Federation Transport U		
138 Sith Infiltrator, Starfighter U	.30	.75
139 Droid Starfighter C	.12	.25
140 Battleship, Trade Federation Transport C	.12	.25

2000 Young Jedi Battle of Naboo Foil

F1 Obi-Wan Kenobi, Jedi Knight UR	2.00	4.00
F2 Qui-Gon Jinn, Jedi Ambassador UR	1.00	2.00
F3 Queen Amidala, Keeper of the Peace SR	1.00	2.00
F4 Yoda, Jedi Elder SR	1.00	2.00
F5 R2-D2, The Queen's Hero SR	1.00	2.00
F6 Queen Amidala, Resolute Negotiator VR	.75	1.50
F7 Mace Windu's Lightsaber VR	.50	1.00
F8 The Will Of The Force VR	.50	1.00
F9 Amidala's Starship, Royal Transport VR	.50	1.00
F10 Darth Maul, Dark Lord of the Sith UR	2.00	4.00
F11 Aurra Sing, Mercenary UR	1.00	2.00
F12 Nute Gunray	.75	1.50
Neimoidian Despot SR		
F13 Destroyer Droid Squad	.75	1.50
Guard Division SR		
F14 Trade Federation Tank	.75	1.50
Guard Division SR		
F15 Battle Droid Squad, Guard Unit VR	.50	1.00
F16 Trade Federation Tank	.50	1.00
Patrol Division VR		
F17 Darth Maul's Lightsaber VR	.50	1.00
F18 Not For A Sith VR	.50	1.00

2000 Young Jedi Duel of the Fates

RELEASED ON NOVEMBER 8, 2000

1 Obi-Wan Kenobi, Jedi Student R	2.00	4.00
2 Qui-Gon Jinn, Jedi Mentor UR	1.50	3.00
3 Anakin Skywalker, Rookie Pilot R	1.00	2.00
4 Captain Panaka, Security Commander R	.75	1.50
5 Mace Windu, Jedi Councilor R	1.00	2.00
6 Queen Amidala, Young Leader R	1.25	2.50
7 Yoda, Jedi Philosopher R	1.25	2.50
8 R2-D2, Repair Droid R	1.00	2.00
9 Ric Olie, Starship Pilot R	.75	1.50
10 Bravo Pilot, Flyer C	.12	.25
11 Valorum, Leader of the Senate C	.12	.25
12 Qui-Gon Jinn's Lightsaber	.75	1.50
Wielded by Obi-Wan Kenobi R		
13 Booma U	.30	.75
14 A Powerful Opponent C	.12	.25
15 Come On, Move! U	.30	.75
16 Critical Confrontation C	.12	.25
17 Gungan Mounted Troops U	.30	.75
18 Naboo Fighter Attack C	.12	.25
19 Qui-Gon's Final Stand C	.12	.25
20 Run The Blockade C	.12	.25
21 Twist Of Fate C	.12	.25
22 You Are Strong With The Force U	.30	.75
23 Gungan Energy Shield U	.30	.75
24 He Can See Things Before They Happen U	.30	.75
25 Jedi Meditation U	.30	.75
26 Jedi Training U	.30	.75
27 Naboo Royal Security Forces U	.30	.75
28 Pounded Unto Death C	.12	.25
29 Senate Guard C	.12	.25
30 Naboo Starfighter C	.12	.25
31 Darth Maul, Student of the Dark Side UR	2.00	4.00
32 Darth Sidious, Master of the Dark Side R	1.25	2.50
33 Aurra Sing, Trophy Collector R	1.00	2.00
34 Tey How, Neimoidian Command Officer R	.75	1.50
35 OWO-1, Battle Droid Command Officer R	.75	1.50
36 Rayno Vaca, Taxi Driver R	.75	1.50
37 Baskol Yeesrim, Gran Senator R	.75	1.50
38 Starfighter Droid, DFS-327 R	.75	1.50
39 Starfighter Droid, DFS-1104 R	.75	1.50
40 Starfighter Droid, DFS-1138 R	.75	1.50
41 Jedi Lightsaber, Stolen by Aurra Sing U	.30	.75
42 Coruscant Taxi U	.30	.75
43 Neimoidian Viewscreen C	.12	.25
44 Battle Droid Patrol U	.30	.75
45 Change In Tactics C	.12	.25
46 Dangerous Encounter C	.12	.25
47 Darth Maul Defiant C	.12	.25
48 Impossible! C	.12	.25
49 It's A Standoff! U	.30	.75
50 Mobile Assassin U	.30	.75
51 Power Of The Sith C	.12	.25
52 Starfighter Screen C	.12	.25
53 To The Death C	.12	.25
54 Use Caution U	.30	.75
55 Blockade U	.30	.75
56 End This Pointless Debate U	.30	.75
57 The Duel Begins U	.30	.75
58 The Jedi Are Involved U	.30	.75
59 Where Are Those Droidekas? U	.30	.75
60 Droid Starfighter C	.12	.25

2000 Young Jedi Enhanced Menace of Darth Maul

P1 Qui-Gon Jinn, Jedi Protector	2.50	5.00
P2 Mace Windu, Jedi Warrior	1.50	3.00
P3 Queen Amidala, Cunning Warrior	5.00	10.00
P4 Darth Maul, Sith Assassin	2.50	5.00
P5 Sebulba, Champion Podracer Pilot	5.00	10.00
P6 Trade Federation Tank, Assault Leader	3.00	6.00

2001 Young Jedi Boonta Eve Podrace

RELEASED ON SEPTEMBER 5, 2001

1 Anakin Skywalker, Boonta Eve Podracer Pilot UR	1.00	2.00
2 Yoda, Jedi Instructor R	1.25	2.50
3 C-3PO, Human-Cyborg Relations Droid R	1.00	2.00
4 Jira, Pallie Vendor R	.75	1.50
5 Kitster, Anakin's Friend R	.75	1.50
6 Wald, Anakin's Friend R	.75	1.50
7 Seek, Anakin's Friend U	.30	.75
8 Amee, Anakin's Friend U	.30	.75
9 Melee, Anakin's Friend U	.30	.75
10 Captain Tarpals, Gungan Leader R	.75	1.50
11 Boles Roor, Podracer Pilot U	.30	.75
12 Elan Mak, Podracer Pilot U	.30	.75
13 Neva Kee, Podracer Pilot U	.30	.75
14 Wan Sandage, Podracer Pilot U	.30	.75
15 Shmi Skywalker, Anakin's Mother R	.75	1.50
16 Boles Roor's Podracer U	.30	.75
17 Elan Mak's Podracer U	.30	.75
18 Neva Kee's Podracer U	.30	.75
19 Wan Sandage's Podracer U	.30	.75
20 Comlink C	.12	.25
21 Hold-Out Blaster C	.12	.25
22 Dis Is Nutsen C	.12	.25
23 Masquerade C	.12	.25
24 No Giben Up, General Jar Jar C	.12	.25
25 What Does Your Heart Tell You? C	.12	.25
26 All-Out Defense U	.30	.75
27 Bravo Squadron C	.12	.25
28 Hologram Projector C	.12	.25
29 Boonta Eve Classic R	.75	1.50
30 Amidala's Starship R	.75	1.50
31 Sebulba, Dug Podracer Pilot UR	.75	1.50
32 Watto, Podrace Sponsor R	.75	1.50
33 Aurra Sing, Formidable Adversary R	1.00	2.00
34 Jabba The Hutt, O Grandio Lust R	.75	1.50
35 TC-14, Protocol Droid R	.75	1.50
36 Orr'UrRuuR'R, Tusken Raider Leader Rare R	.75	1.50
37 UrrOr'RuuR, Tusken Raider Warrior U	.30	.75
38 RuuR'Ur, Tusken Raider Sniper C	.12	.25
39 Sil Unch, Neimoidian Comm Officer U	.30	.75
40 Graxol Kelvyyn and Shakka U	.30	.75
41 Corix Venne, Bith Musician C	.12	.25
42 Reike Th'san, Arms Smuggler R	.75	1.50
43 Meddun, Nikto Mercenary U	.30	.75
44 Rum Sleg, Bounty Hunter R	.75	1.50
45 Aehrrley Rue, Freelance Pilot U	.30	.75
46 Jedwar Seelah, Explorer Scout U	.30	.75
47 Chokk, Klatooinian Explosives Expert C	.12	.25
48 Tatooine Backpack C	.12	.25
49 Gaderffii Stick C	.12	.25
50 Hold-Out Blaster C	.12	.25
51 Watto's Datapad U	.30	.75
52 Colo Claw Fish C	.12	.25
53 He Always Wins! C	.12	.25
54 Bounty Hunter C	.12	.25
55 Two-Pronged Attack C	.12	.25
56 All-Out Attack U	.30	.75
57 Eventually You'll Lose U	.30	.75
58 Gangster's Paradise U	.30	.75
59 Boonta Eve Classic R	.75	1.50
60 Viceroy's Battleship R	.75	1.50
R1 Rule Card 1	.10	.20
R2 Rule Card 2	.10	.20
R3 Rule Card 3	.12	.25

2001 Young Jedi Enhanced Battle of Naboo

RELEASED IN 2001

P8 Obi-Wan Kenobi, Jedi Avenger	5.00	10.00
P9 Anakin Skywalker, Tested By The Jedi Council	12.00	25.00
P10 PadmÈ Naberrie, Loyal Handmaiden	15.00	30.00
P11 Captain Panaka, Royal Defender	2.50	5.00
P12 Yoda, Wise Jedi	5.00	10.00
P13 R2-D2, Starship Maintenance Droid	6.00	12.00
P14 Darth Sidious, The Phantom Menace	2.50	5.00
P15 Watto, Risk Taker	5.00	10.00
P16 Aurra Sing, Scoundrel	5.00	10.00
P17 Jabba The Hutt	5.00	10.00
P18 Nute Gunray, Neimoidean Bureaucrat	3.00	6.00
P19 Rune Haako, Neimoidean Lieutenant	6.00	12.00

2001 Young Jedi Reflections

RELEASED ON JULY 18, 2001

A1 Jar Jar Binks, Bombad Gungan General	1.50	3.00
Jar Jar Binks' Electropole		
A2 Boss Nass, Gungan Chief	2.50	5.00
Fambaa		
A3 Adi Gallia, Corellian Jedi Master	2.00	4.00
Adi Gallia's Lightsaber		
A4 Eeth Koth, Zabrak Jedi Master	2.50	5.00
Eeth Koth's Lightsaber		
A5 Ki-Adi-Mundi, Cerean Jedi Knight	2.50	5.00
Jedi Lightsaber, Constructed by Ki-Adi-Mundi		
A6 Valorum, Supreme Chancellor	1.50	3.00
Planetary Shuttle		
A7 Aurra Sing, Trophy Collector	2.50	5.00
Jedi Lightsaber, Stolen by Aurra Sing		
A8 Nute Gunray, Neimoidian Viceroy	2.00	4.00
Neimoidian Viewscreen		
A9 OOM-9, Battle Droid Commander	2.00	4.00
Battle Droid Blaster Rifle		
A10 OWO-1, Battle Droid Command Officer	2.50	5.00
STAP		
A11 P-59, Destroyer Droid Commander	2.00	4.00
Multi Troop Transport		
A12 Toonbuck Toora, Senator	2.50	5.00
Coruscant Taxi		
C1 Are You An Angel?	1.00	2.00
I've Been Trained In Defense		
C2 Brave Little Droid	.75	1.50
Counterparts		
C3 Celebration	1.00	2.00
Gungan Mounted Troooops		
C4 Enough Of This Pretense	.75	1.50
I Will Not Cooperate		
C5 Fear Attracts The Fearful	1.00	2.00
How Wude!		
C6 I Have A Bad Feeling About This	1.00	2.00

NOOOOOOOOOO!		
C7 Jedi Force Push	1.00	2.00
We're Not In Trouble Yet		
C8 Dos Mackineeks No Comen Here!	1.00	2.00
Bombad General		
C9 At last we will have revenge	.50	1.00
Sith force push		
C10 The Queen's Plan	1.00	2.00
Naboo Royal Security Forces		
C11 The Might Of The Republic	1.00	2.00
Senate Guard		
C12 The Negotiations Were Short	1.00	2.00
Qui-Gon's Final Stand		
C13 Wisdom Of The Council	1.00	2.00
Jedi Training		
C14 Yousa Guys Bombad!	1.00	2.00
Uh-Oh!		
C15 A Thousand Terrible Things & We Are Sending All Troops	.75	1.50
C16 Battle Droid Patrol & In Complete Control	.75	1.50
C17 Boonta Eve Podrace & Kaa Bazza Kundee Hodrudda!	.75	1.50
C18 Podrace Preparation & Yoka To Bantha Poodoo	1.00	2.00
C19 Switch To Bio & Your Little Insurrection Is At An End	.50	1.00
C20 The Phantom Menace & Use Caution	1.00	2.00
D1 Dos Mackineeks No Comen Here!	1.00	2.00
Bombad General		
D2 Gunga City	1.00	2.00
Gungan Energy Shield		
D3 The Queen's Plan	1.00	2.00
Naboo Royal Security Forces		
D4 The Might Of The Republic	1.00	2.00
Senate Guard		
D5 The Negotiations Were Short	1.00	2.00
Qui-Gon's Final Stand		
D6 Wisdom Of The Council	1.00	2.00
Jedi Training		
D7 Yousa Guys Bombad!	1.00	2.00
Uh-Oh!		
D8 Grueling Contest	1.00	2.00
Da Dug Chaaa!		
D9 Let Them Make The First Move	.50	1.00
Very Unusual		
D10 Now There Are Two Of Them	.75	1.50
The Duel Begins		
D11 Opee Sea Killer	1.00	2.00
To The Death		
D12 Starfighter Screen	1.00	2.00
Blockade		
D13 We Have Them On The Run	1.00	2.00
Where Are Those Droidekas?		
D14 You Have Been Well Trained	.50	1.00
After Her!		
2BEP Yoda, Jedi Instructor (foil)	3.00	6.00
2MDM Qui-Gon Jinn, Jedi Master (foil)	12.00	25.00
3BEP C-3PO, Human-Cyborg Relations Droid (foil)	3.00	6.00
4BEP Jira, Pallie Vendor (foil)	1.50	3.00
4BON Anakin Skywalker, Padawan (foil)	4.00	8.00
4TJC Anakin Skywalker, Child of Prophecy (foil)	7.50	15.00
5BEP Kitster, Anakin's Friend (foil)	2.50	5.00
6BEP Wald, Anakin's Friend (foil)	2.00	4.00
7BON Mace Windu, Jedi Speaker (foil)	12.00	25.00
9MDM Queen Amidala, Royal Leader (foil)	4.00	8.00
9TJC Queen Amidala, Voice of Her People (foil)	5.00	10.00
10MDM Yoda, Jedi Master (foil)	2.50	5.00
1DOTF Obi-Wan Kenobi, Jedi Student (foil)	7.50	15.00
2DOTF Qui-Gon Jinn, Jedi Mentor (foil)	4.00	8.00
30BEP Amidala's Starship, Queen's Transport (foil)	2.50	5.00
32BEP Watto, Podrace Sponsor (foil)	2.50	5.00
33BEP Aurra Sing, Formidable Adversary (foil)	5.00	10.00
34BEP Jabba The Hutt, O Grandio Lust (foil)	2.50	5.00
35BEP TC-14, Protocol Droid (foil)	2.50	5.00
36BEP Orr'UrRuuR'R, Tusken Raider Leader (foil)	2.50	5.00
3DOTF Anakin Skywalker, Rookie Pilot (foil)	4.00	8.00
4DOTF Captain Panaka, Security Commander (foil)	2.50	5.00

5DOTF Mace Windu, Jedi Councilor (foil)	3.00	6.00
60BEP Viceroy's Battleship, Trade Federation Transport (foil)	2.00	4.00
6DOTF Queen Amidala, Young Leader (foil)	4.00	8.00
72BON Darth Sidious, Sith Manipulator (foil)	4.00	8.00
73BON Sebulba, Dangerous Podracer Pilot (foil)	10.00	20.00
73TJC Sebulba, Podracer Pilot (foil)	2.00	4.00
74BON Watto, Toydarian Gambler (foil)	1.25	2.50
74MDM Watto, Slave Owner (foil)	2.50	5.00
75MDM Aurra Sing, Bounty Hunter (foil)	5.00	10.00
76BON Jabba The Hutt, Crime Lord (foil)	2.50	5.00
78BON Rune Haako, Neimoidian Deputy (foil)	2.50	5.00
78TJC Destroyer Droid Squad, Defense Division (foil)	4.00	8.00
79TJC Battle Droid Squad, Escort Unit (foil)	2.50	5.00
7DOTF Yoda, Jedi Philosopher (foil)	5.00	10.00
80TJC Trade Federation Tank, Assault Division (foil)	7.50	15.00
88MDM Trade Federation Tank, Armored Division (foil)	2.50	5.00
31DOTF Darth Maul, Student of the Dark Side (foil)	4.00	8.00
32DOTF Darth Sidious, Master of the Dark Side (foil)	12.00	25.00
33DOTF Aurra Sing, Trophy Collector (foil)	2.00	4.00
P1EMDM Qui-Gon Jinn, Jedi Protector (foil)	5.00	10.00
P2EMDM Mace Windu, Jedi Warrior (foil)	5.00	10.00
P3EMDM Queen Amidala, Cunning Warrior (foil)	10.00	20.00
P4EMDM Darth Maul, Sith Assassin (foil)	10.00	20.00
P5EMDM Sebulba, Champion Podracer Pilot (foil)	2.50	5.00
P6EMDM Trade Federation Tank, Assault Leader (foil)	2.00	4.00
P7PREM Shmi Skywalker, Anakin's Mother (foil)	2.00	4.00
P8EBON Obi-Wan Kenobi, Jedi Avenger (foil)	4.00	8.00
P9EBON Anakin Skywalker, Tested by the Jedi Council (foil)	4.00	8.00
P10EBON PadmÈ Naberrie, Loyal Handmaiden (foil)	2.50	5.00
P11EBON Captain Panaka, Royal Defender (foil)	2.50	5.00
P12EBON Yoda, Wise Jedi (foil)	5.00	10.00
P13EBON R2-D2, Starship Maintenance Droid (foil)	4.00	8.00
P14EBON Darth Sidious, The Phantom Menace (foil)	4.00	8.00
P15EBON Watto, Risk Taker (foil)	2.50	5.00
P16EBON Aurra Sing, Scoundrel (foil)	2.00	4.00
P17EBON Jabba The Hutt, Tatooine Tyrant (foil)	2.50	5.00
P18EBON Nute Gunray, Neimoidian Bureaucrat (foil)	2.00	4.00
P19EBON Rune Haako, Neimoidian Lieutenant (foil)	2.50	5.00

2017 Weiss Schwarz Star Wars

SWS49001 Escape From First Order Finn RR	
SWS49001R Escape From First Order Finn RRR FOIL	
SWS49002 Smuggler Han Solo RR	
SWS49002SP Smuggler Han Solo SP FOIL	
SWS49003 Secret Mission Leia RR	
SWS49003S Secret Mission Leia SR FOIL	
SWS49004 Lightsaber in Hand Finn R	
SWS49005 Scoundrel Han Solo R	
SWS49005S Scoundrel Han Solo SR FOIL	
SWS49006 Han Solo R	
SWS49007 Captain of the Millennium Falcon Han Solo R	
SWS49007S Captain of the Millennium Falcon Han Solo SR	
SWS49008 New Name Finn R	
SWS49008S New Name Finn SR FOIL	
SWS49009 Starfighter Pilot Poe R	
SWS49010 Roar of Wookie Chewbacca R	
SWS49011 Bloodline of the Force Leia U	
SWS49012 Reversal of Situation Chewbacca U	
SWS49013 Maz Kanata U	
SWS49014 Rescue Chewbacca U	
SWS49015 Ewoks U	
SWS49016 Lando Calrissian U	
SWS49017 Reunion Poe U	
SWS49018 Thinking of Their Son Han Solo & Leia C	
SWS49019 Wicket C	
SWS49020 Nien Nunb C	
SWS49021 Lobot C	
SWS49022 Neck and Neck Battle Han Solo C	
SWS49023 Princess Leia C	
SWS49024 Rescue Operation Han Solo C	
SWS49025 Wookie' Chewbacca C	
SWS49026 Admiral Ackbar C	
SWS49027 Jakku U	

SWS49028 Dajarik Holochess U
SWS49029 X-wing starfighter C
SWS49030 Millennium Falcon C
SWS49031 Mission! CR
SWS49031SWR Mission! SWR FOIL
SWS49032 Medal Ceremony CC
SWS49032SWR Medal Ceremony SWR FOIL
SWS49033 I can do this! CC
SWS49034 Brilliant battle CC
SWS49035 Boushh's True Form Leia RR
SWS49035R Boushh's True Form Leia RRR FOIL
SWS49036 Jabba the Hut R
SWS49037 Boba Fett R
SWS49038 Message And Present Jabba U
SWS49039 Bib Fortuna U
SWS49040 Crime Lord of the Desert Jabba U
SWS49041 Battle Professional Boba Fett U
SWS49042 Gamorrean C
SWS49043 Hidden Mission R2-D2 C
SWS49044 Unkar Plutt C
SWS49045a Max Rebo Band C
SWS49045b Max Rebo Band C
SWS49045c Max Rebo Band C
SWS49046 Rookie Translator C-3PO C
SWS49047 Eager Lando C
SWS49048 Cantina Band U
SWS49049 Carbon Freezing U
SWS49050 The Sarlacc Pitt C
SWS49051 Jabba's Palace CC
SWS49052 Bounty hunter CC
SWS49053 Reunion And Duel Darth Vader RR
SWS49053R Reunion And Duel Darth Vader RRR FOIL
SWS49054 Kylo Ren RR
SWS49054R Kylo Ren RRR FOIL
SWS49055 Dark Sith Lord Darth Vader RR
SWS49055SP Dark Sith Lord Darth Vader SP FOIL
SWS49056 Dark Side Darth Vader R
SWS49056R Dark Side Darth Vader RRR FOIL
SWS49057 Mask Off Kylo Ren R
SWS49057S Mask Off Kylo Ren SR FOIL
SWS49058 Dark Commander Kylo Ren R
SWS49059 Blitz Darth Vader R
SWS49060 Tainted by Darkness Darth Vader R
SWS49060S Tainted by Darkness Darth Vader SR FOIL
SWS49061 Supreme Leader Snoke R
SWS49062 Emperor R
SWS49063 Stormtrooper U
SWS49063S Stormtrooper SR FOIL
SWS49064 Captain Phasma U
SWS49065 Skillful Strategy Darth Vader U
SWS49066 Persistent About the Outcome Kylo Ren U
SWS49067 General Hux U
SWS49068 Don't Be Overconfident Darth Vader U
SWS49069 Carrying Out the Dying Wish Kylo Ren U
SWS49070 FN-2187 Stormtrooper C
SWS49071 Crowd Tactics Stormtrooper C
SWS49072 First Order Stormtrooper C
SWS49073 Admiral Piett C
SWS49074 Grand Moff Wilhuff Tarkin C
SWS49075 New Vanguard Stormtrooper C
SWS49076 Scout Trooper C
SWS49076S Scout Trooper SR FOIL
SWS49077 Threat of Darkness Darth Vader C
SWS49078 Dictator of the Dark Side Emperor C
SWS49079 Star Destroyer U
SWS49080 The Dark Side U
SWS49081 Death Star U
SWS49082 Lightsaber Duel C
SWS49083 I am your father. CR
SWS49083SWR I am your father. FOIL SWR
SWS49084 You are beaten. CC
SWS49085 Show me CC
SWS49085SWR Show me SWR FOIL
SWS49086 Starkiller CC

SWS49087 R2-D2 RR
SWS49087R R2-D2 RRR FOIL
SWS49088 Awakening Rey RR
SWS49088SP Awakening Rey SP FOIL
SWS49089 Dream-Chasing Youth Luke RR
SWS49089SP Dream-Chasing Youth Luke SP FOIL
SWS49090 Jedi Training Luke R
SWS49090S Jedi Training Luke SR FOIL
SWS49091 Talent of Pilot Rey R
SWS49091R Talent of Pilot Rey RRR FOIL
SWS49092 Brave Supporter C-3PO R
SWS49093 Astromech Droid R2-D2 R
SWS49093S Astromech Droid R2-D2 SR FOIL
SWS49094 Moment of Counterattack Luke R
SWS49095 Yoda R
SWS49095S Yoda SR FOIL
SWS49096 Teaching of the Sage Obi-Wan R
SWS49097 Encounter of Fate Luke R
SWS49097R Encounter of Fate Luke RRR FOIL
SWS49098 Desert Hermit Ben Kenobi U
SWS49099 The Good News Bringer R2-D2 U
SWS49100 Beloved Partner C-3PO U
SWS49101 Obi-Wan Kenobi U
SWS49102 Jedi Master Luke U
SWS49103 Premonition of Friendship BB-8 U
SWS49103S Premonition of Friendship BB-8 SR FOIL
SWS49104 Jedi Master Yoda C
SWS49105 Jedi Knight Luke C
SWS49106 Comrade BB-8 C
SWS49107 Light Side Luke C
SWS49108 Luke Skywalker C
SWS49109 C-3PO C
SWS49110 Sudden Attack Luke C
SWS49111 Shooting Skill Rey C
SWS49112 Jedi Master Obi-wan C
SWS49113 Lightsaber U
SWS49114 Lightsaber U
SWS49115 AT-AT U
SWS49116 Rey's Speeder C
SWS49117 A New Hope CR
SWS49117SWR A New Hope SWR FOIL
SWS49118 The Force Awakens CR
SWS49118SWR The Force Awakens SWR FOIL
SWS49119 Great Mentor CC
SWS49120 Return of the Jedi CC

2017 Weiss Schwarz Star Wars Promo

SWS49P01 Encounter of Fate Rey & BB-8

2017 Weiss Schwarz Star Wars Trial Deck

SWS49T01 The Jacket Left Behind Finn
SWS49T02 Hero Han Solo
SWS49T03 Captured Pilot Poe
SWS49T04 Attack by the Resistance Poe
SWS49T05 Stubborn Tracing Finn
SWS49T06 New Determination Within Him Han Solo
SWS49T07 New Determination Within Him Chewbacca
SWS49T08 Duel in the Forest
SWS49T09 Beginning of Adventure Rey
SWS49T09R Beginning of Adventure Rey RRR FOIL
SWS49T10 Lor San Tekka
SWS49T11 To Jakku BB-8
SWS49T12 Reunion C-3PO
SWS49T13 Long Sleep R2-D2
SWS49T13R Long Sleep R2-D2 RRR FOIL
SWS49T14 For a Small Amount of Food Rey
SWS49T15 Scavenger Days Rey
SWS49T16 Something to Protect
SWS49T16S Something to Protect SR FOIL
SWS49T17 BB Unit
SWS49T18 Escape from Jakku
SWS49T19 Force Wielder
SWS49T19SP Force Wielder SP FOIL

2022 Weiss Schwarz Star Wars Comeback Edition

SWS49001RR Escape from the First Order Finn RR
SWS49001RRRR Escape from the First Order Fin RRR FOIL
SWS49002RR Smuggler Han Solo RR
SWS49002SPSP Smuggler Han Solo SP FOIL
SWS49003reRR Secret Mission Leia RR
SWS49003SreSR Secret Mission Leia SR FOIL
SWS49004R Lightsaber in hand Finn R
SWS49005reR Rogue Han Solo R
SWS49005SreSR Rogue Han Solo SR FOIL
SWS49006R Han Solo R
SWS49007R Captain of the Millennium Falcon Han Solo R
SWS49007SSR Captain of the Millennium Falcon Han Solo SR FOIL
SWS49008R New name Fin R
SWS49008SSR New name Fin SR FOIL
SWS49009R Starfighter Pilot Poe R
SWS49010reR Wookie Roar Chewbacca R
SWS49011U Force Lineage Leia U
SWS49012U Turn the tables Chewbacca U
SWS49013U Maz Kanata U
SWS49014U Rescue Chewbacca U
SWS49015U Ewoks U
SWS49016U Lando Calrissian U
SWS49017U Reunion Po U
SWS49018C Thoughts for my son Han Solo & Leia C
SWS49019C Wicket C
SWS49020C Nine Nan C
SWS49021C Robot C
SWS49022C Back and forth battle Han Solo C
SWS49023C Princess Leia C
SWS49024C Rescue Operation Han Solo C
SWS49025C Wookie Chewbacca C
SWS49026C Admiral Ackbar C
SWS49027U Jakku U
SWS49028U Dejarik Holochess U
SWS49029C X-wing starfighter C
SWS49030C Millennium Falcon C
SWS49031CR Mission! CR
SWS49031SWRSWR Mission! SWR FOIL
SWS49032reCC Medal Ceremony CC
SWS49032SWRreSWR Medal Ceremony SWR
SWS49032SWRreSWR Medal Ceremony SWR FOIL
SWS49033CC I can do this! CC
SWS49034CC Brilliant battle CC
SWS49035RR Bushi's True Identity Leia RR
SWS49035RRRR Bushi's True Identity Leia RRR FOIL
SWS49036R Jabba the Hut R
SWS49037R Boba Fett R
SWS49038U Message and Gift Java U
SWS49039U Bib Fortuna U
SWS49040U Desert Crime King Jabba U
SWS49041U Combat Professional Boba Fett U
SWS49042C Gamorrian C
SWS49043C Hidden Mission R2-D2 C
SWS49044C Anchor platform C
SWS49045aC Max Revo Band C
SWS49045bC Max Revo Band C
SWS49045cC Max Revo Band C
SWS49046C New Rice Flipping System C-3PO C
SWS49047C Tiger Observation Land C
SWS49048U Cantina Band U
SWS49049U Carbon Freezing U
SWS49050C The Sarlacc Pit C
SWS49051CC Jabba's Palace CC
SWS49052CC Bounty hunter CC
SWS49053RR Reunion and Death Struggle Darth Vader RR
SWS49053RRRR Reunion and Deadly Fight Darth Vader RRR FOIL
SWS49054reRR Kylo Ren RR
SWS49054RreRRR Kylo Ren RRR FOIL
SWS49054RrReRRR Kylo Ren RRR FOIL
SWS49055reRR Dark Lord of the Sith Darth Vader RR

SWS49055SPreSP Dark Lord of the Sith Darth Vader SP FOIL
SWS49056R Dark Side Darth Vader R
SWS49056RRRR Dark Side Darth Vader RRR FOIL
SWS49057R Mask Removed Kylo Ren R
SWS49057SSR Mask Removed Kylo Ren SR FOIL
SWS49058R Commander of Darkness Kylo Ren R
SWS49059R Rush Darth Vader R
SWS49060reR The Evil One Darth Vader R
SWS49060SreSR The Evil One Darth Vader SR FOIL
SWS49061R Supreme Leader Snoke R
SWS49062R Emperor R
SWS49063SSR Stormtrooper SR FOIL
SWS49063U Stormtrooper U
SWS49064U Captain Phasma U
SWS49065U Skillful Plot Darth Vader U
SWS49066U Persistence to compete Kylo Ren U
SWS49067U General Hux U
SWS49068U Overconfidence is prohibited Darth Vader U
SWS49069U Heir to the Will Kylo Ren U
SWS49070C FN-2187 Stormtrooper C
SWS49071C Many Soldiers Stormtrooper C
SWS49072C First Order Stormtrooper C
SWS49073C Admiral Piet C
SWS49074C Grand Moff Wilhuff Tarkin C
SWS49075reC New vanguard Stormtrooper C
SWS49076C Scout Trooper C
SWS49076SSR Scout Trooper SR FOIL
SWS49077C Dark Menace Darth Vader C
SWS49078C Ruler of Dark Side Emperor C
SWS49079U Star Destroyer U
SWS49080U The Dark Side U
SWS49081U Death Star U
SWS49082C Lightsaber Duel C
SWS49083reCR I am your father. CR
SWS49083SWRreSWR I am your father. SWR
SWS49084CC You are beaten. CC
SWS49085CC Show me CC
SWS49085SWRSWR Show me SWR
SWS49085SWRSWR Show me SWR FOIL
SWS49086CC Starkiller CC
SWS49087RR R2-D2 RR

SWS49087RRRR R2-D2 RRR FOIL
SWS49088reRR Awakening Rey RR
SWS49088SPreSP Awakening Rey SP FOIL
SWS49089reRR Young man chasing his dreams Luke RR
SWS49089SPreSP Young man chasing his dreams Luke SP FOIL
SWS49090R Jedi Training Luke R
SWS49090SSR Jedi Training Luke SR FOIL
SWS49091R Qualities of a Pilot Ray R
SWS49091RRRR Pilot Qualities Ray RRR FOIL
SWS49092R Courageous Supporter C-3PO R
SWS49093R Astromech Droid R2-D2 R
SWS49093SSR Astromech Droid R2-D2 SR FOIL
SWS49094reR Moment of Counterattack Luke R
SWS49095R Yoda R
SWS49095SSR Yoda SR FOIL
SWS49096R Teachings of the Sage Obi-Wan R
SWS49097R Fateful Encounter Luke R
SWS49097RRRR Fate Encounter Luke RRR FOIL
SWS49098U Desert Recluse Ben Kenobi U
SWS49099U Long-awaited good news R2-D2 U
SWS49100reU Lovable partner C-3PO U
SWS49101U Obi-Wan Kenobi U
SWS49102U Jedi Master Luke U
SWS49103SSR Premonition of Friendship BB-8 SR FOIL
SWS49103U Premonition of Friendship BB-8 U
SWS49104reC Jedi Master Yoda C
SWS49105C Jedi Knight Luke C
SWS49106C Buddy BB-8 C
SWS49107C Light Side Luke C
SWS49108C Luke Skywalker C
SWS49109C C-3PO C
SWS49110C Sudden Attack Luke C
SWS49111C Shooting Skill Rey C
SWS49112C Jedi Master Obi-Wan C
SWS49113reU Lightsaber U
SWS49114reU Lightsaber U
SWS49115U AT-AT U
SWS49116C Reyis Speeder C
SWS49117CR A New Hope CR
SWS49117SWRSWR A New Hope SWR
SWS49117SWRSWR A New Hope SWR FOIL

SWS49118CR The Force Awakens CR
SWS49118SWRSWR The Force Awakens SWR
SWS49118SWRSWR The Force Awakens SWR FOIL
SWS49119CC Great Mentor CC
SWS49120reCC Return of the Jedi CC
SWS49121PR STAR WARS Chewbacca PR
SWS49122PR STAR WARS Kylo Ren PR
SWS49123PR STAR WARS Stormtrooper PR
SWS49124PR STAR WARS Ray PR
SWS49125PR STAR WARS C-3PO/BB-8/R2-D2 PR
COMPLETE SET ()
BOOSTER BOX ()
BOOSTER PACK ()
RELEASED ON

2022 Weiss Schwarz Star Wars Comeback Edition Trial Deck

SWS49T01TD The Leftover Jacket Fin
SWS49T02TD Hero Han Solo
SWS49T03TD Captive Pilot Poe
SWS49T04TD Invasion of the Resistance Poe
SWS49T05TD Relentless Pursuit Finn
SWS49T06TD With a New Determination Han Solo
SWS49T07TD With a New Determination Chewbacca
SWS49T08TD Deadly Combat in the Forest
SWS49T09RRRR The Adventure Begins Rey RRR FOIL
SWS49T09TD The Adventure Begins Ray
SWS49T10TD Lower Sun Tekka
SWS49T11TD To the Land of Jakku BB-8
SWS49T12TD Reunion C-3PO
SWS49T13RRRR Long sleep R2-D2 RRR FOIL
SWS49T13TD Long sleep R2-D2
SWS49T14reTD For a modest meal Ray
SWS49T15TD Days of Garbage Collection Rey
SWS49T16SSR Existence to Protect Rey SR FOIL
SWS49T16TD Existence to be protected Rey
SWS49T17TD BB unit
SWS49T18reTD Escape from Jakku
SWS49T19SPSP Those who have the force SP FOIL
SWS49T19TD One with Force

MINIATURES

2004 Star Wars Rebel Storm Miniatures

RELEASED ON SEPTEMBER 3, 2004

1 4-LOM R		5.00	10.00
2 Bespin Guard C		.30	.75
3 Boba Fett VR		25.00	50.00
4 Bossk R		5.00	10.00
5 Bothan Spy U		.75	1.50
6 C-3PO R		5.00	10.00
7 Chewbacca R		6.00	12.00
8 Commando on Speeder Bike VR		12.00	25.00
9 Darth Vader, Dark Jedi R		6.00	12.00
10 Darth Vader, Sith Lord VR		12.00	25.00
11 Dengar R		5.00	10.00
12 Duros Mercenary U		.75	1.50
13 Elite Hoth Trooper U		.75	1.50
14 Elite Rebel Trooper C		.30	.75
15 Elite Snowtrooper U		.75	1.50
16 Elite Stormtrooper U		.75	1.50
17 Emperor Palpatine VR		15.00	30.00
18 Ewok C		.30	.75
19 Gamorrean Guard U		.75	1.50
20 General Veers R		5.00	10.00
21 Grand Moff Tarkin R		5.00	10.00
22 Greedo R		5.00	10.00
23 Han Solo R		5.00	10.00
24 Heavy Stormtrooper U		.75	1.50
25 Hoth Trooper C		.30	.75
26 IG-88 R		5.00	10.00
27 Imperial Officer U		.75	1.50
28 Ithorian Scout U		.75	1.50
29 Jabba the Hutt VR		12.00	25.00
30 Jawa C		.30	.75
31 Lando Calrissian R		5.00	10.00
32 Luke Skywalker, Jedi Knight VR		15.00	30.00
33 Luke Skywalker, Rebel R		6.00	12.00
34 Mara Jade Emperor's Hand R		5.00	10.00
35 Mon Calamari Mercenary C		.30	.75
36 Obi-Wan Kenobi VR		12.00	25.00
37 Princess Leia, Captive VR		12.00	25.00
38 Princess Leia, Senator R		6.00	12.00
39 Probe Droid VR		10.00	20.00
40 Quarren Assassin U		.75	1.50
41 R2-D2 R		6.00	12.00
42 Rebel Commando U		.75	1.50
43 Rebel Officer U		.75	1.50
44 Rebel Pilot C		.30	.75
45 Rebel Trooper C		.30	.75
46 Rebel Trooper C		.30	.75
47 Royal Guard U		.75	1.50
48 Sandtrooper on Dewback VR		10.00	20.00
49 Scout Trooper on Bike VR		10.00	20.00
50 Scout Trooper U		.75	1.50
51 Snowtrooper C		.30	.75
52 Stormtrooper C		.30	.75
53 Stormtrooper C		.30	.75
54 Stormtrooper C		.30	.75
55 Stormtrooper Officer U		.75	1.50
56 Tusken Raider C		.30	.75

57 Twi'lek Bodyguard U	.75	1.50
58 Twi'lek Scoundrel C	.30	.75
59 Wampa VR	10.00	20.00
60 Wookiee Soldier C	.30	.75

2004 Star Wars Clone Strike Miniatures

RELEASED ON DECEMBER 13, 2004

1 48 Super Battle Droid U	.75	1.50
2 Aayla Secura VR	10.00	20.00
3 Aerial Clone Trooper Captain R	6.00	12.00
4 Agen Kolar R	6.00	12.00
5 Anakin Skywalker VR	12.00	25.00
6 Aqualish Spy C	.30	.75
7 ARC Trooper U	.75	1.50
8 Asajj Ventress R	6.00	12.00
9 Aurra Sing VR	15.00	30.00
10 Battle Droid C	.30	.75
11 Battle Droid C	.30	.75
12 Battle Droid C	.30	.75
13 Battle Droid Officer U	.75	1.50
14 Battle Droid on STAP R	6.00	12.00
15 Captain Typho R	6.00	12.00
16 Clone Trooper C	.30	.75
17 Clone Trooper C	.30	.75
18 Clone Trooper Commander U	.75	1.50
19 Clone Trooper Grenadier C	.30	.75
20 Clone Trooper Sergeant C	.30	.75
21 Count Dooku VR	12.00	25.00
22 Dark Side Acolyte U	.75	1.50
23 Darth Maul VR	15.00	30.00
24 Darth Sidious VR	12.00	25.00
25 Destroyer Droid R	6.00	12.00
26 Devaronian Bounty Hunter C	.30	.75
27 Durge R	6.00	12.00
28 Dwarf Spider Droid R	6.00	12.00
29 General Grievous VR	15.00	30.00
30 General Kenobi R	6.00	12.00
31 Geonosian Drone C	.30	.75
32 Geonosian Overseer U	.75	1.50
33 Geonosian Picador on Orray R	6.00	12.00
34 Geonosian Soldier U	.75	1.50
35 Gran Raider C	.30	.75
36 Gungan Cavalry on Kaadu R	6.00	12.00
37 Gungan Infantry C	.30	.75
38 Ishi Tib Scout U	.75	1.50
39 Jango Fett R	6.00	12.00
40 Jedi Guardian U	.75	1.50
41 Ki-Adi-Mundi R	6.00	12.00
42 Kit Fisto R	6.00	12.00
43 Klatooinian Enforcer C	.30	.75
44 Luminara Unduli R	6.00	12.00
45 Mace Windu VR	12.00	25.00
46 Naboo Soldier U	.75	1.50
47 Nikto Soldier C	.30	.75
48 Padme Amidala VR	10.00	20.00
49 Plo Koon R	6.00	12.00
50 Quarren Raider U	.75	1.50
51 Qui-Gon Jinn VR	10.00	20.00
52 Quinlan Vos VR	10.00	20.00
53 Rodian Mercenary U	.75	1.50
54 Saesee Tiin R	6.00	12.00
55 Security Battle Droid C	.30	.75
56 Super Battle Droid U	.75	1.50
57 Weequay Mercenary C	.30	.75
58 Wookiee Commando U	.75	1.50
59 Yoda VR	15.00	30.00
60 Zam Wesell R	6.00	12.00

2005 Star Wars Revenge of the Sith Miniatures

RELEASED ON APRIL 2, 2005

1 Agen Kolar, Jedi Master R	6.00	12.00
2 Alderaan Trooper U	.75	1.50
3 Anakin Skywalker, Jedi Knight R	6.00	12.00
4 AT-RT VR	12.00	25.00
5 Bail Organa VR	10.00	20.00
6 Captain Antilles R	6.00	12.00
7 Chewbacca of Kashyyk VR	12.00	25.00
8 Clone Trooper C	.30	.75
9 Clone Trooper C	.30	.75
10 Clone Trooper Commander U	.75	1.50
11 Clone Trooper Gunner C	.30	.75
12 Jedi Knight U	.75	1.50
13 Mace Windu, Jedi Master VR	15.00	30.00
14 Mon Mothma VR	10.00	20.00
15 Obi-Wan Kenobi, Jedi Master R	6.00	12.00
16 Polis Massa Medic C	.30	.75
17 R2-D2, Astromech Droid VR	12.00	25.00
18 Senate Guard U	.75	1.50
19 Shaak Ti U	6.00	12.00
20 Stass Allie R	6.00	12.00
21 Tarfful R	6.00	12.00
22 Wookiee Berserker C	.30	.75
23 Wookiee Scout U	.75	1.50
24 Yoda, Jedi Master R	7.50	15.00
25 Battle Droid C	.30	.75
26 Battle Droid C	.30	.75
27 Bodyguard Droid U	.75	1.50
28 Bodyguard Droid U	.75	1.50
29 Darth Tyranus R	6.00	12.00
30 Destroyer Droid R	6.00	12.00
31 General Grievous, Jedi Hunter VR	15.00	30.00
32 General Grievous, Supreme Commander R	6.00	12.00
33 Grievous's Wheel Bike VR	12.00	25.00
34 Muun Guard U	.75	1.50
35 Neimoidian Soldier U	.75	1.50
36 Neimoidian Soldier U	.75	1.50
37 San Hill R	6.00	12.00
38 Separatist Commando C	.30	.75
39 Super Battle Droid C	.30	.75
40 Super Battle Droid C	.30	.75
41 Wat Tambor R	6.00	12.00
42 Boba Fett, Young Mercenary R	6.00	12.00
43 Chagrian Mercenary Commander U	.75	1.50
44 Devaronian Soldier C	.30	.75
45 Gotal Fringer U	.75	1.50
46 Human Mercenary U	.75	1.50
47 Iktotchi Tech Specialist U	.75	1.50
48 Medical Droid R	6.00	12.00
49 Nautolan Soldier C	.30	.75
50 Sly Moore R	6.00	12.00
51 Tion Medon R	6.00	12.00
52 Utapaun Soldier C	.30	.75
53 Utapaun Soldier C	.30	.75
54 Yuzzem C	.30	.75
55 Zabrak Fringer C	.30	.75
56 Anakin Skywalker Sith Apprentice VR	12.00	25.00
57 Dark Side Adept U	.75	1.50
58 Darth Vader VR	15.00	30.00
59 Emperor Palpatine, Sith Lord VR	15.00	30.00
60 Royal Guard U	.75	1.50

2005 Star Wars Universe Miniatures

RELEASED ON AUGUST 19, 2005

1 Abyssin Black Sun Thug C	.30	.75
2 Acklay U	.75	1.50
3 Admiral Ackbar VR	10.00	20.00
4 ASP-7 U	.75	1.50
5 AT-ST R	7.50	15.00
6 B'omarr Monk R	7.50	15.00
7 Baron Fel VR	15.00	30.00
8 Battle Droid U	.75	1.50
9 Battle Droid U	.75	1.50
10 Bith Rebel C	.30	.75
11 Chewbacca, Rebel Hero R	7.50	15.00
12 Clone Trooper C	.30	.75
13 Clone Trooper on BARC Speeder R	10.00	20.00
14 Dark Side Marauder U	.75	1.50
15 Dark Trooper Phase III U	.75	1.50
16 Darth Maul on Speeder VR	12.00	25.00
17 Darth Vader, Jedi Hunter R	7.50	15.00
18 Dash Rendar R	7.50	15.00
19 Dr. Evazan VR	10.00	20.00
20 Dressellian Commando C	.30	.75
21 Elite Clone Trooper U	.75	1.50
22 Flash Speeder U	.75	1.50
23 Gonk Power Droid C	.30	.75
24 Grand Admiral Thrawn VR	15.00	30.00
25 Guri R	7.50	15.00
26 Hailfire Droid U	.75	1.50
27 Han Solo, Rebel Hero R	7.50	15.00
28 Kaminoan Ascetic C	.30	.75
29 Kyle Katarn VR	10.00	20.00
30 Lando Calrissian, Hero of Taanab R	7.50	15.00
31 Lobot R	6.00	12.00
32 Luke Skywalker on Tauntaun R	10.00	20.00
33 Luke Skywalker, Jedi Master VR	15.00	30.00
34 New Republic Commander U	.75	1.50
35 New Republic Trooper C	.30	.75
36 Nexu U	.75	1.50
37 Nien Nunb R	6.00	12.00
38 Nightsister Sith Witch U	.75	1.50
39 Noghri U	.75	1.50
40 Nom Anor R	7.50	15.00
41 Nute Gunray R	6.00	12.00
42 Obi-Wan on Boga VR	12.00	25.00
43 Ponda Baba R	6.00	12.00
44 Prince Xizor VR	10.00	20.00
45 Princess Leia, Rebel Hero VR	10.00	20.00
46 Rancor VR	15.00	30.00
47 Reek U	.75	1.50

48 Rodian Black Sun Vigo U	.75	1.50
49 Shistavanen Pilot U	.75	1.50
50 Stormtrooper C	.30	.75
51 Stormtrooper Commander U	.75	1.50
52 Super Battle Droid C	.30	.75
53 Super Battle Droid Commander U	.75	1.50
54 Tusken Raider on Bantha U	.75	1.50
55 Vornskr C	.30	.75
56 Warmaster Tsavong Lah VR	12.00	25.00
57 Wedge Antilles R	7.50	15.00
58 X-1 Viper Droid U	.75	1.50
59 Young Jedi Knight C	.30	.75
60 Yuuzhan Vong Subaltern U	.75	1.50
61 Yuuzhan Vong Warrior C	.30	.75

2006 Star Wars Champions of the Force Miniatures

RELEASED ON JUNE 6, 2006

1 Arcona Smuggler C	.30	.75
2 Barriss Offee R	6.00	12.00
3 Bastila Shan VR	10.00	20.00
5 Clone Commander Bacara R	6.00	12.00
6 Clone Commander Cody R	7.50	15.00
7 Clone Commander Gree R	6.00	12.00
8 Corran Horn R	6.00	12.00
9 Coruscant Guard C	.30	.75
10 Crab Droid U	.75	1.50
11 Dark Jedi U	.75	1.50
12 Dark Jedi Master U	.75	1.50
13 Dark Side Enforcer U	.75	1.50
14 Dark Trooper Phase I C	.30	.75
15 Dark Trooper Phase II U	.75	1.50
16 Dark Trooper Phase II VR	10.00	20.00
17 Darth Bane VR	12.00	25.00
18 Darth Malak VR	12.00	25.00
19 Darth Maul, Champion of the Sith R	7.50	15.00
20 Darth Nihilus VR	10.00	20.00
21 Darth Sidious, Dark Lord of the Sith R	6.00	12.00
22 Depa Billaba R	6.00	12.00
23 Even Piell R	6.00	12.00
24 Exar Kun VR	12.00	25.00
25 General Windu R	6.00	12.00
26 Gundark Fringe U	.75	1.50
27 HK-47 VR	10.00	20.00
28 Hoth Trooper with Atgar Cannon R	6.00	12.00
29 Jacen Solo VR	10.00	20.00
30 Jaina Solo VR	10.00	20.00
31 Jedi Consular U	.75	1.50
32 Jedi Guardian U	.75	1.50
33 Jedi Padawan U	.75	1.50

34 Jedi Sentinel U	.75	1.50
35 Jedi Weapon Master C	.30	.75
36 Kashyyyk Trooper C	.30	.75
37 Luke Skywalker, Young Jedi VR	12.00	25.00
38 Mas Amedda R	7.50	15.00
39 Massassi Sith Mutant U	.75	1.50
41 Octuparra Droid R	6.00	12.00
42 Old Republic Commander U	.75	1.50
43 Old Republic Trooper U	.75	1.50
44 Old Republic Trooper C	.30	.75
45 Queen Amidala R	6.00	12.00
46 Qui-Gon Jinn, Jedi Master R	7.50	15.00
47 R5 Astromech Droid C	.30	.75
48 Republic Commando Boss U	.75	1.50
49 Republic Commando Fixer C	.30	.75
50 Republic Commando Scorch C	.30	.75
51 Republic Commando Sev C	.30	.75
52 Saleucami Trooper C	.30	.75
53 Sandtrooper C	.30	.75
54 Sith Assault Droid U	.75	1.50
55 Sith Trooper C	.30	.75
56 Sith Trooper C	.30	.75
57 Sith Trooper Commander U	.75	1.50
58 Snowtrooper with E-Web Blaster R	6.00	12.00
59 Ugnaught Demolitionist C	.30	.75
60 Ulic Qel-Droma VR	7.50	15.00
61 Utapau Trooper C	.30	.75
62 Varactyl Wrangler C	.30	.75
63 Yoda of Dagobah VR	12.00	25.00

2006 Star Wars Bounty Hunters Miniatures

RELEASED ON SEPTEMBER 23, 2006

1 4-LOM, Bounty Hunter R	6.00	12.00
2 Aqualish Assassin C	.30	.75
3 Ayy Vida R	6.00	12.00
4 Basilisk War Droid U	.75	1.50
5 Bib Fortuna R	6.00	12.00
6 Bith Black Sun Vigo U	.75	1.50
7 Boba Fett, Bounty Hunter VR	20.00	40.00
8 BoShek R	6.00	12.00
9 Bossk, Bounty Hunter R	7.50	15.00
10 Boushh R	6.00	12.00
11 Calo Nord†R	6.00	12.00
12 Chewbacca w/C-3PO VR	10.00	20.00
13 Commerce Guild Homing Spider Droid U	.75	1.50
14 Corellian Pirate U	.75	1.50
15 Corporate Alliance Tank Droid U	.75	1.50
16 Dannik Jerriko VR	7.50	15.00
17 Dark Hellion Marauder on Swoop Bike U	.75	1.50
18 Dark Hellion Swoop Gang Member C	.30	.75
19 Defel Spy C	.30	.75
20 Dengar, Bounty Hunter R	7.50	15.00
21 Djas Puhr R	6.00	12.00

22 Droid Starfighter in Walking Mode R	7.50	15.00
23 E522 Assassin Droid U	.75	1.50
24 Gamorrean Thug C	.30	.75
25 Garindan R	6.00	12.00
26 Han Solo, Scoundrel VR	7.50	15.00
27 Huge Crab Droid U	.75	1.50
28 Human Blaster-for-Hire C	.30	.75
29 IG-88, Bounty Hunter VR	12.00	25.00
30 ISP Speeder R	6.00	12.00
31 Jango Fett, Bounty Hunter VR	15.00	30.00
32 Klatooinian Hunter C	.30	.75
33 Komari Vosa R	7.50	15.00
34 Lord Vader VR	10.00	20.00
35 Luke Skywalker of Dagobah R	7.50	15.00
36 Mandalore the Indomitable VR	12.00	25.00
37 Mandalorian Blademaster U	.75	1.50
38 Mandalorian Commander U	.75	1.50
39 Mandalorian Soldier C	.30	.75
40 Mandalorian Supercommando C	.30	.75
41 Mandalorian Warrior C	.30	.75
42 Mistryl Shadow Guard U	.75	1.50
43 Mustafarian Flea Rider R	6.00	12.00
44 Mustafarian Soldier C	.30	.75
45 Nikto Gunner on Desert Skiff VR	10.00	20.00
46 Nym VR	7.50	15.00
47 Princess Leia, Hoth Commander R	7.50	15.00
48 Quarren Bounty Hunter C	.30	.75
49 Rebel Captain U	.75	1.50
50 Rebel Heavy Trooper U	.75	1.50
51 Rebel Snowspeeder U	.75	1.50
52 Rodian Hunt Master U	.75	1.50
53 Talon Karrde VR	7.50	15.00
54 Tamtel Skreej VR	7.50	15.00
55 Tusken Raider Sniper C	.30	.75
56 Utapaun on Dactillion VR	7.50	15.00
57 Weequay Leader U	.75	1.50
58 Weequay Thug C	.30	.75
59 Young Krayt Dragon VR	10.00	20.00
60 Zuckuss R	7.50	15.00

2007 Star Wars Alliance and Empire Miniatures

RELEASED IN MAY 2007

1 Admiral Piett R	5.00	10.00
2 Advance Agent, Officer U	.75	1.50
3 Advance Scout C	.30	.75
4 Aurra Sing, Jedi Hunter VR	10.00	20.00
5 Biggs Darklighter VR	7.50	15.00
6 Boba Fett, Enforcer VR	12.00	25.00
7 C-3PO and R2-D2 R	5.00	10.00
8 Chadra-Fan Pickpocket U	.75	1.50
9 Chewbacca, Enraged Wookiee R	5.00	10.00
10 Darth Vader, Imperial Commander VR	12.00	25.00
11 Death Star Gunner U	.75	1.50
12 Death Star Trooper C	.30	.75
13 Duros Explorer C	.30	.75
14 Elite Hoth Trooper C	.30	.75
15 Ephant Mon VR	7.50	15.00
16 Ewok Hang Glider R	5.00	10.00

#	Name		
17	Ewok Warrior C	.30	.75
18	Gamorrean Guard C	.30	.75
19	Han Solo in Stormtrooper Armor R	5.00	10.00
20	Han Solo on Tauntaun VR	10.00	20.00
21	Han Solo Rogue R	5.00	10.00
22	Heavy Stormtrooper U	.75	1.50
23	Human Force Adept C	.30	.75
24	Imperial Governor Tarkin R	5.00	10.00
25	Imperial Officer U	.75	1.50
26	Ithorian Commander U	.75	1.50
27	Jabba, Crime Lord VR	7.50	15.00
28	Jawa on Ronto VR	7.50	15.00
29	Jawa Trader U	.75	1.50
30	Lando Calrissian, Dashing Scoundrel R	5.00	10.00
31	Luke Skywalker, Champion of the Force VR	12.00	25.00
32	Luke Skywalker, Hero of Yavin R	5.00	10.00
33	Luke's Landspeeder VR	7.50	15.00
34	Mara Jade, Jedi R	5.00	10.00
35	Mon Calamari Tech Specialist C	.30	.75
36	Nikto Soldier C	.30	.75
37	Obi-Wan Kenobi, Force Spirit VR	7.50	15.00
38	Princess Leia R	5.00	10.00
39	Quinlan Vos, Infiltrator VR	10.00	20.00
40	Rampaging Wampa VR	7.50	15.00
41	Rebel Commando C	.30	.75
42	Rebel Commando Strike Leader U	.75	1.50
43	Rebel Leader U	.75	1.50
44	Rebel Pilot C	.30	.75
45	Rebel Trooper U	.75	1.50
46	Rodian Scoundrel U	.75	1.50
47	Scout Trooper U	.75	1.50
48	Snivvian Fringer C	.30	.75
49	Snowtrooper C	.30	.75
50	Storm Commando R	5.00	10.00
51	Stormtrooper C	.30	.75
52	Stormtrooper Officer U	.75	1.50
53	Stormtrooper on Repulsor Sled VR	10.00	20.00
54	Talz Spy Fringe U	.75	1.50
55	Trandoshan Mercenary U	.75	1.50
56	Tusken Raider C	.30	.75
57	Twi'lek Rebel Agent U	.75	1.50
58	Wicket R	5.00	10.00
59	Wookiee Freedom Fighter C	.30	.75
60	Yomin Carr R	6.00	12.00

2007 Star Wars The Force Unleashed Miniatures

RELEASED IN 2007

1	Darth Revan VR	50.00	100.00
2	Kazdan Paratus R	5.00	10.00
3	Shaak Ti, Jedi Master VR	10.00	20.00
4	Chewbacca of Hoth VR	5.00	10.00
5	Elite Hoth Trooper C	5.00	10.00
6	Golan Arms DF.9 Anti-Infantry Battery UC	5.00	10.00
7	Han Solo in Carbonite VR	5.00	10.00
8	Han Solo of Hoth VR	5.00	10.00
9	Hoth Trooper Officer UC	5.00	10.00
10	Hoth Trooper with Repeating Blaster Cannon UC	5.00	10.00
11	Juno Eclipse R	5.00	10.00
12	K-3PO R	5.00	10.00
13	Luke Skywalker, Hoth Pilot Unleashed R	5.00	10.00
14	Luke Skywalker and Yoda VR	7.50	15.00
15	Luke's Snowspeeder VR	7.50	15.00
16	Master Kota R	7.50	15.00
17	Mon Calamari Medic C	5.00	10.00
18	Obi-Wan Kenobi, Unleashed R	5.00	10.00
19	Princess Leia of Cloud City R	5.00	10.00
20	Rebel Marksman UC	5.00	10.00
21	Rebel Troop Cart UC	5.00	10.00
22	Rebel Trooper on Tauntaun R	5.00	10.00
23	Rebel Vanguard UC	5.00	10.00
24	2-1B R	5.00	10.00
25	Vader's Secret Apprentice, Redeemed R	10.00	20.00
26	Verpine Tech Rebel C	5.00	10.00
27	Wedge Antilles, Red Two Rebel R	5.00	10.00
28	Wookiee Warrior Rebel C	5.00	10.00
29	Admiral Ozzel R	5.00	10.00
30	AT-AT Driver UC	5.00	10.00
31	Dark trooper UC	5.00	10.00
32	Darth Vader, Unleashed VR	5.00	10.00
33	Emperor's Shadow Guard UC	5.00	10.00
34	Evo Trooper UC	5.00	10.00
35	Felucian Stormtrooper Officer UC	5.00	10.00
36	Gotal Imperial Assassin C	5.00	10.00
37	Imperial Navy trooper C	5.00	10.00
38	Raxus Prime Trooper C	5.00	10.00
39	Snowtrooper C	5.00	10.00
40	Star Destroyer Officer UC	5.00	10.00
41	Stormtrooper UC	5.00	10.00
42	TIE Crawler UC	5.00	10.00
43	Vader's Apprentice, Unleashed VR	5.00	10.00
44	Wookiee Hunter AT-ST R	7.50	15.00
45	Garm Bel Iblis R	5.00	10.00
46	Amanin Scout UC	5.00	10.00
47	Boba Fett, Mercenary VR	25.00	50.00
48	Caamasi Noble C	5.00	10.00
49	Cloud Car Pilot C	5.00	10.00
50	Felucian Warrior on Rancor VR	20.00	40.00
51	Junk golem UC	5.00	10.00
52	Knobby white spider UC	5.00	10.00
53	Maris Brood VR	7.50	15.00
54	Muun Tactics Broker C	5.00	10.00
55	Mynock UC	5.00	10.00
56	PROXY R	5.00	10.00
57	Telosian Tank Droid UC	5.00	10.00
58	Uggernaught R	5.00	10.00
59	Ugnaught Boss UC	5.00	10.00
60	Ugnaught Tech UC	5.00	10.00

2008 Star Wars Knights of the Old Republic Miniatures

RELEASED ON AUGUST 7, 2008

1	Atton Rand VR	5.00	10.00
2	Bao-Dur R	5.00	10.00
3	Carth Onasi VR	10.00	20.00
4	Juggernaut War Droid C	5.00	10.00
5	Master Lucien Draay VR	5.00	10.00
6	Mira VR	15.00	30.00
7	Old Republic Captain UC	5.00	10.00
8	Old Republic Guard C	5.00	10.00
9	Squint VR	5.00	10.00
10	Visas Marr R	5.00	10.00
11	Wookiee Elite Warrior C	5.00	10.00
12	Wookiee Trooper C	5.00	10.00
13	Darth Malak, Dark Lord of the Sith VR	5.00	10.00
14	Darth Sion VR	30.00	60.00
15	Elite Sith Trooper UC	5.00	10.00
16	Sith Assassin UC	5.00	10.00
17	Sith Guard C	12.00	25.00
18	Sith Heavy Assault Droid UC	5.00	10.00
19	Sith Marauder UC	5.00	10.00
20	Sith Operative C	5.00	10.00
21	Sith Trooper Captain UC	5.00	10.00
22	Captain Panaka R	5.00	10.00
23	Captain Tarpals R	5.00	10.00
24	Gungan Artillerist C	5.00	10.00
25	Gungan Shieldbearer UC	5.00	10.00
26	Gungan Soldier C	5.00	10.00
27	Jar Jar Binks VR	15.00	30.00
28	Obi-Wan Kenobi, Padawan VR	5.00	10.00
29	Supreme Chancellor Palpatine R	5.00	10.00
30	Han Solo, Smuggler R	5.00	10.00
31	Leia Organa, Senator VR	5.00	10.00
32	Luke Skywalker, Jedi R	5.00	10.00
33	Darth Vader, Scourge of the Jedi VR	5.00	10.00
34	RA-7 Death Star Protocol Droid UC	5.00	10.00
35	General Wedge Antilles R	5.00	10.00
36	ASN Assassin Droid UC	5.00	10.00
37	Boma UC	5.00	10.00
38	Czerka Scientist C	5.00	10.00
39	Echani Handmaiden C	5.00	10.00
40	GenoHaradan Assassin C	5.00	10.00
41	Jarael R	5.00	10.00
42	Jawa Scout C	5.00	10.00
43	Jolee Bindo VR	5.00	10.00
44	Juhani VR	12.00	25.00
45	Kreia VR	5.00	10.00
46	Massiff UC	5.00	10.00
47	Mission Vao R	10.00	20.00
48	Rakghoul UC	5.00	10.00
49	Shyrack UC	5.00	10.00
50	T1 Series Bulk Loader Droid UC	5.00	10.00
51	T3-M4 R	7.50	15.00
52	Tusken Raider Scout C	5.00	10.00
53	Zaalbar R	5.00	10.00
54	Zayne Carrick R	5.00	10.00
55	Mandalore the Ultimate VR	25.00	50.00
56	Mandalorian Captain UC	5.00	10.00
57	Mandalorian Commando C	5.00	10.00
58	Mandalorian Marauder C	5.00	10.00
59	Mandalorian Quartermaster UC	5.00	10.00
60	Mandalorian Scout C	5.00	10.00

2008 Star Wars Legacy of the Force Miniatures

RELEASED ON MARCH 28, 2008

1	Nomi Sunrider VR	7.50	15.00
2	Old Republic Recruit C	5.00	10.00
3	Old Republic Scout C	5.00	10.00
4	Darth Caedus VR	15.00	30.00
5	Darth Krayt VR	15.00	30.00
6	Darth Nihl VR	5.00	10.00
7	Darth Talon VR	25.00	50.00
8	Lumiya, the Dark Lady R	5.00	10.00
9	Republic Commando Training Sergeant U	5.00	10.00
10	Darth Tyranus, Legacy of the dark side R	5.00	10.00
11	Bothan Noble U	5.00	10.00
12	Deena Shan R	5.00	10.00
13	Elite Rebel Commando U	5.00	10.00
14	General Dodonna R	5.00	10.00
15	Luke Skywalker, Legacy of the Light Side R	5.00	10.00
16	Rebel Honor Guard C	5.00	10.00
17	Twi'lek Scout C	5.00	10.00
18	Antares Draco R	6.00	12.00

19	Emperor Roan Fel VR	5.00	10.00
20	Imperial Knight U	5.00	10.00
21	Imperial Knight U	5.00	10.00
22	Imperial Pilot C	5.00	10.00
23	Imperial Security Officer U	5.00	10.00
24	Jagged Fel R	5.00	10.00
25	Marasiah Fel R	5.00	10.00
26	Moff Morlish Veed VR	5.00	10.00
27	Moff Nyna Calixte R	5.00	10.00
28	Noghri Commando U	5.00	10.00
29	Shadow Stormtrooper U	5.00	10.00
30	Corellian Security Officer U	5.00	10.00
31	Galactic Alliance Scout C	5.00	10.00
32	Galactic Alliance Trooper C	5.00	10.00
33	Han Solo, Galactic Hero R	5.00	10.00
34	Kyle Katarn, Jedi Battlemaster VR	5.00	10.00
35	Leia Organa Solo, Jedi Knight VR	5.00	10.00
36	Luke Skywalker, Force Spirit VR	5.00	10.00
37	Mara Jade Skywalker VR	7.50	15.00
38	Shado Vao R	5.00	10.00
39	Wolf Sazen VR	5.00	10.00
40	Cade Skywalker, Bounty Hunter VR	5.00	10.00
41	Deliah Blue R	5.00	10.00
42	Dug Fringer U	5.00	10.00
43	Duros Scoundrel C	5.00	10.00
44	Gotal Mercenary C	5.00	10.00
45	Guard Droid C	5.00	10.00
46	Human Bodyguard C	5.00	10.00
47	Human Scoundrel C	5.00	10.00
48	Human Scout C	5.00	10.00
49	Jariah Syn R	5.00	10.00
50	Kel Dor Bounty Hunter C	5.00	10.00
51	Rodian Blaster for Hire U	5.00	10.00
52	Trandoshan Mercenary C	5.00	10.00
53	Boba Fett, Mercenary Commander VR	5.00	10.00
54	Canderous Ordo R	5.00	10.00
55	Mandalorian Gunslinger U	5.00	10.00
56	Mandalorian Trooper U	5.00	10.00
57	Yuuzhan Vong Elite Warrior U	5.00	10.00
58	Yuuzhan Vong Jedi Hunter U	5.00	10.00
59	Yuuzhan Vong Shaper U	5.00	10.00
60	Yuuzhan Vong Warrior C	5.00	10.00

2008 Star Wars The Clone Wars Miniatures

RELEASED ON NOVEMBER 4, 2008

1	Darth Sidious Hologram VR	5.00	10.00
2	Ahsoka Tano VR	12.00	25.00
3	Anakin Skywalker Champion of Nelvaan R	5.00	10.00
4	Anakin Skywalker on STAP VR	5.00	10.00
5	ARC Trooper Sniper U	5.00	10.00
6	Barriss Offee, Jedi Knight R	5.00	10.00
7	Captain Rex VR	5.00	10.00
8	Clone Trooper on Gelagrub R	5.00	10.00
9	Commander Gree R	5.00	10.00
10	Elite Clone Trooper Commander U	5.00	10.00
11	Elite Clone Trooper Grenadier C	5.00	10.00
12	Galactic Marine U	5.00	10.00
13	General Aayla Secura R	7.50	15.00
14	Heavy Clone Trooper C	5.00	10.00

15	Mon Calamari Knight U	5.00	10.00
16	Odd Ball R	5.00	10.00
17	Padmé Amidala Senator VR	6.00	12.00
18	Star Corps Trooper U	5.00	10.00
19	Wookiee Scoundrel C	5.00	10.00
20	Yoda on Kybuck VR	5.00	10.00
21	Battle Droid C	5.00	10.00
22	Battle Droid C	5.00	10.00
23	Battle Droid Sniper U	5.00	10.00
24	Chameleon Droid R	5.00	10.00
25	Durge, Jedi Hunter VR	12.00	25.00
26	General Grievous, Droid Army Commander VR	5.00	10.00
27	Heavy Super Battle Droid C	5.00	10.00
28	IG-100 MagnaGuard U	5.00	10.00
29	Neimoidian Warrior C	5.00	10.00
30	Quarren Isolationist U	5.00	10.00
31	Rocket Battle Droid U	5.00	10.00
32	Super Battle Droid C	5.00	10.00
33	Techno Union Warrior C	5.00	10.00
34	Aqualish Warrior C	5.00	10.00
35	Gha Nachkt R	5.00	10.00
36	Human Soldier of Fortune C	5.00	10.00
37	IG-86 Assassin Droid U	5.00	10.00
38	Nelvaanian Warrior U	5.00	10.00
39	Trandoshan Scavenger U	5.00	10.00
40	Utapaun Warrior C	5.00	10.00

2008 Star Wars The Clone Wars Miniatures Starter

RELEASED ON NOVEMBER 4, 2008

1	General Obi-Wan Kenobi	4.00	8.00
2	Clone Trooper	4.00	8.00
3	Clone Trooper Commander	4.00	8.00
4	Count Dooku of Serenno	4.00	8.00
5	Security Battle Droid	4.00	8.00
6	Super Battle Droid Commander	4.00	8.00

2009 Star Wars Galaxy at War Miniatures

RELEASED ON OCTOBER 27, 2009

1	501st Clone Trooper C	2.00	4.00
2	A4-Series Lab Droid U	2.00	4.00
3	Admiral Yularen VR	2.00	4.00
4	Aqualish Technician C	2.00	4.00
5	ARF Trooper C	2.00	4.00
6	Asajj Ventress, Strike Leader R	2.00	4.00
7	AT-TE Driver C	2.00	4.00
8	B3 Ultra Battle Droid U	2.00	4.00
9	Battle Droid C	2.00	4.00
10	Battle Droid Sergeant U	2.00	4.00
11	Cad Bane VR	2.00	4.00
12	Captain Argyus VR	2.00	4.00
13	Captain Mar Tuuk VR	2.00	4.00
14	Captain Rex, 501st Commander R	2.00	4.00
15	Clone Trooper Pilot C	2.00	4.00
16	Clone Trooper Sergeant U	2.00	4.00
17	Clone Trooper with Night Vision C	2.00	4.00
18	Clone Trooper with Repeating Blaster U	2.00	4.00
19	Commander Ahsoka R	2.00	4.00
20	Commander Cody R	2.00	4.00
21	Commando Droid C	2.00	4.00
22	Commando Droid C	2.00	4.00
23	Commando Droid Captain U	2.00	4.00
24	Elite Senate Guard U	2.00	4.00
25	General Grievous, Scourge of the Jedi R	2.00	4.00
26	General Skywalker R	2.00	4.00
27	General Whorm Loathsom VR	2.00	4.00
28	Hondo Ohnaka VR	2.00	4.00
29	IG-100 MagnaGuard Artillerist U	2.00	4.00
30	IG-100 MagnaGuard U	2.00	4.00
31	Jedi Master Kit Fisto R	2.00	4.00
32	LR-57 Combat Droid U	2.00	4.00
33	Nahdar Vebb VR	2.00	4.00
34	Obi-Wan Kenobi, Jedi General R	2.00	4.00
35	R7 Astromech Droid U	2.00	4.00
36	Rodian Trader C	2.00	4.00
37	Senate Commando C	2.00	4.00
38	Treadwell Droid U	2.00	4.00
39	Wat Tambor, Techno Union Foreman VR	2.00	4.00
40	Weequay Pirate C	2.00	4.00

2009 Star Wars Imperial Entanglements Miniatures

RELEASED ON MARCH 17, 2009

1	Bothan Commando C	5.00	10.00
2	C-3PO, Ewok Deity VR	5.00	10.00
3	General Crix Madine R	5.00	10.00
4	General Rieekan VR	6.00	12.00
5	Leia, Bounty Hunter VR	5.00	10.00
6	Luke Skywalker, Rebel Commando VR	10.00	20.00
7	Rebel Commando Pathfinder U	5.00	10.00
8	Rebel Trooper C	5.00	10.00
9	R2-D2 with Extended Sensor R	5.00	10.00
10	Veteran Rebel Commando C	5.00	10.00

11 Arica R	5.00	10.00
12 Darth Vader, Legacy of the Force VR	10.00	20.00
13 Emperor Palpatine on Throne VR	12.00	25.00
14 Imperial Dignitary U	5.00	10.00
15 Moff Tiaan Jerjerrod R	5.00	10.00
16 181st Imperial Pilot U	5.00	10.00
17 Sandtrooper C	5.00	10.00
18 Sandtrooper Officer U	5.00	10.00
19 Scout Trooper C	5.00	10.00
20 Shock Trooper U	5.00	10.00
21 Snowtrooper C	5.00	10.00
22 Snowtrooper Commander U	5.00	10.00
23 Stormtrooper C	5.00	10.00
24 Thrawn Mitth'raw'nuruodo R	5.00	10.00
25 Kyp Durron R	5.00	10.00
26 Bacta Tank U	5.00	10.00
27 Bespin Guard C	5.00	10.00
28 Chiss Mercenary C	5.00	10.00
29 Dash Rendar, Renegade Smuggler VR	7.50	15.00
30 Duros Scout C	5.00	10.00
31 Ewok Scout C	5.00	10.00
32 Jawa Scavenger C	5.00	10.00
33 Lobot, Computer Liaison Officer R	5.00	10.00
34 Logray, Ewok Shaman R	5.00	10.00
35 Mercenary Commander U - resembling Airen Cracken	5.00	10.00
36 Mouse Droid U	5.00	10.00
37 Twi'lek Black Sun Vigo U	5.00	10.00
38 Ugnaught Droid Destroyer U	5.00	10.00
39 Whiphid Tracker U	5.00	10.00
40 Xizor VR	10.00	20.00

2009 Star Wars Jedi Academy Miniatures

RELEASED ON JUNE 30, 2009

1 Anakin Solo R	5.00	10.00
2 Antarian Ranger C	5.00	10.00
3 Cade Skywalker, Padawan R	5.00	10.00
4 Crimson Nova Bounty Hunter UC	5.00	10.00
5 Darth Maul, Sith apprentice VR	12.00	25.00
6 Darth Plagueis VR	12.00	25.00
7 Darth Sidious, Sith Master R	5.00	10.00
8 Death Watch Raider C	5.00	10.00
9 Disciples of Ragnos C	5.00	10.00
10 Exceptional Jedi Apprentice UC	5.00	10.00
11 Felucian UC	5.00	10.00
12 Grand Master Luke Skywalker R	7.50	15.00
13 Grand Master Yoda R	6.00	12.00
14 Heavy Clone Trooper C	5.00	10.00
15 HK-50 Series Assassin Droid UC	5.00	10.00
16 Imperial Sentinel U	5.00	10.00
17 Jedi Battlemaster UC	5.00	10.00
18 Jedi Crusader UC	5.00	10.00

19 Jensaarai Defender UC	5.00	10.00
20 Kol Skywalker VR	5.00	10.00
21 Krath War Droid C	5.00	10.00
22 Kyle Katarn, Combat Instructor R	5.00	10.00
23 Leia Skywalker, Jedi Knight R	5.00	10.00
24 Master K'Kruhk VR	5.00	10.00
25 Naga Sadow VR	7.50	15.00
26 Peace Brigade Thug C	5.00	10.00
27 Praetorite Vong Priest UC	5.00	10.00
28 Praetorite Vong Warrior C	5.00	10.00
29 Qui-Gon Jinn, Jedi Trainer R	5.00	10.00
30 R4 Astromech Droid C	5.00	10.00
31 Reborn C	5.00	10.00
32 Rocket Battle Droid C	5.00	10.00
33 Sith apprentice UC - resembling Darth Bandon	5.00	10.00
34 Sith Lord U	5.00	10.00
35 Stormtrooper C	5.00	10.00
36 The Dark Woman VR	10.00	20.00
37 The Jedi Exile VR	12.00	25.00
38 Vodo-Siosk Baas VR	7.50	15.00
39 Youngling C	5.00	10.00
40 Yuuzhan Vong Ossus Guardian UC	5.00	10.00

2010 Star Wars Dark Times Miniatures

RELEASED ON JANUARY 26, 2010

1 4-LOM, Droid Mercenary R	2.00	4.00
2 501st Legion Clone Commander UC	2.00	4.00
3 501st Legion Clone Trooper C	2.00	4.00
4 501st Legion Stormtrooper C	2.00	4.00
5 ARF Trooper UC	2.00	4.00
6 A'Sharad Hett VR	7.50	15.00
7 Bomo Greenbark VR	2.00	4.00
8 Bossk, Trandoshan Hunter R	2.00	4.00
9 Boushh, Ubese Hunter R	2.00	4.00
10 Chewbacca, Fearless Scout VR	2.00	4.00
11 Dass Jennir VR	5.00	10.00
12 Dengar, Hired Killer R	2.00	4.00
13 EG-5 Jedi Hunter Droid UC	4.00	8.00
14 Elite Sith Assassin UC	2.00	4.00
15 Emperor's Hand UC	2.00	4.00
16 Ferus Olin VR	2.00	4.00
17 Gungan Bounty Hunter C	2.00	4.00
18 Human Engineer C	2.00	4.00
19 IG-88, Assassin Droid	4.00	8.00
20 Imperial Engineer C	2.00	4.00
21 Imperial Inquisitor UC	2.00	4.00
22 Imperial Sovereign Protector UC	2.00	4.00
23 Jax Pavan VR	2.00	4.00
24 Jedi Watchman C	2.00	4.00
25 Kir Kanos VR	5.00	10.00
26 K'Kruhk VR	2.00	4.00

27 Kota's Elite Militia UC	2.00	4.00
28 Kota's Militia C	2.00	4.00
29 Major Maximilian Veers R	2.00	4.00
30 Mandalorian Jedi Hunter UC	2.00	4.00
31 Merumeru R	2.00	4.00
32 Rodian Brute C	2.00	4.00
33 Rodian Raider C	2.00	4.00
34 Talz Chieftain UC	2.00	4.00
35 Talz Warrior C	2.00	4.00
36 Togorian Soldier UC	2.00	4.00
37 Trandoshan Elite Mercenary UC	5.00	10.00
38 Trianii Scout UC	2.00	4.00
39 T'Surr C	2.00	4.00
40 Zuckuss, Bounty Hunter C	6.00	12.00

2010 Star Wars Masters of the Force Miniatures

RELEASED APRIL 6, 2010

1 Cay Qel-Droma VR	7.50	15.00
2 Jedi Healer UC	3.00	6.00
3 Jedi Instructor - resembling Coleman Trebor UC	3.00	6.00
4 Jedi Sith Hunter UC	3.00	6.00
5 Lord Hoth VR	3.00	6.00
6 Freedon Nadd VR	3.00	6.00
7 Kit Fisto, Jedi Master R	3.00	6.00
8 Master Windu R	3.00	6.00
9 Plo Koon, Jedi Master R	5.00	10.00
10 Rodian Diplomat UC	3.00	6.00
11 Saesee Tiin, Jedi Master R	7.50	15.00
12 Voolvif Monn VR	12.00	25.00
13 Battle Droid Officer C	3.00	6.00
14 Anakin Skywalker, Force Spirit R	3.00	6.00
15 General Han Solo R	3.00	6.00
16 Lando Calrissian, Rebel Leader R	3.00	6.00
17 Rebel Soldier C	3.00	6.00
18 Red Hand Trooper UC	3.00	6.00
19 Yoda, Force Spirit VR	3.00	6.00
20 Arden Lyn VR	3.00	6.00
21 Darth Vader, Sith apprentice R	3.00	6.00
22 Ganner Rhysode VR	3.00	6.00
23 Blood Carver Assassin C	3.00	6.00
24 Chiss Trooper UC	3.00	6.00
25 Ewok Warrior C	3.00	6.00
26 Gamorrean Bodyguard C	3.00	6.00
27 Ghhhk UC	4.00	8.00
28 Grievous, Kaleesh Warlord VR	3.00	6.00
29 Houjix C	3.00	6.00
30 K'lor'slug UC	4.00	8.00
31 Kaminoan Medic UC	3.00	6.00
32 Kintan Strider C	3.00	6.00
33 Mantellian Savrip C	3.00	6.00
34 Molator UC	3.00	6.00
35 Monnok UC	3.00	6.00
36 Ng'ok UC	4.00	8.00
37 Sullustan Scout C	3.00	6.00
38 Toydarian Soldier C	3.00	6.00
39 Far-Outsider C	3.00	6.00
40 Taung Warrior C	3.00	6.00

Miscellaneous
PRICE GUIDE

HOT WHEELS

2014 Hot Wheels Star Wars Character Cars Black Cards 1:64

1 Darth Vader	10.00	20.00
2 R2-D2	5.00	10.00
3 Luke Skywalker	5.00	10.00
4 Chewbacca	4.00	8.00
5 Yoda	4.00	8.00
6 Tusken Raider	5.00	10.00
7 501st Clone Trooper	8.00	15.00
8 Stormtrooper	4.00	8.00
9 Darth Maul	4.00	8.00
10 Boba Fett	6.00	12.00
11 Chopper (Star Wars Rebels)	5.00	10.00
12 The Inquisitor (Star Wars Rebels)	4.00	8.00
13 C-3PO	8.00	15.00
14 Wicket the Ewok	5.00	10.00
15 Kanan Jarrus (Star Wars Rebels)	4.00	8.00
16 Zeb (Star Wars Rebels)	4.00	8.00
17 Kylo Ren	5.00	10.00
18 BB-8	8.00	15.00
19 General Grievous	6.00	12.00
20 Han Solo (The Force Awakens)	8.00	15.00
21 First Order Stormtrooper	6.00	12.00
22 Obi-Wan Kenobi	12.00	25.00
23 Rey	8.00	15.00
24 Jabba the Hutt	5.00	10.00
25 Admiral Ackbar	5.00	10.00
26 First Order Flametrooper	6.00	12.00
27 Battle Droid	6.00	12.00
28 Sabine Wren (Star Wars Rebels)	12.50	25.00
29 Clone Shock Trooper/(UER #27)		
30 C-3PO (The Force Awakens)	8.00	15.00
31 Sidon Ithano (The Force Awakens)	8.00	15.00
32 Jango Fett	6.00	12.00

2014 Hot Wheels Star Wars Character Cars Blue Cards 1:64

1 Darth Vader	4.00	8.00
2 R2-D2	4.00	8.00
3 Luke Skywalker	4.00	8.00
4 Chewbacca	6.00	12.00
5 Yoda	7.50	15.00
6 Tusken Raider	4.00	8.00
7 501st Clone Trooper	4.00	8.00
8 Stormtrooper	4.00	8.00
9 Darth Maul	5.00	10.00
10 Boba Fett	4.00	8.00
11 Chopper (Star Wars Rebels)	4.00	8.00
12 The Inquisitor (Star Wars Rebels)	3.00	6.00
13 C-3PO	6.00	12.00
14 Wicket the Ewok	4.00	8.00
15 Kanan Jarrus (Star Wars Rebels)	5.00	10.00
16 Zeb (Star Wars Rebels)		
17 Kylo Ren		
18 BB-8		
19 General Grievous		
20 Han Solo (The Force Awakens)		
21 First Order Stormtrooper	6.00	12.00
22 Obi-Wan Kenobi		
23 Rey		
24 Jabba the Hutt		
25 Admiral Ackbar		
26 First Order Flametrooper		
27 Battle Droid		
28 Sabine Wren (Star Wars Rebels)		
29 Clone Shock Trooper/(UER #27)		
30 C-3PO (The Force Awakens)		
31 Sidon Ithano (The Force Awakens)		
32 Jango Fett		

2014 Hot Wheels Star Wars Saga Walmart Exclusives 1:64

1 Gearonimo (The Phantom Menace)	5.00	10.00
2 Nitro Scorcher (Attack of the Clones)	6.00	12.00
3 Duel Fueler (Revenge of the Sith)	8.00	15.00
4 Motoblade (A New Hope)		
5 Spectyte (Empire Strikes Back)	10.00	20.00
6 Ballistik (Return of the Jedi)	4.00	8.00
7 Brutalistic (The Clone Wars)	4.00	8.00
8 Jet Threat 3.0 (Star Wars Rebels)	12.00	25.00

2014-16 Hot Wheels Star Wars Exclusives 1:64

1 Darth Vader (w/lightsaber box)/(2014 SDCC Exclusive)	80.00	150.00
2 R2-KT/(2015 Star Wars Celebration Make-a-Wish Foundation Exclusive)	40.00	80.00
3 First Order Stormtrooper/(2015 SDCC Exclusive)	25.00	50.00
4 Carships Trench Run Set/(2016 SDCC Exclusive)	50.00	100.00
5 Boba Fett Prototype Armor/(2016 Star Wars Celebration Exclusive)	25.00	50.00

2014-16 Hot Wheels Star Wars Target Exclusive 5-Packs 1:64

1	Character Cars (Battle-Damaged Stormtrooper Luke Skywalker/Darth Vader/Yoda/Chewbacca)	25.00	50.00
2	Light Side vs. Dark Side (Luke Skywalker/Obi-Wan Kenobi Anakin Skywalker/Emperor Palpatine/Kylo Ren)	15.00	30.00
3	Heroes of the Resistance (Chewbacca/Han Solo/Rey Poe Dameron/Maz Kanata)	20.00	40.00

2015 Hot Wheels Star Wars Walmart Exclusives 1:64

1	Obi-Wan Kenobi/(Jedi Order Scorcher)	4.00	8.00
2	Darth Maul/(Sith Scoopa di Fuego)	5.00	10.00
3	Clone Trooper/(Galactic Republic Impavido 1)	4.00	8.00
4	General Grievous/(Separatists Sinistra)	4.00	8.00
5	Luke Skywalker/(Rebel Alliance Enforcer)	4.00	8.00
6	Darth Vader/(Galactic Empire Prototype H-24)	5.00	10.00
7	Poe Dameron/(Resistance Fast Felion)	4.00	8.00
8	Kylo Ren/(First Order Ettorium)	4.00	8.00

2015-16 Hot Wheels Star Wars Character Cars Black Carded 2-Packs 1:64

1	Chewbacca & Han Solo	5.00	10.00
2	R2-D2 & C-3PO (weathered)	4.00	8.00
3	Obi-Wan Kenobi & Darth Vader	20.00	40.00
4	501st Clone Trooper & Battle Droid	4.00	8.00
5	Emperor Palpatine vs. Yoda	8.00	15.00
6	Darth Vader & Princess Leia	10.00	20.00
7	Captain Phasma & First Order Stormtrooper	5.00	10.00
8	Rey vs. First Order Flametrooper	8.00	15.00
9	BB-8 & Poe Dameron	10.00	20.00
10	Han Solo vs. Greedo	12.00	25.00
11	Boba Fett & Bossk		
12	Luke Skywalker vs. Rancor		
13	Stormtrooper & Death Trooper (Rogue One)	8.00	15.00

2015-16 Hot Wheels Star Wars Character Cars Blue Carded 2-Packs 1:64

1	Chewbacca & Han Solo	6.00	12.00
2	R2-D2 & C-3PO (weathered)	6.00	12.00
3	Obi-Wan Kenobi & Darth Vader	6.00	12.00
4	501st Clone Trooper & Battle Droid	8.00	15.00
5	Emperor Palpatine vs. Yoda		
6	Darth Vader & Princess Leia	6.00	12.00
7	Captain Phasma & First Order Stormtrooper		
8	Rey vs. First Order Flametrooper		
9	BB-8 & Poe Dameron		
10	Han Solo vs. Greedo	8.00	15.00
11	Boba Fett & Bossk		
12	Luke Skywalker vs. Rancor		
13	Stormtrooper & Death Trooper (Rogue One)	10.00	20.00

2015-16 Hot Wheels Star Wars Tracksets 1:64

1	TIE Factory Takedown (w/Ezra Bridger car)	12.00	25.00
2	Throne Room Raceway (w/Luke Skywalker car)	12.00	25.00
3	Death Star Battle Blast (w/X-Wing inspired vehicle)	10.00	20.00
4	Blast & Battle Lightsaber Launcher (w/Darth Vader car)	8.00	15.00
5	Starkiller Base Battle (w/Finn car)		
6	Rancor Rumble set (w/Gamorrean Guard car)	15.00	30.00

2017 Hot Wheels Star Wars 40th Anniversary Carships 1:64

NNO	Millennium Falcon	6.00	12.00
NNO	TIE Advanced X1 Prototype	6.00	12.00
NNO	TIE Fighter	5.00	10.00
NNO	X-Wing Fighter	5.00	10.00
NNO	Y-Wing Fighter	8.00	15.00

2017 Hot Wheels Star Wars 40th Anniversary Character Cars 1:64

NNO	Biggs Darklighter/(Celebration Exclusive)	12.00	25.00
NNO	Chewbacca	5.00	10.00
NNO	Darth Vader	6.00	12.00
NNO	Luke Skywalker	4.00	8.00
NNO	Princess Leia	5.00	10.00
NNO	R2-D2	4.00	8.00
NNO	Stormtrooper	4.00	8.00

2017 Hot Wheels Star Wars 40th Anniversary Starships 1:64

NNO	Millennium Falcon	8.00	15.00
NNO	Star Destroyer	10.00	20.00
NNO	TIE Advanced X1 Prototype	6.00	12.00
NNO	TIE Fighter	6.00	12.00
NNO	X-Wing Fighter	6.00	12.00
NNO	Y-Wing Fighter	8.00	15.00

2017 Hot Wheels Star Wars The Last Jedi 2-Packs 1:64

NNO	BB-8 & Poe Dameron	8.00	15.00
NNO	Boba Fett & Bossk	6.00	12.00
NNO	Jabba the Hutt & Han Solo in Carbonite	12.00	25.00
NNO	Kylo Ren & Snoke	15.00	30.00
NNO	R2-D2 & C-3PO	8.00	15.00
NNO	Rey (Jedi Training) & Luke Skywalker	15.00	30.00

2017 Hot Wheels Star Wars The Last Jedi Carships 1:64

NNO	First Order TIE Fighter	6.00	12.00
NNO	Kylo Ren's TIE Silencer		
NNO	Millennium Falcon		
NNO	Poe's X-Wing Fighter		
NNO	Resistance Ski Speeder		
NNO	Y-Wing Fighter		

2017 Hot Wheels Star Wars The Last Jedi Character Cars 1:64

NNO	BB-8	7.50	15.00
NNO	BB-9E	6.00	12.00

NNO	C-3PO	4.00	8.00
NNO	Captain Phasma	4.00	8.00
NNO	Chewbacca	4.00	8.00
NNO	Darth Vader	5.00	10.00
NNO	Elite Praetorian Guard	10.00	20.00
NNO	Finn	7.50	15.00
NNO	First Order Executioner	5.00	10.00
NNO	First Order Stormtrooper		
NNO	Kylo Ren	6.00	12.00
NNO	Luke Skywalker	5.00	10.00
NNO	R2-D2	4.00	8.00
NNO	Rey (Jedi Training)	6.00	12.00

2017 Hot Wheels Star Wars The Last Jedi Character Cars All-Terrain 1:64

NNO	BB-8	10.00	20.00
NNO	Darth Vader		

NNO	Luke Skywalker	
NNO	Stormtrooper	

2017 Hot Wheels Star Wars The Last Jedi Starships 1:64

NNO	First Order Heavy Assault Walker	
NNO	First Order Special Forces TIE Fighter	
NNO	First Order Star Destroyer	
NNO	Kylo Ren's TIE Silencer	
NNO	Kylo Ren's TIE Silencer (boxed)/(SDCC Exclusive)	
NNO	Millennium Falcon	
NNO	Poe's Ski Speeder	
NNO	Resistance Bomber	
NNO	Resistance X-Wing Fighter	

LEGO

1999 LEGO Star Wars Episode I

7101	Lightsaber Duel	50.00	125.00
7111	Droid Fighter	20.00	50.00
7121	Naboo Swamp	50.00	125.00
7131	Anakin's Podracer	60.00	150.00
7141	Naboo Fighter	60.00	150.00
7151	Sith Infiltrator	75.00	200.00
7161	Gungan Sub	125.00	300.00
7171	Mos Espa Podrace	150.00	400.00

1999 LEGO Star Wars Episode IV

7110	Landspeeder	60.00	150.00
7140	X-Wing Fighter	150.00	400.00
7150	TIE Fighter & Y-Wing	150.00	400.00

1999 LEGO Star Wars Episode V

7130	Snowspeeder	75.00	200.00

1999 LEGO Star Wars Episode VI

7128	Speeder Bikes	50.00	125.00

2000 LEGO Star Wars Episode I

7115	Gungan Patrol	50.00	125.00
7124	Flash Speeder	40.00	100.00
7155	Trade Federation AAT	150.00	400.00
7159	Star Wars Bucket	75.00	200.00
7184	Trade Federation MTT	125.00	300.00

2000 LEGO Star Wars Episode IV

7190	Millennium Falcon	250.00	600.00

2000 LEGO Star Wars Episode V

7144	Slave I	100.00	250.00

2000 LEGO Star Wars Episode VI

7104	Desert Skiff	40.00	100.00
7134	A-Wing Fighter	50.00	125.00
7180	B-Wing at Rebel Control Center	100.00	250.00

2000 LEGO Star Wars Minifigure Pack

3340	Emperor Palpatine, Darth Maul and Darth Vader Minifig Pack - Star Wars #1	75.00	200.00
3341	Luke Skywalker, Han Solo and Boba Fett Minifig Pack - Star Wars #2	75.00	200.00
3342	Chewbacca and 2 Biker Scouts Minifig Pack - Star Wars #3	75.00	200.00
3343	2 Battle Droids and Command Officer Minifig Pack - Star Wars #4	75.00	200.00

2000 LEGO Star Wars Technic

8000	Pit Droid	40.00	100.00
8001	Battle Droid	60.00	150.00
8002	Destroyer Droid	100.00	250.00

2000 LEGO Star Wars Ultimate Collector Series

7181	TIE Interceptor	800.00	1,500.00
7191	X-Wing Fighter	500.00	1,200.00

2001 LEGO Star Wars Episode I

7126	Battle Droid Carrier	100.00	250.00
7186	Watto's Junkyard	200.00	500.00

2001 LEGO Star Wars Episode IV

7106	Droid Escape	40.00	100.00
7146	TIE Fighter	75.00	200.00

2001 LEGO Star Wars Episode VI

7127	Imperial AT-ST	60.00	150.00
7166	Imperial Shuttle	100.00	250.00

2001 LEGO Star Wars Technic

8007	C-3PO	60.00	150.00
8008	Stormtrooper	40.00	100.00

2001 LEGO Star Wars Ultimate Collector Series

10018	Darth Maul	1,500.00	4,000.00
10019	Rebel Blockade Runner	800.00	1,500.00

2002 LEGO Star Wars Episode I

7203	Jedi Defense I	50.00	125.00
7204	Jedi Defense II	40.00	100.00

2002 LEGO Star Wars Episode II

7103	Jedi Duel	75.00	150.00
7113	Tusken Raider Encounter	50.00	125.00
7133	Bounty Hunter Pursuit	150.00	400.00
7143	Jedi Starfighter	75.00	200.00
7153	Jango Fett's Slave I	600.00	1,500.00
7163	Republic Gunship	400.00	1,000.00

2002 LEGO Star Wars Episode IV

7142	X-Wing Fighter	200.00	500.00
7152	TIE Fighter & Y-Wing	75.00	200.00

2002 LEGO Star Wars Episode V

7119	Twin-Pod Cloud Car	60.00	150.00

2002 LEGO Star Wars Episode VI

7139	Ewok Attack	60.00	150.00
7200	Final Duel I	60.00	150.00
7201	Final Duel II	40.00	100.00

2002 LEGO Star Wars Miniature Building Set

3219	Mini TIE Fighter	10.00	25.00

2002 LEGO Star Wars Product Collection

2001 continued

65081	R2-D2 & C-3PO Droid Collectors Set	40.00	100.00
65145	X-Wing Fighter TIE Fighter & Y-Wing Fighter Collectors Set		
65153	Jango Fett's Slave I with Bonus Cargo Case	400.00	1,000.00

2002 LEGO Star Wars Technic

8009	R2-D2	40.00	100.00
8010	Darth Vader	60.00	150.00
8011	Jango Fett	50.00	125.00
8012	Super Battle Droid	40.00	100.00

2002 LEGO Star Wars Ultimate Collector Series

7194	Yoda	200.00	500.00
10026	Naboo Starfighter Special Edition	400.00	1,000.00
10030	Imperial Star Destroyer	800.00	1,500.00

2003 LEGO Star Wars Episode II

4482	AT-TE	250.00	600.00
4478	Geonosian Fighter	75.00	200.00
4481	Hailfire Droid	125.00	300.00

2003 LEGO Star Wars Episode IV

4477	T-16 Skyhopper	50.00	125.00

2003 LEGO Star Wars Episode V

4483	AT-AT	200.00	500.00
4479	TIE Bomber	125.00	300.00
10123	Cloud City	3,000.00	8,000.00

2003 LEGO Star Wars Episode VI

4475	Jabba's Message	40.00	100.00
4476	Jabba's Prize	100.00	250.00
4480	Jabba's Palace	150.00	400.00

2003 LEGO Star Wars Miniature Building Set

4484	X-Wing Fighter & TIE Advanced	10.00	25.00
4485	Sebulba's Podracer & Anakin's Podracer	10.00	25.00
4486	AT-ST & Snowspeeder	12.00	30.00
4487	Jedi Starfighter & Slave I	15.00	40.00
4488	Millennium Falcon	20.00	50.00
4489	AT-AT	10.00	25.00
4490	Republic Gunship	15.00	40.00
4491	MTT	8.00	20.00

2003 LEGO Star Wars Product Collection

4207901	Star Wars MINI Bonus Pack	

2003 LEGO Star Wars Ultimate Collector Series

10129	Rebel Snowspeeder	400.00	1,000.00

2004 LEGO Star Wars Episode IV

4501	Mos Eisley Cantina	200.00	500.00
7262	TIE Fighter and Y-Wing	100.00	250.00

2004 LEGO Star Wars Episode V

4500	Rebel Snowspeeder	75.00	200.00
4502	X-Wing Fighter	125.00	300.00
4504	Millennium Falcon	150.00	400.00

2004 LEGO Star Wars Legends

10131	TIE Fighter Collection	60.00	150.00

2004 LEGO Star Wars Miniature Building Set

4492	Star Destroyer	20.00	50.00
4493	Sith Infiltrator	8.00	20.00
4494	Imperial Shuttle	15.00	40.00
4495	AT-TE	25.00	60.00
6963	X-Wing Fighter	20.00	50.00
6964	Boba Fett's Slave I	40.00	100.00
6965	TIE Interceptor	20.00	50.00

2004 LEGO Star Wars Product Collection

65707	Bonus/Value Pack	

2004 LEGO Star Wars Ultimate Collector Series

10134	Y-Wing Attack Starfighter	300.00	800.00

2005 LEGO Star Wars Episode III

6966	Jedi Starfighter	6.00	15.00
6967	ARC Fighter	6.00	15.00
6968	Wookiee Attack		
7250	Clone Scout Walker	75.00	200.00
7251	Darth Vader Transformation	60.00	150.00
7252	Droid Tri-Fighter	40.00	100.00
7255	General Grievous Chase	125.00	300.00
7256	Jedi Starfighter and Vulture Droid	75.00	200.00
7257	Ultimate Lightsaber Duel	150.00	400.00
7258	Wookiee Attack	125.00	300.00
7259	ARC-170 Fighter	150.00	400.00
7260	Wookiee Catamaran	300.00	750.00
7261	Clone Turbo Tank	250.00	600.00
7283	Ultimate Space Battle	300.00	750.00

2005 LEGO Star Wars Episode IV

7263	TIE Fighter	75.00	200.00
10144	Sandcrawler	200.00	500.00

2005 LEGO Star Wars Episode VI

7264	Imperial Inspection	200.00	500.00

2005 LEGO Star Wars Product Collection

65771	Episode III Collectors' Set	100.00	200.00
65828	Bonus/Value Pack		
65844	Bonus/Value Pack		
65845	Bonus/Value Pack		

2005 LEGO Star Wars Exclusives

PROMOSW002 Anakin Skywalker/(2005 International Toy Fair Exclusive)
PROMOSW003 Luminara Unduli (2005 International Toy Fair Exclusive)
SW117PROMO Darth Vader (2005 Nurnberg Toy Fair Exclusive)
TF05 Star Wars V.I.P. Gala Set/(2005 International Toy Fair Exclusive)

2005 LEGO Star Wars Ultimate Collector Series

10143	Death Star II	1,000.00	2,500.00

2006 LEGO Star Wars Episode III

6205	V-wing Fighter	75.00	200.00
72612	Clone Turbo Tank (non-light-up edition)	200.00	500.00

2006 LEGO Star Wars Episode IV

6211	Imperial Star Destroyer	300.00	800.00

2006 LEGO Star Wars Episode V

6209	Slave I	200.00	500.00
6212	X-Wing Fighter	60.00	150.00

2006 LEGO Star Wars Episode VI

6206	TIE Interceptor	75.00	200.00
6207	A-Wing Fighter	40.00	100.00
6208	B-Wing Fighter	125.00	300.00
6210	Jabba's Sail Barge	500.00	1,200.00

2006 LEGO Star Wars Product Collection

66142	Bonus/Value Pack		
66150	Bonus/Value Pack		
66221	Bonus/Value Pack		

2006 LEGO Star Wars Ultimate Collector Series

10174	Imperial AT-ST	300.00	800.00
10175	Vader's TIE Advanced	500.00	1,200.00

2007 LEGO Star Wars Episode I

7660	Naboo N-1 Starfighter with Vulture Droid	75.00	200.00
7662	Trade Federation MTT	400.00	1,000.00
7663	Sith Infiltrator	60.00	150.00
7665	Republic Cruiser	250.00	600.00

2007 LEGO Star Wars Episode III

7654	Droids Battle Pack	75.00	200.00
7655	Clone Troopers Battle Pack	150.00	400.00
7656	General Grievous Starfighter	60.00	150.00
7661	Jedi Starfighter with Hyperdrive Booster Ring	150.00	400.00

2007 LEGO Star Wars Episode IV

7658	Y-Wing Fighter	50.00	125.00
7659	Imperial Landing Craft	100.00	250.00

2007 LEGO Star Wars Episode V

7666	Hoth Rebel Base	75.00	200.00
10178	Motorised Walking AT-AT	250.00	600.00

2007 LEGO Star Wars Episode VI

7657	AT-ST	60.00	150.00

2007 LEGO Star Wars Legends

7664	TIE Crawler	100.00	250.00

2007 LEGO Star Wars Minifigure Pack

4521221	Gold Chrome Plated C-3PO/10,000*	750.00	2,000.00
PROMOSW004	Star Wars Celebration IV Exclusive/500*	2,000.00	5,000.00

2007 LEGO Star Wars Ultimate Collector Series

10179	Ultimate Collector's Millennium Falcon	1,250.00	3,000.00

2008 LEGO Star Wars The Clone Wars

7669	Anakin's Jedi Starfighter	40.00	100.00
7670	Hailfire Droid & Spider Droid	60.00	150.00
7673	MagnaGuard Starfighter	100.00	250.00
7674	V-19 Torrent	150.00	400.00

7675	AT-TE Walker	250.00	600.00
7676	Republic Attack Gunship	500.00	1,200.00
7678	Droid Gunship	75.00	200.00
7679	Republic Fighter Tank	125.00	300.00
7680	The Twilight	125.00	300.00
7681	Separatist Spider Droid	150.00	400.00
8031	V-19 Torrent	6.00	15.00
20006	Clone Turbo Tank		

2008 LEGO Star Wars Episode III

7671	AT-AP Walker	75.00	200.00

2008 LEGO Star Wars Episode V

8029	Mini Snowspeeder	6.00	12.00

2008 LEGO Star Wars Legends

7667	Imperial Dropship	40.00	100.00
7668	Rebel Scout Speeder	30.00	75.00
7672	Rogue Shadow	250.00	600.00

2008 LEGO Star Wars Miniature Building Set

8028	TIE Fighter	6.00	15.00

2008 LEGO Star Wars Miscellaneous

COMCON001	Clone Wars/(2008 SDCC Exclusive)	750.00	2,000.00

2008 LEGO Star Wars Ultimate Collector Series

10186	General Grievous	200.00	500.00
10188	Death Star	600.00	1,500.00

2009 LEGO Star Wars The Clone Wars

7748	Corporate Alliance Tank Droid	60.00	150.00
7751	Ahsoka's Starfighter and Droids	150.00	400.00
7752	Count Dooku's Solar Sailer	125.00	300.00
7753	Pirate Tank	100.00	250.00
8014	Clone Walker Battle Pack	60.00	125.00
8015	Assassin Droids Battle Pack	25.00	60.00
8016	Hyena Droid Bomber	50.00	125.00
8018	Armored Assault Tank (AAT)	100.00	250.00
8019	Republic Attack Shuttle	150.00	400.00
8033	General Grievous' Starfighter	6.00	15.00
8036	Separatist Shuttle	75.00	200.00
8037	Anakin's Y-Wing Starfighter	150.00	400.00
8039	Venator-Class Republic Attack Cruiser	400.00	1,000.00
10195	Republic Dropship with AT-OT Walker	1,200.00	3,000.00
20007	Republic Attack Cruiser	20.00	50.00
20009	AT-TE Walker	20.00	50.00
20010	Republic Gunship	30.00	75.00
30004	Battle Droid on STAP	8.00	20.00
30006	Clone Walker	8.00	20.00

MISCELLANEOUS

COMCON010 Mini Republic Dropship Mini
　　AT-TE Brickmaster Pack/(SDCC 2009 Exclusive)　250.00　600.00

2009 LEGO Star Wars Episode IV

7778	Midi-Scale Millennium Falcon	75.00	200.00
8017	Darth Vader's TIE Fighter	125.00	300.00
10198	Tantive IV	200.00	500.00

2009 LEGO Star Wars Episode V

7749	Echo Base	40.00	100.00

2009 LEGO Star Wars Episode VI

7754	Home One Mon Calamari Star Cruiser	100.00	250.00
8038	The Battle of Endor	150.00	400.00
30005	Imperial Speeder Bike	6.00	15.00

2009 LEGO Star Wars Minifigure Pack

4547551	Chrome Darth Vader	250.00	600.00

2009 LEGO Star Wars SDCC Exclusives

COMCON004	Collectible Display Set 1
COMCON005	Collectible Display Set 2
COMCON006	Collectible Display Set 4
COMCON007	Collectible Display Set 5
COMCON008	Collectible Display Set 3
COMCON009	Collectible Display Set 6
COMCON011	Holo-Brick Archives

2009 LEGO Star Wars Product Collection

66308	3 in 1 Superpack

2010 LEGO Star Wars The Clone Wars

8085	Freeco Speeder	20.00	50.00
8086	Droid Tri-Fighter	30.00	75.00
8093	Plo Koon's Jedi Starfighter	75.00	200.00
8095	General Grievous' Starfighter	60.00	150.00
8098	Clone Turbo Tank	250.00	600.00
8128	Cad Bane's Speeder	100.00	250.00
30050	Republic Attack Shuttle	8.00	20.00

2010 LEGO Star Wars Episode III

8088	ARC-170 Starfighter	150.00	400.00
8091	Republic Swamp Speeder	30.00	100.00
8096	Emperor Palpatine's Shuttle	75.00	200.00

2010 LEGO Star Wars Episode IV

8092	Luke's Landspeeder	25.00	60.00
8099	Midi-Scale Imperial Star Destroyer	50.00	125.00

2010 LEGO Star Wars Episode V

8083	Rebel Trooper Battle Pack	10.00	25.00
8084	Snowtrooper Battle Pack	10.00	25.00
8089	Hoth Wampa Cave	75.00	200.00
8097	Slave I	100.00	250.00
8129	AT-AT Walker	150.00	400.00
20018	AT-AT Walker	15.00	40.00

2010 LEGO Star Wars Legends

8087	TIE Defender	60.00	150.00

2010 LEGO Star Wars Miniature Building Set

20016	Imperial Shuttle	10.00	25.00

2010 LEGO Star Wars Minifigure Pack

2853590	Chrome Stormtrooper	100.00	250.00
2853835	White Boba Fett Figure	150.00	400.00

2010 LEGO Star Wars Miscellaneous

BOBAFETT1	White Boba Fett minifig and Star Wars Book	250.00	600.00

2010 LEGO Star Wars Product Collection

66341	Star Wars Super Pack 3 in 1
66364	Star Wars Super Pack 3 in 1
66366	Star Wars Super Pack 3 in 1
66368	Star Wars Super Pack 3 in 1

2010 LEGO Star Wars Ultimate Collector Series

10212	Imperial Shuttle	750.00	1,500.00
10215	Obi-Wan's Jedi Starfighter	200.00	500.00

2011 LEGO Star Wars The Clone Wars

7868	Mace Windu's Jedi Starfighter	125.00	300.00
7869	Battle for Geonosis	125.00	300.00
7913	Clone Trooper Battle Pack	50.00	125.00
7914	Mandalorian Battle Pack	40.00	100.00
7930	Bounty Hunter Assault Gunship	75.00	200.00
7931	T-6 Jedi Shuttle	200.00	500.00
7957	Sith Nightspeeder	60.00	150.00
7959	Geonosian Starfighter	60.00	150.00
7964	Republic Frigate	200.00	500.00
20021	Bounty Hunter Assault Gunship	12.00	30.00
30053	Republic Attack Cruiser	6.00	15.00

2011 LEGO Star Wars Episode I

7877	Naboo Starfighter	75.00	200.00
7929	The Battle of Naboo	75.00	200.00
7961	Darth Maul's Sith Infiltrator	100.00	250.00
7962	Anakin Skywalker and Sebulba's Podracers	150.00	350.00
30052	AAT	10.00	25.00

2011 LEGO Star Wars Episode IV

7965	Millennium Falcon	150.00	400.00

2011 LEGO Star Wars Episode V

7879	Hoth Echo Base	125.00	300.00
20019	Slave I	25.00	60.00

2011 LEGO Star Wars Episode VI

7956	Ewok Attack	40.00	100.00
30054	AT-ST	8.00	20.00

2011 LEGO Star Wars Legends

7915	Imperial V-wing Starfighter	40.00	100.00

2011 LEGO Star Wars Miniature Building Set

30051	Mini X-Wing	8.00	20.00
30055	Vulture Droid	6.00	15.00

2011 LEGO Star Wars Minifigure Pack

2856197	Shadow ARF Trooper	150.00	400.00

2011 LEGO Star Wars Exclusive

PROMOSW007	Star Wars Miniland Figures		
	(2011 Toy Fair Collector's Party Exclusive)	2,500.00	6,000.00

2011 LEGO Star Wars Product Collection

66377	Star Wars Super Pack 3 in 1	50.00	125.00
66378	Star Wars Super Pack 3 in 1		
66395	Star Wars Super Pack 3 in 1	50.00	125.00
66396	Star Wars Super Pack 3 in 1		

2011 LEGO Star Wars Seasonal Set

COMCON015	Advent calendar/(2011 SDCC Exclusive)/1000*	300.00	750.00
7958	Star Wars Advent Calendar	40.00	100.00

2011 LEGO Star Wars Ultimate Collector Series

10221	Super Star Destroyer	750.00	2,000.00

2012 LEGO Star Wars The Clone Wars

9488	Elite Clone Trooper & Commando Droid Battle Pack	60.00	150.00
9491	Geonosian Cannon	30.00	75.00
9498	Saesee Tiin's Jedi Starfighter	60.00	150.00
9515	Malevolence	200.00	500.00
9525	Pre Vizsla's Mandalorian Fighter	200.00	500.00
30059	MTT	6.00	15.00

2012 LEGO Star Wars Episode I

9499	Gungan Sub	150.00	400.00
30057	Anakin's Pod Racer	6.00	15.00
30058	STAP	15.00	40.00
5000063	Chrome TC-14	60.00	150.00
COMCON019	Sith Infiltrator/(2012 SDCC Exclusive)/1000*	300.00	750.00

2012 LEGO Star Wars Episode III

9494	Anakin's Jedi Interceptor	125.00	300.00
9526	Palpatine's Arrest	300.00	750.00

2012 LEGO Star Wars Episode IV

9490	Droid Escape	30.00	75.00
9492	TIE Fighter	60.00	150.00
9493	X-Wing Starfighter	75.00	200.00
9495	Gold Leader's Y-Wing Starfighter	60.00	150.00
COMCON024	Luke Skywalker's Landspeeder		
	Mini (2012 NYCC Exclusive)	250.00	600.00

2012 LEGO Star Wars Episode V

CELEBVI	Mini Slave I/(2012 Star Wars Celebration VI Exclusive)	125.00	300.00

2012 LEGO Star Wars Episode VI

9489	Endor Rebel Trooper & Imperial Trooper Battle Pack	25.00	60.00
9496	Desert Skiff	50.00	125.00
9516	Jabba's Palace	250.00	600.00

2012 LEGO Star Wars Miniature Building Set

30056	Star Destroyer	6.00	15.00

2012 LEGO Star Wars Minifigure Pack

5000062	Darth Maul	40.00	100.00

2012 LEGO Star Wars The Old Republic

9497	Republic Striker-class Starfighter	100.00	250.00
9500	Sith Fury-class Interceptor	250.00	600.00

2012 LEGO Star Wars Planet Set

9674	Naboo Starfighter & Naboo	15.00	40.00
9675	Sebulba's Podracer & Tatooine	15.00	40.00
9676	TIE Interceptor & Death Star	12.00	30.00
9677	X-Wing Starfighter & Yavin 4	10.00	25.00
9678	Twin-Pod Cloud Car & Bespin	10.00	25.00
9679	AT-ST & Endor	12.00	30.00

2012 LEGO Star Wars Product Collection

66411	Super Pack 3-in-1		
66431	Super Pack 3-in-1		
66432	Super Pack 3-in-1		

2012 LEGO Star Wars Seasonal Set

9509	Star Wars Advent Calendar	50.00	125.00

2012 LEGO Star Wars Ultimate Collector Series

10225	R2-D2	125.00	300.00
10227	B-Wing Starfighter	300.00	800.00

2013 LEGO Star Wars The Clone Wars

11905	Brickmaster Star Wars: Battle for the Stolen Crystals parts	12.00	30.00

30240	Z-95 Headhunter	5.00	12.00
30241	Mandalorian Fighter	6.00	15.00
30242	Republic Frigate	10.00	25.00
30243	Umbaran MHC	5.00	12.00
75002	AT-RT	40.00	100.00
75004	Z-95 Headhunter	125.00	300.00
75012	BARC Speeder with Sidecar	250.00	600.00
75013	Umbaran MHC (Mobile Heavy Cannon)	100.00	250.00
75022	Mandalorian Speeder	125.00	300.00
75024	HH-87 Starhopper	60.00	150.00

2013 LEGO Star Wars Episode II

75000	Clone Troopers vs. Droidekas	30.00	75.00
75015	Corporate Alliance Tank Droid	75.00	200.00
75016	Homing Spider Droid	75.00	200.00
75017	Duel on Geonosis	100.00	250.00
75019	AT-TE	200.00	500.00
75021	Republic Gunship	300.00	800.00
5001709	Clone Trooper Lieutenant	20.00	50.00

2013 LEGO Star Wars Episode V

75014	Battle of Hoth	100.00	250.00
5001621	Han Solo (Hoth)	6.00	15.00

2013 LEGO Star Wars Episode VI

75003	A-Wing Starfighter	40.00	100.00
75005	Rancor Pit	200.00	500.00
75020	Jabba's Sail Barge	300.00	750.00

2013 LEGO Star Wars The Old Republic

75001	Republic Troopers vs. Sith Troopers	30.00	75.00
75025	Jedi Defender-Class Cruiser	250.00	600.00

2013 LEGO Star Wars Originals

75018	JEK-14's Stealth Starfighter	100.00	250.00
COMCON032	Jek-14 Mini Stealth Starfighter		
	(2013 SDCC Exclusive)/1000*	400.00	1,000.00
MAY2013	Holocron Droid	10.00	25.00
TRU03	Mini Jek-14 Stealth Fighter/(2013 Toys R Us Exclusive)	60.00	150.00
YODACHRON	Yoda Chronicles Promotional Set	750.00	2,000.00

2013 LEGO Star Wars Planet Set

75006	Jedi Starfighter & Planet Kamino	25.00	60.00
75007	Republic Assault Ship & Planet Coruscant	20.00	50.00
75008	TIE Bomber & Asteroid Field	15.00	40.00
75009	Snowspeeder & Hoth	30.00	75.00
75010	B-Wing Starfighter & Planet Endor	30.00	75.00
75011	Tantive IV & Planet Alderaan	30.00	75.00

2013 LEGO Star Wars Product Collection

66449 Super Pack 3-in-1	60.00	150.00
66456 Star Wars Value Pack	75.00	200.00
66473 LEGO Star Wars Super Pack	100.00	250.00

2013 LEGO Star Wars Promotional Set

NYCC2013 Yoda display box/(2013 NYCC Exclusive)		
YODA Yoda minifig, NY I Heart Torso	100.00	250.00

2013 LEGO Star Wars Seasonal Set

75023 Star Wars Advent Calendar	60.00	150.00

2013 LEGO Star Wars Ultimate Collector Series

10236 Ewok Village	300.00	800.00
10240 Red Five X-Wing Starfighter	250.00	600.00

2014 LEGO Star Wars The Clone Wars

75045 Republic AV-7 Anti-Vehicle Cannon	150.00	400.00
75046 Coruscant Police Gunship	150.00	400.00

2014 LEGO Star Wars Episode I

75058 MTT	150.00	400.00

2014 LEGO Star Wars Episode III

30244 Anakin's Jedi Interceptor	6.00	15.00
30247 ARC-170 Starfighter	5.00	12.00
75035 Kashyyyk Troopers	50.00	125.00
75036 Utapau Troopers	60.00	150.00
75037 Battle on Saleucami	60.00	150.00
75038 Jedi Interceptor	50.00	125.00
75039 V-Wing Starfighter	40.00	100.00
75040 General Grievous' Wheel Bike	60.00	150.00
75041 Vulture Droid	100.00	250.00
75042 Droid Gunship	60.00	150.00
75043 AT-AP	75.00	200.00
75044 Droid Tri-Fighter	50.00	125.00

2014 LEGO Star Wars Episode IV

75034 Death Star Troopers	15.00	40.00
75052 Mos Eisley Cantina	75.00	200.00
75055 Imperial Star Destroyer	250.00	600.00

2014 LEGO Star Wars Episode V

75049 Snowspeeder	60.00	150.00
75054 AT-AT	125.00	300.00

2014 LEGO Star Wars Episode VI

30246 Imperial Shuttle	6.00	15.00
75050 B-Wing	75.00	200.00

2014 LEGO Star Wars MicroFighters

75028 Clone Turbo Tank	50.00	125.00
75029 AAT	30.00	75.00
75030 Millennium Falcon	15.00	40.00
75031 TIE Interceptor	15.00	40.00
75032 X-Wing Fighter	15.00	40.00
75033 Star Destroyer	15.00	40.00

2014 LEGO Star Wars Minifigure Pack

5002122 TC-4	20.00	50.00

2014 LEGO Star Wars The Old Republic

5002123 Darth Revan	150.00	400.00

2014 LEGO Star Wars Original Content

75051 Jedi Scout Fighter	125.00	300.00

2014 LEGO Star Wars Product Collection

66479 Value Pack		
66495 Star Wars Value Pack		
66512 Rebels Co-Pack		
66514 Microfighter Super Pack 3 in 1		
66515 Microfighter Super Pack 3 in 1		

2014 LEGO Star Wars Toys R Us Exclusives

TRUGHOST The Ghost Micro-Model		
TRUTIE TIE Fighter		
TRUXWING X-Wing		

2014 LEGO Star Wars Rebels

75048 The Phantom	75.00	200.00
75053 The Ghost	400.00	1,000.00
COMCON039 The Ghost Starship/1000*/(2014 SDCC Exclusive)	300.00	800.00
FANEXPO001 The Ghost Starship/(2014 Fan Expo Exclusive)	60.00	150.00

2014 LEGO Star Wars Seasonal Set

75056 Star Wars Advent Calendar	60.00	150.00

2014 LEGO Star Wars Ultimate Collector Series

75059 Sandcrawler	300.00	800.00

2015 LEGO Star Wars Buildable Figures

75107 Jango Fett	30.00	75.00
75108 Clone Commander Cody	30.00	75.00
75109 Obi-Wan Kenobi	30.00	75.00
75110 Luke Skywalker	20.00	50.00
75111 Darth Vader	40.00	100.00
75112 General Grievous	30.00	75.00

2015 LEGO Star Wars The Clone Wars

75087 Anakin's Custom Jedi Starfighter	100.00	250.00

2015 LEGO Star Wars Episode I

75080 AAT	60.00	150.00
75086 Battle Droid Troop Carrier	75.00	200.00
75091 Flash Speeder	50.00	125.00
75092 Naboo Starfighter	100.00	250.00
75096 Sith Infiltrator	100.00	250.00

2015 LEGO Star Wars Episode II

75085 Hailfire Droid	60.00	150.00

2015 LEGO Star Wars Episode IV

75081 T-16 Skyhopper	50.00	125.00
5002947 Admiral Yularen	40.00	100.00

2015 LEGO Star Wars Episode VI

30272 A-Wing Starfighter	10.00	25.00
75093 Death Star Final Duel	60.00	150.00
75094 Imperial Shuttle Tydirium	100.00	250.00

2015 LEGO Star Wars The Force Awakens

30276 First Order Special Forces TIE Fighter	8.00	20.00
75099 Rey's Speeder	25.00	60.00
75100 First Order Snowspeeder	25.00	60.00
75101 First Order Special Forces TIE Fighter	60.00	150.00
75102 Poe's X-Wing Fighter	75.00	200.00
75103 First Order Transporter	100.00	250.00
75104 Kylo Ren's Command Shuttle	75.00	200.00
75105 Millennium Falcon	125.00	300.00
5002948 C-3PO	8.00	20.00
30UNIQUE15 Force Friday Commemorative Brick		

MISCELLANEOUS

2015 LEGO Star Wars Legends

75079	Shadow Troopers	20.00	50.00
75088	Senate Commando Troopers	30.00	75.00
75089	Geonosis Troopers	30.00	75.00

2015 LEGO Star Wars Magazine Gift

SW911506	Snowspeeder
SW911508	Mini Slave I
SW911509	Imperial Shooter
SW911510	Micro Star Destroyer and TIE Fighter
SW911511	Jedi Weapon Stand
SWCOMIC1	Mini X-Wing Starfighter

2015 LEGO Star Wars MicroFighters

75072	ARC-170 Starfighter	15.00	40.00
75073	Vulture Droid	10.00	25.00
75074	Snowspeeder	10.00	25.00
75075	AT-AT	15.00	40.00
75076	Republic Gunship	10.00	25.00
75077	Homing Spider Droid	12.00	30.00

2015 LEGO Star Wars Product Collection

66533	Microfighter 3 in 1 Super Pack	20.00	50.00
66534	Microfighter 3 in 1 Super Pack	12.00	30.00
66535	Battle Pack 2 in 1	50.00	125.00
66536	Luke Skywalker and Darth Vader	50.00	125.00

2015 LEGO Star Wars Exclusives

CELEB2015	Tatooine Mini-Build/1000*		
	(2015 Star Wars Celebration Exclusive)	75.00	200.00
FANEXPO2015	Tatooine Mini Build/(2015 Fan Expo Exclusive)	75.00	200.00
SDCC2015	Dagobah Mini Build/(2015 SDCC Exclusive)	75.00	200.00
TRUWOOKIEE	Wookiee Gunship/(2015 Toys R Us Exclusive)	6.00	15.00
TRUXWING	Poe's X-Wing Fighter/(2015 Toys R Us Exclusive)	8.00	20.00

2015 LEGO Star Wars Rebels

30274	AT-DP	6.00	15.00
30275	TIE Advanced Prototype	6.00	15.00
75078	Imperial Troop Transport	10.00	25.00
75082	TIE Advanced Prototype	15.00	40.00
75083	AT-DP	40.00	100.00
75084	Wookiee Gunship	40.00	100.00
75090	Ezra's Speeder Bike	12.00	30.00
75106	Imperial Assault Carrier	60.00	150.00
5002938	Stormtrooper Sergeant	6.00	15.00
5002939	The Phantom	6.00	15.00

2015 LEGO Star Wars Seasonal Set

75097	Star Wars Advent Calendar	15.00	40.00

2015 LEGO Star Wars Ultimate Collector Series

75060	Slave I	300.00	800.00
75095	TIE Fighter	200.00	500.00

2016 LEGO Star Wars Battlefront

75133	Rebel Alliance Battle Pack	15.00	40.00
75134	Galactic Empire Battle Pack	15.00	40.00

2016 LEGO Star Wars Buildable Figures

75113	Rey	10.00	25.00
75114	First Order Stormtrooper	15.00	40.00
75115	Poe Dameron	10.00	25.00
75116	Finn	8.00	20.00
75117	Kylo Ren	15.00	40.00
75118	Captain Phasma	15.00	40.00
75119	Sergeant Jyn Erso	10.00	25.00
75120	K-2SO	12.00	30.00
75121	Imperial Death Trooper	12.00	30.00

2016 LEGO Star Wars Episode III

75135	Obi-Wan's Jedi Interceptor	40.00	100.00
75142	Homing Spider Droid	50.00	125.00
75151	Clone Turbo Tank	125.00	300.00

2016 LEGO Star Wars Episode IV

75136	Droid Escape Pod	15.00	40.00

2016 LEGO Star Wars Episode V

75137	Carbon-Freezing Chamber	30.00	75.00
75138	Hoth Attack	20.00	50.00

2016 LEGO Star Wars The Force Awakens

30277	First Order Star Destroyer	6.00	15.00
30278	Poe's X-Wing Fighter	5.00	12.00
30279	Kylo Ren's Command Shuttle	5.00	12.00
30602	First Order Stormtrooper	8.00	20.00
30605	Finn (FN-2187)	5.00	12.00

75131	Resistance Trooper Battle Pack	12.00	30.00
75132	First Order Battle Pack	10.00	25.00
75139	Battle on Takodana	15.00	40.00
75140	Resistance Troop Transporter	50.00	125.00
75148	Encounter on Jakku	25.00	60.00
75149	Resistance X-Wing Fighter	60.00	150.00
5004406	First Order General	6.00	15.00

2016 LEGO Star Wars Magazine Gift

SW911607	Millennium Falcon	5.00	12.00
SW911608	Landspeeder	5.00	12.00
SW911609	Naboo Starfighter	5.00	12.00
SW911610	Probe Droid	5.00	12.00
SW911611	AAT	5.00	12.00
SW911612	Acklay	5.00	12.00
SW911613	TIE Bomber	5.00	12.00
SW911614	Yoda's Hut	5.00	12.00
SW911615	AT-AT	5.00	12.00
SW911616	MTT	5.00	12.00
SW911617	Palpatine's Shuttle	6.00	15.00

2016 LEGO Star Wars MicroFighters

75125	Resistance X-Wing Fighter	10.00	25.00
75126	First Order Snowspeeder	8.00	20.00
75127	The Ghost	10.00	25.00
75128	TIE Advanced Prototype	10.00	25.00
75129	Wookiee Gunship	6.00	15.00
75130	AT-DP	10.00	25.00

2016 LEGO Star Wars Miscellaneous

11912	Star Wars: Build Your Own Adventure Parts	12.00	30.00

2016 LEGO Star Wars Originals

75145	Eclipse Fighter	30.00	75.00
75147	StarScavenger	40.00	100.00

2016 LEGO Star Wars Product Collection

66542	Microfighters Super Pack 3 in 1	10.00	25.00

66543	Microfighters Super Pack 3 in 1	12.00	30.00
5005217	Death Star Ultimate Kit		

2016 LEGO Star Wars Promotional Set

6176782	Escape the Space Slug	100.00	250.00
TRUFALCON	Millennium Falcon/(2016 Toys R Us Exclusive)	10.00	25.00

2016 LEGO Star Wars Rebels

75141	Kanan's Speeder Bike	25.00	60.00
75150	Vader's TIE Advanced vs. A-Wing Starfighter	75.00	200.00
75157	Captain Rex's AT-TE	100.00	250.00
75158	Rebel Combat Frigate	150.00	400.00
5004408	Rebel A-Wing Pilot	5.00	12.00

2016 LEGO Star Wars Rogue One

75152	Imperial Assault Hovertank	40.00	100.00
75153	AT-ST Walker	60.00	150.00
75154	TIE Striker	30.00	75.00
75155	Rebel U-Wing Fighter	75.00	200.00
75156	Krennic's Imperial Shuttle	75.00	200.00

2016 LEGO Star Wars Seasonal Set

75146	Star Wars Advent Calendar	25.00	60.00

2016 LEGO Star Wars Ultimate Collector Series

75098	Assault on Hoth	300.00	800.00
75159	Death Star	500.00	1,200.00

2017 LEGO Star Wars BrickHeadz

41498	Boba Fett & Han Solo in Carbonite/NYCC Exclusive	300.00	800.00

2017 LEGO Star Wars Buildable Figures

75523	Scarif Stormtrooper	12.00	30.00
75524	Chirrut Imwe	8.00	20.00
75525	Baze Malbus	8.00	20.00
75526	Elite TIE Fighter Pilot	15.00	40.00
75528	Rey	10.00	25.00
75529	Elite Praetorian Guard	15.00	40.00
75530	Chewbacca	20.00	50.00
75531	Stormtrooper Commander	15.00	40.00
75532	Scout Trooper & Speeder Bike	30.00	75.00

2017 LEGO Star Wars The Clone Wars

75168	Yoda's Jedi Starfighter	30.00	75.00

2017 LEGO Star Wars Episode I

75169	Duel on Naboo	40.00	100.00

2017 LEGO Star Wars Episode II

75191	Jedi Starfighter (w/hyperdrive)	100.00	250.00

2017 LEGO Star Wars Episode III

75183	Darth Vader Transformation	25.00	60.00

2017 LEGO Star Wars Episode IV

75173	Luke's Landspeeder	20.00	50.00

2017 LEGO Star Wars Episode VI

75174	Desert Skiff Escape	30.00	70.00
75175	A-Wing Starfighter	40.00	100.00

2017 LEGO Star Wars The Force Awakens

75166	First Order Transport Speeder Battle Pack	12.00	30.00
75178	Jakku Quadjumper	20.00	50.00
75180	Rathtar Escape	40.00	100.00

2017 LEGO Star Wars The Last Jedi

30497	First Order Heavy Assault Walker	6.00	15.00
75176	Resistance Transport Pod	15.00	40.00
75177	First Order Heavy Scout Walker	30.00	75.00
75179	Kylo Ren's TIE Fighter	40.00	100.00
75187	BB-8	75.00	200.00
75188	Resistance Bomber	60.00	150.00
75189	First Order Heavy Assault Walker	125.00	300.00
75190	First Order Star Destroyer	125.00	300.00

2017 LEGO Star Wars Legends

75182	Republic Fighter Tank	12.00	30.00

2017 LEGO Star Wars Magazine Gift

SW911618	Flash Speeder	6.00	15.00
SW911719	Kanan Jarrus	5.00	12.00
SW911720	The Ghost	6.00	15.00
SW911721	Imperial Combat Driver	8.00	20.00
SW911722	TIE Advanced	8.00	20.00
SW911723	Vulture Droid	6.00	15.00
SW911724	A-Wing	6.00	15.00
SW911725	Sandcrawler	8.00	20.00
SW911726	Imperial Snowtrooper	6.00	15.00
SW911727	Rey's Speeder	8.00	20.00
SW911728	First Order Snowspeeder	6.00	15.00
SW911729	Droid Gunship	6.00	15.00
SW911730	Y-Wing	5.00	12.00

2017 LEGO Star Wars MicroFighters

75160	U-Wing	10.00	25.00
75161	TIE Striker	10.00	25.00
75162	Y-Wing	10.00	25.00
75163	Krennic's Imperial Shuttle	8.00	20.00

2017 LEGO Star Wars Originals

75167	Bounty Hunter Speeder Bike Battle Pack	25.00	60.00
75185	Tracker I	40.00	100.00
75186	The Arrowhead	60.00	150.00

2017 LEGO Star Wars Promotional

30611	R2-D2	12.00	30.00
CELEB2017	Detention Block Rescue	125.00	300.00
SWMF	Millennium Falcon	6.00	15.00
TRUBB8	BB-8	5.00	12.00
TRULEIA	Princess Leia	6.00	15.00

2017 LEGO Star Wars Rebels

75170	The Phantom	40.00	100.00

2017 LEGO Star Wars Rogue One

30496	U-Wing Fighter	6.00	15.00
40176	Scarif Stormtrooper	10.00	25.00
40268	R3-M2	6.00	15.00
75164	Rebel Trooper Battle Pack	15.00	40.00
75165	Imperial Trooper Battle Pack	15.00	40.00
75171	Battle on Scarif	40.00	100.00
75172	Y-Wing Starfighter	60.00	150.00

2017 LEGO Star Wars Seasonal

75184	Star Wars Advent Calendar	15.00	40.00

2017 LEGO Star Wars Ultimate Collector Series

75144	Snowspeeder	200.00	500.00
75192	Millennium Falcon	600.00	1,500.00

2018 LEGO Star Wars Buildable Figures

75533	Boba Fett	30.00	75.00
75534	Darth Vader	25.00	60.00
75535	Han Solo	10.00	25.00
75536	Range Trooper	25.00	60.00
75537	Darth Maul	20.00	50.00
75538	Super Battle Droid		
75539	501st Legion Clone Trooper & AT-RT Walker		

2018 LEGO Star Wars The Clone Wars

75199	General Grievous' Combat Speeder	30.00	80.00
75214	Anakin's Jedi Starfighter	20.00	50.00

2018 LEGO Star Wars Episode II

75206	Jedi and Clone Troopers Battle Pack	20.00	50.00

2018 LEGO Star Wars Episode IV

75198	Tatooine Battle Pack	15.00	40.00
75205	Mos Eisley Cantina	30.00	80.00
75218	X-Wing Starfighter	75.00	200.00
75220	Sandcrawler	125.00	300.00
75221	Imperial Landing Craft	60.00	150.00

2018 LEGO Star Wars Episode V

75203	Hoth Medical Chamber	30.00	75.00
75208	Yoda's Hut	30.00	75.00

2018 LEGO Star Wars The Last Jedi

30380	Kylo Ren's Shuttle	8.00	20.00
40298	DJ	8.00	20.00
75188	Resistance Bomber (Finch Dallow)	125.00	300.00
75197	First Order Specialists Battle Pack	12.00	30.00
75200	Ahch-To Island Training	15.00	40.00
75201	First Order AT-ST	25.00	60.00
75202	Defense of Crait	40.00	100.00
75216	Snoke's Throne Room	30.00	75.00
75230	Porg	60.00	150.00

2018 LEGO Star Wars Legends

75204	Sandspeeder	12.00	30.00

2018 LEGO Star Wars Magazine Gift

SW911831	Kylo Ren's Shuttle	6.00	15.00
SW911832	Imperial Shuttle Pilot	10.00	25.00
SW911833	Imperial Shuttle	5.00	12.00
SW911834	Finn	8.00	20.00

SW911835	Dwarf Spider Droid	8.00	20.00
SW911836	Quadjumper	6.00	15.00
SW911837	AT-ST	10.00	25.00
SW911838	Probe Droid	8.00	20.00
SW911839	Obi-Wan Kenobi	8.00	20.00
SW911840	Droideka	6.00	15.00
SW911841	Poe Dameron's X-Wing Fighter	10.00	25.00
SW911842	Star Destroyer	8.00	20.00
SW911843	Luke Skywalker		

2018 LEGO Star Wars Master Builder

75222	Betrayal at Cloud City	400.00	1,000.00

2018 LEGO Star Wars Microfighters

75193	Millennium Falcon	10.00	25.00
75194	First Order TIE Fighter	8.00	20.00
75195	Ski Speeder vs. First Order Walker	12.00	30.00
75196	A-Wing vs. TIE Silencer	12.00	30.00

2018 LEGO Star Wars Promotional

40288	BB-8	10.00	25.00
75512	Millennium Falcon Cockpit (SDCC Exclusive)	150.00	400.00
5005376	Star Wars Anniversary Pod	12.00	30.00
5005747	Black Card Display Stand	50.00	125.00
6252770	Leia Organa	10.00	25.00
6252808	Chewbacca	10.00	25.00
6252810	Han Solo		
6252811	Obi-Wan Kenobi	6.00	15.00
6252812	Luke Skywalker	10.00	25.00
PORG	Porg		

2018 LEGO Star Wars Seasonal

75213	Star Wars Advent Calendar	20.00	50.00

2018 LEGO Star Wars Solo

30381	Imperial TIE Fighter	6.00	15.00
30498	Imperial AT-Hauler	8.00	20.00
40299	Kessel Mine Worker	10.00	25.00
40300	Han Solo Mudtrooper	20.00	50.00
75207	Imperial Patrol Battle Pack	8.00	20.00
75209	Han Solo's Landspeeder	15.00	40.00
75210	Moloch's Landspeeder	25.00	60.00
75211	Imperial TIE Fighter	100.00	250.00
75212	Kessel Run Millennium Falcon	125.00	300.00
75215	Cloud-Rider Swoop Bikes	20.00	50.00
75217	Imperial Conveyex Transport	40.00	100.00
75219	Imperial AT-Hauler	50.00	125.00

2018 LEGO Star Wars Ultimate Collector Series

75181	Y-Wing Starfighter	300.00	750.00

2019 LEGO Star Wars

11920	Parts for Star Wars: Build Your Own Adventure Galactic Missions		

2019 LEGO Star Wars 4-Plus

75235	X-Wing Starfighter Trench Run	15.00	40.00
75237	TIE Fighter Attack	10.00	25.00
75247	Rebel A-Wing Starfighter	8.00	20.00

2019 LEGO Star Wars Battlefront

75226	Inferno Squad Battle Pack	10.00	25.00

2019 LEGO Star Wars Boost

75253	Droid Commander	125.00	300.00

2019 LEGO Star Wars Episode I

30383	Naboo Starfighter	4.00	10.00
30461	Podracer	6.00	15.00
75258	Anakin's Podracer ñ 20th Anniversary Edition	20.00	50.00

2019 LEGO Star Wars Episode III

75233	Droid Gunship	25.00	60.00
75234	AT-AP Walker	20.00	50.00
75261	Clone Scout Walker ñ 20th Anniversary Edition	15.00	40.00

2019 LEGO Star Wars Episode IV

30624	Obi-Wan Kenobi Mini-Figure	12.00	30.00
75229	Death Star Escape	12.00	30.00
75244	Tantive IV	150.00	400.00
75246	Death Star Cannon	20.00	50.00

2019 LEGO Star Wars Episode V

30384	Snowspeeder	6.00	10.00
75239	Hoth Generator Attack	10.00	25.00
75241	Action Battle Echo Base Defence	15.00	40.00
75243	Slave I ñ 20th Anniversary Edition	60.00	150.00
75259	Snowspeeder ñ 20th Anniversary Edition	40.00	100.00

2019 LEGO Star Wars Episode VI

75238	Action Battle Endor Assault	12.00	30.00

2019 LEGO Star Wars The Force Awakens

75236	Duel on Starkiller Base	12.00	30.00

2019 LEGO Star Wars The Last Jedi

75225	Elite Praetorian Guard Battle Pack	8.00	20.00

2019 Star Wars Legends

75262	Imperial Dropship ñ 20th Anniversary Edition	15.00	40.00

2019 Star Wars Magazine Gift

911943	Luke Skywalker		
911944	Resistance Bomber	3.00	8.00
911945	Slave I	2.50	6.00
911946	U-Wing	3.00	8.00

MISCELLANEOUS

911947	IG-88	2.50	6.00
911948	AT-M6	2.50	6.00
911949	Millennium Falcon	3.00	8.00
911950	B-Wing	2.50	6.00
911951	First Order Stormtrooper	2.50	6.00
911952	Jedi Interceptor	5.00	12.00
911953	First Order SF TIE Fighter		
911954	Kylo Ren's TIE Silencer		

2019 LEGO Star Wars The Mandalorian

75254	AT-ST Raider	40.00	100.00

2019 LEGO Star Wars Microfighters

75223	Naboo Starfighter	6.00	15.00
75224	Sith Infiltrator	5.00	12.00
75228	Escape Pod vs. Dewback	8.00	20.00

2018 LEGO Star Wars Miscellaneous

75251	Darth Vader's Castle	60.00	150.00
75255	Yoda	50.00	120.00

2019 LEGO Star Wars Promotional

40333	Battle of Hoth - 20th Anniversary Edition	20.00	50.00
40362	Battle of Endor	25.00	60.00
75227	Darth Vader Bust	40.00	100.00
75522	Mini Boost Droid Commander	30.00	75.00
LUKE1	Luke Skywalker		
TANTIVEIV	Tantive IV		
XWING1	Mini X-Wing Fighter		
XWING2	X-Wing		

2019 LEGO Star Wars Resistance

75240	Major Vonreg's TIE Fighter	30.00	75.00
75242	Black Ace TIE Interceptor	40.00	100.00

2019 LEGO Star Wars The Rise of Skywalker

75248	Resistance A-Wing Starfighter	20.00	50.00
75249	Resistance Y-Wing Starfighter	30.00	80.00
75250	Pasaana Speeder Chase	20.00	50.00
75256	Kylo Ren's Shuttle	60.00	150.00
75257	Millennium Falcon	75.00	200.00
77901	Sith Trooper Bust SDCC	75.00	200.00

2019 LEGO Star Wars Seasonal

75245	Star Wars Advent Calendar	25.00	60.00

2019 LEGO Star Wars Ultimate Collector Series

75252	Imperial Star Destroyer	500.00	1,200.00

2020 LEGO Star Wars 4-Plus

75268	Snowspeeder	15.00	40.00

2020 LEGO The Clone Wars

75280	501st Legion Clone Troopers	30.00	75.00
75283	Armored Assault Tank (AAT)	30.00	75.00

2020 LEGO Star Wars Episode III

75269	Duel on Mustafar	15.00	40.00
75281	Anakin's Jedi Interceptor	30.00	75.00
75286	General Grievous's Starfighter	40.00	100.00

2020 LEGO Star Wars Episode IV

75270	Obi-Wan's Hut	25.00	60.00
75271	Luke Skywalker's Landspeeder	15.00	40.00

2020 LEGO Star Wars Episode V

75288	AT-AT	125.00	300.00

2020 LEGO Star Wars Episode VI

75291	Death Star Final Duel	60.00	150.00

2020 LEGO Star Wars Galaxy's Edge

75293	Resistance I-TS Transport	60.00	150.00

2020 LEGO Star Wars Helmet Collection

75274	TIE Fighter Pilot	30.00	80.00
75276	Stormtrooper	30.00	80.00
75277	Boba Fett	40.00	100.00

2020 LEGO Star Wars Magazine Gift

912055	Snowspeeder	2.50	6.00
912056	TIE Striker	3.00	8.00
912057	R2-D2 and MSE-6	3.00	8.00
912058	Sith Infiltrator	2.50	6.00
912059	Elite Praetorian Guard	3.00	8.00
912060	A-Wing	2.00	5.00
912061	AT-AT	3.00	8.00
912062	Stormtrooper	4.00	10.00
912063	Resistance X-Wing	6.00	15.00
912064	TIE Dagger	6.00	15.00
912065	Luke Skywalker	8.00	20.00

912066	Jedi Interceptor	4.00	10.00
912067	TIE Interceptor	5.00	12.00

2020 LEGO Star Wars The Mandalorian

75267	Mandalorian Battle Pack	10.00	25.00
75292	The Razor Crest	75.00	200.00
75318	The Child	50.00	125.00

2020 LEGO Star Wars Master Builder

75290	Mos Eisley Cantina	250.00	600.00

2020 LEGO Star Wars Microfighters

75263	Resistance Y-Wing Microfighter	5.00	12.00
75264	Kylo Ren's Shuttle Microfighter	5.00	12.00
75265	T-16 Skyhopper vs Bantha Microfighters	10.00	25.00

2020 LEGO Star Wars Promotional

40407	Death Star II Battle	50.00	125.00
75294	Bespin Duel	12.00	30.00
77904	Nebulon-B Frigate/(SDCC Exclusive)	75.00	200.00
6346097	Yoda's Lightsaber	125.00	300.00
6346098	Yoda's Lightsaber	100.00	250.00

2020 LEGO Star Wars The Rise of Skywalker

30386	Poe Dameron's X-Wing Fighter	5.00	12.00
75266	Sith Troopers Battle Pack	8.00	20.00
75272	Sith TIE Fighter	30.00	80.00
75273	Poe Dameron's X-Wing Fighter	30.00	80.00
75278	D-O	25.00	60.00
75284	Knights of Ren Transport Ship	40.00	100.00

2020 LEGO Star Wars Seasonal

75279	Star Wars Advent Calendar	20.00	50.00

2020 LEGO Star Wars Ultimate Collector Series

75275	A-Wing Starfighter	150.00	400.00

2021 LEGO Star Wars The Bad Batch

75314	The Bad Batch Attack Shuttle	50.00	125.00

2021 LEGO Star Wars The Clone Wars

75310	Duel on Mandalore	20.00	50.00
75316	Mandalorian Starfighter	40.00	100.00

2021 LEGO Star Wars Episode IV

75300	Imperial TIE Fighter	40.00	100.00
75301	Luke Skywalker's X-Wing Fighter	60.00	150.00

2021 LEGO Star Wars Episode V

75296	Darth Vader Meditation Chamber	40.00	100.00
75306	Imperial Probe Droid	30.00	75.00

2021 LEGO Star Wars Episode VI

30388	Imperial Shuttle	6.00	15.00
75302	Imperial Shuttle	40.00	100.00

2021 LEGO Star Wars The Force Awakens

75297	Resistance X-Wing Starfighter	20.00	50.00

2021 LEGO Star Wars Helmet Collection

75304	Darth Vader	40.00	100.00
75305	Scout Trooper	25.00	60.00

2021 LEGO Star Wars Magazine Gift

912168	Mandalorian	8.00	20.00
912169	Emperor Palpatine	6.00	15.00
912170	V-wing	5.00	12.00
912171	TIE Bomber	6.00	15.00
912172	Jedi Starfighter	5.00	12.00
912173	Rey and BB-8	10.00	25.00
912174	Sith Trooper	6.00	15.00
912175	AT-ST Raider	6.00	15.00
912176	Clone Turbo Tank	6.00	15.00
912177	Resistance A-wing	5.00	12.00
912178	Republic Gunship	8.00	20.00
912179	Snowtrooper	6.00	15.00
912280	Millennium Falcon	10.00	25.00

2021 LEGO Star Wars The Mandalorian

75299	Trouble on Tatooine	20.00	50.00
75311	Imperial Armored Marauder	25.00	60.00
75312	Boba Fett's Starship	50.00	125.00
75315	Imperial Light Cruiser	60.00	150.00
75319	The Armorer's Mandalorian Forge	25.00	60.00

2021 LEGO Star Wars Microfighters

75295	Millennium Falcon Microfighter	15.00	40.00
75298	AT-AT vs. Tauntaun Microfighters	12.00	30.00

2021 LEGO Star Wars Miscellaneous

75308	R2-D2	100.00	250.00

2021 LEGO Star Wars Product Collection

66674	Skywalker Adventure Pack	50.00	125.00

2021 LEGO Star Wars Promotional

40451	Tatooine Homestead	20.00	50.00
40483	Luke Skywalker's Lightsaber	75.00	200.00

2021 LEGO Star Wars Seasonal

75307	Star Wars Advent Calendar	30.00	75.00

2021 LEGO Star Wars Ultimate Collector Series

75309	Republic Gunship	250.00	600.00
75313	AT-AT	400.00	1,000.00

2022 Star Wars Andor

75338	Ambush on Ferrix	60.00	150.00

2022 Star Wars The Bad Batch

75323	The Justifier	75.00	200.00

2022 Star Wars The Book of Boba Fett

75325	The Mandalorian's N-1 Starfighter	30.00	75.00
75326	Boba Fett's Throne Room	40.00	100.00

2022 Star Wars The Clone Wars

75342	Republic Fighter Tank	30.00	75.00

2022 Star Wars Diorama Collection

75329	Death Star Trench Run Diorama	40.00	100.00
75330	Dagobah Jedi Training Diorama	50.00	125.00
75339	Death Star Trash Compactor Diorama	50.00	125.00

2022 Star Wars Episode II

40558	Clone Trooper Command Station	20.00	50.00
75333	Obi-Wan Kenobi's Jedi Starfighter	30.00	75.00

2022 Star Wars Episode III

75337	AT-TE Walker	100.00	250.00

2022 Star Wars Episode IV

30625	Luke Skywalker with Blue Milk	30.00	75.00

2022 Star Wars Episode V

30495	AT-ST	4.00	10.00
40557	Defense of Hoth	15.00	40.00
75320	Snowtrooper Battle Pack	15.00	40.00
75322	Hoth AT-ST	25.00	60.00

2022 Star Wars Episode VI

75332	AT-ST	15.00	40.00

2022 Star Wars Helmet Collection

75327	Luke Skywalker (Red Five) Helmet	30.00	75.00
75328	The Mandalorian Helmet	40.00	100.00
75343	Dark Trooper Helmet	50.00	125.00

2022 Star Wars Jedi Fallen Order

75335	BD-1	60.00	150.00

2022 Star Wars Magazine Gift

912281	Clone Trooper	6.00	15.00
912282	AT-AT	6.00	15.00
912283	Tusken Raider	8.00	20.00
912284	Razor Crest	8.00	20.00
912285	Darth Maul	6.00	15.00
912286	Mandalorian Warrior	10.00	25.00
912287	Mandalorian Starfighter	6.00	15.00

2022 Star Wars The Mandalorian

75324	Dark Trooper Attack	20.00	50.00

2022 Star Wars Microfighters

75321	The Razor Crest Microfighter	10.00	25.00

2022 Star Wars Obi-Wan Kenobi

75334	Obi-Wan Kenobi vs. Darth Vader	30.00	75.00
75336	Inquisitor Transport Scythe	60.00	150.00

2022 Star Wars Promotional

40531	Lars Family Homestead Kitchen	30.00	75.00

2022 Star Wars Seasonal

75340	Star Wars Advent Calendar	20.00	50.00

2022 Star Wars Ultimate Collector Series

75331	The Razor Crest		
75341	Luke Skywalker's Landspeeder	100.00	250.00

1993-97 Micro Machines Star Wars Planet Playsets

65872 Ice Planet Hoth	15.00	40.00
65995 Cloud City (w/Twin-Pod Cloud Car)	8.00	20.00
65858A Planet Tatooine (1994)	10.00	25.00
65858B Planet Tatooine (1996)	8.00	20.00
65859A Planet Dagobah (1994)	10.00	25.00
65859B Planet Dagobah (1996)		
65871A Death Star from A New Hope (1994)	10.00	25.00
65871B Death Star from A New Hope (1996)	5.00	12.00
65873A Planet Endor (w/Imperial AT-ST)(1993)	8.00	20.00
65873B Planet Endor (w/Imperial AT-ST)(1997)	6.00	15.00

1993-98 Micro Machines Star Wars Vehicle 3-Packs

65123 Imperial Landing Craft/Death Star/S-Swoop	8.00	20.00
65124 Outrider Tibanna/Gas Refinery/V-35 Landspeeder	6.00	15.00
65886 Star Wars A New Hope (silver)		
65886 Star Wars A New Hope #1	6.00	15.00
65887 Star Wars Empire Strikes Back #2		
65887 Star Wars Empire Strikes Back (silver)	5.00	12.00
65888 Star Wars Return of the Jedi (silver)		
65888 Star Wars Return of the Jedi #3		
65897 Star Wars A New Hope #4		
65898 Star Wars Empire Strikes Back #5	5.00	12.00
65899 Star Wars Return of the Jedi #6		
66111 TIE Interceptor/Imperial Star Destroyer/Rebel Blockade Runner	5.00	12.00
66112 Landspeeder/Millennium Falcon/Jawa Sandcrawler	8.00	20.00
66113 Darth Vader's TIE Fighter/Y-Wing Starfighter/X-Wing Starfighter	5.00	12.00
66114 Snowspeeder/Imperial AT-AT/Imperial Probot	15.00	40.00
66115 Rebel Transport/TIE Bomber/Imperial AT-ST	6.00	15.00
66116 Escort Frigate/Slave I/Twin-Pod Cloud Car	5.00	12.00
66117 Desert Sail Barge/Mon Calamari Star Cruiser/Speeder Bike and Rebel Pilot		
66118 Speeder Bike and Imperial Pilot/Imperial Shuttle Tydirium/TIE Starfighter		
66119 Super Star Destroyer Executor		
A-Wing Starfighter/B-Wing Starfighter	10.00	25.00
66137 Lars Family Landspeeder/Death Star II/T-16 Skyhopper	8.00	20.00
66138 Bespin Cloud City/Mon Calamari Rebel Cruiser/Escape Pod	6.00	15.00
66139 A-Wing Starfighter/Y-Wing Starfighter/TIE Starfighter	10.00	25.00
66155 2 Red Squad X-Wings/Green Squad X-Wing		

1994 Micro Machines Star Wars Fan Club Pieces

18279 Han Solo and the Millennium Falcon	6.00	15.00
28450 Darth Vader and Imperial Star Destroyer	6.00	15.00

1994-96 Micro Machines Star Wars Gift Sets

64624 Bronze Finish Collector's Gift Set	12.00	30.00
65836 Rebel Force Gift Set	6.00	15.00
65837 Imperial Force Gift Set	5.00	12.00
65847 11-Piece Collector's Gift Set	10.00	25.00
65851 A New Hope	5.00	12.00
65852 Empire Strikes Back		
65853 Return of the Jedi	8.00	20.00
65856 Rebel Force Gift Set 2nd Edition	6.00	15.00
65857 Imperial Force Gift Set 2nd Edition		
67079 Star Wars Trilogy Gift Set	15.00	40.00
68042 Rebel vs. Imperial Forces		

1994-97 Micro Machines Star Wars Collector's Sets

64598 Galaxy Battle Collector's Set 2nd Edition	8.00	20.00
64601 Master Collector's Edition (19 Items)	15.00	40.00
64602 Galaxy Battle Collector's Set	10.00	25.00
66090 Droids	10.00	25.00
68048 Master Collector's Edition (40 Items)	8.00	20.00

1994-99 Micro Machines Star Wars Transforming Action Sets

65694 TIE Fighter Pilot/Academy	10.00	25.00
65695 Royal Guard/Death Star II	15.00	40.00

65811 C-3PO/Cantina	10.00	25.00
65812 Darth Vader/Bespin	10.00	25.00
65813 R2-D2/Jabba's Palace	12.00	30.00
65814 Stormtrooper/Death Star	12.00	30.00
65815 Chewbacca/Endor	10.00	25.00
65816 Boba Fett/Cloud City	15.00	40.00
65817 Luke Skywalker/Hoth	10.00	25.00
66551 Jar Jar Binks/Naboo	6.00	15.00
66552 Battle Droid/Trade Federation Droid Control Ship		
66553 Darth Maul/Theed Generator	30.00	80.00
66554 Gungan Sub/Otoh Gunga		
67094 Star Destroyer/Space Fortress	15.00	40.00
67095 Slave I/Tatooine	10.00	25.00
68063 Yoda/Dagobah	12.00	30.00
68064 Jabba/Mos Eisley Spaceport	15.00	40.00

1995 Micro Machines Star Wars Action Fleet Playsets

67091 Ice Planet Hoth (w/Battle-Damaged Snow Speeder Luke Skywalker on Tauntaun	10.00	25.00
Wampa Ice Creature/Rebel Pilot/Princess Leia/2-1B Droid)		
67092 The Death Star (w/Darth Vader's Battle-Damaged TIE Fighter/Imperial Pilot	10.00	25.00
Imperial Gunner/Darth Vader/Stormtrooper/Imperial Royal Guard/Emperor Palpatine)		
67093 Yavin Rebel Base (w/Battle-Damaged X-Wing Wedge Antilles/R2 Unit	12.00	30.00
Luke Skywalker/Han Solo/Princess Leia/Rebel Sentry)		
68177 Naboo Hangar Final Combat (w/Obi-Wan Kenobi Darth Maul/Qui-Gon Jinn)	20.00	50.00

1995 Micro Machines Star Wars Gold Classic

67085 X-Wing Fighter and Slave I	12.00	30.00
67086 Imperial Shuttle		
67088 Millennium Falcon and TIE Fighter	30.00	80.00

1995-03 Micro Machines Star Wars Action Fleet Vehicles

46846 AT-TE		
46848 Solar Sailer		
46849 Millennium Falcon	12.00	30.00
46850 X-Wingfighter		
47045 Luke Skywalker's Snowspeeder		
47224 Imperial AT-AT	8.00	20.00
47287 Republic Gunship		
47305 Slave I	5.00	12.00
47356 TIE Advance X1		
47414 Naboo N-1 Starfighter		
47425 Republic Assault Ship	30.00	80.00
47766 Anakin's Speeder		
47767 Zam Wessel Speeder		

47768	Homing Spider Droid	4.00	10.00
47994	Jedi Starfighter	8.00	20.00
47995	Star Destroyer		
47997	Mon Calamari Cruiser	8.00	20.00
66989	Rancor (w/Gamorrean Guard and Luke Skywalker)	10.00	25.00
66990	Virago (w/Prince Xizor and Guri)	10.00	25.00
66991	X-Wing Starfighter (w/Wedge and R2 Unit)		
66992	Y-Wing Starfighter (red)(w/Gold Leader and R2 Unit)		
66993	A-Wing Starfighter (green)(w/Rebel pilot and Mon Mothma)	8.00	20.00
66994	B-Wing Starfighter (w/Rebel pilot and Admiral Ackbar)	10.00	25.00
66995	TIE Fighter (w/Imperial pilot and Grand Moff Tarkin)		
66996	Bespin Twin-Pod Cloud Car (w/Cloud Car pilot and Lobot)		
66997	Y-Wing Starfighter (blue)(w/Blue Leader and R2 Unit)	10.00	25.00
66998	X-Wing Starfighter (w/Jek Porkins and R2 Unit)		
67014	Jabba's Sail Barge (w/Jabba the Hutt/Saelt Marae and R2-D2	12.00	30.00
67031	Luke's X-Wing Starfighter (w/Luke and R2-D2)	15.00	40.00
67032	Darth Vader's TIE Fighter (w/Darth Vader and Imperial pilot)		
67033	Imperial AT-AT (w/Imperial drive and snowtrooper)	10.00	25.00
67034	A-Wing Starfighter (w/C-3PO and Rebel pilot)	6.00	15.00
67035	Imperial Shuttle Tydirium (w/Han Solo and Chewbacca)		
67036	Rebel Snowspeeder (w/Luke Skywalker and Rebel gunner)		
67039	Jawa Sandcrawler (w/Jawa and scavenger droid)	8.00	20.00
67040	Y-Wing Starfighter (w/Gold Leader and R2 Unit)	8.00	20.00
67041	Slave I (w/Boba Fett and Han Solo)	12.00	30.00
67058	TIE Interceptor (w/2 Imperial pilots)	8.00	20.00
67059	TIE Bomber (w/Imperial pilot and Imperial Naval pilot)	10.00	25.00
67077	Landspeeder and Imperial AT-ST 2-Pack	10.00	25.00
	(w/Luke Skywalker/Obi-Wan Kenobi/Imperial Driver/Stormtrooper)		
67098	Luke's X-Wing from Dagobah (w/Luke Skywalker and R2-D2)	8.00	20.00
	(1998 Toy Fair Magazine Exclusive)		
67100	Millennium Falcon (w/Han Solo and Chewbacca)		
67101	Rebel Blockade Runner (w/Princess Leia and Rebel trooper)	8.00	20.00
67102	Incom T-16 Skyhopper (w/Luke Skywalker and Biggs Darklighter)	6.00	15.00
67103	Imperial Landing Craft (w/Sandtrooper and Imperial Officer)	15.00	40.00
67105	TIE Defender (w/Imperial pilot and Moff Jerjerrod)	30.00	80.00
67106	E-Wing Starfighter (w/Rebel pilot and R7 Unit)		
68131	Naboo Starfighter (w/Anakin)		
68132	Trade Federation MTT (w/Battle Droid)	25.00	60.00
68133	Sebulba's Pod Racer (w/Sebulba)		
68134	Republic Cruiser (w/Qui-Gon Jinn)	12.00	30.00
68135	Droid Fighter (w/Daultry Dofine)		
68136	Gungan Sub (w/Qui-Gon Jinn)	4.00	10.00
68137	Flash Speeder (w/Naboo Royal Guard)		
68138	Trade Federation Landing Ship (w/Battle Droid)		
68140	Mars Guo's Pod Racer (w/Mars Guo)		
68180	Gian Speeder and Theed Palace (w		
	Captain Panaka/Naboo Foot Soldier/2 Battle Droids)		
79050	Anakin's Pod Racer (w/Anakin)		
79967	Royal Starship (w/Rick Olie)	25.00	60.00
79968	Droid Control Ship (w/Neimoidian Commander)		
79971	Trade Federation Tank (w/Battle Droid)	12.00	30.00
79972	Sith Infiltrator (w/Darth Maul)	30.00	80.00
1327CM6	Darth Vader's TIE Fighter (w/Darth Vader and Imperial pilot)		

1996 Micro Machines Star Wars Adventure Gear

68031	Vader's Lightsaber (w/Death Star Trench/X-Wing	8.00	20.00
	Imperial Gunner/Grand Moff Tarkin/Darth Vader		
68032	Luke's Binoculars (w/Yavin Rebel Base/Y-Wing	8.00	20.00
	Luke Skywalker/R5 Droid/Wedge Antilles		

1996 Micro Machines Star Wars Epic Collections

66281	Heir to the Empire	8.00	20.00
66282	Jedi Search	6.00	15.00
66283	The Truce at Bakura	8.00	20.00

1996 Micro Machines Star Wars Exclusives

66091	Balance of Power (Special Offer)		
68060	Star Wars Trilogy (Special Giveaway)	20.00	50.00

1996 Micro Machines Star Wars Shadows of the Empire

66194	Stinger/IG-2000/Guri/Darth Vader/Asp	5.00	12.00
66195	Virago/Swoop with Rider/Prince Xizor/Emperor Palpatine	6.00	15.00
66196	Outrider/Hound's Tooth/Dash Rendar/LE-B02D9	10.00	25.00

1996 Micro Machines Star Wars X-Ray Fleet

67071	Darth Vader's TIE Fighter/A-Wing Starfighter		
67072	X-Wing Starfighter/Imperial AT-AT		
67073	Millennium Falcon/Jawa Sandcrawler	6.00	15.00
67074	Boba Fett's Slave I/Y-Wing Starfighter		

1996-97 Micro Machines Star Wars Action Sets

65878	Millennium Falcon (w/Y-Wing/Mynock/Han Solo/Chewbacca	20.00	50.00
	Lando Calrissian/Nien Nunb/Leia		
65996	Rebel Transport (w/X-Wing/Rebel mechanic/General Rieekan/Major Derlin		

1996-98 Micro Machines Star Wars Character Sets

66081	Imperial Stormtroopers	10.00	25.00
66082	Ewoks	10.00	25.00
66083	Rebel Pilots	6.00	15.00
66084	Imperial Pilots	6.00	15.00
66096	Jawas	5.00	12.00
66097	Imperial Officers	6.00	15.00
66098	Echo Base Troops	5.00	12.00
66099	Imperial Naval Troops	8.00	20.00
66108	Rebel Fleet Troops	8.00	20.00
66109	Tusken Raiders	6.00	15.00
66158	Classic Characters	8.00	20.00

67112	Endor Rebel Strike Force	10.00	25.00
67113	Imperial Scout Troopers	5.00	12.00
67114	Bounty Hunters	10.00	25.00

1996-98 Micro Machines Star Wars Mini Heads

68021	Boba Fett/Admiral Ackbar/Gamorrean Guard	5.00	12.00
68022	Greedo/Nien Nunb/Tusken Raider	5.00	12.00
68023	Jawa/Yoda/Leia	5.00	12.00
68024	Bib Fortuna/Figrin D'an/Scout Trooper	4.00	10.00
68038	Darth Vader Set	5.00	10.00
68046	C-3PO Set		
NNO	Pizza Hut Set		

1996-99 Micro Machines Star Wars Battle Packs

68011	Rebel Alliance	6.00	15.00
68012	Galactic Empire	6.00	15.00
68013	Aliens and Creatures	6.00	15.00
68014	Galactic Hunters	6.00	15.00
68015	Shadow of the Empire	6.00	15.00
68016	Dune Sea	6.00	15.00
68017	Droid Escape	6.00	15.00
68018	Desert Palace	6.00	15.00
68035	Endor Adventure	8.00	20.00
68036	Mos Eisley Spaceport	12.00	30.00
68037	Cantina Encounter	6.00	15.00
68090	Cantina Smugglers and Spies	8.00	20.00
68091	Hoth Attack	10.00	25.00
68092	Death Star Escape	6.00	15.00
68093	Endor Victory	12.00	30.00
68094	Lars Family Homestead	8.00	20.00
68095	Imperial Troops	15.00	40.00
68096	Rebel Troops	10.00	25.00

1996-99 Micro Machines Star Wars Die-Cast Vehicles

66267	Death Star	10.00	25.00
66268	A-Wing Starfighter		
66269	Snowspeeder		
66270	TIE Bomber	8.00	20.00
66271	Landspeeder		
66272	Executor (w/Star Destroyer)	6.00	15.00
66273	Slave I		
66520	Royal Starship	5.00	12.00
66523	Gian Speeder		
66524	Trade Federation Battleship	6.00	15.00
66525	Sith Infiltrator	4.00	10.00
66526	Republic Cruiser		
66527	Trade Federation Tank	6.00	15.00
66528	Sebulba's Pod Racer		
79021	Trade Federation Droid Starfighter		
66261A	X-Wing Starfighter (bubble)		
66261B	X-Wing Starfighter (stripe)		

66262A	Millennium Falcon (bubble)	5.00	12.00
66262B	Millennium Falcon (stripe)	8.00	20.00
66263A	Imperial Star Destroyer (bubble)	4.00	10.00
66263B	Imperial Star Destroyer (stripe)	4.00	10.00
66264A	TIE Fighter (bubble)		
66264B	TIE Fighter (stripe)		
66265A	Y-Wing Starfighter (bubble)		
66265B	Y-Wing Starfighter (stripe)		
66266A	Jawa Sandcrawler (bubble)	6.00	15.00
66266B	Jawa Sandcrawler (stripe)	4.00	10.00

1996-99 Micro Machines Star Wars Electronic Action Fleet Vehicles

73419	AT-AT (w/Snowtrooper and Imperial Driver)	15.00	40.00
79072	FAMBAA		
79073	Trade Federation Tank		

1996-99 Micro Machines Star Wars Series Alpha

73421	X-Wing Starfighter	8.00	20.00
73422	Imperial Shuttle	10.00	25.00
73423	Rebel Snowspeeder	6.00	15.00
73424	Imperial AT-AT	8.00	20.00
73430	Twin-Pod Cloud Car		
73431	Y-Wing Starfighter		
73432	B-Wing Starfighter		
97033	Naboo Fighter		
97034	Droid Fighter		
97035	Sith Infiltrator	25.00	60.00
97036	Royal Starship		

1997 Micro Machines Star Wars Classic Duels

68301	TIE Fighter vs. X-Wing Starfighter	
68302	TIE Interceptor vs. Millennium Falcon	

1997 Micro Machines Star Wars Double Takes

75118	Death Star (w/Millennium Falcon/Obi-Wan Kenobi/Owen Lars	30.00	80.00
	Ronto and Jawas/Beru Lars/2 Scurriers		

1997-98 Micro Machines Star Wars Flight Controllers

73417	Luke Skywalker's X-Wing Starfighter		
73418	Darth Vader's TIE Fighter	10.00	25.00
73440	Y-Wing Starfighter	8.00	20.00
73441	TIE Interceptor	8.00	20.00

1998-99 Micro Machines Star Wars Action Fleet Mini Scenes

68121	STAP Invasion (w/STAP/Jar Jar Binks/Battle Droid)	5.00	12.00
68122	Destroyer Droid Ambush (w/Destroyer Droid/Obi-Wan Kenobi/TC-14)	4.00	10.00
68123	Gungan Assault (w/Gungan/Kaadu/Battle Droid)	4.00	10.00
68124	Sith Pursuit (w/Sith speeder/Darth Maul/Qui-Gon Jinn)		
79025	Trade Federation Raid (w/Trade Federation MTT Ikopi/Jar Jar Binks/Qui-Gon Jinn)	5.00	12.00
79026	Throne Room Reception (w/Throne Room Sio Bibble/Nute Gunray)	6.00	15.00
79027	Watto's Deal (w/Watto's Shop/Anakin/Pit droid)		
79028	Generator Core Duel (w/generator core Darth Maul/Obi-Wan Kenobi)	8.00	20.00

1998-99 Micro Machines Star Wars Platform Action Sets

66541	Pod Race Arena	8.00	20.00
66542	Naboo Temple Ruins	6.00	15.00
66543	Galactic Senate	6.00	15.00
66544	Galactic Dogfight	10.00	25.00
66545	Theed Palace		
66546	Tatooine Desert		

1999 Micro Machines Star Wars Deluxe Platform Action Sets

66561	Royal Starship Repair	30.00	80.00
66562	Theed Palace Assault	100.00	200.00

1999 Micro Machines Star Wars Deluxe Action Sets

68156	Pod Racer Hangar Bay (w/pit droid and pit mechanic)		
68157	Mos Espa Market (w/Anakin Skywalker and C-3PO)	8.00	20.00
68158	Otoh Gunga (w/Obi-Wan Kenobi and Jar Jar Binks)		
68159	Theed Palace		

1999 Micro Machines Star Wars Mega Platform Set

66566	Trade Federation MTT/Naboo Battlefield	25.00	60.00

1999 Micro Machines Star Wars Pod Racer

66531	Pack 1 (w/Anakin and Ratts Tyrell)	5.00	12.00

66532	Pack 2 (w/Sebulba and Clegg Holdfast)	5.00	12.00
66533	Pack 3 (w/Dud Bolt and Mars Guo)	5.00	12.00
66534	Pack 4 (w/Boles Roor and Neva Kee)	5.00	12.00
66548A	Build Your Own Pod Racer Green (Galoob)	5.00	12.00
66548B	Build Your Own Pod Racer Yellow (Galoob)	5.00	12.00
97023A	Build Your Own Pod Racer Black (Hasbro)	5.00	12.00
97023B	Build Your Own Pod Racer Blue (Hasbro)	5.00	12.00

1999 Micro Machines Star Wars Pod Racing Gravity Track

66566	Beggar's Canyon Challenge		
66570	Boonta Eve Challenge	15.00	40.00
66577	Arch Canyon Adventure		

1999 Micro Machines Star Wars Turbo Pod Racers

68148	Gasgano	
68149	Ody Mandrell	

2002 Micro Machines Star Wars Action Fleet Movie Scenes

32549	Dune Sea Ambush (w/Tusken Raider/Bantha/Luke's Landspeeder)	5.00	12.00
32553	Tatooine Droid Hunter (w/Dewback/Sandtrooper/Escape Pod)	6.00	15.00
32554	Imperial Endor Pursuit (w/Luke Skywalker Scout Trooper/2 speeder bikes/AT-ST)	6.00	15.00
32557	Mos Eisley Encounter (w/Ranto/Jawa/Black Landspeeder)	5.00	12.00

2015 Micro Machines Star Wars The Force Awakens Playsets

1	First Order Stormtrooper (w/Poe Dameron and transport)	6.00	15.00
2	Millennium Falcon (w/smaller Millennium Falcon and stormtrooper)	8.00	20.00
3	R2-D2 (w/Chewbacca/2 snowtroopers and transport)	5.00	12.00
4	Star Destroyer (w/Kylo Ren/Finn/X-Wing/TIE Fighter)	12.00	30.00

2015 Micro Machines Star Wars The Force Awakens Vehicles

1	Battle of Hoth (ESB)	5.00	12.00
2	Clone Army Raid (AOTC)	4.00	10.00
3	Desert Invasion	4.00	10.00
4	Droid Army (ROTS)	5.00	12.00
5	Endor Forest Battle (ROTJ)	6.00	15.00
6	First Order Attacks	4.00	10.00
7	First Order TIE Fighter Attack	4.00	10.00
8	Galactic Showdown	5.00	12.00
9	Imperial Pursuit (ANH)	4.00	10.00
10	Inquisitor's Hunt (Rebels)	4.00	10.00
11	Speeder Chase	5.00	12.00
12	Trench Run (ANH)	6.00	15.00

2005-09 Star Wars Titanium Series 3-Inch Die-Cast

1 A-Wing Fighter
2 A-Wing Fighter (blue)
3 A-Wing Fighter (green)
4 Aayla Secura's Jedi Starfighter
5 Amidala's Star Skiff
6 Anakin Skywalker's Pod Racer
7 Anakin's Jedi Starfighter (Coruscant)
8 Anakin's Jedi Starfighter (Mustafar)
9 Anakin's Jedi Starfighter with Hyperspace Ring
10 Anakin Skywalker's Jedi Starfighter (The Clone Wars)
11 Anakin's Modified Jedi Starfighter (Clone Wars)
12 ARC-170 Fighter
13 ARC-170 Fighter (green)
14 ARC-170 Fighter (Clone Wars deco)
15 ARC-170 Starfighter (The Clone Wars)
16 ARC-170 Fighter (Flaming Wampa)
17 ARC-170 Starfighter (Lucky Lekku)
18 AT-AP
19 AT-AP (The Clone Wars)
20 AT-AT Walker
21 AT-AT Walker (Endor)
22 AT-AT Walker (Shadow)
23 AT-OT
24 AT-OT (The Clone Wars)
25 AT-RT
26 AT-RT (Kashyyyk)
27 AT-RT (Utapau)
28 AT-ST
29 AT-ST (Hoth deco)
30 AT-ST (dirty)
31 AT-TE
32 AT-TE (The Clone Wars)
33 Jedi Starfighter with Hyperdrive Ring (green/black)
34 Jedi Starfighter with Hyperdrive Ring (green/blue)
35 B-Wing Starfighter
36 B-Wing Starfighter (orange)
37 B-Wing Starfighter (Dagger Squadron)
38 BARC Speeder
39 Clone Turbo Tank
40 Clone Turbo Tank (Snow deco)
41 Cloud Car
42 Darth Maul's Sith Speeder
43 Darth Vader's Sith Starfighter
44 Darth Vader's TIE Advanced x1 Starfighter
45 Darth Vader's TIE Advanced x1 Starfighter (white)
46 Death Star
47 Dewback with Stormtrooper
48 Droid Gunship

49 Droid Tri-Fighter
50 Droid Tri-Fighter (Battle Damage)
51 Executor
52 Firespray Interceptor
53 General Grievous' Starfighter
54 Hailfire Droid
55 Hound's Tooth
56 Hyena Droid Bomber
57 IG-2000
58 Imperial Attack Cruiser
59 Imperial Landing Craft
60 Imperial Shuttle
61 Imperial Shuttle (Emperor's Hand)
62 Invisible Hand
63 Jabba's Desert Skiff
64 Jabba's Sail Barge
65 Jedi Starfighter (Hot Rod)
66 Kit Fisto's Jedi Starfighter
67 Landspeeder
68 Mace Windu's Jedi Starfighter
69 Mace Windu's Jedi Starfighter (repaint)
70 Mace Windu's Jedi Starfighter with Hyperdrive Ring
71 Malevolence
72 Millennium Falcon
73 Millennium Falcon (Battle Ravaged)
74 Millennium Falcon (Episode III)
75 Mist Hunter
76 Mon Calamari Star Cruiser
77 Naboo Fighter
78 Naboo Patrol Fighter
79 Naboo Royal Cruiser
80 Naboo Royal Starship
81 Nebulon-B Escort Frigate
82 Neimoidian Shuttle
83 Obi-Wan's Jedi Starfighter (Coruscant)
84 Obi-Wan's Jedi Starfighter (Utapau)
85 Obi-Wan's Jedi Starfighter with Hyperspace Ring
86 Obi-Wan's Jedi Starfighter (The Clone Wars)
87 Outrider
88 P-38 Starfighter / Magnaguard Starfighter
89 Plo Koon's Jedi Starfighter with Hyperspace Ring
90 Punishing One
91 Rebel Blockade Runner
92 Rebel Transport
93 Republic Attack Cruiser
94 Republic Attack Cruiser (The Clone Wars)
95 Republic Attack Shuttle
96 Republic Cruiser
97 Republic Fighter Tank
98 Republic Gunship
99 Republic Gunship – Clone Wars (Titanium Limited)
100 Republic Gunship (Closed Doors)
101 Republic Gunship (Command Gunship deco)
102 Republic Gunship (The Clone Wars)
103 Republic Gunship (Lucky Lekku)
104 Republic V-Wing Fighter
105 Rogue Shadow
106 Saesee Tiin's Jedi Starfighter with Hyperspace Ring
107 Sandcrawler
108 Sandspeeder
109 Sebulba's Pod Racer
110 Shadow Scout on Speeder Bike
111 Shadow Trooper Gunship

112 Sith Infiltrator
113 Slave 1 - Boba Fett
114 Slave 1 – Jango Fett
115 Slave 1 – Jango Fett (Battle Damage)
116 Slave 1 - Silver (Titanium Limited)
117 Snowspeeder
118 Snowspeeder (Luke's)
119 Snowspeeder (Vintage deco)
120 Speeder Bike - Blizzard Force
121 Speeder Bike - Kashyyyk
122 Speeder Bike - Leia
123 Speeder Bike - Luke Skywalker
124 Speeder Bike - Paploo
125 Speeder Bike - Scout Trooper
126 Star Destroyer
127 Star Destroyer (repaint)
128 Swamp Speeder
129 Swamp Speeder (Dirty deco)
130 T-16 Skyhopper
131 TIE Bomber
132 TIE Bomber (Battle Damage)
133 TIE Defender
134 TIE Fighter
135 TIE Fighter (Battle Damage)
136 TIE Fighter – White (Titanium Limited)
137 TIE Fighter (Ecliptic Evader)
138 TIE Interceptor
139 TIE Interceptor (Royal Guard)
140 TIE Interceptor (Baron Fel)
141 Tantive IV
142 Trade Federation AAT
143 Trade Federation AAT (Clone Wars deco)
144 Trade Federation AAT (The Clone Wars)
145 Trade Federation Battleship
146 Trade Federation Landing Craft
147 Trade Federation MTT
148 The Twilight
149 V-19 Torrent Starfighter
150 V-Wing Starfighter
151 V-Wing Starfighter (Imperial)
152 Virago
153 Vulture Droid
154 Vulture Droid (The Clone Wars)
155 Wookiee Flyer
156 X-Wing Fighter
157 X-Wing Starfighter (Biggs Darklighter's Red 3)
158 X-Wing Fighter (Dagobah)
159 X-Wing Starfighter (John Branon's Red 4)
160 X-Wing Fighter (Luke Skywalker's Red 5)
161 X-Wing Starfighter (Red Leader's Red 1)
162 X-Wing Fighter (Wedge Antilles)
163 X-Wing Starfighter (Wedge Antilles' Red 2)
164 Xanadu Blood
165 XP-34 Landspeeder
166 Y-Wing Bomber
167 Y-Wing Bomber (Anakin's)
168 Y-Wing Fighter
169 Y-Wing Fighter (Davish Krail's Gold 5)
170 Y-Wing Fighter (Gold Leader)
171 Y-Wing Starfighter (green deco)
172 Y-Wing Fighter (Red deco)
173 Z-95 Headhunter

Comics
PRICE GUIDE

Marvel STAR WARS (1977-1986)

1 July 1977		
"Star Wars: A New Hope" adaptation Part 1	75.00	200.00
1 July 1977		
Star Wars 35-cent price variant	3,000.00	6,000.00
2 August 1977		
"Star Wars: A New Hope" adaptation Part 2	30.00	80.00
2 August 1977		
Star Wars 35-cent price variant	1,000.00	3,000.00
3 September 1977		
"Star Wars: A New Hope" adaptation Part 3	15.00	40.00
3 September 1977		
Star Wars 35-cent price variant	500.00	1,000.00
4 October 1977		
"Star Wars: A New Hope" adaptation Part 4	15.00	40.00
4 October 1977		
Star Wars 35-cent price variant	500.00	1,000.00
5 November 1977		
"Star Wars: A New Hope" adaptation Part 5	15.00	40.00
6 December 1977		
"Star Wars: A New Hope" adaptation Part 6	15.00	40.00
7 January 1978	10.00	25.00
8 February 1978	10.00	25.00
9 March 1978	8.00	20.00
10 April 1978	8.00	20.00
11 May 1978	8.00	20.00
12 June 1978		
1st appearance of Governor Quarg	8.00	20.00
13 July 1978		
John Byrne & Terry Austin cover	10.00	25.00
14 August 1978	8.00	20.00
15 September 1978	8.00	20.00
16 October 1978		
1st appearance of Valance	8.00	20.00
17 November 1978	6.00	15.00
18 December 1978	6.00	15.00
19 January 1979	6.00	15.00
20 February 1979	6.00	15.00
21 March 1979	6.00	15.00
22 April 1979	6.00	15.00
23 May 1979		
Darth Vader appearance	6.00	15.00
24 June 1979	6.00	15.00
25 July 1979	6.00	15.00
26 August 1979	6.00	15.00
27 September 1979	6.00	15.00
28 October 1979	6.00	15.00

29 November 1979		
1st appearance of Tyler Lucian	6.00	15.00
30 December 1979	5.00	12.00
31 January 1980	5.00	12.00
32 February 1980	5.00	12.00
33 March 1980	5.00	12.00
34 April 1980	5.00	12.00
35 May 1980		
Darth Vader cover	6.00	15.00
36 June 1980	5.00	12.00
37 July 1980	5.00	12.00
38 August 1980	5.00	12.00
39 September 1980		
"The Empire Strikes Back" adaptation - Part 1	8.00	20.00
40 October 1980		
"The Empire Strikes Back" adaptation - Part 2	8.00	20.00
41 November 1980		
"The Empire Strikes Back" adaptation - Part 3	8.00	20.00
42 December 1980		
"The Empire Strikes Back" adaptation - Part 4, "Bounty Hunters" cover w/Boba Fett	75.00	200.00
43 January 1981		
"The Empire Strikes Back" adaptation - Part 5	12.00	30.00
44 February 1981		
"The Empire Strikes Back" adaptation - Part 6	8.00	20.00
45 March 1981	5.00	12.00
46 April 1981	5.00	12.00
47 May 1981		
1st appearance Captain Kligson	5.00	12.00
48 June 1981		
Princess Leia vs. Darth Vader	8.00	20.00
49 July 1981		
"The Last Jedi" story title on cover	6.00	15.00
50 August 1981		
Giant-Size issue	6.00	15.00
51 September 1981	5.00	12.00
52 October 1981		
Darth Vader cover	6.00	15.00
53 November 1981	5.00	12.00
54 December 1981	5.00	12.00
55 January 1982		
1st appearance Plif	5.00	12.00
56 February 1982	5.00	12.00
57 March 1982	5.00	12.00
58 April 1982	5.00	12.00
59 May 1982	5.00	12.00
60 June 1982	5.00	12.00
61 July 1982	5.00	12.00
62 August 1982	5.00	12.00
63 September 1982	5.00	12.00
64 October 1982	5.00	12.00
65 November 1982	5.00	12.00
66 December 1982	5.00	12.00
67 January 1983	5.00	12.00
68 February 1983		
Boba Fett cover	60.00	150.00
69 March 1983	5.00	12.00
70 April 1983	5.00	12.00
71 May 1983	5.00	12.00
72 June 1983	5.00	12.00
73 July 1983	5.00	12.00
74 August 1983	5.00	12.00
75 September 1983	5.00	12.00
76 October 1983	5.00	12.00
77 November 1983	5.00	12.00
78 December 1983	5.00	12.00
79 January 1984	5.00	12.00

80 February 1984	5.00	12.00
81 March 1984		
Boba Fett appearance	30.00	80.00
82 April 1984	5.00	12.00
83 May 1984	5.00	12.00
84 June 1984	5.00	12.00
85 July 1984	5.00	12.00
86 August 1984	5.00	12.00
87 September 1984	5.00	12.00
88 October 1984		
1st appearance of Lumiya	6.00	15.00
89 November 1984	5.00	12.00
90 December 1984	5.00	12.00
91 January 1985	6.00	15.00
92 February 1985		
Giant-Size issue	8.00	20.00
93 March 1985	6.00	15.00
94 April 1985	6.00	15.00
95 May 1985	6.00	15.00
96 June 1985	6.00	15.00
97 July 1985	6.00	15.00
98 August 1985	6.00	15.00
99 September 1985	6.00	15.00
100 October 1985		
Giant-Size issue	10.00	25.00
101 November 1985	8.00	20.00
102 December 1985	8.00	20.00
103 January 1986	8.00	20.00
104 March 1986	8.00	20.00
105 May 1986	8.00	20.00
106 July 1986	10.00	25.00
107 September 1986		
Final issue	25.00	60.00

Marvel STAR WARS Annual

1 Star Wars Annual 1979	6.00	15.00
2 Star Wars Annual 1982	6.00	15.00
3 Star Wars Annual 1983	6.00	15.00

STAR WARS: RETURN OF THE JEDI MINI-SERIES (1983-1984)

1 October 1983		
"Return of the Jedi" adaptation Part 1	4.00	10.00
2 November 1983		
"Return of the Jedi" adaptation Part 2	3.00	8.00

COMICS

3 December 1983
"Return of the Jedi" adaptation Part 3   3.00   8.00
4 January 1984
"Return of the Jedi" adaptation Part 4   3.00   8.00

JOURNEY TO STAR WARS: THE FORCE AWAKENS - SHATTERED EMPIRE (2015)

1 November 2015   2.00   5.00
1 November 2015
Blank Cover Variant   4.00   10.00
1 November 2015
1:20 Hyperspace Variant   6.00   15.00
1 November 2015
1:25 Movie Photo Variant   8.00   20.00
1 November 2015
1:25 Marco Checchetto Variant   8.00   20.00
2 December 2015   1.50   4.00
2 December 2015
1:25 Movie Photo Variant   6.00   15.00
2 December 2015
1:25 Kris Anka Variant   6.00   15.00
3 December 2015   1.50   4.00
3 December 2015
1:25 Movie Photo Variant   6.00   15.00
3 December 2015
1:25 Mike Deodato Jr. Variant   6.00   15.00
4 December 2015   1.50   4.00
4 December 2015
1:25 Movie Photo Variant   6.00   15.00
4 December 2015
1:25 Sara Pichelli Variant   6.00   15.00

Marvel STAR WARS (2015-)

1 March 2015   3.00   8.00
1 March 2015
Blank Cover Variant   12.00   30.00
1 March 2015
Skottie Young "Baby" Variant   3.00   8.00
1 March 2015
Luke Skywalker Action Figure Variant   10.00   25.00
1 March 2015
1:15 Movie Photo Variant   4.00   10.00
1 March 2015
1:20 Sara Pichelli Variant   4.00   10.00
1 March 2015
1:25 "Two Suns" Variant   3.00   8.00
1 March 2015
1:25 Bob McLeod Variant   4.00   10.00
1 March 2015
1:50 Alex Ross Variant   20.00   50.00
1 March 2015
1:50 J. Scott Campbell Variant   15.00   40.00
1 March 2015
1:100 Joe Quesada Variant   15.00   40.00
1 March 2015
1:200 Alex Ross Sketch Variant   30.00   80.00
1 March 2015
1:500 Joe Quesada Sketch Variant   75.00   200.00

1 April 2015
2nd printing   4.00   10.00
1 April 2015
3rd printing   4.00   10.00
1 June 2015
4th printing   4.00   10.00
1 July 2015
5th printing   4.00   10.00
1 September 2015
6th printing (double cover)   6.00   15.00
1 7th printing   4.00   10.00
2 April 2015   4.00   10.00
2 April 2015
Han Solo Action Figure Variant   15.00   40.00
2 April 2015
Sergio Aragones Variant   3.00   8.00
2 April 2015
1:25 Leinil Francis Yu Variant   6.00   15.00
2 April 2015
1:25 Howard Chaykin Variant   6.00   15.00
2 April 2015
1:100 John Cassaday Sketch Variant   20.00   50.00
2 May 2015
2nd printing   4.00   10.00
2 June 2015
3rd printing   3.00   8.00
2 July 2015
4th printing   3.00   8.00
2 August 2015
5th printing   3.00   8.00
2 6th printing   3.00   8.00
3 May 2015   2.50   6.00
3 May 2015
Obi-Wan Kenobi Action Figure Variant   2.50   6.00
3 May 2015
1:25 Leinil Francis Yu Variant   6.00   15.00
3 May 2015
1:100 John Cassaday Sketch Variant   15.00   40.00
3 July 2015
2nd printing   2.00   5.00
3 July 2015
3rd printing   2.00   5.00
3 4th printing   2.00   5.00
4 June 2015   12.00   30.00
4 June 2015
Chewbacca Action Figure Variant   8.00   20.00
4 June 2015
1:25 Giuseppe Camuncoli Variant   12.00   30.00
4 June 2015
1:100 John Cassaday Sketch Variant   40.00   100.00
4 2nd printing   20.00   50.00
5 July 2015   3.00   8.00
5 July 2015
C-3PO Action Figure Variant   4.00   10.00
5 July 2015
1:100 John Cassaday Sketch Variant   20.00   50.00
5 2nd printing   4.00   10.00
6 August 2015   10.00   25.00
6 August 2015
R2-D2 Action Figure Variant   8.00   20.00
6 2nd printing   15.00   40.00
6 3rd printing   15.00   40.00
7 September 2015   2.00   5.00
7 September 2015
Stormtrooper Action Figure Variant   2.50   6.00
7 September 2015
1:25 Simone Bianchi Variant Cover   3.00   8.00
7 September 2015
1:25 Tony Moore Variant Cover   3.00   8.00
7 September 2015
1:100 John Cassaday Sketch Variant   15.00   40.00
8 October 2015   2.00   5.00
8 October 2015
Tusken Raider Action Figure Variant   2.50   6.00
8 October 2015
1:50 John Cassaday Variant   6.00   15.00
8 October 2015
1:100 Stuart Immonen Sketch Variant   15.00   40.00

9 November 2015   2.00   5.00
9 November 2015
Star Destroyer Commander Action Figure Variant   2.50   6.00
9 November 2015
1:100 Stuart Immonen Sketch Variant   15.00   40.00
10 December 2015   2.00   5.00
10 December 2015
Jawa Action Figure Variant   2.50   6.00
10 December 2015
1:100 Stuart Immonen Sketch Variant   25.00   60.00
11 January 2016   2.00   5.00
11 January 2016
Luke Skywalker: X-Wing Pilot Action Figure Variant   2.50   6.00
11 January 2016
1:100 Stuart Immonen Sketch Variant   15.00   40.00
12 January 2016   2.00   5.00
12 January 2016
Greedo Action Figure Variant   2.50   6.00
12 January 2016
1:100 Stuart Immonen Sketch Variant   15.00   40.00
13 February 2016   2.50   6.00
13 February 2016
R5-D4 Action Figure Variant   3.00   8.00
13 February 2016
Clay Mann Variant   8.00   20.00
13 March 2016
2nd printing   2.00   5.00
14 March 2016   4.00   10.00
14 March 2016
Hammerhead Action Figure Variant   2.50   6.00
14 March 2016
Clay Mann Variant   2.50   6.00
14 April 2016
2nd printing   5.00   12.00
15 March 2016   2.00   5.00
15 March 2016
Snaggletooth Action Figure Variant   2.50   6.00
15 March 2016
1:100 Mike Mayhew Sketch Variant   15.00   40.00
15 May 2016
2nd printing   2.00   5.00
16 April 2016   2.00   5.00
16 April 2016
Death Star Droid Action Figure Variant   2.50   6.00
16 April 2016
1:25 Stuart Immonen Variant   4.00   10.00
16 April 2016
1:25 Leinil Francis Yu Variant   4.00   10.00
16 April 2016
1:100 Terry Dodson Sketch Variant   15.00   40.00
17 May 2016   2.00   5.00
17 May 2016
Walrus Man Action Figure Variant   2.50   6.00
17 May 2016
1:25 Leinil Francis Yu Variant   4.00   10.00
17 May 2016
1:100 Terry Dodson Sketch Variant   15.00   40.00
18 June 2016   2.00   5.00
18 June 2016
Power Droid Action Figure Variant   2.50   6.00
18 June 2016
1:100 Leinil Francis Yu Sketch Variant   20.00   50.00
19 July 2016   2.00   5.00
19 July 2016
Leia Organa: Bespin Gown Action Figure Variant   3.00   8.00
19 July 2016
1:100 Leinil Francis Yu Sketch Variant   15.00   40.00
20 August 2016   6.00   15.00
20 August 2016
Yoda Action Figure Variant   12.00   30.00
20 August 2016
1:100 Mike Mayhew Sketch Variant   15.00   40.00
21 September 2016   2.00   5.00
21 September 2016
Stormtrooper: Hoth Battle Gear Action Figure Variant   3.00   8.00
21 September 2016
1:100 David Aja Sketch Variant   60.00   150.00
22 October 2016   2.00   5.00

COMICS

22 October 2016
Dengar Action Figure Variant 2.50 6.00
22 October 2016
1:100 Mike Deodato Sketch Variant 20.00 50.00
23 November 2016 2.00 5.00
23 November 2016
Rebel Soldier: Hoth Battle Gear Action Figure Variant 2.50 6.00
23 November 2016
1:25 Jorge Molina Variant 5.00 12.00
23 November 2016
1:100 Mike Deodato Sketch Variant 20.00 50.00
24 December 2016' 2.00 5.00
24 December 2016
Lobot Action Figure Variant 2.50 6.00
24 December 2016
1:100 Mike Deodato Sketch Variant 20.00 50.00
25 January 2017 2.00 5.00
25 January 2017
IG-88 Action Figure Variant 2.50 6.00
25 January 2017
1:100 Mike Deodato Sketch Variant 20.00 50.00
26 February 2017' 2.00 5.00
26 February 2017
2-1B Action Figure Variant 2.50 6.00
26 February 2017
Qui-Gon Jinn Action Figure Variant 20.00 50.00
26 February 2017'
1:100 Mike Deodato Sketch Variant 20.00 50.00
27 March 2017' 2.00 5.00
27 March 2017
R2-D2 with Sensorscope Action Figure Variant 2.50 6.00
27 March 2017
Star Wars 40th Anniversary Variant 6.00 15.00
28 April 2017' 2.00 5.00
28 April 2017
C-3PO Removable Limbs Action Figure Variant 2.50 6.00
28 April 2017
Star Wars 40th Anniversary Variant 4.00 10.00
29 May 2017' 2.00 5.00
29 May 2017
Luke Skywalker: Hoth Battle Gear Action Figure Variant 2.50 6.00
29 May 2017
Star Wars 40th Anniversary Variant 3.00 8.00
30 June 2017' 2.00 5.00
30 June 2017
AT-AT Commander Action Figure Variant 2.50 6.00
30 June 2017
Star Wars 40th Anniversary Variant 3.00 8.00
31 July 2017' 2.00 5.00
31 July 2017
Luke Skywalker: Bespin Fatigues Action Figure Variant 2.50 6.00
31 July 2017
Star Wars 40th Anniversary Variant 3.00 8.00
32 August 2017' 2.00 5.00
32 August 2017
FX-7 Medical Droid Action Figure Variant 2.50 6.00
32 August 2017
Star Wars 40th Anniversary Variant 3.00 8.00
33 September 2017' 2.00 5.00
33 September 2017
Bespin Security Guard Action Figure Variant 2.50 6.00
33 September 2017
Star Wars 40th Anniversary Variant 3.00 8.00
34 October 2017' 2.00 5.00
34 October 2017
Han Solo: Hoth Outfit Action Figure Variant 2.50 6.00
34 October 2017
Star Wars 40th Anniversary Variant 3.00 8.00
35 October 2017' 2.00 5.00
35 October 2017
Ugnaught Action Figure Variant 2.50 6.00
35 October 2017
Star Wars 40th Anniversary Variant 3.00 8.00
36 November 2017' 2.00 5.00
36 November 2017
Leia Organa: Hoth Outfit Action Figure Variant 3.00 8.00
36 November 2017
Star Wars 40th Anniversary Variant 3.00 8.00

37 December 2017' 2.00 5.00
37 December 2017
Rebel Commander Action Figure Variant 2.50 6.00
37 December 2017
Star Wars 40th Anniversary Variant 3.00 8.00
38 January 2018' 2.00 5.00
38 January 2018
Michael Walsh Variant 2.00 5.00
38 January 2018
AT-AT Driver Action Figure Variant 3.00 8.00
38 January 2018
1:25 Pepe Larraz Variant 5.00 12.00
38 January 2018
1:50 Terry Dodson Variant 12.00 30.00
38 January 2018
Star Wars 40th Anniversary Variant 3.00 8.00
39 January 2018' 2.00 5.00
39 January 2018
Imperial Commander Action Figure Variant 3.00 8.00
40 February 2018' 2.00 5.00
40 February 2018
Star Wars 40th Anniversary Variant 3.00 8.00
40 February 2018
Luke Skywalker: Yavin Fatigues Action Figure Variant 20.00 50.00
41 March 2018' 2.00 5.00
41 March 2018
Zuckuss Action Figure Variant 3.00 8.00
41 March 2018
Rey Galactic Icons Variant 6.00 15.00
42 March 2018' 2.00 5.00
42 March 2018
4-LOM Action Figure Variant 3.00 8.00
43 April 2018' 2.00 5.00
43 April 2018
Imperial TIE Fighter Pilot Action Figure Variant 3.00 8.00
43 April 2018
Poe Dameron Galactic Icons Variant 2.50 6.00
44 May 2018' 2.00 5.00
44 May 2018
(Twin Pod) Cloud Car Pilot Action Figure Variant 3.00 8.00
44 May 2018
Captain Phasma Galactic Icons Variant 2.50 6.00
45 May 2018' 2.00 5.00
45 May 2018
Bib Fortune Action Figure Variant 3.00 8.00
46 June 2018' 2.00 5.00
46 June 2018
Ree-Yees Action Figure Variant 3.00 8.00
46 June 2018
Han Solo Galactic Icons Variant 2.50 6.00
47 July 2018' 2.00 5.00
47 July 2018
Weequay Action Figure Variant 3.00 8.00
47 July 2018
Qi'ra Galactic Icons Variant 2.50 6.00
48 July 2018' 2.00 5.00
48 July 2018
Bespin Security Guard Action Figure Variant 3.00 8.00
49 August 2018' 2.00 5.00
49 August 2018
Emperor's Royal Guard Action Figure Variant 3.00 8.00
49 August 2018
Sheev Palpatine Galactic Icons Variant 2.50 6.00
50 September 2018' 2.50 6.00
50 September 2018
David Marquez Variant 2.50 6.00
50 September 2018
The Emperor Action Figure Variant 4.00 10.00
50 September 2018
Thrawn Galactic Icons Variant 4.00 10.00
50 September 2018
1:25 Phil Noto Variant 5.00 12.00
50 September 2018
1:50 Terry Dodson Variant 12.00 30.00
50 September 2018
1:100 Terry Dodson Virgin Variant 30.00 80.00
50 October 2018
2nd printing 2.50 6.00

51 September 2018' 2.00 5.00
51 September 2018
Chief Chirpa Action Figure Variant 3.00 8.00
51 September 2018
Jabba the Hutt Action Figure Variant 20.00 50.00
52 October 2018' 2.00 5.00
52 October 2018
Lando Calrissian: Skiff Guard Disguise Action Figure Variant 3.00 8.00
52 October 2018
Ben Kenobi Galactic Icons Variant 2.50 6.00
53 November 2018' 2.00 5.00
53 November 2018
Logray (Ewok Shaman) Action Figure Variant 3.00 8.00
54 November 2018' 2.00 5.00
54 November 2018
Squid Head Action Figure Variant 3.00 8.00
55 December 2018' 2.00 5.00
55 December 2018
Klaatu Action Figure Variant 3.00 8.00
55 December 2018
Cad Bane Galactic Icons Variant 2.50 6.00

Marvel STAR WARS ANNUAL (2015-)

1 February 2016 2.00 5.00
1 February 2016
Blank Cover Variant 3.00 8.00
2 January 2017' 2.00 5.00
2 January 2017
Elsa Charretier Variant 2.00 5.00
3 November 2017' 2.00 5.00
3 November 2017
Rod Reis Variant 2.00 5.00
4 July 2018' 2.50 6.00
4 July 2018
1:25 John Tyler Christopher Variant 200.00 500.00

Marvel DARTH VADER (2015-2016)

1 April 2015		
1st appearance Black Krrsantan	20.00	50.00
1 April 2015		
Blank Cover Variant	8.00	20.00
1 April 2015		
Skottie Young "Baby" Variant	25.00	60.00
1 April 2015		
Darth Vader Action Figure Variant	15.00	40.00
1 April 2015		
1:15 Movie Photo Variant	10.00	25.00
1 April 2015		
1:25 John Cassaday Variant	12.00	30.00
1 April 2015		
1:25 Whilce Portacio Variant	20.00	50.00
1 April 2015		
1:25 Mike Del Mundo Variant	25.00	60.00
1 April 2015		
1:50 J. Scott Campbell Variant	40.00	100.00
1 April 2015		
1:50 Alex Ross Variant	40.00	100.00
1 April 2015		
1:200 Alex Ross Sketch Variant	75.00	200.00
1 2nd printing	15.00	40.00
1 3rd printing	20.00	50.00
1 4th printing	25.00	60.00
1 5th printing	30.00	80.00
2 April 2015	5.00	12.00
2 April 2015		
1:25 Dave Dorman Variant	12.00	30.00
2 April 2015		
1:25 Salvador Larroca Variant	12.00	30.00
2 2nd printing	8.00	20.00
2 3rd printing	10.00	25.00
2 4th printing	12.00	30.00
2 5th printing	12.00	30.00
3 May 2015		
1st appearance of Dr. Aphra, 0-0-0 & BT-1	60.00	150.00
3 May 2015		
1:25 Salvador Larroca Variant	300.00	600.00
3 2nd printing	50.00	120.00
3 3rd printing	75.00	200.00
3 4th printing	125.00	300.00
4 June 2015	4.00	10.00
4 June 2015		
1:25 Salvador Larroca Variant	12.00	30.00
4 2nd printing	8.00	20.00
4 3rd printing	12.00	30.00
4 4th printing	15.00	40.00
5 July 2015	2.50	6.00
5 July 2015		
1:25 Salvador Larroca Variant	10.00	25.00
5 2nd printing	5.00	12.00
6 August 2015	20.00	50.00
6 2nd printing	5.00	12.00
7 September 2015	2.50	6.00
8 October 2015	2.50	6.00
9 November 2015	2.50	6.00
9 November 2015		
1:25 Adi Granov Variant	10.00	25.00
10 December 2015	2.50	6.00
11 December 2015	2.50	6.00
12 January 2016	2.50	6.00
13 January 2016	2.50	6.00
13 January 2016		
Clay Mann Variant	2.50	6.00
13 2nd printing	5.00	12.00
14 February 2016	2.50	6.00
14 February 2016		
Clay Mann Variant	2.50	6.00
14 2nd printing	5.00	12.00
15 March 2016	2.50	6.00
15 April 2016		
Clay Mann Variant	2.50	6.00
15 May 2016		
1:25 Francesco Francavilla Variant	12.00	30.00

15 June 2016		
1:100 Mark Brooks Sketch Variant	40.00	100.00
15 2nd printing	5.00	12.00
16 April 2016	2.50	6.00
16 2nd printing	5.00	12.00
17 May 2016	2.50	6.00
18 May 2016	2.50	6.00
19 June 2016	2.50	6.00
20 July 2016	2.50	6.00
20 July 2016		
Inspector Thanoth Action Figure Variant	2.50	6.00
20 July 2016		
"The Story Thus Far" Reilly Brown Variant	2.50	6.00
20 2nd printing	5.00	12.00
21 August 2016	2.50	6.00
21 August 2016		
Tulon Action Figure Variant	2.50	6.00
21 2nd printing	5.00	12.00
22 August 2016	2.50	6.00
22 August 2016		
Cylo Action Figure Variant	2.50	6.00
22 2nd printing	5.00	12.00
23 September 2016	2.50	6.00
23 September 2016		
BT-1 Action Figure Variant	2.50	6.00
23 2nd printing	5.00	12.00
24 October 2016	2.50	6.00
24 0-0-0 (Triple-Zero) Action Figure Variant	5.00	12.00
25 December 2016		
final issue	5.00	12.00
25 December 2016		
Doctor Aphra Action Figure Variant	8.00	20.00
25 December 2016		
Adi Granov Variant	4.00	10.00
25 December 2016		
Jamie McKelvie Variant	4.00	10.00
25 December 2016		
Karmome Shirahama Variant	4.00	10.00
25 December 2016		
Salvador Larroca Variant	4.00	10.00
25 December 2016		
1:25 Chris Samnee Variant	10.00	25.00
25 December 2016		
1:25 Sara Pichelli Variant	10.00	25.00
25 December 2016		
1:25 Cliff Chiang Variant	20.00	50.00
25 December 2016		
1:50 Michael Cho Variant	25.00	60.00
25 December 2016		
1:100 Joe Quesada Variant	60.00	150.00
25 December 2016		
1:200 Joe Quesada Sketch Variant	125.00	300.00

Marvel DARTH VADER ANNUAL (2015-2016)

1 February 2015	3.00	8.00
1 February 2015		
Blank Cover Variant	6.00	15.00

Marvel STAR WARS: THE FORCE AWAKENS (2016-2017)

1 August 2016		
"Star Wars: The Force Awakens " adaptation Part 1	6.00	15.00
1 August 2016		
Blank Cover Variant	12.00	30.00
1 August 2016		
1:15 Movie Photo Variant	20.00	50.00
1 August 2016		
1:25 Phil Noto Variant	10.00	25.00
1 August 2016		
1:50 John Cassaday Variant	12.00	30.00
1 August 2016		
1:75 Esad Ribic Sketch Variant	20.00	50.00
1 August 2016		
1:100 Joe Quesada Variant	125.00	300.00
1 August 2016		
1:200 John Cassaday Sketch Variant	25.00	60.00
1 August 2016		
1:300 Joe Quesada Sketch Variant	200.00	500.00
2 September 2016		
"Star Wars: The Force Awakens " adaptation Part 2	3.00	8.00
2 September 2016		
1:15 Movie Photo Variant	4.00	10.00
2 September 2016		
1:25 Chris Samnee Variant	6.00	15.00
2 September 2016		
1:75 Mike Mayhew Sketch Variant	30.00	80.00
3 October 2016		
"Star Wars: The Force Awakens" adaptation Part 3	3.00	8.00
3 October 2016		
1:15 Movie Photo Variant	5.00	12.00
3 October 2016		
1:75 Mike Deodato Jr. Sketch Variant	30.00	80.00
4 November 2016		
"Star Wars: The Force Awakens" adaptation Part 4	2.00	5.00
4 November 2016		
1:15 Movie Photo Variant	15.00	40.00
4 November 2016		
1:75 Mike Del Mundo Sketch Variant	30.00	80.00
5 December 2016		
"Star Wars: The Force Awakens" adaptation Part 5	2.00	5.00
5 December 2016		
1:15 Movie Photo Variant	6.00	15.00
5 December 2016		
1:75 Rafael Albuquerque Sketch Variant	50.00	120.00
6 January 2017		
"Star Wars: The Force Awakens" adaptation Part 6	2.00	5.00
6 January 2017		
1:15 Movie Photo Variant	40.00	100.00
6 January 2017		
1:25 Esad Ribic Variant	10.00	25.00
6 January 2017		
1:75 Paolo Rivera Variant	30.00	80.00